AF179493

fedora

Fedora 15

Deployment Guide

Deployment, Configuration and Administration of Fedora 15

❖

Fultus™ Books

Fedora 15

Deployment Guide

Deployment, Configuration and Administration of Fedora 15

ISBN-10: 1-59682-232-5
ISBN-13: 978-1-59682-232-0

Copyright © 2011 Red Hat, Inc. and others. All rights reserved.

Cover design and book layout by Fultus Corporation

Published by Fultus Corporation

Publisher Web: *www.fultus.com*
Linbrary™ - Linux Library: *www.linbrary.com*
Online Bookstore: *store.fultus.com*
email: *production@fultus.com*

This material may only be distributed subject to the terms and conditions set forth in the Creative Commons ShareAlike 3.0 License (CC-BY-SA),
(the latest version is presently available at *http://creativecommons.org/licenses/by-sa/3.0/legalcode*).

Fedora and the Fedora Infinity Design logo are trademarks or registered trademarks of Red Hat, Inc., in the U.S. and other countries. Red Hat and the Red Hat "Shadow Man" logo are registered trademarks of Red Hat Inc. in the United States and other countries. All product names and services identified throughout this manual are trademarks or registered trademarks of their respective companies.

The author and publisher have made every effort in the preparation of this book to ensure the accuracy of the information. However, the information contained in this book is offered without warranty, either express or implied. Neither the author nor the publisher nor any dealer or distributor will be held liable for any damages caused or alleged to be caused either directly or indirectly by this book.

Table of Contents

List of Figures

List of Tables

Legal Notice

Copyright © 2011 Red Hat, Inc.

The text of and illustrations in this document are licensed by Red Hat under a Creative Commons Attribution–Share Alike 3.0 Unported license ("CC-BY-SA"). An explanation of CC-BY-SA is available at *http://creativecommons.org/licenses/by-sa/3.0/*. The original authors of this document, and Red Hat, designate the Fedora Project as the "Attribution Party" for purposes of CC-BY-SA. In accordance with CC-BY-SA, if you distribute this document or an adaptation of it, you must provide the URL for the original version.

Red Hat, as the licensor of this document, waives the right to enforce, and agrees not to assert, Section 4d of CC-BY-SA to the fullest extent permitted by applicable law.

Red Hat, Red Hat Enterprise Linux, the Shadowman logo, JBoss, MetaMatrix, Fedora, the Infinity Logo, and RHCE are trademarks of Red Hat, Inc., registered in the United States and other countries.

For guidelines on the permitted uses of the Fedora trademarks, refer to *https://fedoraproject.org/wiki/Legal:Trademark_guidelines*.

Linux® is the registered trademark of Linus Torvalds in the United States and other countries.

Java® is a registered trademark of Oracle and/or its affiliates.

XFS® is a trademark of Silicon Graphics International Corp. or its subsidiaries in the United States and/or other countries.

MySQL® is a registered trademark of MySQL AB in the United States, the European Union and other countries.

All other trademarks are the property of their respective owners.

Abstract

The *Deployment Guide* documents relevant information regarding the deployment, configuration, and administration of Fedora 15. It is oriented towards system administrators with a basic understanding of the system.

Preface

The *Deployment Guide* contains information on how to customize the Fedora 15 system to fit your needs. If you are looking for a comprehensive, task-oriented guide for configuring and customizing your system, this is the manual for you.

This manual discusses many intermediate topics such as the following:

- Installing and managing packages using the graphical **PackageKit** and command line **Yum** package managers
- Setting up a network—from establishing an Ethernet connection using **NetworkManager** to configuring channel bonding interfaces to increase server bandwidth
- Configuring `DHCP`, **BIND**, **Apache HTTP Server**, **Postfix**, **Sendmail** and other enterprise-class servers and software
- Gathering information about your system, including obtaining user-space crash data with the **Automatic Bug Reporting Tool**, and kernel-space crash data with `kdump`
- Easily working with kernel modules and upgrading the kernel

1. Target Audience

The *Deployment Guide* assumes you have a basic understanding of the Fedora operating system. If you need help with the installation of this system, refer to the *Fedora 15 Installation Guide*.

2. How to Read this Book

This manual is divided into the following main categories:

Part I, *Basic System Configuration* (page 35)

This part covers basic system administration tasks such as keyboard configuration, date and time configuration, and managing users and groups.

Chapter 1, *Language and Keyboard Configuration* (page 36) covers basic language and keyboard setup. Read this chapter if you need to configure the language of your desktop, change the keyboard layout, or add the keyboard layout indicator to the panel.

Chapter 2, *Date and Time Configuration* (page 39) covers the configuration of the system date and time. Read this chapter if you need to change the date and time setup, or configure the system to synchronize the clock with a remote Network Time Protocol (NTP) server.

Chapter 3, *Managing Users and Groups* (page 44) covers the management of users and groups in a graphical user interface and on the command line. Read this chapter if you need to manage users and groups on your system, or enable password aging.

Part II, *Package Management* (page 69)

This part describes how to manage software packages on Fedora using both **Yum** and the **PackageKit** suite of graphical package management tools.

Chapter 4, *Yum* (page 70) describes the **Yum** package manager. Read this chapter for information how to search, install, update, and uninstall packages on the command line.

Chapter 5, *PackageKit* (page 91) describes the **PackageKit** suite of graphical package management tools. Read this chapter for information how to search, install, update, and uninstall packages using a graphical user interface.

Part III, *Networking* (page 103)

This part describes how to configure the network on Fedora.

Chapter 6, *Network Interfaces* (page 104) explores various interface configuration files, interface control scripts, and network function files located in the `/etc/sysconfig/network-scripts/` directory. Read this chapter for information how to use these files to configure network interfaces.

Part IV, *Infrastructure Services* (page 119)

This part provides information how to configure services and daemons, configure authentication, and enable remote logins.

Chapter 7, *Services and Daemons* (page 120) explains the concept of runlevels, and describes how to set the default one. It also covers the configuration of the services to be run in each of these runlevels, and provides information on how to start, stop, and restart a service. Read this chapter to learn how to manage services on your system.

Chapter 8, *Configuring Authentication* (page 125) describes how to configure user information retrieval from Lightweight Directory Access Protocol (LDAP), Network Information Service (NIS), and Winbind user account databases, and provides an introduction to the System Security Services Daemon (SSSD). Read this chapter if you need to configure authentication on your system.

Chapter 9, *OpenSSH* (page 168) describes how to enable a remote login via the SSH protocol. It covers the configuration of the `sshd` service, as well as a basic usage of the `ssh`, `scp`, `sftp` client utilities. Read this chapter if you need a remote access to a machine.

Part V, *Servers* (page 185)

This part discusses various topics related to servers such as how to set up a Web server or share files and directories over the network.

Chapter 10, *DHCP Servers* (page 186) guides you through the installation of a Dynamic Host Configuration Protocol (DHCP) server and client. Read this chapter if you need to configure DHCP on your system.

Chapter 11, *DNS Servers* (page 198) introduces you to Domain Name System (DNS), explains how to install, configure, run, and administer the **BIND** DNS server. Read this chapter if you need to configure a DNS server on your system.

Chapter 12, *Web Servers* (page 225) focuses on the **Apache HTTP Server 2.2**, a robust, full-featured open source web server developed by the Apache Software Foundation. Read this chapter if you need to configure a web server on your system.

Chapter 13, *Mail Servers* (page 272) reviews modern email protocols in use today, and some of the programs designed to send and receive email, including **Postfix**, **Sendmail**, **Fetchmail**, and **Procmail**. Read this chapter if you need to configure a mail server on your system.

Chapter 14, *Directory Servers* (page 302) covers the installation and configuration of **OpenLDAP 2.4**, an open source implementation of the LDAPv2 and LDAPv3 protocols. Read this chapter if you need to configure a directory server on your system.

Chapter 15, *File Servers* (page 317) guides you through the installation and configuration of **Samba**, an open source implementation of the Server Message Block (SMB) protocol, and **vsftpd**, the primary FTP server shipped with Fedora. Read this chapter if you need to configure a file server on your system.

Part VI, *Monitoring and Automation* (page 358)

This part describes various tools that allow system administrators to monitor system performance, automate system tasks, and report bugs.

Chapter 16, *System Monitoring Tools* (page 359) discusses applications and commands that can be used to retrieve important information about the system. Read this chapter to learn how to gather essential system information.

Chapter 17, *Viewing and Managing Log Files* (page 366) describes the configuration of the `rsyslog` daemon, and explains how to locate, view, and monitor log files. Read this chapter to learn how to work with log files.

Chapter 18, *Automating System Tasks*(page 388) provides an overview of the `cron`, `at`, and `batch` utilities. Read this chapter to learn how to use these utilities to perform automated tasks.

Chapter 19, *Automatic Bug-Reporting Tool (ABRT)* (page 397) concentrates on **ABRT**, a system service and a set of tools to collect crash data and send a report to the relevant issue tracker. Read this chapter to learn how to use **ABRT** on your system.

Part VII, *Kernel, Module and Driver Configuration* (page 412)

This part covers various tools that assist administrators with kernel customization.

Chapter 20, *Manually Upgrading the Kernel* (page 413) provides important information how to manually update a kernel package using the `rpm` command instead of `yum`. Read this chapter if you cannot update a kernel package with the **Yum** package manager.

Chapter 21, *Working with Kernel Modules* (page 422) explains how to display, query, load, and unload kernel modules and their dependencies, and how to set module parameters. Additionally, it covers specific kernel module capabilities such as using multiple Ethernet cards and using channel bonding. Read this chapter if you need to work with kernel modules.

Chapter 22, *The kdump Crash Recovery Service* (page 439) explains how to configure, test, and use the `kdump` service in Fedora, and provides a brief overview of how to analyze the resulting core dump using the **crash** debugging utility. Read this chapter to learn how to enable `kdump` on your system.

Appendix A, *RPM* (page 456)

This appendix concentrates on the RPM Package Manager (RPM), an open packaging system used by Fedora, and the use of the `rpm` utility. Read this appendix if you need to use `rpm` instead of `yum`.

Appendix B, *The sysconfig Directory* (page 470)

This appendix outlines some of the files and directories located in the `/etc/sysconfig/` directory. Read this appendix if you want to learn more about these files and directories, their function, and their contents.

Appendix C, *The proc File System* (page 488)

This appendix explains the concept of a virtual file system, and describes some of the top-level files and directories within the `proc` file system (that is, the `/proc/` directory). Read this appendix if you want to learn more about this file system.

3. Document Conventions

This manual uses several conventions to highlight certain words and phrases and draw attention to specific pieces of information.

In PDF and paper editions, this manual uses typefaces drawn from the *Liberation Fonts*[1] set. The Liberation Fonts set is also used in HTML editions if the set is installed on your system. If not, alternative but equivalent typefaces are displayed. Note: Red Hat Enterprise Linux 5 and later includes the Liberation Fonts set by default.

3.1. Typographic Conventions

Four typographic conventions are used to call attention to specific words and phrases. These conventions, and the circumstances they apply to, are as follows.

`Mono-spaced Bold`

Used to highlight system input, including shell commands, file names and paths. Also used to highlight key caps and key-combinations. For example:

> To see the contents of the file `my_next_bestselling_novel` in your current working directory, enter the `cat my_next_bestselling_novel` command at the shell prompt and press **Enter** to execute the command.

The above includes a file name, a shell command and a key cap, all presented in Mono-spaced Bold and all distinguishable thanks to context.

Key-combinations can be distinguished from key caps by the hyphen connecting each part of a key-combination. For example:

> Press **Enter** to execute the command.
>
> Press **Ctrl+Alt+F2** to switch to the first virtual terminal. Press **Ctrl+Alt+F1** to return to your X-Windows session.

The first sentence highlights the particular key cap to press. The second highlights two sets of three key caps, each set pressed simultaneously.

If source code is discussed, class names, methods, functions, variable names and returned values mentioned within a paragraph will be presented as above, in `Mono-spaced Bold`. For example:

> File-related classes include `filesystem` for file systems, `file` for files, and `dir` for directories. Each class has its own associated set of permissions.

Proportional Bold

This denotes words or phrases encountered on a system, including application names; dialogue box text; labelled buttons; check-box and radio button labels; menu titles and sub-menu titles. For example:

[1] *https://fedorahosted.org/liberation-fonts/*

> Choose **System > Preferences > Mouse** from the main menu bar to launch **Mouse Preferences**. In the **Buttons** tab, click the **Left-handed mouse** check box and click **Close** to switch the primary mouse button from the left to the right (making the mouse suitable for use in the left hand).
>
> To insert a special character into a **gedit** file, choose **Applications > Accessories > Character Map** from the main menu bar. Next, choose **Search > Find...** from the **Character Map** menu bar, type the name of the character in the **Search** field and click **Next**. The character you sought will be highlighted in the **Character Table**. Double-click this highlighted character to place it in the **Text to copy** field and then click the **Copy** button. Now switch back to your document and choose **Edit > Paste** from the **gedit** menu bar.

The above text includes application names; system-wide menu names and items; application-specific menu names; and buttons and text found within a GUI interface, all presented in Proportional Bold and all distinguishable by context.

Note the > shorthand used to indicate traversal through a menu and its sub-menus. This is to avoid the difficult-to-follow 'Select **Mouse** from the **Preferences** sub-menu in the **System** menu of the main menu bar' approach.

`Mono-spaced Bold Italic` or *`Proportional Bold Italic`*

Whether Mono-spaced Bold or Proportional Bold, the addition of Italics indicates replaceable or variable text. Italics denotes text you do not input literally or displayed text that changes depending on circumstance. For example:

> To connect to a remote machine using ssh, type `ssh` *`username@domain.name`* at a shell prompt. If the remote machine is `example.com` and your username on that machine is john, type `ssh john@example.com`.
>
> The `mount -o remount` *`file-system`* command remounts the named file system. For example, to remount the `/home` file system, the command is `mount -o remount /home`.
>
> To see the version of a currently installed package, use the `rpm -q` *`package`* command. It will return a result as follows: *`package-version-release`*.

Note the words in bold italics above — username, domain.name, file-system, package, version and release. Each word is a placeholder, either for text you enter when issuing a command or for text displayed by the system.

Aside from standard usage for presenting the title of a work, italics denotes the first use of a new and important term. For example:

> When the Apache HTTP Server accepts requests, it dispatches child processes or threads to handle them. This group of child processes or threads is known as a *server-pool*. Under

Apache HTTP Server 2.0, the responsibility for creating and maintaining these server-pools has been abstracted to a group of modules called *Multi-Processing Modules (MPMs)*. Unlike other modules, only one module from the MPM group can be loaded by the Apache HTTP Server.

3.2. Pull-quote Conventions

Two, commonly multi-line, data types are set off visually from the surrounding text.

Output sent to a terminal is set in `Mono-spaced Roman` and presented thus:

```
books        Desktop   documentation  drafts  mss    photos   stuff  svn
books_tests  Desktop1  downloads      images  notes  scripts  svgs
```

Source-code listings are also set in `Mono-spaced Roman` but are presented and highlighted as follows:

```
package org.jboss.book.jca.ex1;

import javax.naming.InitialContext;

public class ExClient
{
   public static void main(String args[])
       throws Exception
   {
      InitialContext iniCtx = new InitialContext();
      Object         ref    = iniCtx.lookup("EchoBean");
      EchoHome       home   = (EchoHome) ref;
      Echo           echo   = home.create();

      System.out.println("Created Echo");

      System.out.println("Echo.echo('Hello') = " + echo.echo("Hello"));
   }
}
```

3.3. Notes and Warnings

Finally, we use three visual styles to draw attention to information that might otherwise be overlooked.

Note

A note is a tip or shortcut or alternative approach to the task at hand. Ignoring a note should have no negative consequences, but you might miss out on a trick that makes your life easier.

Important

Important boxes detail things that are easily missed: configuration changes that only apply to the current session, or services that need restarting before an update will apply. Ignoring Important boxes will not cause data loss but may cause irritation and frustration.

Warning

A Warning should not be ignored. Ignoring warnings will most likely cause data loss.

4. Feedback

If you find a typographical error in this manual, or if you have thought of a way to make this manual better, we would love to hear from you! Please submit a report in *Bugzilla*[2] against the product **Fedora Documentation.**

When submitting a bug report, be sure to provide the following information:

- Manual's identifier: `deployment-guide`
- Version number: `15`

If you have a suggestion for improving the documentation, try to be as specific as possible when describing it. If you have found an error, please include the section number and some of the surrounding text so we can find it easily.

5. Acknowledgements

Certain portions of this text first appeared in the *Deployment Guide*, copyright © 2007 Red Hat, Inc., available at *http://docs.redhat.com/docs/en-US/Red_Hat_Enterprise_Linux/5/html/Deployment_Guide/index.html*

The authors of this book would like to thank the following people for their valuable contributions: Adam Tkáč, Andrew Fitzsimon, Andrius Benokraitis, Brian Cleary Edward Bailey, Garrett LeSage, Jeffrey Fearn, Joe Orton, Joshua Wulf, KarstenWade, Lucy Ringland, Marcela Mašláňová, Mark Johnson, Michael Behm, Michael Behm, Miroslav Lichvár, Radek Vokál, Rahul Kavalapara, Rahul Sundaram, Sandra Moore, Zbyšek Mráz and Jan Včelák, among many others.

[2] *http://bugzilla.redhat.com/*

Part I.
Basic System Configuration

This part covers basic system administration tasks such as keyboard configuration, date and time configuration, and managing users and groups.

Chapter 1.
Language and Keyboard Configuration

This chapter describes how to change the language of your desktop, configure the keyboard layout, and allow a user to switch between different keyboard layouts using the **Region and Language** configuration tool.

1.1. Changing the Language

To configure the language of your desktop, open the **System Settings** dialog window by selecting **Applications** → **System Tools** → **System Settings** from the **Activities** menu, click **Region and Language**, and select the **Language** tab. You will be presented with a list of available languages.

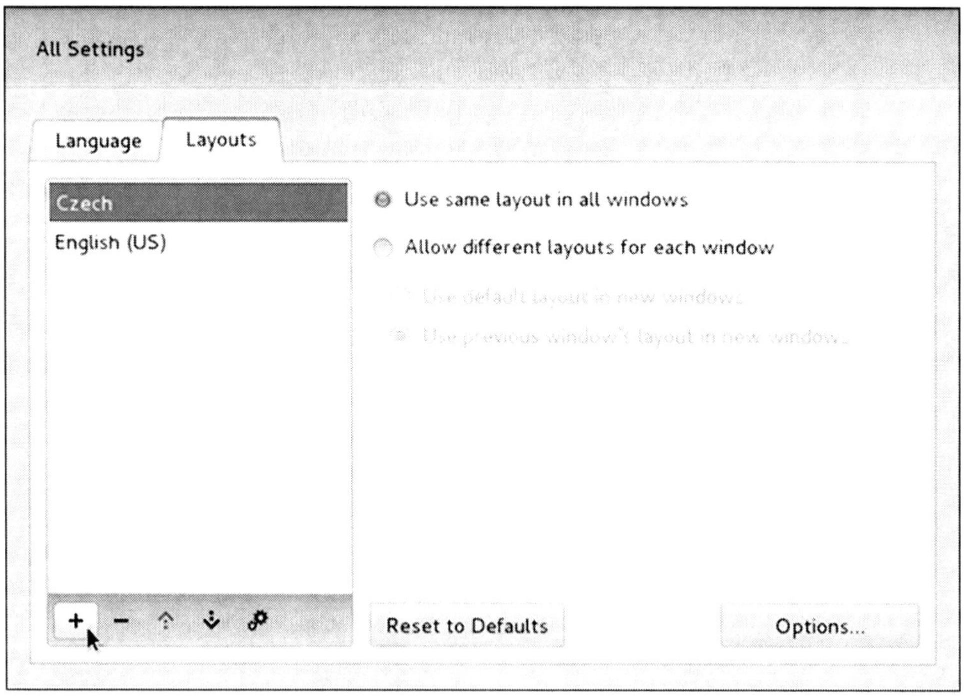

Figure 1.1. Changing the language

To choose a particular language, select it from the list and either close the window, or click the **All Settings** button in the upper-left corner of the window to return to the **System Settings** window. The changes will take effect the next time you log in to your system.

1.2. Changing the Keyboard Layout

Although the installation program allows a system administrator to configure a keyboard layout during the system installation, the default settings may not always suit your current needs. To add a new keyboard layout, open the **System Settings** window by selecting **Applications** → **System Tools** → **System Settings** from the **Activities** menu, click the **Region and Language** icon, and select the **Layouts** tab.

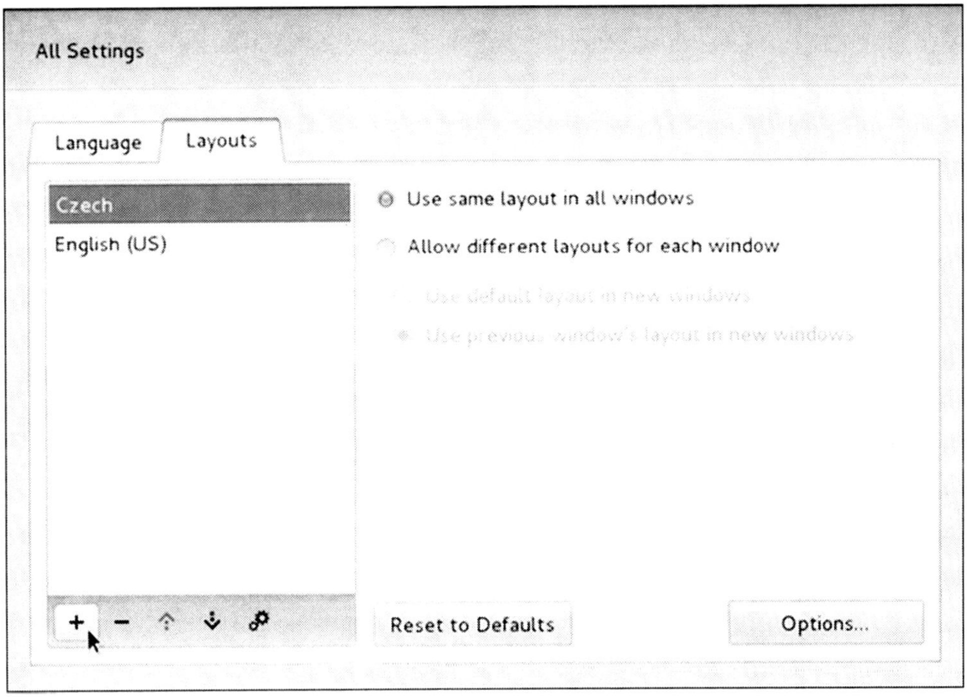

Figure 1.2. Changing the keyboard layout

The left part of the window provides a list of currently enabled layouts, while the right part allows you to choose whether to use the same keyboard layout for all windows, or if you prefer to use a different layout for each window.

To add a keyboard layout, click the + (that is, the plus sign) button below the list. A dialog box will appear, allowing you to select the desired layout. The input field in the bottom part of the dialog box allows you to reduce the number of displayed items by typing part of the layout name (such as "slov" for Slovak layouts) in it. Once you are done, click the **Add** button to confirm your choice.

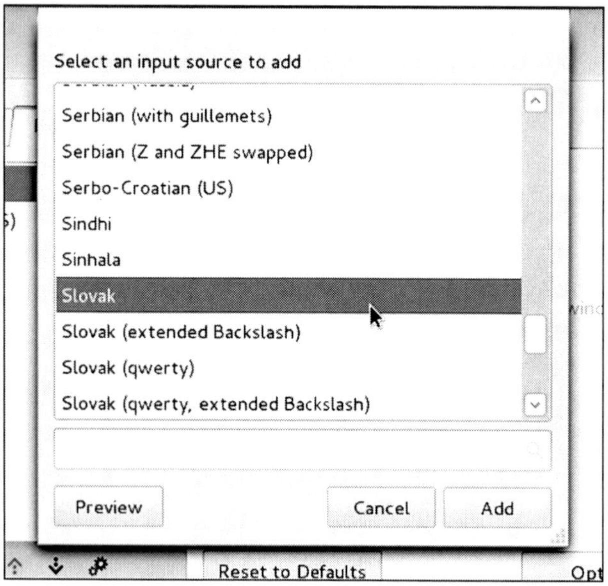

Figure 1.3. Adding a keyboard layout

To remove a keyboard layout, click the – (that is, the minus sign) button below the list.

When more than one layout is enabled, a keyboard indicator appears on the panel in order to allow you to switch between the layouts, and the first layout in the list is considered the default. To move a particular layout up or down in the list, select it from the list and click the ↑ (the upwards arrow) or ↓ (the downwards arrow) buttons respectively.

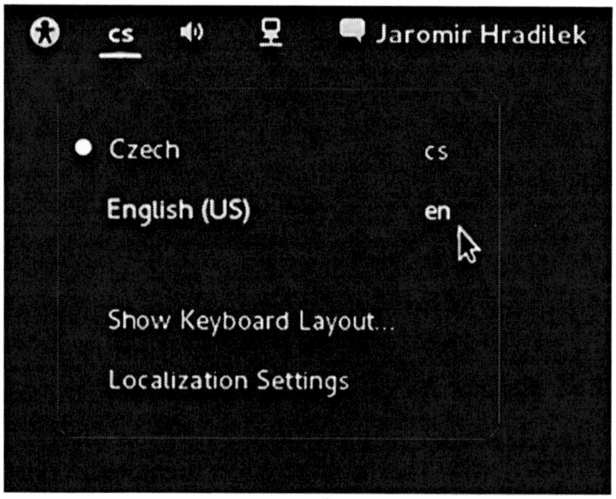

Figure 1.4. The keyboard layout indicator

The changes take effect immediately.

Chapter 2.

Date and Time Configuration

This chapter covers setting the system date and time in Fedora, both manually and using the Network Time Protocol (NTP), as well as setting the adequate time zone. Two methods are covered: setting the date and time using the **Date and Time** configuration tool, and doing so on the command line.

2.1. Date and Time Configuration Tool

The **Date and Time** configuration tool allows a user to change the system date and time, to configure the time zone used by the system, and to set up the Network Time Protocol daemon to synchronize the system clock with a time server.

To start the tool, select **Applications → System Tools → System Settings** from the **Activities** menu and click the **Date and Time** icon, or click the time in the panel and select **Date and Time Settings** from the drop-down menu.

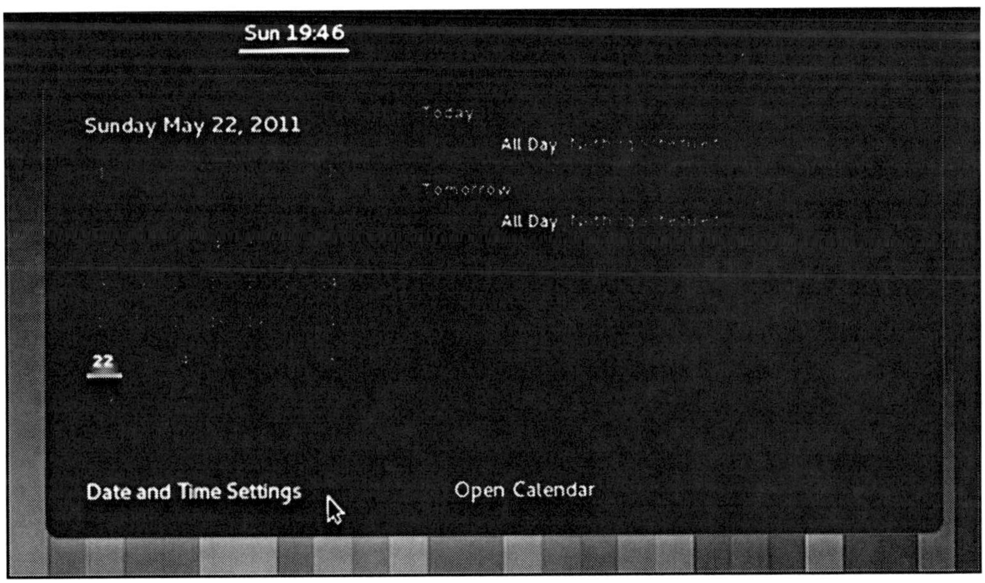

Figure 2.1. Running the Date and Time configuration tool

By default, the tool only allows you to review the current settings. This is because only `root` is allowed to set the system date and time. To unlock the configuration tool for changes, click the **Unlock** button in the bottom-left corner of the window, and provide the root password when prompted.

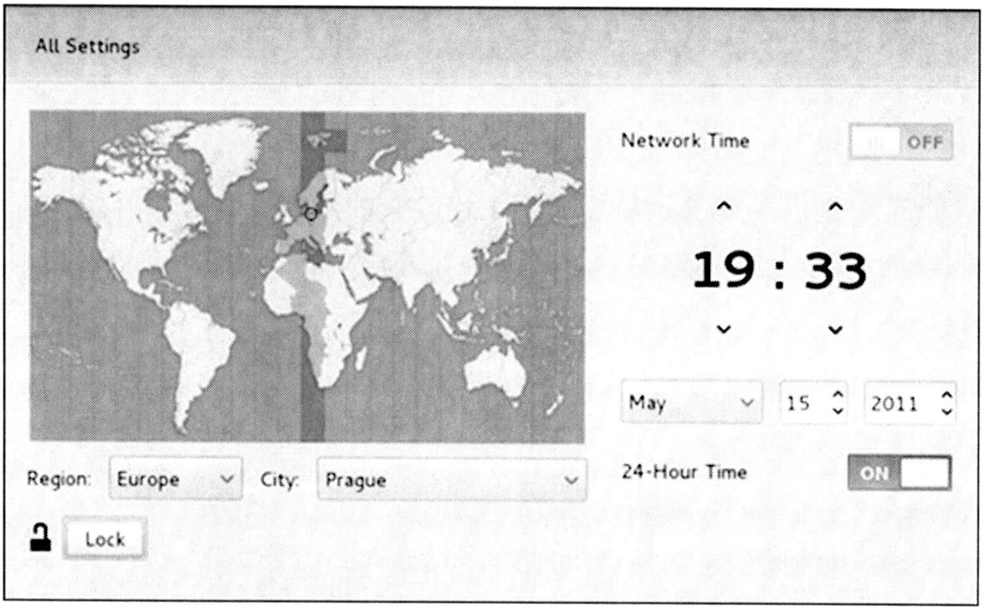

Figure 2.2. The Date and Time configuration tool

As you can see in *Figure 2.2. The Date and Time configuration tool* above, the main window of the **Date and Time** configuration tool is divided into two parts: while the left side of the window is dedicated to the time zone settings, the right part allows you to configure the date and time itself.

To change the time zone, click on the map, or select the region and city from the **Region** and **City** drop-down lists.

To change the current time of your system, either configure the system to synchronize it over the network by clicking the **Network Time** switch, or set it manually by clicking the up and down arrows above and below the numbers. Use the **24-Hour Time** switch to enable or disable the 24-hour time format.

To change the current date of your system, select a month from the drop-down list below the time, and use the up and down arrows to choose the day and year.

The changes take effect immediately.

2.2. Command Line Configuration

In case your system does not have the **Date/Time Properties** tool installed, or the *X Window Server* is not running, you can change the system date and time on the command line. Note that in order to perform actions described in this section, you have to be logged in as `root`. To do so, type the following at a shell prompt:

```
su -
```

2.2.1. Configuring the Date and Time

The `date` command allows the superuser to set the system date and time manually:

1. To change the current date, type the command in the following form at a shell prompt, replacing the *YYYY* with a four-digit year, *MM* with a two-digit month, and *DD* with a two-digit day of the month:

   ```
   date +%D -s YYYY-MM-DD
   ```

   For example, to set the date to 2 June 2010, type:

   ```
   ~]# date +%D -s 2010-06-02
   ```

2. To change the current date, use the following command, where *HH* stands for an hour, *MM* is a minute, and *SS* is a second, all typed in a two-digit form:

   ```
   date +%T -s HH:MM:SS
   ```

   If your system clock is set to use UTC (Coordinated Universal Time), add the following option:

   ```
   date +%T -s HH:MM:SS -u
   ```

   For instance, to set the system clock to 11:26 PM using the UTC, type:

   ```
   ~]# date +%T -s 23:26:00 -u
   ```

You can check your current settings by typing `date` without any additional argument, for example:

```
~]$ date
Wed Jun  2 11:58:48 CEST 2010
```

2.2.2. Configuring the Network Time Protocol

As opposed to the manual setup described above, you can also synchronize the system clock with a remote server over the Network Time Protocol (NTP). For the one-time synchronization only, use the **ntpdate** command:

1. Check whether the selected NTP server is accessible by using the `ntpdate` command in the following form:

   ```
   ntpdate -q server_address
   ```

For example, to connect to `0.fedora.pool.ntp.org`, type:

```
~]# ntpdate -q 0.fedora.pool.ntp.org
server 204.15.208.61, stratum 2, offset -39.275438, delay 0.16083
server 69.65.40.29, stratum 2, offset -39.269122, delay 0.17191
server 148.167.132.201, stratum 2, offset -39.270239, delay 0.20482
23 May 01:05:54 ntpdate[10619]: step time server 204.15.208.61 offset -
39.275438 sec
```

2. When you find a satisfactory server, run the **ntpdate** command followed with one or more server addresses:

   ```
   ntpdate server_address...
   ```

   For instance:

   ```
   ~]# ntpdate 0.fedora.pool.ntp.org 1.fedora.pool.ntp.org
   23 May 01:07:13 ntpdate[10669]: step time server 204.15.208.61 offset -
   39.275436 sec
   ```

   Unless an error message is displayed, the system time should now be set. You can check the current by setting typing `date` without any additional arguments as shown in Section 2.2.1, *Configuring the Date and Time* (page 41).

3. In most cases, these steps are sufficient. Only if you really need one or more system services to always use the correct time, enable running the **ntpdate** at boot time:

   ```
   systemctl enable ntpdate.service
   ```

   For more information about system services and their setup, refer to Chapter 7, *Services and Daemons* (page 120).

Note

If the synchronization with the time server at boot time keeps failing, that is, you find a relevant error message in the `/var/log/boot.log` system log, try to add the following line to `/etc/sysconfig/network`:

```
NETWORKWAIT=1
```

However, the more convenient way is to set the `ntpd` daemon to synchronize the time at boot time automatically:

1. Open the NTP configuration file `/etc/ntp.conf` in a text editor, creating a new one if it does not already exist.
2. Add or edit the list of public NTP servers. If you are using Fedora 15, the file should already contain the following lines, but feel free to change or expand these according to your needs:

   ```
   server 0.fedora.pool.ntp.org iburst
   server 1.fedora.pool.ntp.org iburst
   server 2.fedora.pool.ntp.org iburst
   ```

Speeding up initial synchronization

To speed the initial synchronization up, it is recommended that the `iburst` directive is added at the end of each server line.

3. In the same file, set the proper permissions, giving the unrestricted access to localhost only:

```
restrict default kod nomodify notrap nopeer noquery
restrict -6 default kod nomodify notrap nopeer noquery
restrict 127.0.0.1
restrict -6 ::1
```

4. Save the changes, exit the editor, and restart the NTP daemon:

```
systemctl restart ntpd.service
```

5. Additionally, make sure that `ntpd` daemon is started at boot time:

```
systemctl enable ntpd.service
```

2.3. Additional Resources

For more information about the date and time configuration, refer to the following resources.

2.3.1. Additional Resources

- `date`(1) — The manual page for the **date** utility.
- `ntpdate`(8) — The manual page for the **ntpdate** utility.
- `ntpd`(8) — The manual page for the `ntpd` service.

Chapter 3.

Managing Users and Groups

The control of *users* and *groups* is a core element of Fedora system administration. Users can be either people (meaning accounts tied to physical users) or accounts which exist for specific applications to use. Groups are logical expressions of organization, tying users together for a common purpose. Users within a group can read, write, or execute files owned by that group.

Each user is associated with a unique numerical identification number called a *userid* (*UID*); likewise, each group is associated with a *groupid* (*GID*).

A user who creates a file is also the owner and group owner of that file. The file is assigned separate read, write, and execute permissions for the owner, the group, and everyone else. The file owner can be changed only by the `root` user, and access permissions can be changed by both the `root` user and file owner.

Fedora also supports *access control lists* (*ACLs*) for files and directories which allow permissions for specific users outside of the owner to be set. For more information about ACLs, refer to the *Access Control Lists* chapter of the Fedora *Storage Administration Guide*.

3.1. User Accounts Tool

The **User Accounts** configuration tool allows you to view, modify, add, and delete local users. To run the utility, either select **Applications** → **System Tools** → **System Settings** from the **Activities** menu and click the **User Accounts** icon, or click your name on the panel and choose **My Account** from the drop-down menu.

The main window of the **User Accounts** configuration tool is divided into two parts: The left side of the window contains a list of available user accounts. The right side provides details on a particular account.

By default, the tool only allows you to change certain settings regarding your account. This is because only `root` is allowed to configure users and groups. To unlock the configuration tool for all kinds of changes, click the **Unlock** button in the bottom-left corner of the window, and provide the root password when prompted.

Figure 3.1. The User Accounts configuration tool

3.1.1. Configuring an Account

To change the image associated with an account, click the icon next to the account name and either select a picture from the drop-down list, or click **Browse for more pictures...** to use an image from your local drive.

To change the name associated with an account, click the name next to the icon to edit it.

To change the account type, use the **Account type** drop-down list. However, this change requires the configuration tool to be unlocked even if it is your account.

To change the default language for an account, click the button next to the **Language** label, and select the desired language from the list.

To change the password, click the button next to the **Password** label. A dialog box will appear, allowing you to set the new password. Note that the current password must be provided in order to confirm the change. Once done, click the **Change** button to save the change.

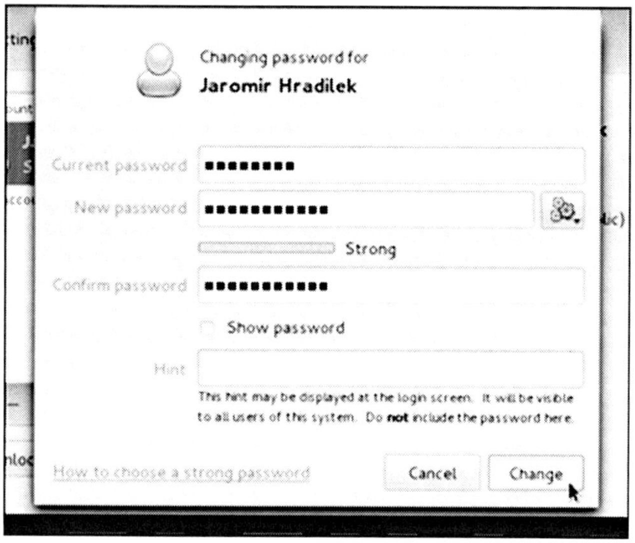

Figure 3.2. Changing the password

Password security advice

It is advisable to use a much longer password, as this makes it more difficult for an intruder to guess it and access the account without permission. It is also recommended that the password not be based on a dictionary term: use a combination of letters, numbers and special characters.

Finally, to set up automatic login for a particular account, enable the **Automatic Login** switch. The configuration tool must be unlocked to make this change.

3.1.2. Adding a New User

To add a new user, make sure the configuration tool is unlocked, and click the **+** button (that is, the plus sign) below the account list. A dialog box as shown in *Figure 3.3. Creating a new account* below will appear.

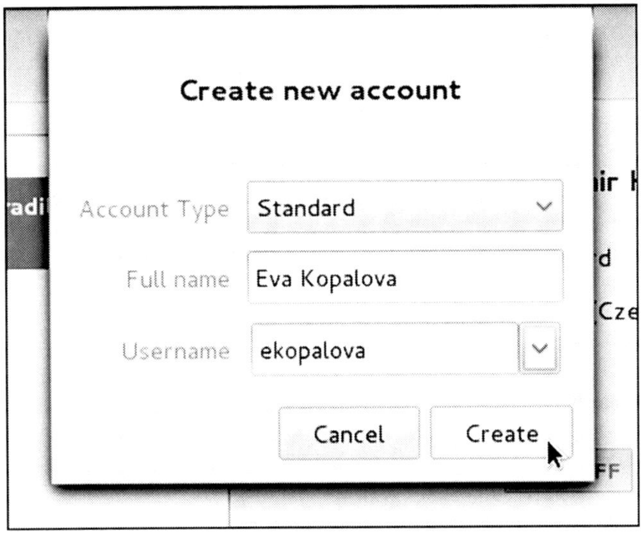

Figure 3.3. Creating a new account

Take the followign steps to create an account:

1. Select an account type from the **Account type** drop-down list. Available account types are `Administrator` and `Standard` (the default option).
2. Fill in the **Full name** input field to set the name associated with the account. This name will be used by the login manager, and will be displayed on the panel.
3. Either select a suggested username from the **Username** drop-down list, or fill in the corresponding input field.
4. Click the **Create** button to confirm the settings.

Fedora uses a *user private group* (UPG) scheme. The UPG scheme does not add or change anything in the standard UNIX way of handling groups; it offers a new convention. Whenever you create a new user, a unique group with the same name as the user is created.

When a new account is created, default configuration files are copied from the `/etc/skel/` directory into the new home directory.

3.1.3. Removing a User

To remove a user, make sure the configuration tool is unlocked, select the desired account from the account list, and click the – button (that is, the minus sign) below the account list. A dialog box as shown in *Figure 3.4. Removing an account* below will appear.

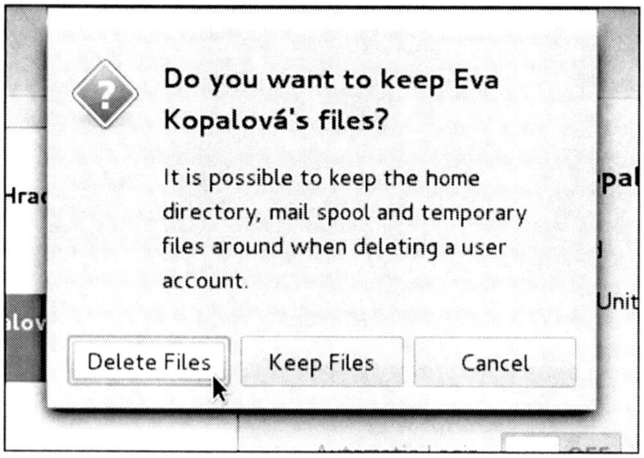

Figure 3.4. Removing an account

To delete files and directories that belong to the user (that is, the home directory, mail spool, and temporary files), click the **Delete Files** button. To keep these files intact and only delete the user account, click **Keep Files**. To abort the deletion, click **Cancel**.

3.2. User Manager Tool

The **User Manager** allows you to view, modify, add, and delete local users and groups.

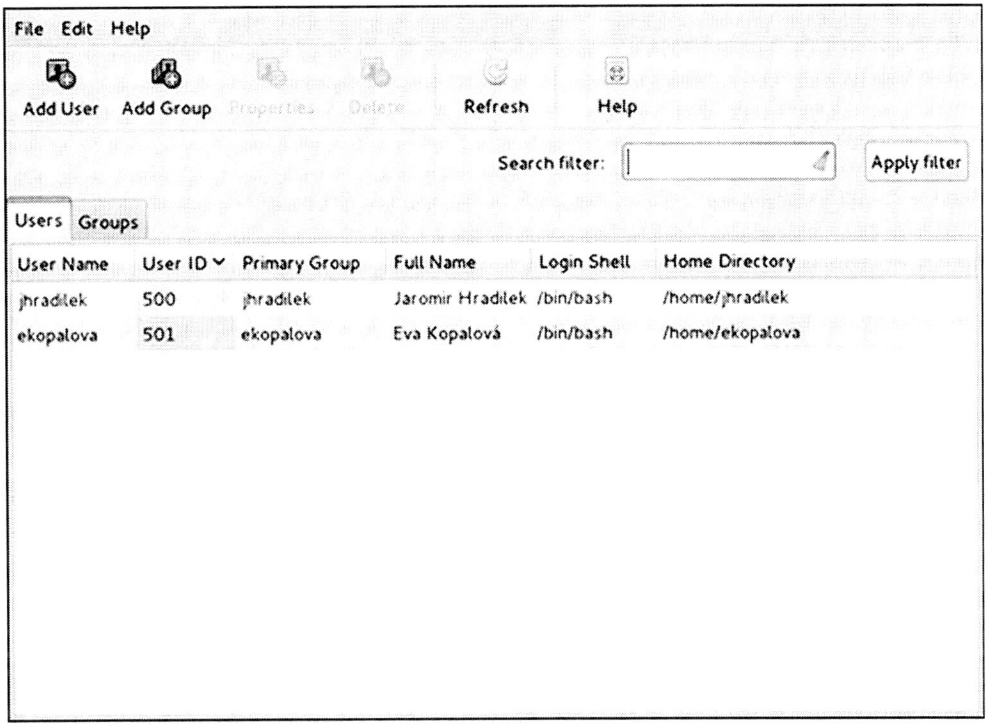

Figure 3.5. The GNOME User Manager

You can start the **User Manager** by clicking **Applications → Other → Users and Groups** from the **Activities** menu. Alternatively, you can enter `system-config-users` at the shell prompt to open the **User Manager**. Viewing and modifying user and group information requires superuser privileges. If you are not the superuser when you open the **User Manager**, it will prompt you for the superuser password.

To view a list of local users on the system, click the **Users** tab. To view a list of local groups on the system, click the **Groups** tab.

To find a specific user or group, type the first few letters of the name in the **Search filter** field. Press **Enter** or click the **Apply filter** button. The filtered list is displayed.

To sort the users, click on the column User Name and for groups click on Group Name. The users or groups are sorted according to the value of that column.

Fedora reserves user IDs below 500 for system users. By default, the **User Manager** does not display system users. To view all users, including the system users, go to **Edit → Preferences** and uncheck **Hide system users and groups** from the dialog box.

3.2.1. Adding a New User

To add a new user, click the **Add User** button. A window as shown in *Figure 3.6. Creating a new user* below appears. Type the username and full name for the new user in the appropriate fields. Type the user's password in the **Password** and **Confirm Password** fields. The password must be at least six characters.

Password security advice

It is advisable to use a much longer password, as this makes it more difficult for an intruder to guess it and access the account without permission. It is also recommended that the password not be based on a dictionary term: use a combination of letters, numbers and special characters.

Select a login shell from the pulldown list. If you are not sure which shell to select, accept the default value of `/bin/bash`. The default home directory is `/home/`*`username`*`/`. You can change the home directory that is created for the user, or you can choose not to create the home directory by unselecting **Create home directory**.

If you select to create the home directory, default configuration files are copied from the `/etc/skel/` directory into the new home directory.

Fedora uses a *user private group* (UPG) scheme. The UPG scheme does not add or change anything in the standard UNIX way of handling groups; it offers a new convention. Whenever you create a new user, by default, a unique group with the same name as the user is created. If you do not want to create this group, unselect **Create a private group for the user**.

To specify a user ID for the user, select **Specify user ID manually**. If the option is not selected, the next available user ID above 500 is assigned to the new user. Because Fedora reserves user IDs below 500 for system users, it is not advisable to manually assign user IDs 1-499.

Click **OK** to create the user.

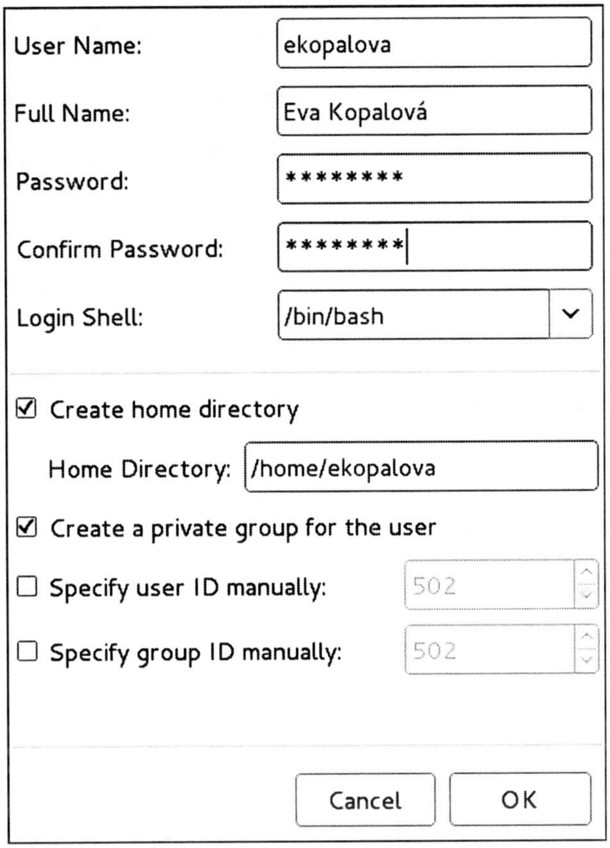

Figure 3.6. Creating a new user

To configure more advanced user properties, such as password expiration, modify the user's properties after adding the user.

Modifying User Properties

To view the properties of an existing user, click on the **Users** tab, select the user from the user list, and click **Properties** from the menu (or choose **File** → **Properties** from the pulldown menu). A window similar to *Figure 3.7. User Properties* below appears.

Figure 3.7. User Properties

The **User Properties** window is divided into multiple tabbed pages:

- **User Data** — Shows the basic user information configured when you added the user. Use this tab to change the user's full name, password, home directory, or login shell.
- **Account Info** — Select **Enable account expiration** if you want the account to expire on a certain date. Enter the date in the provided fields. Select **Local password is locked** to lock the user account and prevent the user from logging into the system.
- **Password Info** — Displays the date that the user's password last changed. To force the user to change passwords after a certain number of days, select **Enable password expiration** and enter a desired value in the **Days before change required:** field. The number of days before the user's password expires, the number of days before the user is warned to change passwords, and days before the account becomes inactive can also be changed.
- **Groups** — Allows you to view and configure the Primary Group of the user, as well as other groups that you want the user to be a member of.

3.2.2. Adding a New Group

To add a new user group, select **Add Group** from the toolbar. A window similar to *Figure 3.8. New Group* below appears. Type the name of the new group. To specify a group ID for the new group, select **Specify group ID manually** and select the GID. Note that Fedora also reserves group IDs lower than 500 for system groups.

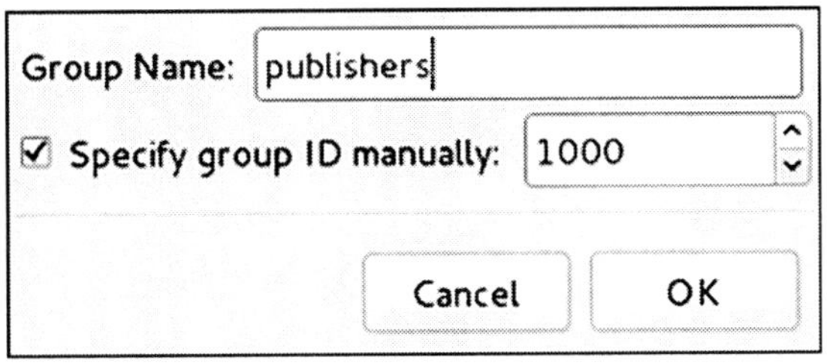

Figure 3.8. New Group

Click **OK** to create the group. The new group appears in the group list.

3.2.3. Modifying Group Properties

To view the properties of an existing group, select the group from the group list and click **Properties** from the menu (or choose **File** → **Properties** from the pulldown menu). A window similar to *Figure 3.9. Group Properties* below appears.

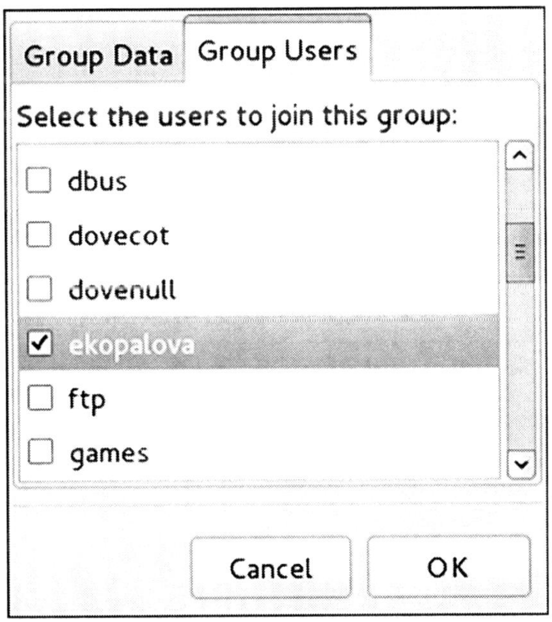

Figure 3.9. Group Properties

The **Group Users** tab displays which users are members of the group. Use this tab to add or remove users from the group. Click **OK** to save your changes.

3.3. User and Group Management Tools

Managing users and groups can be tiresome; this is why Fedora provides tools and conventions to make this task easier to manage.

The easiest way to manage users and groups is through the graphical application, **User Manager** (`system-config-users`). For more information on **User Manager**, refer to Section 3.2, *User Manager Tool* (page 49).

The following command line tools can also be used to manage users and groups:

- `useradd`, `usermod`, and `userdel` — Industry-standard methods of adding, deleting and modifying user accounts
- `groupadd`, `groupmod`, and `groupdel` — Industry-standard methods of adding, deleting, and modifying user groups
- `gpasswd` — Industry-standard method of administering the `/etc/group` file
- `pwck`, `grpck` — Tools used for the verification of the password, group, and associated shadow files
- `pwconv`, `pwunconv` — Tools used for the conversion of passwords to shadow passwords and back to standard passwords

3.3.1. Command Line Configuration

If you prefer command line tools or do not have the X Window System installed, use following to configure users and groups.

Adding a User

To add a user to the system:

1. Issue the `useradd` command to create a locked user account:
   `useradd` *`username`*
2. Unlock the account by issuing the `passwd` command to assign a password and set password aging guidelines:
   `passwd` *`username`*

Command line options for `useradd` are detailed in *Table 3.1. `useradd` Command Line Options* below.

Option	Description
-c '*comment*'	*comment* can be replaced with any string. This option is generally used to specify the full name of a user.
-d *home_directory*	Home directory to be used instead of default /home/*username*/.
-e *date*	Date for the account to be disabled in the format YYYY-MM-DD.
-f *days*	Number of days after the password expires until the account is disabled. If 0 is specified, the account is disabled immediately after the password expires. If -1 is specified, the account is not be disabled after the password expires.
-g *group_name*	Group name or group number for the user's default group. The group must exist prior to being specified here.
-G *group_list*	List of additional (other than default) group names or group numbers, separated by commas, of which the user is a member. The groups must exist prior to being specified here.
-m	Create the home directory if it does not exist.
-M	Do not create the home directory.
-N	Do not create a user private group for the user.
-p *password*	The password encrypted with crypt.
-r	Create a system account with a UID less than 500 and without a home directory.
-s	User's login shell, which defaults to /bin/bash.
-u *uid*	User ID for the user, which must be unique and greater than 499.

Table 3.1. useradd Command Line Options

Adding a Group

To add a group to the system, use the command groupadd:

```
groupadd group_name
```

Command line options for groupadd are detailed in *Table 3.2. groupadd Command Line Options* below.

Option	Description
-f, --force	When used with -g *gid* and *gid* already exists, groupadd will choose another unique *gid* for the group.
-g *gid*	Group ID for the group, which must be unique and greater than 499.
-K, --key *key*=*value*	Override /etc/login.defs defaults.

Option	Description
`-o`, `--non-unique`	Allow to create groups with duplicate.
`-p`, `--password` *`password`*	Use this encrypted password for the new group.
`-r`	Create a system group with a GID less than 500.

Table 3.2. `groupadd` Command Line Options

Password Aging

For security reasons, it is advisable to require users to change their passwords periodically. This can be done when adding or editing a user on the **Password Info** tab of the **User Manager**.

To configure password expiration for a user from a shell prompt, use the `chage` command with an option from *Table 3.3. `chage` Command Line Options* below, followed by the username.

> **Shadow passwords must be enabled to use chage**
>
> Shadow passwords must be enabled to use the `chage` command. For more information, see Section 3.7, *Shadow Passwords* (page 66).

Option	Description
`-d` *`days`*	Specifies the number of days since January 1, 1970 the password was changed.
`-E` *`date`*	Specifies the date on which the account is locked, in the format YYYY-MM-DD. Instead of the date, the number of days since January 1, 1970 can also be used.
`-I` *`days`*	Specifies the number of inactive days after the password expiration before locking the account. If the value is `0`, the account is not locked after the password expires.
`-l`	Lists current account aging settings.
`-m` *`days`*	Specify the minimum number of days after which the user must change passwords. If the value is `0`, the password does not expire.
`-M` *`days`*	Specify the maximum number of days for which the password is valid. When the number of days specified by this option plus the number of days specified with the `-d` option is less than the current day, the user must change passwords before using the account.
`-W` *`days`*	Specifies the number of days before the password expiration date to warn the user.

Table 3.3. `chage` Command Line Options

chage interactivity

If the `chage` command is followed directly by a username (with no options), it displays the current password aging values and allows them to be changed interactively.

You can configure a password to expire the first time a user logs in. This forces users to change passwords immediately.

1. *Set up an initial password* — There are two common approaches to this step: the administrator can assign a default password, or he can use a null password.

   To assign a default password, type the following at a shell prompt:

   ```
   passwd username
   ```

   To assign a null password instead, use the following command:

   ```
   passwd -d username
   ```

Avoid using null passwords whenever possible

Using a null password, while convenient, is a highly insecure practice, as any third party can log in first and access the system using the insecure username. Always make sure that the user is ready to log in before unlocking an account with a null password.

2. *Force immediate password expiration* — Type the following command:

   ```
   chage -d 0 username
   ```

   This command sets the value for the date the password was last changed to the epoch (January 1, 1970). This value forces immediate password expiration no matter what password aging policy, if any, is in place.

Upon the initial log in, the user is now prompted for a new password.

3.3.2. Explaining the Process

The following steps illustrate what happens if the command `useradd juan` is issued on a system that has shadow passwords enabled:

1. A new line for `juan` is created in `/etc/passwd`:

   ```
   juan:x:501:501::/home/juan:/bin/bash
   ```

   The line has the following characteristics:

   - It begins with the username `juan`.
   - There is an `x` for the password field indicating that the system is using shadow passwords.

    - A UID greater than 499 is created. Under Fedora, UIDs and GIDs below 500 are reserved for system use. These should not be assigned to users.
    - A GID greater than 499 is created.
    - The optional GECOS information is left blank.
    - The home directory for `juan` is set to `/home/juan/`.
    - The default shell is set to `/bin/bash`.

2. A new line for `juan` is created in `/etc/shadow`:

   ```
   juan:!!:14798:0:99999:7:::
   ```

   The line has the following characteristics:

    - It begins with the username `juan`.
    - Two exclamation marks (`!!`) appear in the password field of the `/etc/shadow` file, which locks the account.

   Note

   If an encrypted password is passed using the `-p` flag, it is placed in the `/etc/shadow` file on the new line for the user.

    - The password is set to never expire.

3. A new line for a group named `juan` is created in `/etc/group`:

   ```
   juan:x:501:
   ```

   A group with the same name as a user is called a *user private group*. For more information on user private groups, refer to Section 3.2.1, *Adding a New User* (page 50).

   The line created in `/etc/group` has the following characteristics:

    - It begins with the group name `juan`.
    - An `x` appears in the password field indicating that the system is using shadow group passwords.
    - The GID matches the one listed for user `juan` in `/etc/passwd`.

4. A new line for a group named `juan` is created in `/etc/gshadow`:

   ```
   juan:!::
   ```

   The line has the following characteristics:

    - It begins with the group name `juan`.
    - An exclamation mark (`!`) appears in the password field of the `/etc/gshadow` file, which locks the group.
    - All other fields are blank.

5. A directory for user `juan` is created in the `/home/` directory:

   ```
   ~]# ls -l /home
   total 4
   drwx------. 4 juan juan 4096 Mar  3 18:23 juan
   ```

   This directory is owned by user `juan` and group `juan`. It has *read*, *write*, and *execute* privileges *only* for the user `juan`. All other permissions are denied.

6. The files within the `/etc/skel/` directory (which contain default user settings) are copied into the new `/home/juan/` directory:

   ```
   ~]# ls -la /home/juan
   total 28
   drwx------. 4 juan juan 4096 Mar  3 18:23 .
   drwxr-xr-x. 5 root root 4096 Mar  3 18:23 ..
   -rw-r--r--. 1 juan juan   18 Jun 22  2010 .bash_logout
   -rw-r--r--. 1 juan juan  176 Jun 22  2010 .bash_profile
   -rw-r--r--. 1 juan juan  124 Jun 22  2010 .bashrc
   drwxr-xr-x. 2 juan juan 4096 Jul 14  2010 .gnome2
   drwxr-xr-x. 4 juan juan 4096 Nov 23 15:09 .mozilla
   ```

At this point, a locked account called `juan` exists on the system. To activate it, the administrator must next assign a password to the account using the `passwd` command and, optionally, set password aging guidelines.

3.4. Standard Users

Table 3.4. Standard Users below lists the standard users configured in the `/etc/passwd` file by an **Everything** installation. The group ID (GID) in this table is the *primary group* for the user. See Section 3.5, *Standard Groups* (page 63) for a listing of standard groups.

User	UID	GID	Home Directory	Shell	Packages
root	0	0	/root	/bin/bash	setup
bin	1	1	/bin	/sbin/nologin	setup
daemon	2	2	/sbin	/sbin/nologin	setup
sys	–	3	–	–	setup
adm	3	4	/var/adm	/bin/bash	setup
tty	–	5	–	–	setup
disk	–	6	–	–	setup
lp	4	7	/var/spool/lpd	/sbin/nologin	setup
mem	–	8	–	–	setup
kmem	–	9	–	–	setup
wheel	–	10	–	–	setup
cdrom	–	11	–	–	udev, MAKEDEV

User	UID	GID	Home Directory	Shell	Packages
sync	5	(0)	/sbin	/bin/sync	setup
shutdown	6	(0)	/sbin	/sbin/shutdown	setup
halt	7	(0)	/sbin	/sbin/halt	setup
mail	8	12	/var/spool/mail	/sbin/nologin	setup
news	9	13	/var/spool/news	/sbin/nologin	setup
uucp	10	14	/var/spool/uucp	/sbin/nologin	setup
operator	11	(0)	/root	/sbin/nologin	setup
games	12	(100)	/usr/games	/sbin/nologin	setup
gopher	13	30	/usr/lib/gopher-data	/sbin/nologin	setup
ftp	14	50	/var/ftp	/sbin/nologin	setup
man	–	15	–	–	setup
oprofile	16	16	/home/oprofile	/sbin/nologin	oprofile
pkiuser	17	17	/usr/share/pki	/sbin/nologin	pki-ca, rhpki-ca
dialout	–	18	–	–	udev, MAKEDEV
floppy	–	19	–	–	dev, MAKEDEV
games	–	20	–	–	setup
slocate	–	21	–	–	slocate
utmp	–	22	–	–	initscripts, libutempter
squid	23	23	/var/spool/squid	/dev/null	squid
pvm	24	24	/usr/share/pvm3	/bin/bash	pvm
named	25	25	/var/named	/bin/false	bind
postgres	26	26	/var/lib/pgsql	/bin/bash	postgresql-server
mysql	27	27	/var/lib/mysql	/bin/bash	mysql
nscd	28	28	/	/bin/false	nscd
rpcuser	29	29	/var/lib/nfs	/bin/false	nfs-utils
console	–	31	–	–	dev
rpc	32	32	/	/bin/false	portmap
amanda	33	(6)	/var/lib/amanda	/bin/false	amanda
tape	–	33	–	–	udev, MAKEDEV
netdump	34	34	/var/crash	/bin/bash	netdump-client, netdump-server
utempter	–	35	–	–	libutempter

User	UID	GID	Home Directory	Shell	Packages
vdsm	36	–	/	/bin/bash	kvm, vdsm
kvm	–	36	–	–	kvm, vdsm, libvirt
rpm	37	37	/var/lib/rpm	/bin/bash	rpm
ntp	38	38	/etc/ntp	/sbin/nologin	ntp
video	–	39	–	–	setup
dip	–	40	–	–	setup
mailman	41	41	/var/mailman	/bin/false	mailman
gdm	42	42	/var/gdm	/bin/bash	gdm
xfs	43	43	/etc/X11/fs	/bin/false	XFree86-xfs
pppusers	–	44	–	–	linuxconf
popusers	–	45	–	–	linuxconf
slipusers	–	46	–	–	linuxconf
mailnull	47	47	/var/spool/mqueue	/dev/null	sendmail
apache	48	48	/var/www	/bin/false	apache
wnn	49	49	/home/wnn	/bin/bash	FreeWnn
smmsp	51	51	/var/spool/mqueue	/dev/null	sendmail
puppet	52	52	/var/lib/puppet	/sbin/nologin	puppet
tomcat	53	53	/var/lib/tomcat	/sbin/nologin	tomcat
lock	–	54	–	–	lockdev
ldap	55	55	/var/lib/ldap	/bin/false	openldap-servers
frontpage	56	56	/var/www	/bin/false	mod_frontpage
nut	57	57	/var/lib/ups	/bin/false	nut
beagleindex	58	58	/var/cache/beagle	/bin/false	beagle
tss	59	59	–	/sbin/nologin	trousers
piranha	60	60	/etc/sysconfig/ha	/dev/null	piranha
prelude-manager	61	61	–	/sbin/nologin	prelude-manager
snortd	62	62	–	/sbin/nologin	snortd
audio	–	63	–	–	setup
condor	64	64	/var/lib/condor	/sbin/nologin	condord
nslcd	65	(55)	/	/sbin/nologin	nslcd
wine	–	66	–	–	wine
pegasus	66	65	/var/lib/Pegasus	/sbin/nologin	tog-pegasus

User	UID	GID	Home Directory	Shell	Packages
webalizer	67	67	/var/www/html/usage	/sbin/nologin	webalizer
haldaemon	68	68	/	/sbin/nologin	hal
vcsa	69	69	–	/sbin/nologin	dev, MAKEDEV
avahi	70	70	/var/run/avahi-daemon	/sbin/nologin	avahi
realtime	–	71	–	–	–
tcpdump	72	72	/	/sbin/nologin	tcpdump
privoxy	73	73	/etc/privoxy	/bin/bash	privoxy
sshd	74	74	/var/empty/sshd	/sbin/nologin	openssh-server
radvd	75	75	/	/bin/false	radvd
cyrus	76	(12)	/var/imap	/bin/bash	cyrus-imapd
saslauth	–	76	–	–	cyrus-imapd
arpwatch	77	77	/var/lib/arpwatch	/sbin/nologin	arpwatch
fax	78	78	/var/spool/fax	/sbin/nologin	mgetty
nocpulse	79	79	/etc/sysconfig/nocpulse	/bin/bash	nocpulse
desktop	80	80	–	/sbin/nologin	desktop-file-utils
dbus	81	81	/	/sbin/nologin	dbus
jonas	82	82	/var/lib/jonas	/sbin/nologin	jonas
clamav	83	83	/tmp	/sbin/nologin	clamav
screen	–	84	–	–	screen
quaggavt	–	85	–	–	quagga
sabayon	86	86	–	/sbin/nologin	sabayon
polkituser	87	87	/	/sbin/nologin	PolicyKit
wbpriv	–	88	–	–	samba-common
postfix	89	89	/var/spool/postfix	/bin/true	postfix
postdrop	–	90	–	–	postfix
majordomo	91	91	/usr/lib/majordomo	/bin/bash	majordomo
quagga	92	92	/	/sbin/nologin	quagga
exim	93	93	/var/spool/exim	/sbin/nologin	exim
distcache	94	94	/	/sbin/nologin	distcache
radiusd	95	95	/	/bin/false	freeradius
hsqldb	96	96	/var/lib/hsqldb	/sbin/nologin	hsqldb
dovecot	97	97	/usr/libexec/dovecot	/sbin/nologin	dovecot
ident	98	98	/	/sbin/nologin	ident

User	UID	GID	Home Directory	Shell	Packages
nobody	99	99	/	/sbin/nologin	setup
users	–	100	–	–	setup
qemu	107	107	/	/sbin/nologin	libvirt
ovirt	108	108	/	/sbin/nologin	libvirt
saned	111	111	/	/sbin/nologin	sane-backends
vhostmd	112	112	/usr/share/vhostmd	/sbin/nologin	vhostmd
usbmuxd	113	113	/	/sbin/nologin	usbmuxd
bacula	133	133	/var/spool/bacula	/sbin/nologin	bacula
ricci	140	140	/var/lib/ricci	/sbin/nologin	ricci
luci	141	141	/var/lib/luci	/sbin/nologin	luci
stap-server	155	155	/var/lib/stap-server	/sbin/nologin	systemtap
avahi-autoipd	170	170	/var/lib/avahi-autoipd	/sbin/nologin	avahi
pulse	171	171	/var/run/pulse	/sbin/nologin	pulseaudio
rtkit	172	172	/proc	/sbin/nologin	rtkit
nfsnobody	65534[1]	65534	/var/lib/nfs	/sbin/nologin	nfs-utils

Table 3.4. Standard Users

3.5. Standard Groups

Table 3.5. Standard Groups below lists the standard groups configured by an **Everything** installation. Groups are stored in the `/etc/group` file.

Group	GID	Members
root	0	root
bin	1	root, bin, daemon
daemon	2	root, bin, daemon
sys	3	root, bin, adm
adm	4	root, adm, daemon
tty	5	–
disk	6	root
lp	7	daemon, lp
mem	8	–

[1] nfsnobdy is 4294967294 on 64-bit platforms

Group	GID	Members
kmem	9	–
wheel	10	root
mail	12	mail,postfix
uucp	14	uucp
man	15	–
games	20	–
gopher	30	–
video	39	–
dip	40	–
ftp	50	–
lock	54	–
audio	63	–
nobody	99	–
users	100	–
dbus	81	–
usbmuxd	113	–
utmp	22	–
utempter	35	–
avahi-autoipd	170	–
floppy	19	–
vcsa	69	–
rpc	32	–
rtkit	499	–
abrt	498	–
nscd	28	–
desktop_admin_r	497	–
desktop_user_r	496	–
cdrom	11	–
tape	33	–
dialout	18	–
haldaemon	68	haldaemon
apache	48	–
ldap	55	–

Group	GID	Members
saslauth	495	–
postdrop	90	–
postfix	89	–
avahi	70	–
ntp	38	–
rpcuser	29	–
nfsnobody	65534	–
pulse	494	–
pulse-access	493	–
fuse	492	–
gdm	42	–
stapdev	491	–
stapusr	490	–
sshd	74	–
tcpdump	72	–
slocate	21	–
dovecot	97	–
dovenull	489	–
mailnull	47	–
smmsp	51	–

Table 3.5. Standard Groups

3.6. User Private Groups

Fedora uses a *user private group* (*UPG*) scheme, which makes UNIX groups easier to manage. A UPG is created whenever a new user is added to the system. It has the same name as the user for which it was created and that user is the only member of the UPG.

UPGs make it safe to set default permissions for a newly created file or directory, allowing both the user and *the group of that user* to make modifications to the file or directory.

The setting which determines what permissions are applied to a newly created file or directory is called a *umask* and is configured in the `/etc/bashrc` file. Traditionally on UNIX systems, the `umask` is set to `022`, which allows only the user who created the file or directory to make modifications. Under this scheme, all other users, *including members of the creator's group*, are not allowed to make any modifications. However, under the UPG scheme, this "group protection" is not necessary since every user has their own private group.

3.6.1. Group Directories

System administrators usually like to create a group for each major project and assign people to the group when they need to access that project's files. With this traditional scheme, file managing is difficult; when someone creates a file, it is associated with the primary group to which they belong. When a single person works on multiple projects, it becomes difficult to associate the right files with the right group. However, with the UPG scheme, groups are automatically assigned to files created within a directory with the *setgid* bit set. The setgid bit makes managing group projects that share a common directory very simple because any files a user creates within the directory are owned by the group which owns the directory.

For example, a group of people need to work on files in the `/opt/myproject/` directory. Some people are trusted to modify the contents of this directory, but not everyone.

1. As `root`, create the `/opt/myproject/` directory by typing the following at a shell prompt:
   ```
   mkdir /opt/myproject
   ```
2. Add the `myproject` group to the system:
   ```
   groupadd myproject
   ```
3. Associate the contents of the `/opt/myproject/` directory with the `myproject` group:
   ```
   chown root:myproject /opt/myproject
   ```
4. Allow users to create files within the directory, and set the setgid bit:
   ```
   chmod 2775 /opt/myproject
   ```

At this point, all members of the `myproject` group can create and edit files in the `/opt/myproject/` directory without the administrator having to change file permissions every time users write new files. To verify that the permissions have been set correctly, run the following command:

```
~]# ls -l /opt
total 4
drwxrwsr-x. 3 root myproject 4096 Mar  3 18:31 myproject
```

3.7. Shadow Passwords

In multiuser environments it is very important to use *shadow passwords* (provided by the `shadow-utils` package). Doing so enhances the security of system authentication files. For this reason, the installation program enables shadow passwords by default.

The following list shows the advantages shadow passwords have over the traditional way of storing passwords on UNIX-based systems:

- Improves system security by moving encrypted password hashes from the world-readable `/etc/passwd` file to `/etc/shadow`, which is readable only by the `root` user.
- Stores information about password aging.
- Allows the `/etc/login.defs` file to enforce security policies.

Most utilities provided by the `shadow-utils` package work properly whether or not shadow passwords are enabled. However, since password aging information is stored exclusively in the `/etc/shadow` file, any commands which create or modify password aging information do not work.

The following is a list of commands which do not work without first enabling shadow passwords:

- `chage`
- `gpasswd`
- `usermod -e` or `-f` options
- `useradd -e` or `-f` options

3.8. Additional Resources

For more information about users and groups, and tools to manage them, refer to the following resources.

3.8.1. Installed Documentation

- Related man pages — There are a number of man pages for the various applications and configuration files involved with managing users and groups. Some of the more important man pages have been listed here:

  User and Group Administrative Applications

  - `man chage` — A command to modify password aging policies and account expiration.
  - `man gpasswd` — A command to administer the `/etc/group` file.
  - `man groupadd` — A command to add groups.
  - `man grpck` — A command to verify the `/etc/group` file.
  - `man groupdel` — A command to remove groups.
  - `man groupmod` — A command to modify group membership.
  - `man pwck` — A command to verify the `/etc/passwd` and `/etc/shadow` files.
  - `man pwconv` — A tool to convert standard passwords to shadow passwords.
  - `man pwunconv` — A tool to convert shadow passwords to standard passwords.

- `man useradd` — A command to add users.
- `man userdel` — A command to remove users.
- `man usermod` — A command to modify users.

Configuration Files

- `man 5 group` — The file containing group information for the system.
- `man 5 passwd` — The file containing user information for the system.
- `man 5 shadow` — The file containing passwords and account expiration information for the system.

Part II.
Package Management

All software on a Fedora system is divided into RPM packages, which can be installed, upgraded, or removed. This part describes how to manage packages on Fedora using both **Yum** and the **PackageKit** suite of graphical package management tools.

Chapter 4.
Yum

Yum is the The Fedora Project package manager that is able to query for information about packages, fetch packages from repositories, install and uninstall packages using automatic dependency resolution, and update an entire system to the latest available packages. **Yum** performs automatic dependency resolution on packages you are updating, installing or removing, and thus is able to automatically determine, fetch and install all available dependent packages. **Yum** can be configured with new, additional repositories, or *package sources*, and also provides many plugins which enhance and extend its capabilities. **Yum** is able to perform many of the same tasks that **RPM** can; additionally, many of the command line options are similar. **Yum** enables easy and simple package management on a single machine or on groups of them.

Secure package management with GPG-signed packages

Yum provides secure package management by enabling GPG (Gnu Privacy Guard; also known as GnuPG) signature verification on GPG-signed packages to be turned on for all package repositories (i.e. package sources), or for individual repositories. When signature verification is enabled, **Yum** will refuse to install any packages not GPG-signed with the correct key for that repository. This means that you can trust that the **RPM** packages you download and install on your system are from a trusted source, such as The Fedora Project, and were not modified during transfer. Refer to Section 4.3, *Configuring Yum and Yum Repositories* (page 80) for details on enabling signature-checking with **Yum**, or Section A.3, *Checking a Package's Signature* (page 465) for information on working with and verifying GPG-signed **RPM** packages in general.

Yum also enables you to easily set up your own repositories of **RPM** packages for download and installation on other machines.

Learning **Yum** is a worthwhile investment because it is often the fastest way to perform system administration tasks, and it provides capabilities beyond those provided by the **PackageKit** graphical package management tools. Refer to Chapter 5, *PackageKit* (page 91) for details on using **PackageKit**.

Yum and superuser privileges

You must have superuser privileges in order to use `yum` to install, update or remove packages on your system. All examples in this chapter assume that you have already obtained superuser privileges by using either the `su` or `sudo` command.

4.1. Checking For and Updating Packages

4.1.1. Checking For Updates

You can use the `yum check-update` command to see which installed packages on your system have updates available:

```
~]# yum check-update
Loaded plugins: langpacks, presto, refresh-packagekit

PackageKit.x86_64                     0.6.14-2.fc15               fedora
PackageKit-command-not-found.x86_64   0.6.14-2.fc15               fedora
PackageKit-device-rebind.x86_64       0.6.14-2.fc15               fedora
PackageKit-glib.x86_64                0.6.14-2.fc15               fedora
PackageKit-gstreamer-plugin.x86_64    0.6.14-2.fc15               fedora
PackageKit-gtk-module.x86_64          0.6.14-2.fc15               fedora
PackageKit-gtk3-module.x86_64         0.6.14-2.fc15               fedora
PackageKit-yum.x86_64                 0.6.14-2.fc15               fedora
PackageKit-yum-plugin.x86_64          0.6.14-2.fc15               fedora
gdb.x86_64                            7.2.90.20110429-36.fc15     fedora
kernel.x86_64                         2.6.38.6-26.fc15            fedora
rpm.x86_64                            4.9.0-6.fc15                fedora
rpm-libs.x86_64                       4.9.0-6.fc15                fedora
rpm-python.x86_64                     4.9.0-6.fc15                fedora
yum.noarch                            3.2.29-5.fc15               fedora
```

The packages in the above output are listed as having updates available. The first package in the list is **PackageKit**, the graphical package manager. The line in the example output tells us:

- `PackageKit` — the name of the package
- `x86_64` — the CPU architecture the package was built for
- `0.6.14` — the version of the updated package to be installed
- `fedora` — the repository in which the updated package is located

The output also shows us that we can update the kernel (the kernel package), **Yum** and **RPM** themselves (the `yum` and `rpm` packages), as well as their dependencies (such as the rpm-libs and rpm-python packages), all using `yum`.

4.1.2. Updating Packages

You can choose to update a single package, multiple packages, or all packages at once. If any dependencies of the package (or packages) you update have updates available themselves, then they are updated too.

Updating a Single Package

To update a single package, enter `yum update` *`package_name`*, for example:

```
~]# yum update gdb
Loaded plugins: langpacks, presto, refresh-packagekit
Setting up Update Process
Resolving Dependencies
--> Running transaction check
---> Package gdb.x86_64 0:7.2.90.20110411-34.fc15 will be updated
---> Package gdb.x86_64 0:7.2.90.20110429-36.fc15 will be an update
--> Finished Dependency Resolution

Dependencies Resolved

================================================================================
 Package     Arch         Version                          Repository       Size
================================================================================
Updating:
 gdb         x86_64       7.2.90.20110429-36.fc15          fedora          1.9 M

Transaction Summary
================================================================================
Upgrade       1 Package(s)

Total download size: 1.9 M
Is this ok [y/N]:
```

This output contains several items of interest:

1. `Loaded plugins:` — `yum` always informs you which **Yum** plugins are installed and enabled. Here, `yum` is using the **langpacks**, **presto**, and **refresh-packagekit** plugins. Refer to Section 4.4, *Yum Plugins* (page 88) for general information on **Yum** plugins, or to Section 4.4.3, *Plugin Descriptions* (page 89) for descriptions of specific plugins.
2. `gdb.x86_64` — you can download and install new gdb package.
3. `yum` presents the update information and then prompts you as to whether you want it to perform the update; `yum` runs interactively by default. If you already know which transactions `yum` plans to perform, you can use the `-y` option to automatically answer `yes` to any questions `yum` may ask (in which case it runs non-interactively). However, you should always examine which changes `yum` plans to make to the system so that you can easily troubleshoot any problems that might arise.

If a transaction does go awry, you can view **Yum**'s log of transactions by typing the `cat /var/log/yum.log` command at a shell prompt. The most recent transactions are listed at the end of the log file.

Updating and installing kernels with Yum

`yum` always *installs* a new kernel in the same sense that **RPM** installs a new kernel when you use the command `rpm -i kernel`. Therefore, you do not need to worry about the distinction between *installing* and *upgrading* a kernel package when you use `yum`: it will do the right thing, regardless of whether you are using the `yum update` or `yum install` command.

When using **RPM**, on the other hand, it is important to use the `rpm -i kernel` command (which installs a new kernel) instead of `rpm -u kernel` (which *replaces* the current kernel). Refer to Section A.2.2, *Installing and Upgrading* (page 459) for more information on installing/updating kernels with **RPM**.

Updating All Packages and Their Dependencies

To update all packages and their dependencies, simply enter the `yum update` command (without any arguments):

```
~]# yum update
```

Updating Security-Related Packages

Discovering which packages have security updates available and then updating those packages quickly and easily is important. **Yum** provides the plugin for this purpose. The **security** plugin extends the `yum` command with a set of highly-useful security-centric commands, subcommands and options. Refer to Section 4.4.3, *Plugin Descriptions* (page 89) for specific information.

4.1.3. Preserving Configuration File Changes

You will inevitably make changes to the configuration files installed by packages as you use your Fedora system. **RPM**, which **Yum** uses to perform changes to the system, provides a mechanism for ensuring their integrity. Refer to Section A.2.2, *Installing and Upgrading* (page 459) for details on how to manage changes to configuration files across package upgrades.

4.2. Packages and Package Groups

4.2.1. Searching Packages

You can search all RPM package names, descriptions and summaries by using the `yum search term [more_terms]` command. `yum` displays the list of matches for each term, for example:

```
~]# yum search meld kompare
Loaded plugins: langpacks, presto, refresh-packagekit
=============================== N/S Matched: meld ===============================
meld.noarch : Visual diff and merge tool
python-meld3.x86_64 : HTML/XML templating system for Python

============================== N/S Matched: kompare ==============================
komparator.x86_64 : Kompare and merge two folders

  Name and summary matches only, use "search all" for everything.
```

The `yum search` command is useful for searching for packages you do not know the name of, but for which you know a related term.

4.2.2. Listing Packages

`yum list` and related commands provide information about packages, package groups, and repositories.

All of **Yum**'s list commands allow you to filter the results by appending one or more *glob expressions* as arguments. Glob expressions are normal strings of characters which contain one or more of the wildcard characters `*` (which expands to match any character multiple times) and `?` (which expands to match any one character).

Filtering results with glob expressions

Be careful to escape the glob expressions when passing them as arguments to a `yum` command, otherwise the Bash shell will interpret these expressions as *pathname expansions*, and potentially pass all files in the current directory that match the globs to `yum`. To make sure the glob expressions are passed to `yum` as intended, either:

- escape the wildcard characters by preceding them with a backslash character
- double-quote or single-quote the entire glob expression.

Refer to *Example 4.1. Listing all ABRT addons and plugins using glob expressions* below and *Example 4.4. Listing available packages using a single glob expression with escaped wildcard characters* below for an example usage of both these methods.

`yum list glob_expr [more_glob_exprs]`

Lists information on installed and available packages matching all glob expressions.

```
~]# yum list abrt-addon\* abrt-plugin\*
Loaded plugins: langpacks, presto, refresh-packagekit
Installed Packages
abrt-addon-ccpp.x86_64                2.0.2-5.fc15      @fedora
abrt-addon-kerneloops.x86_64          2.0.2-5.fc15      @fedora
abrt-addon-python.x86_64              2.0.2-5.fc15      @fedora
abrt-plugin-bugzilla.x86_64           2.0.2-5.fc15      @fedora
abrt-plugin-logger.x86_64             2.0.2-5.fc15      @fedora
Available Packages
abrt-plugin-mailx.x86_64              2.0.2-5.fc15      updates
abrt-plugin-reportuploader.x86_64     2.0.2-5.fc15      updates
abrt-plugin-rhtsupport.x86_64         2.0.2-5.fc15      updates
```

Example 4.1. Listing all ABRT addons and plugins using glob expressions

`yum list all`

Lists all installed *and* available packages.

```
~]# yum list all
Loaded plugins: langpacks, presto, refresh-packagekit
Installed Packages
ConsoleKit.x86_64                     0.4.4-1.fc15                    @fedora
ConsoleKit-libs.x86_64                0.4.4-1.fc15                    @fedora
ConsoleKit-x11.x86_64                 0.4.4-1.fc15                    @fedora
GConf2.x86_64                         2.32.3-1.fc15                   @fedora
GConf2-gtk.x86_64                     2.32.3-1.fc15                   @fedora
ModemManager.x86_64                   0.4-7.git20110201.fc15          @fedora
NetworkManager.x86_64                 1:0.8.998-4.git20110427.fc15    @fedora
NetworkManager-glib.x86_64            1:0.8.998-4.git20110427.fc15    @fedora
NetworkManager-gnome.x86_64           1:0.8.998-4.git20110427.fc15    @fedora
NetworkManager-openconnect.x86_64     0.8.1-9.git20110419.fc15        @fedora
[output truncated]
```

Example 4.2. Listing all installed and available packages

`yum list installed`

Lists all packages installed on your system. The rightmost column in the output lists the repository from which the package was retrieved.

```
~]# yum list installed "krb?-*"
Loaded plugins: langpacks, presto, refresh-packagekit
Installed Packages
krb5-libs.x86_64              1.9-7.fc15              @fedora
```

Example 4.3. Listing installed packages using a double-quoted glob expression

`yum list available`

Lists all available packages in all enabled repositories.

```
~]# yum list available gstreamer\*plugin\*
Loaded plugins: langpacks, presto, refresh-packagekit
Available Packages
gstreamer-plugin-crystalhd.x86_64              3.5.1-1.fc14     fedora
gstreamer-plugins-bad-free.x86_64              0.10.22-1.fc15   updates
gstreamer-plugins-bad-free-devel.x86_64        0.10.22-1.fc15   updates
gstreamer-plugins-bad-free-devel-docs.x86_64   0.10.22-1.fc15   updates
gstreamer-plugins-bad-free-extras.x86_64       0.10.22-1.fc15   updates
gstreamer-plugins-base.x86_64                  0.10.33-1.fc15   updates
gstreamer-plugins-base-devel.x86_64            0.10.33-1.fc15   updates
gstreamer-plugins-base-devel-docs.noarch       0.10.33-1.fc15   updates
gstreamer-plugins-base-tools.x86_64            0.10.33-1.fc15   updates
gstreamer-plugins-espeak.x86_64                0.3.3-3.fc15     fedora
gstreamer-plugins-fc.x86_64                    0.2-2.fc15       fedora
gstreamer-plugins-good.x86_64                  0.10.29-1.fc15   updates
gstreamer-plugins-good-devel-docs.noarch       0.10.29-1.fc15   updates
```

Example 4.4. Listing available packages using a single glob expression with escaped wildcard characters

`yum grouplist`

Lists all package groups.

```
~]# yum grouplist
Loaded plugins: langpacks, presto, refresh-packagekit
Setting up Group Process
Installed Groups:
   Administration Tools
   Design Suite
   Dial-up Networking Support
   Fonts
   GNOME Desktop Environment
[output truncated]
```

Example 4.5. Listing all package groups

`yum repolist`

Lists the repository ID, name, and number of packages it provides for each *enabled* repository.

```
~]# yum repolist
Loaded plugins: langpacks, presto, refresh-packagekit
repo id                  repo name                                    status
fedora                   Fedora 15 - i386                             19,365
updates                  Fedora 15 - i386 - Updates                   3,848
repolist: 23,213
```

Example 4.6. Listing enabled repositories

4.2.3. Displaying Package Information

The `yum info` *package_name* [*more_names*] command displays information about one or more packages (glob expressions are valid here as well). For example, to display information about the abrt package, type:

```
~]# yum info abrt
Loaded plugins: langpacks, presto, refresh-packagekit
Installed Packages
Name        : abrt
Arch        : x86_64
Version     : 2.0.1
Release     : 2.fc15
Size        : 806 k
Repo        : installed
From repo   : fedora
Summary     : Automatic bug detection and reporting tool
URL         : https://fedorahosted.org/abrt/
License     : GPLv2+
Description : abrt is a tool to help users to detect defects in applications and
            : to create a bug report with all informations needed by maintainer
            : to fix it. It uses plugin system to extend its functionality.
```

`yum info` *package_name* is similar to the `rpm -q --info` *package_name* command, but provides as additional information the ID of the **Yum** repository the RPM package is found in (look for the `From repo` line in the output).

The `yumdb info` *package_name* [*more_names*] command can be used to query the **Yum** database for alternative and useful information about a package, including the checksum of the package (and algorithm used to produce it, such as SHA-256), the command given on the command line that was invoked to install the package (if any), and the reason that the package is installed on the system (where `user` indicates it was installed by the user, and `dep` means it was brought in as a dependency). For example, to display additional information about the yum package, type:

```
~]# yumdb info yum
Loaded plugins: langpacks, presto, refresh-packagekit
yum-3.2.29-4.fc15.noarch
   checksum_data = 249f21fb43c41381c8c9b0cd98d2ea5fa0aa165e81ed2009cfda74c05af67246
   checksum_type = sha256
   from_repo = fedora
   from_repo_revision = 1304429533
   from_repo_timestamp = 1304442346
   installed_by = 0
   reason = user
   releasever = $releasever
```

For more information on the `yumdb` command, see `man yumdb`.

Finally, the `yum history` command can be used to show a timeline of **Yum** transactions, the dates and times on when they occurred, the number of packages affected, whether transactions succeeded or were aborted, and if the RPM database was changed between transactions. Refer to the `history` section of `man yum` for details.

4.2.4. Installing Packages

You can install a package and all of its non-installed dependencies by entering:

```
yum install package_name
```

You can install multiple packages simultaneously by appending their names as arguments:

```
yum install package_name [more_names]
```

If you are installing packages on a *multilib* system, such as an AMD64 or Intel 64 machine, you can specify the architecture of the package (as long as it is available in an enabled repository) by appending *.arch* to the package name. For example, to install the sqlite2 package for `i686`, type:

```
~]# yum install sqlite2.i686
```

You can use glob expressions to quickly install multiple similarly-named packages:

```
~]# yum install audacious-plugins-\*
```

In addition to package names and glob expressions, you can also provide file names to `yum install`. If you know the name of the binary you want to install, but not its package name, you can give `yum install` the path name:

```
~]# yum install /usr/sbin/named
```

`yum` then searches through its package lists, finds the package which provides `/usr/sbin/named`, if any, and prompts you as to whether you want to install it.

Finding which package owns a file

If you know you want to install the package that contains the `named` binary, but you do not know in which `bin` or `sbin` directory is the file installed, use the `yum provides` command with a glob expression:

```
~]# yum provides "*bin/named"
Loaded plugins: langpacks, presto, refresh-packagekit
32:bind-9.8.0-3.P1.fc15.i686 : The Berkeley Internet Name Domain (BIND) DNS
                             : (Domain Name System) server
Repo        : fedora
Matched from:
Filename    : /usr/sbin/named
```

`yum provides "*/file_name"` is a common and useful trick to find the packages that contain *`file_name`*.

Installing a Package Group

A package group is similar to a package: it is not useful by itself, but installing one pulls a group of dependent packages that serve a common purpose. A package group has a name and a *groupid*. The `yum grouplist -v` command lists the names of all package groups, and, next to each of them, their groupid in parentheses. The groupid is always the term in the last pair of parentheses, such as `kde-desktop` in the following example:

```
~]# yum -v grouplist kde\*
Not loading "blacklist" plugin, as it is disabled
Loading "langpacks" plugin
Loading "presto" plugin
Loading "refresh-packagekit" plugin
Not loading "whiteout" plugin, as it is disabled
Adding en_US to language list
Config time: 0.900
Yum Version: 3.2.29
Setting up Group Process
rpmdb time: 0.002
group time: 0.995
Available Groups:
   KDE Software Compilation (kde-desktop)
   KDE Software Development (kde-software-development)
Done
```

You can install a package group by passing its full group name (without the groupid part) to `groupinstall`, for example:

```
~]# yum groupinstall "KDE Software Compilation"
```

You can also install by groupid:

```
~]# yum groupinstall kde-desktop
```

You can even pass the groupid (or quoted name) to the `install` command if you prepend it with an @-symbol (which tells `yum` that you want to perform a `groupinstall`):

```
~]# yum install @kde-desktop
```

4.2.5. Removing Packages

The `yum remove` *`package_name`* uninstalls (removes in **RPM** and **Yum** terminology) the package, as well as any packages that depend on it. As when you install multiple packages, you can remove several at once by adding more package names to the command. For example, to remove totem, rhythmbox, and sound-juicer, type the following at a shell prompt:

```
~]# yum remove totem rhythmbox sound-juicer
```

Similar to `install`, `remove` can take these arguments:

- package names
- glob expressions
- file lists
- package provides

Removing a package when other packages depend on it

Yum is not able to remove a package without also removing packages which depend on it. This type of operation can only be performed by **RPM**, is not advised, and can potentially leave your system in a non-functioning state or cause applications to misbehave and/or crash. For further information, refer to Section A.2.4, *Uninstalling* (page 462) in the **RPM** chapter.

4.2.5.1. Removing a Package Group

You can remove a package group using syntax congruent with the `install` syntax. The following are alternative but equivalent ways of removing the `KDE Software Compilation` group:

```
~]# yum groupremove "KDE Software Compilation"
~]# yum groupremove kde-desktop
~]# yum remove @kde-desktop
```

Intelligent package group removal

When you tell **yum** to remove a package group, it will remove every package in that group, even if those packages are members of other package groups or dependencies of other installed packages. However, you can instruct `yum` to remove only those packages which are not required by any other packages or groups by adding the `groupremove_leaf_only=1` directive to the `[main]` section of the `/etc/yum.conf` configuration file. For more information on this directive, refer to Section 4.3.1, *Setting [main] Options* (page 81).

4.3. Configuring Yum and Yum Repositories

This section shows you how to:

- set global **Yum** options by editing the `[main]` section of the `/etc/yum.conf` configuration file;
- set options for individual repositories by editing the `[`*`repository`*`]` sections in `/etc/yum.conf` and `.repo` files in the `/etc/yum.repos.d/` directory;

- use **Yum** variables in `/etc/yum.conf` and files in `/etc/yum.repos.d/` so that dynamic version and architecture values are handled correctly; and,
- set up your own custom **Yum** repository.

The `/etc/yum.conf` configuration file contains one mandatory `[main]` section under which you can set **Yum** options. The values that you define in the `[main]` section of `yum.conf` have global effect, and may override values set in individual `[repository]` sections. You can also add `[repository]` sections to `/etc/yum.conf`; however, best practice is to define individual repositories in new or existing `.repo` files in the `/etc/yum.repos.d/`directory. Refer to Section 4.3.2, *Setting [repository] Options* (page 85) if you need to add or edit repository-specific information.

4.3.1. Setting [main] Options

The `/etc/yum.conf` configuration file contains exactly one `[main]` section. You can add many additional options under the `[main]` section heading in `/etc/yum.conf`. Some of the key-value pairs in the `[main]` section affect how `yum` operates; others affect how **Yum** treats repositories. The best source of information for all **Yum** options is in the `[main] OPTIONS` and `[repository] OPTIONS` sections of `man yum.conf`.

A sample `/etc/yum.conf` configuration file can look like this:

```
[main]
cachedir=/var/cache/yum/$basearch/$releasever
keepcache=0
debuglevel=2
logfile=/var/log/yum.log
exactarch=1
obsoletes=1
gpgcheck=1
plugins=1
installonly_limit=3
[comments abridged]
# PUT YOUR REPOS HERE OR IN separate files named file.repo
# in /etc/yum.repos.d
```

The following is a list of the most commonly-used options in the `[main]` section, and descriptions for each:

assumeyes=*value*

...where *value* is one of:

`0` — `yum` should prompt for confirmation of critical actions it performs. This is the default.

`1` — Do not prompt for confirmation of critical `yum` actions. If `assumeyes=1` is set, `yum` behaves in the same way that the command line option `-y` does.

cachedir=`/var/cache/yum/$basearch/$releasever`

This option specifies the directory where **Yum** should store its cache and database files. By default, **Yum**'s cache directory is `/var/cache/yum/$basearch/$releasever`. See Section 4.3.3, *Using Yum Variables* (page 86) for descriptions of the `$basearch` and `$releasever` **Yum** variables.

debuglevel=*`value`*

...where *`value`* is an integer between `1` and `10`. Setting a higher `debuglevel` value causes `yum` to display more detailed debugging output. `debuglevel=0` disables debugging output, while `debuglevel=2` is the default.

exactarch=*`value`*

...where *`value`* is one of:

`0` — Do not take into account the exact architecture when updating packages.

`1` — Consider the exact architecture when updating packages. With this setting, `yum` will not install an i686 package to update an i386 package already installed on the system. This is the default.

exclude=*`package_name`* [*`more_package_names`*]

This option allows you to exclude packages by keyword during installation/updates. Listing multiple packages for exclusion can be accomplished by quoting a space-delimited list of packages. Shell globs using wildcards (for example, `*` and `?`) are allowed.

gpgcheck=*`value`*

...where *`value`* is one of:

`0` — Disable GPG signature-checking on packages in all repositories, including local package installation.

`1` — Enable GPG signature-checking on all packages in all repositories, including local package installation. `gpgcheck=1` is the default, and thus all packages' signatures are checked.

If this option is set in the `[main]` section of the `/etc/yum.conf` file, it sets the GPG-checking rule for all repositories. However, you can also set `gpgcheck=`*`value`* for individual repositories instead; i.e., you can enable GPG-checking on one repository while disabling it on another. Setting `gpgcheck=`*`value`* for an individual repository in its corresponding `.repo` file overrides the default if it is present in `/etc/yum.conf`. Refer to Section A.3, *Checking a Package's Signature* (page 465) for further information on GPG signature-checking.

groupremove_leaf_only=*value*

...where *value* is one of:

0 — yum should *not* check the dependencies of each package when removing a package group. With this setting, yum removes all packages in a package group, regardless of whether those packages are required by other packages or groups. groupremove_leaf_only=0 is the default.

1 — yum should check the dependencies of each package when removing a package group, and remove only those packages which are not not required by any other package or group.

For more information on removing packages, refer to *Intelligent package group removal* (page 80).

installonlypkgs=*space separated list of packages*

Here you can provide a space-separated list of packages which yum can *install*, but will never *update*. Refer to man yum.conf for the list of packages which are install-only by default. If you add the installonlypkgs directive to /etc/yum.conf, you should ensure that you list *all* of the packages that should be install-only, including any of those listed under the installonlypkgs section of man yum.conf. In particular, kernel packages should always be listed in installonlypkgs (as they are by default), and installonly_limit should always be set to a value greater than 2 so that a backup kernel is always available in case the default one fails to boot. Refer to *installonly_limit*=*value* (see Section 4.3.1, *Setting [main] Options* - page 81) for details on the installonly_limit directive.

installonly_limit=*value*

...where *value* is an integer representing the maximum number of versions that can be installed simultaneously for any single package listed in the installonlypkgs directive. The defaults for the installonlypkgs directive include several different kernel packages, so be aware that changing the value of installonly_limit will also affect the maximum number of installed versions of any single kernel package. The default value listed in /etc/yum.conf is installonly_limit=3, and it is not recommended to decrease this value, particularly below 2.

keepcache=*value*

...where *value* is one of:

0 — Do not retain the cache of headers and packages after a successful installation. This is the default.

1 — Retain the cache after a successful installation.

logfile=`/var/log/yum.log`

This option specifies where `yum` should send its logging output. By default, `yum` logs to `/var/log/yum.log`.

multilib_policy=*`value`*

...where *`value`* is one of:

`best` — install the best-choice architecture for this system. For example, setting `multilib_policy=best` on an AMD64 system causes `yum` to install 64-bit versions of all packages.

`all` — always install every possible architecture for every package. For example, with `multilib_policy` set to `all` on an AMD64 system, `yum` would install both the i686 and AMD64 versions of a package, if both were available.

obsoletes=*`value`*

...where *`value`* is one of:

`0` — Disable `yum`'s obsoletes processing logic when performing updates.

`1` — Enable `yum`'s obsoletes processing logic when performing updates. When one package declares in its spec file that it *obsoletes* another package, the latter package will be replaced by the former package when the former package is installed. Obsoletes are declared, for example, when a package is renamed. `obsoletes=1` the default.

plugins=*`value`*

...where *`value`* is one of:

`0` — Disable all **Yum** plugins globally.

Disabling all plugins is not advised

Disabling all plugins is not advised, because certain plugins provide important `Yum` services. Disabling plugins globally is provided as a convenience option, and is generally only recommended when diagnosing a potential problem with `Yum`.

`1` — Enable all **Yum** plugins globally. With `plugins=1`, you can still disable a specific **Yum** plugin by setting `enabled=0` in that plugin's configuration file. Refer to Section 4.4, *Yum Plugins* (page 88) for more information about various **Yum** plugins, or to Section 4.4.1, *Enabling, Configuring and Disabling Yum Plugins* (page 88) for further information on controlling plugins.

reposdir=*`/absolute/path/to/directory/containing/repo/files`*

This option allows you to specify a directory where `.repo` files are located. All `.repo` files contain repository information (similar to the `[`*`repository`*`]` sections of

`/etc/yum.conf`). `yum` collects all repository information from `.repo` files and the `[repository]` section of the `/etc/yum.conf` file to create a master list of repositories to use for transactions. Refer to Section 4.3.2, *Setting [repository] Options* (page 85) for more information about options you can use for both the `[repository]` section and `.repo` files. If `reposdir` is not set, `yum` uses the default directory `/etc/yum.repos.d/`.

retries=*value*

...where *value* is an integer `0` or greater. This value sets the number of times `yum` should attempt to retrieve a file before returning an error. Setting this to `0` makes `yum` retry forever. The default value is `10`.

4.3.2. Setting [repository] Options

The `[repository]` sections (where *repository* is a unique repository ID, such as `my_personal_repo`) allow you to define individual **Yum** repositories. To define a new repository, either add this section to the `/etc/yum.conf` file, or to a `.repo` file in the `/etc/yum.repos.d/` directory.

All `.repo` files in `/etc/yum.repos.d/`are read by `yum`, which allows you to create new, custom `.repo` files in this directory. Best practice is to define your repositories here instead of in `/etc/yum.conf`.

The following is a (bare-minimum) example of the form a `.repo` file takes:

```
[repository_ID]
name=A Repository Name
baseurl=http://path/to/repo or ftp://path/to/repo or file:///path/to/local/repo
```

Every `[repository]` section must contain the following minimum directives:

[*repository_ID*]

The repository ID is a unique, one-word (no spaces; underscores are allowed) string of characters (enclosed by brackets) that serves as a repository identifier.

name=*A Repository Name*

This is a human-readable string describing the repository.

baseurl=*http://path/to/repo, ftp://path/to/repo, file:///path/to/local/repo*

This is a URL to the directory where the repodata directory of a repository is located. Usually this URL is an HTTP link, such as:

```
baseurl=http://path/to/repo/releases/$releasever/server/$basearch/os/
```

Note that **Yum** always expands the `$releasever`, `$arch` and `$basearch` variables in URLs. See Section 4.3.3, *Using Yum Variables* (page 86) for explanations of all **Yum** variables.

- If the repository is available over FTP, use: `ftp://path/to/repo`
- If the repository is local to the machine, use `file:///path/to/local/repo`
- If a specific online repository requires basic HTTP authentication, you can specify your username and password in the `http://path/to/repo` by prepending it as *`username:password@link`*. For example, if a repository on http://www.example.com/repo/ requires a username of "user" and a password of "password", then the `baseurl` link could be specified as:

  ```
  baseurl=http://user:password@www.example.com/repo/
  ```

The following is another useful `[repository]` directive:

enabled=*`value`*

...where *`value`* is one of:

`0` — do not include this repository as a package source when performing updates and installs. This is an easy way of quickly turning repositories on and off, which is useful when you desire a single package from a repository that you do not want to enable for updates or installs.

`1` — include this repository as a package source.

Turning repositories on and off can also be performed by passing either the `--enablerepo=`*`repo_name`* or `--disablerepo=`*`repo_name`* option to `yum`, or through the **Add/Remove Software** window of the **PackageKit** utility.

Many more `[repository]` options exist. Refer to the `[repository] OPTIONS` section of `man yum.conf` for the exhaustive list and descriptions for each.

4.3.3. Using Yum Variables

You can use and reference the following built-in variables in `yum` commands and in all **Yum** configuration files (that is, `/etc/yum.conf` and all `.repo` files in the `/etc/yum.repos.d/` directory):

`$releasever`

You can use this variable to reference the release version of Fedora. **Yum** obtains the value of `$releasever` from the `distroverpkg=`*`value`* line in the `/etc/yum.conf` configuration file. If there is no such line in `/etc/yum.conf`, then `yum` infers the correct value by deriving the version number from the redhat-release package.

`$arch`

You can use this variable to refer to the system's CPU architecture as returned when calling Python's `os.uname()` function. Valid values for `$arch` include: `i586`, `i686`, and `x86_64`.

`$basearch`

You can use `$basearch` to reference the base architecture of the system. For example, i686 and i586 machines both have a base architecture of `i386`, and AMD64 and Intel 64 machines have a base architecture of `x86_64`.

`$uuid`

You can use this variable to refer to a *universally unique identifier* (UUID) for the machine.

`$YUM0-9`

These ten variables are each replaced with the value of any shell environment variables with the same name. If one of these variables is referenced (in `/etc/yum.conf` for example) and a shell environment variable with the same name does not exist, then the configuration file variable is not replaced.

To define a custom variable or to override the value of an existing one, create a file with the same name as the variable (without the "`$`" sign) in the `/etc/yum/vars/` directory, and add the desired value on its first line.

Repository descriptions often include the operating system name. To define a new variable called `$osname`, create a new file with "Fedora" on the first line and save it as `/etc/yum/vars/osname`. For example:

```
~]# echo "Fedora" > /etc/yum/vars/osname
```

Instead of "Fedora 15", you can now use the following in the `.repo` files:

```
name=$osname $releasever
```

Example 4.7. Using a custom Yum variable

4.3.4. Creating a Yum Repository

To set up a **Yum** repository, follow these steps:

1. Install the createrepo package:

   ```
   ~]# yum install createrepo
   ```

2. Copy all of the packages into one directory, such as `/mnt/local_repo/`.
3. Run the `createrepo --database` command on that directory:

   ```
   ~]# createrepo --database /mnt/local_repo/
   ```

This will create the necessary metadata for your **Yum** repository, as well as the **sqlite** database for speeding up `yum` operations.

4.4. Yum Plugins

Yum provides plugins that extend and enhance its operations. Certain plugins are installed by default. **Yum** always informs you which plugins, if any, are loaded and active whenever you call any `yum` command:

```
~]# yum info yum
Loaded plugins: langpacks, presto, refresh-packagekit
[output truncated]
```

Note that the plugin names which follow `Loaded plugins` are the names you can provide to the `--disableplugins=`*`plugin_name`* option.

4.4.1. Enabling, Configuring and Disabling Yum Plugins

To enable **Yum** plugins, ensure that a line beginning with `plugins=` is present in the `[main]` section of `/etc/yum.conf`, and that its value is set to `1`:

```
plugins=1
```

You can disable all plugins by changing this line to `plugins=0`.

Disabling all plugins is not advised

Disabling all plugins is not advised because certain plugins provide important `Yum` services. Disabling plugins globally is provided as a convenience option, and is generally only recommended when diagnosing a potential problem with `Yum`.

Every installed plugin has its own configuration file in the `/etc/yum/pluginconf.d/` directory. You can set plugin-specific options in these files. For example, the following is the content of `refresh-packagekit.conf`, the configuration file for the **refresh-packagekit** plugin:

```
[main]
enabled=1
```

Plugin configuration files always contain a `[main]` section (similar to **Yum**'s `/etc/yum.conf` file) in which there is (or you can place if it is missing) an `enabled=` option that controls whether the plugin is enabled when you run `yum` commands.

If you disable all plugins by setting `enabled=0` in `/etc/yum.conf`, then all plugins are disabled regardless of whether they are enabled in their individual configuration files.

If you merely want to disable all **Yum** plugins for a single `yum` command, use the `--noplugins` option.

If you want to disable one or more **Yum** plugins for a single `yum` command, add the `--disableplugin=`*`plugin_name`* option to the command. For example, to disable the **presto** plugin while updating a system, type:

```
~]# yum update --disableplugin=presto
```

The plugin names you provide to the `--disableplugin=` option are the same names listed after the `Loaded plugins` line in the output of any `yum` command. You can disable multiple plugins by separating their names with commas. In addition, you can match multiple plugin names or shorten long ones by using glob expressions:

```
~]# yum update --disableplugin=presto,refresh-pack*
```

4.4.2. Installing Additional Yum Plugins

Yum plugins usually adhere to the `yum-plugin-`*`plugin_name`* package-naming convention, but not always: the package which provides the **presto** plugin is named `yum-presto`, for example. You can install a **Yum** plugin in the same way you install other packages. For instance, to install the **security** plugin, type the following at a shell prompt:

```
~]# yum install yum-plugin-security
```

4.4.3. Plugin Descriptions

The following are descriptions of a few commonly installed **Yum** plugins:

presto (yum-presto)

The **presto** plugin adds support to **Yum** for downloading *delta RPM* packages, during updates, from repositories which have **presto** metadata enabled. Delta RPMs contain only the differences between the version of the package installed on the client requesting the RPM package and the updated version in the repository.

Downloading a delta RPM is much quicker than downloading the entire updated package, and can speed up updates considerably. Once the delta RPMs are downloaded, they must be rebuilt to apply the difference to the currently-installed package and thus create the full, updated package. This process takes CPU time on the installing machine. Using delta RPMs is therefore a tradeoff between time-to-download, which depends on the network connection, and time-to-rebuild, which is CPU-bound. Using the **presto** plugin is recommended for fast machines and systems with slower network connections, while slower machines on very fast connections *may* benefit more from downloading normal RPM packages, that is, by disabling **presto**.

refresh-packagekit (PackageKit-yum-plugin)

The **refresh-packagekit** plugin updates metadata for **PackageKit** whenever `yum` is run. The **refresh-packagekit** plugin is installed by default.

rhnplugin (yum-rhn-plugin)

The **rhnplugin** provides support for connecting to `RHN Classic`. This allows systems registered with `RHN Classic` to update and install packages from this system.

Refer to `man rhnplugin` for more information about the plugin.

security (yum-plugin-security)

Discovering information about and applying security updates easily and often is important to all system administrators. For this reason **Yum** provides the **security** plugin, which extends `yum` with a set of highly-useful security-related commands, subcommands and options.

You can check for security-related updates as follows:

```
~]# yum check-update --security
Loaded plugins: langpacks, presto, refresh-packagekit, security
Limiting package lists to security relevant ones
updates-testing/updateinfo                              | 329 kB     00:00
9 package(s) needed for security, out of 270 available

ConsoleKit.x86_64                    0.4.5-1.fc15                    updates
ConsoleKit-libs.x86_64               0.4.5-1.fc15                    updates
ConsoleKit-x11.x86_64                0.4.5-1.fc15                    updates
NetworkManager.x86_64                1:0.8.999-2.git20110509.fc15    updates
NetworkManager-glib.x86_64           1:0.8.999-2.git20110509.fc15    updates
[output truncated]
```

You can then use either `yum update --security` or `yum update-minimal --security` to update those packages which are affected by security advisories. Both of these commands update all packages on the system for which a security advisory has been issued. `yum update-minimal --security` updates them to the latest packages which were released as part of a security advisory, while `yum update --security` will update all packages affected by a security advisory *to the latest version of that package available*.

In other words, if:

- the *kernel-2.6.38.4-20* package is installed on your system;
- the *kernel-2.6.38.6-22* package was released as a security update;
- then *kernel-2.6.38.6-26* was released as a bug fix update,

...then `yum update-minimal --security` will update you to kernel-2.6.38.6-22, and `yum update --security` will update you to kernel-2.6.38.6-26. Conservative system administrators may want to use `update-minimal` to reduce the risk incurred by updating packages as much as possible.

Refer to `man yum-security` for usage details and further explanation of the enhancements the **security** plugin adds to `yum`.

4.5. Additional Resources

http://yum.baseurl.org/wiki/Guides

The `Yum Guides` section of the **Yum** wiki contains more documentation.

Chapter 5.

PackageKit

Fedora provides **PackageKit** for viewing, managing, updating, installing and uninstalling packages compatible with your system. **PackageKit** consists of several graphical interfaces that can be opened from the GNOME panel menu, or from the Notification Area when **PackageKit** alerts you that updates are available. For more information on **PackageKit's** architecture and available front ends, refer to Section 5.3, *PackageKit Architecture* (page 101).

5.1. Updating Packages with Software Update

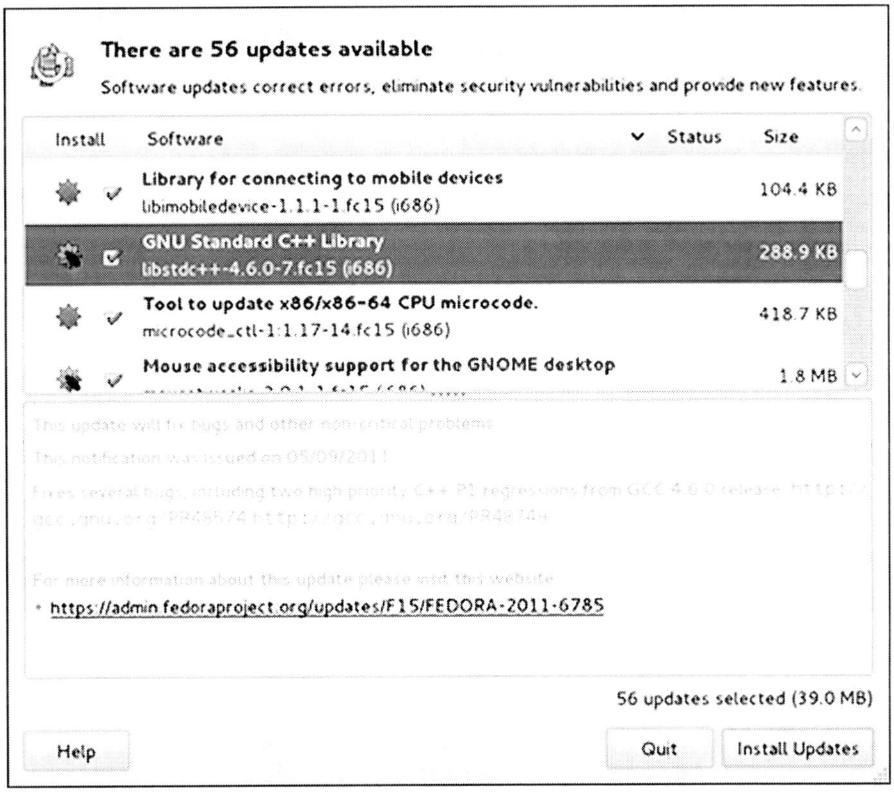

Figure 5.1. Installing updates with Software Update

You can open **Software Updates** by clicking **Applications** → **System Tools** → **Software Update** from the **Activities** menu, or running the `gpk-update-viewer` command at the shell prompt. In the **Software Updates** window, all available updates are listed along with the names of the packages being updated (minus the `.rpm` suffix, but including the CPU architecture), a short summary of the package, and, usually, short descriptions of the changes the update provides. Any updates you do not wish to install can be de-selected here by unchecking the checkbox corresponding to the update.

The updates presented in the **Software Updates** window only represent the currently-installed packages on your system for which updates are available; dependencies of those packages, whether they are existing packages on your system or new ones, are not shown until you click **Install Updates**.

PackageKit utilizes the fine-grained user authentication capabilities provided by the **PolicyKit** toolkit whenever you request it to make changes to the system. Whenever you instruct **PackageKit** to update, install or remove packages, you will be prompted to enter the superuser password before changes are made to the system.

If you instruct **PackageKit** to update the `kernel` package, then it will prompt you after installation, asking you whether you want to reboot the system and thereby boot into the newly-installed kernel.

5.1.1. Setting the Update-Checking Interval

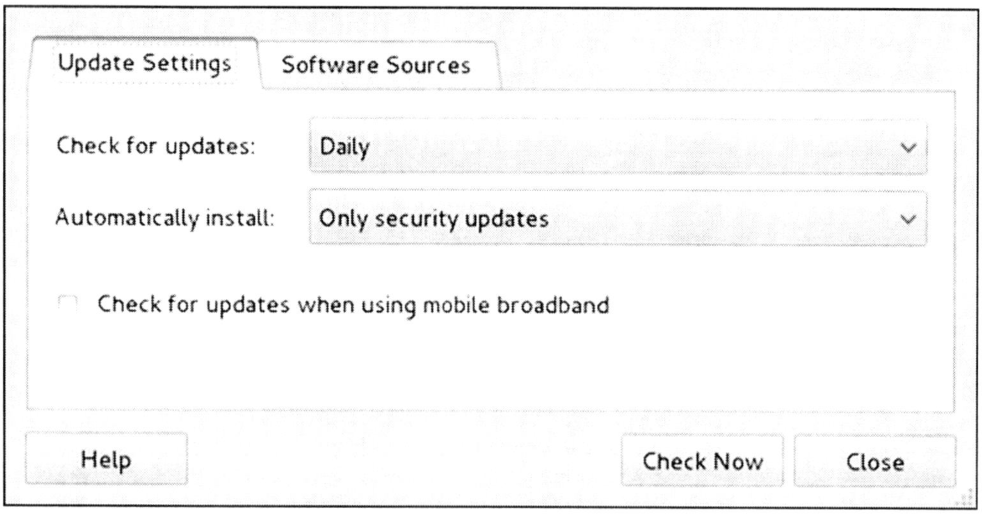

Figure 5.2. Setting PackageKit's update-checking interval

Selecting **Applications** → **Other** → **Software Updates** from the **Activities** menu opens the **Software Update Preferences** window. The **Update Settings** tab allows you to define the interval at which **PackageKit** checks for package updates, as well as whether or not to automatically install all updates or only security updates. Leaving the **Check for updates when using mobile broadband** box unchecked is handy for avoiding extraneous bandwidth usage when using a wireless connection on which you are charged for the amount of data you download.

5.1.2. Setting the Software Sources

To select which package repositories to use to install software updates, select **Applications → Other → Software Updates** from the **Activities** menu, and click the **Software Sources** tab of the **Software Update Preferences** window.

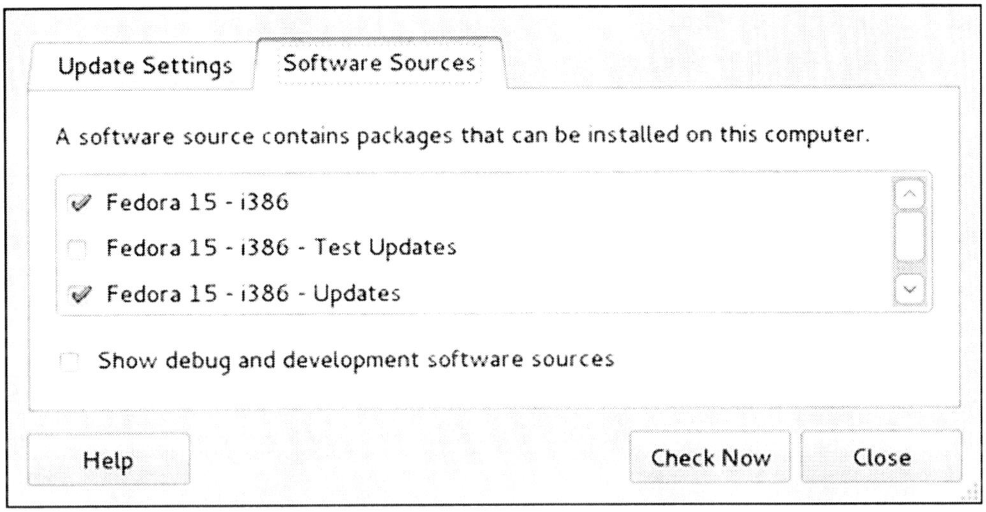

Figure 5.3. Setting PackageKit's software sources

PackageKit refers to **Yum** repositories as software sources. It obtains all packages from enabled software sources.The **Software Sources** tab shows the repository name, as written on the `name=`*`My Repository Name`* field of all [*`repository`*] sections in the `/etc/yum.conf` configuration file, and in all *`repository`*`.repo` files in the `/etc/yum.repos.d/` directory.

Entries which are checked in the **Enabled** column indicate that the corresponding repository will be used to locate packages to satisfy all update and installation requests (including dependency resolution). The **Enabled** column corresponds to the `enabled=`*`<1 or 0>`* field in [*`repository`*] sections. Checking an unchecked box enables the Yum repository, and unchecking it disables it. Performing either function causes **PolicyKit** to prompt for superuser authentication to enable or disable the repository. **PackageKit** actually inserts the `enabled=`*`<1 or 0>`* line into the correct [*`repository`*] section if it does not exist, or changes the value if it does. This means that enabling or disabling a repository through the **Software**

Sources window causes that change to persist after closing the window or rebooting the system. The ability to quickly enable and disable repositories based on our needs is a highly-convenient feature of **PackageKit**.

Note that it is not possible to add or remove **Yum** repositories through **PackageKit**.

Showing source RPM, test, and debuginfo repositories

Checking the box at the bottom of the **Software Sources** tab causes **PackageKit** to display source RPM, testing and debuginfo repositories as well. This box is unchecked by default.

5.2. Using Add/Remove Software

PackageKit's **Software Update** GUI window is a separate application from its **Add/Remove Software** application, although the two have intuitively similar interfaces. To find and install a new package, select **Applications → System Tools → Add/Remove Software** from the **Activities** menu, or run the `gpk-application` command at the shell prompt.

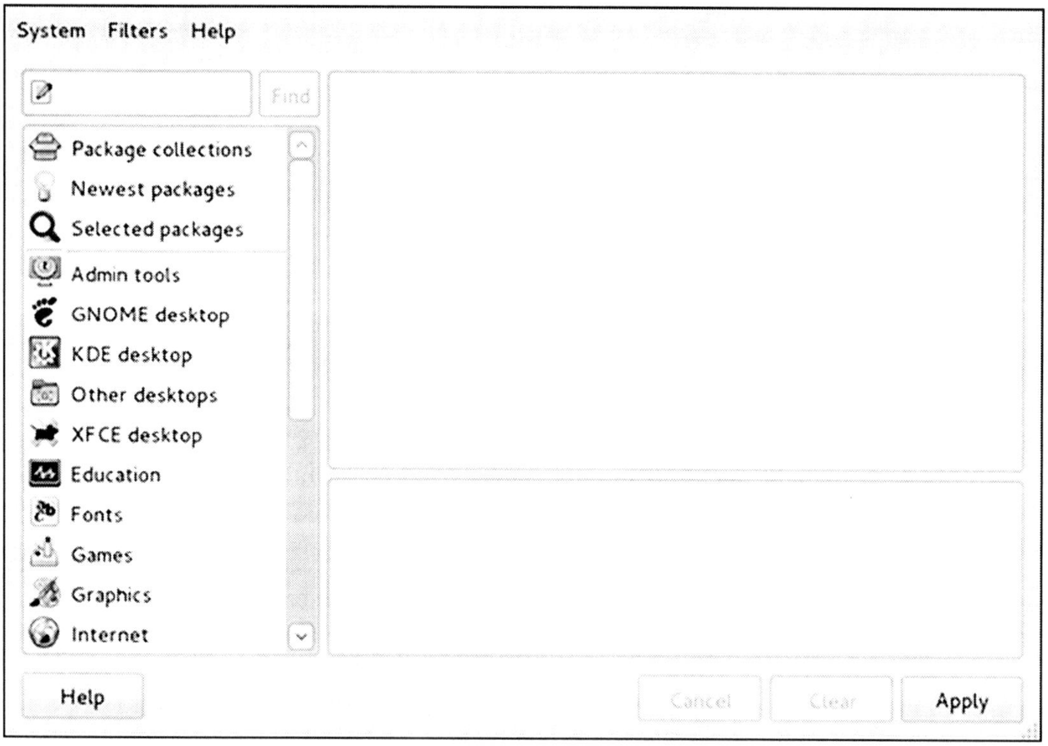

Figure 5.4. PackageKit's Add/Remove Software window

5.2.1. Refreshing Software Sources (Yum Repositories)

To enable or disable a **Yum** repository, open a dialog box by sclicking **System → Software Sources**, and select the **Software Sources** tab. Refer to Section 5.1.2, *Setting the Software Sources* (page 93) for more information on available configuration options.

After enabling and/or disabling the correct **Yum** repositories, make sure that you have the latest list of available packages. Click on **System → Refresh Package Lists** and **PackageKit** will obtain the latest lists of packages from all enabled software sources, that is, **Yum** repositories.

5.2.2. Finding Packages with Filters

You can view the list of all *configured* and unfiltered (see below) **Yum** repositories by opening **Add/Remove Software** and clicking **System → Software Sources**. Once the software sources have been updated, it is often beneficial to apply some filters so that **PackageKit** retrieves the results of our **Find** queries faster. This is especially helpful when performing many package searches. Four of the filters in the **Filters** drop-down menu are used to split results by matching or not matching a single criterion. By default when **PackageKit** starts, these filters are all unapplied (**No Filter**), but once you do filter by one of them, that filter remains set until you either change it or close **PackageKit**.

Because you are usually searching for available packages that are *not* installed on the system, click **Filters → Installed** and select the **Only Available** radio button.

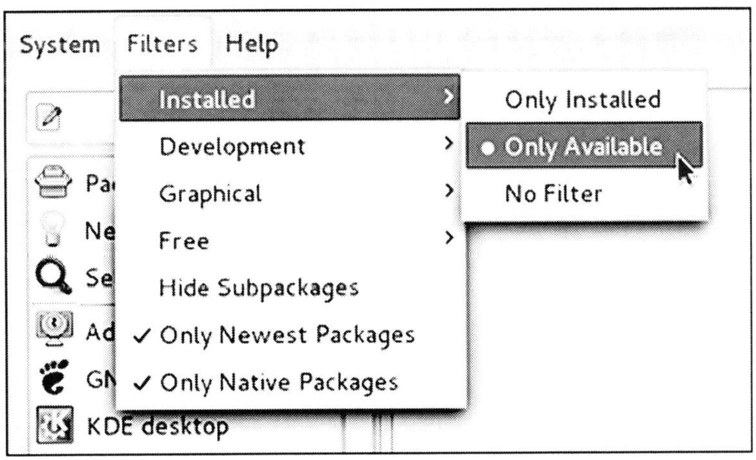

Figure 5.5. Filtering out already-installed packages

Also, unless we require development files such as C header files, we can filter for **Only End User Files** and, in doing so, filter out all of the `package_name-devel` packages we are not interested in.

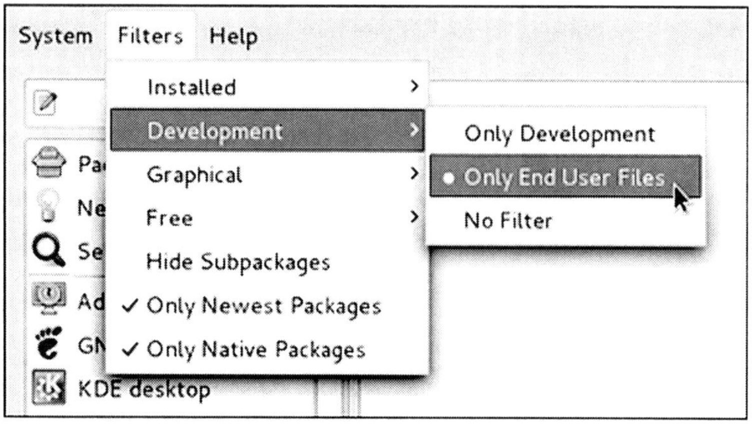

Figure 5.6. Filtering out development packages from the list of Find results

The two remaining filters with submenus are:

Graphical

Narrows the search to either applications which provide a GUI interface (**Only Graphical**) or those that do not. This filter is useful when browsing for GUI applications that perform a specific function.

Free

Search for packages which are considered to be free software Refer to the *Fedora Licensing List*[1] for details on approved licenses.

The remaining checkbox filters are always either checked or unchecked. They are:

Hide Subpackages

Checking the **Hide Subpackages** checkbox filters out generally-uninteresting packages that are typically only dependencies of other packages that we want. For example, checking **Hide Subpackages** and searching for `package` would cause the following related packages to be filtered out of the **Find** results (if it exists):

- `package-devel`
- `package-libs`
- `package-libs-devel`
- `package-debuginfo`

[1] *https://fedoraproject.org/wiki/Licensing#SoftwareLicenses*

Only Newest Packages

Checking **Only Newest Packages** filters out all older versions of the same package from the list of results, which is generally what we want.

> **Using the Only Newest Packages filter**
>
> Checking **Only Newest Packages** filters out all but the most recent version of any package from the results list. This filter is often combined with the **Only Available** filter to search for the latest available versions of new (not installed) packages.

Only native packages

Checking the **Only Native Packages** box on a multilib system causes **PackageKit** to omit listing results for packages compiled for the architecture that runs in *compatibility mode*. For example, enabling this filter on a 64-bit system with an AMD64 CPU would cause all packages built for the 32-bit x86 CPU architecture not to be shown in the list of results, even though those packages are able to run on an AMD64 machine. Packages which are architecture-agnostic (i.e. *noarch* packages such as `crontabs-1.10-32.1.el6.noarch.rpm`) are never filtered out by checking **Only Native Packages**. This filter has no affect on non-multilib systems, such as x86 machines.

5.2.3. Installing and Removing Packages (and Dependencies)

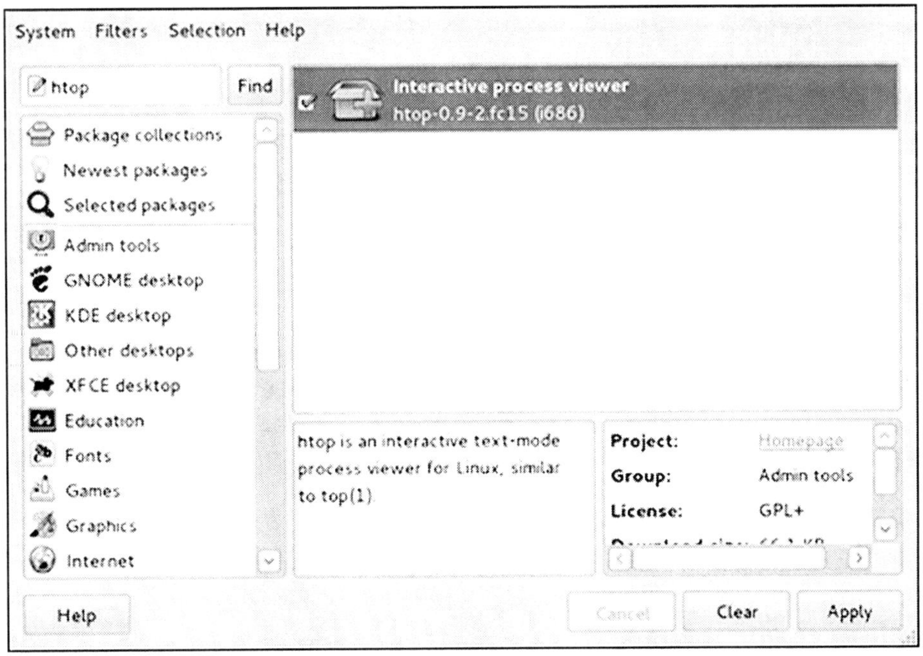

Figure 5.7. Viewing and installing a package with PackageKit's Add/Remove Software window

With the two filters selected, **Only Available** and **Only End User Files**, search for the **htop** interactive process viewer and highlight the package. You now have access to some very useful information about it, including: a clickable link to the project homepage; the **Yum** package group it is found in, if any; the license of the package; a pointer to the GNOME menu location from where the application can be opened, if applicable; and the size of the package, which is relevant when we download and install it.

When the checkbox next to a package or group is checked, then that item is already installed on the system. Checking an unchecked box causes it to be *marked* for installation, which only occurs when the **Apply** button is clicked. In this way, you can search for and select multiple packages or package groups before performing the actual installation transactions. Additionally, you can remove installed packages by unchecking the checked box, and the removal will occur along with any pending installations when **Apply** is pressed. Dependency resolution , which may add additional packages to be installed or removed, is performed after pressing **Apply**. **PackageKit** will then display a window listing those additional packages to install or remove, and ask for confirmation to proceed.

Check **htop** and click the **Apply** button. You will then be prompted for the superuser password; enter it, and **PackageKit** will install **htop**. One nice feature of **PackageKit** is that, following installation, it sometimes presents you with a list of your newly-installed applications and offer you the choice of running them immediately. Alternatively, you will remember that finding a package and selecting it in the **Add/Remove Software** window shows you the **Location** of where in the GNOME menus its application shortcut is located, which is helpful when you want to run it.

Once it is installed, you can run `htop`, a colorful and enhanced version of the `top` process viewer, by opening a shell prompt and entering:

```
htop
```

htop is nifty, but we decide that `top` is good enough for us and we want to uninstall it. Remembering that we need to change the **Only Available** filter we recently used to install it to **Only Installed** in **Filters** → **Installed**, we search for **htop** again and uncheck it. The program did not install any dependencies of its own; if it had, those would be automatically removed as well, as long as they were not also dependencies of any other packages still installed on our system.

Removing a package when other packages depend on it

Although **PackageKit** automatically resolves dependencies during package installation and removal, it is unable to remove a package without also removing packages which depend on it. This type of operation can only be performed by **RPM**, is not advised, and can potentially leave your system in a non-functioning state or cause applications to misbehave and/or crash.

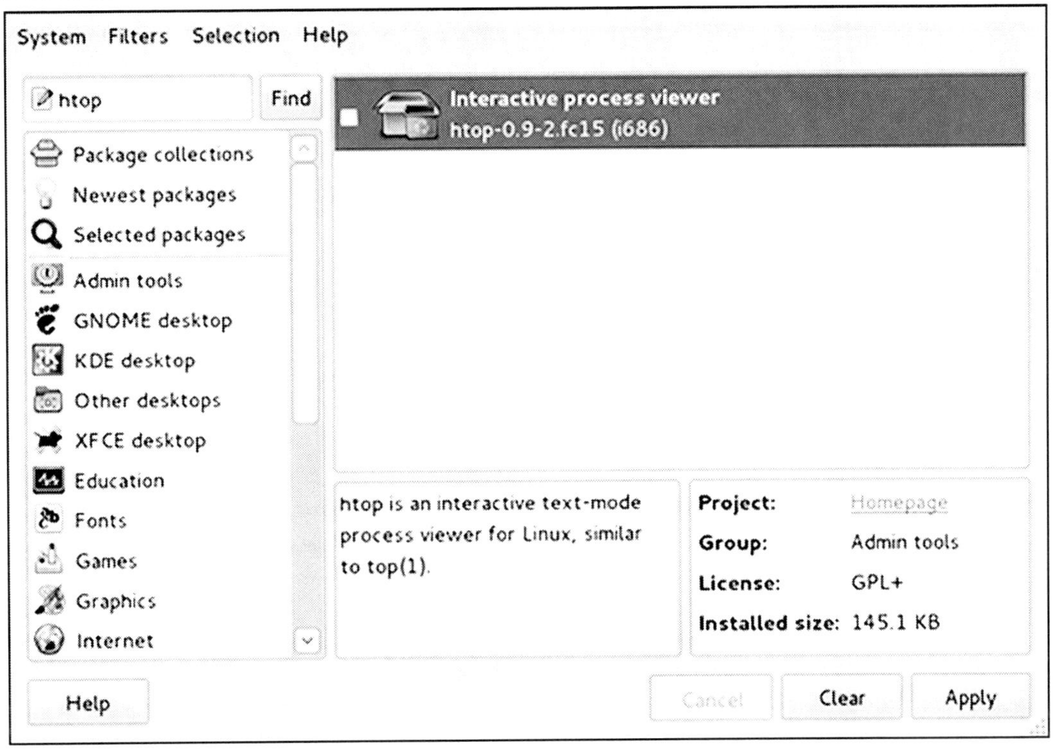

Figure 5.8. Removing a package with PackageKit's Add/Remove Software window

5.2.4. Installing and Removing Package Groups

PackageKit also has the ability to install **Yum** package groups, which it calls **Package collections**. Clicking on **Package collections** in the top-left list of categories in the **Software Updates** window allows us to scroll through and find the package group we want to install. In this case, we want to install Czech language support (the **Czech Support** group). Checking the box and clicking **Apply** informs us how many *additional* packages must be installed in order to fulfill the dependencies of the package group.

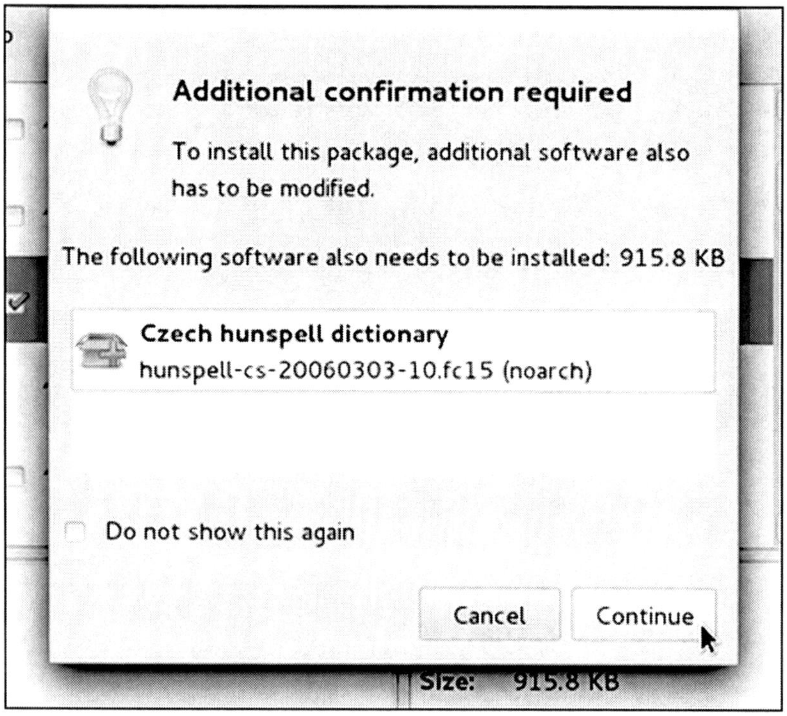

Figure 5.9. Installing the Czech Support package group

Similarly, installed package groups can be uninstalled by selecting **Package collections**, unchecking the appropriate checkbox, and applying.

5.2.5. Viewing the Transaction Log

PackageKit maintains a log of the transactions that it performs. To view the log, from the **Add/Remove Software** window, click **System** → **Software Log**, or run the `gpk-log` command at the shell prompt.

The **Software Log Viewer** shows the **Action**, such as `Updated Packages` or `Installed Packages`, the **Date** on which that action was performed, the **Username** of the user who performed the action, and the front end **Application** the user used (such as `Add/Remove Software`, or `Update System`). The **Details** column provides the types of the transactions, such as `Updated`, `Installed`, or `Removed`, as well as the list of packages the transactions were performed on.

Typing the name of a package in the top text entry field filters the list of transactions to those which affected that package.

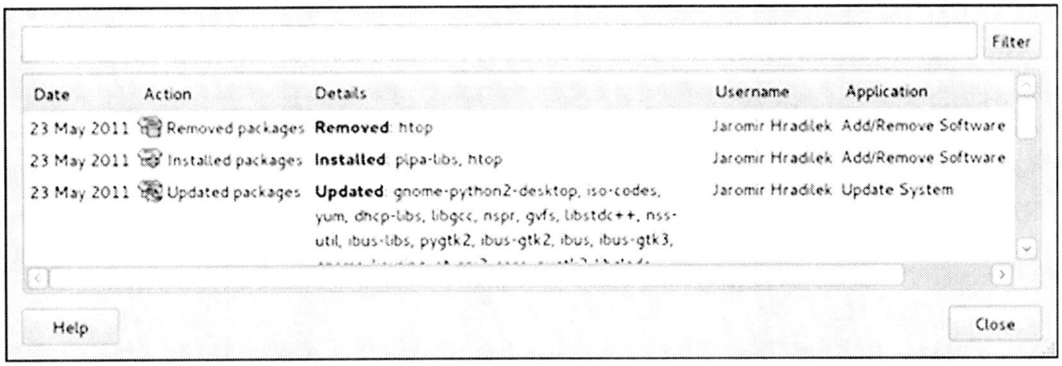

Figure 5.10. Viewing the log of package management transactions with the Software Log Viewer

5.3. PackageKit Architecture

Fedora provides the **PackageKit** suite of applications for viewing, updating, installing and uninstalling packages and package groups compatible with your system. Architecturally, **PackageKit** consists of several graphical front ends that communicate with the `packagekitd` daemon back end, which communicates with a package manager-specific back end that utilizes **Yum** to perform the actual transactions, such as installing and removing packages, etc.

Table 5.1. PackageKit GUI windows, menu locations, and shell prompt commands below shows the name of the GUI window, how to start the window from the GNOME desktop or from the **Add/Remove Software** window, and the name of the command line application that opens that window.

Window Title	Function	How to Open	Shell Command
Add/Remove Software	Install, remove or view package info	From the GNOME panel: **System** → **Administration** → **Add/Remove Software**	gpk-application
Software Update	Perform package updates	From the GNOME panel: **System** → **Administration** → **Software Update**	gpk-update-viewer
Software Sources	Enable and disable **Yum** repositories	From **Add/Remove Software**: **System** → **Software Sources**	gpk-repo
Software Log Viewer	View the transaction log	From **Add/Remove Software**: **System** → **Software Log**	gpk-log
Software Update Preferences	Set **PackageKit** preferences		gpk-prefs
(Notification Area Alert)	Alerts you when updates are available	From the GNOME panel: **System** → **Preferences** → **Startup Applications**, **Startup Programs** tab	gpk-update-icon

Table 5.1. PackageKit GUI windows, menu locations, and shell prompt commands

The `packagekitd` daemon runs outside the user session and communicates with the various graphical front ends. The `packagekitd` daemon[2] communicates via the **DBus** system message bus with another back end, which utilizes **Yum**'s Python API to perform queries and make changes to the system. On Linux systems other than Red Hat Enterprise Linux and Fedora, `packagekitd` can communicate with other back ends that are able to utilize the native package manager for that system. This modular architecture provides the abstraction necessary for the graphical interfaces to work with many different package managers to perform essentially the same types of package management tasks. Learning how to use the **PackageKit** front ends means that you can use the same familiar graphical interface across many different Linux distributions, even when they utilize a native package manager other than **Yum**.

In addition, **PackageKit**'s separation of concerns provides reliability in that a crash of one of the GUI windows—or even the user's X Window session—will not affect any package management tasks being supervised by the `packagekitd` daemon, which runs outside of the user session.

All of the front end graphical applications discussed in this chapter are provided by the `gnome-packagekit` package instead of by **PackageKit** and its dependencies. Users working in a KDE environment may prefer to install the `kpackagekit` package, which provides a KDE interface for **PackageKit**.

Finally, **PackageKit** also comes with a console-based front end called `pkcon`.

5.4. Additional Resources

PackageKit home page — *http://www.packagekit.org/index.html*

Information about and mailing lists for **PackageKit**.

PackageKit FAQ — *http://www.packagekit.org/pk-faq.html*

An informative list of Frequently Asked Questions for the **PackageKit** software suite.

PackageKit Feature Matrix — *http://www.packagekit.org/pk-matrix.html*

Cross-reference **PackageKit**-provided features with the long list of package manager back ends.

---

[2] System daemons are typically long-running processes that provide services to the user or to other programs, and which are started, often at boot time. Daemons respond to the `systemctl` command and can be turned on or off permanently by using the `systemctl enable` or `systemctl disable`commands. They can typically be recognized by a "*d*" appended to their name, such as the `packagekitd` daemon. Refer to Chapter 7, *Services and Daemons* (page 109) for information about system services.

Part III.
Networking

This part describes how to configure the network on Fedora.

Chapter 6.
Network Interfaces

Under Fedora, all network communications occur between configured software *interfaces* and *physical networking devices* connected to the system.

The configuration files for network interfaces are located in the `/etc/sysconfig/network-scripts/` directory. The scripts used to activate and deactivate these network interfaces are also located here. Although the number and type of interface files can differ from system to system, there are three categories of files that exist in this directory:

1. *Interface configuration files*
2. *Interface control scripts*
3. *Network function files*

The files in each of these categories work together to enable various network devices.

This chapter explores the relationship between these files and how they are used.

6.1. Network Configuration Files

Before delving into the interface configuration files, let us first itemize the primary configuration files used in network configuration. Understanding the role these files play in setting up the network stack can be helpful when customizing a Fedora system.

The primary network configuration files are as follows:

`/etc/hosts`

The main purpose of this file is to resolve hostnames that cannot be resolved any other way. It can also be used to resolve hostnames on small networks with no DNS server. Regardless of the type of network the computer is on, this file should contain a line specifying the IP address of the loopback device (`127.0.0.1`) as `localhost.localdomain`. For more information, refer to the `hosts` man page.

`/etc/resolv.conf`

This file specifies the IP addresses of DNS servers and the search domain. Unless configured to do otherwise, the network initialization scripts populate this file. For more information about this file, refer to the `resolv.conf` man page.

`/etc/sysconfig/network`

This file specifies routing and host information for all network interfaces. For more information about this file and the directives it accepts, refer to Section B.1.13, */etc/sysconfig/network* (page 481).

`/etc/sysconfig/network-scripts/ifcfg-interface-name`

For each network interface, there is a corresponding interface configuration script. Each of these files provide information specific to a particular network interface. Refer to Section 6.2, *Interface Configuration Files* (page 105) for more information on this type of file and the directives it accepts.

Warning

The `/etc/sysconfig/networking/` directory is used by the **Network Administration Tool** (`system-config-network`) and its contents should **not** be edited manually. Using only one method for network configuration is strongly encouraged, due to the risk of configuration deletion.

6.2. Interface Configuration Files

Interface configuration files control the software interfaces for individual network devices. As the system boots, it uses these files to determine what interfaces to bring up and how to configure them. These files are usually named `ifcfg-name` , where *`name`* refers to the name of the device that the configuration file controls.

6.2.1. Ethernet Interfaces

One of the most common interface files is `ifcfg-eth0`, which controls the first Ethernet *network interface card* or *NIC* in the system. In a system with multiple NICs, there are multiple `ifcfg-ethX` files (where *`X`* is a unique number corresponding to a specific interface). Because each device has its own configuration file, an administrator can control how each interface functions individually.

The following is a sample `ifcfg-eth0` file for a system using a fixed IP address:

```
DEVICE=eth0
BOOTPROTO=none
ONBOOT=yes
NETMASK=255.255.255.0
IPADDR=10.0.1.27
USERCTL=no
```

The values required in an interface configuration file can change based on other values. For example, the `ifcfg-eth0` file for an interface using DHCP looks different because IP information is provided by the DHCP server:

```
DEVICE=eth0
BOOTPROTO=dhcp
ONBOOT=yes
```

The **Network Administration Tool** (`system-config-network`) is an easy way to make changes to the various network interface configuration files.

However, it is also possible to manually edit the configuration files for a given network interface.

Below is a listing of the configurable parameters in an Ethernet interface configuration file:

`BONDING_OPTS=`*`parameters`*

sets the configuration parameters for the bonding device, and is used in `/etc/sysconfig/network-scripts/ifcfg-bond`*`N`* (see Section 6.2.2, *Channel Bonding Interfaces* - page 109). These parameters are identical to those used for bonding devices in `/sys/class/net/`*`bonding device`*`/bonding`, and the module parameters for the bonding driver as described in *`bonding` Module Directives*.

This configuration method is used so that multiple bonding devices can have different configurations. It is highly recommended to place all of your bonding options after the `BONDING_OPTS` directive in `ifcfg-`*`name`*. Do *not* specify options for the bonding device in `/etc/modprobe.d/`*`bonding`*`.conf`, or in the deprecated `/etc/modprobe.conf` file.

`BOOTPROTO=`*`protocol`*

where *`protocol`* is one of the following:

- `none` — No boot-time protocol should be used.
- `bootp` — The BOOTP protocol should be used.
- `dhcp` — The DHCP protocol should be used.

`BROADCAST=`*`address`*

where *`address`* is the broadcast address. This directive is deprecated, as the value is calculated automatically with `ipcalc`.

`DEVICE=`*`name`*

where *`name`* is the name of the physical device (except for dynamically-allocated PPP devices where it is the *logical name*).

`DHCP_HOSTNAME`

Use this option only if the DHCP server requires the client to specify a hostname before receiving an IP address.

`DNS`*`{1,2}`*`=`*`address`*

where *`address`* is a name server address to be placed in `/etc/resolv.conf` if the `PEERDNS` directive is set to `yes`.

`ETHTOOL_OPTS=`*`options`*

where *`options`* are any device-specific options supported by `ethtool`. For example, if you wanted to force 100Mb, full duplex:

`ETHTOOL_OPTS="autoneg off speed 100 duplex full"`

Instead of a custom initscript, use `ETHTOOL_OPTS` to set the interface speed and duplex settings. Custom initscripts run outside of the network init script lead to unpredictable results during a post-boot network service restart.

Set "autoneg off" before changing speed or duplex settings

Changing speed or duplex settings almost always requires disabling autonegotiation with the `autoneg off` option. This needs to be stated first, as the option entries are order-dependent.

`GATEWAY=`*`address`*

where *`address`* is the IP address of the network router or gateway device (if any).

`HOTPLUG=`*`answer`*

where *`answer`* is one of the following:

- `yes` — This device should be activated when it is hot-plugged (this is the default option).
- `no` — This device should *not* be activated when it is hot-plugged.

The `HOTPLUG=no` option can be used to prevent a channel bonding interface from being activated when a bonding kernel module is loaded.

Refer to Section 6.2.2, *Channel Bonding Interfaces* (page 109) for more information about channel bonding interfaces.

`HWADDR=`*`MAC-address`*

where *`MAC-address`* is the hardware address of the Ethernet device in the form *`AA:BB:CC:DD:EE:FF`*. This directive must be used in machines containing more than one NIC to ensure that the interfaces are assigned the correct device names regardless of the configured load order for each NIC's module. This directive should **not** be used in conjunction with `MACADDR`.

`IPADDR=`*`address`*

where *`address`* is the IP address.

`MACADDR=`*`MAC-address`*

where *`MAC-address`* is the hardware address of the Ethernet device in the form *`AA:BB:CC:DD:EE:FF`*. This directive is used to assign a MAC address to an interface, overriding the one assigned to the physical NIC. This directive should **not** be used in conjunction with `HWADDR`.

`MASTER=`*`bond-interface`*

where *`bond-interface`* is the channel bonding interface to which the Ethernet interface is linked.

This directive is used in conjunction with the `SLAVE` directive.

Refer to Section 6.2.2, *Channel Bonding Interfaces* (page 109) for more information about channel bonding interfaces.

`NETMASK=`*`mask`*

where *`mask`* is the netmask value.

`NETWORK=`*`address`*

where *`address`* is the network address. This directive is deprecated, as the value is calculated automatically with `ipcalc`.

`ONBOOT=`*`answer`*

where *`answer`* is one of the following:

- `yes` — This device should be activated at boot-time.
- `no` — This device should not be activated at boot-time.

`PEERDNS=`*`answer`*

where *`answer`* is one of the following:

- `yes` — Modify `/etc/resolv.conf` if the DNS directive is set. If using DHCP, then `yes` is the default.
- `no` — Do not modify `/etc/resolv.conf`.

`SLAVE=`*`answer`*

where *`answer`* is one of the following:

- `yes` — This device is controlled by the channel bonding interface specified in the `MASTER` directive.
- `no` — This device is *not* controlled by the channel bonding interface specified in the `MASTER` directive.

This directive is used in conjunction with the `MASTER` directive.

Refer to Section 6.2.2, *Channel Bonding Interfaces* (page 109) for more about channel bonding interfaces.

`SRCADDR=`*`address`*

where *`address`* is the specified source IP address for outgoing packets.

```
USERCTL=answer
```

where *answer* is one of the following:

- `yes` — Non-`root` users are allowed to control this device.
- `no` — Non-`root` users are not allowed to control this device.

6.2.2. Channel Bonding Interfaces

Fedora allows administrators to bind multiple network interfaces together into a single channel using the `bonding` kernel module and a special network interface called a *channel bonding interface*. Channel bonding enables two or more network interfaces to act as one, simultaneously increasing the bandwidth and providing redundancy.

To create a channel bonding interface, create a file in the `/etc/sysconfig/network-scripts/` directory called `ifcfg-bondN` , replacing *N* with the number for the interface, such as `0`.

The contents of the file can be identical to whatever type of interface is getting bonded, such as an Ethernet interface. The only difference is that the `DEVICE=` directive must be `bondN` , replacing *N* with the number for the interface.

The following is a sample channel bonding configuration file:

```
DEVICE=bond0
IPADDR=192.168.1.1
NETMASK=255.255.255.0
ONBOOT=yes
BOOTPROTO=none
USERCTL=no
BONDING_OPTS="bonding parameters separated by spaces"
```

Example 6.1. Sample ifcfg-bond0 interface configuration file

After the channel bonding interface is created, the network interfaces to be bound together must be configured by adding the `MASTER=` and `SLAVE=` directives to their configuration files. The configuration files for each of the channel-bonded interfaces can be nearly identical.

For example, if two Ethernet interfaces are being channel bonded, both `eth0` and `eth1` may look like the following example:

```
DEVICE=ethN
BOOTPROTO=none
ONBOOT=yes
MASTER=bond0
SLAVE=yes
USERCTL=no
```

In this example, replace *N* with the numerical value for the interface.

For a channel bonding interface to be valid, the kernel module must be loaded. To ensure that the module is loaded when the channel bonding interface is brought up, create a new file as `root` named *bonding*`.conf` in the `/etc/modprobe.d/` directory. Note that you can name this file anything you like as long as it ends with a `.conf` extension. Insert the following line in this new file:

```
alias bondN bonding
```

Replace *N* with the interface number, such as `0`. For each configured channel bonding interface, there must be a corresponding entry in your new `/etc/modprobe.d/`*bonding*`.conf` file.

Put all bonding module parameters in ifcfg-bondN files

Parameters for the bonding kernel module must be specified as a space-separated list in the *BONDING_OPTS="bonding parameters"* directive in the ifcfg-bond*N* interface file. Do *not* specify options for the bonding device in `/etc/modprobe.d/`*bonding*`.conf`, or in the deprecated `/etc/modprobe.conf` file. For further instructions and advice on configuring the bonding module and to view the list of bonding parameters, refer to Section 21.7.2, *Using Channel Bonding* (page 430).

6.2.3. Alias and Clone Files

Two lesser-used types of interface configuration files are *alias* and *clone* files.

Alias interface configuration files, which are used to bind multiple addresses to a single interface, use the `ifcfg-`*`if-name`*`:`*`alias-value`* naming scheme.

For example, an `ifcfg-eth0:0` file could be configured to specify `DEVICE=eth0:0` and a static IP address of 10.0.0.2, serving as an alias of an Ethernet interface already configured to receive its IP information via DHCP in `ifcfg-eth0`. Under this configuration, `eth0` is bound to a dynamic IP address, but the same physical network card can receive requests via the fixed, 10.0.0.2 IP address.

Caution

Alias interfaces do not support DHCP.

A clone interface configuration file should use the following naming convention: `ifcfg-`*`if-name`*`-`*`clone-name`* . While an alias file allows multiple addresses for an existing interface, a clone file is used to specify additional options for an interface. For example, a standard DHCP Ethernet interface called `eth0`, may look similar to this:

```
DEVICE=eth0
ONBOOT=yes
BOOTPROTO=dhcp
```

Since the default value for the `USERCTL` directive is `no` if it is not specified, users cannot bring this interface up and down. To give users the ability to control the interface, create a clone by copying `ifcfg-eth0` to `ifcfg-eth0-user` and add the following line to `ifcfg-eth0-user`:

```
USERCTL=yes
```

This way a user can bring up the `eth0` interface using the `/sbin/ifup eth0-user` command because the configuration options from `ifcfg-eth0` and `ifcfg-eth0-user` are combined. While this is a very basic example, this method can be used with a variety of options and interfaces.

The easiest way to create alias and clone interface configuration files is to use the graphical **Network Administration Tool**.

6.2.4. Dialup Interfaces

If you are connecting to the Internet via a dialup connection, a configuration file is necessary for the interface.

PPP interface files are named using the following format:

`ifcfg-ppp`*`X`*

where *`X`* is a unique number corresponding to a specific interface.

The PPP interface configuration file is created automatically when `wvdial`, the **Network Administration Tool** or **Kppp** is used to create a dialup account. It is also possible to create and edit this file manually.

The following is a typical `ifcfg-ppp0` file:

```
DEVICE=ppp0
NAME=test
WVDIALSECT=test
MODEMPORT=/dev/modem
LINESPEED=115200
PAPNAME=test
USERCTL=true
ONBOOT=no
PERSIST=no
DEFROUTE=yes
PEERDNS=yes
DEMAND=no
IDLETIMEOUT=600
```

Serial Line Internet Protocol (SLIP) is another dialup interface, although it is used less frequently. SLIP files have interface configuration file names such as `ifcfg-sl0`.

Other options that may be used in these files include:

`DEFROUTE=`*`answer`*

where *`answer`* is one of the following:

- `yes` — Set this interface as the default route.
- `no` — Do not set this interface as the default route.

`DEMAND=`*`answer`*

where *`answer`* is one of the following:

- `yes` — This interface allows `pppd` to initiate a connection when someone attempts to use it.
- `no` — A connection must be manually established for this interface.

`IDLETIMEOUT=`*`value`*

where *`value`* is the number of seconds of idle activity before the interface disconnects itself.

`INITSTRING=`*`string`*

where *`string`* is the initialization string passed to the modem device. This option is primarily used in conjunction with SLIP interfaces.

`LINESPEED=`*`value`*

where *`value`* is the baud rate of the device. Possible standard values include `57600`, `38400`, `19200`, and `9600`.

`MODEMPORT=`*`device`*

where *`device`* is the name of the serial device that is used to establish the connection for the interface.

`MTU=`*`value`*

where *`value`* is the *Maximum Transfer Unit (MTU)* setting for the interface. The MTU refers to the largest number of bytes of data a frame can carry, not counting its header information. In some dialup situations, setting this to a value of `576` results in fewer packets dropped and a slight improvement to the throughput for a connection.

`NAME=`*`name`*

where *`name`* is the reference to the title given to a collection of dialup connection configurations.

`PAPNAME=name`

where `name` is the username given during the *Password Authentication Protocol (PAP)* exchange that occurs to allow connections to a remote system.

`PERSIST=answer`

where `answer` is one of the following:

- `yes` — This interface should be kept active at all times, even if deactivated after a modem hang up.
- `no` — This interface should not be kept active at all times.

`REMIP=address`

where `address` is the IP address of the remote system. This is usually left unspecified.

`WVDIALSECT=name`

where `name` associates this interface with a dialer configuration in `/etc/wvdial.conf`. This file contains the phone number to be dialed and other important information for the interface.

6.2.5. Other Interfaces

Other common interface configuration files include the following:

`ifcfg-lo`

A local *loopback interface* is often used in testing, as well as being used in a variety of applications that require an IP address pointing back to the same system. Any data sent to the loopback device is immediately returned to the host's network layer.

Do not manually edit the ifcfg-lo script

The loopback interface script, `/etc/sysconfig/network-scripts/ifcfg-lo`, should never be edited manually. Doing so can prevent the system from operating correctly.

`ifcfg-irlan0`

An *infrared interface* allows information between devices, such as a laptop and a printer, to flow over an infrared link. This works in a similar way to an Ethernet device except that it commonly occurs over a peer-to-peer connection.

`ifcfg-plip0`

A *Parallel Line Interface Protocol (PLIP)* connection works much the same way as an Ethernet device, except that it utilizes a parallel port.

6.3. Interface Control Scripts

The interface control scripts activate and deactivate system interfaces. There are two primary interface control scripts that call on control scripts located in the `/etc/sysconfig/network-scripts/` directory: `/sbin/ifdown` and `/sbin/ifup`.

The `ifup` and `ifdown` interface scripts are symbolic links to scripts in the `/sbin/` directory. When either of these scripts are called, they require the value of the interface to be specified, such as:

```
ifup eth0
```

Use the ifup and ifdown interface scripts

The `ifup` and `ifdown` interface scripts are the only scripts that the user should use to bring up and take down network interfaces.
The following scripts are described for reference purposes only.

Two files used to perform a variety of network initialization tasks during the process of bringing up a network interface are `/etc/rc.d/init.d/functions` and `/etc/sysconfig/network-scripts/network-functions`. Refer to Section 6.5, *Network Function Files* (page 117) for more information.

After verifying that an interface has been specified and that the user executing the request is allowed to control the interface, the correct script brings the interface up or down. The following are common interface control scripts found within the `/etc/sysconfig/network-scripts/` directory:

`ifup-aliases`

Configures IP aliases from interface configuration files when more than one IP address is associated with an interface.

`ifup-ippp` and `ifdown-ippp`

Brings ISDN interfaces up and down.

`ifup-ipv6` and `ifdown-ipv6`

Brings IPv6 interfaces up and down.

`ifup-plip`

Brings up a PLIP interface.

`ifup-plusb`

Brings up a USB interface for network connections.

`ifup-post` and `ifdown-post`

Contains commands to be executed after an interface is brought up or down.

`ifup-ppp` and `ifdown-ppp`

Brings a PPP interface up or down.

`ifup-routes`

Adds static routes for a device as its interface is brought up.

`ifdown-sit` and `ifup-sit`

Contains function calls related to bringing up and down an IPv6 tunnel within an IPv4 connection.

`ifup-wireless`

Brings up a wireless interface.

Be careful when removing or modifying network scripts!

Removing or modifying any scripts in the `/etc/sysconfig/network-scripts/` directory can cause interface connections to act irregularly or fail. Only advanced users should modify scripts related to a network interface.

The easiest way to manipulate all network scripts simultaneously is to use the `systemctl` command on the network service (`/etc/rc.d/init.d/network`), as illustrated the following command:

```
systemctl action network.service
```

Here, *`action`* can be either `start`, `stop`, or `restart`.

To view a list of configured devices and currently active network interfaces, use the following command:

```
service network status
```

6.4. Configuring Static Routes

If static routes are required, they can be configured for each interface. This can be useful if you have multiple interfaces in different subnets. Use the `route` command to display the IP routing table.

Static route configuration is stored in a `/etc/sysconfig/network-scripts/route-`*`interface`* file. For example, static routes for the eth0 interface would be stored in the `/etc/sysconfig/network-scripts/route-eth0` file. The `route-`*`interface`* file has two formats: IP command arguments and network/netmask directives.

IP Command Arguments Format

Define a default gateway on the first line. This is only required if the default gateway is not set via DHCP:

```
default via X.X.X.X dev interface
```

`X.X.X.X` is the IP address of the default gateway. The *`interface`* is the interface that is connected to, or can reach, the default gateway.

Define a static route. Each line is parsed as an individual route:

```
X.X.X.X/X via X.X.X.X dev interface
```

`X.X.X.X/X` is the network number and netmask for the static route. `X.X.X.X` and *`interface`* are the IP address and interface for the default gateway respectively. The `X.X.X.X` address does not have to be the default gateway IP address. In most cases, `X.X.X.X` will be an IP address in a different subnet, and *`interface`* will be the interface that is connected to, or can reach, that subnet. Add as many static routes as required.

The following is a sample `route-eth0` file using the IP command arguments format. The default gateway is 192.168.0.1, interface eth0. The two static routes are for the 10.10.10.0/24 and 172.16.1.0/24 networks:

```
default via 192.168.0.1 dev eth0
10.10.10.0/24 via 192.168.0.1 dev eth0
172.16.1.0/24 via 192.168.0.1 dev eth0
```

Static routes should only be configured for other subnets. The above example is not necessary, since packets going to the 10.10.10.0/24 and 172.16.1.0/24 networks will use the default gateway anyway. Below is an example of setting static routes to a different subnet, on a machine in a 192.168.0.0/24 subnet. The example machine has an eth0 interface in the 192.168.0.0/24 subnet, and an eth1 interface (10.10.10.1) in the 10.10.10.0/24 subnet:

```
10.10.10.0/24 via 10.10.10.1 dev eth1
```

Duplicate default gateways

If the default gateway is already assigned from DHCP, the IP command arguments format can cause one of two errors during start-up, or when bringing up an interface from the down state using the `ifup` command: "RTNETLINK answers: File exists" or 'Error: either "to" is a duplicate, or "`X.X.X.X`" is a garbage.', where `X.X.X.X` is the gateway, or a different IP address. These errors can also occur if you have another route to another network using the default gateway. Both of these errors are safe to ignore.

Network/Netmask Directives Format

You can also use the network/netmask directives format for `route-interface` files. The following is a template for the network/netmask format, with instructions following afterwards:

```
ADDRESS0=X.X.X.X
NETMASK0=X.X.X.X
GATEWAY0=X.X.X.X
```

- `ADDRESS0=X.X.X.X` is the network number for the static route.
- `NETMASK0=X.X.X.X` is the netmask for the network number defined with `ADDRESS0=X.X.X.X` .
- `GATEWAY0=X.X.X.X` is the default gateway, or an IP address that can be used to reach `ADDRESS0=X.X.X.X`

The following is a sample `route-eth0` file using the network/netmask directives format. The default gateway is 192.168.0.1, interface eth0. The two static routes are for the 10.10.10.0/24 and 172.16.1.0/24 networks. However, as mentioned before, this example is not necessary as the 10.10.10.0/24 and 172.16.1.0/24 networks would use the default gateway anyway:

```
ADDRESS0=10.10.10.0
NETMASK0=255.255.255.0
GATEWAY0=192.168.0.1
ADDRESS1=172.16.1.0
NETMASK1=255.255.255.0
GATEWAY1=192.168.0.1
```

Subsequent static routes must be numbered sequentially, and must not skip any values. For example, `ADDRESS0`, `ADDRESS1`, `ADDRESS2`, and so on.

Below is an example of setting static routes to a different subnet, on a machine in the 192.168.0.0/24 subnet. The example machine has an eth0 interface in the 192.168.0.0/24 subnet, and an eth1 interface (10.10.10.1) in the 10.10.10.0/24 subnet:

```
ADDRESS0=10.10.10.0
NETMASK0=255.255.255.0
GATEWAY0=10.10.10.1
```

Note that if DHCP is used, it can assign these settings automatically.

6.5. Network Function Files

Fedora makes use of several files that contain important common functions used to bring interfaces up and down. Rather than forcing each interface control file to contain these functions, they are grouped together in a few files that are called upon when necessary.

The `/etc/sysconfig/network-scripts/network-functions` file contains the most commonly used IPv4 functions, which are useful to many interface control scripts. These functions include contacting running programs that have requested information about changes in the status of an interface, setting hostnames, finding a gateway device, verifying whether or not a particular device is down, and adding a default route.

As the functions required for IPv6 interfaces are different from IPv4 interfaces, a `/etc/sysconfig/network-scripts/network-functions-ipv6` file exists specifically to hold this information. The functions in this file configure and delete static IPv6 routes, create and remove tunnels, add and remove IPv6 addresses to an interface, and test for the existence of an IPv6 address on an interface.

6.6. Additional Resources

The following are resources which explain more about network interfaces.

6.6.1. Installed Documentation

`/usr/share/doc/initscripts-`*`version`*`/sysconfig.txt`

A guide to available options for network configuration files, including IPv6 options not covered in this chapter.

`/usr/share/doc/iproute-`*`version`*`/ip-cref.ps`

This file contains a wealth of information about the `ip` command, which can be used to manipulate routing tables, among other things. Use the **ggv** or **kghostview** application to view this file.

Part IV. Infrastructure Services

This part provides information how to configure services and daemons, configure authentication, and enable remote logins.

Chapter 7.

Services and Daemons

Maintaining security on your system is extremely important, and one approach for this task is to manage access to system services carefully. Your system may need to provide open access to particular services (for example, `httpd` if you are running a web server). However, if you do not need to provide a service, you should turn it off to minimize your exposure to possible bug exploits.

This chapter covers the configuration of the services to be run when a system is started, and provides information on how to start, stop, and restart the services on the command line using the **systemctl** utility.

Keep the system secure

When you allow access for new services, always remember that both the firewall and **SELinux** need to be configured as well. One of the most common mistakes committed when configuring a new service is neglecting to implement the necessary firewall configuration and SELinux policies to allow access for it. Refer to the Fedora *Security Guide* (see Section 7.3, *Additional Resources* - page 124) for more information.

7.1. Configuring Services

To allow you to configure which services are started at boot time, Fedora is shipped with the **systemctl** command line tool.

Do not use the ntsysv and chkconfig utilities

Although it is still possible to use the **ntsysv** and **chkconfig** utilities to manage services that have init scripts installed in the `/etc/rc.d/init.d/` directory, it is advised that you use the **systemctl** utility.

Enabling the irqbalance service

To ensure optimal performance on POWER architecture, it is recommended that the `irqbalance` service is enabled. In most cases, this service is installed and configured to run during the Fedora 15 installation. To verify that `irqbalance` is running, type the following at a shell prompt:

```
systemctl status irqbalance.service
```

7.1.1. Enabling the Service

To configure a service to be automatically started at boot time, use the `systemctl` command in the following form:

```
systemctl enable service_name.service
```

The service will be started the next time you boot the system. For information on how to start the service immediately, refer to Section 7.2.2, *Running the Service* (page 123).

Imagine you want to run the Apache HTTP Server on your system. Provided that you have the httpd package installed, you can enable the `httpd` service by typing the following at a shell prompt as `root`:

```
~]# systemctl enable httpd.service
```

Example 7.1. Enabling the httpd service

7.1.2. Disabling the Service

To disable starting a service at boot time, use the `systemctl` command in the following form:

```
systemctl disable service_name.service
```

The next time you boot the system, the service will *not* be started. For information on how to stop the service immediately, refer to Section 7.2.3, *Stopping the Service* (page 123).

In order to secure the system, users are advised to disable insecure connection protocols such as Telnet. You can make sure that the `telnet` service is disabled by running the following command as `root`:

```
~]# systemctl disable telnet.service
```

Example 7.2. Disabling the telnet service

7.2. Running Services

The **systemctl** utility also allows you to determine the status of a particular service, as well as to start, stop, or restart a service.

Do not use the service utility

Although it is still possible to use the **service** utility to manage services that have init scripts installed in the `/etc/rc.d/init.d/` directory, it is advised that you use the **systemctl** utility.

7.2.1. Checking the Service Status

To determine the status of a particular service, use the `systemctl` command in the following form:

```
systemctl status service_name.service
```

This command provides detailed information on the service's status. However, if you merely need to verify that a service is running, you can use the `systemctl` command in the following form instead:

```
systemctl is-active service_name.service
```

Finally, to display a list of all active system services, type:

```
systemctl list-units --type=service
```

This command provides a tabular output with each line consisting of the following columns:

- `UNIT` — A `systemd` unit name. In this case, a service name.
- `LOAD` — Information whether the `systemd` unit was properly loaded.
- `ACTIVE` — A high-level unit activation state.
- `SUB` — A low-level unit activation state.
- `JOB` — A pending job for the unit.
- `DESCRIPTION` — A brief description of the unit.

Example 7.1. Enabling the httpd service above illustrated how to enable starting the `httpd` service at boot time. Imagine that the system has been restarted and you need to verify that the service is really running. You can do so by typing the following at a shell prompt:

```
~]$ systemctl is-active httpd.service
active
```

You can also display detailed information about the service by running the following command:

```
~]$ systemctl status httpd.service
httpd.service - LSB: start and stop Apache HTTP Server
     Loaded: loaded (/etc/rc.d/init.d/httpd)
     Active: active (running) since Mon, 23 May 2011 21:38:57 +0200; 27s ago
    Process: 2997 ExecStart=/etc/rc.d/init.d/httpd start (code=exited, status=0/SUCCESS
   Main PID: 3002 (httpd)
     CGroup: name=systemd:/system/httpd.service
             ├ 3002 /usr/sbin/httpd
             ├ 3004 /usr/sbin/httpd
             ├ 3005 /usr/sbin/httpd
             ├ 3006 /usr/sbin/httpd
             ├ 3007 /usr/sbin/httpd
             ├ 3008 /usr/sbin/httpd
```

```
        ├ 3009 /usr/sbin/httpd
        ├ 3010 /usr/sbin/httpd
        └ 3011 /usr/sbin/httpd
```

Example 7.3. Checking the status of the httpd service

You can list all active services by using the following command:

```
~]$ systemctl list-units --type=service
UNIT                      LOAD   ACTIVE SUB     JOB DESCRIPTION
abrt-ccpp.service         loaded active exited      LSB: Installs coredump handler
                                                           which saves segfault data
abrt-oops.service         loaded active running     LSB: Watches system log for oops
                               messages, creates ABRT dump directories for each oops
abrtd.service             loaded active running     ABRT Automated Bug Reporting Tool
accounts-daemon.service   loaded active running     Accounts Service
atd.service               loaded active running     Job spooling tools
[output truncated]
```

In the example above, the `abrtd` service is loaded, active, and running, and it does not have any pending jobs.

Example 7.4. Listing all active services

7.2.2. Running the Service

To run a service, use the `systemctl` command in the following form:

```
systemctl start service_name.service
```

This will start the service in the current session. To configure the service to be started at boot time, refer to Section 7.1.1, *Enabling the Service* (page 121).

Example 7.1. Enabling the httpd service above illustrated how to run the `httpd` service at boot time. You can start the service immediately by typing the following at a shell prompt as `root`:

```
~]# systemctl start httpd.service
```

Example 7.5. Running the httpd service

7.2.3. Stopping the Service

To stop a service, use the `systemctl` command in the following form:

```
systemctl stop service_name.service
```

This will stop the service in the current session. To disable starting the service at boot time, refer to Section 7.1.1, *Enabling the Service* (page 121).

Example 7.2. Disabling the telnet service above illustrated how to disable starting the `telnet` service at boot time. You can stop the service immediately by running the following command as `root`:

```
~]# systemctl stop telnet.service
```

Example 7.6. Stopping the telnet service

7.2.4. Restarting the Service

To restart a service, use the `systemctl` command in the following form:

```
systemctl restart service_name.service
```

For any changes in the `/etc/ssh/sshd_config` configuration file to take effect, it is required that you restart the `sshd` service. You can do so by typing the following at a shell prompt as `root`:

```
~]# systemctl restart httpd.service
```

Example 7.7. Restarting the sshd service

7.3. Additional Resources

7.3.1. Installed Documentation

- `systemctl`(1) — The manual page for the **systemctl** utility.

7.3.2. Related Books

Security Guide

A guide to securing Fedora. It contains valuable information on how to set up the firewall, as well as the configuration of **SELinux**.

Chapter 8.
Configuring Authentication

8.1. The Authentication Configuration Tool

When a user logs in to a Fedora system, the username and password combination must be verified, or *authenticated*, as a valid and active user. Sometimes the information to verify the user is located on the local system, and other times the system defers the authentication to a user database on a remote system.

The **Authentication Configuration Tool** provides a graphical interface for configuring user information retrieval from *Lightweight Directory Access Protocol* (LDAP), *Network Information Service* (NIS), and *Winbind* user account databases. This tool also allows you to configure Kerberos to be used as the authentication protocol when using LDAP or NIS.

Using a high or medium security level

If you configured a medium or high security level during installation (or with the **Security Level Configuration Tool**), then the firewall will prevent NIS authentication. For more information about firewalls, refer to the "*Firewalls*" section of the Fedora *Security Guide*.

To start the graphical version of the **Authentication Configuration** tool from the desktop, select **Applications** → **Other** → **Authentication** form the **Activities** menu or type the command `system-config-authentication` at a shell prompt (for example, in an **XTerm** or a **GNOME** terminal).

Your changes are immediately applied

After exiting the authentication program, any changes you made take effect immediately.

8.1.1. Identity & Authentication

The **Identity & Authentication** tab allows you to configure how users should be authenticated, and has several options for each method of authentication. To select which user account database should be used, select an option from the drop-down list.

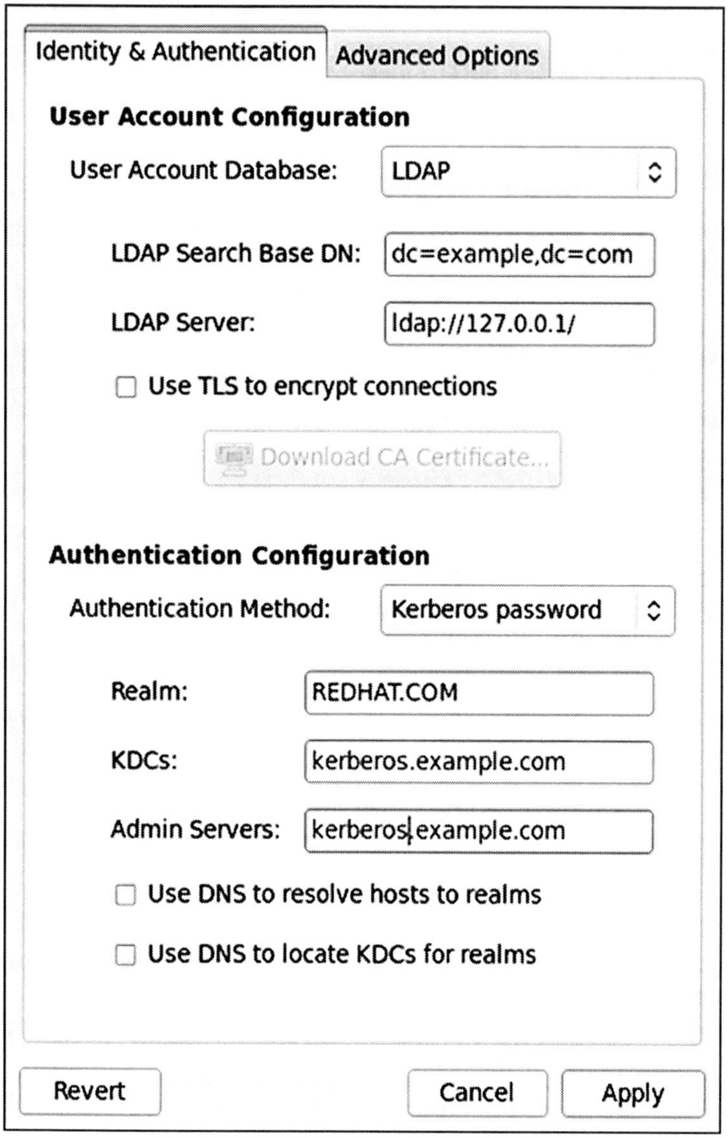

Figure 8.1. Identity & Authentication; changing the option in the User Account Database drop-down list changes the contents of the tab

The following list explains what each option configures:

LDAP

The **LDAP** option instructs the system to retrieve user information via LDAP. It contains the following specifications:

- **LDAP Search Base DN** — Specifies that user information should be retrieved using the listed Distinguished Name (DN).
- **LDAP Server** — Specifies the address of the `LDAP` server.
- **Use TLS to encrypt connections** — When enabled, `Transport Layer Security` (TLC) will be used to encrypt passwords sent to the `LDAP` server. The **Download CA Certificate** option allows you to specify a URL from which to download a valid *Certificate Authority certificate* (CA). A valid CA certificate must be in the *Privacy Enhanced Mail* (PEM) format.

Using ldaps:// in the LDAP Server field

The **Use TLS to encrypt connections** option must not be ticked if an `ldaps://` server address is specified in the **LDAP Server** field.

For more information about CA Certificates, refer to Section 12.1.8.1, *An Overview of Certificates and Security* (page 261).

The `openldap-clients` package must be installed for this option to work.

For more information about LDAP, refer to Section 14.1, *OpenLDAP* (page 302).

LDAP provides the following methods of authentication:

- **Kerberos password** — This option enables Kerberos authentication. It contains the following specifications:
  - **Realm** — Configures the realm for the Kerberos server. The realm is the network that uses Kerberos, composed of one or more KDCs and a potentially large number of clients.
  - **KDCs** — Defines the Key Distribution Centers (KDC), which are servers that issue Kerberos tickets.
  - **Admin Servers** — Specifies the administration server(s) running `kadmind`.

  The **Kerberos Settings** dialog also allows you to use DNS to resolve hosts to realms and locate KDCs for realms.

  The `krb5-libs` and `krb5-workstation` packages must be installed for this option to work. For more information about Kerberos, refer to section *Using Kerberos* of the Fedora 15 *Managing Single Sign-On and Smart Cards* guide.
- **LDAP password** — This option instructs standard PAM-enabled applications to use LDAP authentication with options specified in the User Account Configuration of LDAP. When using this option, you must provide an `ldaps://` server address or use TLS for LDAP authentication.

Setting up the SSSD service

The SSSD service is used as a client for LDAP and Kerberos servers. Thus, offline login is enabled and supported by default. No user interaction is needed to set up the SSSD service with the **Authentication Configuration Tool**. For more information about the SSSD service, refer to Section 8.2, *The System Security Services Daemon (SSSD)* (page 134).

NIS

The **NIS** option configures the system to connect to a NIS server (as an NIS client) for user and password authentication. To configure this option, specify the NIS domain and NIS server. If the NIS server is not specified, the daemon attempts to find it via broadcast.

The ypbind package must be installed for this option to work. If the NIS user account database is used, the `portmap` and `ypbind` services are started and are also enabled to start at boot time.

For more information about NIS, refer to section "*Securing NIS*" of the Fedora *Security Guide*.

NIS provides the following methods of authentication:

- **Kerberos password** — This option enables Kerberos authentication. For more information about configuration of the Kerberos authentication method, refer to the previous section on LDAP.
- **NIS password** — This option enables NIS authentication. NIS can provide authentication information to outside processes to authenticate users.

Winbind

The **Winbind** option configures the system to connect to a Windows Active Directory or a Windows domain controller. User information from the specified directory or domain controller can then be accessed, and server authentication options can be configured. It contains the following specifications:

- **Winbind Domain** — Specifies the Windows Active Directory or domain controller to connect to.
- **Security Model** — Allows you to select a security model, which configures the Samba client mode of operation. The drop-down list allows you to select any of the following:
  - **ads** — This mode instructs Samba to act as a domain member in an Active Directory Server (ADS) realm. To operate in this mode, the `krb5-server` package must be installed, and Kerberos must be configured properly.

  - **domain** — In this mode, Samba will attempt to validate the username/password by authenticating it through a Windows NT Primary or Backup Domain Controller, similar to how a Windows NT Server would.
  - **server** — In this mode, Samba will attempt to validate the username/password by authenticating it through another SMB server (for example, a Windows NT Server). If the attempt fails, the **user** mode will take effect instead.
  - **user** — This is the default mode. With this level of security, a client must first log in with a valid username and password. Encrypted passwords can also be used in this security mode.
- **Winbind ADS Realm** — When the **ads** Security Model is selected, this allows you to specify the ADS Realm the Samba server should act as a domain member of.
- **Winbind Domain Controllers** — Use this option to specify which domain controller `winbind` should use. For more information about domain controllers, please refer to Section 15.1.6.3, *Domain Controller* (page 328).
- **Template Shell** — When filling out the user information for a Windows NT user, the `winbindd` daemon uses the value chosen here to specify the login shell for that user.
- **Allow offline login** — By checking this option, you allow authentication information to be stored in a local cache (provided by SSSD). This information is then used when a user attempts to authenticate while offline.

For more information about the `winbindd` service, refer to Section 15.1.2, *Samba Daemons and Related Services* (page 318).

Winbind provides only one method of authentication, **Winbind password**. This method of authentication uses the options specified in the User Account Configuration of Winbind to connect to a Windows Active Directory or a Windows domain controller.

8.1.2. Advanced Options

This tab allows you to configure advanced options, as listed below.

Local Authentication Options

- **Enable fingerprint reader support** — By checking this option, you enable fingerprint authentication to log in by scanning your finger with the fingerprint reader.
- **Enable local access control** — When enabled, `/etc/security/access.conf` is consulted for authorization of a user.
- **Password Hashing Algorithm** — This option lets you specify which hashing or cryptographic algorithm should be used to encrypt locally stored passwords.

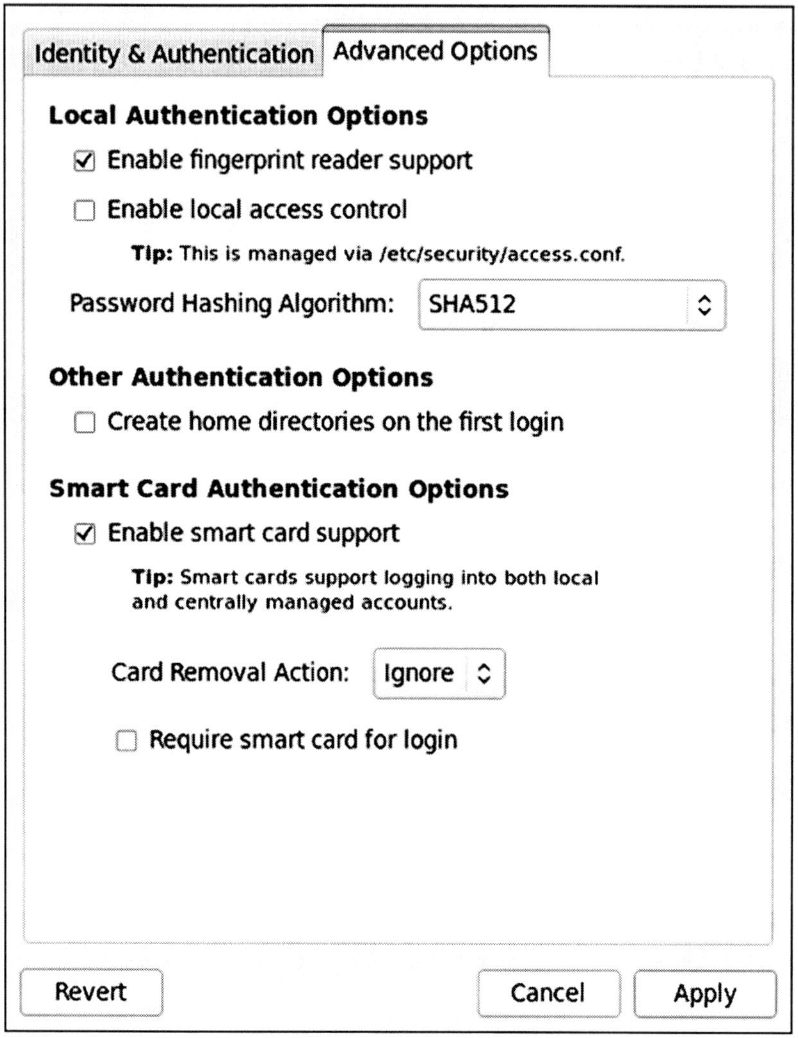

Figure 8.2. Advanced Options

Other Authentication Options

Create home directories on the first login – When enabled, the user's home directory is automatically created when they log in if it does not already exist.

Smart Card Authentication Options

Enable smart card support – This option enables smart card authentication. Smart card authentication allows you to log in using a certificate and a key associated with a smart card.

When the **Enable smart card support** option is checked, the following options can be specified:

- **Card Removal Action** — This option defines what action the system performs when the card is removed from the card reader during an active session. Two alternatives are available:
    - **Ignore** — The card removal is ignored and the system continues to function as normal.
    - **Lock** — The current session is immediately locked.
- **Require smart card login** — Requires the user to login and authenticate with a smart card. It essentially disables any other type of password authentication. This option should not be selected until after you have successfully logged in using a smart card.

The pam_pkcs11 and the coolkey packages must be installed for this option to work. For more information about smart cards, refer to the Red Hat Enterprise Linux 6 *Managing Single Sign-On and Smart Cards Guide*[1].

Click Revert to restore the previous configuration

You can restore all of the options specified in the **Authentication Configuration Tool** to the previous configuration setup by clicking **Revert**.

8.1.3. Command Line Version

The **Authentication Configuration** tool also supports a command line interface. The command line version can be used in a configuration script or a kickstart script. The authentication options are summarized in *Table 8.1. Command line options* below.

Getting the list of supported authentication options

These options can also be found in the `authconfig` man page or by typing `authconfig --help` at the shell prompt.

Option	Description
`--enableshadow, --useshadow`	Enable shadow passwords
`--disableshadow`	Disable shadow passwords
`--passalgo=`*`descrypt|bigcrypt|md5|sha256|sha512`*	Hash/crypt algorithm to be used
`--enablenis`	Enable NIS for user account configuration
`--disablenis`	Disable NIS for user account configuration
`--nisdomain=`*`domain`*	Specify an NIS domain

[1] *http://docs.redhat.com/docs/en-US/Red_Hat_Enterprise_Linux/6/html/Managing_Smart_Cards/enabling-smart-card-login.html*

Option	Description
`--nisserver=`*`server`*	Specify an NIS server
`--enableldap`	Enable LDAP for user account configuration
`--disableldap`	Disable LDAP for user account configuration
`--enableldaptls`	Enable use of TLS with LDAP
`--disableldaptls`	Disable use of TLS with LDAP
`--enablerfc2307bis`	Enable use of RFC-2307bis schema for LDAP user information lookups
`--disablerfc2307bis`	Disable use of RFC-2307bis schema for LDAP user information lookups
`--enableldapauth`	Enable LDAP for authentication
`--disableldapauth`	Disable LDAP for authentication
`--ldapserver=`*`server`*	Specify an LDAP server
`--ldapbasedn=`*`dn`*	Specify an LDAP base DN (Distinguished Name)
`--ldaploadcacert=`*`URL`*	Load a CA certificate from the specified URL
`--enablekrb5`	Enable Kerberos for authentication
`--disablekrb5`	Disable Kerberos for authentication
`--krb5kdc=`*`server`*	Specify Kerberos KDC server
`--krb5adminserver=`*`server`*	Specify Kerberos administration server
`--krb5realm=`*`realm`*	Specify Kerberos realm
`--enablekrb5kdcdns`	Enable use of DNS to find Kerberos KDCs
`--disablekrb5kdcdns`	Disable use of DNS to find Kerberos KDCs
`--enablekrb5realmdns`	Enable use of DNS to find Kerberos realms
`--disablekrb5realmdns`	Disable use of DNS to find Kerberos realms
`--enablewinbind`	Enable winbind for user account configuration
`--disablewinbind`	Disable winbind for user account configuration
`--enablewinbindauth`	Enable winbindauth for authentication
`--disablewinbindauth`	Disable winbindauth for authentication
`--winbindseparator=\`	Character used to separate the domain and user part of winbind usernames if `winbindusedefaultdomain` is not enabled
`--winbindtemplatehomedir=`*`/home/%D/%U`*	Directory that winbind users have as their home
`--winbindtemplateprimarygroup=`*`nobody`*	Group that winbind users have as their primary group

Option	Description
`--winbindtemplateshell=`*`/bin/false`*	Shell that winbind users have as their default login shell
`--enablewinbindusedefaultdomain`	Configures winbind to assume that users with no domain in their usernames are domain users
`--disablewinbindusedefaultdomain`	Configures winbind to assume that users with no domain in their usernames are not domain users
`--winbindjoin=`*`Administrator`*	Joins the winbind domain or ADS realm as the specified administrator
`--enablewinbindoffline`	Configures winbind to allow offline login
`--disablewinbindoffline`	Configures winbind to prevent offline login
`--smbsecurity=`*`user|server|domain|ads`*	Security mode to use for the Samba and Winbind services
`--smbrealm=`*`realm`*	Default realm for Samba and Winbind services when **security** is set to **ads**
`--enablewins`	Enable Wins for hostname resolution
`--disablewins`	Disable Wins for hostname resolution
`--enablesssd`	Enable SSSD for user information
`--disablesssd`	Disable SSSD for user information
`--enablecache`	Enable `nscd`
`--disablecache`	Disable `nscd`
`--enablelocauthorize`	Local authorization is sufficient for local users
`--disablelocauthorize`	Local users are also authorized through a remote service
`--enablesysnetauth`	Authenticate system accounts with network services
`--disablesysnetauth`	Authenticate system accounts with local files only
`--enablepamaccess`	Check `/etc/security/access.conf` during account authorization
`--disablepamaccess`	Do not check `/etc/security/access.conf` during account authorization
`--enablemkhomedir`	Create a home directory for a user on the first login
`--disablemkhomedir`	Do not create a home directory for a user on the first login
`--enablesmartcard`	Enable authentication with a smart card

Option	Description
`--disablesmartcard`	Disable authentication with a smart card
`--enablerequiresmartcard`	Require smart card for authentication
`--disablerequiresmartcard`	Do not require smart card for authentication
`--smartcardmodule=`*module*	Default smart card module to use
`--smartcardaction=`*0=Lock|1=Ignore*	Action to be taken when smart card removal is detected
`--enablefingerprint`	Enable fingerprint authentication
`--disablefingerprint`	Disable fingerprint authentication
`--nostart`	Do not start or stop the `portmap`, `ypbind`, or `nscd` services even if they are configured
`--test`	Do not update the configuration files, only print the new settings
`--update, --kickstart`	Opposite of `--test`, update configuration files with changed settings
`--updateall`	Update all configuration files
`--probe`	Probe and display network defaults
`--savebackup=`*name*	Save a backup of all configuration files
`--restorebackup=`*name*	Restore a backup of all configuration files
`--restorelastbackup`	Restore the backup of configuration files saved before the previous configuration change

Table 8.1. Command line options

8.2. The System Security Services Daemon (SSSD)

This section provides an introduction to the *System Security Services Daemon (SSSD)*, the main features that it provides, and discusses the requirements and any limitations of a typical SSSD deployment.

This section also describes how to configure SSSD, and how to use the features that it provides. It provides information on the types of services that it supports and how to configure them, and introduces and describes the most important configuration options. Sample configuration files are also provided to help you optimize your deployment.

8.2.1. What is SSSD?

The System Security Services Daemon (SSSD) is a service which provides access to different identity and authentication providers. You can configure SSSD to use a native LDAP domain (that is, an LDAP identity provider with LDAP authentication), or an LDAP identity provider with Kerberos authentication. It provides an NSS and PAM interface to the system, and a pluggable back-end system to connect to multiple different account sources.

SSSD is also extensible; you can configure it to use new identity sources and authentication mechanisms should they arise. In addition, SSSD is fully IPv6-compatible, provided that it is built against c-ares 1.7.1 or later and krb5-libs 1.8.1 or later.

8.2.2. SSSD Features

8.2.2.1. Offline Authentication

One of the primary benefits of SSSD is offline authentication. This solves the case of users having a separate corporate account and a local machine account because of the common requirement to implement a Virtual Private Network (VPN).

SSSD can cache remote identities and authentication credentials. This means that you can still authenticate with these remote identities even when a machine is offline. In an SSSD system, you only need to manage one account.

8.2.2.2. Server Load Reduction

The use of SSSD also helps to reduce the load on identification servers. For example, using nss_ldap, every client application that needs to request user information opens its own connection to the LDAP server. Managing these multiple connections can lead to a heavy load on the LDAP server. In an SSSD system, only the SSSD Data Provider process actually communicates with the LDAP server, reducing the load to one connection per client system.

8.2.2.3. Support for Multiple Domains

You can use SSSD to specify multiple domains of the same type. Compare this to an `nsswitch.conf` file configuration, with which you can only request user information from a single server of any particular type (LDAP, NIS, etc.). With SSSD, you can create multiple domains of the same, or of different types of identity provider.

Beginning with version 0.6.0, SSSD maintains a separate database file for each domain. This means that each domain has its own cache, and in the event that problems occur and maintenance is necessary, it is very easy to purge the cache for a single domain, by stopping `sssd` and deleting the corresponding cache file. These cache files are stored in the `/var/lib/sss/db/` directory.

All cache files are named according to the domain that they represent, for example `cache_`*`DOMAINNAME`*`.ldb`.

Considerations Associated with Deleting Cache Files

Deleting a domain's cache file can have some unexpected side effects. You should be aware of the following before you proceed:

- Deleting the cache file also deletes all user data (both identification and cached credentials). Consequently, you should not proceed unless you are online and can authenticate with your username against the domain's servers, because offline authentication will fail.
- If you are online and change your configuration to reference a different identity provider, SSSD will recognize users from both providers until the cached entries from the original provider time out.

  To avoid this situation, you can either purge the cache or use a different domain name for the new provider (this is the recommended practice). Changing the domain name means that when you restart SSSD it will create a new cache file (with the new name) and the old file will be ignored.

8.2.2.4. Support for LDAP Referrals

SSSD supports two types of LDAP referrals: object-level referrals and subtree referrals. These referral types and the extent of SSSD support is outlined below.

8.2.2.4.1. Object-level Referrals

SSSD provides full support for object-level referrals within the same LDAP server, correctly handling any differences in the distinguished name (DN) that might exist as part of the LDAP server referral configuration.

SSSD provides partial support for object-level referrals between different LDAP servers, and requires that the full DN of an LDAP request be identical on each server. SSSD does not support referrals to different DN paths on other servers.

8.2.2.4.2. Subtree Referrals

SSSD provides a similar level of support for subtree referrals as it does for object-level referrals. That is, it supports referrals to a changed DN on the local system or to an identical DN on a remote system. The difference with subtree referrals, however, is the ability to set up identical subtrees on each LDAP server and to then configure referrals between these subtrees.

8.2.2.4.3. Enabling LDAP Referrals

To take advantage of the SSSD LDAP referral functionality, you need to set the `ldap_referrals` option to `TRUE` in the LDAP domain configuration section of the `/etc/sssd/sssd.conf` file. This will enable anonymous access to the second LDAP server.

Make sure SSSD is compiled with OpenLDAP version 2.4.13 or later

SSSD only supports LDAP referrals when it is compiled with OpenLDAP version 2.4.13 or later.

8.2.2.5. Differentiating Like-named Users

SSSD supports the differentiation of like-named users in different domains. For example, you can differentiate the user `kate` in the `ldap.example.com` domain from the user `kate` in the `ldap.myhome.com` domain. You can use SSSD to make requests using fully-qualified usernames. If you request information for `kate`, you will receive the information from whichever domain is listed first in the look-up order. If you request information for `kate@ldap.myhome.com`, however, you will receive the correct user information.

SSSD also provides a `filter_users` option, which you can use to exclude certain users from being fetched from the database. Refer to the *sssd.conf(5)* manual page for full details about this option.

8.2.2.6. Integration with IPA

Beyond the offline authentication, multiple domain management and other features already described, SSSD is also designed to integrate with and enhance the functionality of IPA clients. In an environment with the latest version of IPA installed, SSSD provides additional functionality, including support for dynamic DNS updates, host-based access control, and password migration from an LDAP-only environment into the LDAP/Kerberos 5 environment employed by IPA.

8.2.2.6.1. Support for Dynamic DNS Updates

Because the IP address of IPA clients can change, SSSD provides the ability to dynamically update the client's DNS entry on the IPA server. Using a combination of Kerberos and GSS-TSIG (Generic Security Service Algorithm for Secret Key Transaction), IPA can determine the identity of the host machine, authenticate it, and allow that machine to edit its own DNS record. These changes are then stored in the LDAP back end.

Each IPA client can only edit its own DNS record

Using this authentication system means that each IPA client can only edit its own DNS record; it cannot edit the DNS record of any other client.

Setting up Dynamic DNS Updates

The SSSD configuration file provides two options used for setting up dynamic DNS updates: `ipa_dyndns_update`, used to enable dynamic DNS updates; and ipa_dyndns_iface, which specifies the interface whose IP address should be used for dynamic DNS updates.

Refer to the *sssd-ipa* manual page for more information about these options, and how to configure dynamic DNS updates.

Support for dynamic DNS updates

Support for dynamic DNS updates is only available on IPA version 2 or later, and with DNS correctly configured.

8.2.3. Setting Up SSSD

This section describes how to install SSSD, how to run the service, and how to configure it for each type of supported information provider.

8.2.3.1. Installing SSSD

Run the following command to install SSSD and any dependencies, including the SSSD client:

```
# yum install sssd
```

SSSD requires very few dependencies and should install very quickly, depending on the speed of your network connection.

8.2.3.1.1. Upgrading from a Previous Version

Upgrading Using RPM Packages

If you are upgrading using RPM packages, the script will run automatically when you upgrade to the new version. This will upgrade the /etc/sssd/sssd.conf file to the new format, and copy the existing version to /etc/sssd/sssd.conf.bak.

Upgrading Manually

It may be necessary to run the upgrade script manually, either because you built SSSD from source files, or because you are using a platform that does not support the use of RPM packages. The synopsis for the script is as follows:

```
upgrade_config.py [ -f INFILE ] [ -o OUTFILE ] [ -verbose ] [ --no-backup ]
```

- *-f INFILE* — the configuration file to upgrade. If not specified, this defaults to /etc/sssd/sssd.conf
- *-o OUTFILE* — the name of the upgraded configuration file. If not specified, this defaults to /etc/sssd/sssd.conf

- *-verbose* — produce more verbose output during the upgrade process
- *--no-backup* — do not produce a back-up file. If not specified, this defaults to *INFILE*.bak

8.2.3.1.2. Starting and Stopping SSSD

Starting SSSD for the first time

Before you start SSSD for the first time, you need to configure at least one domain. Refer to Section 8.2.5, *Configuring Domains* (page 147) for information on how to configure an SSSD domain.

You can use either the `service` command or the `/etc/init.d/sssd` script to control SSSD. For example, run the following command to start `sssd`:

```
# systemctl start sssd.service
```

By default, SSSD is configured not to start automatically. There are two ways to change this behavior; if you use the Authentication Configuration tool to configure SSSD, it will reconfigure the default behavior so that SSSD starts when the machine boots. Alternatively, you can use the `systemctl` command, as follows:

```
# systemctl enable sssd.service
```

8.2.3.2. Configuring SSSD

The global configuration of SSSD is stored in the `/etc/sssd/sssd.conf` file. This file consists of various sections, each of which contains a number of key/value pairs. Some keys accept multiple values; use commas to separate multiple values for such keys. This configuration file uses data types of string (no quotes required), integer and Boolean (with values of `TRUE` or `FALSE`). Comments are indicated by either a hash sign (#) or a semicolon (;) in the first column. The following example illustrates some of this syntax:

```
[section]
# Keys with single values
key1 = value
key2 = val2

# Keys with multiple values
key10 = val10,val11
```

Specifying a different configuration file

You can use the *-c* (or *--config*) parameter on the command line to specify a different configuration file for SSSD.

The format of the configuration file is described in Section 8.2.9, *SSSD Configuration File Format* (page 166).

Refer to the *sssd.conf(5)* manual page for more information on global SSSD configuration options.

8.2.3.2.1. Configuring NSS

SSSD provides a new NSS module, `sssd_nss`, so that you can configure your system to use SSSD to retrieve user information. Edit the `/etc/nsswitch.conf` file for your system to use the `sss` name database. For example:

```
passwd: files sss
group: files sss
```

8.2.3.2.2. Configuring PAM

Be careful when changing your PAM configuration

Use extreme care when changing your PAM configuration. A mistake in the PAM configuration file can lock you out of the system completely. Always back up your configuration files before performing any changes, and keep a session open so that you can revert any changes you make should the need arise.

To enable your system to use SSSD for PAM, you need to edit the default PAM configuration file. On Fedora—based systems, this is the `/etc/pam.d/system-auth` file. Edit this file to reflect the following example, and then restart `sssd`:

```
#%PAM-1.0
# This file is auto-generated.
# User changes will be destroyed the next time authconfig is run.
auth        required      pam_env.so
auth        sufficient    pam_unix.so nullok try_first_pass
auth        requisite     pam_succeed_if.so uid >= 500 quiet
auth        sufficient    pam_sss.so use_first_pass
auth        required      pam_deny.so

account     required      pam_unix.so broken_shadow
account     sufficient    pam_localuser.so
account     sufficient    pam_succeed_if.so uid < 500 quiet
account [default=bad success=ok user_unknown=ignore] pam_sss.so
account     required      pam_permit.so

password    requisite     pam_cracklib.so try_first_pass retry=3
password    sufficient    pam_unix.so sha512 shadow nullok try_first_pass use_authtok
password    sufficient    pam_sss.so use_authtok
password    required      pam_deny.so

session     required      pam_mkhomedir.so umask=0022 skel=/etc/skel/
session     optional      pam_keyinit.so revoke
session     required      pam_limits.so
session     [success=1 default=ignore] pam_succeed_if.so service in crond quiet use_uid
session     sufficient    pam_sss.so
session     required      pam_unix.so
```

8.2.3.2.2.1. Using Custom Home Directories with SSSD

If your LDAP users have home directories that are not in /home, and if your system is configured to create home directories the first time your users log in, then these directories will be created with the wrong permissions. For example, instead of a typical home directory such as /home/<username>, your users might have home directories that include their locale, such as /home/<locale>/<username>. If this is true for your system, the following steps need to be taken (preemptively):

1. Apply the correct SELinux context and permissions from the /home directory to the home directory that you use on your system. In the example above, the following command would achieve this result (replace the directory names with those that apply to your system):

   ```
   # semanage fcontext -a -e /home /home/locale
   ```

2. Ensure the oddjob-mkhomedir package is installed on your system and then re-run the Authentication Configuration tool.

   This package provides the pam_oddjob_mkhomedir.so library, which the Authentication Configuration tool will then use to create your custom home directories. You need to use this library to create your home directories, and not the default pam_mkhomedir.so library, because the latter cannot create SELinux labels.

The pam_oddjob_mkhomedir and pam_mkhomedir libraries

The Authentication Configuration tool will automatically use the pam_oddjob_mkhomedir.so library if it is available. Otherwise, it will default to using pam_mkhomedir.so.

If the preceding steps were not performed before the custom home directories were created, you can use the following commands to correct the permissions and SELinux contexts (again, replace the directory names with those that apply to your system):

```
# semanage fcontext -a -e /home /home/locale
# restorecon -R -v /home/locale
```

8.2.3.2.2.2. Using "include" Statements in PAM Configurations

Recent PAM implementations allow you to use include statements in PAM configurations. For example:

```
...
session     include     system-auth
session     optional    pam_console.so
...
```

In the preceding example, if a *sufficient* condition from system-auth returns PAM_SUCCESS, pam_console.so will not be executed.

8.2.3.2.3. Configuring Access Control

SSSD provides a rudimentary access control mechanism, offering two solutions based on the value of the access_provider option in the [domain/<*NAME*>] section in the /etc/sssd/sssd.conf file.

8.2.3.2.3.1. The Simple Access Provider

The first of these solutions is known as the *Simple Access Provider*, and is based on the implementation of access or deny lists of usernames. To enable the Simple Access Provider, you need to set the access_provider option to simple, and then add usernames as a comma-separated list to either the simple_allow_users or simple_deny_users options.

Using the Simple Access Provider

By using the Simple Access Provider, you can continue to support a number of network logins to maintain common network accounts on company or department laptops, but you might want to restrict the use of a particular laptop to one or two users. This means that even if a different user authenticated successfully against the same authentication provider, the Simple Access Provider would prevent that user from gaining access.

The following example demonstrates the use of the Simple Access Provider to grant access to two users. This example assumes that SSSD is correctly configured and example.com is one of the domains specified in the [sssd] section, and only shows the Simple Access Provider-specific options.

```
[domain/example.com]
access_provider = simple
simple_allow_users = user1, user2
```

Using the Local ID provider

The Local ID provider does not support simple as an access provider.

Access Control Rules

The Simple Access Provider adheres to the following three rules to determine which users should or should not be granted access:

- If both lists are empty, access is granted.
- If simple_allow_users is set, only users from this list are allowed access. This setting supersedes the simple_deny_users list (which would be redundant).
- If the simple_allow_users list is empty, users are allowed access unless they appear in the simple_deny_users list.

Do not define both simple_allow_users and simple_deny_users

Defining both `simple_allow_users` and `simple_deny_users` is a configuration error. If this occurs, SSSD will output an error to the `/var/log/sssd/sssd_default.log` log file when loading the back end, but continue to start normally. Future versions of SSSD will output an error and fail to start.

8.2.3.2.3.2. The LDAP Access Provider

The second access control solution uses the LDAP server itself as the access provider (`access_provider=ldap`) and the associated filter option (`ldap_access_filter`) to specify which users are granted access to the specified host. Note that these two options are codependent; if you use LDAP as your access provider then you must specify a value for the `ldap_access_filter` option, otherwise all users will be denied access. If you are not using LDAP as your access provider, then the `ldap_access_filter` option has no effect.

Using the LDAP Access Provider

The following example demonstrates the use of the LDAP Access Provider to grant access to members of the "allowedusers" group in LDAP. This example assumes that SSSD is correctly configured and `example.com` is one of the domains specified in the `[sssd]` section, and only shows the LDAP Access Provider-specific options.

```
[domain/example.com]
access_provider = ldap
ldap_access_filter = memberOf=cn=allowedusers,ou=Groups,dc=example,dc=com
```

Using offline caching

Offline caching for this feature is limited to determining whether or not the user's last online login attempt was successful. If they were granted access during their last login, they will continue to be granted access while offline, and vice-versa.

Refer to the *sssd-ldap* manual page for more information about using the LDAP Access Provider.

8.2.3.2.4. Configuring Failover

The failover feature allows back ends to automatically switch to a different server if the primary server fails. These servers are entered as a case-insensitive, comma-separated list in the `[domain/<NAME>]` sections of the `/etc/sssd/sssd.conf` file, and listed in order of preference. This list can contain any number of servers.

For example, if you have configured a native LDAP domain, you could specify the following as your *`ldap_uri`* values:

```
ldap_uri = ldap://ldap0.mydomain.org, ldap://ldap1.mydomain.org,
                                          ldap://ldap2.mydomain.org
```

In this configuration, `ldap://ldap0.mydomain.org` functions as the primary server. If this server fails, the SSSD failover mechanism first attempts to connect to `ldap1.mydomain.org`, and if that server is unavailable, it then attempts to connect to `ldap2.mydomain.org`.

If the parameter that specifies which server to connect to for the specific domain (for example, *`ldap_uri`*, *`krb5_server`*, …) is not specified, the back end defaults to using *`Use service discovery`*. Refer to Section 8.2.3.2.4.1, *Using SRV Records with Failover* (page 144) for more information on service discovery.

Do not use multiple ldap_uri parameters

Do not use multiple *`ldap_uri`* parameters to specify your failover servers. The failover servers must be entered as a comma-separated list of values for a single *`ldap_uri`* parameter. If you enter multiple *`ldap_uri`* parameters, SSSD only recognizes the last entry.

Future versions of SSSD will throw an error upon receiving additional *`ldap_uri`* entries.

8.2.3.2.4.1. Using SRV Records with Failover

SSSD also supports the use of SRV records in its failover configuration. This means that you can specify a server that is later resolved into a list of specific servers using SRV requests. The *`priority`* and *`weight`* attributes of SRV records provide further opportunity for specifying which servers should be contacted first in the event that the primary server fails.

For every service with which you want to use service discovery, you need to add a special DNS record to your DNS server using the following form:

```
_service._protocol._domain TTL priority weight port hostname
```

A typical configuration would contain multiple such records, each with a different priority (for failover) and different weights (for load balancing).

The client then makes an SRV DNS query to retrieve a list of host names, their priorities, and weights. These queries are of the form *`_service._protocol._domain`*, for example, `_ldap._tcp._redhat.com`. The client then sorts this list according to the priorities and weights, and connects to the first server in this sorted list.

For more information on SRV records, refer to *RFC 2782*[2].

[2] *http://tools.ietf.org/html/rfc2782*

8.2.3.2.4.2. How the Failover Mechanism Works

The failover mechanism distinguishes between machines and services. The back end first tries to resolve the hostname of a given machine; if this resolution attempt fails, the machine is considered offline. No further attempts are made to connect to this machine for any other service. If the resolution attempt succeeds, the back end tries to connect to a service on this machine. If the service connection attempt fails, then only this particular service is considered offline and the back end automatically switches over to the next service. The machine is still considered online and might still be tried for another service.

The failover mechanism does not handle DNS A records with multiple IP addresses; instead it only uses the first address. DNS round-robin cannot be used for failover. Further, providing multiple A records does not provide failover. Only the first A record is used, and if a lookup attempt on the first record fails then the system attempts no further lookups. To find multiple servers with a single request, and thus implementing failover, SSSD relies on SRV resource records, as explained in Section 8.2.3.2.4.1, *Using SRV Records with Failover* (page 144).

Further connection attempts are made to machines or services marked as offline after a specified period of time; this is currently hard coded to 30 seconds. If there are no more machines to try, the back end as a whole switches to offline mode, and then attempts to reconnect every 30 seconds.

8.2.4. Configuring Services

Individual pieces of SSSD functionality are provided by special SSSD services that are started and stopped together with SSSD. The services provided by SSSD have their own configuration sections. The `[sssd]` section also lists the services that are active and should be started when `sssd` starts within the `services` directive.

SSSD currently provides several services:

- `NSS` — An NSS provider service that answers NSS requests from the `sssd_nss` module.
- `PAM` — A PAM provider service that manages a PAM conversation through the `sssd_pam` PAM module.
- `monitor` — A special service that monitors all other SSSD services, and starts or restarts them as needed. Its options are specified in the `[sssd]` section of the `/etc/sssd/sssd.conf` configuration file.

8.2.4.1. Configuration Options

The following sections cover the most important SSSD configuration options. Refer to the *sssd.conf(5)* manual page that ships with SSSD for information on all the available configuration options.

8.2.4.1.1. General Configuration Options

- `debug_level (integer)`

  Sets the debug level for a particular service. This is a per-service setting (that is, it can appear in any of the `[service/<NAME>]` sections in the SSSD configuration file).

- `reconnection_retries (integer)`

  In the event of a data provider crash or restart, this specifies the number of times that a service should attempt to reconnect.

DNS lookup of IPv6 addresses

If a `DNS` lookup fails to return an `IPv4` address for a hostname, SSSD attempts to look up an `IPv6` address before returning a failure. Note that this only ensures that the async resolver identifies the correct address; there is currently a bug in the LDAP code that prevents SSSD from connecting to an LDAP server over IPv6. This is being investigated separately.

8.2.4.1.2. NSS Configuration Options

Use the following options to configure the `Name Service Switch (NSS)` service. Refer to the *sssd.conf(5)* manual page for full details about each option.

- `enum_cache_timeout (integer)`

  Specifies for how long (in seconds) sssd_nss should cache enumerations (requests for information about all users).

- `entry_cache_nowait_percentage (integer)`

  Specifies for how long sssd_nss should return cached entries before initiating an out-of-band cache refresh (`0` disables this feature).

  You can configure the entry cache to automatically update entries in the background if they are requested beyond a percentage of the `entry_cache_timeout` value for the domain.

  Valid values for this option are `0-99`, and represent a percentage of the `entry_cache_timeout` value for each domain.

- `entry_negative_timeout (integer)`

Specifies for how long (in seconds) sssd_nss should cache negative cache hits (that is, queries for invalid database entries, such as nonexistent ones) before asking the back end again.

- `filter_users, filter_groups (string)`

  Exclude certain users from being fetched from the sss NSS database. This is particularly useful for system accounts such as `root`.

- `filter_users_in_groups (Boolean)`

  If set to `TRUE`, specifies that users listed in the `filter_users` list do not appear in group memberships when performing group lookups. If set to `FALSE`, group lookups return all users that are members of that group. If not specified, defaults to `TRUE`.

8.2.4.1.3. PAM Configuration Options

Use the following options to configure the `Pluggable Authentication Module (PAM)` service.

- `offline_credentials_expiration (integer)`

  If the authentication provider is offline, specifies for how long to allow cached log-ins (in days). This value is measured from the last successful online log-in. If not specified, defaults to `0` (no limit).

- `offline_failed_login_attempts (integer)`

  If the authentication provider is offline, specifies how many failed log in attempts are allowed. If not specified, defaults to `0` (no limit).

- `offline_failed_login_delay (integer)`

  Specifies the time in minutes after the value of `offline_failed_login_attempts` has been reached before a new log in attempt is possible.

  If set to `0`, the user cannot authenticate offline if the value of `offline_failed_login_attempts` has been reached. Only a successful online authentication can re-enable offline authentication. If not specified, defaults to `5`.

8.2.5. Configuring Domains

A domain is a database of user information. SSSD can use more than one domain at the same time, but at least one must be configured for SSSD to start. Using SSSD domains, it is possible to use several LDAP servers providing several unique namespaces. You can specify not only where users' identity information is stored, but how users authenticate against each of the specified domains.

SSSD supports the following identity and authentication combinations:

LDAP/LDAP

This combination uses an LDAP back end as both the identity and authentication provider. For more information, refer to Section 8.2.5.2, *Configuring an LDAP Domain* (page 152).

LDAP/KRB5

This combination uses an LDAP back end as the identity provider, and uses Kerberos to provide authentication. For more information, refer to Section 8.2.6, *Setting Up Kerberos Authentication* (page 157).

proxy

Specifying a proxy identity or an authentication provider uses an existing NSS library or a customized PAM stack, but takes advantage of the SSSD caching mechanism. For more information, refer to Section 8.2.7, *Configuring a Proxy Domain* (page 160).

The following example assumes that SSSD is correctly configured and FOO is one of the domains in the `[sssd]` section. This example shows only the configuration of Kerberos authentication; it does not include any identity provider.

```
[domain/FOO]
auth_provider = krb5
krb5_server = 192.168.1.1
krb5_realm = EXAMPLE.COM
```

8.2.5.1. Domain Configuration Options

You can add new domain configurations to the `[domain/<NAME>]` sections of the `/etc/sssd/sssd.conf` file, and then add the list of domains to the *`domains`* attribute of the `[sssd]` section, in the order you want them to be queried.

8.2.5.1.1. General Domain Configuration Options

You can use the following configuration options in a domain configuration section:

- `min_id,max_id (integer)`

  Specifies the UID and GID limits for the domain. If a domain contains entries that are outside these limits, they are ignored.

  The default value for `min_id` is `1`; the default value for `max_id` is `0` (unbounded).

Avoid conflicts with users in /etc/passwd

If `min_id` is unspecified, it defaults to `1` for any back end. This default was chosen to provide compatibility with existing systems and to ease any migration attempts. LDAP administrators should be aware that granting identities in this range may conflict with users in the local `/etc/passwd` file. To avoid these conflicts, `min_id` should be set to `1000` or higher wherever possible.

The `min_id` option determines the minimum acceptable value for both UID and GID numbers. Accounts with either UID or GID values below the `min_id` value are filtered out and not made available on the client.

- `enumerate (Boolean)`

  Specifies whether or not to enumerate (list) the users and groups of a domain.

  Enumeration means that the entire set of available users and groups on the remote source is cached on the local machine. When enumeration is disabled, users and groups are only cached as they are requested.

Disable enumeration for domains with many users and groups

If a client has enumeration enabled, reinitialization of the client results in a complete refresh of the entire set of available users and groups from the remote source. Similarly, when SSSD is connected to a new server, the entire set of available users and groups from the remote source is pulled and cached on the local machine. In a domain with a large amount of clients connected to a remote source, both aforementioned cases can affect the network performance due to frequent queries from the clients. If the set of available users and groups is large enough, it will affect the performance of clients as well. For performance reasons, it is recommended that you disable enumeration for domains with many users and groups.

The default value for this parameter is `FALSE`. Set this value to `TRUE` to enable enumeration of users and groups of a domain.

- `timeout (integer)`

  Specifies the timeout in seconds for this particular domain.

  This is used to ensure that the back end process is alive and capable of answering requests. The default value for this parameter is `10` seconds. Raising this timeout might prove useful for slower back ends, such as distant LDAP servers.

Changing the timeout value to 0

If you set `timeout = 0`, SSSD reverts to the default value; you cannot force a timeout value of zero, because this would force the `sssd` daemon into a loop.

- `cache_credentials (Boolean)`

  Specifies whether or not to store user credentials in the local SSSD domain database cache.

  The default value for this parameter is `FALSE`. You should set this value to `TRUE` for domains other than local if you want to enable offline authentication.

- `id_provider (string)`

  Specifies the data provider identity back end to use for this domain. Currently supported identity back ends are:

  - proxy — Support a legacy NSS provider (for example, nss_nis).

Changing the id_provider value to proxy

SSSD needs to know which legacy NSS library to load in order to start successfully. If you set `id_provider` to `proxy`, ensure that you also specify a value for `proxy_lib_name`. Refer to Section 8.2.7, *Configuring a Proxy Domain* (page 160) for information on this attribute.

  - local — SSSD internal local provider.
  - ldap — LDAP provider.

- `entry_cache_timeout (integer)`

  Specifies for how long the domain's data provider should cache positive cache hits (that is, queries for valid database entries) before asking the database again.

- `use_fully_qualified_names (Boolean)`

  Specifies whether or not requests to this domain require fully-qualified domain names.

  If set to `TRUE`, all requests to this domain must use fully-qualified domain names. It also means that the output from the request displays the fully-qualified name.

  The ability to restrict requests in this way means that if you know you have multiple domains with conflicting usernames, then there is no doubt about which username the query will resolve.

  Consider the following examples, in which the IPA domain database contains a user named `ipauser01`, and the *`use_fully_qualified_names`* attribute is set to `TRUE`:

```
# getent passwd ipauser01
[no output]
# getent passwd ipauser01@IPA
ipauser01@IPA:x:937315651:937315651:ipauser01:/home/ipauser01:/bin/sh
```

  In the following examples, using the same IPA domain and user, the *`use_fully_qualified_names`* attribute is set to `FALSE`:

```
# getent passwd ipauser01
ipauser01:x:937315651:937315651:ipauser01:/home/ipauser01:/bin/sh
# getent passwd ipauser01@IPA
ipauser01:x:937315651:937315651:ipauser01:/home/ipauser01:/bin/sh
```

Changing the use_fully_qualified_names value to FALSE

If `use_fully_qualified_names` is set to `FALSE`, you can continue to use the fully-qualified name in your requests, but only the simplified version is displayed in the output.

SSSD can only parse `name@domain`, not `name@realm`. You can, however, use the same name for both your domain and your realm.

- `auth_provider (string)`

  The authentication provider used for the domain. The default value for this option is the value of `id_provider` if it is set and can handle authentication requests.

  Currently supported authentication providers are:

  - ldap — for native LDAP authentication. Refer to the sssd-ldap(5) manual page for more information on configuring LDAP.
  - krb5 — for Kerberos authentication. Refer to the sssd-krb5(5) manual page for more information on configuring Kerberos.
  - proxy — for relaying authentication to some other PAM target.
  - none — explicitly disables authentication.

8.2.5.1.2. Proxy Configuration Options

- `proxy_pam_target` (string)

  This option is only used when the `auth_provider` option is set to `proxy`, and specifies the target to which PAM must proxy.

  This option has no default value. If proxy authentication is required, you need to specify your own PAM target. This corresponds to a file containing PAM stack information in the system's default PAM configuration directory. On Fedora based systems, this is the `/etc/pam.d/` directory.

Avoid recursive inclusion of pam_sss

Ensure that your proxy PAM stack does *not* recursively include `pam_sss.so`.

- `proxy_lib_name` (string)

  This option is only used when the `id_provider` option is set to `proxy`, and specifies which existing NSS library to proxy identity requests through.

  This option has no default value. You need to manually specify an existing library to take advantage of this option. For example, set this value to `nis` to use the existing `libnss_nis.so` file.

8.2.5.2. Configuring an LDAP Domain

An LDAP domain is one where the `id_provider` option is set to `ldap` (`id_provider = ldap`). Such a domain requires a running LDAP server against which to authenticate. This can be an open source LDAP server such as OpenLDAP or Microsoft Active Directory. SSSD currently supports Microsoft Active Directory 2003 (+Services for UNIX) and Active Directory 2008 (+Subsystem for UNIX-based Applications). In all cases, the client configuration is stored in the `/etc/sssd/sssd.conf` file.

How to Authenticate Against an LDAP Server

SSSD does not support authentication over an unencrypted channel. Consequently, if you want to authenticate against an LDAP server, either `TLS/SSL` or `LDAPS` is required. If the LDAP server is used only as an identity provider, an encrypted channel is not needed.

Edit your `/etc/sssd/sssd.conf` file to include the following settings:

```
# A native LDAP domain
[domain/LDAP]
enumerate = false
cache_credentials = TRUE

id_provider = ldap
auth_provider = ldap
ldap_schema = rfc2307
chpass_provider = ldap

ldap_uri = ldap://ldap.mydomain.org
ldap_search_base = dc=mydomain,dc=org
ldap_tls_reqcert = demand
ldap_tls_cacert = /etc/pki/tls/certs/ca-bundle.crt
```

Creating a certificate with an IP address instead of the server name

If you wish to use an IP address in the `ldap_uri` option instead of the server name, for example, if `GSSAPI` is used to avoid time consuming `DNS` lookups, the `TSL/SSL` setup might fail. This is due to the fact that `TSL/SSL` certificates contain the server name only. However, a special field in the certificate, called *Subject Alternative Name* (`subjectAltName`), can be used to additionally set the IP address of the server.

The following steps show how to create a certificate with a Subject Alternative Name being the IP address of your server:

1. Using your command line, execute the following command to convert an existing certificate (previously signed by the *`key.pem`* key) into a certificate request:

```
openssl x509 -x509toreq -in old_cert.pem -out req.pem -signkey key.pem
```

Alternatively, if you are using a self-signed certificate(for example, one created by the Fedora OpenLDAP package in `/etc/pki/tls/certs/slapd.pem`), execute the following command:

```
openssl x509 -x509toreq -in old_cert.pem -out req.pem -signkey old_cert.pem
```

2. Edit your `/etc/pki/tls/openssl.cnf` configuration file to include the following line under the *[v3_ca]* section:

```
subjectAltName = IP:10.0.0.10
```

Replace the IP address with one of your choice.

3. By executing the following command, use the previously generated certificate request to generate a new self-signed certificate that will contain your desired IP address:

```
openssl x509 -req -in req.pem -out new_cert.pem -extfile ./openssl.cnf -
                                    extensions v3_ca -signkey old_cert.pem
```

where:

- The `openssl x509` command creates the new certificate.
- The `-req` option tells the command to expect a certificate request as an input.
- The `-in` and `-out` options specify the input and output files.
- The `-extfile` option expects a file containing certificate extensions to use (in our case the `subjectAltName` extension).
- The `-extensions` option specifies the section of the `openssl.cnf` file to add certificate extensions from (in this case, the *[v3_ca]* section).
- The `-signkey` option tells the command to self-sign the input file using the supplied private key.

For more information on the **x509** utility and its parameters, refer to `man x509`.

4. Lastly, copy the private key block from the `old_cert.pem` file into the `new_cert.pem` file to keep all relevant information in one file.

When creating a certificate through the **certutil** utility provided by the nss-utils package, note that **certutil** supports `DNS` subject alternative names for certificate creation only.

It is advisable to use a Certificate Authority to issue your certificate. Consider using the Red Hat Certificate System; for more information on managing subject names and subject alternative names in your certificate, refer to the *Red Hat Certificate System Admin Guide*[3].

---

[3] *http://docs.redhat.com/docs/en-US/Red_Hat_Certificate_System/8.0/html/Admin_Guide/Managing_Subject_Names_and_Subject_Alternative_Names.html*

Selecting an LDAP Schema

You can set the `ldap_schema` attribute to either `rfc2307` or `rfc2307bis`. These schema define how groups in LDAP are specified. In *RFC 2307*, group objects use a multi-valued attribute, `memberuid`, which lists the names of the users that belong to that group. In *RFC 2307bis*, instead of the `memberuid`, group objects use the `member` attribute. Rather than just the name of the user, this attribute contains the full Distinguished Name (DN) of another object in the LDAP database. This means that groups can have other groups as members. That is, it adds support for nested groups.

SSSD assumes that your LDAP server is using *RFC 2307*. If your LDAP server is using *RFC 2307bis*, and you do not update the `/etc/sssd/sssd.conf` file accordingly, this can impact how your users and groups are displayed. It also means that some groups will not be available and network resources may be inaccessible even though you have permissions to use them.

For example, when using *RFC 2307bis* and you have configured both primary and secondary groups, or are using nested groups, you can use the `id` command to display these groups:

```
[f12server@ipaserver ~]$ id
uid=500(f12server) gid=500(f12server) groups=500(f12server),510(f12tester)
```

If instead you have configured your client to use *RFC 2307* then only the primary group is displayed.

Changes to this setting only affect how SSSD determines the groups to which a user belongs; there is no negative effect on the actual user data. If you do not know the correct value for this attribute, consult your System Administrator.

Specifying Timeout Values

SSSD supports a number of timeout values that apply when configuring an LDAP domain. These are described below.

- `ldap_search_timeout (integer)` — Specifies the timeout (in seconds) that LDAP searches are allowed to run before they are canceled and cached results are returned (and offline mode is entered). If not specified:

  Defaults to five when `enumerate` = `False`

  Defaults to 30 when `enumerate` = `True`. This option is forced to a minimum of 30 in this case.

The ldap_network_timeout option is going to be changed

This option is subject to change in future versions of SSSD, where it may be replaced by a series of timeouts for specific look-up types.

- `ldap_network_timeout (integer)` — Specifies the timeout (in seconds) after which the `poll(2)/select(2)` following a `connect(2)` returns in case of no activity.

  If not specified, defaults to five.

- `ldap_opt_timeout (integer)` — Specifies the timeout (in seconds) after which calls to synchronous LDAP APIs will abort if no response is received. This option also controls the timeout when communicating with the KDC in case of a SASL bind.

  If not specified, defaults to five.

DNS Service Discovery

The DNS service discovery feature allows the LDAP back end to automatically find the appropriate DNS servers to connect to using a special DNS query. For more information on the DNS service discovery feature, refer to Section 8.2.3.2.4.1, *Using SRV Records with Failover* (page 144).

8.2.5.3. Configuring a Microsoft Active Directory Domain

You can configure SSSD to use Microsoft Active Directory as an LDAP back end, providing both identity and authentication services. If you are using Active Directory 2003, SSSD requires that you install Windows Services for UNIX (SFU) on the machine where Active Directory is installed. If instead you are using Active Directory 2008, you need to install the Subsystem for UNIX-based Applications (SUA) on the Active Directory machine.

SFU is not supported on 64-bit systems

SFU is not supported on 64-bit operating systems. Refer to *http://support.microsoft.com/kb/920751* for more information about which Windows systems can provide a suitable platform for an SSSD LDAP back end.

8.2.5.3.1. Configuring Active Directory 2003 as an LDAP Back End

The example `/etc/sssd/sssd.conf` file that ships with SSSD contains the following sample configuration for Active Directory 2003:

```
# Example LDAP domain where the LDAP server is an Active Directory 2003 server.

[domain/AD]
description = LDAP domain with AD server
enumerate = false
min_id = 1000
;
id_provider = ldap
auth_provider = ldap
ldap_uri = ldap://your.ad.server.com
```

```
ldap_schema = rfc2307bis
ldap_search_base = dc=example,dc=com
ldap_default_bind_dn = cn=Administrator,cn=Users,dc=example,dc=com
ldap_default_authtok_type = password
ldap_default_authtok = YOUR_PASSWORD
ldap_user_object_class = person
ldap_user_name = msSFU30Name
ldap_user_uid_number = msSFU30UidNumber
ldap_user_gid_number = msSFU30GidNumber
ldap_user_home_directory = msSFU30HomeDirectory
ldap_user_shell = msSFU30LoginShell
ldap_user_principal = userPrincipalName
ldap_group_object_class = group
ldap_group_name = msSFU30Name
ldap_group_gid_number = msSFU30GidNumber
```

This configuration is specific to Windows Active Directory 2003. Refer to Section 8.2.5.3.2, *Configuring Active Directory 2003 R2 and 2008 as LDAP Back Ends* (page 156) for information on how to configure Active Directory 2003 R2 and Active Directory 2008.

Note that the above configuration assumes that the certificates are stored in the default location (that is, in `/etc/openldap/cacerts`) and that the `c_rehash` function has been used to create the appropriate symlinks.

More Information

Refer to the *sssd-ldap(5)* manual page for a full description of all the options that apply to LDAP domains.

8.2.5.3.2. Configuring Active Directory 2003 R2 and 2008 as LDAP Back Ends

The configuration of `/etc/sssd/sssd.conf` to support Active Directory 2003 R2 or Active Directory 2008 as a back end is similar to that for AD 2003. The following example configuration highlights the necessary changes.

```
# Example LDAP domain where the LDAP server is an Active Directory 2003 R2 or an
                                                    Active Directory 2008 server.

[domain/AD]
description = LDAP domain with AD server
; debug_level = 9
enumerate = false

id_provider = ldap
auth_provider = ldap
chpass_provider = ldap

ldap_uri = ldap://your.ad.server.com
ldap_tls_cacertdir = /etc/openldap/cacerts
ldap_tls_cacert = /etc/openldap/cacerts/test.cer
```

```
ldap_search_base = dc=example,dc=com
ldap_default_bind_dn = cn=Administrator,cn=Users,dc=example,dc=com
ldap_default_authtok_type = password
ldap_default_authtok = YOUR_PASSWORD
ldap_pwd_policy = none
ldap_user_object_class = user
ldap_group_object_class = group
```

Note that the above configuration assumes that the certificates are stored in the default location (that is, in `/etc/openldap/cacerts`) and that the `c_rehash` function has been used to create the appropriate symlinks.

8.2.6. Setting Up Kerberos Authentication

In order to set up Kerberos authentication, you need to know the address of your *key distribution center* (KDC) and the Kerberos domain. The client configuration is then stored in the `/etc/sssd/sssd.conf` file.

The Kerberos 5 authentication back end does not contain an identity provider and must be paired with one in order to function properly (for example, `id_provider = ldap`). Some information required by the Kerberos 5 authentication back end must be supplied by the identity provider, such as the user's *Kerberos Principal Name* (UPN). The identity provider configuration should contain an entry to specify this UPN. Refer to the manual page for the applicable identity provider for details on how to configure the UPN.

If the UPN is not available in the identity back end, SSSD will construct a UPN using the format `username@krb5_realm`.

SSSD assumes that the Kerberos KDC is also a Kerberos kadmin server. However, it is very common for production environments to have multiple, read-only replicas of the KDC, but only a single kadmin server (because password changes and similar procedures are comparatively rare). To manage this type of configuration, you can use the `krb5_kpasswd` option to specify where your password changing service is running, or if it is running on a non-default port. If the `krb5_kpasswd` option is not defined, SSSD tries to use the Kerberos KDC in order to change the password. Refer to the *sssd-krb5(5)* manual page for more information about this and all Kerberos configuration options.

How to Set Up Kerberos Authentication

Edit your `/etc/sssd/sssd.conf` file to include the following settings:

```
# A domain with identities provided by LDAP and authentication by Kerberos
[domain/KRBDOMAIN]
enumerate = false
id_provider = ldap
chpass_provider = krb5
ldap_uri = ldap://ldap.mydomain.org
```

```
ldap_search_base = dc=mydomain,dc=org
tls_reqcert = demand
ldap_tls_cacert = /etc/pki/tls/certs/ca-bundle.crt

auth_provider = krb5
krb5_server = 192.168.1.1
krb5_realm = EXAMPLE.COM
krb5_changepw_principal = kadmin/changepw
krb5_ccachedir = /tmp
krb5_ccname_template = FILE:%d/krb5cc_%U_XXXXXX
krb5_auth_timeout = 15
```

This example describes the minimum options that must be configured when using Kerberos authentication. Refer to the *sssd-krb5(5)* manual page for a full description of all the options that apply to configuring Kerberos authentication.

DNS Service Discovery

The DNS service discovery feature allows the Kerberos 5 authentication back end to automatically find the appropriate DNS servers to connect to using a special DNS query. For more information on the DNS service discovery feature, refer to Section 8.2.3.2.4.1, *Using SRV Records with Failover* (page 144).

8.2.6.1. Setting up SASL/GSSAPI Authentication

GSSAPI (Generic Security Services Application Programming Interface) is a supported *SASL* (Simple Authentication and Security Layer) authentication method. Kerberos is currently the only commonly used GSSAPI implementation. An LDAP client and an LDAP server use SASL to take advantage of GSSAPI as the authentication method (an alternative to plain text passwords, etc.). The GSSAPI plug-in for SASL is then invoked on the client and server side to use Kerberos to communicate.

Using GSSAPI protected communication for LDAP is an advanced configuration not supported by the Authentication Configuration tool; the following steps show how to manually configure it.

Setting up the SASL/GSSAPI authentication on Fedora 6.0

The following setup works correctly on all Fedora 6.1 systems and any systems released after it. However, when using Fedora 6.0, you must correctly configure the `default_realm` option in the `[libdefaults]` section and `kdc` option for your realm in the `[realms]` section in the `/etc/krb5.conf` configuration file not only on the directory server and the KDC but also on the client running SSSD. For more information on various `/etc/krb5.conf` options, refer to `man krb5.conf`

On the KDC

1. Using **kadmin**, set up a Kerberos service principal for the directory server. Use the `-randkey` option for the **kadmin**'s `addprinc` command to create the principal and assign it a random key:
   ```
   kadmin: addprinc -randkey ldap/server.example.com
   ```
2. Use the `ktadd` command to write the service principal to a file:
   ```
   kadmin: ktadd -k /root/ldap.keytab ldap/server.example.com
   ```
3. Using **kadmin**, set up a Kerberos host principal for the client running SSSD. Use the `-randkey` option for the **kadmin**'s `addprinc` command to create the principal and assign it a random key:
   ```
   kadmin: addprinc -randkey host/client.example.com
   ```
4. Use the `ktadd` command to write the host principal to a file:
   ```
   kadmin: ktadd -k /root/client.keytab host/client.example.com
   ```

On the Directory Server

Complete the following steps for a directory server of your choice:

OpenLDAP

1. Copy the previously created `/root/ldap.keytab` file from the KDC to the `/etc/openldap/` directory and name it `ldap.keytab`.
2. Make the `/etc/openldap/ldap.keytab` file read-writable for the `ldap` user and readable for the `ldap` group only.

Red Hat Directory Server

1. Copy the previously created `/root/ldap.keytab` file from the KDC to the `/etc/dirsrv/` directory and name it `ldap.keytab`.
2. Uncomment the `KRB5_KTNAME` line in the `/etc/sysconfig/dirsrv` (or instance-specific) file, and set the keytab location for the `KRB5_KTNAME` variable. For example:
   ```
   # In order to use SASL/GSSAPI the directory
   # server needs to know where to find its keytab
   # file - uncomment the following line and set
   # the path and filename appropriately
   KRB5_KTNAME=/etc/dirsrv/ldap.keytab; export KRB5_KTNAME
   ```

On the Client

1. Copy the previously created `/root/client.keytab` file from the KDC to the `/etc/` directory and name it `krb5.keytab`. If the `/etc/krb5.keytab` file exists already, use

the **ktutil** utility to merge both files properly. For more information on the **ktutil** utility, refer to `man ktutil`.

2. Modify your /etc/sssd/sssd.conf file to include the following settings:

```
ldap_sasl_mech = gssapi
ldap_sasl_authid = host/client.example.com@EXAMPLE.COM
ldap_krb5_keytab = /etc/krb5.keytab (default)
ldap_krb5_init_creds = true (default)
ldap_krb5_ticket_lifetime = 86400 (default)
krb5_realm = EXAMPLE.COM
```

8.2.7. Configuring a Proxy Domain

SSSD currently only supports LDAP and Kerberos as authentication providers. If you prefer to use SSSD (for example, to take advantage of its caching functionality), but SSSD does not support your authentication method, you can set up a proxy authentication provider. This could be the case if you use fingerprint scanners or smart cards as part of your authentication process. Similarly, you can set up proxy to serve as an identity provider.

The following sections cover combinations of identity and authentication providers in which the proxy server takes the role of one.

8.2.7.1. proxy/KRB5

The following configuration is an example of a combination of a proxy identity provider used with Kerberos authentication:

Edit the `/etc/sssd/sssd.conf` configuration file to include the following settings:

```
[domain/PROXY_KRB5]
auth_provider = krb5
krb5_server = 192.168.1.1
krb5_realm = EXAMPLE.COM

id_provider = proxy
proxy_lib_name = nis
enumerate = true
cache_credentials = true
```

For more information on various Kerberos configuration options, refer to Section 8.2.6, *Setting Up Kerberos Authentication* (page 157).

8.2.7.2. LDAP/proxy

An example of a combination of an LDAP identity provider and a proxy authentication provider is the use of the LDAP with a custom PAM stack. To enable authentication via the PAM stack, complete the following steps:

1. Edit the `/etc/sssd/sssd.conf` configuration file to include the following settings:

```
[domain/LDAP_PROXY]
id_provider = ldap
ldap_uri = ldap://example.com
ldap_search_base = dc=example,dc=com

auth_provider = proxy
proxy_pam_target = sssdpamproxy
enumerate = true
cache_credentials = true
```

By specifying the options above, authentication requests will be proxied via the `/etc/pam.d/sssdpamproxy` file which provides the needed module interfaces. Note that the `pam_ldap.so` file can be substituted with a PAM module of your choice.

For more information on various LDAP configuration options, refer to Section 8.2.5.2, *Configuring an LDAP Domain* (page 152).

2. Create a `/etc/pam.d/sssdpamproxy` file (if not already created) and specify the following settings in it:

```
auth        required      pam_ldap.so
account     required      pam_ldap.so
password    required      pam_ldap.so
session     required      pam_ldap.so
```

8.2.7.3. proxy/proxy

An example of a combination of an proxy identity provider and a proxy authentication provider is the use of the proxy identity provider with a custom PAM stack. To enable authentication via the PAM stack, complete the following steps:

Make sure the nss-pam-ldapd package is installed

In order to use the proxy identity provider, you must have the nss-pam-ldapd package installed.

1. Edit the `/etc/sssd/sssd.conf` configuration file to include the following settings:

```
[domain/PROXY_PROXY]
auth_provider = proxy
id_provider = proxy
proxy_lib_name = ldap
proxy_pam_target = sssdproxyldap
enumerate = true
cache_credentials = true
```

By specifying the options above, authentication requests will be proxied via the `/etc/pam.d/sssdproxyldap` file which provides the needed module interfaces.

For more information on the options used in the configuration example above, refer to `man sssd.conf`

2. Create a `/etc/pam.d/sssdproxyldap` file (if not already created) and specify the following settings in it:

```
auth          required       pam_ldap.so
account       required       pam_ldap.so
password      required       pam_ldap.so
session       required       pam_ldap.so
```

3. Edit the `/etc/nslcd.conf` file (the default configuration file for the LDAP name service daemon) to include the following settings:

```
uid nslcd
gid ldap
uri ldaps://ldap.mydomain.org:636
base dc=mydomain,dc=org
ssl on
tls_cacertdir /etc/openldap/cacerts
```

   For more information on the options used in the configuration example above, refer to `man nslcd.conf`

8.2.8. Troubleshooting

This section lists some of the issues you may encounter when implementing SSSD, the possible causes of these issues, and how to resolve them. If you find further issues that are not covered here, refer to the *We Need Feedback* section in the *Preface* for information on how to file a bug report.

8.2.8.1. Using SSSD Log Files

SSSD uses a number of log files to report information about its operation, and this information can help to resolve issues in the event of SSSD failure or unexpected behavior. The default location for these log files on Fedora—based systems is the `/var/log/sssd/` directory.

SSSD produces a log file for each back end (that is, one log file for each domain specified in the `/etc/sssd/sssd.conf` file), as well as an `sssd_pam.log` and an `sssd_nss.log` file. This level of granularity can help you to quickly isolate and resolve any errors or issues you might experience with SSSD.

You should also examine the `/var/log/secure` file, which logs authentication failures and the reason for the failure. For example, if you see Reason 4: System Error reported against any failure, you should increase the debug level of the log files.

Producing More Verbose Log Files

If you are unable to identify and resolve any problems with SSSD after inspection of the default log files, you can configure SSSD to produce more verbose files. You can set the `debug_level` option in the `/etc/sssd/sssd.conf` for the domain that is causing concern, and then restart SSSD. Refer to the *sssd.conf(5)* manual page for more information on how to set the `debug_level` for a specific domain.

All log files include timestamps on debug messages by default. This can make it easier to understand any errors that may occur, why they occurred, and how to address them. If necessary, you can disable these timestamps by setting the appropriate parameter to `FALSE` in the `/etc/sssd/sssd.conf` file:

```
--debug-timestamps=FALSE
```

8.2.8.2. Problems with SSSD Configuration

- SSSD fails to start
    - SSSD requires at least one properly configured domain before the service will start. Without such a domain, you might see the following error message when trying to start SSSD with the following command:

      ```
      # sssd -d4

      [sssd] [ldb] (3): server_sort:Unable to register control with rootdse!

      [sssd] [confdb_get_domains] (0): No domains configured, fatal error!
      [sssd] [get_monitor_config] (0): No domains configured.
      ```

      You can ignore the "Unable to register control with rootdse!" message, as it is erroneous. The other messages, however, indicate that SSSD is unable to locate any properly configured domains.

      Edit your `/etc/sssd/sssd.conf` file and ensure you have at least one properly configured domain, and then try to start SSSD.
    - SSSD requires at least one available service provider before it will start. With no available service providers, you might see the following error message when trying to start SSSD with the following command:

      ```
      # sssd -d4

      [sssd] [ldb] (3): server_sort:Unable to register control with rootdse!

      [sssd] [get_monitor_config] (0): No services configured!
      ```

      You can ignore the "Unable to register control with rootdse!" message, as it is erroneous. The other message, however, indicates that SSSD is unable to locate any available service providers.

      Edit your `/etc/sssd/sssd.conf` file and ensure you have at least one available service providers, and then try to start SSSD.

Important

SSSD requires that service providers be configured as a comma-separated list in a single `services` entry in the `/etc/sssd/sssd.conf` file. If services are listed in multiple entries, only the last entry is recognized by SSSD.

- Refer to the *sssd.conf(5)* manual page for more options that might assist in troubleshooting issues with SSSD.

8.2.8.3. Problems with SSSD Service Configuration

8.2.8.3.1. Problems with NSS

This section describes some common problems with `NSS`, their symptoms, and how to resolve them.

- `NSS` fails to return user information
  - Ensure that NSS is running

    ```
    # systemctl is-active sssd.service
    ```

    This command should return results similar to the following:

    ```
    sssd (pid 21762) is running...
    ```
  - Ensure that you have correctly configured the `[nss]` section of the `/etc/sssd/sssd.conf` file. For example, ensure that you have not misconfigured the *`filter_users`* or *`filter_groups`* attributes. Refer to the *NSS configuration options* section of the *sssd.conf(5)* manual page for information on how to configure these attributes.
  - Ensure that you have included `nss` in the list of services that `sssd` should start
  - Ensure that you have correctly configured the `/etc/nsswitch.conf` file. Refer to the section Section 8.2.3.2.1, *Configuring NSS* (page 140) for information on how to correctly configure this file.

8.2.8.3.2. Problems with PAM

This section describes some common problems with `PAM`, their symptoms, and how to resolve them.

- Setting the password for the local SSSD user prompts twice for the password

  When attempting to change a local SSSD user's password, you might see output similar to the following:

  ```
  [root@clientF11 tmp]# passwd user1000
  Changing password for user user1000.
  ```

```
New password:
Retype new password:
New Password:
Reenter new Password:
passwd: all authentication tokens updated successfully.
```

This is the result of an incorrect PAM configuration. Refer to Section 8.2.3.2.2, *Configuring PAM* (page 140), and ensure that the *use_authtok* option is correctly configured in your /etc/pam.d/system-auth file.

8.2.8.3.3. Problems with NFS and NSCD

SSSD is not designed to be used with the nscd daemon, and will likely generate warnings in the SSSD log files. Even though SSSD does not directly conflict with nscd, the use of both at the same time can result in unexpected behavior (specifically with how long entries are being cached).

If you are using Network Manager to manage your network connections, it may take several minutes for the network interface to come up. During this time, various services will attempt to start. If these services start before the network is up (that is, the DNS servers cannot yet be reached) they will fail to identify the forward or reverse DNS entries they might need. These services will be reading an incorrect or possibly empty resolv.conf file. This file is typically only read once, and so any changes made to this file are not automatically applied.

This can result in the failure of some system services, and in particular can cause NFS locking to fail on the machine where the nscd service is running, unless that service is manually restarted.

One method of working around this problem is to enable caching for *hosts* and *services* in the /etc/nscd.conf file, and to rely on the SSSD cache for the *passwd* and *group* entries. With nscd answering *hosts* and *services* requests, these entries would have been cached and returned by nscd during the boot process.

NSCD and later versions of SSSD

Later versions of SSSD should negate any need for NSCD.

8.2.8.4. Problems with SSSD Domain Configuration

- NSS returns incorrect user information
    - If your search for user information returns incorrect data, ensure that you do not have conflicting usernames in separate domains. If you use multiple domains, it is recommended that you set the *use_fully_qualified_domains* attribute to TRUE in the /etc/sssd/sssd.conf file.

8.2.8.5. Additional Resources

8.2.8.5.1. Manual Pages

SSSD ships with a number of manual pages, all of which provide additional information about specific aspects of SSSD, such as configuration files, commands, and available options. SSSD currently provides the following manual pages:

- `sssd.conf(5)`
- `sssd-ipa(5)`
- `sssd-krb5(5)`
- `sssd-ldap(5)`
- `sssd(8)`
- `sssd_krb5_locator_plugin(8)`
- `pam_sss(8)`

You should refer to these manual pages for detailed information about all aspects of SSSD, its configuration, and associated tools and commands.

8.2.8.5.2. Mailing Lists

You can subscribe to the SSSD mailing list to follow and become involved in the development of SSSD, or to ask questions about any issues you may be experiencing with your SSSD deployment.

Visit *https://fedorahosted.org/mailman/listinfo/sssd-devel* to subscribe to this mailing list.

8.2.9. SSSD Configuration File Format

The following listing describes the current version (Version 2) of the SSSD configuration file format.

```
[sssd]
config_file_version = 2
services = nss, pam
domains = mybox.example.com, ldap.example.com, ipa.example.com, nis.example.com
# sbus_timeout = 300

[nss]
nss_filter_groups = root
nss_filter_users = root
nss_entry_cache_timeout = 30
nss_enum_cache_timeout = 30

[domain/mybox.example.com]
domain_type = local
```

```
enumerate = true
min_id = 1000
# max_id = 2000

local_default_shell = /bin/bash
local_default_homedir = /home

# Possible overrides
# id_provider = local
# auth_provider = local
# authz_provider = local
# passwd_provider = local

[domain/ldap.example.com]
domain_type = ldap
server = ldap.example.com, ldap3.example.com, 10.0.0.2
# ldap_uri = ldaps://ldap.example.com:9093
# ldap_use_tls = ssl
ldap_search_base = dc=ldap,dc=example,dc=com
enumerate = false

# Possible overrides
# id_provider = ldap
# id_server = ldap2.example.com
# auth_provider = krb5
# auth_server = krb5.example.com
# krb5_realm = KRB5.EXAMPLE.COM

[domain/ipa.example.com]
domain_type = ipa
server = ipa.example.com, ipa2.example.com
enumerate = false

# Possible overrides
# id_provider = ldap
# id_server = ldap2.example.com
# auth_provider = krb5
# auth_server = krb5.example.com
# krb5_realm = KRB5.EXAMPLE.COM

[domain/nis.example.com]
id_provider = proxy
proxy_lib = nis
auth_provider = proxy
proxy_auth_target = nis_pam_proxy
```

Chapter 9.
OpenSSH

`SSH` (Secure Shell) is a protocol which facilitates secure communications between two systems using a client/server architecture and allows users to log into server host systems remotely. Unlike other remote communication protocols, such as `FTP` or `Telnet`, SSH encrypts the login session, rendering the connection difficult for intruders to collect unencrypted passwords.

The **ssh** program is designed to replace older, less secure terminal applications used to log into remote hosts, such as `telnet` or `rsh`. A related program called `scp` replaces older programs designed to copy files between hosts, such as `rcp`. Because these older applications do not encrypt passwords transmitted between the client and the server, avoid them whenever possible. Using secure methods to log into remote systems decreases the risks for both the client system and the remote host.

Fedora includes the general OpenSSH package (openssh) as well as the OpenSSH server (openssh-server) and client (openssh-clients) packages. Note that the OpenSSH packages require the OpenSSL package (openssl), which installs several important cryptographic libraries, enabling OpenSSH to provide encrypted communications.

9.1. The SSH Protocol

9.1.1. Why Use SSH?

Potential intruders have a variety of tools at their disposal enabling them to disrupt, intercept, and re-route network traffic in an effort to gain access to a system. In general terms, these threats can be categorized as follows:

Interception of communication between two systems

The attacker can be somewhere on the network between the communicating parties, copying any information passed between them. He may intercept and keep the information, or alter the information and send it on to the intended recipient.

This attack is usually performed using a *packet sniffer*, a rather common network utility that captures each packet flowing through the network, and analyzes its content.

Impersonation of a particular host

Attacker's system is configured to pose as the intended recipient of a transmission. If this strategy works, the user's system remains unaware that it is communicating with the wrong host.

This attack can be performed using a technique known as *DNS poisoning*, or via so-called *IP spoofing*. In the first case, the intruder uses a cracked DNS server to point client systems to a maliciously duplicated host. In the second case, the intruder sends falsified network packets that appear to be from a trusted host.

Both techniques intercept potentially sensitive information and, if the interception is made for hostile reasons, the results can be disastrous. If SSH is used for remote shell login and file copying, these security threats can be greatly diminished. This is because the SSH client and server use digital signatures to verify their identity. Additionally, all communication between the client and server systems is encrypted. Attempts to spoof the identity of either side of a communication does not work, since each packet is encrypted using a key known only by the local and remote systems.

9.1.2. Main Features

The SSH protocol provides the following safeguards:

No one can pose as the intended server

After an initial connection, the client can verify that it is connecting to the same server it had connected to previously.

No one can capture the authentication information

The client transmits its authentication information to the server using strong, 128-bit encryption.

No one can intercept the communication

All data sent and received during a session is transferred using 128-bit encryption, making intercepted transmissions extremely difficult to decrypt and read.

Additionally, it also offers the following options:

It provides secure means to use graphical applications over a network

Using a technique called *X11 forwarding*, the client can forward *X11* (*X Window System*) applications from the server.

It provides a way to secure otherwise insecure protocols

The SSH protocol encrypts everything it sends and receives. Using a technique called *port forwarding*, an SSH server can become a conduit to securing otherwise insecure protocols, like POP, and increasing overall system and data security.

It can be used to create a secure channel

The OpenSSH server and client can be configured to create a tunnel similar to a virtual private network for traffic between server and client machines.

It supports the Kerberos authentication

OpenSSH servers and clients can be configured to authenticate using the GSSAPI (Generic Security Services Application Program Interface) implementation of the Kerberos network authentication protocol.

9.1.3. Protocol Versions

Two varieties of SSH currently exist: version 1, and newer version 2. The OpenSSH suite under Fedora uses SSH version 2, which has an enhanced key exchange algorithm not vulnerable to the known exploit in version 1. However, for compatibility reasons, the OpenSSH suite does support version 1 connections as well.

Avoid using SSH version 1

To ensure maximum security for your connection, it is recommended that only SSH version 2-compatible servers and clients are used whenever possible.

9.1.4. Event Sequence of an SSH Connection

The following series of events help protect the integrity of SSH communication between two hosts.

1. A cryptographic handshake is made so that the client can verify that it is communicating with the correct server.
2. The transport layer of the connection between the client and remote host is encrypted using a symmetric cipher.
3. The client authenticates itself to the server.
4. The remote client interacts with the remote host over the encrypted connection.

9.1.4.1. Transport Layer

The primary role of the transport layer is to facilitate safe and secure communication between the two hosts at the time of authentication and during subsequent communication. The transport layer accomplishes this by handling the encryption and decryption of data, and by providing integrity protection of data packets as they are sent and received. The transport layer also provides compression, speeding the transfer of information.

Once an SSH client contacts a server, key information is exchanged so that the two systems can correctly construct the transport layer. The following steps occur during this exchange:

- Keys are exchanged
- The public key encryption algorithm is determined
- The symmetric encryption algorithm is determined
- The message authentication algorithm is determined
- The hash algorithm is determined

During the key exchange, the server identifies itself to the client with a unique *host key*. If the client has never communicated with this particular server before, the server's host key is unknown to the client and it does not connect. OpenSSH gets around this problem by accepting the server's host key. This is done after the user is notified and has both accepted and verified the new host key. In subsequent connections, the server's host key is checked against the saved version on the client, providing confidence that the client is indeed communicating with the intended server. If, in the future, the host key no longer matches, the user must remove the client's saved version before a connection can occur.

Always verify the integrity of a new SSH server

It is possible for an attacker to masquerade as an SSH server during the initial contact since the local system does not know the difference between the intended server and a false one set up by an attacker. To help prevent this, verify the integrity of a new SSH server by contacting the server administrator before connecting for the first time or in the event of a host key mismatch.

SSH is designed to work with almost any kind of public key algorithm or encoding format. After an initial key exchange creates a hash value used for exchanges and a shared secret value, the two systems immediately begin calculating new keys and algorithms to protect authentication and future data sent over the connection.

After a certain amount of data has been transmitted using a given key and algorithm (the exact amount depends on the SSH implementation), another key exchange occurs, generating another set of hash values and a new shared secret value. Even if an attacker is able to determine the hash and shared secret value, this information is only useful for a limited period of time.

9.1.4.2. Authentication

Once the transport layer has constructed a secure tunnel to pass information between the two systems, the server tells the client the different authentication methods supported, such as using a private key-encoded signature or typing a password. The client then tries to authenticate itself to the server using one of these supported methods.

SSH servers and clients can be configured to allow different types of authentication, which gives each side the optimal amount of control. The server can decide which encryption methods it supports based on its security model, and the client can choose the order of authentication methods to attempt from the available options.

9.1.4.3. Channels

After a successful authentication over the SSH transport layer, multiple channels are opened via a technique called *multiplexing*[1]. Each of these channels handles communication for different terminal sessions and for forwarded X11 sessions.

Both clients and servers can create a new channel. Each channel is then assigned a different number on each end of the connection. When the client attempts to open a new channel, the clients sends the channel number along with the request. This information is stored by the server and is used to direct communication to that channel. This is done so that different types of sessions do not affect one another and so that when a given session ends, its channel can be closed without disrupting the primary SSH connection.

Channels also support *flow-control*, which allows them to send and receive data in an orderly fashion. In this way, data is not sent over the channel until the client receives a message that the channel is open.

The client and server negotiate the characteristics of each channel automatically, depending on the type of service the client requests and the way the user is connected to the network. This allows great flexibility in handling different types of remote connections without having to change the basic infrastructure of the protocol.

9.2. An OpenSSH Configuration

In order to perform tasks described in this section, you must have superuser privileges. To obtain them, log in as `root` by typing:

```
su -
```

9.2.1. Configuration Files

There are two different sets of configuration files: those for client programs (that is, `ssh`, `scp`, and `sftp`), and those for the server (the `sshd` daemon).

System-wide SSH configuration information is stored in the `/etc/ssh/` directory. See *Table 9.1. System-wide configuration files* below for a description of its content.

[1] A multiplexed connection consists of several signals being sent over a shared, common medium. With SSH, different channels are sent over a common secure connection.

Configuration File	Description
/etc/ssh/moduli	Contains Diffie-Hellman groups used for the Diffie-Hellman key exchange which is critical for constructing a secure transport layer. When keys are exchanged at the beginning of an SSH session, a shared, secret value is created which cannot be determined by either party alone. This value is then used to provide host authentication.
/etc/ssh/ssh_config	The default SSH client configuration file. Note that it is overridden by ~/.ssh/config if it exists.
/etc/ssh/sshd_config	The configuration file for the sshd daemon.
/etc/ssh/ssh_host_dsa_key	The DSA private key used by the sshd daemon.
/etc/ssh/ssh_host_dsa_key.pub	The DSA public key used by the sshd daemon.
/etc/ssh/ssh_host_key	The RSA private key used by the sshd daemon for version 1 of the SSH protocol.
/etc/ssh/ssh_host_key.pub	The RSA public key used by the sshd daemon for version 1 of the SSH protocol.
/etc/ssh/ssh_host_rsa_key	The RSA private key used by the sshd daemon for version 2 of the SSH protocol.
/etc/ssh/ssh_host_rsa_key.pub	The RSA public key used by the sshd for version 2 of the SSH protocol.

Table 9.1. System-wide configuration files

User-specific SSH configuration information is stored in the user's home directory within the `~/.ssh/` directory. See *Table 9.2. User-specific configuration files* below for a description of its content.

Configuration File	Description
~/.ssh/authorized_keys	Holds a list of authorized public keys for servers. When the client connects to a server, the server authenticates the client by checking its signed public key stored within this file.
~/.ssh/id_dsa	Contains the DSA private key of the user.
~/.ssh/id_dsa.pub	The DSA public key of the user.
~/.ssh/id_rsa	The RSA private key used by ssh for version 2 of the SSH protocol.
~/.ssh/id_rsa.pub	The RSA public key used by ssh for version 2 of the SSH protocol
~/.ssh/identity	The RSA private key used by ssh for version 1 of the SSH protocol.
~/.ssh/identity.pub	The RSA public key used by ssh for version 1 of the SSH protocol.
~/.ssh/known_hosts	Contains DSA host keys of SSH servers accessed by the user. This file is very important for ensuring that the SSH client is connecting the correct SSH server.

Table 9.2. User-specific configuration files

Refer to the `ssh_config` and `sshd_config` man pages for information concerning the various directives available in the SSH configuration files.

9.2.2. Starting an OpenSSH Server

Make sure you have relevant packages installed

To run an OpenSSH server, you must have the openssh-server and openssh packages installed. Refer to Section 4.2.4, *Installing Packages* (page 78) for more information on how to install new packages in Fedora.

To start the `sshd` daemon, type the following at a shell prompt:

```
systemctl start sshd.service
```

To stop the running `sshd` daemon, use the following command:

```
systemctl stop sshd.service
```

If you want the daemon to start automatically at the boot time, type:

```
systemctl enable sshd.service
```

Refer to Chapter 7, *Services and Daemons* (page 120) for more information on how to configure services in Fedora.

Note that if you reinstall the system, a new set of identification keys will be created. As a result, clients who had connected to the system with any of the OpenSSH tools before the reinstall will see the following message:

```
@@@@@@@@@@@@@@@@@@@@@@@@@@@@@@@@@@@@@@@@@@@@@@@@@@@@@@@@@@@
@    WARNING: REMOTE HOST IDENTIFICATION HAS CHANGED!     @
@@@@@@@@@@@@@@@@@@@@@@@@@@@@@@@@@@@@@@@@@@@@@@@@@@@@@@@@@@@
IT IS POSSIBLE THAT SOMEONE IS DOING SOMETHING NASTY!
Someone could be eavesdropping on you right now (man-in-the-middle attack)!
It is also possible that the RSA host key has just been changed.
```

To prevent this, you can back up the relevant files from the `/etc/ssh/` directory (see *Table 9.1. System-wide configuration files* above for a complete list), and restore them whenever you reinstall the system.

9.2.3. Requiring SSH for Remote Connections

For SSH to be truly effective, using insecure connection protocols should be prohibited. Otherwise, a user's password may be protected using SSH for one session, only to be captured later while logging in using Telnet. Some services to disable include `telnet`, `rsh`, `rlogin`, and `vsftpd`.

To make sure these services are not running, type the following commands at a shell prompt:

```
systemctl stop telnet.service
systemctl stop rsh.service
systemctl stop rlogin.service
systemctl stop vsftpd.service
```

To disable running these services at startup, type:

```
systemctl disable telnet.service
systemctl disable rsh.service
systemctl disable rlogin.service
systemctl disable vsftpd.service
```

Refer to Chapter 7, *Services and Daemons* (page 120) for more information on how to configure services in Fedora.

9.2.4. Using a Key-Based Authentication

To improve the system security even further, you can enforce the key-based authentication by disabling the standard password authentication. To do so, open the `/etc/ssh/sshd_config` configuration file in a text editor, and change the `PasswordAuthentication` option as follows:

```
PasswordAuthentication no
```

To be able to use `ssh`, `scp`, or `sftp` to connect to the server from a client machine, generate an authorization key pair by following the steps below. Note that keys must be generated for each user separately.

Fedora 15 uses SSH Protocol 2 and RSA keys by default (see Section 9.1.3, *Protocol Versions* - page 170) for more information).

Do not generate key pairs as root

If you complete the steps as `root`, only `root` will be able to use the keys.

Backup your ~/.ssh/ directory

If you reinstall your system and want to keep previously generated key pair, backup the `~/.ssh/` directory. After reinstalling, copy it back to your home directory. This process can be done for all users on your system, including `root`.

9.2.4.1. Generating Key Pairs

To generate an RSA key pair for version 2 of the SSH protocol, follow these steps:

1. Generate an RSA key pair by typing the following at a shell prompt:

```
~]$ ssh-keygen -t rsa
Generating public/private rsa key pair.
Enter file in which to save the key (/home/john/.ssh/id_rsa):
```

2. Press **Enter** to confirm the default location (that is, `~/.ssh/id_rsa`) for the newly created key.
3. Enter a passphrase, and confirm it by entering it again when prompted to do so. For security reasons, avoid using the same password as you use to log in to your account.

   After this, you will be presented with a message similar to this:

```
Your identification has been saved in /home/john/.ssh/id_rsa.
Your public key has been saved in /home/john/.ssh/id_rsa.pub.
The key fingerprint is:
e7:97:c7:e2:0e:f9:0e:fc:c4:d7:cb:e5:31:11:92:14 john@penguin.example.com
The key's randomart image is:
+--[ RSA 2048]----+
|             E.  |
|             . . |
|             o . |
|              . .|
|        S .    . |
|         + o o ..|
|          * * +oo|
|           O +..=|
|           o*  o.|
+-----------------+
```

4. Change the permissions of the `~/.ssh/` directory:

```
~]$ chmod 755 ~/.ssh
```

5. Copy the content of `~/.ssh/id_rsa.pub` into the `~/.ssh/authorized_keys` on the machine to which you want to connect, appending it to its end if the file already exists.
6. Change the permissions of the `~/.ssh/authorized_keys` file using the following command:

```
~]$ chmod 644 ~/.ssh/authorized_keys
```

To generate a DSA key pair for version 2 of the SSH protocol, follow these steps:

1. Generate a DSA key pair by typing the following at a shell prompt:

```
~]$ ssh-keygen -t dsa
Generating public/private dsa key pair.
Enter file in which to save the key (/home/john/.ssh/id_dsa):
```

2. Press **Enter** to confirm the default location (that is, `~/.ssh/id_dsa`) for the newly created key.

3. Enter a passphrase, and confirm it by entering it again when prompted to do so. For security reasons, avoid using the same password as you use to log in to your account.

   After this, you will be presented with a message similar to this:

```
Your identification has been saved in /home/john/.ssh/id_dsa.
Your public key has been saved in /home/john/.ssh/id_dsa.pub.
The key fingerprint is:
81:a1:91:a8:9f:e8:c5:66:0d:54:f5:90:cc:bc:cc:27 john@penguin.example.com
The key's randomart image is:
+--[ DSA 1024]----+
|    .oo*o.       |
|   ...o Bo       |
| .. . + o.       |
|.  .    E o      |
| o..o    S       |
|. o= .           |
|. +              |
| .               |
|                 |
+-----------------+
```

4. Change the permissions of the `~/.ssh/` directory:

```
~]$ chmod 775 ~/.ssh
```

5. Copy the content of `~/.ssh/id_dsa.pub` into the `~/.ssh/authorized_keys` on the machine to which you want to connect, appending it to its end if the file already exists.

6. Change the permissions of the `~/.ssh/authorized_keys` file using the following command:

```
~]$ chmod 644 ~/.ssh/authorized_keys
```

To generate an RSA key pair for version 1 of the SSH protocol, follow these steps:

1. Generate an RSA key pair by typing the following at a shell prompt:

```
~]$ ssh-keygen -t rsa1
Generating public/private rsa1 key pair.
Enter file in which to save the key (/home/john/.ssh/identity):
```

2. Press **Enter** to confirm the default location (that is, `~/.ssh/identity`) for the newly created key.

3. Enter a passphrase, and confirm it by entering it again when prompted to do so. For security reasons, avoid using the same password as you use to log into your account.

   After this, you will be presented with a message similar to this:

```
Your identification has been saved in /home/john/.ssh/identity.
Your public key has been saved in /home/john/.ssh/identity.pub.
The key fingerprint is:
cb:f6:d5:cb:6e:5f:2b:28:ac:17:0c:e4:62:e4:6f:59 john@penguin.example.com
The key's randomart image is:
```

```
+--[RSA1 2048]----+
|                 |
|     . .         |
|    o o          |
|     + o E       |
|    . o S        |
|       = +   .   |
|      . = . o . .|
|       . = o o..o|
|       .o o  o=o.|
+-----------------+
```

4. Change the permissions of the `~/.ssh/` directory:

   ```
   ~]$ chmod 755 ~/.ssh
   ```

5. Copy the content of `~/.ssh/identity.pub` into the `~/.ssh/authorized_keys` on the machine to which you want to connect, appending it to its end if the file already exists.

6. Change the permissions of the `~/.ssh/authorized_keys` file using the following command:

   ```
   ~]$ chmod 644 ~/.ssh/authorized_keys
   ```

Refer to Section 9.2.4.2, *Configuring ssh-agent* (page 178) for information on how to set up your system to remember the passphrase.

Never share your private key

The private key is for your personal use only, and it is important that you never give it to anyone.

9.2.4.2. Configuring ssh-agent

To store your passphrase so that you do not have to enter it each time you initiate a connection with a remote machine, you can use the `ssh-agent` authentication agent. To save your passphrase for a certain shell prompt, use the following command:

```
~]$ ssh-add
Enter passphrase for /home/john/.ssh/id_rsa:
```

Note that when you log out, your passphrase will be forgotten. You must execute the command each time you log in to a virtual console or a terminal window.

9.3. OpenSSH Clients

Make sure you have relevant packages installed

To connect to an OpenSSH server from a client machine, you must have the openssh-clients and openssh packages installed. Refer to Section 4.2.4, *Installing Packages* (page 78) for more information on how to install new packages in Fedora.

9.3.1. Using the ssh Utility

`ssh` allows you to log in to a remote machine and execute commands there. It is a secure replacement for the `rlogin`, `rsh`, and `telnet` programs.

Similarly to `telnet`, to log in to a remote machine named `penguin.example.com`, type the following command at a shell prompt:

```
~]$ ssh penguin.example.com
```

This will log you in with the same username you are using on a local machine. If you want to specify a different one, use a command in the `ssh` *`username@hostname`* form. For example, to log in as `john`, type:

```
~]$ ssh john@penguin.example.com
```

The first time you initiate a connection, you will be presented with a message similar to this:

```
The authenticity of host 'penguin.example.com' can't be established.
RSA key fingerprint is 94:68:3a:3a:bc:f3:9a:9b:01:5d:b3:07:38:e2:11:0c.
Are you sure you want to continue connecting (yes/no)?
```

Type **`yes`** to confirm. You will see a notice that the server has been added to the list of known hosts, and a prompt asking for your password:

```
Warning: Permanently added 'penguin.example.com' (RSA) to the list of known hosts.
john@penguin.example.com's password:
```

Updating the host key of an SSH server

If the SSH server's host key changes, the client notifies the user that the connection cannot proceed until the server's host key is deleted from the `~/.ssh/known_hosts` file. To do so, open the file in a text editor, and remove a line containing the remote machine name at the beginning. Before doing this, however, contact the system administrator of the SSH server to verify the server is not compromised.

After entering the password, you will be provided with a shell prompt for the remote machine.

Alternatively, the `ssh` program can be used to execute a command on the remote machine without logging in to a shell prompt. The syntax for that is `ssh` [*`username`*`@`] *`hostname`* *`command`*. For example, if you want to execute the `whoami` command on `penguin.example.com`, type:

```
~]$ ssh john@penguin.example.com whoami
john@penguin.example.com's password:
john
```

After you enter the correct password, the username will be displayed, and you will return to your local shell prompt.

9.3.2. Using the `scp` Utility

`scp` can be used to transfer files between machines over a secure, encrypted connection. In its design, it is very similar to `rcp`.

To transfer a local file to a remote system, use a command in the following form:

```
scp localfile username@hostname:remotefile
```

For example, if you want to transfer `taglist.vim` to a remote machine named `penguin.example.com`, type the following at a shell prompt:

```
~]$ scp taglist.vim john@penguin.example.com:.vim/plugin/taglist.vim
john@penguin.example.com's password:
taglist.vim                                   100%  144KB 144.5KB/s   00:00
```

Multiple files can be specified at once. To transfer the contents of `.vim/plugin/` to the same directory on the remote machine `penguin.example.com`, type the following command:

```
~]$ scp .vim/plugin/* john@penguin.example.com:.vim/plugin/
john@penguin.example.com's password:
closetag.vim                                  100%   13KB  12.6KB/s   00:00
snippetsEmu.vim                               100%   33KB  33.1KB/s   00:00
taglist.vim                                   100%  144KB 144.5KB/s   00:00
```

To transfer a remote file to the local system, use the following syntax:

```
scp username@hostname:remotefile localfile
```

For instance, to download the `.vimrc` configuration file from the remote machine, type:

```
~]$ scp john@penguin.example.com:.vimrc .vimrc
john@penguin.example.com's password:
.vimrc                                        100% 2233     2.2KB/s   00:00
```

9.3.3. Using the `sftp` Utility

The `sftp` utility can be used to open a secure, interactive FTP session. In its design, it is similar to `ftp` except that it uses a secure, encrypted connection.

To connect to a remote system, use a command in the following form:

```
sftp username@hostname
```

For example, to log in to a remote machine named `penguin.example.com` with `john` as a username, type:

```
~]$ sftp john@penguin.example.com
john@penguin.example.com's password:
Connected to penguin.example.com.
sftp>
```

After you enter the correct password, you will be presented with a prompt. The `sftp` utility accepts a set of commands similar to those used by `ftp` (see *Table 9.3. A selection of available sftp commands* below).

Command	Description
`ls` [*`directory`*]	List the content of a remote *`directory`*. If none is supplied, a current working directory is used by default.
`cd` *`directory`*	Change the remote working directory to *`directory`*.
`mkdir` *`directory`*	Create a remote *`directory`*.
`rmdir` *`path`*	Remove a remote *`directory`*.
`put` *`localfile`* [*`remotefile`*]	Transfer *`localfile`* to a remote machine.
`get` *`remotefile`* [*`localfile`*]	Transfer *`remotefile`* from a remote machine.

Table 9.3. A selection of available sftp commands

For a complete list of available commands, refer to the `sftp` man page.

9.4. More Than a Secure Shell

A secure command line interface is just the beginning of the many ways SSH can be used. Given the proper amount of bandwidth, X11 sessions can be directed over an SSH channel. Or, by using TCP/IP forwarding, previously insecure port connections between systems can be mapped to specific SSH channels.

9.4.1. X11 Forwarding

To open an X11 session over an SSH connection, use a command in the following form:

```
ssh -Y username@hostname
```

For example, to log in to a remote machine named `penguin.example.com` with `john` as a username, type:

```
~]$ ssh -Y john@penguin.example.com
john@penguin.example.com's password:
```

When an X program is run from the secure shell prompt, the SSH client and server create a new secure channel, and the X program data is sent over that channel to the client machine transparently.

X11 forwarding can be very useful. For example, X11 forwarding can be used to create a secure, interactive session of the **Printer Configuration** utility. To do this, connect to the server using **ssh** and type:

```
~]$ system-config-printer &
```

The **Printer Configuration Tool** will appear, allowing the remote user to safely configure printing on the remote system.

9.4.2. Port Forwarding

SSH can secure otherwise insecure `TCP/IP` protocols via port forwarding. When using this technique, the SSH server becomes an encrypted conduit to the SSH client.

Port forwarding works by mapping a local port on the client to a remote port on the server. SSH can map any port from the server to any port on the client. Port numbers do not need to match for this technique to work.

Using reserved port numbers

Setting up port forwarding to listen on ports below 1024 requires root level access.

To create a TCP/IP port forwarding channel which listens for connections on the `localhost`, use a command in the following form:

```
ssh -L local-port:remote-hostname:remote-port username@hostname
```

For example, to check email on a server called `mail.example.com` using `POP3` through an encrypted connection, use the following command:

```
~]$ ssh -L 1100:mail.example.com:110 mail.example.com
```

Once the port forwarding channel is in place between the client machine and the mail server, direct a POP3 mail client to use port `1100` on the `localhost` to check for new email. Any requests sent to port `1100` on the client system will be directed securely to the `mail.example.com` server.

If `mail.example.com` is not running an SSH server, but another machine on the same network is, SSH can still be used to secure part of the connection. However, a slightly different command is necessary:

```
~]$ ssh -L 1100:mail.example.com:110 other.example.com
```

In this example, POP3 requests from port `1100` on the client machine are forwarded through the SSH connection on port `22` to the SSH server, `other.example.com`. Then, `other.example.com` connects to port `110` on `mail.example.com` to check for new email. Note that when using this technique, only the connection between the client system and `other.example.com` SSH server is secure.

Port forwarding can also be used to get information securely through network firewalls. If the firewall is configured to allow SSH traffic via its standard port (that is, port 22) but blocks access to other ports, a connection between two hosts using the blocked ports is still possible by redirecting their communication over an established SSH connection.

A connection is only as secure as a client system

Using port forwarding to forward connections in this manner allows any user on the client system to connect to that service. If the client system becomes compromised, the attacker also has access to forwarded services.

System administrators concerned about port forwarding can disable this functionality on the server by specifying a `No` parameter for the `AllowTcpForwarding` line in `/etc/ssh/sshd_config` and restarting the `sshd` service.

9.5. Additional Resources

The OpenSSH and OpenSSL projects are in constant development, and the most up-to-date information for them is available from their websites. The man pages for OpenSSH and OpenSSL tools are also good sources of detailed information.

9.5.1. Installed Documentation

`man ssh`
: The manual page for **ssh** containing the full documentation on its usage.

`man scp`
: The manual page for **scp** containing the full documentation on its usage.

`man sftp`
: The manual page for **sftp** containing the full documentation on its usage.

`man sshd`
: The manual page for **sshd** containing the full documentation on its usage.

`man ssh-keygen`
: The manual page for **ssh-keygen** containing the full documentation on its usage.

`man ssh_config`
: The manual page with full description of available SSH client configuration options.

`man sshd_config`
: The manual page with full description of available SSH daemon configuration options.

9.5.2. Useful Websites

http://www.openssh.com/
: The OpenSSH home page containing further documentation, frequently asked questions, links to the mailing lists, bug reports, and other useful resources.

http://www.openssl.org/
: The OpenSSL home page containing further documentation, frequently asked questions, links to the mailing lists, and other useful resources.

http://www.freesshd.com/

Another implementation of an SSH server.

Part V.
Servers

This part discusses various topics related to servers such as how to set up a Web server or share files and directories over the network.

Chapter 10.
DHCP Servers

Dynamic Host Configuration Protocol (DHCP) is a network protocol that automatically assigns TCP/IP information to client machines. Each DHCP client connects to the centrally located DHCP server, which returns that client's network configuration (including the IP address, gateway, and DNS servers).

10.1. Why Use DHCP?

DHCP is useful for automatic configuration of client network interfaces. When configuring the client system, the administrator chooses DHCP instead of specifying an IP address, netmask, gateway, or DNS servers. The client retrieves this information from the DHCP server. DHCP is also useful if an administrator wants to change the IP addresses of a large number of systems. Instead of reconfiguring all the systems, he can just edit one DHCP configuration file on the server for the new set of IP addresses. If the DNS servers for an organization changes, the changes are made on the DHCP server, not on the DHCP clients. When the administrator restarts the network or reboots the clients, the changes will go into effect.

If an organization has a functional DHCP server properly connected to a network, laptops and other mobile computer users can move these devices from office to office.

10.2. Configuring a DHCP Server

The `dhcp` package contains an ISC DHCP server. First, install the package as `root`:

```
yum install dhcp
```

Installing the `dhcp` package creates a file, `/etc/dhcp/dhcpd.conf`, which is merely an empty configuration file:

```
#
# DHCP Server Configuration file.
#    see /usr/share/doc/dhcp*/dhcpd.conf.sample
#    see dhcpd.conf(5) man page
#
```

The sample configuration file can be found at `/usr/share/doc/dhcp-version/dhcpd.conf.sample`. You should use this file to help you configure `/etc/dhcp/dhcpd.conf`, which is explained in detail below.

DHCP also uses the file `/var/lib/dhcpd/dhcpd.leases` to store the client lease database. Refer to Section 10.2.2, *Lease Database* (page 190) for more information.

10.2.1. Configuration File

The first step in configuring a DHCP server is to create the configuration file that stores the network information for the clients. Use this file to declare options and global options for client systems.

The configuration file can contain extra tabs or blank lines for easier formatting. Keywords are case-insensitive and lines beginning with a hash sign (#) are considered comments.

There are two types of statements in the configuration file:

- Parameters — State how to perform a task, whether to perform a task, or what network configuration options to send to the client.
- Declarations — Describe the topology of the network, describe the clients, provide addresses for the clients, or apply a group of parameters to a group of declarations.

The parameters that start with the keyword option are referred to as *options*. These options control DHCP options; whereas, parameters configure values that are not optional or control how the DHCP server behaves.

Parameters (including options) declared before a section enclosed in curly brackets ({ }) are considered global parameters. Global parameters apply to all the sections below it.

Restart the DHCP daemon for the changes to take effect

If the configuration file is changed, the changes do not take effect until the DHCP daemon is restarted. To do so, type the following at a shell prompt as `root`:

```
systemctl restart dhcpd.service
```

Use the omshell command

Instead of changing a DHCP configuration file and restarting the service each time, using the `omshell` command provides an interactive way to connect to, query, and change the configuration of a DHCP server. By using `omshell`, all changes can be made while the server is running. For more information on `omshell`, refer to the `omshell` man page.

In *Example 10.1. Subnet declaration* below, the `routers`, `subnet-mask`, `domain-search`, `domain-name-servers`, and `time-offset` options are used for any `host` statements declared below it.

Additionally, a `subnet` can be declared, a `subnet` declaration must be included for every subnet in the network. If it is not, the DHCP server fails to start.

In this example, there are global options for every DHCP client in the subnet and a `range` declared. Clients are assigned an IP address within the `range`.

```
subnet 192.168.1.0 netmask 255.255.255.0 {
        option routers                  192.168.1.254;
        option subnet-mask              255.255.255.0;
        option domain-search              "example.com";
        option domain-name-servers       192.168.1.1;
        option time-offset              -18000;     # Eastern Standard Time
        range 192.168.1.10 192.168.1.100;
}
```

Example 10.1. Subnet declaration

To configure a DHCP server that leases a dynamic IP address to a system within a subnet, modify *Example 10.2. Range parameter* below with your values. It declares a default lease time, maximum lease time, and network configuration values for the clients. This example assigns IP addresses in the `range` 192.168.1.10 and 192.168.1.100 to client systems.

```
default-lease-time 600;
max-lease-time 7200;
option subnet-mask 255.255.255.0;
option broadcast-address 192.168.1.255;
option routers 192.168.1.254;
option domain-name-servers 192.168.1.1, 192.168.1.2;
option domain-search "example.com";
subnet 192.168.1.0 netmask 255.255.255.0 {
   range 192.168.1.10 192.168.1.100;
}
```

Example 10.2. Range parameter

To assign an IP address to a client based on the MAC address of the network interface card, use the `hardware ethernet` parameter within a `host` declaration. As demonstrated in *Example 10.3. Static IP address using DHCP* below, the `host apex` declaration specifies that the network interface card with the MAC address 00:A0:78:8E:9E:AA always receives the IP address 192.168.1.4.

Note that the optional parameter `host-name` can also be used to assign a host name to the client.

```
host apex {
   option host-name "apex.example.com";
   hardware ethernet 00:A0:78:8E:9E:AA;
   fixed-address 192.168.1.4;
}
```

Example 10.3. Static IP address using DHCP

All subnets that share the same physical network should be declared within a `shared-network` declaration as shown in *Example 10.4. Shared-network declaration* below. Parameters within the `shared-network`, but outside the enclosed `subnet` declarations, are considered to be global parameters. The name of the `shared-network` must be a descriptive title for the network, such as using the title 'test-lab' to describe all the subnets in a test lab environment.

```
shared-network name {
    option domain-search              "test.redhat.com";
    option domain-name-servers       ns1.redhat.com, ns2.redhat.com;
    option routers                   192.168.0.254;
    more parameters for EXAMPLE shared-network
    subnet 192.168.1.0 netmask 255.255.252.0 {
        parameters for subnet
        range 192.168.1.1 192.168.1.254;
    }
    subnet 192.168.2.0 netmask 255.255.252.0 {
        parameters for subnet
        range 192.168.2.1 192.168.2.254;
    }
}
```

Example 10.4. Shared-network declaration

As demonstrated in *Example 10.5. Group declaration* below, the `group` declaration is used to apply global parameters to a group of declarations. For example, shared networks, subnets, and hosts can be grouped.

```
group {
   option routers                  192.168.1.254;
   option subnet-mask              255.255.255.0;
   option domain-search              "example.com";
   option domain-name-servers       192.168.1.1;
   option time-offset              -18000;     # Eastern Standard Time
   host apex {
      option host-name "apex.example.com";
      hardware ethernet 00:A0:78:8E:9E:AA;
      fixed-address 192.168.1.4;
   }
   host raleigh {
      option host-name "raleigh.example.com";
      hardware ethernet 00:A1:DD:74:C3:F2;
      fixed-address 192.168.1.6;
   }
}
```

Example 10.5. Group declaration

Using the sample configuration file

The sample configuration file provided can be used as a starting point and custom configuration options can be added to it. To copy it to the proper location, use the following command:

```
cp /usr/share/doc/dhcp-version-number/dhcpd.conf.sample
                                              /etc/dhcp/dhcpd.conf
```

... where *version-number* is the DHCP version number.

For a complete list of option statements and what they do, refer to the `dhcp-options` man page.

10.2.2. Lease Database

On the DHCP server, the file `/var/lib/dhcpd/dhcpd.leases` stores the DHCP client lease database. Do not change this file. DHCP lease information for each recently assigned IP address is automatically stored in the lease database. The information includes the length of the lease, to whom the IP address has been assigned, the start and end dates for the lease, and the MAC address of the network interface card that was used to retrieve the lease.

All times in the lease database are in Coordinated Universal Time (UTC), not local time.

The lease database is recreated from time to time so that it is not too large. First, all known leases are saved in a temporary lease database. The `dhcpd.leases` file is renamed `dhcpd.leases~` and the temporary lease database is written to `dhcpd.leases`.

The DHCP daemon could be killed or the system could crash after the lease database has been renamed to the backup file but before the new file has been written. If this happens, the `dhcpd.leases` file does not exist, but it is required to start the service. Do not create a new lease file. If you do, all old leases are lost which causes many problems. The correct solution is to rename the `dhcpd.leases~` backup file to `dhcpd.leases` and then start the daemon.

10.2.3. Starting and Stopping the Server

Starting the DHCP server for the first time

When the DHCP server is started for the first time, it fails unless the `dhcpd.leases` file exists. Use the command `touch /var/lib/dhcpd/dhcpd.leases` to create the file if it does not exist.

If the same server is also running BIND as a DNS server, this step is not necessary, as starting the `named` service automatically checks for a `dhcpd.leases` file.

To start the DHCP service, use the following command:

```
systemctl start dhcpd.service
```

To stop the DHCP server, type:

```
systemctl stop dhcpd.service
```

By default, the DHCP service does not start at boot time. To configure the daemon to start automatically at boot time, run:

```
systemctl enable dhcpcd.service
```

Refer to Chapter 7, *Services and Daemons* (page 120) for more information on how to configure services in Fedora.

If more than one network interface is attached to the system, but the DHCP server should only be started on one of the interfaces, configure the DHCP server to start only on that device. In `/etc/sysconfig/dhcpd`, add the name of the interface to the list of `DHCPDARGS`:

```
# Command line options here
DHCPDARGS=eth0
```

This is useful for a firewall machine with two network cards. One network card can be configured as a DHCP client to retrieve an IP address to the Internet. The other network card can be used as a DHCP server for the internal network behind the firewall. Specifying only the network card connected to the internal network makes the system more secure because users can not connect to the daemon via the Internet.

Other command line options that can be specified in `/etc/sysconfig/dhcpd` include:

- `-p` *`portnum`* — Specifies the UDP port number on which `dhcpd` should listen. The default is port 67. The DHCP server transmits responses to the DHCP clients at a port number one greater than the UDP port specified. For example, if the default port 67 is used, the server listens on port 67 for requests and responses to the client on port 68. If a port is specified here and the DHCP relay agent is used, the same port on which the DHCP relay agent should listen must be specified. Refer to Section 10.2.4, *DHCP Relay Agent* (page 192) for details.
- `-f` — Runs the daemon as a foreground process. This is mostly used for debugging.
- `-d` — Logs the DHCP server daemon to the standard error descriptor. This is mostly used for debugging. If this is not specified, the log is written to `/var/log/messages`.
- `-cf` *`filename`* — Specifies the location of the configuration file. The default location is `/etc/dhcp/dhcpd.conf`.
- `-lf` *`filename`* — Specifies the location of the lease database file. If a lease database file already exists, it is very important that the same file be used every time the DHCP server is started. It is strongly recommended that this option only be used for debugging purposes on non-production machines. The default location is `/var/lib/dhcpd/dhcpd.leases`.
- `-q` — Do not print the entire copyright message when starting the daemon.

10.2.4. DHCP Relay Agent

The DHCP Relay Agent (`dhcrelay`) allows for the relay of DHCP and BOOTP requests from a subnet with no DHCP server on it to one or more DHCP servers on other subnets.

When a DHCP client requests information, the DHCP Relay Agent forwards the request to the list of DHCP servers specified when the DHCP Relay Agent is started. When a DHCP server returns a reply, the reply is broadcast or unicast on the network that sent the original request.

The DHCP Relay Agent listens for DHCP requests on all interfaces unless the interfaces are specified in `/etc/sysconfig/dhcrelay` with the `INTERFACES` directive.

To start the DHCP Relay Agent, use the following command:

```
systemctl start dhcrelay.service
```

10.3. Configuring a DHCP Client

To configure a DHCP client manually, modify the `/etc/sysconfig/network` file to enable networking and the configuration file for each network device in the `/etc/sysconfig/network-scripts` directory. In this directory, each device should have a configuration file named `ifcfg-eth0`, where `eth0` is the network device name.

The `/etc/sysconfig/network-scripts/ifcfg-eth0` file should contain the following lines:

```
DEVICE=eth0
BOOTPROTO=dhcp
ONBOOT=yes
```

A configuration file is needed for each device to be configured to use DHCP.

Other options for the network script includes:

- `DHCP_HOSTNAME` — Only use this option if the DHCP server requires the client to specify a hostname before receiving an IP address. (The DHCP server daemon in Fedora does not support this feature.)
- `PEERDNS=`*`answer`* , where *`answer`* is one of the following:
  - `yes` — Modify `/etc/resolv.conf` with information from the server. If using DHCP, then `yes` is the default.
  - `no` — Do not modify `/etc/resolv.conf`.

Advanced configurations

For advanced configurations of client DHCP options such as protocol timing, lease requirements and requests, dynamic DNS support, aliases, as well as a wide variety of values to override, prepend, or append to client-side configurations, refer to the `dhclient` and `dhclient.conf` man pages.

10.4. Configuring a Multihomed DHCP Server

A multihomed DHCP server serves multiple networks, that is, multiple subnets. The examples in these sections detail how to configure a DHCP server to serve multiple networks, select which network interfaces to listen on, and how to define network settings for systems that move networks.

Before making any changes, back up the existing `/etc/sysconfig/dhcpd` and `/etc/dhcp/dhcpd.conf` files.

The DHCP daemon listens on all network interfaces unless otherwise specified. Use the `/etc/sysconfig/dhcpd` file to specify which network interfaces the DHCP daemon listens on. The following `/etc/sysconfig/dhcpd` example specifies that the DHCP daemon listens on the `eth0` and `eth1` interfaces:

```
DHCPDARGS="eth0 eth1";
```

If a system has three network interfaces cards -- `eth0`, `eth1`, and `eth2` -- and it is only desired that the DHCP daemon listens on `eth0`, then only specify `eth0` in `/etc/sysconfig/dhcpd`:

```
DHCPDARGS="eth0";
```

The following is a basic `/etc/dhcp/dhcpd.conf` file, for a server that has two network interfaces, `eth0` in a 10.0.0.0/24 network, and `eth1` in a 172.16.0.0/24 network. Multiple `subnet` declarations allow different settings to be defined for multiple networks:

```
default-lease-time 600;
max-lease-time 7200;
subnet 10.0.0.0 netmask 255.255.255.0 {
      option subnet-mask 255.255.255.0;
      option routers 10.0.0.1;
      range 10.0.0.5 10.0.0.15;
}
subnet 172.16.0.0 netmask 255.255.255.0 {
      option subnet-mask 255.255.255.0;
      option routers 172.16.0.1;
      range 172.16.0.5 172.16.0.15;
}
```

`subnet` *`10.0.0.0`* `netmask` *`255.255.255.0`*`;`

A `subnet` declaration is required for every network your DHCP server is serving. Multiple subnets require multiple `subnet` declarations. If the DHCP server does not have a network interface in a range of a `subnet` declaration, the DHCP server does not serve that network.

If there is only one `subnet` declaration, and no network interfaces are in the range of that subnet, the DHCP daemon fails to start, and an error such as the following is logged to `/var/log/messages`:

```
dhcpd: No subnet declaration for eth0 (0.0.0.0).
dhcpd: ** Ignoring requests on eth0.  If this is not what
dhcpd:    you want, please write a subnet declaration
dhcpd:    in your dhcpd.conf file for the network segment
dhcpd:    to which interface eth1 is attached. **
dhcpd:
dhcpd:
dhcpd: Not configured to listen on any interfaces!
```

`option subnet-mask` *`255.255.255.0;`*

The `option subnet-mask` option defines a subnet mask, and overrides the `netmask` value in the `subnet` declaration. In simple cases, the subnet and netmask values are the same.

`option routers` *`10.0.0.1;`*

The `option routers` option defines the default gateway for the subnet. This is required for systems to reach internal networks on a different subnet, as well as external networks.

`range` *`10.0.0.5 10.0.0.15;`*

The `range` option specifies the pool of available IP addresses. Systems are assigned an address from the range of specified IP addresses.

For further information, refer to the `dhcpd.conf(5)` man page.

Do not use alias interfaces

Alias interfaces are not supported by DHCP. If an alias interface is the only interface, in the only subnet specified in `/etc/dhcp/dhcpd.conf`, the DHCP daemon fails to start.

10.4.1. Host Configuration

Before making any changes, back up the existing `/etc/sysconfig/dhcpd` and `/etc/dhcp/dhcpd.conf` files.

Configuring a single system for multiple networks

The following `/etc/dhcp/dhcpd.conf` example creates two subnets, and configures an IP address for the same system, depending on which network it connects to:

```
default-lease-time 600;
max-lease-time 7200;
```

```
subnet 10.0.0.0 netmask 255.255.255.0 {
        option subnet-mask 255.255.255.0;
        option routers 10.0.0.1;
        range 10.0.0.5 10.0.0.15;
}
subnet 172.16.0.0 netmask 255.255.255.0 {
        option subnet-mask 255.255.255.0;
        option routers 172.16.0.1;
        range 172.16.0.5 172.16.0.15;
}
host example0 {
        hardware ethernet 00:1A:6B:6A:2E:0B;
        fixed-address 10.0.0.20;
}
host example1 {
        hardware ethernet 00:1A:6B:6A:2E:0B;
        fixed-address 172.16.0.20;
}
```

`host` *`example0`*

The `host` declaration defines specific parameters for a single system, such as an IP address. To configure specific parameters for multiple hosts, use multiple `host` declarations.

Most DHCP clients ignore the name in `host` declarations, and as such, this name can anything, as long as it is unique to other `host` declarations. To configure the same system for multiple networks, use a different name for each `host` declaration, otherwise the DHCP daemon fails to start. Systems are identified by the `hardware ethernet` option, not the name in the `host` declaration.

`hardware ethernet` *`00:1A:6B:6A:2E:0B;`*

The `hardware ethernet` option identifies the system. To find this address, run the `ip link` command.

`fixed-address` *`10.0.0.20;`*

The `fixed-address` option assigns a valid IP address to the system specified by the `hardware ethernet` option. This address must be outside the IP address pool specified with the `range` option.

If `option` statements do not end with a semicolon, the DHCP daemon fails to start, and an error such as the following is logged to `/var/log/messages`:

```
/etc/dhcp/dhcpd.conf line 20: semicolon expected.
dhcpd: }
dhcpd: ^
dhcpd: /etc/dhcp/dhcpd.conf line 38: unexpected end of file
dhcpd:
dhcpd: ^
dhcpd: Configuration file errors encountered -- exiting
```

Configuring systems with multiple network interfaces

The following host declarations configure a single system, that has multiple network interfaces, so that each interface receives the same IP address. This configuration will not work if both network interfaces are connected to the same network at the same time:

```
host interface0 {
        hardware ethernet 00:1a:6b:6a:2e:0b;
        fixed-address 10.0.0.18;
}
host interface1 {
        hardware ethernet 00:1A:6B:6A:27:3A;
        fixed-address 10.0.0.18;
}
```

For this example, `interface0` is the first network interface, and `interface1` is the second interface. The different `hardware ethernet` options identify each interface.

If such a system connects to another network, add more `host` declarations, remembering to:

- assign a valid `fixed-address` for the network the host is connecting to.
- make the name in the `host` declaration unique.

When a name given in a `host` declaration is not unique, the DHCP daemon fails to start, and an error such as the following is logged to `/var/log/messages`:

```
dhcpd: /etc/dhcp/dhcpd.conf line 31: host interface0: already exists
dhcpd: }
dhcpd: ^
dhcpd: Configuration file errors encountered -- exiting
```

This error was caused by having multiple `host interface0` declarations defined in `/etc/dhcp/dhcpd.conf`.

10.5. DHCP for IPv6 (DHCPv6)

The ISC DHCP includes support for IPv6 (DHCPv6) since the 4.x release with a DHCPv6 server, client and relay agent functionality. The server, client and relay agents support both IPv4 and IPv6. However, the client and the server can only manage one protocol at a time — for dual support they must be started separately for IPv4 and IPv6.

The DHCPv6 server configuration file can be found at `/etc/dhcp/dhcpd6.conf`.

The sample server configuration file can be found at `/usr/share/doc/dhcp-version/dhcpd6.conf.sample`.

To start the DHCPv6 service, use the following command:

```
systemctl start dhcpd6.service
```

A simple DHCPv6 server configuration file can look like this:

```
subnet6 2001:db8:0:1::/64 {
        range6 2001:db8:0:1::129 2001:db8:0:1::254;
        option dhcp6.name-servers fec0:0:0:1::1;
        option dhcp6.domain-search "domain.example";
}
```

10.6. Additional Resources

For additional information, refer to *The DHCP Handbook; Ralph Droms and Ted Lemon; 2003* or the following resources.

10.6.1. Installed Documentation

- `dhcpd` man page — Describes how the DHCP daemon works.
- `dhcpd.conf` man page — Explains how to configure the DHCP configuration file; includes some examples.
- `dhcpd.leases` man page — Describes a persistent database of leases.
- `dhcp-options` man page — Explains the syntax for declaring DHCP options in `dhcpd.conf`; includes some examples.
- `dhcrelay` man page — Explains the DHCP Relay Agent and its configuration options.
- `/usr/share/doc/dhcp-*version*/` — Contains sample files, README files, and release notes for current versions of the DHCP service.

Chapter 11.
DNS Servers

DNS (Domain Name System), also known as a *nameserver*, is a network system that associates hostnames with their respective IP addresses. For users, this has the advantage that they can refer to machines on the network by names that are usually easier to remember than the numerical network addresses. For system administrators, using the nameserver allows them to change the IP address for a host without ever affecting the name-based queries, or to decide which machines handle these queries.

11.1. Introduction to DNS

DNS is usually implemented using one or more centralized servers that are authoritative for certain domains. When a client host requests information from a nameserver, it usually connects to port 53. The nameserver then attempts to resolve the name requested. If it does not have an authoritative answer, or does not already have the answer cached from an earlier query, it queries other nameservers, called *root nameservers*, to determine which nameservers are authoritative for the name in question, and then queries them to get the requested name.

11.1.1. Nameserver Zones

In a DNS server such as BIND, all information is stored in basic data elements called *resource records* (RR). The resource record is usually a *fully qualified domain name* (FQDN) of a host, and is broken down into multiple sections organized into a tree-like hierarchy. This hierarchy consists of a main trunk, primary branches, secondary branches, and so on. The following is an example of a resource record:

```
bob.sales.example.com
```

Each level of the hierarchy is divided by a period (that is, `.`). In the example above, `com` defines the *top-level domain*, `example` its subdomain, and `sales` the subdomain of `example`. In this case, `bob` identifies a resource record that is part of the `sales.example.com` domain. With the exception of the part furthest to the left (that is, `bob`), each of these sections is called a *zone* and defines a specific *namespace*.

Zones are defined on authoritative nameservers through the use of *zone files*, which contain definitions of the resource records in each zone. Zone files are stored on *primary nameservers* (also called *master nameservers*), where changes are made to the files, and *secondary nameservers* (also called *slave nameservers*), which receive zone definitions from the primary nameservers. Both primary and secondary nameservers are authoritative for the zone and look the same to clients. Depending on the configuration, any nameserver can also serve as a primary or secondary server for multiple zones at the same time.

11.1.2. Nameserver Types

There are two nameserver configuration types:

authoritative

Authoritative nameservers answer to resource records that are part of their zones only. This category includes both primary (master) and secondary (slave) nameservers.

recursive

Recursive nameservers offer resolution services, but they are not authoritative for any zone. Answers for all resolutions are cached in a memory for a fixed period of time, which is specified by the retrieved resource record.

Although a nameserver can be both authoritative and recursive at the same time, it is recommended not to combine the configuration types. To be able to perform their work, authoritative servers should be available to all clients all the time. On the other hand, since the recursive lookup takes far more time than authoritative responses, recursive servers should be available to a restricted number of clients only, otherwise they are prone to distributed denial of service (DDoS) attacks.

11.1.3. BIND as a Nameserver

BIND consists of a set of DNS-related programs. It contains a monolithic nameserver called `named`, an administration utility called `rndc`, and a debugging tool called `dig`. Refer to Chapter 7, *Services and Daemons* (page 120) for more information on how to configure services in Fedora.

11.2. BIND

This chapter covers `BIND` (Berkeley Internet Name Domain), the DNS server included in Fedora. It focuses on the structure of its configuration files, and describes how to administer it both locally and remotely.

11.2.1. Configuring the named Service

When the `named` service is started, it reads the configuration from the files as described in *Table 11.1. The named service configuration files* below.

Path	Description
`/etc/named.conf`	The main configuration file.
`/etc/named/`	An auxiliary directory for configuration files that are included in the main configuration file.

Table 11.1. The named service configuration files

The configuration file consists of a collection of statements with nested options surrounded by opening and closing curly brackets (that is, { and }). Note that when editing the file, you have to be careful not to make any syntax error, otherwise the `named` service will not start. A typical `/etc/named.conf` file is organized as follows:

```
statement-1 ["statement-1-name"] [statement-1-class] {
  option-1;
  option-2;
  option-N;
};
statement-2 ["statement-2-name"] [statement-2-class] {
  option-1;
  option-2;
  option-N;
};
statement-N ["statement-N-name"] [statement-N-class] {
  option-1;
  option-2;
  option-N;
};
```

Running BIND in a chroot environment

If you have installed the bind-chroot package, the BIND service will run in the `/var/named/chroot` environment. In that case, the initialization script will mount the above configuration files using the `mount --bind` command, so that you can manage the configuration outside this environment.

11.2.1.1. Common Statement Types

The following types of statements are commonly used in `/etc/named.conf`:

`acl`

The `acl` (Access Control List) statement allows you to define groups of hosts, so that they can be permitted or denied access to the nameserver. It takes the following form:

```
acl acl-name {
  match-element;
  ...
};
```

The `acl-name` statement name is the name of the access control list, and the `match-element` option is usually an individual IP address (such as `10.0.1.1`) or a CIDR network notation (for example, `10.0.1.0/24`). For a list of already defined keywords, see *Table 11.2. Predefined access control lists* below.

Keyword	Description
`any`	Matches every IP address.
`localhost`	Matches any IP address that is in use by the local system.
`localnets`	Matches any IP address on any network to which the local system is connected.
`none`	Does not match any IP address.

Table 11.2. Predefined access control lists

The `acl` statement can be especially useful with conjunction with other statements such as `options`. *Example 11.1. Using acl in conjunction with options* below defines two access control lists, `black-hats` and `red-hats`, and adds `black-hats` on the blacklist while granting `red-hats` a normal access.

```
acl black-hats {
  10.0.2.0/24;
  192.168.0.0/24;
  1234:5678::9abc/24;
};
acl red-hats {
  10.0.1.0/24;
};
options {
  blackhole { black-hats; };
  allow-query { red-hats; };
  allow-query-cache { red-hats; };
};
```

Example 11.1. Using acl in conjunction with options

`include`

The `include` statement allows you to include files in the `/etc/named.conf`, so that potentially sensitive data can be placed in a separate file with restricted permissions. It takes the following form:

```
include "file-name"
```

The `file-name` statement name is an absolute path to a file.

```
include "/etc/named.rfc1912.zones";
```

Example 11.2. Including a file to /etc/named.conf

`options`

The `options` statement allows you to define global server configuration options as well as to set defaults for other statements. It can be used to specify the location of the `named` working directory, the types of queries allowed, and much more. It takes the following form:

```
options {
  option;
  ...
};
```

For a list of frequently used `option` directives, see *Table 11.3. Commonly used options* below.

Option	Description
`allow-query`	Specifies which hosts are allowed to query the nameserver for authoritative resource records. It accepts an access control lists, a collection of IP addresses, or networks in the CIDR notation. All hosts are allowed by default.
`allow-query-cache`	Specifies which hosts are allowed to query the nameserver for non-authoritative data such as recursive queries. Only `localhost` and `localnets` are allowed by default.
`blackhole`	Specifies which hosts are *not* allowed to query the nameserver. This option should be used when particular host or network floods the server with requests. The default option is `none`.
`directory`	Specifies a working directory for the `named` service. The default option is `/var/named/`.
`dnssec-enable`	Specifies whether to return DNSSEC related resource records. The default option is `yes`.
`dnssec-validation`	Specifies whether to prove that resource records are authentic via DNSSEC. The default option is `yes`.
`forwarders`	Specifies a list of valid IP addresses for nameservers to which the requests should be forwarded for resolution.
`forward`	Specifies the behavior of the `forwarders` directive. It accepts the following options: `first` — The server will query the nameservers listed in the `forwarders` directive before attempting to resolve the name on its own. `only` — When unable to query the nameservers listed in the `forwarders` directive, the server will not attempt to resolve the name on its own.
`listen-on`	Specifies the IPv4 network interface on which to listen for queries. On a DNS server that also acts as a gateway, you can use this option to answer queries originating from a single network only. All IPv4 interfaces are used by default.

Option	Description
`listen-on-v6`	Specifies the IPv6 network interface on which to listen for queries. On a DNS server that also acts as a gateway, you can use this option to answer queries originating from a single network only. All IPv6 interfaces are used by default.
`max-cache-size`	Specifies the maximum amount of memory to be used for server caches. When the limit is reached, the server causes records to expire prematurely so that the limit is not exceeded. In a server with multiple views, the limit applies separately to the cache of each view. The default option is `32M`.
`notify`	Specifies whether to notify the secondary nameservers when a zone is updated. It accepts the following options: `yes` — The server will notify all secondary nameservers. `no` — The server will *not* notify any secondary nameserver. `master-only` — The server will notify primary server for the zone only. `explicit` — The server will notify only the secondary servers that are specified in the `also-notify` list within a zone statement.
`pid-file`	Specifies the location of the process ID file created by the `named` service.
`recursion`	Specifies whether to act as a recursive server. The default option is `yes`.
`statistics-file`	Specifies an alternate location for statistics files. The `/var/named/named.stats` file is used by default.

Table 11.3. Commonly used options

Restrict recursive servers to selected clients only

To prevent distributed denial of service (DDoS) attacks, it is recommended that you use the `allow-query-cache` option to restrict recursive DNS services for a particular subset of clients only.

Refer to the *BIND 9 Administrator Reference Manual* referenced in Section 11.2.7.1, *Installed Documentation* (page 223), and the `named.conf` manual page for a complete list of available options.

```
options {
  allow-query       { localhost; };
  listen-on port    53 { 127.0.0.1; };
  listen-on-v6 port 53 { ::1; };
  max-cache-size    256M;
  directory         "/var/named";
  statistics-file   "/var/named/data/named_stats.txt";

  recursion         yes;
  dnssec-enable     yes;
  dnssec-validation yes;
};
```

Example 11.3. Using the options statement

`zone`

The `zone` statement allows you to define the characteristics of a zone, such as the location of its configuration file and zone-specific options, and can be used to override the global `options` statements. It takes the following form:

```
zone zone-name [zone-class] {
  option;
  ...
};
```

The *`zone-name`* attribute is the name of the zone, *`zone-class`* is the optional class of the zone, and *`option`* is a `zone` statement option as described in *Table 11.4. Commonly used options* below.

The *`zone-name`* attribute is particularly important, as it is the default value assigned for the `$ORIGIN` directive used within the corresponding zone file located in the `/var/named/` directory. The `named` daemon appends the name of the zone to any non-fully qualified domain name listed in the zone file. For example, if a `zone` statement defines the namespace for `example.com`, use `example.com` as the *`zone-name`* so that it is placed at the end of hostnames within the `example.com` zone file.

For more information about zone files, refer to Section 11.2.2, *Editing Zone Files* (page 208).

Option	Description
`allow-query`	Specifies which clients are allowed to request information about this zone. This option overrides global `allow-query` option. All query requests are allowed by default.
`allow-transfer`	Specifies which secondary servers are allowed to request a transfer of the zone's information. All transfer requests are allowed by default.
`allow-update`	Specifies which hosts are allowed to dynamically update information in their zone. The default option is to deny all dynamic update requests. Note that you should be careful when allowing hosts to update information about their zone. Do not set IP addresses in this option unless the server is in the trusted network. Instead, use TSIG key as described in Section 11.2.5.3, *Transaction SIGnatures (TSIG)* (page 221).
`file`	Specifies the name of the file in the `named` working directory that contains the zone's configuration data.
`masters`	Specifies from which IP addresses to request authoritative zone information. This option is used only if the zone is defined as `type slave`.
`notify`	Specifies whether to notify the secondary nameservers when a zone is updated. It accepts the following options: • `yes` — The server will notify all secondary nameservers. • `no` — The server will *not* notify any secondary nameserver. • `master-only` — The server will notify primary server for the zone only.

Option	Description
	• `explicit` – The server will notify only the secondary servers that are specified in the `also-notify` list within a zone statement.
`type`	Specifies the zone type. It accepts the following options: • `delegation-only` – Enforces the delegation status of infrastructure zones such as COM, NET, or ORG. Any answer that is received without an explicit or implicit delegation is treated as `NXDOMAIN`. This option is only applicable in TLDs or root zone files used in recursive or caching implementations. • `forward` – Forwards all requests for information about this zone to other nameservers. • `hint` – A special type of zone used to point to the root nameservers which resolve queries when a zone is not otherwise known. No configuration beyond the default is necessary with a `hint` zone. • `master` – Designates the nameserver as authoritative for this zone. A zone should be set as the `master` if the zone's configuration files reside on the system. • `slave` – Designates the nameserver as a slave server for this zone. Master server is specified in `masters` directive.

Table 11.4. Commonly used options

Most changes to the `/etc/named.conf` file of a primary or secondary nameserver involve adding, modifying, or deleting `zone` statements, and only a small subset of `zone` statement options is usually needed for a nameserver to work efficiently.

In *Example 11.4. A zone statement for a primary nameserver* below, the zone is identified as `example.com`, the type is set to `master`, and the `named` service is instructed to read the `/var/named/example.com.zone` file. It also allows only a secondary nameserver (`192.168.0.2`) to transfer the zone.

```
zone "example.com" IN {
  type master;
  file "example.com.zone";
  allow-transfer { 192.168.0.2; };
};
```

Example 11.4. A zone statement for a primary nameserver

A secondary server's `zone` statement is slightly different. The type is set to `slave`, and the `masters` directive is telling `named` the IP address of the master server.

In *Example 11.5. A zone statement for a secondary nameserver* below, the `named` service is configured to query the primary server at the `192.168.0.1` IP address for information about the `example.com` zone. The received information is then saved to the `/var/named/slaves/example.com.zone` file. Note that you have to put all slave zones to `/var/named/slaves` directory, otherwise the service will fail to transfer the zone.

```
zone "example.com" {
  type slave;
  file "slaves/example.com.zone";
  masters { 192.168.0.1; };
};
```

Example 11.5. A zone statement for a secondary nameserver

11.2.1.2. Other Statement Types

The following types of statements are less commonly used in `/etc/named.conf`:

`controls`

The `controls` statement allows you to configure various security requirements necessary to use the `rndc` command to administer the `named` service.

Refer to Section 11.2.3, *Using the rndc Utility* (page 215) for more information on the `rndc` utility and its usage.

`key`

The `key` statement allows you to define a particular key by name. Keys are used to authenticate various actions, such as secure updates or the use of the `rndc` command. Two options are used with `key`:

- `algorithm` *`algorithm-name`* — The type of algorithm to be used (for example, `hmac-md5`).
- `secret "`*`key-value`*`"` — The encrypted key.

Refer to Section 11.2.3, *Using the rndc Utility* (page 215) for more information on the `rndc` utility and its usage.

`logging`

The `logging` statement allows you to use multiple types of logs, so called *channels*. By using the `channel` option within the statement, you can construct a customized type of log with its own file name (`file`), size limit (`size`), versioning (`version`), and level of importance (`severity`). Once a customized channel is defined, a `category` option is used to categorize the channel and begin logging when the `named` service is restarted.

By default, `named` sends standard messages to the `rsyslog` daemon, which places them in `/var/log/messages`. Several standard channels are built into BIND with various severity levels, such as `default_syslog` (which handles informational logging messages) and `default_debug` (which specifically handles debugging messages). A default category, called `default`, uses the built-in channels to do normal logging without any special configuration.

Customizing the logging process can be a very detailed process and is beyond the scope of this chapter. For information on creating custom BIND logs, refer to the *BIND 9 Administrator Reference Manual* referenced in Section 11.2.7.1, *Installed Documentation* (page 223).

`server`

The `server` statement allows you to specify options that affect how the `named` service should respond to remote nameservers, especially with regard to notifications and zone transfers.

The `transfer-format` option controls the number of resource records that are sent with each message. It can be either `one-answer` (only one resource record), or `many-answers` (multiple resource records). Note that while the `many-answers` option is more efficient, it is not supported by older versions of BIND.

`trusted-keys`

The `trusted-keys` statement allows you to specify assorted public keys used for secure DNS (DNSSEC). Refer to Section 11.2.5.4, *DNS Security Extensions (DNSSEC)* (page 221) for more information on this topic.

`view`

The `view` statement allows you to create special views depending upon which network the host querying the nameserver is on. This allows some hosts to receive one answer regarding a zone while other hosts receive totally different information. Alternatively, certain zones may only be made available to particular trusted hosts while non-trusted hosts can only make queries for other zones.

Multiple views can be used as long as their names are unique. The `match-clients` option allows you to specify the IP addresses that apply to a particular view. If the `options` statement is used within a view, it overrides the already configured global options. Finally, most `view` statements contain multiple `zone` statements that apply to the `match-clients` list.

Note that the order in which the `view` statements are listed is important, as the first statement that matches a particular client's IP address is used. For more information on this topic, refer to Section 11.2.5.1, *Multiple Views* (page 221).

11.2.1.3. Comment Tags

Additionally to statements, the `/etc/named.conf` file can also contain comments. Comments are ignored by the `named` service, but can prove useful when providing additional information to a user. The following are valid comment tags:

//

Any text after the // characters to the end of the line is considered a comment. For example:

```
notify yes;  // notify all secondary nameservers
```

#

Any text after the # character to the end of the line is considered a comment. For example:

```
notify yes;  # notify all secondary nameservers
```

/* and */

Any block of text enclosed in /* and */ is considered a comment. For example:

```
notify yes;  /* notify all secondary nameservers */
```

11.2.2. Editing Zone Files

As outlined in Section 11.1.1, *Nameserver Zones* (page 198), zone files contain information about a namespace. They are stored in the `named` working directory located in `/var/named/` by default, and each zone file is named according to the `file` option in the `zone` statement, usually in a way that relates to the domain in question and identifies the file as containing zone data, such as `example.com.zone`.

Path	Description
`/var/named/`	The working directory for the `named` service. The nameserver is *not* allowed to write to this directory.
`/var/named/slaves/`	The directory for secondary zones. This directory is writable by the `named` service.
`/var/named/dynamic/`	The directory for other files, such as dynamic DNS (DDNS) zones or managed DNSSEC keys. This directory is writable by the `named` service.
`/var/named/data/`	The directory for various statistics and debugging files. This directory is writable by the `named` service.

Table 11.5. The named service zone files

A zone file consists of directives and resource records. Directives tell the nameserver to perform tasks or apply special settings to the zone, resource records define the parameters of the zone and assign identities to individual hosts. While the directives are optional, the resource records are required in order to provide name service to a zone.

All directives and resource records should be entered on individual lines.

11.2.2.1. Common Directives

Directives begin with the dollar sign character (that is, `$`) followed by the name of the directive, and usually appear at the top of the file. The following directives are commonly used in zone files:

`$INCLUDE`

The `$INCLUDE` directive allows you to include another file at the place where it appears, so that other zone settings can be stored in a separate zone file.

```
$INCLUDE /var/named/penguin.example.com
```

Example 11.6. Using the $INCLUDE directive

`$ORIGIN`

The `$ORIGIN` directive allows you to append the domain name to unqualified records, such as those with the hostname only. Note that the use of this directive is not necessary if the zone is specified in `/etc/named.conf`, since the zone name is used by default.

In *Example 11.7. Using the $ORIGIN directive* below, any names used in resource records that do not end in a trailing period (that is, the `.` character) are appended with `example.com`.

```
$ORIGIN example.com.
```

Example 11.7. Using the $ORIGIN directive

`$TTL`

The `$TTL` directive allows you to set the default *Time to Live* (TTL) value for the zone, that is, how long is a zone record valid. Each resource record can contain its own TTL value, which overrides this directive.

Increasing this value allows remote nameservers to cache the zone information for a longer period of time, reducing the number of queries for the zone and lengthening the amount of time required to proliferate resource record changes.

```
$TTL 1D
```

Example 11.8. Using the $TTL directive

11.2.2.2. Common Resource Records

The following resource records are commonly used in zone files:

`A`

The *Address* record specifies an IP address to be assigned to a name. It takes the following form:

hostname `IN A` *IP-address*

If the `hostname` value is omitted, the record will point to the last specified `hostname`.

In *Example 11.9. Using the A resource record* below, the requests for `server1.example.com` are pointed to `10.0.1.3` or `10.0.1.5`.

```
server1  IN  A  10.0.1.3
         IN  A  10.0.1.5
```

Example 11.9. Using the A resource record

`CNAME`

The *Canonical Name* record maps one name to another. Because of this, this type of record is sometimes referred to as an *alias record*. It takes the following form:

`alias-name IN CNAME real-name`

`CNAME` records are most commonly used to point to services that use a common naming scheme, such as `www` for Web servers. However, there are multiple restrictions for their usage:

- CNAME records should not point to other CNAME records. This is mainly to avoid possible infinite loops.
- CNAME records should not contain other resource record types (such as A, NS, MX, etc.). The only exception are DNSSEC related records (that is, RRSIG, NSEC, etc.) when the zone is signed.
- Other resource record that point to the fully qualified domain name (FQDN) of a host (that is, NS, MX, PTR) should not point to a CNAME record.

In *Example 11.10. Using the CNAME resource record* below, the `A` record binds a hostname to an IP address, while the `CNAME` record points the commonly used `www` hostname to it.

```
server1  IN  A      10.0.1.5
www      IN  CNAME  server1
```

Example 11.10. Using the CNAME resource record

`MX`

The *Mail Exchange* record specifies where the mail sent to a particular namespace controlled by this zone should go. It takes the following form:

`IN MX preference-value email-server-name`

The `email-server-name` is a fully qualified domain name (FQDN). The `preference-value` allows numerical ranking of the email servers for a namespace, giving preference to some email systems over others. The `MX` resource record with the lowest `preference-value` is preferred over the others. However, multiple email servers can possess the same value to distribute email traffic evenly among them.

In *Example 11.11. Using the MX resource record* below, the first `mail.example.com` email server is preferred to the `mail2.example.com` email server when receiving email destined for the `example.com` domain.

```
example.com.   IN  MX  10  mail.example.com.
               IN  MX  20  mail2.example.com.
```

Example 11.11. Using the MX resource record

`NS`

The *Nameserver* record announces authoritative nameservers for a particular zone. It takes the following form:

`IN NS` *`nameserver-name`*

The *`nameserver-name`* should be a fully qualified domain name (FQDN). Note that when two nameservers are listed as authoritative for the domain, it is not important whether these nameservers are secondary nameservers, or if one of them is a primary server. They are both still considered authoritative.

```
IN  NS  dns1.example.com.
IN  NS  dns2.example.com.
```

Example 11.12. Using the NS resource record

`PTR`

The *Pointer* record points to another part of the namespace. It takes the following form:

`last-IP-digit` `IN PTR` *`FQDN-of-system`*

The *`last-IP-digit`* directive is the last number in an IP address, and the *`FQDN-of-system`* is a fully qualified domain name (FQDN).

`PTR` records are primarily used for reverse name resolution, as they point IP addresses back to a particular name. Refer to Section 11.2.2.4.2, *A Reverse Name Resolution Zone File* (page 214) for more examples of `PTR` records in use.

`SOA`

The *Start of Authority* record announces important authoritative information about a namespace to the nameserver. Located after the directives, it is the first resource record in a zone file. It takes the following form:

```
@   IN   SOA  primary-name-server hostmaster-email (
          serial-number
          time-to-refresh
          time-to-retry
          time-to-expire
          minimum-TTL )
```

The directives are as follows:

- The `@` symbol places the `$ORIGIN` directive (or the zone's name if the `$ORIGIN` directive is not set) as the namespace being defined by this `SOA` resource record.
- The *`primary-name-server`* directive is the hostname of the primary nameserver that is authoritative for this domain.
- The *`hostmaster-email`* directive is the email of the person to contact about the namespace.
- The *`serial-number`* directive is a numerical value incremented every time the zone file is altered to indicate it is time for the `named` service to reload the zone.
- The *`time-to-refresh`* directive is the numerical value secondary nameservers use to determine how long to wait before asking the primary nameserver if any changes have been made to the zone.
- The *`time-to-retry`* directive is a numerical value used by secondary nameservers to determine the length of time to wait before issuing a refresh request in the event that the primary nameserver is not answering. If the primary server has not replied to a refresh request before the amount of time specified in the *`time-to-expire`* directive elapses, the secondary servers stop responding as an authority for requests concerning that namespace.
- In BIND 4 and 8, the *`minimum-TTL`* directive is the amount of time other nameservers cache the zone's information. In BIND 9, it defines how long negative answers are cached for. Caching of negative answers can be set to a maximum of 3 hours (that is, `3H`).

When configuring BIND, all times are specified in seconds. However, it is possible to use abbreviations when specifying units of time other than seconds, such as minutes (`M`), hours (`H`), days (`D`), and weeks (`W`). *Table 11.6. Seconds compared to other time units* below shows an amount of time in seconds and the equivalent time in another format.

Seconds	Other Time Units
60	`1M`
1800	`30M`
3600	`1H`
10800	`3H`
21600	`6H`
43200	`12H`
86400	`1D`
259200	`3D`

Seconds	Other Time Units
604800	`1W`
31536000	`365D`

Table 11.6. Seconds compared to other time units

```
@   IN   SOA  dns1.example.com.   hostmaster.example.com. (
         2001062501   ; serial
         21600        ; refresh after 6 hours
         3600         ; retry after 1 hour
         604800       ; expire after 1 week
         86400 )      ; minimum TTL of 1 day
```

Example 11.13. Using the SOA resource record

11.2.2.3. Comment Tags

Additionally to resource records and directives, a zone file can also contain comments. Comments are ignored by the `named` service, but can prove useful when providing additional information to the user. Any text after the semicolon character (that is, `;`) to the end of the line is considered a comment. For example:

```
604800  ; expire after 1 week
```

11.2.2.4. Example Usage

The following examples show the basic usage of zone files.

11.2.2.4.1. A Simple Zone File

Example 11.14. A simple zone file below demonstrates the use of standard directives and `SOA` values.

```
$ORIGIN example.com.
$TTL 86400
@         IN  SOA  dns1.example.com.  hostmaster.example.com. (
              2001062501  ; serial
              21600       ; refresh after 6 hours
              3600        ; retry after 1 hour
              604800      ; expire after 1 week
              86400 )     ; minimum TTL of 1 day
;
;
          IN  NS     dns1.example.com.
          IN  NS     dns2.example.com.
dns1      IN  A      10.0.1.1
          IN  AAAA   aaaa:bbbb::1
dns2      IN  A      10.0.1.2
          IN  AAAA   aaaa:bbbb::2
```

```
;
;
@           IN  MX     10  mail.example.com.
            IN  MX     20  mail2.example.com.
mail        IN  A      10.0.1.5
            IN  AAAA   aaaa:bbbb::5
mail2       IN  A      10.0.1.6
            IN  AAAA   aaaa:bbbb::6
;
;
; This sample zone file illustrates sharing the same IP addresses
; for multiple services:
;
services    IN  A      10.0.1.10
            IN  AAAA   aaaa:bbbb::10
            IN  A      10.0.1.11
            IN  AAAA   aaaa:bbbb::11

ftp         IN  CNAME  services.example.com.
www         IN  CNAME  services.example.com.
;
;
```

Example 11.14. A simple zone file

In this example, the authoritative nameservers are set as `dns1.example.com` and `dns2.example.com`, and are tied to the `10.0.1.1` and `10.0.1.2` IP addresses respectively using the `A` record.

The email servers configured with the `MX` records point to `mail` and `mail2` via `A` records. Since these names do not end in a trailing period (that is, the `.` character), the `$ORIGIN` domain is placed after them, expanding them to `mail.example.com` and `mail2.example.com`.

Services available at the standard names, such as `www.example.com` (WWW), are pointed at the appropriate servers using the `CNAME` record.

This zone file would be called into service with a `zone` statement in the `/etc/named.conf` similar to the following:

```
zone "example.com" IN {
  type master;
  file "example.com.zone";
  allow-update { none; };
};
```

11.2.2.4.2. A Reverse Name Resolution Zone File

A reverse name resolution zone file is used to translate an IP address in a particular namespace into an fully qualified domain name (FQDN). It looks very similar to a standard zone file, except that the `PTR` resource records are used to link the IP addresses to a fully qualified domain name as shown in *Example 11.15. A reverse name resolution zone file* below

```
$ORIGIN 1.0.10.in-addr.arpa.
$TTL 86400
@   IN   SOA  dns1.example.com.  hostmaster.example.com. (
         2001062501   ; serial
         21600        ; refresh after 6 hours
         3600         ; retry after 1 hour
         604800       ; expire after 1 week
         86400 )      ; minimum TTL of 1 day
;
@   IN   NS   dns1.example.com.
;
1   IN   PTR  dns1.example.com.
2   IN   PTR  dns2.example.com.
;
5   IN   PTR  server1.example.com.
6   IN   PTR  server2.example.com.
;
3   IN   PTR  ftp.example.com.
4   IN   PTR  ftp.example.com.
```

Example 11.15. A reverse name resolution zone file

In this example, IP addresses `10.0.1.1` through `10.0.1.6` are pointed to the corresponding fully qualified domain name.

This zone file would be called into service with a `zone` statement in the `/etc/named.conf` file similar to the following:

```
zone "1.0.10.in-addr.arpa" IN {
  type master;
  file "example.com.rr.zone";
  allow-update { none; };
};
```

There is very little difference between this example and a standard `zone` statement, except for the zone name. Note that a reverse name resolution zone requires the first three blocks of the IP address reversed followed by `.in-addr.arpa`. This allows the single block of IP numbers used in the reverse name resolution zone file to be associated with the zone.

11.2.3. Using the rndc Utility

The `rndc` utility is a command line tool that allows you to administer the `named` service, both locally and from a remote machine. Its usage is as follows:

```
rndc [option...] command [command-option]
```

11.2.3.1. Configuring the Utility

To prevent unauthorized access to the service, `named` must be configured to listen on the selected port (that is, `953` by default), and an identical key must be used by both the service and the `rndc` utility.

Path	Description
`/etc/named.conf`	The default configuration file for the `named` service.
`/etc/rndc.conf`	The default configuration file for the `rndc` utility.
`/etc/rndc.key`	The default key location.

Table 11.7. Relevant files

The `rndc` configuration is located in `/etc/rndc.conf`. If the file does not exist, the utility will use the key located in `/etc/rndc.key`, which was generated automatically during the installation process using the `rndc-confgen -a` command.

The `named` service is configured using the `controls` statement in the `/etc/named.conf` configuration file as described in Section 11.2.1.2, *Other Statement Types* (page 206). Unless this statement is present, only the connections from the loopback address (that is, `127.0.0.1`) will be allowed, and the key located in `/etc/rndc.key` will be used.

For more information on this topic, refer to manual pages and the *BIND 9 Administrator Reference Manual* listed in Section 11.2.7, *Additional Resources* (page 222).

Set the correct permissions

To prevent unprivileged users from sending control commands to the service, make sure only root is allowed to read the `/etc/rndc.key` file:

```
~]# chmod o-rwx /etc/rndc.key
```

11.2.3.2. Checking the Service Status

To check the current status of the `named` service, use the following command:

```
~]# rndc status
version: 9.7.0-P2-RedHat-9.7.0-5.P2.el6
CPUs found: 1
worker threads: 1
number of zones: 16
debug level: 0
xfers running: 0
xfers deferred: 0
soa queries in progress: 0
query logging is OFF
recursive clients: 0/0/1000
tcp clients: 0/100
server is up and running
```

11.2.3.3. Reloading the Configuration and Zones

To reload both the configuration file and zones, type the following at a shell prompt:

```
~]# rndc reload
server reload successful
```

This will reload the zones while keeping all previously cached responses, so that you can make changes to the zone files without losing all stored name resolutions.

To reload a single zone, specify its name after the `reload` command, for example:

```
~]# rndc reload localhost
zone reload up-to-date
```

Finally, to reload the configuration file and newly added zones only, type:

```
~]# rndc reconfig
```

Modifying zones with dynamic DNS

If you intend to manually modify a zone that uses Dynamic DNS (DDNS), make sure you run the `freeze` command first:

```
~]# rndc freeze localhost
```

Once you are finished, run the `thaw` command to allow the DDNS again and reload the zone:

```
~]# rndc thaw localhost
The zone reload and thaw was successful.
```

11.2.3.4. Updating Zone Keys

To update the DNSSEC keys and sign the zone, use the `sign` command. For example:

```
~]# rndc sign localhost
```

Note that to sign a zone with the above command, the `auto-dnssec` option has to be set to `maintain` in the zone statement. For instance:

```
zone "localhost" IN {
  type master;
  file "named.localhost";
  allow-update { none; };
  auto-dnssec maintain;
};
```

11.2.3.5. Enabling the DNSSEC Validation

To enable the DNSSEC validation, type the following at a shell prompt:

```
~]# rndc validation on
```

Similarly, to disable this option, type:

```
~]# rndc validation off
```

Refer to the `options` statement described in Section 11.2.1.1, *Common Statement Types* (page 200) for information on how configure this option in `/etc/named.conf`.

11.2.3.6. Enabling the Query Logging

To enable (or disable in case it is currently enabled) the query logging, run the following command:

```
~]# rndc querylog
```

To check the current setting, use the `status` command as described in Section 11.2.3.2, *Checking the Service Status* (page 216).

11.2.4. Using the dig Utility

The `dig` utility is a command line tool that allows you to perform DNS lookups and debug a nameserver configuration. Its typical usage is as follows:

```
dig [@server] [option...] name type
```

Refer to Section 11.2.2.2, *Common Resource Records* (page 209) for a list of common *types*.

11.2.4.1. Looking Up a Nameserver

To look up a nameserver for a particular domain, use the command in the following form:

```
dig name NS
```

In *Example 11.16. A sample nameserver lookup* below, the `dig` utility is used to display nameservers for `example.com`.

```
~]$ dig example.com NS

; <<>> DiG 9.7.1-P2-RedHat-9.7.1-2.P2.fc13 <<>> example.com NS
;; global options: +cmd
;; Got answer:
;; ->>HEADER<<- opcode: QUERY, status: NOERROR, id: 57883
;; flags: qr rd ra; QUERY: 1, ANSWER: 2, AUTHORITY: 0, ADDITIONAL: 0

;; QUESTION SECTION:
;example.com.                   IN      NS

;; ANSWER SECTION:
example.com.            99374   IN      NS      a.iana-servers.net.
example.com.            99374   IN      NS      b.iana-servers.net.

;; Query time: 1 msec
```

```
;; SERVER: 10.34.255.7#53(10.34.255.7)
;; WHEN: Wed Aug 18 18:04:06 2010
;; MSG SIZE  rcvd: 77
```

Example 11.16. A sample nameserver lookup

11.2.4.2. Looking Up an IP Address

To look up an IP address assigned to a particular domain, use the command in the following form:

`dig` *`name`* `A`

In *Example 11.17. A sample IP address lookup* below, the `dig` utility is used to display the IP address of `example.com`.

```
~]$ dig example.com A

; <<>> DiG 9.7.1-P2-RedHat-9.7.1-2.P2.fc13 <<>> example.com A
;; global options: +cmd
;; Got answer:
;; ->>HEADER<<- opcode: QUERY, status: NOERROR, id: 4849
;; flags: qr rd ra; QUERY: 1, ANSWER: 1, AUTHORITY: 2, ADDITIONAL: 0

;; QUESTION SECTION:
;example.com.                   IN      A

;; ANSWER SECTION:
example.com.            155606  IN      A       192.0.32.10

;; AUTHORITY SECTION:
example.com.            99175   IN      NS      a.iana-servers.net.
example.com.            99175   IN      NS      b.iana-servers.net.

;; Query time: 1 msec
;; SERVER: 10.34.255.7#53(10.34.255.7)
;; WHEN: Wed Aug 18 18:07:25 2010
;; MSG SIZE  rcvd: 93
```

Example 11.17. A sample IP address lookup

11.2.4.3. Looking Up a Hostname

To look up a hostname for a particular IP address, use the command in the following form:

`dig -x` *`address`*

In *Example 11.18. A sample hostname lookup* below, the `dig` utility is used to display the hostname assigned to `192.0.32.10`.

```
~]$ dig -x 192.0.32.10
```

```
; <<>> DiG 9.7.1-P2-RedHat-9.7.1-2.P2.fc13 <<>> -x 192.0.32.10
;; global options: +cmd
;; Got answer:
;; ->>HEADER<<- opcode: QUERY, status: NOERROR, id: 29683
;; flags: qr rd ra; QUERY: 1, ANSWER: 1, AUTHORITY: 5, ADDITIONAL: 6

;; QUESTION SECTION:
;10.32.0.192.in-addr.arpa.       IN      PTR

;; ANSWER SECTION:
10.32.0.192.in-addr.arpa. 21600 IN      PTR     www.example.com.

;; AUTHORITY SECTION:
32.0.192.in-addr.arpa.  21600   IN      NS      b.iana-servers.org.
32.0.192.in-addr.arpa.  21600   IN      NS      c.iana-servers.net.
32.0.192.in-addr.arpa.  21600   IN      NS      d.iana-servers.net.
32.0.192.in-addr.arpa.  21600   IN      NS      ns.icann.org.
32.0.192.in-addr.arpa.  21600   IN      NS      a.iana-servers.net.

;; ADDITIONAL SECTION:
a.iana-servers.net.     13688   IN      A       192.0.34.43
b.iana-servers.org.     5844    IN      A       193.0.0.236
b.iana-servers.org.     5844    IN      AAAA    2001:610:240:2::c100:ec
c.iana-servers.net.     12173   IN      A       139.91.1.10
c.iana-servers.net.     12173   IN      AAAA    2001:648:2c30::1:10
ns.icann.org.           12884   IN      A       192.0.34.126

;; Query time: 156 msec
;; SERVER: 10.34.255.7#53(10.34.255.7)
;; WHEN: Wed Aug 18 18:25:15 2010
;; MSG SIZE  rcvd: 310
```

Example 11.18. A sample hostname lookup

11.2.5. Advanced Features of BIND

Most BIND implementations only use the `named` service to provide name resolution services or to act as an authority for a particular domain. However, BIND version 9 has a number of advanced features that allow for a more secure and efficient DNS service.

Make sure the feature is supported

Before attempting to use advanced features like DNSSEC, TSIG, or IXFR, make sure that the particular feature is supported by all nameservers in the network environment, especially when you use older versions of BIND or non-BIND servers.

All of the features mentioned are discussed in greater detail in the *BIND 9 Administrator Reference Manual* referenced in Section 11.2.7.1, *Installed Documentation* (page 223).

11.2.5.1. Multiple Views

Optionally, different information can be presented to a client depending on the network a request originates from. This is primarily used to deny sensitive DNS entries from clients outside of the local network, while allowing queries from clients inside the local network.

To configure multiple views, add the `view` statement to the `/etc/named.conf` configuration file. Use the `match-clients` option to match IP addresses or entire networks and give them special options and zone data.

11.2.5.2. Incremental Zone Transfers (IXFR)

Incremental Zone Transfers (*IXFR*) allow a secondary nameserver to only download the updated portions of a zone modified on a primary nameserver. Compared to the standard transfer process, this makes the notification and update process much more efficient.

Note that IXFR is only available when using dynamic updating to make changes to master zone records. If manually editing zone files to make changes, *Automatic Zone Transfer* (*AXFR*) is used.

11.2.5.3. Transaction SIGnatures (TSIG)

Transaction SIGnatures (TSIG) ensure that a shared secret key exists on both primary and secondary nameserver before allowing a transfer. This strengthens the standard IP address-based method of transfer authorization, since attackers would not only need to have access to the IP address to transfer the zone, but they would also need to know the secret key.

Since version 9, BIND also supports *TKEY*, which is another shared secret key method of authorizing zone transfers.

Secure the transfer

When communicating over an insecure network, do not rely on IP address-based authentication only.

11.2.5.4. DNS Security Extensions (DNSSEC)

Domain Name System Security Extensions (*DNSSEC*) provide origin authentication of DNS data, authenticated denial of existence, and data integrity. When a particular domain is marked as secure, the `SERFVAIL` response is returned for each resource record that fails the validation.

Note that to debug a DNSSEC-signed domain or a DNSSEC-aware resolver, you can use the `dig` utility as described in Section 11.2.4, *Using the dig Utility* (page 218). Useful options are `+dnssec` (requests DNSSEC-related resource records by setting the DNSSEC OK bit), `+cd` (tells recursive nameserver not to validate the response), and `+bufsize=512` (changes the packet size to 512B to get through some firewalls).

11.2.5.5. Internet Protocol version 6 (IPv6)

Internet Protocol version 6 (*IPv6*) is supported through the use of `AAAA` resource records, and the `listen-on-v6` directive as described in *Table 11.3. Commonly used options* above.

11.2.6. Common Mistakes to Avoid

The following is a list of advices how to avoid common mistakes users make when configuring a nameserver:

Use semicolons and curly brackets correctly

An omitted semicolon or unmatched curly bracket in the `/etc/named.conf` file can prevent the `named` service from starting.

Use period (that is, the `.` character) correctly

In zone files, a period at the end of a domain name denotes a fully qualified domain name. If omitted, the `named` service will append the name of the zone or the value of `$ORIGIN` to complete it.

Increment the serial number when editing a zone file

If the serial number is not incremented, the primary nameserver will have the correct, new information, but the secondary nameservers will never be notified of the change, and will not attempt to refresh their data of that zone.

Configure the firewall

If a firewall is blocking connections from the `named` service to other nameservers, the recommended best practice is to change the firewall settings whenever possible.

Avoid using fixed UDP source ports

According to the recent research in DNS security, using a fixed UDP source port for DNS queries is a potential security vulnerability that could allow an attacker to conduct cache-poisoning attacks more easily. To prevent this, configure your firewall to allow queries from a random UDP source port.

11.2.7. Additional Resources

The following sources of information provide additional resources regarding BIND.

11.2.7.1. Installed Documentation

BIND features a full range of installed documentation covering many different topics, each placed in its own subject directory. For each item below, replace *version* with the version of the bind package installed on the system:

`/usr/share/doc/bind-version/`

The main directory containing the most recent documentation.

`/usr/share/doc/bind-version/arm/`

The directory containing the *BIND 9 Administrator Reference Manual* in HTML and SGML formats, which details BIND resource requirements, how to configure different types of nameservers, how to perform load balancing, and other advanced topics. For most new users of BIND, this is the best place to start.

`/usr/share/doc/bind-version/draft/`

The directory containing assorted technical documents that review issues related to the DNS service, and propose some methods to address them.

`/usr/share/doc/bind-version/misc/`

The directory designed to address specific advanced issues. Users of BIND version 8 should consult the `migration` document for specific changes they must make when moving to BIND 9. The `options` file lists all of the options implemented in BIND 9 that are used in `/etc/named.conf`.

`/usr/share/doc/bind-version/rfc/`

The directory providing every RFC document related to BIND.

There is also a number of man pages for the various applications and configuration files involved with BIND:

`man rndc`

The manual page for `rndc` containing the full documentation on its usage.

`man named`

The manual page for `named` containing the documentation on assorted arguments that can be used to control the BIND nameserver daemon.

`man lwresd`

The manual page for `lwresd` containing the full documentation on the lightweight resolver daemon and its usage.

`man named.conf`

The manual page with a comprehensive list of options available within the `named` configuration file.

`man rndc.conf`

The manual page with a comprehensive list of options available within the `rndc` configuration file.

11.2.7.2. Useful Websites

http://www.isc.org/software/bind

The home page of the BIND project containing information about current releases as well as a PDF version of the *BIND 9 Administrator Reference Manual*.

11.2.7.3. Related Books

DNS and BIND by Paul Albitz and Cricket Liu; O'Reilly & Associates

A popular reference that explains both common and esoteric BIND configuration options, and provides strategies for securing a DNS server.

The Concise Guide to DNS and BIND by Nicolai Langfeldt; Que

Looks at the connection between multiple network services and BIND, with an emphasis on task-oriented, technical topics.

Chapter 12.

Web Servers

HTTP (Hypertext Transfer Protocol) server, or a *web server*, is a network service that serves content to a client over the web. This typically means web pages, but any other documents can be served as well.

12.1. The Apache HTTP Server

This section focuses on the **Apache HTTP Server 2.2**, a robust, full-featured open source web server developed by the *Apache Software Foundation*[1], that is included in Fedora 15. It describes the basic configuration of the `httpd` service, and covers advanced topics such as adding server modules, setting up virtual hosts, or configuring the secure HTTP server.

There are important differences between the Apache HTTP Server 2.2 and version 2.0, and if you are upgrading from a previous release of Fedora, you will need to update the `httpd` service configuration accordingly. This section reviews some of the newly added features, outlines important changes, and guides you through the update of older configuration files.

12.1.1. New Features

The Apache HTTP Server version 2.2 introduces the following enhancements:

- Improved caching modules, that is, `mod_cache` and `mod_disk_cache`.
- Support for proxy load balancing, that is, the `mod_proxy_balancer` module.
- Support for large files on 32-bit architectures, allowing the web server to handle files greater than 2GB.
- A new structure for authentication and authorization support, replacing the authentication modules provided in previous versions.

12.1.2. Notable Changes

Since version 2.0, few changes have been made to the default `httpd` service configuration:

---

[1] *http://www.apache.org/*

- The following modules are no longer loaded by default: `mod_cern_meta` and `mod_asis`.
- The following module is newly loaded by default: `mod_ext_filter`.

12.1.3. Updating the Configuration

To update the configuration files from the Apache HTTP Server version 2.0, take the following steps:

1. Make sure all module names are correct, since they may have changed. Adjust the `LoadModule` directive for each module that has been renamed.
2. Recompile all third party modules before attempting to load them. This typically means authentication and authorization modules.
3. If you use the `mod_userdir` module, make sure the `UserDir` directive indicating a directory name (typically `public_html`) is provided.
4. If you use the Apache HTTP Secure Server, edit the `/etc/httpd/conf.d/ssl.conf` to enable the Secure Sockets Layer (SSL) protocol.

Note that you can check the configuration for possible errors by using the following command:

```
service httpd configtest
```

For more information on upgrading the Apache HTTP Server configuration from version 2.0 to 2.2, refer to *http://httpd.apache.org/docs/2.2/upgrading.html*.

12.1.4. Running the httpd Service

This section describes how to start, stop, restart, and check the current status of the Apache HTTP Server. To be able to use the `httpd` service, make sure you have the httpd installed. You can do so by using the following command as `root`:

```
yum install httpd
```

For more information on the concept of runlevels and how to manage system services in Fedora in general, refer to Chapter 7, *Services and Daemons* (page 120).

12.1.4.1. Starting the Service

To run the `httpd` service, type the following at a shell prompt as `root`:

```
systemctl start httpd.service
```

If you want the service to start automatically at the boot time, use the following command:

```
systemctl enable httpd.service
```

Refer to Chapter 7, *Services and Daemons* (page 120) for more information on how to configure services in Fedora.

Using the secure server

If running the Apache HTTP Server as a secure server, a password may be required after the machine boots if using an encrypted private SSL key.

12.1.4.2. Stopping the Service

To stop the running `httpd` service, type the following at a shell prompt as `root`:

```
systemctl stop httpd.service
```

To prevent the service from starting automatically at the boot time, type:

```
systemctl disable httpd.service
```

Refer to Chapter 7, *Services and Daemons* (page 120) for more information on how to configure services in Fedora.

12.1.4.3. Restarting the Service

There are two different ways to restart the running `httpd` service:

1. To restart the service completely, type the following at a shell prompt as `root`:

   ```
   systemctl restart httpd.service
   ```

   This will stop the running `httpd` service, and then start it again. Use this command after installing or removing a dynamically loaded module such as PHP.

2. To only reload the configuration, as `root`, type:

   ```
   systemctl reload httpd.service
   ```

   This will cause the running `httpd` service to reload the configuration file. Note that any requests being currently processed will be interrupted, which may cause a client browser to display an error message or render a partial page.

3. To reload the configuration without affecting active requests, run the following command as `root`:

   ```
   service httpd graceful
   ```

   This will cause the running `httpd` service to reload the configuration file. Note that any requests being currently processed will use the old configuration.

Refer to Chapter 7, *Services and Daemons* (page 120) for more information on how to configure services in Fedora.

12.1.4.4. Checking the Service Status

To check whether the service is running, type the following at a shell prompt:

```
systemctl is-active httpd.service
```

Refer to Chapter 7, *Services and Daemons* (page 120) for more information on how to configure services in Fedora.

12.1.5. Editing the Configuration Files

When the `httpd` service is started, by default, it reads the configuration from locations that are listed in *Table 12.1. The httpd service configuration files* below.

Path	Description
`/etc/httpd/conf/httpd.conf`	The main configuration file.
`/etc/httpd/conf.d/`	An auxiliary directory for configuration files that are included in the main configuration file.

Table 12.1. The httpd service configuration files

Although the default configuration should be suitable for most situations, it is a good idea to become at least familiar with some of the more important configuration options. Note that for any changes to take effect, the web server has to be restarted first. Refer to Section 12.1.4.3, *Restarting the Service* (page 227) for more information on how to restart the `httpd` service.

To check the configuration for possible errors, type the following at a shell prompt:

```
service httpd configtest
```

To make the recovery from mistakes easier, it is recommended that you make a copy of the original file before editing it.

12.1.5.1. Common httpd.conf Directives

The following directives are commonly used in the `/etc/httpd/conf/httpd.conf` configuration file:

`<Directory>`

The `<Directory>` directive allows you to apply certain directives to a particular directory only. It takes the following form:

```
<Directory directory>
  directive
  …
</Directory>
```

The *directory* can be either a full path to an existing directory in the local file system, or a wildcard expression.

This directive can be used to configure additional `cgi-bin` directories for server-side scripts located outside the directory that is specified by `ScriptAlias`. In this case, the `ExecCGI` and `AddHandler` directives must be supplied, and the permissions on the target directory must be set correctly (that is, `0755`).

```
<Directory /var/www/html>
  Options Indexes FollowSymLinks
  AllowOverride None
  Order allow,deny
  Allow from all
</Directory>
```

Example 12.1. Using the <Directory> directive

`<IfDefine>`

The `IfDefine` directive allows you to use certain directives only when a particular parameter is supplied on the command line. It takes the following form:

```
<IfDefine [!]parameter>
  directive
  …
</IfDefine>
```

The *parameter* can be supplied at a shell prompt using the `-Dparameter` command line option (for example, `httpd -DEnableHome`). If the optional exclamation mark (that is, `!`) is present, the enclosed directives are used only when the parameter is *not* specified.

```
<IfDefine EnableHome>
  UserDir public_html
</IfDefine>
```

Example 12.2. Using the <IfDefine> directive

`<IfModule>`

The `<IfModule>` directive allows you to use certain directive only when a particular module is loaded. It takes the following form:

```
<IfModule [!]module>
  directive
  …
</IfModule>
```

The *module* can be identified either by its name, or by the file name. If the optional exclamation mark (that is, `!`) is present, the enclosed directives are used only when the module is *not* loaded.

```
<IfModule mod_disk_cache.c>
  CacheEnable disk /
  CacheRoot /var/cache/mod_proxy
</IfModule>
```

Example 12.3. Using the <IfModule> directive

`<Location>`

The `<Location>` directive allows you to apply certain directives to a particular URL only. It takes the following form:

```
<Location url>
  directive
  …
</Location>
```

The *url* can be either a path relative to the directory specified by the `DocumentRoot` directive (for example, `/server-info`), or an external URL such as `http://example.com/server-info`.

```
<Location /server-info>
  SetHandler server-info
  Order deny,allow
  Deny from all
  Allow from .example.com
</Location>
```

Example 12.4. Using the <Location> directive

`<Proxy>`

The `<Proxy>` directive allows you to apply certain directives to the proxy server only. It takes the following form:

```
<Proxy pattern>
  directive
  …
</Proxy>
```

The *pattern* can be an external URL, or a wildcard expression (for example, `http://example.com/*`).

```
<Proxy *>
  Order deny,allow
  Deny from all
  Allow from .example.com
</Proxy>
```

Example 12.5. Using the <Proxy> directive

`<VirtualHost>`

The `<VirtualHost>` directive allows you apply certain directives to particular virtual hosts only. It takes the following form:

```
<VirtualHost address[:port]…>
  directive
  …
</VirtualHost>
```

The *address* can be an IP address, a fully qualified domain name, or a special form as described in *Table 12.2. Available <VirtualHost> options* below.

Option	Description
*	Represents all IP addresses.
default	Represents unmatched IP addresses.

Table 12.2. Available <VirtualHost> options

```
<VirtualHost *:80>
  ServerAdmin webmaster@penguin.example.com
  DocumentRoot /www/docs/penguin.example.com
  ServerName penguin.example.com
  ErrorLog logs/penguin.example.com-error_log
  CustomLog logs/penguin.example.com-access_log common
</VirtualHost>
```

Example 12.6. Using the <VirtualHost> directive

`AccessFileName`

The `AccessFileName` directive allows you to specify the file to be used to customize access control information for each directory. It takes the following form:

```
AccessFileName filename…
```

The *filename* is a name of the file to look for in the requested directory. By default, the server looks for `.htaccess`.

For security reasons, the directive is typically followed by the `Files` tag to prevent the files beginning with `.ht` from being accessed by web clients. This includes the `.htaccess` and `.htpasswd` files.

```
AccessFileName .htaccess

<Files ~ "^\.ht">
  Order allow,deny
  Deny from all
  Satisfy All
</Files>
```

Example 12.7. Using the AccessFileName directive

`Action`

The `Action` directive allows you to specify a CGI script to be executed when a certain media type is requested. It takes the following form:

```
Action content-type path
```

The *`content-type`* has to be a valid MIME type such as `text/html`, `image/png`, or `application/pdf`. The *`path`* refers to an existing CGI script, and must be relative to the directory specified by the `DocumentRoot` directive (for example, `/cgi-bin/process-image.cgi`).

```
Action image/png /cgi-bin/process-image.cgi
```

Example 12.8. Using the Action directive

`AddDescription`

The `AddDescription` directive allows you to specify a short description to be displayed in server-generated directory listings for a given file. It takes the following form:

```
AddDescription "description" filename…
```

The *`description`* should be a short text enclosed in double quotes (that is, `"`). The *`filename`* can be a full file name, a file extension, or a wildcard expression.

```
AddDescription "GZIP compressed tar archive" .tgz
```

Example 12.9. Using the AddDescription directive

`AddEncoding`

The `AddEncoding` directive allows you to specify an encoding type for a particular file extension. It takes the following form:

```
AddEncoding encoding extension…
```

The *`encoding`* has to be a valid MIME encoding such as `x-compress`, `x-gzip`, etc. The *`extension`* is a case sensitive file extension, and is conventionally written with a leading dot (for example, `.gz`).

This directive is typically used to instruct web browsers to decompress certain file types as they are downloaded.

```
AddEncoding x-gzip .gz .tgz
```

Example 12.10. Using the AddEncoding directive

`AddHandler`

The `AddHandler` directive allows you to map certain file extensions to a selected handler. It takes the following form:

```
AddHandler handler extension…
```

The *handler* has to be a name of previously defined handler. The *extension* is a case sensitive file extension, and is conventionally written with a leading dot (for example, `.cgi`).

This directive is typically used to treat files with the `.cgi` extension as CGI scripts regardless of the directory they are in. Additionally, it is also commonly used to process server-parsed HTML and image-map files.

```
AddHandler cgi-script .cgi
```

Example 12.11. Using the AddHandler option

`AddIcon`

The `AddIcon` directive allows you to specify an icon to be displayed for a particular file in server-generated directory listings. It takes the following form:

`AddIcon` *path pattern...*

The *path* refers to an existing icon file, and must be relative to the directory specified by the `DocumentRoot` directive (for example, `/icons/folder.png`). The *pattern* can be a file name, a file extension, a wildcard expression, or a special form as described in the following table:

Option	Description
`^^DIRECTORY^^`	Represents a directory.
`^^BLANKICON^^`	Represents a blank line.

Table 12.3. Available AddIcon options

```
AddIcon /icons/text.png .txt README
```

Example 12.12. Using the AddIcon directive

`AddIconByEncoding`

The `AddIconByEncoding` directive allows you to specify an icon to be displayed for a particular encoding type in server-generated directory listings. It takes the following form:

`AddIconByEncoding` *path encoding...*

The *path* refers to an existing icon file, and must be relative to the directory specified by the `DocumentRoot` directive (for example, `/icons/compressed.png`). The *encoding* has to be a valid MIME encoding such as `x-compress`, `x-gzip`, etc.

```
AddIconByEncoding /icons/compressed.png x-compress x-gzip
```

Example 12.13. Using the AddIconByEncoding directive

`AddIconByType`

The `AddIconByType` directive allows you to specify an icon to be displayed for a particular media type in server-generated directory listings. It takes the following form:

`AddIconByType` *`path content-type...`*

The *`path`* refers to an existing icon file, and must be relative to the directory specified by the `DocumentRoot` directive (for example, `/icons/text.png`). The *`content-type`* has to be either a valid MIME type (for example, `text/html` or `image/png`), or a wildcard expression such as `text/*`, `image/*`, etc.

```
AddIconByType /icons/video.png video/*
```

Example 12.14. Using the AddIconByType directive

`AddLanguage`

The `AddLanguage` directive allows you to associate a file extension with a specific language. It takes the following form:

`AddLanguage` *`language extension...`*

The *`language`* has to be a valid MIME language such as `cs`, `en`, or `fr`. The *`extension`* is a case sensitive file extension, and is conventionally written with a leading dot (for example, `.cs`).

This directive is especially useful for web servers that serve content in multiple languages based on the client's language settings.

```
AddLanguage cs .cs .cz
```

Example 12.15. Using the AddLanguage directive

`AddType`

The `AddType` directive allows you to define or override the media type for a particular file extension. It takes the following form:

`AddType` *`content-type extension...`*

The *`content-type`* has to be a valid MIME type such as `text/html`, `image/png`, etc. The *`extension`* is a case sensitive file extension, and is conventionally written with a leading dot (for example, `.cs`).

```
AddType application/x-gzip .gz .tgz
```

Example 12.16. Using the AddType directive

`Alias`

The `Alias` directive allows you to refer to files and directories outside the default directory specified by the `DocumentRoot` directive. It takes the following form:

`Alias` *`url-path real-path`*

The *url-path* must be relative to the directory specified by the `DocumentRoot` directive (for example, `/images/`). The *real-path* is a full path to a file or directory in the local file system.

This directive is typically followed by the `Directory` tag with additional permissions to access the target directory. By default, the `/icons/` alias is created so that the icons from `/var/www/icons/` are displayed in server-generated directory listings.

```
Alias /icons/ /var/www/icons/

<Directory "/var/www/icons">
  Options Indexes MultiViews FollowSymLinks
  AllowOverride None
  Order allow,deny
  Allow from all
<Directory>
```

Example 12.17. Using the Alias directive

`Allow`

The `Allow` directive allows you to specify which clients have permission to access a given directory. It takes the following form:

`Allow from` *`client`*...

The *client* can be a domain name, an IP address (both full and partial), a *network*/*netmask* pair, or `all` for all clients.

```
Allow from 192.168.1.0/255.255.255.0
```

Example 12.18. Using the Allow directive

`AllowOverride`

The `AllowOverride` directive allows you to specify which directives in a `.htaccess` file can override the default configuration. It takes the following form:

`AllowOverride` *`type`*...

The *type* has to be one of the available grouping options as described in *Table 12.4. Available AllowOverride options* below.

Option	Description
`All`	All directives in `.htaccess` are allowed to override earlier configuration settings.
`None`	No directive in `.htaccess` is allowed to override earlier configuration settings.
`AuthConfig`	Allows the use of authorization directives such as `AuthName`, `AuthType`, or `Require`.
`FileInfo`	Allows the use of file type, metadata, and `mod_rewrite` directives such as `DefaultType`, `RequestHeader`, or `RewriteEngine`, as well as the `Action` directive.

Option	Description
`Indexes`	Allows the use of directory indexing directives such as `AddDescription`, `AddIcon`, or `FancyIndexing`.
`Limit`	Allows the use of host access directives, that is, `Allow`, `Deny`, and `Order`.
`Options[=`*option*,...]	Allows the use of the `Options` directive. Additionally, you can provide a comma-separated list of options to customize which options can be set using this directive.

Table 12.4. Available AllowOverride options

```
AllowOverride FileInfo AuthConfig Limit
```

Example 12.19. Using the AllowOverride directive

`BrowserMatch`

The `BrowserMatch` directive allows you to modify the server behavior based on the client's web browser type. It takes the following form:

`BrowserMatch` *`pattern variable`*...

The *`pattern`* is a regular expression to match the User-Agent HTTP header field. The *`variable`* is an environment variable that is set when the header field matches the pattern.

By default, this directive is used to deny connections to specific browsers with known issues, and to disable keepalives and HTTP header flushes for browsers that are known to have problems with these actions.

```
BrowserMatch "Mozilla/2" nokeepalive
```

Example 12.20. Using the BrowserMatch directive

`CacheDefaultExpire`

The `CacheDefaultExpire` option allows you to set how long to cache a document that does not have any expiration date or the date of its last modification specified. It takes the following form:

`CacheDefaultExpire` *`time`*

The *`time`* is specified in seconds. The default option is `3600` (that is, one hour).

```
CacheDefaultExpire 3600
```

Example 12.21. Using the CacheDefaultExpire directive

`CacheDisable`

The `CacheDisable` directive allows you to disable caching of certain URLs. It takes the following form:

`CacheDisable` *`path`*

The *path* must be relative to the directory specified by the `DocumentRoot` directive (for example, `/files/`).

```
CacheDisable /temporary
```

Example 12.22. Using the CacheDisable directive

`CacheEnable`

The `CacheEnable` directive allows you to specify a cache type to be used for certain URLs. It takes the following form:

```
CacheEnable type url
```

The *type* has to be a valid cache type as described in *Table 12.5. Available cache types* below. The *url* can be a path relative to the directory specified by the `DocumentRoot` directive (for example, `/images/`), a protocol (for example, `ftp://`), or an external URL such as `http://example.com/`.

Type	Description
`mem`	The memory-based storage manager.
`disk`	The disk-based storage manager.
`fd`	The file descriptor cache.

Table 12.5. Available cache types

```
CacheEnable disk /
```

Example 12.23. Using the CacheEnable directive

`CacheLastModifiedFactor`

The `CacheLastModifiedFactor` directive allows you to customize how long to cache a document that does not have any expiration date specified, but that provides information about the date of its last modification. It takes the following form:

```
CacheLastModifiedFactor number
```

The *number* is a coefficient to be used to multiply the time that passed since the last modification of the document. The default option is `0.1` (that is, one tenth).

```
CacheLastModifiedFactor 0.1
```

Example 12.24. Using the CacheLastModifiedFactor directive

`CacheMaxExpire`

The `CacheMaxExpire` directive allows you to specify the maximum amount of time to cache a document. It takes the following form:

```
CacheMaxExpire time
```

The *time* is specified in seconds. The default option is `86400` (that is, one day).

```
CacheMaxExpire 86400
```

Example 12.25. Using the CacheMaxExpire directive

`CacheNegotiatedDocs`

The `CacheNegotiatedDocs` directive allows you to enable caching of the documents that were negotiated on the basis of content. It takes the following form:

```
CacheNegotiatedDocs option
```

The *option* has to be a valid keyword as described in *Table 12.6. Available CacheNegotiatedDocs options* below. Since the content-negotiated documents may change over time or because of the input from the requester, the default option is `Off`.

Option	Description
`On`	Enables caching the content-negotiated documents.
`Off`	Disables caching the content-negotiated documents.

Table 12.6. Available CacheNegotiatedDocs options

```
CacheNegotiatedDocs On
```

Example 12.26. Using the CacheNegotiatedDocs directive

`CacheRoot`

The `CacheRoot` directive allows you to specify the directory to store cache files in. It takes the following form:

```
CacheRoot directory
```

The *directory* must be a full path to an existing directory in the local file system. The default option is `/var/cache/mod_proxy/`.

```
CacheRoot /var/cache/mod_proxy
```

Example 12.27. Using the CacheRoot directive

`CustomLog`

The `CustomLog` directive allows you to specify the log file name and the log file format. It takes the following form:

```
CustomLog path format
```

The *path* refers to a log file, and must be relative to the directory that is specified by the `ServerRoot` directive (that is, `/etc/httpd/` by default). The *format* has to be either an explicit format string, or a format name that was previously defined using the `LogFormat` directive.

```
CustomLog logs/access_log combined
```

Example 12.28. Using the CustomLog directive

`DefaultIcon`

The `DefaultIcon` directive allows you to specify an icon to be displayed for a file in server-generated directory listings when no other icon is associated with it. It takes the following form:

`DefaultIcon` *`path`*

The *`path`* refers to an existing icon file, and must be relative to the directory specified by the `DocumentRoot` directive (for example, `/icons/unknown.png`).

```
DefaultIcon /icons/unknown.png
```

Example 12.29. Using the DefaultIcon directive

`DefaultType`

The `DefaultType` directive allows you to specify a media type to be used in case the proper MIME type cannot be determined by the server. It takes the following form:

`DefaultType` *`content-type`*

The *`content-type`* has to be a valid MIME type such as `text/html`, `image/png`, `application/pdf`, etc.

```
DefaultType text/plain
```

Example 12.30. Using the DefaultType directive

`Deny`

The `Deny` directive allows you to specify which clients are denied access to a given directory. It takes the following form:

`Deny from` *`client`*…

The *`client`* can be a domain name, an IP address (both full and partial), a *`network`*/*`netmask`* pair, or `all` for all clients.

```
Deny from 192.168.1.1
```

Example 12.31. Using the Deny directive

`DirectoryIndex`

The `DirectoryIndex` directive allows you to specify a document to be served to a client when a directory is requested (that is, when the URL ends with the / character). It takes the following form:

```
DirectoryIndex filename...
```

The *filename* is a name of the file to look for in the requested directory. By default, the server looks for `index.html`, and `index.html.var`.

```
DirectoryIndex index.html index.html.var
```

Example 12.32. Using the DirectoryIndex directive

`DocumentRoot`

The `DocumentRoot` directive allows you to specify the main directory from which the content is served. It takes the following form:

```
DocumentRoot directory
```

The *directory* must be a full path to an existing directory in the local file system. The default option is `/var/www/html/`.

```
DocumentRoot /var/www/html
```

Example 12.33. Using the DocumentRoot directive

`ErrorDocument`

The `ErrorDocument` directive allows you to specify a document or a message to be displayed as a response to a particular error. It takes the following form:

```
ErrorDocument error-code action
```

The *error-code* has to be a valid code such as `403` (Forbidden), `404` (Not Found), or `500` (Internal Server Error). The *action* can be either a URL (both local and external), or a message string enclosed in double quotes (that is, `"`).

```
ErrorDocument 403 "Access Denied"
ErrorDocument 404 /404-not_found.html
```

Example 12.34. Using the ErrorDocument directive

`ErrorLog`

The `ErrorLog` directive allows you to specify a file to which the server errors are logged. It takes the following form:

```
ErrorLog path
```

The *path* refers to a log file, and can be either absolute, or relative to the directory that is specified by the `ServerRoot` directive (that is, `/etc/httpd/` by default). The default option is `logs/error_log`

```
ErrorLog logs/error_log
```

Example 12.35. Using the ErrorLog directive

`ExtendedStatus`

The `ExtendedStatus` directive allows you to enable detailed server status information. It takes the following form:

```
ExtendedStatus option
```

The *option* has to be a valid keyword as described in *Table 12.7. Available ExtendedStatus options* below. The default option is `Off`.

Option	Description
`On`	Enables generating the detailed server status.
`Off`	Disables generating the detailed server status.

Table 12.7. Available ExtendedStatus options

```
ExtendedStatus On
```

Example 12.36. Using the ExtendedStatus directive

`Group`

The `Group` directive allows you to specify the group under which the `httpd` service will run. It takes the following form:

```
Group group
```

The *group* has to be an existing UNIX group. The default option is `apache`.

Note that `Group` is no longer supported inside `<VirtualHost>`, and has been replaced by the `SuexecUserGroup` directive.

```
Group apache
```

Example 12.37. Using the Group directive

`HeaderName`

The `HeaderName` directive allows you to specify a file to be prepended to the beginning of the server-generated directory listing. It takes the following form:

```
HeaderName filename
```

The *filename* is a name of the file to look for in the requested directory. By default, the server looks for `HEADER.html`.

```
HeaderName HEADER.html
```

Example 12.38. Using the HeaderName directive

`HostnameLookups`

The `HostnameLookups` directive allows you to enable automatic resolving of IP addresses. It takes the following form:

```
HostnameLookups option
```

The `option` has to be a valid keyword as described in *Table 12.8. Available HostnameLookups options* below. To conserve resources on the server, the default option is `Off`.

Option	Description
`On`	Enables resolving the IP address for each connection so that the hostname can be logged. However, this also adds a significant processing overhead.
`Double`	Enables performing the double-reverse DNS lookup. In comparison to the above option, this adds even more processing overhead.
`Off`	Disables resolving the IP address for each connection.

Table 12.8. Available HostnameLookups options

Note that when the presence of hostnames is required in server log files, it is often possible to use one of the many log analyzer tools that perform the DNS lookups more efficiently.

```
HostnameLookups Off
```

Example 12.39. Using the HostnameLookups directive

`Include`

The `Include` directive allows you to include other configuration files. It takes the following form:

```
Include filename
```

The `filename` can be an absolute path, a path relative to the directory specified by the `ServerRoot` directive, or a wildcard expression. All configuration files from the `/etc/httpd/conf.d/` directory are loaded by default.

```
Include conf.d/*.conf
```

Example 12.40. Using the Include directive

`IndexIgnore`

The `IndexIgnore` directive allows you to specify a list of file names to be omitted from the server-generated directory listings. It takes the following form:

```
IndexIgnore filename…
```

The *filename* option can be either a full file name, or a wildcard expression.

```
IndexIgnore .??* *~ *# HEADER* README* RCS CVS *,v *,t
```

Example 12.41. Using the IndexIgnore directive

`IndexOptions`

The `IndexOptions` directive allows you to customize the behavior of server-generated directory listings. It takes the following form:

`IndexOptions` *`option`*…

The *`option`* has to be a valid keyword as described in *Table 12.9. Available directory listing options* below. The default options are `Charset=UTF-8`, `FancyIndexing`, `HTMLTable`, `NameWidth=*`, and `VersionSort`.

Option	Description
`Charset=`*`encoding`*	Specifies the character set of a generated web page. The *`encoding`* has to be a valid character set such as `UTF-8` or `ISO-8859-2`.
`Type=`*`content-type`*	Specifies the media type of a generated web page. The *`content-type`* has to be a valid MIME type such as `text/html` or `text/plain`.
`DescriptionWidth=`*`value`*	Specifies the width of the description column. The *`value`* can be either a number of characters, or an asterisk (that is, `*`) to adjust the width automatically.
`FancyIndexing`	Enables advanced features such as different icons for certain files or possibility to re-sort a directory listing by clicking on a column header.
`FolderFirst`	Enables listing directories first, always placing them above files.
`HTMLTable`	Enables the use of HTML tables for directory listings.
`IconsAreLinks`	Enables using the icons as links.
`IconHeight=`*`value`*	Specifies an icon height. The *`value`* is a number of pixels.
`IconWidth=`*`value`*	Specifies an icon width. The *`value`* is a number of pixels.
`IgnoreCase`	Enables sorting files and directories in a case-sensitive manner.
`IgnoreClient`	Disables accepting query variables from a client.
`NameWidth=`*`value`*	Specifies the width of the file name column. The *`value`* can be either a number of characters, or an asterisk (that is, `*`) to adjust the width automatically.
`ScanHTMLTitles`	Enables parsing the file for a description (that is, the `title` element) in case it is not provided by the `AddDescription` directive.
`ShowForbidden`	Enables listing the files with otherwise restricted access.
`SuppressColumnSorting`	Disables re-sorting a directory listing by clicking on a column header.
`SuppressDescription`	Disables reserving a space for file descriptions.

Option	Description
`SuppressHTMLPreamble`	Disables the use of standard HTML preamble when a file specified by the `HeaderName` directive is present.
`SuppressIcon`	Disables the use of icons in directory listings.
`SuppressLastModified`	Disables displaying the date of the last modification field in directory listings.
`SuppressRules`	Disables the use of horizontal lines in directory listings.
`SuppressSize`	Disables displaying the file size field in directory listings.
`TrackModified`	Enables returning the `Last-Modified` and `ETag` values in the HTTP header.
`VersionSort`	Enables sorting files that contain a version number in the expected manner.
`XHTML`	Enables the use of XHTML 1.0 instead of the default HTML 3.2.

Table 12.9. Available directory listing options

```
IndexOptions FancyIndexing VersionSort NameWidth=* HTMLTable Charset=UTF-8
```

Example 12.42. Using the IndexOptions directive

`KeepAlive`

The `KeepAlive` directive allows you to enable persistent connections. It takes the following form:

`KeepAlive option`

The `option` has to be a valid keyword as described in *Table 12.10. Available KeepAlive options* below. The default option is `Off`.

Option	Description
`On`	Enables the persistent connections. In this case, the server will accept more than one request per connection.
`Off`	Disables the keep-alive connections.

Table 12.10. Available KeepAlive options

Note that when the persistent connections are enabled, on a busy server, the number of child processes can increase rapidly and eventually reach the maximum limit, slowing down the server significantly. To reduce the risk, it is recommended that you set `KeepAliveTimeout` to a low number, and monitor the `/var/log/httpd/logs/error_log` log file carefully.

```
KeepAlive Off
```

Example 12.43. Using the KeepAlive directive

`KeepAliveTimeout`

The `KeepAliveTimeout` directive allows you to specify the amount of time to wait for another request before closing the connection. It takes the following form:

`KeepAliveTimeout` *`time`*

The *`time`* is specified in seconds. The default option is `15`.

```
KeepAliveTimeout 15
```

Example 12.44. Using the KeepAliveTimeout directive

`LanguagePriority`

The `LanguagePriority` directive allows you to customize the precedence of languages. It takes the following form:

`LanguagePriority` *`language...`*

The *`language`* has to be a valid MIME language such as `cs`, `en`, or `fr`.

This directive is especially useful for web servers that serve content in multiple languages based on the client's language settings.

```
LanguagePriority sk cs en
```

Example 12.45. Using the LanguagePriority directive

`Listen`

The *`Listen`* directive allows you to specify IP addresses or ports to listen to. It takes the following form:

`Listen [`*`ip-address`*`:]`*`port`*` [`*`protocol`*`]`

The *`ip-address`* is optional and unless supplied, the server will accept incoming requests on a given *`port`* from all IP addresses. Since the *`protocol`* is determined automatically from the port number, it can be usually omitted. The default option is to listen to port `80`.

Note that if the server is configured to listen to a port under 1024, only superuser will be able to start the `httpd` service.

```
Listen 80
```

Example 12.46. Using the Listen directive

`LoadModule`

The `LoadModule` directive allows you to load a *Dynamic Shared Object* (DSO) module. It takes the following form:

`LoadModule` *`name path`*

The `name` has to be a valid identifier of the required module. The `path` refers to an existing module file, and must be relative to the directory in which the libraries are placed (that is, `/usr/lib/httpd/` on 32-bit and `/usr/lib64/httpd/` on 64-bit systems by default).

Refer to Section 12.1.6, *Working with Modules* (page 259) for more information on the Apache HTTP Server's DSO support.

```
LoadModule php5_module modules/libphp5.so
```

Example 12.47. Using the LoadModule directive

`LogFormat`

The *`LogFormat`* directive allows you to specify a log file format. It takes the following form:

`LogFormat` *`format name`*

The *`format`* is a string consisting of options as described in *Table 12.11. Common LogFormat options* below. The `name` can be used instead of the format string in the `CustomLog` directive.

Option	Description
`%b`	Represents the size of the response in bytes.
`%h`	Represents the IP address or hostname of a remote client.
`%l`	Represents the remote log name if supplied. If not, a hyphen (that is, -) is used instead.
`%r`	Represents the first line of the request string as it came from the browser or client.
`%s`	Represents the status code.
`%t`	Represents the date and time of the request.
`%u`	If the authentication is required, it represents the remote user. If not, a hyphen (that is, -) is used instead.
`%{`*`field`*`}`	Represents the content of the HTTP header *`field`*. The common options include `%{Referer}` (the URL of the web page that referred the client to the server) and `%{User-Agent}` (the type of the web browser making the request).

Table 12.11. Common LogFormat options

```
LogFormat "%h %l %u %t \"%r\" %>s %b" common
```

Example 12.48. Using the LogFormat directive

`LogLevel`

The `LogLevel` directive allows you to customize the verbosity level of the error log. It takes the following form:

```
LogLevel option
```

The `option` has to be a valid keyword as described in *Table 12.12. Available LogLevel options* below. The default option is `warn`.

Option	Description
`emerg`	Only the emergency situations when the server cannot perform its work are logged.
`alert`	All situations when an immediate action is required are logged.
`crit`	All critical conditions are logged.
`error`	All error messages are logged.
`warn`	All warning messages are logged.
`notice`	Even normal, but still significant situations are logged.
`info`	Various informational messages are logged.
`debug`	Various debugging messages are logged.

Table 12.12. Available LogLevel options

```
LogLevel warn
```

Example 12.49. Using the LogLevel directive

`MaxKeepAliveRequests`

The `MaxKeepAliveRequests` directive allows you to specify the maximum number of requests for a persistent connection. It takes the following form:

```
MaxKeepAliveRequests number
```

A high `number` can improve the performance of the server. Note that using `0` allows unlimited number of requests. The default option is `100`.

```
MaxKeepAliveRequests 100
```

Example 12.50. Using the MaxKeepAliveRequests option

`NameVirtualHost`

The `NameVirtualHost` directive allows you to specify the IP address and port number for a name-based virtual host. It takes the following form:

```
NameVirtualHost ip-address[:port]
```

The `ip-address` can be either a full IP address, or an asterisk (that is, `*`) representing all interfaces. Note that IPv6 addresses have to be enclosed in square brackets (that is, `[` and `]`). The *port* is optional.

Name-based virtual hosting allows one Apache HTTP Server to serve different domains without using multiple IP addresses.

Using secure HTTP connections

Name-based virtual hosts *only* work with non-secure HTTP connections. If using virtual hosts with a secure server, use IP address-based virtual hosts instead.

```
NameVirtualHost *:80
```

Example 12.51. Using the NameVirtualHost directive

`Options`

The `Options` directive allows you to specify which server features are available in a particular directory. It takes the following form:

`Options option…`

The *option* has to be a valid keyword as described in *Table 12.13. Available server features* below.

Option	Description
`ExecCGI`	Enables the execution of CGI scripts.
`FollowSymLinks`	Enables following symbolic links in the directory.
`Includes`	Enables server-side includes.
`IncludesNOEXEC`	Enables server-side includes, but does not allow the execution of commands.
`Indexes`	Enables server-generated directory listings.
`MultiViews`	Enables content-negotiated "MultiViews".
`SymLinksIfOwnerMatch`	Enables following symbolic links in the directory when both the link and the target file have the same owner.
`All`	Enables all of the features above with the exception of `MultiViews`.
`None`	Disables all of the features above.

Table 12.13. Available server features

```
Options Indexes FollowSymLinks
```

Example 12.52. Using the Options directive

`Order`

The `Order` directive allows you to specify the order in which the `Allow` and `Deny` directives are evaluated. It takes the following form:

```
Order option
```

The *option* has to be a valid keyword as described in *Table 12.14. Available Order options* below. The default option is `allow,deny`.

Option	Description
`allow,deny`	`Allow` directives are evaluated first.
`deny,allow`	`Deny` directives are evaluated first.

Table 12.14. Available Order options

```
Order allow,deny
```

Example 12.53. Using the Order directive

`PidFile`

The `PidFile` directive allows you to specify a file to which the *process ID* (PID) of the server is stored. It takes the following form:

```
PidFile path
```

The *path* refers to a pid file, and can be either absolute, or relative to the directory that is specified by the `ServerRoot` directive (that is, `/etc/httpd/` by default). The default option is `run/httpd.pid`.

```
PidFile run/httpd.pid
```

Example 12.54. Using the PidFile directive

`ProxyRequests`

The `ProxyRequests` directive allows you to enable forward proxy requests. It takes the following form:

```
ProxyRequests option
```

The *option* has to be a valid keyword as described in *Table 12.15. Available ProxyRequests options* below. The default option is `Off`.

Option	Description
`On`	Enables forward proxy requests.
`Off`	Disables forward proxy requests.

Table 12.15. Available ProxyRequests options

```
ProxyRequests On
```

Example 12.55. Using the ProxyRequests directive

`ReadmeName`

The `ReadmeName` directive allows you to specify a file to be appended to the end of the server-generated directory listing. It takes the following form:

`ReadmeName filename`

The *`filename`* is a name of the file to look for in the requested directory. By default, the server looks for `README.html`.

```
ReadmeName README.html
```

Example 12.56. Using the ReadmeName directive

`Redirect`

The `Redirect` directive allows you to redirect a client to another URL. It takes the following form:

`Redirect [status] path url`

The *`status`* is optional, and if provided, it has to be a valid keyword as described in *Table 12.16. Available status options* below. The *`path`* refers to the old location, and must be relative to the directory specified by the `DocumentRoot` directive (for example, `/docs`). The *`url`* refers to the current location of the content (for example, `http://docs.example.com`).

Status	Description
`permanent`	Indicates that the requested resource has been moved permanently. The `301` (Moved Permanently) status code is returned to a client.
`temp`	Indicates that the requested resource has been moved only temporarily. The `302` (Found) status code is returned to a client.
`seeother`	Indicates that the requested resource has been replaced. The `303` (See Other) status code is returned to a client.
`gone`	Indicates that the requested resource has been removed permanently. The `410` (Gone) status is returned to a client.

Table 12.16. Available status options

Note that for more advanced redirection techniques, you can use the `mod_rewrite` module that is part of the Apache HTTP Server installation.

```
Redirect permanent /docs http://docs.example.com
```

Example 12.57. Using the Redirect directive

`ScriptAlias`

The `ScriptAlias` directive allows you to specify the location of CGI scripts. It takes the following form:

`ScriptAlias` *`url-path real-path`*

The *`url-path`* must be relative to the directory specified by the `DocumentRoot` directive (for example, `/cgi-bin/`). The *`real-path`* is a full path to a file or directory in the local file system.

This directive is typically followed by the `Directory` tag with additional permissions to access the target directory. By default, the `/cgi-bin/` alias is created so that the scripts located in the `/var/www/cgi-bin/` are accessible.

The `ScriptAlias` directive is used for security reasons to prevent CGI scripts from being viewed as ordinary text documents.

```
ScriptAlias /cgi-bin/ /var/www/cgi-bin/

<Directory "/var/www/cgi-bin">
  AllowOverride None
  Options None
  Order allow,deny
  Allow from all
</Directory>
```

Example 12.58. Using the ScriptAlias directive

`ServerAdmin`

The `ServerAdmin` directive allows you to specify the email address of the server administrator to be displayed in server-generated web pages. It takes the following form:

`ServerAdmin` *`email`*

The default option is `root@localhost`.

This directive is commonly set to `webmaster@`*`hostname`*, where *`hostname`* is the address of the server. Once set, alias `webmaster` to the person responsible for the web server in `/etc/aliases`, and as superuser, run the `newaliases` command.

```
ServerAdmin webmaster@penguin.example.com
```

Example 12.59. Using the ServerAdmin directive

`ServerName`

The `ServerName` directive allows you to specify the hostname and the port number of a web server. It takes the following form:

`ServerName` *`hostname`*`[:`*`port`*`]`

The *hostname* has to be a *fully qualified domain name* (FQDN) of the server. The *port* is optional, but when supplied, it has to match the number specified by the `Listen` directive.

When using this directive, make sure that the IP address and server name pair are included in the `/etc/hosts` file.

```
ServerName penguin.example.com:80
```

Example 12.60. Using the ServerName directive

`ServerRoot`

The `ServerRoot` directive allows you to specify the directory in which the server operates. It takes the following form:

```
ServerRoot directory
```

The *directory* must be a full path to an existing directory in the local file system. The default option is `/etc/httpd/`.

```
ServerRoot /etc/httpd
```

Example 12.61. Using the ServerRoot directive

`ServerSignature`

The `ServerSignature` directive allows you to enable displaying information about the server on server-generated documents. It takes the following form:

```
ServerSignature option
```

The *option* has to be a valid keyword as described in *Table 12.17. Available ServerSignature options* below. The default option is `On`.

Option	Description
`On`	Enables appending the server name and version to server-generated pages.
`Off`	Disables appending the server name and version to server-generated pages.
`EMail`	Enables appending the server name, version, and the email address of the system administrator as specified by the `ServerAdmin` directive to server-generated pages.

Table 12.17. Available ServerSignature options

```
ServerSignature On
```

Example 12.62. Using the ServerSignature directive

`ServerTokens`

The `ServerTokens` directive allows you to customize what information are included in the Server response header. It takes the following form:

`ServerTokens` *`option`*

The *`option`* has to be a valid keyword as described in *Table 12.18. Available ServerTokens options* below. The default option is `OS`.

Option	Description
`Prod`	Includes the product name only (that is, `Apache`).
`Major`	Includes the product name and the major version of the server (for example, `2`).
`Minor`	Includes the product name and the minor version of the server (for example, `2.2`).
`Min`	Includes the product name and the minimal version of the server (for example, `2.2.15`).
`OS`	Includes the product name, the minimal version of the server, and the type of the operating system it is running on (for example, `Red Hat`).
`Full`	Includes all the information above along with the list of loaded modules.

Table 12.18. Available ServerTokens options

Note that for security reasons, it is recommended to reveal as little information about the server as possible.

```
ServerTokens Prod
```

Example 12.63. Using the ServerTokens directive

`SuexecUserGroup`

The `SuexecUserGroup` directive allows you to specify the user and group under which the CGI scripts will be run. It takes the following form:

`SuexecUserGroup` *`user group`*

The *`user`* has to be an existing user, and the *`group`* must be a valid UNIX group.

For security reasons, the CGI scripts should not be run with `root` privileges. Note that in `<VirtualHost>`, `SuexecUserGroup` replaces the `User` and `Group` directives.

```
SuexecUserGroup apache apache
```

Example 12.64. Using the SuexecUserGroup directive

`Timeout`

The `Timeout` directive allows you to specify the amount of time to wait for an event before closing a connection. It takes the following form:

`Timeout time`

The *time* is specified in seconds. The default option is `60`.

```
Timeout 60
```

Example 12.65. Using the Timeout directive

`TypesConfig`

The `TypesConfig` allows you to specify the location of the MIME types configuration file. It takes the following form:

`TypesConfig path`

The *path* refers to an existing MIME types configuration file, and can be either absolute, or relative to the directory that is specified by the `ServerRoot` directive (that is, `/etc/httpd/` by default). The default option is `/etc/mime.types`.

Note that instead of editing `/etc/mime.types`, the recommended way to add MIME type mapping to the Apache HTTP Server is to use the `AddType` directive.

```
TypesConfig /etc/mime.types
```

Example 12.66. Using the TypesConfig directive

`UseCanonicalName`

The `UseCanonicalName` allows you to specify the way the server refers to itself. It takes the following form:

`UseCanonicalName option`

The *option* has to be a valid keyword as described in *Table 12.19. Available UseCanonicalName options* below. The default option is `Off`.

Option	Description
`On`	Enables the use of the name that is specified by the `ServerName` directive.
`Off`	Disables the use of the name that is specified by the `ServerName` directive. The hostname and port number provided by the requesting client are used instead.
`DNS`	Disables the use of the name that is specified by the `ServerName` directive. The hostname determined by a reverse DNS lookup is used instead.

Table 12.19. Available UseCanonicalName options

```
UseCanonicalName Off
```

Example 12.67. Using the UseCanonicalName directive

`User`

The `User` directive allows you to specify the user under which the `httpd` service will run. It takes the following form:

`User` *`user`*

The *`user`* has to be an existing UNIX user. The default option is `apache`.

For security reasons, the `httpd` service should not be run with `root` privileges. Note that `User` is no longer supported inside `<VirtualHost>`, and has been replaced by the `SuexecUserGroup` directive.

```
User apache
```

Example 12.68. Using the User directive

`UserDir`

The `UserDir` directive allows you to enable serving content from users' home directories. It takes the following form:

`UserDir` *`option`*

The *`option`* can be either a name of the directory to look for in user's home directory (typically `public_html`), or a valid keyword as described in *Table 12.20. Available UserDir options* below. The default option is `disabled`.

Option	Description
`enabled` *`user`*...	Enables serving content from home directories of given *`user`*s.
`disabled` [*`user`*...]	Disables serving content from home directories, either for all users, or, if a space separated list of *`user`*s is supplied, for given users only.

Table 12.20. Available UserDir options

Set the correct permissions

In order for the web server to access the content, the permissions on relevant directories and files must be set correctly. Make sure that all users are able to access the home directories, and that they can access and read the content of the directory specified by the `UserDir` directive. For example, to allow access to `public_html/` in the home directory of user `joe`, type the following at a shell prompt as `root`:

```
~]# chmod a+x /home/joe/
~]# chmod a+rx /home/joe/public_html/
```

All files in this directory must be set accordingly.

```
UserDir public_html
```

Example 12.69. Using the UserDir directive

12.1.5.2. Common ssl.conf Directives

The *Secure Sockets Layer* (SSL) directives allow you to customize the behavior of the Apache HTTP Secure Server, and in most cases, they are configured appropriately during the installation. Be careful when changing these settings, as incorrect configuration can lead to security vulnerabilities.

The following directive is commonly used in `/etc/httpd/conf.d/ssl.conf`:

`SetEnvIf`

The `SetEnvIf` directive allows you to set environment variables based on the headers of incoming connections. It takes the following form:

```
SetEnvIf option pattern [!]variable[=value]…
```

The *`option`* can be either a HTTP header field, a previously defined environment variable name, or a valid keyword as described in *Table 12.21. Available SetEnvIf options* below. The *`pattern`* is a regular expression. The *`variable`* is an environment variable that is set when the option matches the pattern. If the optional exclamation mark (that is, `!`) is present, the variable is removed instead of being set.

Option	Description
`Remote_Host`	Refers to the client's hostname.
`Remote_Addr`	Refers to the client's IP address.
`Server_Addr`	Refers to the server's IP address.
`Request_Method`	Refers to the request method (for example, `GET`).
`Request_Protocol`	Refers to the protocol name and version (for example, `HTTP/1.1`).
`Request_URI`	Refers to the requested resource.

Table 12.21. Available SetEnvIf options

The `SetEnvIf` directive is used to disable HTTP keepalives, and to allow SSL to close the connection without a closing notification from the client browser. This is necessary for certain web browsers that do not reliably shut down the SSL connection.

```
SetEnvIf User-Agent ".*MSIE.*" \
         nokeepalive ssl-unclean-shutdown \
         downgrade-1.0 force-response-1.0
```

Example 12.70. Using the SetEnvIf directive

Note that for the `/etc/httpd/conf.d/ssl.conf` file to be present, the mod_ssl needs to be installed. Refer to Section 12.1.8, *Setting Up an SSL Server* (page 260) for more information on how to install and configure an SSL server.

12.1.5.3. Common Multi-Processing Module Directives

The *Multi-Processing Module* (MPM) directives allow you to customize the behavior of a particular MPM specific server-pool. Since its characteristics differ depending on which MPM is used, the directives are embedded in `IfModule`. By default, the server-pool is defined for both the `prefork` and `worker` MPMs.

The following MPM directives are commonly used in `/etc/httpd/conf/httpd.conf`:

`MaxClients`

The `MaxClients` directive allows you to specify the maximum number of simultaneously connected clients to process at one time. It takes the following form:

`MaxClients` *`number`*

A high *`number`* can improve the performance of the server, although it is not recommended to exceed `256` when using the `prefork` MPM.

```
MaxClients 256
```

Example 12.71. Using the MaxClients directive

`MaxRequestsPerChild`

The `MaxRequestsPerChild` directive allows you to specify the maximum number of request a child process can serve before it dies. It takes the following form:

`MaxRequestsPerChild` *`number`*

Setting the *`number`* to `0` allows unlimited number of requests.

The `MaxRequestsPerChild` directive is used to prevent long-lived processes from causing memory leaks.

```
MaxRequestsPerChild 4000
```

Example 12.72. Using the MaxRequestsPerChild directive

`MaxSpareServers`

The `MaxSpareServers` directive allows you to specify the maximum number of spare child processes. It takes the following form:

`MaxSpareServers` *`number`*

This directive is used by the `prefork` MPM only.

```
MaxSpareServers 20
```

Example 12.73. Using the MaxSpareServers directive

`MaxSpareThreads`

The `MaxSpareThreads` directive allows you to specify the maximum number of spare server threads. It takes the following form:

```
MaxSpareThreads number
```

The *`number`* must be greater than or equal to the sum of `MinSpareThreads` and `ThreadsPerChild`. This directive is used by the `worker` MPM only.

```
MaxSpareThreads 75
```

Example 12.74. Using the MaxSpareThreads directive

`MinSpareServers`

The `MinSpareServers` directive allows you to specify the minimum number of spare child processes. It takes the following form:

```
MinSpareServers number
```

Note that a high *`number`* can create a heavy processing load on the server. This directive is used by the `prefork` MPM only.

```
MinSpareServers 5
```

Example 12.75. Using the MinSpareServers directive

`MinSpareThreads`

The `MinSpareThreads` directive allows you to specify the minimum number of spare server threads. It takes the following form:

```
MinSpareThreads number
```

This directive is used by the `worker` MPM only.

```
MinSpareThreads 75
```

Example 12.76. Using the MinSpareThreads directive

`StartServers`

The `StartServers` directive allows you to specify the number of child processes to create when the service is started. It takes the following form:

```
StartServers number
```

Since the child processes are dynamically created and terminated according to the current traffic load, it is usually not necessary to change this value.

```
StartServers 8
```

Example 12.77. Using the StartServers directive

`ThreadsPerChild`

The `ThreadsPerChild` directive allows you to specify the number of threads a child process can create. It takes the following form:

```
ThreadsPerChild number
```

This directive is used by the `worker` MPM only.

```
ThreadsPerChild 25
```

Example 12.78. Using the ThreadsPerChild directive

12.1.6. Working with Modules

Being a modular application, the `httpd` service is distributed along with a number of *Dynamic Shared Objects* (DSOs), which can be dynamically loaded or unloaded at runtime as necessary. By default, these modules are located in `/usr/lib/httpd/modules/` on 32-bit and in `/usr/lib64/httpd/modules/` on 64-bit systems.

12.1.6.1. Loading a Module

To load a particular DSO module, use the `LoadModule` directive as described in Section 12.1.5.1, *Common httpd.conf Directives* (page 228). Note that modules provided by a separate package often have their own configuration file in the `/etc/httpd/conf.d/` directory.

```
LoadModule ssl_module modules/mod_ssl.so
```

Example 12.79. Loading the mod_ssl DSO

Once you are finished, restart the web server to reload the configuration. Refer to Section 12.1.4.3, *Restarting the Service* (page 227) for more information on how to restart the `httpd` service.

12.1.6.2. Writing a Module

If you intend to create a new DSO module, make sure you have the httpd-devel package installed. To do so, type the following at a shell prompt as `root`:

```
yum install httpd-devel
```

This package contains the include files, the header files, and the **APache eXtenSion** (`apxs`) utility required to compile a module.

Once written, you can build the module with the following command:

```
apxs -i -a -c module_name.c
```

If the build was successful, you should be able to load the module the same way as any other module that is distributed with the Apache HTTP Server.

12.1.7. Setting Up Virtual Hosts

The Apache HTTP Server's built in virtual hosting allows the server to provide different information based on which IP address, hostname, or port is being requested.

To create a name-based virtual host, find the virtual host container provided in `/etc/httpd/conf/httpd.conf` as an example, remove the hash sign (that is, `#`) from the beginning of each line, and customize the options according to your requirements as shown in *Example 12.80. Sample virtual host configuration* below.

```
NameVirtualHost penguin.example.com:80

<VirtualHost penguin.example.com:80>
    ServerAdmin webmaster@penguin.example.com
    DocumentRoot /www/docs/penguin.example.com
    ServerName penguin.example.com:80
    ErrorLog logs/penguin.example.com-error_log
    CustomLog logs/penguin.example.com-access_log common
</VirtualHost>
```

Example 12.80. Sample virtual host configuration

Note that `ServerName` must be a valid DNS name assigned to the machine. The `<VirtualHost>` container is highly customizable, and accepts most of the directives available within the main server configuration. Directives that are *not* supported within this container include `User` and `Group`, which were replaced by `SuexecUserGroup`.

Changing the port number

If you configure a virtual host to listen on a non-default port, make sure you update the `Listen` directive in the global settings section of the `/etc/httpd/conf/httpd.conf` file accordingly.

To activate a newly created virtual host, the web server has to be restarted first. Refer to Section 12.1.4.3, *Restarting the Service* (page 227) for more information on how to restart the `httpd` service.

12.1.8. Setting Up an SSL Server

Secure Sockets Layer (SSL) is a cryptographic protocol that allows a server and a client to communicate securely. Along with its extended and improved version called *Transport Layer Security* (TLS), it ensures both privacy and data integrity. The Apache HTTP Server in combination with `mod_ssl`, a module that uses the OpenSSL toolkit to provide the SSL/TLS support, is commonly referred to as the *SSL server*.

Unlike a regular HTTP connection that can be read and possibly modified by anybody who is able to intercept it, the use of `mod_ssl` prevents any inspection or modification of the transmitted content. This section provides basic information on how to enable this module in the Apache HTTP Server configuration, and guides you through the process of generating private keys and self-signed certificates.

12.1.8.1. An Overview of Certificates and Security

Secure communication is based on the use of keys. In conventional or *symmetric cryptography*, both ends of the transaction have the same key they can use to decode each other's transmissions. On the other hand, in public or *asymmetric cryptography*, two keys co-exist: a *private key* that is kept a secret, and a *public key* that is usually shared with the public. While the data encoded with the public key can only be decoded with the private key, data encoded with the private key can in turn only be decoded with the public key.

To provide secure communications using SSL, an SSL server must use a digital certificate signed by a *Certificate Authority* (CA). The certificate lists various attributes of the server (that is, the server hostname, the name of the company, its location, etc.), and the signature produced using the CA's private key. This signature ensures that a particular certificate authority has issued the certificate,and that the certificate has not been modified in any way.

When a web browser establishes a new SSL connection, it checks the certificate provided by the web server. If the certificate does not have a signature from a trusted CA, or if the hostname listed in the certificate does not match the hostname used to establish the connection, it refuses to communicate with the server and usually presents a user with an appropriate error message.

By default, most web browsers are configured to trust a set of widely used certificate authorities. Because of this, an appropriate CA should be chosen when setting up a secure server, so that target users can trust the connection, otherwise they will be presented with an error message, and will have to accept the certificate manually. Since encouraging users to override certificate errors can allow an attacker to intercept the connection, you should use a trusted CA whenever possible. For more information on this, see *Table 12.22. CA lists for most common web browsers* below.

Web Browser	**Link**
Mozilla Firefox	*Mozilla root CA list*[2]
Opera	*The Opera Rootstore*[3]
Internet Explorer	*Windows root certificate program members*[4]

Table 12.22. CA lists for most common web browsers

[2] *http://www.mozilla.org/projects/security/certs/included/*

[3] *http://my.opera.com/rootstore/blog/*

[4] *http://support.microsoft.com/kb/931125*

When setting up an SSL server, you need to generate a certificate request and a private key, and then send the certificate request, proof of the company's identity, and payment to a certificate authority. Once the CA verifies the certificate request and your identity, it will send you a signed certificate you can use with your server. Alternatively, you can create a self-signed certificate that does not contain a CA signature, and thus should be used for testing purposes only.

12.1.8.2. Enabling the mod_ssl Module

If you intend to set up an SSL server, make sure you have the mod_ssl (the `mod_ssl` module) and openssl (the OpenSSL toolkit) packages installed. To do so, type the following at a shell prompt as `root`:

```
yum install mod_ssl openssl
```

This will create the `mod_ssl` configuration file at `/etc/httpd/conf.d/ssl.conf`, which is included in the main Apache HTTP Server configuration file by default. For the module to be loaded, restart the `httpd` service as described in Section 12.1.4.3, *Restarting the Service* (page 227).

12.1.8.3. Using an Existing Key and Certificate

If you have a previously created key and certificate, you can configure the SSL server to use these files instead of generating new ones. There are only two situations where this is not possible:

1. *You are changing the IP address or domain name.*

   Certificates are issued for a particular IP address and domain name pair. If one of these values changes, the certificate becomes invalid.

2. *You have a certificate from VeriSign, and you are changing the server software.*

   VeriSign, a widely used certificate authority, issues certificates for a particular software product, IP address, and domain name. Changing the software product renders the certificate invalid.

In either of the above cases, you will need to obtain a new certificate. For more information on this topic, refer to Section 12.1.8.4, *Generating a New Key and Certificate* (page 263).

If you wish to use an existing key and certificate, move the relevant files to the `/etc/pki/tls/private/` and `/etc/pki/tls/certs/` directories respectively. You can do so by running the following commands as `root`:

```
mv key_file.key /etc/pki/tls/private/hostname.key
mv certificate.crt /etc/pki/tls/certs/hostname.crt
```

Then add the following lines to the `/etc/httpd/conf.d/ssl.conf` configuration file:

```
SSLCertificateFile /etc/pki/tls/certs/hostname.crt
SSLCertificateKeyFile /etc/pki/tls/private/hostname.key
```

To load the updated configuration, restart the `httpd` service as described in Section 12.1.4.3, *Restarting the Service* (page 227).

```
~]# mv /etc/httpd/conf/httpsd.key
/etc/pki/tls/private/penguin.example.com.key
~]# mv /etc/httpd/conf/httpsd.crt
/etc/pki/tls/certs/penguin.example.com.crt
```

Example 12.81. Using a key and certificate from the Red Hat Secure Web Server

12.1.8.4. Generating a New Key and Certificate

In order to generate a new key and certificate pair, you must to have the crypto-utils package installed in your system. As `root`, you can install it by typing the following at a shell prompt:

```
yum install crypto-utils
```

This package provides a set of tools to generate and manage SSL certificates and private keys, and includes **genkey**, the Red Hat Keypair Generation utility that will guide you through the key generation process.

Replacing an existing certificate

If the server already has a valid certificate and you are replacing it with a new one, specify a different serial number. This ensures that client browsers are notified of this change, update to this new certificate as expected, and do not fail to access the page. To create a new certificate with a custom serial number, as `root`, use the following command instead of **genkey**:

```
openssl req -x509 -new -set_serial number -key hostname.key
                                              -out hostname.crt
```

Remove a previously created key

If there already is a key file for a particular hostname in your system, **genkey** will refuse to start. In this case, remove the existing file using the following command as `root`:

```
rm /etc/pki/tls/private/hostname.key
```

To run the utility, as `root`, run the `genkey` command followed by the appropriate hostname (for example, `penguin.example.com`):

```
genkey hostname
```

To complete the key and certificate creation, take the following steps:

1. Review the target locations in which the key and certificate will be stored.

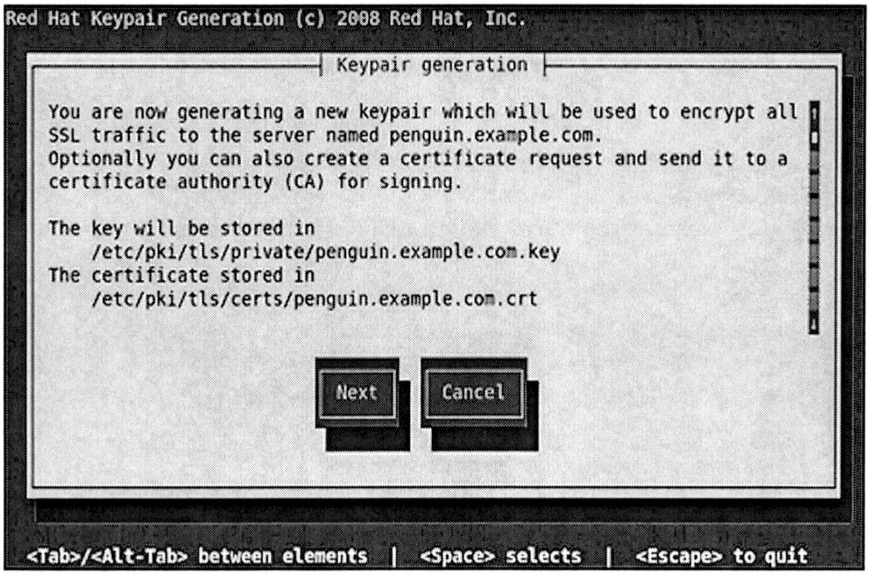

Figure 12.1. Running the genkey utility

Use the **Tab** key to select the **Next** button, and press **Enter** to proceed to the next screen.

2. Using the **Up** and **down** arrow keys, select the suitable key size. Note that while the large key increases the security, it also increases the response time of your server. Because of this, the recommended option is `1024 bits`.

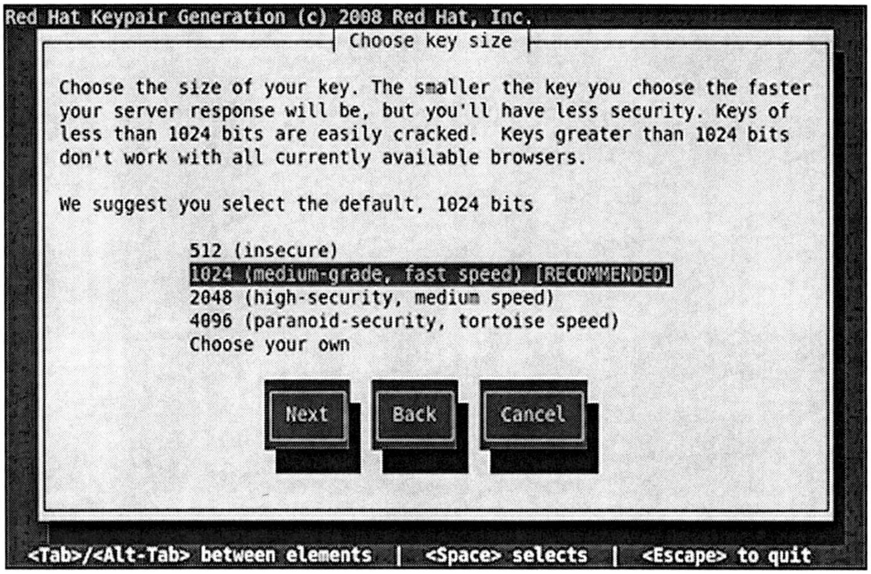

Figure 12.2. Selecting the key size

Once finished, use the **Tab** key to select the **Next** button, and press **Enter** to initiate the random bits generation process. Depending on the selected key size, this may take some time.

3. Decide whether you wish to send a certificate request to a certificate authority.

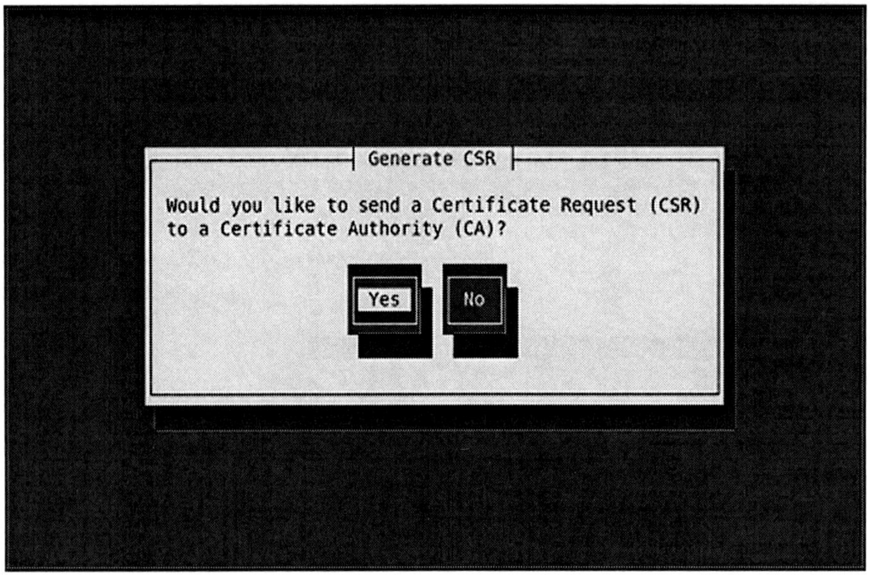

Figure 12.3. Generating a certificate request

Use the **Tab** key to select **Yes** to compose a certificate request, or **No** to generate a self-signed certificate. Then press **Enter** to confirm your choice.

4. Using the **Spacebar** key, enable (`[*]`) or disable (`[ ]`) the encryption of the private key.

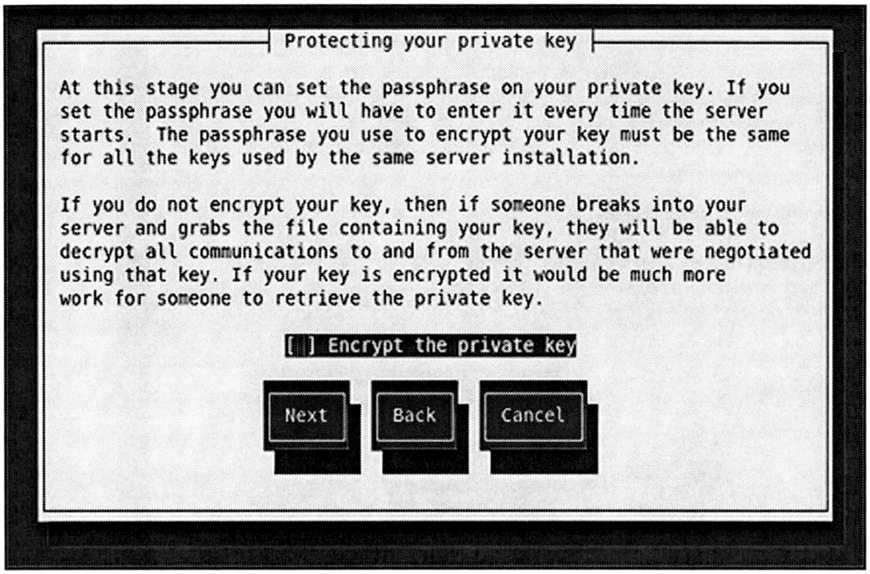

Figure 12.4. Encrypting the private key

Use the **Tab** key to select the **Next** button, and press **Enter** to proceed to the next screen.

5. If you have enabled the private key encryption, enter an adequate passphrase. Note that for security reasons, it is not displayed as you type, and it must be at least five characters long.

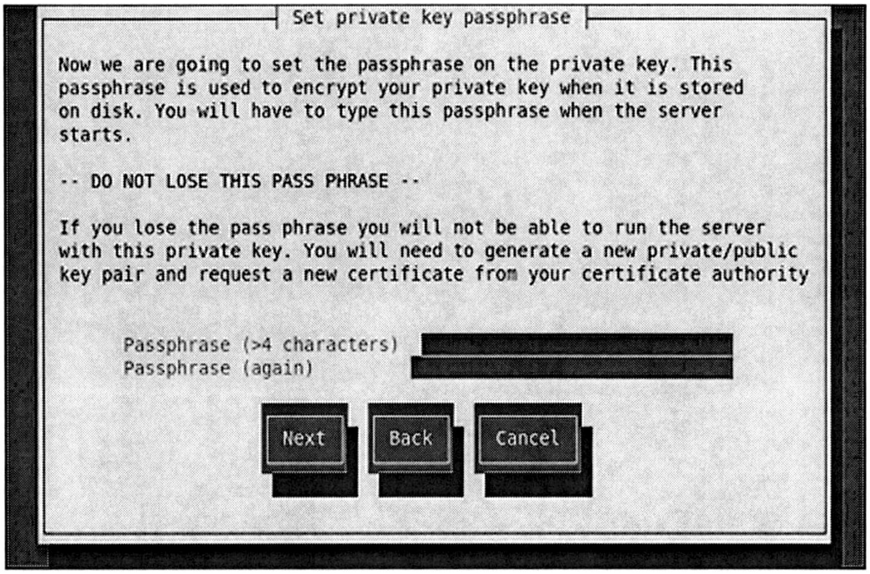

Figure 12.5. Entering a passphrase

Use the **Tab** key to select the **Next** button, and press **Enter** to proceed to the next screen.

Do not forget the passphrase

Entering the correct passphrase is required in order for the server to start. If you lose it, you will need to generate a new key and certificate.

6. Customize the certificate details.

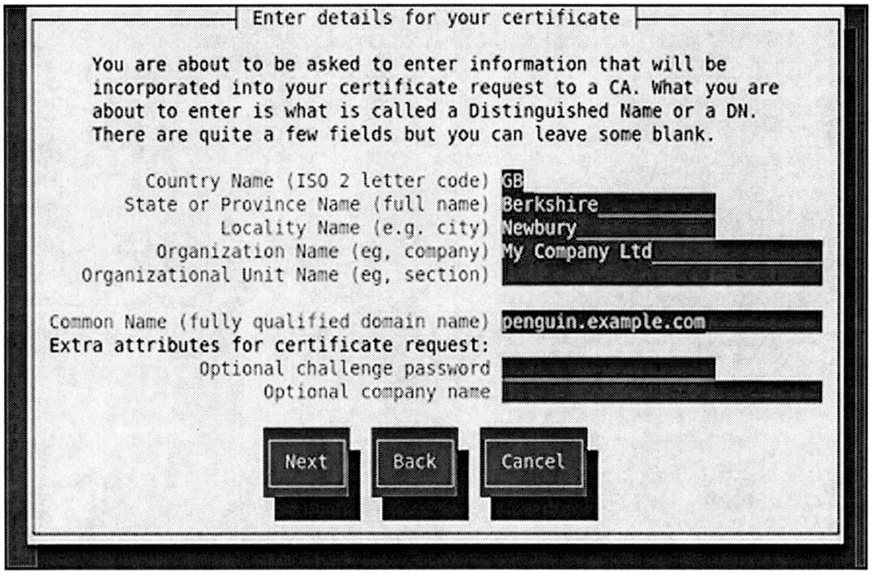

Figure 12.6. Specifying certificate information

Use the **Tab** key to select the **Next** button, and press **Enter** to finish the key generation.

7. If you have previously enabled the certificate request generation, you will be prompted to send it to a certificate authority.

```
You now need to submit your CSR and documentation to your certificate
authority. Submitting your CSR may involve pasting it into an online
web form, or mailing it to a specific address. In either case, you
should include the BEGIN and END lines.

-----BEGIN NEW CERTIFICATE REQUEST-----
MIIBqjCCARMCAQAwajELMAkGA1UEBhMCR0IxEjAQBgNVBAgTCUJlcmtzaGlyZTEQ
MA4GA1UEBxMHTmV3YnVyeTEXMBUGA1UEChMOTXkgQ29tcGFueSBMdGQxHDAaBgNV
BAMTE3BlbmdlaW4uZXhhbXBsZS5jb20wgZ8wDQYJKoZIhvcNAQEBBQADgY0AMIGJ
AoGBAJjw8bXq7wKGGXNZsNZltEe9849wUMc4uAh+X8251b8x+ptJQCanGeNhLlXU
xiL5srY2TjoTSQ5DvyFgPQmFFe3cn7v//bKNgNqd4h0EbRFGaj/hDUG3fXnjujkX
hP+9iY/eIAQZlHQSkABh/2egtIllpfDeRvsTUX376TnkIWLhAgMBAAGgADANBgkq
hkiG9w0BAQQFAAOBgQBUTjgjcntslhZKO70c5j+b4IfsBCwm4lnvGx3jOwpLdRq/
rHpx5cbHV99vcKnF3CwDrze9DgpTdjdbAccSCVgSG5GE8JZXWYD8EK8p2naJNQl1
YVX1KPi5MPLZuZ9cTb+k4K0cbug0IQiYaKNLNI/0zLE1VEWZXYFXOUBFM2gXYw==
-----END NEW CERTIFICATE REQUEST-----


A copy of this CSR has been saved in the file
/etc/pki/tls/certs/penguin.example.com.1.csr

Press return when ready to continue
█
```

Figure 12.7. Instructions on how to send a certificate request

Press **Enter** to return to a shell prompt.

Once generated, add the key and certificate locations to the `/etc/httpd/conf.d/ssl.conf` configuration file:

```
SSLCertificateFile /etc/pki/tls/certs/hostname.crt
SSLCertificateKeyFile /etc/pki/tls/private/hostname.key
```

Finally, restart the `httpd` service as described in Section 12.1.4.3, *Restarting the Service* (page 227), so that the updated configuration is loaded.

12.1.9. Additional Resources

To learn more about the Apache HTTP Server, refer to the following resources.

12.1.9.1. Installed Documentation

http://localhost/manual/

The official documentation for the Apache HTTP Server with the full description of its directives and available modules. Note that in order to access this documentation, you must have the httpd-manual package installed, and the web server must be running.

`man httpd`

The manual page for the `httpd` service containing the complete list of its command line options.

`man genkey`

The manual page for `genkey` containing the full documentation on its usage.

12.1.9.2. Useful Websites

http://httpd.apache.org/

The official website for the Apache HTTP Server with documentation on all the directives and default modules.

http://www.modssl.org/

The official website for the **mod_ssl** module.

http://www.openssl.org/

The OpenSSL home page containing further documentation, frequently asked questions, links to the mailing lists, and other useful resources.

Chapter 13.

Mail Servers

Email was born in the 1960s. The mailbox was a file in a user's home directory that was readable only by that user. Primitive mail applications appended new text messages to the bottom of the file, making the user wade through the constantly growing file to find any particular message. This system was only capable of sending messages to users on the same system.

The first network transfer of an electronic mail message file took place in 1971 when a computer engineer named Ray Tomlinson sent a test message between two machines via ARPANET—the precursor to the Internet. Communication via email soon became very popular, comprising 75 percent of ARPANET's traffic in less than two years.

Today, email systems based on standardized network protocols have evolved into some of the most widely used services on the Internet. Fedora offers many advanced applications to serve and access email.

This chapter reviews modern email protocols in use today, and some of the programs designed to send and receive email.

13.1. Email Protocols

Today, email is delivered using a client/server architecture. An email message is created using a mail client program. This program then sends the message to a server. The server then forwards the message to the recipient's email server, where the message is then supplied to the recipient's email client.

To enable this process, a variety of standard network protocols allow different machines, often running different operating systems and using different email programs, to send and receive email.

The following protocols discussed are the most commonly used in the transfer of email.

13.1.1. Mail Transport Protocols

Mail delivery from a client application to the server, and from an originating server to the destination server, is handled by the *Simple Mail Transfer Protocol* (*SMTP*).

13.1.1.1. SMTP

The primary purpose of SMTP is to transfer email between mail servers. However, it is critical for email clients as well. To send email, the client sends the message to an outgoing mail server, which in turn contacts the destination mail server for delivery. For this reason, it is necessary to specify an SMTP server when configuring an email client.

Under Fedora, a user can configure an SMTP server on the local machine to handle mail delivery. However, it is also possible to configure remote SMTP servers for outgoing mail.

One important point to make about the SMTP protocol is that it does not require authentication. This allows anyone on the Internet to send email to anyone else or even to large groups of people. It is this characteristic of SMTP that makes junk email or *spam* possible. Imposing relay restrictions limits random users on the Internet from sending email through your SMTP server, to other servers on the internet. Servers that do not impose such restrictions are called *open relay* servers.

Fedora provides the Postfix and Sendmail SMTP programs.

13.1.2. Mail Access Protocols

There are two primary protocols used by email client applications to retrieve email from mail servers: the *Post Office Protocol* (*POP*) and the *Internet Message Access Protocol* (*IMAP*).

13.1.2.1. POP

The default POP server under Fedora is **Dovecot** and is provided by the dovecot package.

Installing the dovecot package

In order to use **Dovecot**, first ensure the `dovecot` package is installed on your system by running, as `root`:

```
yum install dovecot
```

For more information on installing packages with Yum, refer to Section 4.2.4, *Installing Packages* (page 78).

When using a `POP` server, email messages are downloaded by email client applications. By default, most `POP` email clients are automatically configured to delete the message on the email server after it has been successfully transferred, however this setting usually can be changed.

`POP` is fully compatible with important Internet messaging standards, such as *Multipurpose Internet Mail Extensions* (*MIME*), which allow for email attachments.

`POP` works best for users who have one system on which to read email. It also works well for users who do not have a persistent connection to the Internet or the network containing the mail server. Unfortunately for those with slow network connections, `POP` requires client programs upon authentication to download the entire content of each message. This can take a long time if any messages have large attachments.

The most current version of the standard `POP` protocol is `POP3`.

There are, however, a variety of lesser-used `POP` protocol variants:

- *APOP* — `POP3` with `MDS` (Monash Directory Service) authentication. An encoded hash of the user's password is sent from the email client to the server rather then sending an unencrypted password.
- *KPOP* — `POP3` with Kerberos authentication.
- *RPOP* — `POP3` with `RPOP` authentication. This uses a per-user ID, similar to a password, to authenticate POP requests. However, this ID is not encrypted, so `RPOP` is no more secure than standard `POP`.

For added security, it is possible to use *Secure Socket Layer* (*SSL*) encryption for client authentication and data transfer sessions. This can be enabled by using the `pop3s` service, or by using the `/usr/sbin/stunnel` application. For more information on securing email communication, refer to Section 13.5.1, *Securing Communication* (page 297).

13.1.2.2. IMAP

The default `IMAP` server under Fedora is **Dovecot** and is provided by the dovecot package. Refer to Section 13.1.2.1, *POP* (page 273) for information on how to install **Dovecot**.

When using an `IMAP` mail server, email messages remain on the server where users can read or delete them. `IMAP` also allows client applications to create, rename, or delete mail directories on the server to organize and store email.

`IMAP` is particularly useful for users who access their email using multiple machines. The protocol is also convenient for users connecting to the mail server via a slow connection, because only the email header information is downloaded for messages until opened, saving bandwidth. The user also has the ability to delete messages without viewing or downloading them.

For convenience, `IMAP` client applications are capable of caching copies of messages locally, so the user can browse previously read messages when not directly connected to the `IMAP` server.

`IMAP`, like `POP`, is fully compatible with important Internet messaging standards, such as MIME, which allow for email attachments.

For added security, it is possible to use `SSL` encryption for client authentication and data transfer sessions. This can be enabled by using the `imaps` service, or by using the

/usr/sbin/stunnel program. For more information on securing email communication, refer to Section 13.5.1, *Securing Communication* (page 297).

Other free, as well as commercial, IMAP clients and servers are available, many of which extend the IMAP protocol and provide additional functionality.

13.1.2.3. Dovecot

The imap-login and pop3-login processes which implement the IMAP and POP3 protocols are spawned by the master dovecot daemon included in the dovecot package. The use of IMAP and POP is configured through the /etc/dovecot/dovecot.conf configuration file; by default dovecot runs IMAP and POP3 together with their secure versions using SSL. To configure dovecot to use POP, complete the following steps:

1. Edit the /etc/dovecot/dovecot.conf configuration file to make sure the protocols variable is uncommented (remove the hash sign (#) at the beginning of the line) and contains the pop3 argument. For example:

   ```
   protocols = imap imaps pop3 pop3s
   ```

   When the protocols variable is left commented out, dovecot will use the default values specified for this variable.
2. Make that change operational for the current session by running the following command as root:

   ```
   systemctl restart dovecot.service
   ```

3. Make that change operational after the next reboot by running the command:

   ```
   systemctl enable dovecot.service
   ```

The dovecot service starts the POP3 server

Please note that dovecot only reports that it started the IMAP server, but also starts the POP3 server.

Unlike SMTP, both IMAP and POP3 require connecting clients to authenticate using a username and password. By default, passwords for both protocols are passed over the network unencrypted.

To configure SSL on dovecot:

- Edit the /etc/pki/dovecot/dovecot-openssl.conf configuration file as you prefer. However, in a typical installation, this file does not require modification.
- Rename, move or delete the files /etc/pki/dovecot/certs/dovecot.pem and /etc/pki/dovecot/private/dovecot.pem.
- Execute the /usr/libexec/dovecot/mkcert.sh script which creates the dovecot self signed certificates. These certificates are copied in the /etc/pki/dovecot/certs

and /etc/pki/dovecot/private directories. To implement the changes, restart dovecot by typing the following at a shell prompt as root:

```
systemctl restart dovecot.service
```

More details on dovecot can be found online at *http://www.dovecot.org*.

13.2. Email Program Classifications

In general, all email applications fall into at least one of three classifications. Each classification plays a specific role in the process of moving and managing email messages. While most users are only aware of the specific email program they use to receive and send messages, each one is important for ensuring that email arrives at the correct destination.

13.2.1. Mail Transport Agent

A *Mail Transport Agent* (*MTA*) transports email messages between hosts using SMTP. A message may involve several MTAs as it moves to its intended destination.

While the delivery of messages between machines may seem rather straightforward, the entire process of deciding if a particular MTA can or should accept a message for delivery is quite complicated. In addition, due to problems from spam, use of a particular MTA is usually restricted by the MTA's configuration or the access configuration for the network on which the MTA resides.

Many modern email client programs can act as an MTA when sending email. However, this action should not be confused with the role of a true MTA. The sole reason email client programs are capable of sending email like an MTA is because the host running the application does not have its own MTA. This is particularly true for email client programs on non-UNIX-based operating systems. However, these client programs only send outbound messages to an MTA they are authorized to use and do not directly deliver the message to the intended recipient's email server.

Since Fedora offers two MTAs—*Postfix* and *Sendmail*—email client programs are often not required to act as an MTA. Fedora also includes a special purpose MTA called *Fetchmail*.

For more information on Postfix, Sendmail, and Fetchmail, refer to Section 13.3, *Mail Transport Agents* (page 277).

13.2.2. Mail Delivery Agent

A *Mail Delivery Agent* (*MDA*) is invoked by the MTA to file incoming email in the proper user's mailbox. In many cases, the MDA is actually a *Local Delivery Agent* (*LDA*), such as mail or Procmail.

Any program that actually handles a message for delivery to the point where it can be read by an email client application can be considered an MDA. For this reason, some MTAs (such as Sendmail and Postfix) can fill the role of an MDA when they append new email messages to a local user's mail spool file. In general, MDAs do not transport messages between systems nor do they provide a user interface; MDAs distribute and sort messages on the local machine for an email client application to access.

13.2.3. Mail User Agent

A *Mail User Agent* (*MUA*) is synonymous with an email client application. An MUA is a program that, at the very least, allows a user to read and compose email messages. Many MUAs are capable of retrieving messages via the `POP` or `IMAP` protocols, setting up mailboxes to store messages, and sending outbound messages to an MTA.

MUAs may be graphical, such as **Evolution**, or have simple text-based interfaces, such as **pine**.

13.3. Mail Transport Agents

Fedora offers two primary MTAs: Postfix and Sendmail. Postfix is configured as the default MTA, although it is easy to switch the default MTA to Sendmail. To switch the default MTA to Sendmail, as `root`, you can either uninstall Postfix or use the following command to switch to Sendmail:

```
alternatives --config mta
```

You can also use the following command to enable/disable the desired service:

```
systemctl enable|disable service.service
```

13.3.1. Postfix

Originally developed at IBM by security expert and programmer Wietse Venema, Postfix is a Sendmail-compatible MTA that is designed to be secure, fast, and easy to configure.

To improve security, Postfix uses a modular design, where small processes with limited privileges are launched by a *master* daemon. The smaller, less privileged processes perform very specific tasks related to the various stages of mail delivery and run in a change rooted environment to limit the effects of attacks.

Configuring Postfix to accept network connections from hosts other than the local computer takes only a few minor changes in its configuration file. Yet for those with more complex needs, Postfix provides a variety of configuration options, as well as third party add-ons that make it a very versatile and full-featured MTA.

The configuration files for Postfix are human readable and support upward of 250 directives. Unlike Sendmail, no macro processing is required for changes to take effect and the majority of the most commonly used options are described in the heavily commented files.

13.3.1.1. The Default Postfix Installation

The Postfix executable is `/usr/sbin/postfix`. This daemon launches all related processes needed to handle mail delivery.

Postfix stores its configuration files in the `/etc/postfix/` directory. The following is a list of the more commonly used files:

- `access` — Used for access control, this file specifies which hosts are allowed to connect to Postfix.
- `main.cf` — The global Postfix configuration file. The majority of configuration options are specified in this file.
- `master.cf` — Specifies how Postfix interacts with various processes to accomplish mail delivery.
- `transport` — Maps email addresses to relay hosts.

The `aliases` file can be found in the `/etc/` directory. This file is shared between Postfix and Sendmail. It is a configurable list required by the mail protocol that describes user ID aliases.

Configuring Postfix as a server for other clients

The default `/etc/postfix/main.cf` file does not allow Postfix to accept network connections from a host other than the local computer. For instructions on configuring Postfix as a server for other clients, refer to Section 13.3.1.2, *Basic Postfix Configuration* (page 278).

Restart the `postfix` service after changing any options in the configuration files under the `/etc/postfix` directory in order for those changes to take effect. To do so, run the following command as `root`:

```
systemctl restart postfix.service
```

13.3.1.2. Basic Postfix Configuration

By default, Postfix does not accept network connections from any host other than the local host. Perform the following steps as `root` to enable mail delivery for other hosts on the network:

- Edit the `/etc/postfix/main.cf` file with a text editor, such as `vi`.
- Uncomment the `mydomain` line by removing the hash sign (`#`), and replace *`domain.tld`* with the domain the mail server is servicing, such as `example.com`.
- Uncomment the `myorigin = $mydomain` line.
- Uncomment the `myhostname` line, and replace *`host.domain.tld`* with the hostname for the machine.
- Uncomment the `mydestination = $myhostname, localhost.$mydomain` line.
- Uncomment the `mynetworks` line, and replace *`168.100.189.0/28`* with a valid network setting for hosts that can connect to the server.
- Uncomment the `inet_interfaces = all` line.
- Comment the `inet_interfaces = localhost` line.
- Restart the `postfix` service.

Once these steps are complete, the host accepts outside emails for delivery.

Postfix has a large assortment of configuration options. One of the best ways to learn how to configure Postfix is to read the comments within the `/etc/postfix/main.cf` configuration file. Additional resources including information about Postfix configuration, SpamAssassin integration, or detailed descriptions of the `/etc/postfix/main.cf` parameters are available online at *http://www.postfix.org/*.

13.3.1.3. Using Postfix with LDAP

Postfix can use an `LDAP` directory as a source for various lookup tables (e.g.: `aliases`, `virtual`, `canonical`, etc.). This allows `LDAP` to store hierarchical user information and Postfix to only be given the result of `LDAP` queries when needed. By not storing this information locally, administrators can easily maintain it.

13.3.1.3.1. The /etc/aliases lookup example

The following is a basic example for using `LDAP` to look up the `/etc/aliases` file. Make sure your `/etc/postfix/main.cf` contains the following:

```
alias_maps = hash:/etc/aliases, ldap:/etc/postfix/ldap-aliases.cf
```

Create a `/etc/postfix/ldap-aliases.cf` file if you do not have one created already and make sure it contains the following:

```
server_host = ldap.example.com
search_base = dc=example, dc=com
```

where *`ldap.example.com`*, *`example`*, and *`com`* are parameters that need to be replaced with specification of an existing available `LDAP` server.

The /etc/postfix/ldap-aliases.cf file

The `/etc/postfix/ldap-aliases.cf` file can specify various parameters, including parameters that enable LDAP SSL and STARTTLS. For more information, refer to the `ldap_table(5)` man page.

For more information on LDAP, refer to Section 14.1, *OpenLDAP* (page 302).

13.3.2. Sendmail

Sendmail's core purpose, like other MTAs, is to safely transfer email among hosts, usually using the SMTP protocol. However, Sendmail is highly configurable, allowing control over almost every aspect of how email is handled, including the protocol used. Many system administrators elect to use Sendmail as their MTA due to its power and scalability.

13.3.2.1. Purpose and Limitations

It is important to be aware of what Sendmail is and what it can do, as opposed to what it is not. In these days of monolithic applications that fulfill multiple roles, Sendmail may seem like the only application needed to run an email server within an organization. Technically, this is true, as Sendmail can spool mail to each users' directory and deliver outbound mail for users. However, most users actually require much more than simple email delivery. Users usually want to interact with their email using an MUA, that uses POP or IMAP, to download their messages to their local machine. Or, they may prefer a Web interface to gain access to their mailbox. These other applications can work in conjunction with Sendmail, but they actually exist for different reasons and can operate separately from one another.

It is beyond the scope of this section to go into all that Sendmail should or could be configured to do. With literally hundreds of different options and rule sets, entire volumes have been dedicated to helping explain everything that can be done and how to fix things that go wrong. Refer to the Section 13.6, *Additional Resources* (page 299) for a list of Sendmail resources.

This section reviews the files installed with Sendmail by default and reviews basic configuration changes, including how to stop unwanted email (spam) and how to extend Sendmail with the *Lightweight Directory Access Protocol (LDAP)*.

13.3.2.2. The Default Sendmail Installation

In order to use Sendmail, first ensure the sendmail package is installed on your system by running, as `root`:

```
yum install sendmail
```

In order to configure Sendmail, ensure the sendmail-cf package is installed on your system by running, as `root`:

```
yum install sendmail-cf
```

For more information on installing packages with Yum, refer to Section 4.2.4, *Installing Packages* (page 78).

Before using Sendmail, the default MTA has to be switched from Postfix. For more information how to switch the default MTA refer to Section 13.3, *Mail Transport Agents* (page 277).

The Sendmail executable is `/usr/sbin/sendmail`.

Sendmail's lengthy and detailed configuration file is `/etc/mail/sendmail.cf`. Avoid editing the `sendmail.cf` file directly. To make configuration changes to Sendmail, edit the `/etc/mail/sendmail.mc` file, back up the original `/etc/mail/sendmail.cf`, and use the following alternatives to generate a new configuration file:

- Use the included makefile in `/etc/mail/` (`~]# make all -C /etc/mail/`) to create a new `/etc/mail/sendmail.cf` configuration file. All other generated files in `/etc/mail` (db files) will be regenerated if needed. The old makemap commands are still usable. The make command will automatically be used by `systemctl start|restart|reload sendmail.service`.
- Alternatively you may use the `m4` macro processor to create a new `/etc/mail/sendmail.cf`. The `m4` macro processor is not installed by default. Before using it to create `/etc/mail/sendmail.cf`, install the m4 package as `root`:
  ```
  yum install m4
  ```

More information on configuring Sendmail can be found in Section 13.3.2.3, *Common Sendmail Configuration Changes* (page 282).

Various Sendmail configuration files are installed in the `/etc/mail/` directory including:

- `access` — Specifies which systems can use Sendmail for outbound email.
- `domaintable` — Specifies domain name mapping.
- `local-host-names` — Specifies aliases for the host.
- `mailertable` — Specifies instructions that override routing for particular domains.
- `virtusertable` — Specifies a domain-specific form of aliasing, allowing multiple virtual domains to be hosted on one machine.

Several of the configuration files in `/etc/mail/`, such as `access`, `domaintable`, `mailertable` and `virtusertable`, must actually store their information in database files before Sendmail can use any configuration changes. To include any changes made to these configurations in their database files, run the following command, as `root`:

```
makemap hash /etc/mail/name < /etc/mail/name
```

where *name* represents the name of the configuration file to be updated. You may also restart the `sendmail` service for the changes to take effect by running:

```
systemctl restart sendmail.service
```

For example, to have all emails addressed to the `example.com` domain delivered to *bob@other-example.com*, add the following line to the `virtusertable` file:

```
@example.com bob@other-example.com
```

To finalize the change, the `virtusertable.db` file must be updated:

```
makemap hash /etc/mail/virtusertable < /etc/mail/virtusertable
```

Sendmail will create an updated `virtusertable.db` file containing the new configuration.

13.3.2.3. Common Sendmail Configuration Changes

When altering the Sendmail configuration file, it is best not to edit an existing file, but to generate an entirely new `/etc/mail/sendmail.cf` file.

Backup the sendmail.cf file before changing its content

Before changing the `sendmail.cf` file, it is a good idea to create a backup copy.

To add the desired functionality to Sendmail, edit the `/etc/mail/sendmail.mc` file as `root`. Once you are finished, restart the `sendmail` service and, if the m4 package is installed, the `m4` macro processor will automatically generate a new `sendmail.cf` configuration file:

```
systemctl restart sendmail.service
```

Configuring Sendmail as a server for other clients

The default `sendmail.cf` file does not allow Sendmail to accept network connections from any host other than the local computer. To configure Sendmail as a server for other clients, edit the `/etc/mail/sendmail.mc` file, and either change the address specified in the `Addr=` option of the `DAEMON_OPTIONS` directive from `127.0.0.1` to the IP address of an active network device or comment out the `DAEMON_OPTIONS` directive all together by placing `dnl` at the beginning of the line. When finished, regenerate `/etc/mail/sendmail.cf` by restarting the service:

```
systemctl restart sendmail.service
```

The default configuration which ships with Fedora works for most SMTP-only sites. However, it does not work for *UUCP* (*UNIX-to-UNIX Copy Protocol*) sites. If using UUCP mail transfers, the `/etc/mail/sendmail.mc` file must be reconfigured and a new `/etc/mail/sendmail.cf` file must be generated.

Consult the `/usr/share/sendmail-cf/README` file before editing any files in the directories under the `/usr/share/sendmail-cf` directory, as they can affect the future configuration of the `/etc/mail/sendmail.cf` file.

13.3.2.4. Masquerading

One common Sendmail configuration is to have a single machine act as a mail gateway for all machines on the network. For instance, a company may want to have a machine called `mail.example.com` that handles all of their email and assigns a consistent return address to all outgoing mail.

In this situation, the Sendmail server must masquerade the machine names on the company network so that their return address is `user@example.com` instead of `user@host.example.com`.

To do this, add the following lines to `/etc/mail/sendmail.mc`:

```
FEATURE(always_add_domain)dnl
FEATURE(`masquerade_entire_domain')dnl
FEATURE(`masquerade_envelope')dnl
FEATURE(`allmasquerade')dnl
MASQUERADE_AS(`bigcorp.com.')dnl
MASQUERADE_DOMAIN(`bigcorp.com.')dnl
MASQUERADE_AS(bigcorp.com)dnl
```

After generating a new `sendmail.cf` using the `m4` macro processor, this configuration makes all mail from inside the network appear as if it were sent from `bigcorp.com`.

13.3.2.5. Stopping Spam

Email spam can be defined as unnecessary and unwanted email received by a user who never requested the communication. It is a disruptive, costly, and widespread abuse of Internet communication standards.

Sendmail makes it relatively easy to block new spamming techniques being employed to send junk email. It even blocks many of the more usual spamming methods by default. Main anti-spam features available in sendmail are *header checks, relaying denial* (default from version 8.9), *access database and sender information checks.*

For example, forwarding of SMTP messages, also called relaying, has been disabled by default since Sendmail version 8.9. Before this change occurred, Sendmail directed the mail host (`x.edu`) to accept messages from one party (`y.com`) and sent them to a different party (`z.net`). Now, however, Sendmail must be configured to permit any domain to relay mail through the server. To configure relay domains, edit the `/etc/mail/relay-domains` file and restart Sendmail:

```
systemctl restart sendmail.service
```

However, many times users are bombarded with spam from other servers throughout the Internet. In these instances, Sendmail's access control features available through the `/etc/mail/access` file can be used to prevent connections from unwanted hosts. The following example illustrates how this file can be used to both block and specifically allow access to the Sendmail server:

```
badspammer.com ERROR:550 "Go away and do not spam us" tux.badspammer.com OK 10.0 RELAY
```

This example shows that any email sent from `badspammer.com` is blocked with a 550 RFC-821 compliant error code, with a message sent back to the spammer. Email sent from the `tux.badspammer.com` sub-domain, is accepted. The last line shows that any email sent from the 10.0.*.* network can be relayed through the mail server.

Because the `/etc/mail/access.db` file is a database, use the `makemap` command to update any changes. Do this using the following command as `root`:

```
makemap hash /etc/mail/access < /etc/mail/access
```

Message header analysis allows you to reject mail based on header contents. SMTP servers store information about an email's journey in the message header. As the message travels from one MTA to another, each puts in a `Received` header above all the other `Received` headers. It is important to note that this information may be altered by spammers.

The above examples only represent a small part of what Sendmail can do in terms of allowing or blocking access. Refer to the `/usr/share/sendmail-cf/README` for more information and examples.

Since Sendmail calls the Procmail MDA when delivering mail, it is also possible to use a spam filtering program, such as SpamAssassin, to identify and file spam for users. Refer to Section 13.4.2.6, *Spam Filters* (page 296) for more information about using SpamAssassin.

13.3.2.6. Using Sendmail with LDAP

Using LDAP is a very quick and powerful way to find specific information about a particular user from a much larger group. For example, an LDAP server can be used to look up a particular email address from a common corporate directory by the user's last name. In this kind of implementation, LDAP is largely separate from Sendmail, with LDAP storing the hierarchical user information and Sendmail only being given the result of LDAP queries in pre-addressed email messages.

However, Sendmail supports a much greater integration with LDAP, where it uses LDAP to replace separately maintained files, such as `/etc/aliases` and `/etc/mail/virtusertables`, on different mail servers that work together to support a medium- to enterprise-level organization. In short, LDAP abstracts the mail routing level from Sendmail and its separate configuration files to a powerful LDAP cluster that can be leveraged by many different applications.

The current version of Sendmail contains support for LDAP. To extend the Sendmail server using LDAP, first get an LDAP server, such as **OpenLDAP**, running and properly configured. Then edit the `/etc/mail/sendmail.mc` to include the following:

```
LDAPROUTE_DOMAIN('yourdomain.com')dnl
FEATURE('ldap_routing')dnl
```

Advanced configuration

This is only for a very basic configuration of Sendmail with LDAP. The configuration can differ greatly from this depending on the implementation of LDAP, especially when configuring several Sendmail machines to use a common LDAP server.

Consult `/usr/share/sendmail-cf/README` for detailed LDAP routing configuration instructions and examples.

Next, recreate the `/etc/mail/sendmail.cf` file by running the `m4` macro processor and again restarting Sendmail. Refer to Section 13.3.2.3, *Common Sendmail Configuration Changes* (page 282) for instructions.

For more information on LDAP, refer to Section 14.1, *OpenLDAP* (page 302).

13.3.3. Fetchmail

Fetchmail is an MTA which retrieves email from remote servers and delivers it to the local MTA. Many users appreciate the ability to separate the process of downloading their messages located on a remote server from the process of reading and organizing their email in an MUA. Designed with the needs of dial-up users in mind, Fetchmail connects and quickly downloads all of the email messages to the mail spool file using any number of protocols, including POP3 and IMAP. It can even forward email messages to an SMTP server, if necessary.

Installing the fetchmail package

In order to use **Fetchmail**, first ensure the fetchmail package is installed on your system by running, as `root`:

```
yum install fetchmail
```

For more information on installing packages with Yum, refer to Section 4.2.4, *Installing Packages* (page 78).

Fetchmail is configured for each user through the use of a `.fetchmailrc` file in the user's home directory. If it does not already exist, create the `.fetchmailrc` file in your home directory

Using preferences in the `.fetchmailrc` file, Fetchmail checks for email on a remote server and downloads it. It then delivers it to port `25` on the local machine, using the local MTA to place the email in the correct user's spool file. If Procmail is available, it is launched to filter the email and place it in a mailbox so that it can be read by an MUA.

13.3.3.1. Fetchmail Configuration Options

Although it is possible to pass all necessary options on the command line to check for email on a remote server when executing Fetchmail, using a `.fetchmailrc` file is much easier. Place any desired configuration options in the `.fetchmailrc` file for those options to be used each time the `fetchmail` command is issued. It is possible to override these at the time Fetchmail is run by specifying that option on the command line.

A user's `.fetchmailrc` file contains three classes of configuration options:

- *global options* — Gives Fetchmail instructions that control the operation of the program or provide settings for every connection that checks for email.
- *server options* — Specifies necessary information about the server being polled, such as the hostname, as well as preferences for specific email servers, such as the port to check or number of seconds to wait before timing out. These options affect every user using that server.
- *user options* — Contains information, such as username and password, necessary to authenticate and check for email using a specified email server.

Global options appear at the top of the `.fetchmailrc` file, followed by one or more server options, each of which designate a different email server that Fetchmail should check. User options follow server options for each user account checking that email server. Like server options, multiple user options may be specified for use with a particular server as well as to check multiple email accounts on the same server.

Server options are called into service in the `.fetchmailrc` file by the use of a special option verb, `poll` or `skip`, that precedes any of the server information. The `poll` action tells Fetchmail to use this server option when it is run, which checks for email using the specified user options. Any server options after a `skip` action, however, are not checked unless this server's hostname is specified when Fetchmail is invoked. The `skip` option is useful when testing configurations in the `.fetchmailrc` file because it only checks skipped servers when specifically invoked, and does not affect any currently working configurations.

The following is a sample example of a `.fetchmailrc` file:

```
set postmaster "user1"
set bouncemail

poll pop.domain.com proto pop3
    user 'user1' there with password 'secret' is user1 here

poll mail.domain2.com
    user 'user5' there with password 'secret2' is user1 here
    user 'user7' there with password 'secret3' is user1 here
```

In this example, the global options specify that the user is sent email as a last resort (`postmaster` option) and all email errors are sent to the postmaster instead of the sender (bouncemail option). The set action tells Fetchmail that this line contains a global option. Then, two email servers are specified, one set to check using POP3, the other for trying various protocols to find one that works. Two users are checked using the second server option, but all email found for any user is sent to user1's mail spool. This allows multiple mailboxes to be checked on multiple servers, while appearing in a single MUA inbox. Each user's specific information begins with the user action.

Omitting the password from the configuration

Users are not required to place their password in the .fetchmailrc file. Omitting the with password '*password*' section causes Fetchmail to ask for a password when it is launched.

Fetchmail has numerous global, server, and local options. Many of these options are rarely used or only apply to very specific situations. The fetchmail man page explains each option in detail, but the most common ones are listed in the following three sections.

13.3.3.2. Global Options

Each global option should be placed on a single line after a set action.

- daemon *seconds* — Specifies daemon-mode, where Fetchmail stays in the background. Replace *seconds* with the number of seconds Fetchmail is to wait before polling the server.
- postmaster — Specifies a local user to send mail to in case of delivery problems.
- syslog — Specifies the log file for errors and status messages. By default, this is /var/log/maillog.

13.3.3.3. Server Options

Server options must be placed on their own line in .fetchmailrc after a poll or skip action.

- auth *auth-type* — Replace *auth-type* with the type of authentication to be used. By default, password authentication is used, but some protocols support other types of authentication, including kerberos_v5, kerberos_v4, and ssh. If the any authentication type is used, Fetchmail first tries methods that do not require a password, then methods that mask the password, and finally attempts to send the password unencrypted to authenticate to the server.
- interval *number* — Polls the specified server every *number* of times that it checks for email on all configured servers. This option is generally used for email servers where the user rarely receives messages.

- `port` *`port-number`* — Replace *`port-number`* with the port number. This value overrides the default port number for the specified protocol.
- `proto` *`protocol`* — Replace *`protocol`* with the protocol, such as `pop3` or `imap`, to use when checking for messages on the server.
- `timeout` *`seconds`* — Replace *`seconds`* with the number of seconds of server inactivity after which Fetchmail gives up on a connection attempt. If this value is not set, a default of `300` seconds is assumed.

13.3.3.4. User Options

User options may be placed on their own lines beneath a server option or on the same line as the server option. In either case, the defined options must follow the `user` option (defined below).

- `fetchall` — Orders Fetchmail to download all messages in the queue, including messages that have already been viewed. By default, Fetchmail only pulls down new messages.
- `fetchlimit` *`number`* — Replace *`number`* with the number of messages to be retrieved before stopping.
- `flush` — Deletes all previously viewed messages in the queue before retrieving new messages.
- `limit` *`max-number-bytes`* — Replace *`max-number-bytes`* with the maximum size in bytes that messages are allowed to be when retrieved by Fetchmail. This option is useful with slow network links, when a large message takes too long to download.
- `password '`*`password`*`'` — Replace *`password`* with the user's password.
- `preconnect "`*`command`*`"` — Replace *`command`* with a command to be executed before retrieving messages for the user.
- `postconnect "`*`command`*`"` — Replace *`command`* with a command to be executed after retrieving messages for the user.
- `ssl` — Activates SSL encryption.
- `user "`*`username`*`"` — Replace *`username`* with the username used by Fetchmail to retrieve messages. *This option must precede all other user options.*

13.3.3.5. Fetchmail Command Options

Most Fetchmail options used on the command line when executing the `fetchmail` command mirror the `.fetchmailrc` configuration options. In this way, Fetchmail may be used with or without a configuration file. These options are not used on the command line by most users because it is easier to leave them in the `.fetchmailrc` file.

There may be times when it is desirable to run the `fetchmail` command with other options for a particular purpose. It is possible to issue command options to temporarily override a `.fetchmailrc` setting that is causing an error, as any options specified at the command line override configuration file options.

13.3.3.6. Informational or Debugging Options

Certain options used after the `fetchmail` command can supply important information.

- `--configdump` — Displays every possible option based on information from `.fetchmailrc` and Fetchmail defaults. No email is retrieved for any users when using this option.
- `-s` — Executes Fetchmail in silent mode, preventing any messages, other than errors, from appearing after the `fetchmail` command.
- `-v` — Executes Fetchmail in verbose mode, displaying every communication between Fetchmail and remote email servers.
- `-V` — Displays detailed version information, lists its global options, and shows settings to be used with each user, including the email protocol and authentication method. No email is retrieved for any users when using this option.

13.3.3.7. Special Options

These options are occasionally useful for overriding defaults often found in the `.fetchmailrc` file.

- `-a` — Fetchmail downloads all messages from the remote email server, whether new or previously viewed. By default, Fetchmail only downloads new messages.
- `-k` — Fetchmail leaves the messages on the remote email server after downloading them. This option overrides the default behavior of deleting messages after downloading them.
- `-l` *`max-number-bytes`* — Fetchmail does not download any messages over a particular size and leaves them on the remote email server.
- `--quit` — Quits the Fetchmail daemon process.

More commands and `.fetchmailrc` options can be found in the `fetchmail` man page.

13.3.4. Mail Transport Agent (MTA) Configuration

A *Mail Transport Agent* (MTA) is essential for sending email. A *Mail User Agent* (MUA) such as **Evolution**, **Thunderbird**, and **Mutt**, is used to read and compose email. When a user sends an email from an MUA, the message is handed off to the MTA, which sends the message through a series of MTAs until it reaches its destination.

Even if a user does not plan to send email from the system, some automated tasks or system programs might use the `/bin/mail` command to send email containing log messages to the `root` user of the local system.

Fedora 15 provides two MTAs: Postfix and Sendmail. If both are installed, Postfix is the default MTA.

13.4. Mail Delivery Agents

Fedora includes two primary MDAs, Procmail and `mail`. Both of the applications are considered LDAs and both move email from the MTA's spool file into the user's mailbox. However, Procmail provides a robust filtering system.

This section details only Procmail. For information on the `mail` command, consult its man page (`man mail`).

Procmail delivers and filters email as it is placed in the mail spool file of the localhost. It is powerful, gentle on system resources, and widely used. Procmail can play a critical role in delivering email to be read by email client applications.

Procmail can be invoked in several different ways. Whenever an MTA places an email into the mail spool file, Procmail is launched. Procmail then filters and files the email for the MUA and quits. Alternatively, the MUA can be configured to execute Procmail any time a message is received so that messages are moved into their correct mailboxes. By default, the presence of `/etc/procmailrc` or of a `~/.procmailrc` file (also called an *rc* file) in the user's home directory invokes Procmail whenever an MTA receives a new message.

By default, no system-wide `rc` files exist in the `/etc/` directory and no `.procmailrc` files exist in any user's home directory. Therefore, to use Procmail, each user must construct a `.procmailrc` file with specific environment variables and rules.

Whether Procmail acts upon an email message depends upon whether the message matches a specified set of conditions or *recipes* in the `rc` file. If a message matches a recipe, then the email is placed in a specified file, is deleted, or is otherwise processed.

When Procmail starts, it reads the email message and separates the body from the header information. Next, Procmail looks for a `/etc/procmailrc` file and `rc` files in the `/etc/procmailrcs` directory for default, system-wide, Procmail environmental variables and recipes. Procmail then searches for a `.procmailrc` file in the user's home directory. Many users also create additional `rc` files for Procmail that are referred to within the `.procmailrc` file in their home directory.

13.4.1. Procmail Configuration

The Procmail configuration file contains important environmental variables. These variables specify things such as which messages to sort and what to do with the messages that do not match any recipes.

These environmental variables usually appear at the beginning of the `~/.procmailrc` file in the following format:

`env-variable="value"`

In this example, *`env-variable`* is the name of the variable and *`value`* defines the variable.

There are many environment variables not used by most Procmail users and many of the more important environment variables are already defined by a default value. Most of the time, the following variables are used:

- `DEFAULT` — Sets the default mailbox where messages that do not match any recipes are placed.

  The default `DEFAULT` value is the same as `$ORGMAIL`.

- `INCLUDERC` — Specifies additional `rc` files containing more recipes for messages to be checked against. This breaks up the Procmail recipe lists into individual files that fulfill different roles, such as blocking spam and managing email lists, that can then be turned off or on by using comment characters in the user's `~/.procmailrc` file.

  For example, lines in a user's `.procmailrc` file may look like this:

  `MAILDIR=$HOME/Msgs INCLUDERC=$MAILDIR/lists.rc INCLUDERC=$MAILDIR/spam.rc`

  To turn off Procmail filtering of email lists but leaving spam control in place, comment out the first `INCLUDERC` line with a hash sign (`#`).

- `LOCKSLEEP` — Sets the amount of time, in seconds, between attempts by Procmail to use a particular lockfile. The default is `8` seconds.

- `LOCKTIMEOUT` — Sets the amount of time, in seconds, that must pass after a lockfile was last modified before Procmail assumes that the lockfile is old and can be deleted. The default is `1024` seconds.

- `LOGFILE` — The file to which any Procmail information or error messages are written.

- `MAILDIR` — Sets the current working directory for Procmail. If set, all other Procmail paths are relative to this directory.

- `ORGMAIL` — Specifies the original mailbox, or another place to put the messages if they cannot be placed in the default or recipe-required location.

  By default, a value of `/var/spool/mail/$LOGNAME` is used.

- `SUSPEND` — Sets the amount of time, in seconds, that Procmail pauses if a necessary resource, such as swap space, is not available.

- `SWITCHRC` — Allows a user to specify an external file containing additional Procmail recipes, much like the `INCLUDERC` option, except that recipe checking is actually stopped on the referring configuration file and only the recipes on the `SWITCHRC`-specified file are used.

- `VERBOSE` — Causes Procmail to log more information. This option is useful for debugging.

Other important environmental variables are pulled from the shell, such as `LOGNAME`, which is the login name; `HOME`, which is the location of the home directory; and `SHELL`, which is the default shell.

A comprehensive explanation of all environments variables, as well as their default values, is available in the `procmailrc` man page.

13.4.2. Procmail Recipes

New users often find the construction of recipes the most difficult part of learning to use Procmail. To some extent, this is understandable, as recipes do their message matching using *regular expressions*, which is a particular format used to specify qualifications for a matching string. However, regular expressions are not very difficult to construct and even less difficult to understand when read. Additionally, the consistency of the way Procmail recipes are written, regardless of regular expressions, makes it easy to learn by example. To see example Procmail recipes, refer to Section 13.4.2.5, *Recipe Examples* (page 294).

Procmail recipes take the following form:

```
:0flags: lockfile-name * special-condition-character
       condition-1 * special-condition-character
       condition-2 * special-condition-character
       condition-N
       special-action-character
       action-to-perform
```

The first two characters in a Procmail recipe are a colon and a zero. Various flags can be placed after the zero to control how Procmail processes the recipe. A colon after the *`flags`* section specifies that a lockfile is created for this message. If a lockfile is created, the name can be specified by replacing *`lockfile-name`* .

A recipe can contain several conditions to match against the message. If it has no conditions, every message matches the recipe. Regular expressions are placed in some conditions to facilitate message matching. If multiple conditions are used, they must all match for the action to be performed. Conditions are checked based on the flags set in the recipe's first line. Optional special characters placed after the asterisk character (`*`) can further control the condition.

The *`action-to-perform`* argument specifies the action taken when the message matches one of the conditions. There can only be one action per recipe. In many cases, the name of a mailbox is used here to direct matching messages into that file, effectively sorting the email. Special action characters may also be used before the action is specified. Refer to Section 13.4.2.4, *Special Conditions and Actions* (page 294) for more information.

13.4.2.1. Delivering vs. Non-Delivering Recipes

The action used if the recipe matches a particular message determines whether it is considered a *delivering* or *non-delivering* recipe. A delivering recipe contains an action that writes the message to a file, sends the message to another program, or forwards the message to another email address. A non-delivering recipe covers any other actions, such as a *nesting block*. A nesting block is a set of actions, contained in braces `{ }`, that are performed on messages which match the recipe's conditions. Nesting blocks can be nested inside one another, providing greater control for identifying and performing actions on messages.

When messages match a delivering recipe, Procmail performs the specified action and stops comparing the message against any other recipes. Messages that match non-delivering recipes continue to be compared against other recipes.

13.4.2.2. Flags

Flags are essential to determine how or if a recipe's conditions are compared to a message. The following flags are commonly used:

- `A` — Specifies that this recipe is only used if the previous recipe without an `A` or `a` flag also matched this message.
- `a` — Specifies that this recipe is only used if the previous recipe with an `A` or `a` flag also matched this message *and* was successfully completed.
- `B` — Parses the body of the message and looks for matching conditions.
- `b` — Uses the body in any resulting action, such as writing the message to a file or forwarding it. This is the default behavior.
- `c` — Generates a carbon copy of the email. This is useful with delivering recipes, since the required action can be performed on the message and a copy of the message can continue being processed in the `rc` files.
- `D` — Makes the `egrep` comparison case-sensitive. By default, the comparison process is not case-sensitive.
- `E` — While similar to the `A` flag, the conditions in the recipe are only compared to the message if the immediately preceding the recipe without an `E` flag did not match. This is comparable to an *else* action.
- `e` — The recipe is compared to the message only if the action specified in the immediately preceding recipe fails.
- `f` — Uses the pipe as a filter.
- `H` — Parses the header of the message and looks for matching conditions. This is the default behavior.
- `h` — Uses the header in a resulting action. This is the default behavior.

- `w` — Tells Procmail to wait for the specified filter or program to finish, and reports whether or not it was successful before considering the message filtered.
- `W` — Is identical to `w` except that "Program failure" messages are suppressed.

For a detailed list of additional flags, refer to the `procmailrc` man page.

13.4.2.3. Specifying a Local Lockfile

Lockfiles are very useful with Procmail to ensure that more than one process does not try to alter a message simultaneously. Specify a local lockfile by placing a colon (`:`) after any flags on a recipe's first line. This creates a local lockfile based on the destination file name plus whatever has been set in the `LOCKEXT` global environment variable.

Alternatively, specify the name of the local lockfile to be used with this recipe after the colon.

13.4.2.4. Special Conditions and Actions

Special characters used before Procmail recipe conditions and actions change the way they are interpreted.

The following characters may be used after the asterisk character (`*`) at the beginning of a recipe's condition line:

- `!` — In the condition line, this character inverts the condition, causing a match to occur only if the condition does not match the message.
- `<` — Checks if the message is under a specified number of bytes.
- `>` — Checks if the message is over a specified number of bytes.

The following characters are used to perform special actions:

- `!` — In the action line, this character tells Procmail to forward the message to the specified email addresses.
- `$` — Refers to a variable set earlier in the `rc` file. This is often used to set a common mailbox that is referred to by various recipes.
- `|` — Starts a specified program to process the message.
- { and } — Constructs a nesting block, used to contain additional recipes to apply to matching messages.

If no special character is used at the beginning of the action line, Procmail assumes that the action line is specifying the mailbox in which to write the message.

13.4.2.5. Recipe Examples

Procmail is an extremely flexible program, but as a result of this flexibility, composing Procmail recipes from scratch can be difficult for new users.

The best way to develop the skills to build Procmail recipe conditions stems from a strong understanding of regular expressions combined with looking at many examples built by others. A thorough explanation of regular expressions is beyond the scope of this section. The structure of Procmail recipes and useful sample Procmail recipes can be found at various places on the Internet (such as *http://www.iki.fi/era/procmail/links.html*). The proper use and adaptation of regular expressions can be derived by viewing these recipe examples. In addition, introductory information about basic regular expression rules can be found in the `grep` man page.

The following simple examples demonstrate the basic structure of Procmail recipes and can provide the foundation for more intricate constructions.

A basic recipe may not even contain conditions, as is illustrated in the following example:

```
:0: new-mail.spool
```

The first line specifies that a local lockfile is to be created but does not specify a name, so Procmail uses the destination file name and appends the value specified in the `LOCKEXT` environment variable. No condition is specified, so every message matches this recipe and is placed in the single spool file called `new-mail.spool`, located within the directory specified by the `MAILDIR` environment variable. An MUA can then view messages in this file.

A basic recipe, such as this, can be placed at the end of all `rc` files to direct messages to a default location.

The following example matched messages from a specific email address and throws them away.

```
:0 * ^From: spammer@domain.com /dev/null
```

With this example, any messages sent by `spammer@domain.com` are sent to the `/dev/null` device, deleting them.

Sending messages to /dev/null

Be certain that rules are working as intended before sending messages to `/dev/null` for permanent deletion. If a recipe inadvertently catches unintended messages, and those messages disappear, it becomes difficult to troubleshoot the rule.

A better solution is to point the recipe's action to a special mailbox, which can be checked from time to time to look for false positives. Once satisfied that no messages are accidentally being matched, delete the mailbox and direct the action to send the messages to `/dev/null`.

The following recipe grabs email sent from a particular mailing list and places it in a specified folder.

```
:0: * ^(From|Cc|To).*tux-lug tuxlug
```

Any messages sent from the `tux-lug@domain.com` mailing list are placed in the `tuxlug` mailbox automatically for the MUA. Note that the condition in this example matches the message if it has the mailing list's email address on the `From`, `Cc`, or `To` lines.

Consult the many Procmail online resources available in Section 13.6, *Additional Resources* (page 299) for more detailed and powerful recipes.

13.4.2.6. Spam Filters

Because it is called by Sendmail, Postfix, and Fetchmail upon receiving new emails, Procmail can be used as a powerful tool for combating spam.

This is particularly true when Procmail is used in conjunction with SpamAssassin. When used together, these two applications can quickly identify spam emails, and sort or destroy them.

SpamAssassin uses header analysis, text analysis, blacklists, a spam-tracking database, and self-learning Bayesian spam analysis to quickly and accurately identify and tag spam.

Installing the spamassassin package

In order to use **SpamAssassin**, first ensure the spamassassin package is installed on your system by running, as `root`:

```
yum install spamassassin
```

For more information on installing packages with Yum, refer to Section 4.2.4, *Installing Packages* (page 78).

The easiest way for a local user to use SpamAssassin is to place the following line near the top of the `~/.procmailrc` file:

```
INCLUDERC=/etc/mail/spamassassin/spamassassin-default.rc
```

The `/etc/mail/spamassassin/spamassassin-default.rc` contains a simple Procmail rule that activates SpamAssassin for all incoming email. If an email is determined to be spam, it is tagged in the header as such and the title is prepended with the following pattern:

```
*****SPAM*****
```

The message body of the email is also prepended with a running tally of what elements caused it to be diagnosed as spam.

To file email tagged as spam, a rule similar to the following can be used:

```
:0 Hw * ^X-Spam-Status: Yes spam
```

This rule files all email tagged in the header as spam into a mailbox called `spam`.

Since SpamAssassin is a Perl script, it may be necessary on busy servers to use the binary SpamAssassin daemon (`spamd`) and the client application (**spamc**). Configuring SpamAssassin this way, however, requires `root` access to the host.

To start the `spamd` daemon, type the following command:

```
systemctl start spamassassin.service
```

To start the SpamAssassin daemon when the system is booted, run:

```
systemctl enable spamassassin.service
```

Refer to Chapter 7, *Services and Daemons* (page 120) for more information on how to configure services in Fedora.

To configure Procmail to use the SpamAssassin client application instead of the Perl script, place the following line near the top of the `~/.procmailrc` file. For a system-wide configuration, place it in `/etc/procmailrc`:

```
INCLUDERC=/etc/mail/spamassassin/spamassassin-spamc.rc
```

13.5. Mail User Agents

Fedora offers a variety of email programs, both, graphical email client programs, such as **Evolution**, and text-based email programs such as `mutt`.

The remainder of this section focuses on securing communication between a client and a server.

13.5.1. Securing Communication

Popular MUAs included with Fedora, such as **Evolution** and `mutt` offer SSL-encrypted email sessions.

Like any other service that flows over a network unencrypted, important email information, such as usernames, passwords, and entire messages, may be intercepted and viewed by users on the network. Additionally, since the standard `POP` and `IMAP` protocols pass authentication information unencrypted, it is possible for an attacker to gain access to user accounts by collecting usernames and passwords as they are passed over the network.

13.5.1.1. Secure Email Clients

Most Linux MUAs designed to check email on remote servers support SSL encryption. To use SSL when retrieving email, it must be enabled on both the email client and the server.

SSL is easy to enable on the client-side, often done with the click of a button in the MUA's configuration window or via an option in the MUA's configuration file. Secure `IMAP` and `POP` have known port numbers (`993` and `995`, respectively) that the MUA uses to authenticate and download messages.

13.5.1.2. Securing Email Client Communications

Offering SSL encryption to `IMAP` and `POP` users on the email server is a simple matter.

First, create an SSL certificate. This can be done in two ways: by applying to a *Certificate Authority* (*CA*) for an SSL certificate or by creating a self-signed certificate.

Avoid using self-signed certificates

Self-signed certificates should be used for testing purposes only. Any server used in a production environment should use an SSL certificate granted by a CA.

To create a self-signed SSL certificate for `IMAP` or `POP`, change to the `/etc/pki/dovecot/` directory, edit the certificate parameters in the `/etc/pki/dovecot/dovecot-openssl.conf` configuration file as you prefer, and type the following commands, as `root`:

```
dovecot]# rm -f certs/dovecot.pem private/dovecot.pem
dovecot]# /usr/libexec/dovecot/mkcert.sh
```

Once finished, make sure you have the following configurations in your `/etc/dovecot/conf.d/10-ssl.conf` file:

```
ssl_cert = </etc/pki/dovecot/certs/dovecot.pem
ssl_key = </etc/pki/dovecot/private/dovecot.pem
```

Execute the `systemctl restart dovecot.service` command to restart the `dovecot` daemon.

Alternatively, the `stunnel` command can be used as an SSL encryption wrapper around the standard, non-secure connections to `IMAP` or `POP` services.

The `stunnel` utility uses external OpenSSL libraries included with Fedora to provide strong cryptography and to protect the network connections. It is recommended to apply to a CA to obtain an SSL certificate, but it is also possible to create a self-signed certificate.

Installing the stunnel package

In order to use `stunnel`, first ensure the stunnel package is installed on your system by running, as `root`:

```
yum install stunnel
```

For more information on installing packages with Yum, refer to Section 4.2.4, *Installing Packages* (page 78).

To create a self-signed SSL certificate, change to the `/etc/pki/tls/certs/` directory, and type the following command:

```
certs]# make stunnel.pem
```

Answer all of the questions to complete the process.

Once the certificate is generated, create an `stunnel` configuration file, for example `/etc/stunnel/mail.conf`, with the following content:

```
cert = /etc/pki/tls/certs/stunnel.pem

[pop3s]
accept  = 995
connect = 110

[imaps]
accept  = 993
connect = 143
```

Once you start `stunnel` with the created configuration file using the `/usr/bin/stunnel /etc/stunnel/mail.conf` command, it will be possible to use an `IMAP` or a `POP` email client and connect to the email server using SSL encryption.

For more information on `stunnel`, refer to the `stunnel` man page or the documents in the `/usr/share/doc/stunnel-`*`version-number`* / directory, where *`version-number`* is the version number of `stunnel`.

13.6. Additional Resources

The following is a list of additional documentation about email applications.

13.6.1. Installed Documentation

- Information on configuring Sendmail is included with the `sendmail` and `sendmail-cf` packages.
  - `/usr/share/sendmail-cf/README` — Contains information on the `m4` macro processor, file locations for Sendmail, supported mailers, how to access enhanced features, and more.

  In addition, the `sendmail` and `aliases` man pages contain helpful information covering various Sendmail options and the proper configuration of the Sendmail `/etc/mail/aliases` file.
- `/usr/share/doc/postfix-`*`version-number`* — Contains a large amount of information about ways to configure Postfix. Replace *`version-number`* with the version number of Postfix.
- `/usr/share/doc/fetchmail-`*`version-number`* — Contains a full list of Fetchmail features in the `FEATURES` file and an introductory `FAQ` document. Replace *`version-number`* with the version number of Fetchmail.
- `/usr/share/doc/procmail-`*`version-number`* — Contains a `README` file that provides an overview of Procmail, a `FEATURES` file that explores every program

feature, and an `FAQ` file with answers to many common configuration questions. Replace *`version-number`* with the version number of Procmail.

When learning how Procmail works and creating new recipes, the following Procmail man pages are invaluable:

- `procmail` — Provides an overview of how Procmail works and the steps involved with filtering email.
- `procmailrc` — Explains the `rc` file format used to construct recipes.
- `procmailex` — Gives a number of useful, real-world examples of Procmail recipes.
- `procmailsc` — Explains the weighted scoring technique used by Procmail to match a particular recipe to a message.
- `/usr/share/doc/spamassassin-`*`version-number`*`/` — Contains a large amount of information pertaining to SpamAssassin. Replace *`version-number`* with the version number of the `spamassassin` package.

13.6.2. Useful Websites

- *http://www.sendmail.org/* — Offers a thorough technical breakdown of Sendmail features, documentation and configuration examples.
- *http://www.sendmail.com/* — Contains news, interviews and articles concerning Sendmail, including an expanded view of the many options available.
- *http://www.postfix.org/* — The Postfix project home page contains a wealth of information about Postfix. The mailing list is a particularly good place to look for information.
- *http://fetchmail.berlios.de/* — The home page for Fetchmail, featuring an online manual, and a thorough FAQ.
- *http://www.procmail.org/* — The home page for Procmail with links to assorted mailing lists dedicated to Procmail as well as various FAQ documents.
- *http://partmaps.org/era/procmail/mini-faq.html* — An excellent Procmail FAQ, offers troubleshooting tips, details about file locking, and the use of wildcard characters.
- *http://www.uwasa.fi/~ts/info/proctips.html* — Contains dozens of tips that make using Procmail much easier. Includes instructions on how to test `.procmailrc` files and use Procmail scoring to decide if a particular action should be taken.
- *http://www.spamassassin.org/* — The official site of the SpamAssassin project.

13.6.3. Related Books

- *Sendmail Milters: A Guide for Fighting Spam* by Bryan Costales and Marcia Flynt; Addison-Wesley — A good Sendmail guide that can help you customize your mail filters.
- *Sendmail* by Bryan Costales with Eric Allman et al.; O'Reilly & Associates — A good Sendmail reference written with the assistance of the original creator of Delivermail and Sendmail.
- *Removing the Spam: Email Processing and Filtering* by Geoff Mulligan; Addison-Wesley Publishing Company — A volume that looks at various methods used by email administrators using established tools, such as Sendmail and Procmail, to manage spam problems.
- *Internet Email Protocols: A Developer's Guide* by Kevin Johnson; Addison-Wesley Publishing Company — Provides a very thorough review of major email protocols and the security they provide.
- *Managing IMAP* by Dianna Mullet and Kevin Mullet; O'Reilly & Associates — Details the steps required to configure an IMAP server.

Chapter 14.

Directory Servers

14.1. OpenLDAP

`LDAP` (Lightweight Directory Access Protocol) is a set of open protocols used to access centrally stored information over a network. It is based on the `X.500` standard for directory sharing, but is less complex and resource-intensive. For this reason, LDAP is sometimes referred to as "X.500 Lite".

Like X.500, LDAP organizes information in a hierarchical manner using directories. These directories can store a variety of information such as names, addresses, or phone numbers, and can even be used in a manner similar to the *Network Information Service* (NIS), enabling anyone to access their account from any machine on the LDAP enabled network.

LDAP is commonly used for centrally managed users and groups, user authentication, or system configuration. It can also serve as a virtual phone directory, allowing users to easily access contact information for other users. Additionally, it can refer a user to other LDAP servers throughout the world, and thus provide an ad-hoc global repository of information. However, it is most frequently used within individual organizations such as universities, government departments, and private companies.

This section covers the installation and configuration of **OpenLDAP 2.4**, an open source implementation of the LDAPv2 and LDAPv3 protocols.

14.1.1. Introduction to LDAP

Using a client/server architecture, LDAP provides reliable means to create a central information directory accessible from the network. When a client attempts to modify information within this directory, the server verifies the user has permission to make the change, and then adds or updates the entry as requested. To ensure the communication is secure, the *Secure Sockets Layer* (SSL) or *Transport Layer Security* (TLS) cryptographic protocols can be used to prevent an attacker from intercepting the transmission.

Using Mozilla NSS

The OpenLDAP suite in Fedora 15 no longer uses OpenSSL. Instead, it uses the

Mozilla implementation of *Network Security Services* (NSS). OpenLDAP continues to work with existing certificates, keys, and other TLS configuration. For more information on how to configure it to use Mozilla certificate and key database, refer to *How do I use TLS/SSL with Mozilla NSS*[1].

The LDAP server supports several database systems, which gives administrators the flexibility to choose the best suited solution for the type of information they are planning to serve. Because of a well-defined client *Application Programming Interface* (API), the number of applications able to communicate with an LDAP server is numerous, and increasing in both quantity and quality.

14.1.1.1. LDAP Terminology

The following is a list of LDAP-specific terms that are used within this chapter:

entry

A single unit within an LDAP directory. Each entry is identified by its unique *Distinguished Name* (DN).

attribute

Information directly associated with an entry. For example, if an organization is represented as an LDAP entry, attributes associated with this organization might include an address, a fax number, etc. Similarly, people can be represented as entries with common attributes such as personal telephone number or email address.

An attribute can either have a single value, or an unordered space-separated list of values. While certain attributes are optional, other are required. Required attributes are specified using the `objectClass` definition, and can be found in schema files located in the `/etc/openldap/slapd.d/cn=config/cn=schema/` directory.

The assertion of an attribute and its corresponding value is also referred to as a *Relative Distinguished Name* (RDN). Unlike distinguished names that are unique globally, a relative distinguished name is only unique per entry.

LDIF

The *LDAP Data Interchange Format* (LDIF) is a plain text representation of an LDAP entry. It takes the following form:

```
[id] dn: distinguished_name
attribute_type: attribute_value…
attribute_type: attribute_value…
…
```

[1] *http://www.openldap.org/faq/index.cgi?file=1514*

The optional `id` is a number determined by the application that is used to edit the entry. Each entry can contain as many `attribute_type` and `attribute_value` pairs as needed, as long as they are all defined in a corresponding schema file. A blank line indicates the end of an entry.

14.1.1.2. OpenLDAP Features

OpenLDAP suite provides a number of important features:

- *LDAPv3 Support* — Many of the changes in the protocol since LDAP version 2 are designed to make LDAP more secure. Among other improvements, this includes the support for Simple Authentication and Security Layer (SASL), Transport Layer Security (TLS), and Secure Sockets Layer (SSL) protocols.
- *LDAP Over IPC* — The use of inter-process communication (IPC) enhances security by eliminating the need to communicate over a network.
- *IPv6 Support* — OpenLDAP is compliant with Internet Protocol version 6 (IPv6), the next generation of the Internet Protocol.
- *LDIFv1 Support* — OpenLDAP is fully compliant with LDIF version 1.
- *Updated C API* — The current C API improves the way programmers can connect to and use LDAP directory servers.
- *Enhanced Standalone LDAP Server* — This includes an updated access control system, thread pooling, better tools, and much more.

14.1.1.3. OpenLDAP Server Setup

The typical steps to set up an LDAP server on Fedora are as follows:

1. Install the OpenLDAP suite. Refer to Section 14.1.2, *Installing the OpenLDAP Suite* (page 304) for more information on required packages.
2. Customize the configuration as described in Section 14.1.3, *Configuring an OpenLDAP Server* (page 307).
3. Start the `slapd` service as described in Section 14.1.4, *Running an OpenLDAP Server* (page 312).
4. Use the `ldapadd` utility to add entries to the LDAP directory.
5. Use the `ldapsearch` utility to verify that the `slapd` service is accessing the information correctly.

14.1.2. Installing the OpenLDAP Suite

The suite of OpenLDAP libraries and tools is provided by the following packages:

Package	Description
openldap	A package containing the libraries necessary to run the OpenLDAP server and client applications.
openldap-clients	A package containing the command line utilities for viewing and modifying directories on an LDAP server.
openldap-servers	A package containing both the services and utilities to configure and run an LDAP server. This includes the *Standalone LDAP Daemon*, `slapd`.
openldap-servers-sql	A package containing the SQL support module.

Table 14.1. List of OpenLDAP packages

Additionally, the following packages are commonly used along with the LDAP server:

Package	Description
nss-pam-ldapd	A package containing `nslcd`, a local LDAP name service that allows a user to perform local LDAP queries.
mod_authz_ldap	A package containing `mod_authz_ldap`, the LDAP authorization module for the Apache HTTP Server. This module uses the short form of the distinguished name for a subject and the issuer of the client SSL certificate to determine the distinguished name of the user within an LDAP directory. It is also capable of authorizing users based on attributes of that user's LDAP directory entry, determining access to assets based on the user and group privileges of the asset, and denying access for users with expired passwords. Note that the `mod_ssl` module is required when using the `mod_authz_ldap` module.

Table 14.2. List of commonly installed additional LDAP packages

To install these packages, use the `yum` command in the following form:

```
yum install package...
```

For example, to perform the basic LDAP server installation, type the following at a shell prompt as `root`:

```
yum install openldap openldap-clients openldap-servers
```

Note that you must have superuser privileges (that is, you must be logged in as `root`) to run this command. For more information on how to install new packages in Fedora, refer to Section 4.2.4, *Installing Packages* (page 78).

14.1.2.1. Overview of OpenLDAP Server Utilities

To perform administrative tasks, the openldap-servers package installs the following utilities along with the `slapd` service:

Command	Description
`slapacl`	Allows you to check the access to a list of attributes.
`slapadd`	Allows you to add entries from an LDIF file to an LDAP directory.
`slapauth`	Allows you to check a list of IDs for authentication and authorization permissions.
`slapcat`	Allows you to pull entries from an LDAP directory in the default format and save them in an LDIF file.
`slapdn`	Allows you to check a list of Distinguished Names (DNs) based on available schema syntax.
`slapindex`	Allows you to re-index the `slapd` directory based on the current content. Run this utility whenever you change indexing options in the configuration file.
`slappasswd`	Allows you to create an encrypted user password to be used with the `ldapmodify` utility, or in the `slapd` configuration file.
`slapschema`	Allows you to check the compliance of a database with the corresponding schema.
`slaptest`	Allows you to check the LDAP server configuration.

Table 14.3. List of OpenLDAP server utilities

For a detailed description of these utilities and their usage, refer to the corresponding manual pages as referred to in Section 14.1.6.1, *Installed Documentation* (page 314).

Make sure the files have correct owner

Although only `root` can run `slapadd`, the `slapd` service runs as the `ldap` user. Because of this, the directory server is unable to modify any files created by `slapadd`. To correct this issue, after running the `slapd` utility, type the following at a shell prompt:

```
chown -R ldap:ldap /var/lib/ldap
```

Stop slapd before using these utilities

To preserve the data integrity, stop the `slapd` service before using `slapadd`, `slapcat`, or `slapindex`. You can do so by typing the following at a shell prompt as `root`:

```
systemctl stop slapd.service
```

For more information on how to start, stop, restart, and check the current status of the `slapd` service, refer to Section 14.1.4, *Running an OpenLDAP Server* (page 312).

14.1.2.2. Overview of OpenLDAP Client Utilities

The openldap-clients package installs the following utilities which can be used to add, modify, and delete entries in an LDAP directory:

Command	Description
`ldapadd`	Allows you to add entries to an LDAP directory, either from a file, or from standard input. It is a symbolic link to `ldapmodify -a`.
`ldapcompare`	Allows you to compare given attribute with an LDAP directory entry.
`ldapdelete`	Allows you to delete entries from an LDAP directory.
`ldapexop`	Allows you to perform extended LDAP operations.
`ldapmodify`	Allows you to modify entries in an LDAP directory, either from a file, or from standard input.
`ldapmodrdn`	Allows you to modify the RDN value of an LDAP directory entry.
`ldappasswd`	Allows you to set or change the password for an LDAP user.
`ldapsearch`	Allows you to search LDAP directory entries.
`ldapurl`	Allows you to compose or decompose LDAP URLs.
`ldapwhoami`	Allows you to perform a `whoami` operation on an LDAP server.

Table 14.4. List of OpenLDAP client utilities

With the exception of `ldapsearch`, each of these utilities is more easily used by referencing a file containing the changes to be made rather than typing a command for each entry to be changed within an LDAP directory. The format of such a file is outlined in the man page for each utility.

14.1.2.3. Overview of Common LDAP Client Applications

Although there are various graphical LDAP clients capable of creating and modifying directories on the server, none of them is included in Fedora. Popular applications that can access directories in a read-only mode include **Mozilla Thunderbird**, **Evolution**, or **Ekiga**.

14.1.3. Configuring an OpenLDAP Server

By default, the OpenLDAP configuration is stored in the `/etc/openldap/` directory. The following table highlights the most important directories and files within this directory:

Path	Description
`/etc/openldap/ldap.conf`	The configuration file for client applications that use the OpenLDAP libraries. This includes `ldapadd`, `ldapsearch`, **Evolution**, etc.
`/etc/openldap/slapd.d/`	The directory containing the `slapd` configuration.

Table 14.5. List of OpenLDAP configuration files and directories

Note that OpenLDAP no longer reads its configuration from the `/etc/openldap/slapd.conf` file. Instead, it uses a configuration database located in the `/etc/openldap/slapd.d/` directory. If you have an existing `slapd.conf` file from a previous installation, you can convert it to the new format by running the following command as `root`:

```
slaptest -f /etc/openldap/slapd.conf -F /etc/openldap/slapd.d/
```

The `slapd` configuration consists of LDIF entries organized in a hierarchical directory structure, and the recommended way to edit these entries is to use the server utilities described in Section 14.1.2.1, *Overview of OpenLDAP Server Utilities* (page 305).

Do not edit LDIF files directly

An error in an LDIF file can render the `slapd` service unable to start. Because of this, it is strongly advised that you avoid editing the LDIF files within the `/etc/openldap/slapd.d/` directly.

14.1.3.1. Changing the Global Configuration

Global configuration options for the LDAP server are stored in the `/etc/openldap/slapd.d/cn=config.ldif` file. The following directives are commonly used:

`olcAllows`

The `olcAllows` directive allows you to specify which features to enable. It takes the following form:

```
olcAllows: feature…
```

It accepts a space-separated list of features as described in *Table 14.6. Available olcAllows options* below. The default option is `bind_v2`.

Option	Description
bind_v2	Enables the acceptance of LDAP version 2 bind requests.
bind_anon_cred	Enables an anonymous bind when the Distinguished Name (DN) is empty.
bind_anon_dn	Enables an anonymous bind when the Distinguished Name (DN) is *not* empty.
update_anon	Enables processing of anonymous update operations.
proxy_authz_anon	Enables processing of anonymous proxy authorization control.

Table 14.6. Available olcAllows options

```
olcAllows: bind_v2 update_anon
```

Example 14.1. Using the olcAllows directive

`olcConnMaxPending`

The `olcConnMaxPending` directive allows you to specify the maximum number of pending requests for an anonymous session. It takes the following form:

`olcConnMaxPending: number`

The default option is `100`.

```
olcConnMaxPending: 100
```

Example 14.2. Using the olcConnMaxPending directive

`olcConnMaxPendingAuth`

The `olcConnMaxPendingAuth` directive allows you to specify the maximum number of pending requests for an authenticated session. It takes the following form:

`olcConnMaxPendingAuth: number`

The default option is `1000`.

```
olcConnMaxPendingAuth: 1000
```

Example 14.3. Using the olcConnMaxPendingAuth directive

`olcDisallows`

The `olcDisallows` directive allows you to specify which features to disable. It takes the following form:

`olcDisallows: feature…`

It accepts a space-separated list of features as described in *Table 14.7. Available olcDisallows options* below. No features are disabled by default.

Option	Description
`bind_anon`	Disables the acceptance of anonymous bind requests.
`bind_simple`	Disables the simple bind authentication mechanism.
`tls_2_anon`	Disables the enforcing of an anonymous session when the STARTTLS command is received.
`tls_authc`	Disallows the STARTTLS command when authenticated.

Table 14.7. Available olcDisallows options

```
olcDisallows: bind_anon
```

Example 14.4. Using the olcDisallows directive

`olcIdleTimeout`

The `olcIdleTimeout` directive allows you to specify how many seconds to wait before closing an idle connection. It takes the following form:

`olcIdleTimeout: *number*`

This option is disabled by default (that is, set to `0`).

```
olcIdleTimeout: 180
```

Example 14.5. Using the olcIdleTimeout directive

`olcLogFile`

The `olcLogFile` directive allows you to specify a file in which to write log messages. It takes the following form:

`olcLogFile: *file_name*`

The log messages are written to standard error by default.

```
olcLogFile: /var/log/slapd.log
```

Example 14.6. Using the olcLogFile directive

`olcReferral`

The `olcReferral` option allows you to specify a URL of a server to process the request in case the server is not able to handle it. It takes the following form:

`olcReferral: *URL*`

This option is disabled by default.

```
olcReferral: ldap://root.openldap.org
```

Example 14.7. Using the olcReferral directive

`olcWriteTimeout`

The `olcWriteTimeout` option allows you to specify how many seconds to wait before closing a connection with an outstanding write request. It takes the following form:

`olcWriteTimeout`

This option is disabled by default (that is, set to `0`).

```
olcWriteTimeout: 180
```

Example 14.8. Using the olcWriteTimeout directive

14.1.3.2. Changing the Database-Specific Configuration

By default, the OpenLDAP server uses Berkeley DB (BDB) as a database back end. The configuration for this database is stored in the `/etc/openldap/slapd.d/cn=config/olcDatabase={1}bdb.ldif` file. The following directives are commonly used in a database-specific configuration:

`olcReadOnly`

The `olcReadOnly` directive allows you to use the database in a read-only mode. It takes the following form:

`olcReadOnly: *boolean*`

It accepts either `TRUE` (enable the read-only mode), or `FALSE` (enable modifications of the database). The default option is `FALSE`.

```
olcReadOnly: TRUE
```

Example 14.9. Using the olcReadOnly directive

`olcRootDN`

The `olcRootDN` directive allows you to specify the user that is unrestricted by access controls or administrative limit parameters set for operations on the LDAP directory. It takes the following form:

`olcRootDN: *distinguished_name*`

It accepts a *Distinguished Name* (DN). The default option is `cn=Manager,dn=my-domain,dc=com`.

```
olcRootDN: cn=root,dn=example,dn=com
```

Example 14.10. Using the olcRootDN directive

`olcRootPW`

The `olcRootPW` directive allows you to set a password for the user that is specified using the `olcRootDN` directive. It takes the following form:

`olcRootPW: *password*`

It accepts either a plain text string, or a hash. To generate a hash, use the `slappaswd` utility, for example:

```
~]$ slappaswd
New password:
Re-enter new password:
{SSHA}WczWsyPEnMchFf1GRTweq2q7XJcvmSxD
olcRootPW: {SSHA}WczWsyPEnMchFf1GRTweq2q7XJcvmSxD
```

Example 14.11. Using the olcRootPW directive

`olcSuffix`

The `olcSuffix` directive allows you to specify the domain for which to provide information. It takes the following form:

`olcSuffix: *domain_name*`

It accepts a *fully qualified domain name* (FQDN). The default option is `dc=my-domain,dc=com`.

```
olcSuffix: dc=example,dc=com
```

Example 14.12. Using the olcSuffix directive

14.1.3.3. Extending Schema

Since OpenLDAP 2.3, the `/etc/openldap/slapd.d/` directory also contains LDAP definitions that were previously located in `/etc/openldap/schema/`. It is possible to extend the schema used by OpenLDAP to support additional attribute types and object classes using the default schema files as a guide. However, this task is beyond the scope of this chapter. For more information on this topic, refer to *http://www.openldap.org/doc/admin/schema.html*.

14.1.4. Running an OpenLDAP Server

This section describes how to start, stop, restart, and check the current status of the **Standalone LDAP Daemon**. For more information on how to manage system services in general, refer to Chapter 7, *Services and Daemons* (page 120).

14.1.4.1. Starting the Service

To run the `slapd` service, type the following at a shell prompt as `root`:

```
systemctl start slapd.service
```

If you want the service to start automatically at the boot time, use the following command:

```
systemctl enable slapd.service
```

Refer to Chapter 7, *Services and Daemons* (page 120) for more information on how to configure services in Fedora.

14.1.4.2. Stopping the Service

To stop the running `slapd` service, type the following at a shell prompt as `root`:

```
systemctl stop slapd.service
```

To prevent the service from starting automatically at the boot time, type:

```
systemctl disable slapd.service
```

Refer to Chapter 7, *Services and Daemons* (page 120) for more information on how to configure services in Fedora.

14.1.4.3. Restarting the Service

To restart the running `slapd` service, type the following at a shell prompt as `root`:

```
systemctl restart slapd.service
```

This stops the service, and then starts it again. Use this command to reload the configuration.

14.1.4.4. Checking the Service Status

To check whether the service is running, type the following at a shell prompt:

```
systemctl is-active slapd.service
```

14.1.5. Configuring a System to Authenticate Using OpenLDAP

In order to configure a system to authenticate using OpenLDAP, make sure that the appropriate packages are installed on both LDAP server and client machines. For information on how to set up the server, follow the instructions in Section 14.1.2, *Installing the OpenLDAP Suite* (page 304) and Section 14.1.3, *Configuring an OpenLDAP Server* (page 307). On a client, type the following at a shell prompt as `root`:

```
yum install openldap openldap-clients nss-pam-ldapd
```

Chapter 8, *Configuring Authentication* (page 125) provides detailed instructions on how to configure applications to use LDAP for authentication.

14.1.5.1. Migrating Old Authentication Information to LDAP Format

The migrationtools package provides a set of shell and Perl scripts to help you migrate authentication information into an LDAP format. To install this package, type the following at a shell prompt as `root`:

```
yum install migrationtools
```

This will install the scripts to the `/usr/share/migrationtools/` directory. Once installed, edit the `/usr/share/migrationtools/migrate_common.ph` file and change the following lines to reflect the correct domain, for example:

```
# Default DNS domain
$DEFAULT_MAIL_DOMAIN = "example.com";

# Default base
$DEFAULT_BASE = "dc=example,dc=com";
```

Alternatively, you can specify the environment variables directly on the command line. For example, to run the `migrate_all_online.sh` script with the default base set to `dc=example,dc=com`, type:

```
export DEFAULT_BASE="dc=example,dc=com" \
/usr/share/migrationtools/migrate_all_online.sh
```

To decide which script to run in order to migrate the user database, refer to *Table 14.8. Commonly used LDAP migration scripts* below.

Existing Name Service	Is LDAP Running?	Script to Use
`/etc` flat files	yes	`migrate_all_online.sh`
`/etc` flat files	no	`migrate_all_offline.sh`
NetInfo	yes	`migrate_all_netinfo_online.sh`
NetInfo	no	`migrate_all_netinfo_offline.sh`
NIS (YP)	yes	`migrate_all_nis_online.sh`
NIS (YP)	no	`migrate_all_nis_offline.sh`

Table 14.8. Commonly used LDAP migration scripts

For more information on how to use these scripts, refer to the `README` and the `migration-tools.txt` files in the `/usr/share/doc/migrationtools-`*`version`*`/` directory.

14.1.6. Additional Resources

The following resources offer additional information on the Lightweight Directory Access Protocol. Before configuring LDAP on your system, it is highly recommended that you review these resources, especially the *OpenLDAP Software Administrator's Guide*.

14.1.6.1. Installed Documentation

The following documentation is installed with the openldap-servers package:

`/usr/share/doc/openldap-servers-`*`version`*`/guide.html`
: A copy of the *OpenLDAP Software Administrator's Guide*.

`/usr/share/doc/openldap-servers-`*`version`*`/README.schema`
: A README file containing the description of installed schema files.

Additionally, there is also a number of manual pages that are installed with the openldap, openldap-servers, and openldap-clients packages:

Client Applications

- `man ldapadd` — Describes how to add entries to an LDAP directory.
- `man ldapdelete` — Describes how to delete entries within an LDAP directory.
- `man ldapmodify` — Describes how to modify entries within an LDAP directory.

- `man ldapsearch` — Describes how to search for entries within an LDAP directory.
- `man ldappasswd` — Describes how to set or change the password of an LDAP user.
- `man ldapcompare` — Describes how to use the `ldapcompare` tool.
- `man ldapwhoami` — Describes how to use the `ldapwhoami` tool.
- `man ldapmodrdn` — Describes how to modify the RDNs of entries.

Server Applications

- `man slapd` — Describes command line options for the LDAP server.

Administrative Applications

- `man slapadd` — Describes command line options used to add entries to a `slapd` database.
- `man slapcat` — Describes command line options used to generate an LDIF file from a `slapd` database.
- `man slapindex` — Describes command line options used to regenerate an index based upon the contents of a `slapd` database.
- `man slappasswd` — Describes command line options used to generate user passwords for LDAP directories.

Configuration Files

- `man ldap.conf` — Describes the format and options available within the configuration file for LDAP clients.
- `man slapd-config` — Describes the format and options available within the configuration directory.

14.1.6.2. Useful Websites

http://www.openldap.org/doc/admin24/
The current version of the *OpenLDAP Software Administrator's Guide*.

http://www.kingsmountain.com/ldapRoadmap.shtml
Jeff Hodges' *LDAP Roadmap & FAQ* containing links to several useful resources and emerging news concerning the LDAP protocol.

http://www.ldapman.org/articles/
A collection of articles that offer a good introduction to LDAP, including methods to design a directory tree and customizing directory structures.

http://www.padl.com/
A website of developers of several useful LDAP tools.

14.1.6.3. Related Books

OpenLDAP by Example by John Terpstra and Benjamin Coles; Prentice Hall.
A collection of practical exercises in the OpenLDAP deployment.

Implementing LDAP by Mark Wilcox; Wrox Press, Inc.
A book covering LDAP from both the system administrator's and software developer's perspective.

Understanding and Deploying LDAP Directory Services by Tim Howes et al.; Macmillan Technical Publishing.
A book covering LDAP design principles, as well as its deployment in a production environment.

Chapter 15.
File Servers

15.1. Samba

Samba is an open source implementation of the *Server Message Block* (SMB) protocol. It allows the networking of Microsoft Windows®, Linux, UNIX, and other operating systems together, enabling access to Windows-based file and printer shares. Samba's use of SMB allows it to appear as a Windows server to Windows clients.

Installing the samba package

In order to use **Samba**, first ensure the samba package is installed on your system by running, as `root`:

```
yum install samba
```

For more information on installing packages with Yum, refer to Section 4.2.4, *Installing Packages* (page 78).

15.1.1. Introduction to Samba

The third major release of Samba, version 3.0.0, introduced numerous improvements from prior versions, including:

- The ability to join an Active Directory domain by means of the *Lightweight Directory Access Protocol* (LDAP) and *Kerberos*
- Built in Unicode support for internationalization
- Support for all recent Microsoft Windows server and client versions to connect to Samba servers without needing local registry hacking
- Two new documents developed by the Samba.org team, which include a 400+ page reference manual, and a 300+ page implementation and integration manual. For more information about these published titles, refer to Section 15.1.12.2, *Related Books* (page 342).

15.1.1.1. Samba Features

Samba is a powerful and versatile server application. Even seasoned system administrators must know its abilities and limitations before attempting installation and configuration.

What Samba can do:

- Serve directory trees and printers to Linux, UNIX, and Windows clients
- Assist in network browsing (with or without NetBIOS)
- Authenticate Windows domain logins
- Provide *Windows Internet Name Service* (`WINS`) name server resolution
- Act as a Windows NT®-style *Primary Domain Controller* (PDC)
- Act as a *Backup Domain Controller* (BDC) for a Samba-based PDC
- Act as an Active Directory domain member server
- Join a Windows NT/2000/2003/2008 PDC

What Samba cannot do:

- Act as a BDC for a Windows PDC (and vice versa)
- Act as an Active Directory domain controller

15.1.2. Samba Daemons and Related Services

The following is a brief introduction to the individual Samba daemons and services.

15.1.2.1. Samba Daemons

Samba is comprised of three daemons (`smbd`, `nmbd`, and `winbindd`). Three services (`smb`, `nmb`, and `winbind`) control how the daemons are started, stopped, and other service-related features. These services act as different init scripts. Each daemon is listed in detail below, as well as which specific service has control over it.

`smbd`

The `smbd` server daemon provides file sharing and printing services to Windows clients. In addition, it is responsible for user authentication, resource locking, and data sharing through the `SMB` protocol. The default ports on which the server listens for `SMB` traffic are `TCP` ports `139` and `445`.

The `smbd` daemon is controlled by the `smb` service.

`nmbd`

The `nmbd` server daemon understands and replies to NetBIOS name service requests such as those produced by SMB/*Common Internet File System* (CIFS) in Windows-based systems. These systems include Windows 95/98/ME, Windows NT, Windows 2000, Windows XP, and LanManager clients. It also participates in the browsing protocols that make up the Windows **Network Neighborhood** view. The default port that the server listens to for `NMB` traffic is `UDP` port `137`.

The `nmbd` daemon is controlled by the `nmb` service.

`winbindd`

The `winbind` service resolves user and group information on a server running Windows NT, 2000, 2003 or Windows Server 2008. This makes Windows user / group information understandable by UNIX platforms. This is achieved by using Microsoft RPC calls, *Pluggable Authentication Modules* (PAM), and the *Name Service Switch* (NSS). This allows Windows NT domain users to appear and operate as UNIX users on a UNIX machine. Though bundled with the Samba distribution, the `winbind` service is controlled separately from the `smb` service.

The `winbindd` daemon is controlled by the `winbind` service and does not require the `smb` service to be started in order to operate. `winbindd` is also used when Samba is an Active Directory member, and may also be used on a Samba domain controller (to implement nested groups and/or interdomain trust). Because `winbind` is a client-side service used to connect to Windows NT-based servers, further discussion of `winbind` is beyond the scope of this chapter.

Obtaining a list of utilities that are shipped with Samba

You may refer to Section 15.1.11, *Samba Distribution Programs* (page 336) for a list of utilities included in the Samba distribution.

15.1.3. Connecting to a Samba Share

You can use **Nautilus** to view available Samba shares on your network. To view a list of Samba workgroups and domains on your network, select **Applications** → **Accessories** → **Files** from the **Activities** menu, and click **Browse Network** at the sidebar.

An icon appears for each available SMB workgroup or domain on the network. Double-click one of the workgroup/domain icons to view a list of computers within the workgroup/domain.

Each machine within the workgroup is represented by its own icon. Double-click on an icon to view the Samba shares on the machine. If a username and password combination is required, you are prompted for them.

Alternately, you can also specify the Samba server and sharename in the **Location:** bar for **Nautilus** using the following syntax (replace *`servername`* and *`sharename`* with the appropriate values):

```
smb://servername/sharename
```

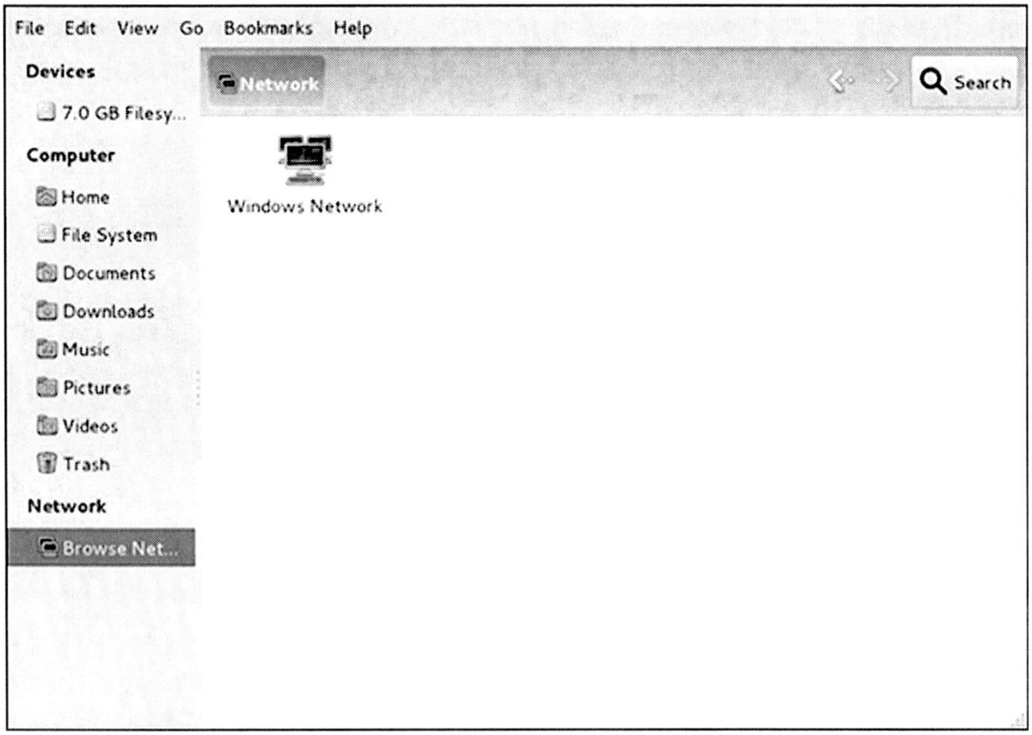

Figure 15.1. Browsing a network in Nautilus

15.1.3.1. Command Line

To query the network for Samba servers, use the `findsmb` command. For each server found, it displays its `IP` address, NetBIOS name, workgroup name, operating system, and `SMB` server version.

To connect to a Samba share from a shell prompt, type the following command:

```
smbclient //hostname/sharename -U username
```

Replace *`hostname`* with the hostname or `IP` address of the Samba server you want to connect to, *`sharename`* with the name of the shared directory you want to browse, and *`username`* with the Samba username for the system. Enter the correct password or press **Enter** if no password is required for the user.

If you see the `smb:\>` prompt, you have successfully logged in. Once you are logged in, type **`help`** for a list of commands. If you wish to browse the contents of your home directory, replace *`sharename`* with your username. If the `-U` switch is not used, the username of the current user is passed to the Samba server.

To exit `smbclient`, type **`exit`** at the `smb:\>` prompt.

15.1.3.2. Mounting the Share

Sometimes it is useful to mount a Samba share to a directory so that the files in the directory can be treated as if they are part of the local file system.

To mount a Samba share to a directory, create a directory to mount it to (if it does not already exist), and execute the following command as `root`:

```
mount -t cifs //servername/sharename /mnt/point/ -o
username=username,password=password
```

This command mounts *`sharename`* from *`servername`* in the local directory `/mnt/point/`.

Installing cifs-utils package

The **mount.cifs** utility is a separate RPM (independent from Samba). In order to use **mount.cifs**, first ensure the cifs-utils package is installed on your system by running, as `root`:

```
yum install cifs-utils
```

For more information on installing packages with Yum, refer to Section 4.2.4, *Installing Packages* (page 78).

Note that the cifs-utils package also contains the **cifs.upcall** binary called by the kernel in order to perform kerberized CIFS mounts. For more information on **cifs.upcall**, refer to `man cifs.upcall`.

For more information about mounting a samba share, refer to `man mount.cifs`.

CIFS servers that require plain text passwords

Some CIFS servers require plain text passwords for authentication. Support for plain text password authentication can be enabled using the following command as `root`:

```
echo 0x37 > /proc/fs/cifs/SecurityFlags
```

WARNING: This operation can expose passwords by removing password encryption.

15.1.4. Configuring a Samba Server

The default configuration file (`/etc/samba/smb.conf`) allows users to view their home directories as a Samba share. It also shares all printers configured for the system as Samba shared printers. In other words, you can attach a printer to the system and print to it from the Windows machines on your network.

15.1.4.1. Graphical Configuration

To configure Samba using a graphical interface, use one of the available Samba graphical user interfaces. A list of available GUIs can be found at *http://www.samba.org/samba/GUI/*.

15.1.4.2. Command Line Configuration

Samba uses /etc/samba/smb.conf as its configuration file. If you change this configuration file, the changes do not take effect until you restart the Samba daemon with the following command, as root:

```
systemctl restart smb.service
```

To specify the Windows workgroup and a brief description of the Samba server, edit the following lines in your /etc/samba/smb.conf file:

```
workgroup = WORKGROUPNAME
server string = BRIEF COMMENT ABOUT SERVER
```

Replace *WORKGROUPNAME* with the name of the Windows workgroup to which this machine should belong. The *BRIEF COMMENT ABOUT SERVER* is optional and is used as the Windows comment about the Samba system.

To create a Samba share directory on your Linux system, add the following section to your /etc/samba/smb.conf file (after modifying it to reflect your needs and your system):

```
[sharename]
comment = Insert a comment here
path = /home/share/
valid users = tfox carole
public = no
writable = yes
printable = no
create mask = 0765
```

The above example allows the users tfox and carole to read and write to the directory /home/share, on the Samba server, from a Samba client.

15.1.4.3. Encrypted Passwords

Encrypted passwords are enabled by default because it is more secure to do so. To create a user with an encrypted password, use the command smbpasswd -a *username* .

15.1.5. Starting and Stopping Samba

To start a Samba server, type the following command in a shell prompt, as root:

```
systemctl start smb.service
```

Setting up a domain member server

To set up a domain member server, you must first join the domain or Active Directory using the net join command *before* starting the smb service.

To stop the server, type the following command in a shell prompt, as `root`:

```
systemctl stop smb.service
```

The `restart` option is a quick way of stopping and then starting Samba. This is the most reliable way to make configuration changes take effect after editing the configuration file for Samba. Note that the restart option starts the daemon even if it was not running originally.

To restart the server, type the following command in a shell prompt, as `root`:

```
systemctl restart smb.service
```

The `condrestart` (*conditional restart*) option only starts `smb` on the condition that it is currently running. This option is useful for scripts, because it does not start the daemon if it is not running.

Applying the changes to the configuration

When the `/etc/samba/smb.conf` file is changed, Samba automatically reloads it after a few minutes. Issuing a manual `restart` or `reload` is just as effective.

To conditionally restart the server, type the following command, as `root`:

```
systemctl condrestart smb.service
```

A manual reload of the `/etc/samba/smb.conf` file can be useful in case of a failed automatic reload by the `smb` service. To ensure that the Samba server configuration file is reloaded without restarting the service, type the following command, as `root`:

```
systemctl reload smb.service
```

By default, the `smb` service does *not* start automatically at boot time. To configure Samba to start at boot time, use a service manager such as `systemctl`. Refer to Chapter 7, *Services and Daemons* (page 120) for more information regarding this tool.

15.1.6. Samba Server Types and the `smb.conf` File

Samba configuration is straightforward. All modifications to Samba are done in the `/etc/samba/smb.conf` configuration file. Although the default `smb.conf` file is well documented, it does not address complex topics such as LDAP, Active Directory, and the numerous domain controller implementations.

The following sections describe the different ways a Samba server can be configured. Keep in mind your needs and the changes required to the `/etc/samba/smb.conf` file for a successful configuration.

15.1.6.1. Stand-alone Server

A stand-alone server can be a workgroup server or a member of a workgroup environment. A stand-alone server is not a domain controller and does not participate in a domain in any way. The following examples include several anonymous share-level security configurations and one user-level security configuration. For more information on share-level and user-level security modes, refer to Section 15.1.7, *Samba Security Modes* (page 331).

15.1.6.1.1. Anonymous Read-Only

The following `/etc/samba/smb.conf` file shows a sample configuration needed to implement anonymous read-only file sharing. The `security = share` parameter makes a share anonymous. Note, security levels for a single Samba server cannot be mixed. The `security` directive is a global Samba parameter located in the `[global]` configuration section of the `/etc/samba/smb.conf` file.

```
[global]
workgroup = DOCS
netbios name = DOCS_SRV
security = share
[data]
comment = Documentation Samba Server
path = /export
read only = Yes
guest only = Yes
```

15.1.6.1.2. Anonymous Read/Write

The following `/etc/samba/smb.conf` file shows a sample configuration needed to implement anonymous read/write file sharing. To enable anonymous read/write file sharing, set the `read only` directive to `no`. The `force user` and `force group` directives are also added to enforce the ownership of any newly placed files specified in the share.

Do not use anonymous read/write servers

Although having an anonymous read/write server is possible, it is not recommended. Any files placed in the share space, regardless of user, are assigned the user/group combination as specified by a generic user (`force user`) and group (`force group`) in the `/etc/samba/smb.conf` file.

```
[global]
workgroup = DOCS
netbios name = DOCS_SRV
security = share
[data]
comment = Data
path = /export
force user = docsbot
force group = users
read only = No
guest ok = Yes
```

15.1.6.1.3. Anonymous Print Server

The following /etc/samba/smb.conf file shows a sample configuration needed to implement an anonymous print server. Setting browseable to no as shown does not list the printer in Windows **Network Neighborhood**. Although hidden from browsing, configuring the printer explicitly is possible. By connecting to DOCS_SRV using NetBIOS, the client can have access to the printer if the client is also part of the DOCS workgroup. It is also assumed that the client has the correct local printer driver installed, as the use client driver directive is set to Yes. In this case, the Samba server has no responsibility for sharing printer drivers to the client.

```
[global]
workgroup = DOCS
netbios name = DOCS_SRV
security = share
printcap name = cups
disable spools= Yes
show add printer wizard = No
printing = cups
[printers]
comment = All Printers
path = /var/spool/samba
guest ok = Yes
printable = Yes
use client driver = Yes
browseable = Yes
```

15.1.6.1.4. Secure Read/Write File and Print Server

The following /etc/samba/smb.conf file shows a sample configuration needed to implement a secure read/write print server. Setting the security directive to user forces Samba to authenticate client connections. Notice the [homes] share does not have a force user or force group directive as the [public] share does. The [homes] share uses the authenticated user details for any files created as opposed to the force user and force group in [public].

```
[global]
workgroup = DOCS
netbios name = DOCS_SRV
security = user
printcap name = cups
disable spools = Yes
show add printer wizard = No
printing = cups
[homes]
comment = Home Directories
valid users = %S
read only = No
browseable = No
```

```
[public]
comment = Data
path = /export
force user = docsbot
force group = users
guest ok = Yes
[printers]
comment = All Printers
path = /var/spool/samba
printer admin = john, ed, @admins
create mask = 0600
guest ok = Yes
printable = Yes
use client driver = Yes
browseable = Yes
```

15.1.6.2. Domain Member Server

A domain member, while similar to a stand-alone server, is logged into a domain controller (either Windows or Samba) and is subject to the domain's security rules. An example of a domain member server would be a departmental server running Samba that has a machine account on the Primary Domain Controller (PDC). All of the department's clients still authenticate with the PDC, and desktop profiles and all network policy files are included. The difference is that the departmental server has the ability to control printer and network shares.

15.1.6.2.1. Active Directory Domain Member Server

The following `/etc/samba/smb.conf` file shows a sample configuration needed to implement an Active Directory domain member server. In this example, Samba authenticates users for services being run locally but is also a client of the Active Directory. Ensure that your kerberos `realm` parameter is shown in all caps (for example `realm = EXAMPLE.COM`). Since Windows 2000/2003/2008 requires Kerberos for Active Directory authentication, the `realm` directive is required. If Active Directory and Kerberos are running on different servers, the `password server` directive may be required to help the distinction.

```
[global]
realm = EXAMPLE.COM
security = ADS
encrypt passwords = yes
# Optional. Use only if Samba cannot determine the Kerberos server automatically.
password server = kerberos.example.com
```

In order to join a member server to an Active Directory domain, the following steps must be completed:

- Configuration of the `/etc/samba/smb.conf` file on the member server
- Configuration of Kerberos, including the `/etc/krb5.conf` file, on the member server

- Creation of the machine account on the Active Directory domain server
- Association of the member server to the Active Directory domain

To create the machine account and join the Windows 2000/2003/2008 Active Directory, Kerberos must first be initialized for the member server wishing to join the Active Directory domain. To create an administrative Kerberos ticket, type the following command as `root` on the member server:

```
kinit administrator@EXAMPLE.COM
```

The `kinit` command is a Kerberos initialization script that references the Active Directory administrator account and Kerberos realm. Since Active Directory requires Kerberos tickets, `kinit` obtains and caches a Kerberos ticket-granting ticket for client/server authentication. For more information on Kerberos, the `/etc/krb5.conf` file, and the `kinit` command, refer to the *Using Kerberos* section of the Red Hat Enterprise Linux 6 *Managing Single Sign-On and Smart Cards* guide.

To join an Active Directory server (windows1.example.com), type the following command as `root` on the member server:

```
net ads join -S windows1.example.com -U administrator%password
```

Since the machine `windows1` was automatically found in the corresponding Kerberos realm (the `kinit` command succeeded), the `net` command connects to the Active Directory server using its required administrator account and password. This creates the appropriate machine account on the Active Directory and grants permissions to the Samba domain member server to join the domain.

The security option

Since `security = ads` and not `security = user` is used, a local password back end such as `smbpasswd` is not needed. Older clients that do not support `security = ads` are authenticated as if `security = domain` had been set. This change does not affect functionality and allows local users not previously in the domain.

15.1.6.2.2. Windows NT4-based Domain Member Server

The following `/etc/samba/smb.conf` file shows a sample configuration needed to implement a Windows NT4-based domain member server. Becoming a member server of an NT4-based domain is similar to connecting to an Active Directory. The main difference is NT4-based domains do not use Kerberos in their authentication method, making the `/etc/samba/smb.conf` file simpler. In this instance, the Samba member server functions as a pass through to the NT4-based domain server.

```
[global]
workgroup = DOCS
```

```
netbios name = DOCS_SRV
security = domain
[homes]
comment = Home Directories
valid users = %S
read only = No
browseable = No
[public]
comment = Data
path = /export
force user = docsbot
force group = users
guest ok = Yes
```

Having Samba as a domain member server can be useful in many situations. There are times where the Samba server can have other uses besides file and printer sharing. It may be beneficial to make Samba a domain member server in instances where Linux-only applications are required for use in the domain environment. Administrators appreciate keeping track of all machines in the domain, even if not Windows-based. In the event the Windows-based server hardware is deprecated, it is quite easy to modify the `/etc/samba/smb.conf` file to convert the server to a Samba-based PDC. If Windows NT-based servers are upgraded to Windows 2000/2003/2008, the `/etc/samba/smb.conf` file is easily modifiable to incorporate the infrastructure change to Active Directory if needed.

Make sure you join the domain before starting Samba

After configuring the `/etc/samba/smb.conf` file, join the domain *before* starting Samba by typing the following command as `root`:

```
net rpc join -U administrator%password
```

Note that the `-S` option, which specifies the domain server hostname, does not need to be stated in the `net rpc join` command. Samba uses the hostname specified by the `workgroup` directive in the `/etc/samba/smb.conf` file instead of it being stated explicitly.

15.1.6.3. Domain Controller

A domain controller in Windows NT is functionally similar to a Network Information Service (NIS) server in a Linux environment. Domain controllers and NIS servers both host user/group information databases as well as related services. Domain controllers are mainly used for security, including the authentication of users accessing domain resources. The service that maintains the user/group database integrity is called the *Security Account Manager* (SAM). The SAM database is stored differently between Windows and Linux Samba-based systems, therefore SAM replication cannot be achieved and platforms cannot be mixed in a PDC/BDC environment.

In a Samba environment, there can be only one PDC and zero or more BDCs.

A mixed Samba/Windows domain controller environment

Samba cannot exist in a mixed Samba/Windows domain controller environment (Samba cannot be a BDC of a Windows PDC or vice versa). Alternatively, Samba PDCs and BDCs *can* coexist.

15.1.6.3.1. Primary Domain Controller (PDC) using `tdbsam`

The simplest and most common implementation of a Samba PDC uses the new default `tdbsam` password database back end. Replacing the aging `smbpasswd` back end, `tdbsam` has numerous improvements that are explained in more detail in Section 15.1.8, *Samba Account Information Databases* (page 332). The `passdb backend` directive controls which back end is to be used for the PDC.

The following `/etc/samba/smb.conf` file shows a sample configuration needed to implement a `tdbsam` password database back end.

```
[global]
workgroup = DOCS
netbios name = DOCS_SRV
passdb backend = tdbsam
security = user
add user script = /usr/sbin/useradd -m "%u"
delete user script = /usr/sbin/userdel -r "%u"
add group script = /usr/sbin/groupadd "%g"
delete group script = /usr/sbin/groupdel "%g"
add user to group script = /usr/sbin/usermod -G "%g" "%u"
add machine script = /usr/sbin/useradd -s /bin/false -d /dev/null  -g machines "%u"
# The following specifies the default logon script
# Per user logon scripts can be specified in the user
# account using pdbedit logon script = logon.bat
# This sets the default profile path.
# Set per user paths with pdbedit
logon drive = H:
domain logons = Yes
os level = 35
preferred master = Yes
domain master = Yes
[homes]
     comment = Home Directories
     valid users = %S
     read only = No
[netlogon]
     comment = Network Logon Service
     path = /var/lib/samba/netlogon/scripts
     browseable = No
     read only = No
# For profiles to work, create a user directory under the
# path shown.
mkdir -p /var/lib/samba/profiles/john
```

```
[Profiles]
      comment = Roaming Profile Share
      path = /var/lib/samba/profiles
      read only = No
      browseable = No
      guest ok = Yes
      profile acls = Yes
# Other resource shares ... ...
```

To provide a functional PDC system which uses the `tdbsam` follow these steps:

1. Use a configuration of the `smb.conf` file as shown in the example above.
2. Add the `root` user to the Samba password database:

   ```
   smbpasswd -a root
   ```

3. Start the `smb` service.
4. Make sure all profile, user, and netlogon directories are created.
5. Add groups that users can be members of:

   ```
   groupadd -f users
   groupadd -f nobody
   groupadd -f ntadmins
   ```

6. Associate the UNIX groups with their respective Windows groups:

   ```
   net groupmap add ntgroup="Domain Users" unixgroup=users
   net groupmap add ntgroup="Domain Guests" unixgroup=nobody
   net groupmap add ntgroup="Domain Admins" unixgroup=ntadmins
   ```

7. Grant access rights to a user or a group. For example, to grant the right to add client machines to the domain on a Samba domain controller, to the members to the Domain Admins group, execute the following command:

   ```
   net rpc rights grant 'DOCS\Domain Admins'
                              SetMachineAccountPrivilege -S PDC -U root
   ```

Keep in mind that Windows systems prefer to have a primary group which is mapped to a domain group such as Domain Users.

Windows groups and users use the same namespace thus not allowing the existence of a group and a user with the same name like in UNIX.

Limitations of the tdbsam authentication back end

If you need more than one domain controller or have more than 250 users, do *not* use a `tdbsam` authentication back end. LDAP is recommended in these cases.

15.1.6.3.2. Primary Domain Controller (PDC) with Active Directory

Although it is possible for Samba to be a member of an Active Directory, it is not possible for Samba to operate as an Active Directory domain controller.

15.1.7. Samba Security Modes

There are only two types of security modes for Samba, *share-level* and *user-level*, which are collectively known as *security levels* . Share-level security can only be implemented in one way, while user-level security can be implemented in one of four different ways. The different ways of implementing a security level are called *security modes*.

15.1.7.1. User-Level Security

User-level security is the default setting for Samba. Even if the `security = user` directive is not listed in the `/etc/samba/smb.conf` file, it is used by Samba. If the server accepts the client's username/password, the client can then mount multiple shares without specifying a password for each instance. Samba can also accept session-based username/password requests. The client maintains multiple authentication contexts by using a unique UID for each logon.

In the `/etc/samba/smb.conf` file, the `security = user` directive that sets user-level security is:

```
[GLOBAL]
...
security = user
...
```

The following sections describe other implementations of user-level security.

15.1.7.1.1. Domain Security Mode (User-Level Security)

In domain security mode, the Samba server has a machine account (domain security trust account) and causes all authentication requests to be passed through to the domain controllers. The Samba server is made into a domain member server by using the following directives in the `/etc/samba/smb.conf` file:

```
[GLOBAL]
...
security = domain
workgroup = MARKETING
...
```

15.1.7.1.2. Active Directory Security Mode (User-Level Security)

If you have an Active Directory environment, it is possible to join the domain as a native Active Directory member. Even if a security policy restricts the use of NT-compatible authentication protocols, the Samba server can join an ADS using Kerberos. Samba in Active Directory member mode can accept Kerberos tickets.

In the `/etc/samba/smb.conf` file, the following directives make Samba an Active Directory member server:

```
[GLOBAL]
...
security = ADS
realm = EXAMPLE.COM
password server = kerberos.example.com
...
```

15.1.7.1.3. Server Security Mode (User-Level Security)

Server security mode was previously used when Samba was not capable of acting as a domain member server.

Avoid using the server security mode

It is highly recommended to *not* use this mode since there are numerous security drawbacks.

In the `/etc/samba/smb.conf`, the following directives enable Samba to operate in server security mode:

```
[GLOBAL]
...
encrypt passwords = Yes
security = server
password server = "NetBIOS_of_Domain_Controller"
...
```

15.1.7.2. Share-Level Security

With share-level security, the server accepts only a password without an explicit username from the client. The server expects a password for each share, independent of the username. There have been recent reports that Microsoft Windows clients have compatibility issues with share-level security servers. Samba developers strongly discourage use of share-level security.

In the `/etc/samba/smb.conf` file, the `security = share` directive that sets share-level security is:

```
[GLOBAL]
...
security = share
...
```

15.1.8. Samba Account Information Databases

The latest release of Samba offers many new features including new password database back ends not previously available. Samba version 3.0.0 fully supports all databases used in previous versions of Samba. However, although supported, many back ends may not be suitable for production use.

The following is a list different back ends you can use with Samba. Other back ends not listed here may also be available.

Plain Text

Plain text back ends are nothing more than the `/etc/passwd` type back ends. With a plain text back end, all usernames and passwords are sent unencrypted between the client and the Samba server. This method is very unsecure and is not recommended for use by any means. It is possible that different Windows clients connecting to the Samba server with plain text passwords cannot support such an authentication method.

`smbpasswd`

A popular back end used in previous Samba packages, the `smbpasswd` back end utilizes a plain ASCII text layout that includes the MS Windows LanMan and NT account, and encrypted password information. The `smbpasswd` back end lacks the storage of the Windows NT/2000/2003 SAM extended controls. The `smbpasswd` back end is not recommended because it does not scale well or hold any Windows information, such as RIDs for NT-based groups. The `tdbsam` back end solves these issues for use in a smaller database (250 users), but is still not an enterprise-class solution.

`ldapsam_compat`

The `ldapsam_compat` back end allows continued OpenLDAP support for use with upgraded versions of Samba. This option is normally used when migrating to Samba 3.0.

`tdbsam`

The new default `tdbsam` password back end provides an ideal database back end for local servers, servers that do not need built-in database replication, and servers that do not require the scalability or complexity of LDAP. The `tdbsam` back end includes all of the `smbpasswd` database information as well as the previously-excluded SAM information. The inclusion of the extended SAM data allows Samba to implement the same account and system access controls as seen with Windows NT/2000/2003/2008 based systems.

The `tdbsam` back end is recommended for 250 users at most. Larger organizations should require Active Directory or LDAP integration due to scalability and possible network infrastructure concerns.

`ldapsam`

The `ldapsam` back end provides an optimal distributed account installation method for Samba. LDAP is optimal because of its ability to replicate its database to any number of servers such as the **Red Hat Directory Server** or an **OpenLDAP Server**. LDAP databases are light-weight and scalable, and as such are preferred by large enterprises. Installation and configuration of directory servers is beyond the scope of this chapter. For more information on the **Red Hat Directory Server**, refer to the *Red Hat Directory Server 8.2 Deployment Guide*. For more information on LDAP, refer to Section 14.1, *OpenLDAP* (page 302).

If you are upgrading from a previous version of Samba to 3.0, note that the OpenLDAP schema file (`/usr/share/doc/samba-version/LDAP/samba.schema`) and the Red Hat Directory Server schema file (`/usr/share/doc/samba-version/LDAP/samba-schema-FDS.ldif`) have changed. These files contain the *attribute syntax definitions* and *objectclass definitions* that the `ldapsam` back end needs in order to function properly.

As such, if you are using the `ldapsam` back end for your Samba server, you will need to configure `slapd` to include one of these schema file. Refer to Section 14.1.3.3, *Extending Schema* (page 312) for directions on how to do this.

Make sure the openldap-server package is installed

You need to have the `openldap-server` package installed if you want to use the `ldapsam` back end.

15.1.9. Samba Network Browsing

Network browsing enables Windows and Samba servers to appear in the Windows **Network Neighborhood**. Inside the **Network Neighborhood**, icons are represented as servers and if opened, the server's shares and printers that are available are displayed.

Network browsing capabilities require NetBIOS over `TCP/IP`. NetBIOS-based networking uses broadcast (`UDP`) messaging to accomplish browse list management. Without NetBIOS and WINS as the primary method for `TCP/IP` hostname resolution, other methods such as static files (`/etc/hosts`) or `DNS`, must be used.

A domain master browser collates the browse lists from local master browsers on all subnets so that browsing can occur between workgroups and subnets. Also, the domain master browser should preferably be the local master browser for its own subnet.

15.1.9.1. Domain Browsing

By default, a Windows server PDC for a domain is also the domain master browser for that domain. A Samba server must *not* be set up as a domain master server in this type of situation

For subnets that do not include the Windows server PDC, a Samba server can be implemented as a local master browser. Configuring the `/etc/samba/smb.conf` file for a local master browser (or no browsing at all) in a domain controller environment is the same as workgroup configuration.

15.1.9.2. WINS (Windows Internet Name Server)

Either a Samba server or a Windows NT server can function as a WINS server. When a WINS server is used with NetBIOS enabled, UDP unicasts can be routed which allows name resolution across networks. Without a WINS server, the UDP broadcast is limited to the local subnet and therefore cannot be routed to other subnets, workgroups, or domains. If WINS replication is necessary, do not use Samba as your primary WINS server, as Samba does not currently support WINS replication.

In a mixed NT/2000/2003/2008 server and Samba environment, it is recommended that you use the Microsoft WINS capabilities. In a Samba-only environment, it is recommended that you use *only one* Samba server for WINS.

The following is an example of the `/etc/samba/smb.conf` file in which the Samba server is serving as a WINS server:

```
[global]
wins support = Yes
```

Using WINS

All servers (including Samba) should connect to a WINS server to resolve NetBIOS names. Without WINS, browsing only occurs on the local subnet. Furthermore, even if a domain-wide list is somehow obtained, hosts cannot be resolved for the client without WINS.

15.1.10. Samba with CUPS Printing Support

Samba allows client machines to share printers connected to the Samba server. In addition, Samba also allows client machines to send documents built in Linux to Windows printer shares. Although there are other printing systems that function with Fedora, CUPS (Common UNIX Print System) is the recommended printing system due to its close integration with Samba.

15.1.10.1. Simple `smb.conf` Settings

The following example shows a very basic `/etc/samba/smb.conf` configuration for CUPS support:

```
[global]
load printers = Yes
printing = cups
printcap name = cups
[printers]
comment = All Printers
path = /var/spool/samba
browseable = No
```

```
public = Yes
guest ok = Yes
writable = No
printable = Yes
printer admin = @ntadmins
[print$]
comment = Printer Drivers Share
path = /var/lib/samba/drivers
write list = ed, john
printer admin = ed, john
```

Other printing configurations are also possible. To add additional security and privacy for printing confidential documents, users can have their own print spooler not located in a public path. If a job fails, other users would not have access to the file.

The `print$` directive contains printer drivers for clients to access if not available locally. The `print$` directive is optional and may not be required depending on the organization.

Setting `browseable` to `Yes` enables the printer to be viewed in the Windows Network Neighborhood, provided the Samba server is set up correctly in the domain/workgroup.

15.1.11. Samba Distribution Programs

findsmb

`findsmb` *`subnet_broadcast_address`*

The `findsmb` program is a Perl script which reports information about SMB-aware systems on a specific subnet. If no subnet is specified the local subnet is used. Items displayed include IP address, NetBIOS name, workgroup or domain name, operating system, and version.

The following example shows the output of executing `findsmb` as any valid user on a system:

```
~]$ findsmb
IP ADDR         NETBIOS NAME   WORKGROUP/OS/VERSION
---------------------------------------------------------------------
10.1.59.25      VERVE           [MYGROUP] [Unix] [Samba 3.0.0-15]
10.1.59.26      STATION22       [MYGROUP] [Unix] [Samba 3.0.2-7.FC1]
10.1.56.45      TREK           +[WORKGROUP] [Windows 5.0] [Windows 2000 LAN Manager]
10.1.57.94      PIXEL           [MYGROUP] [Unix] [Samba 3.0.0-15]
10.1.57.137     MOBILE001       [WORKGROUP] [Windows 5.0] [Windows 2000 LAN Manager]
10.1.57.141     JAWS           +[KWIKIMART] [Unix] [Samba 2.2.7a-security-rollup-fix]
10.1.56.159     FRED           +[MYGROUP] [Unix] [Samba 3.0.0-14.3E]
10.1.59.192     LEGION         *[MYGROUP] [Unix] [Samba 2.2.7-security-rollup-fix]
10.1.56.205     NANCYN         +[MYGROUP] [Unix] [Samba 2.2.7a-security-rollup-fix]
```

net

`net` *`protocol function misc_options target_options`*

The `net` utility is similar to the `net` utility used for Windows and MS-DOS. The first argument is used to specify the protocol to use when executing a command. The *protocol* option can be `ads`, `rap`, or `rpc` for specifying the type of server connection. Active Directory uses `ads`, Win9x/NT3 uses `rap`, and Windows NT4/2000/2003/2008 uses `rpc`. If the protocol is omitted, `net` automatically tries to determine it.

The following example displays a list the available shares for a host named `wakko`:

```
~]$ net -l share -S wakko
Password:
Enumerating shared resources (exports) on remote server:
Share name   Type    Description
----------   ----    -----------
data         Disk    Wakko data share
tmp          Disk    Wakko tmp share
IPC$         IPC     IPC Service (Samba Server)
ADMIN$       IPC     IPC Service (Samba Server)
```

The following example displays a list of Samba users for a host named `wakko`:

```
~]$ net -l user -S wakko
root password:
User name            Comment
-----------------------------
andriusb             Documentation
joe                  Marketing
lisa                 Sales
```

nmblookup

`nmblookup` *options netbios_name*

The `nmblookup` program resolves NetBIOS names into `IP` addresses. The program broadcasts its query on the local subnet until the target machine replies.

Here is an example:

```
~]$ nmblookup trek
querying trek on 10.1.59.255
10.1.56.45 trek<00>
```

pdbedit

`pdbedit` *options*

The `pdbedit` program manages accounts located in the SAM database. All back ends are supported including `smbpasswd`, LDAP, and the `tdb` database library.

The following are examples of adding, deleting, and listing users:

```
~]$ pdbedit -a kristin
new password:
retype new password:
```

```
Unix username:        kristin
NT username:
Account Flags:        [U         ]
User SID:             S-1-5-21-1210235352-3804200048-1474496110-2012
Primary Group SID:    S-1-5-21-1210235352-3804200048-1474496110-2077
Full Name: Home Directory:       \\wakko\kristin
HomeDir Drive:
Logon Script:
Profile Path:         \\wakko\kristin\profile
Domain:               WAKKO
Account desc:
Workstations: Munged
dial:
Logon time:           0
Logoff time:          Mon, 18 Jan 2038 22:14:07 GMT
Kickoff time:         Mon, 18 Jan 2038 22:14:07 GMT
Password last set:    Thu, 29 Jan 2004 08:29:28
GMT Password can change:  Thu, 29 Jan 2004 08:29:28 GMT
Password must change: Mon, 18 Jan 2038 22:14:07 GMT
~]$ pdbedit -v -L kristin
Unix username:        kristin
NT username:
Account Flags:        [U          ]
User SID:             S-1-5-21-1210235352-3804200048-1474496110-2012
Primary Group SID:    S-1-5-21-1210235352-3804200048-1474496110-2077
Full Name:
Home Directory:       \\wakko\kristin
HomeDir Drive:
Logon Script:
Profile Path:         \\wakko\kristin\profile
Domain:               WAKKO
Account desc:
Workstations: Munged
dial:
Logon time:           0
Logoff time:          Mon, 18 Jan 2038 22:14:07 GMT
Kickoff time:         Mon, 18 Jan 2038 22:14:07 GMT
Password last set:    Thu, 29 Jan 2004 08:29:28 GMT
Password can change:  Thu, 29 Jan 2004 08:29:28 GMT
Password must change: Mon, 18 Jan 2038 22:14:07 GMT
~]$ pdbedit -L
andriusb:505:
joe:503:
lisa:504:
kristin:506:
~]$ pdbedit -x joe
~]$ pdbedit -L
andriusb:505: lisa:504: kristin:506:
```

rpcclient

rpcclient *server options*

The `rpcclient` program issues administrative commands using Microsoft RPCs, which provide access to the Windows administration graphical user interfaces (GUIs) for systems management. This is most often used by advanced users that understand the full complexity of Microsoft RPCs.

smbcacls

`smbcacls //server/share filename options`

The `smbcacls` program modifies Windows ACLs on files and directories shared by a Samba server or a Windows server.

smbclient

`smbclient //server/share password options`

The `smbclient` program is a versatile UNIX client which provides functionality similar to `ftp`.

smbcontrol

```
smbcontrol -i options
smbcontrol options destination messagetype parameters
```

The `smbcontrol` program sends control messages to running `smbd`, `nmbd`, or `winbindd` daemons. Executing `smbcontrol -i` runs commands interactively until a blank line or a *'q'* is entered.

smbpasswd

`smbpasswd options username password`

The `smbpasswd` program manages encrypted passwords. This program can be run by a superuser to change any user's password as well as by an ordinary user to change their own Samba password.

smbspool

`smbspool job user title copies options filename`

The `smbspool` program is a CUPS-compatible printing interface to Samba. Although designed for use with CUPS printers, `smbspool` can work with non-CUPS printers as well.

smbstatus

`smbstatus options`

The `smbstatus` program displays the status of current connections to a Samba server.

smbtar

```
smbtar options
```

The `smbtar` program performs backup and restores of Windows-based share files and directories to a local tape archive. Though similar to the `tar` command, the two are not compatible.

testparm

```
testparm options filename hostname IP_address
```

The `testparm` program checks the syntax of the `/etc/samba/smb.conf` file. If your `/etc/samba/smb.conf` file is in the default location (`/etc/samba/smb.conf`) you do not need to specify the location. Specifying the hostname and IP address to the `testparm` program verifies that the `hosts.allow` and `host.deny` files are configured correctly. The `testparm` program also displays a summary of your `/etc/samba/smb.conf` file and the server's role (stand-alone, domain, etc.) after testing. This is convenient when debugging as it excludes comments and concisely presents information for experienced administrators to read.

For example:

```
~]$ testparm
Load smb config files from /etc/samba/smb.conf
Processing section "[homes]"
Processing section "[printers]"
Processing section "[tmp]"
Processing section "[html]"
Loaded services file OK.
Server role: ROLE_STANDALONE
Press enter to see a dump of your service definitions
<enter>
# Global parameters
[global]
      workgroup = MYGROUP
      server string = Samba Server
      security = SHARE
      log file = /var/log/samba/%m.log
      max log size = 50
      socket options = TCP_NODELAY SO_RCVBUF=8192 SO_SNDBUF=8192
      dns proxy = No
[homes]
      comment = Home Directories
      read only = No
      browseable = No
[printers]
      comment = All Printers
      path = /var/spool/samba
      printable = Yes
```

```
      browseable = No
[tmp]
      comment = Wakko tmp
      path = /tmp
      guest only = Yes
[html]
      comment = Wakko www
      path = /var/www/html
      force user = andriusb
      force group = users
      read only = No
      guest only = Yes
```

wbinfo

`wbinfo` *`options`*

The `wbinfo` program displays information from the `winbindd` daemon. The `winbindd` daemon must be running for `wbinfo` to work.

15.1.12. Additional Resources

The following sections give you the means to explore Samba in greater detail.

15.1.12.1. Installed Documentation

- `/usr/share/doc/samba-`*`version-number`*`/` — All additional files included with the Samba distribution. This includes all helper scripts, sample configuration files, and documentation. This directory also contains online versions of *The Official Samba-3 HOWTO-Collection* and *Samba-3 by Example*, both of which are cited below.

Make sure you have the samba-doc package installed

In order to use the **Samba** documentation, first ensure the samba-doc package is installed on your system by running, as `root`:

```
yum install samba-doc
```

For more information on installing packages with Yum, refer to Section 4.2.4, *Installing Packages* (page 78).

Refer to the following manual pages for detailed information specific **Samba** features:

- `smb.conf`
- `samba`
- `smbd`
- `nmbd`
- `winbind`

15.1.12.2. Related Books

- *The Official Samba-3 HOWTO-Collection* by John H. Terpstra and Jelmer R. Vernooij; Prentice Hall — The official Samba-3 documentation as issued by the Samba development team. This is more of a reference guide than a step-by-step guide.
- *Samba-3 by Example* by John H. Terpstra; Prentice Hall — This is another official release issued by the Samba development team which discusses detailed examples of OpenLDAP, DNS, DHCP, and printing configuration files. This has step-by-step related information that helps in real-world implementations.
- *Using Samba, 2nd Edition* by Jay T's, Robert Eckstein, and David Collier-Brown; O'Reilly — A good resource for novice to advanced users, which includes comprehensive reference material.

15.1.12.3. Useful Websites

- *http://www.samba.org/* — Homepage for the Samba distribution and all official documentation created by the Samba development team. Many resources are available in HTML and PDF formats, while others are only available for purchase. Although many of these links are not Fedora specific, some concepts may apply.
- *http://samba.org/samba/archives.html* — Active email lists for the Samba community. Enabling digest mode is recommended due to high levels of list activity.
- Samba newsgroups — Samba threaded newsgroups, such as gmane.org, that use the NNTP protocol are also available. This an alternative to receiving mailing list emails.

15.2. FTP

File Transfer Protocol (`FTP`) is one of the oldest and most commonly used protocols found on the Internet today. Its purpose is to reliably transfer files between computer hosts on a network without requiring the user to log directly into the remote host or have knowledge of how to use the remote system. It allows users to access files on remote systems using a standard set of simple commands.

This section outlines the basics of the `FTP` protocol, as well as configuration options for the primary `FTP` server shipped with Fedora, `vsftpd`.

15.2.1. The File Transfer Protocol

However, because `FTP` is so prevalent on the Internet, it is often required to share files to the public. System administrators, therefore, should be aware of the `FTP` protocol's unique characteristics.

15.2.1.1. Multiple Ports, Multiple Modes

Unlike most protocols used on the Internet, FTP requires multiple network ports to work properly. When an FTP client application initiates a connection to an FTP server, it opens port 21 on the server — known as the *command port*. This port is used to issue all commands to the server. Any data requested from the server is returned to the client via a *data port*. The port number for data connections, and the way in which data connections are initialized, vary depending upon whether the client requests the data in *active* or *passive* mode.

The following defines these modes:

active mode

Active mode is the original method used by the FTP protocol for transferring data to the client application. When an active mode data transfer is initiated by the FTP client, the server opens a connection from port 20 on the server to the IP address and a random, unprivileged port (greater than 1024) specified by the client. This arrangement means that the client machine must be allowed to accept connections over any port above 1024. With the growth of insecure networks, such as the Internet, the use of firewalls to protect client machines is now prevalent. Because these client-side firewalls often deny incoming connections from active mode FTP servers, passive mode was devised.

passive mode

Passive mode, like active mode, is initiated by the FTP client application. When requesting data from the server, the FTP client indicates it wants to access the data in passive mode and the server provides the IP address and a random, unprivileged port (greater than 1024) on the server. The client then connects to that port on the server to download the requested information.

While passive mode resolves issues for client-side firewall interference with data connections, it can complicate administration of the server-side firewall. You can reduce the number of open ports on a server by limiting the range of unprivileged ports on the FTP server. This also simplifies the process of configuring firewall rules for the server. Refer to Section 15.2.5.8, *Network Options* (page 354) for more information about limiting passive ports.

15.2.2. FTP Servers

Fedora ships with two different FTP servers:

- **Red Hat Content Accelerator** — A kernel-based Web server that delivers high performance Web server and FTP services. Since speed is its primary design goal, it has limited functionality and runs only as an anonymous FTP server. For more information about configuring and administering **Red Hat Content Accelerator**,

consult the documentation available online at
http://www.redhat.com/docs/manuals/tux/.

- `vsftpd` — A fast, secure FTP daemon which is the preferred FTP server for Fedora. The remainder of this section focuses on `vsftpd`.

15.2.2.1. vsftpd

The Very Secure FTP Daemon (`vsftpd`) is designed from the ground up to be fast, stable, and, most importantly, secure. `vsftpd` is the only stand-alone FTP server distributed with Fedora, due to its ability to handle large numbers of connections efficiently and securely.

The security model used by `vsftpd` has three primary aspects:

- *Strong separation of privileged and non-privileged processes* — Separate processes handle different tasks, and each of these processes run with the minimal privileges required for the task.
- *Tasks requiring elevated privileges are handled by processes with the minimal privilege necessary* — By leveraging compatibilities found in the `libcap` library, tasks that usually require full `root` privileges can be executed more safely from a less privileged process.
- *Most processes run in a `chroot` jail* — Whenever possible, processes are change-rooted to the directory being shared; this directory is then considered a `chroot` jail. For example, if the directory `/var/ftp/` is the primary shared directory, `vsftpd` reassigns `/var/ftp/` to the new root directory, known as `/`. This disallows any potential malicious hacker activities for any directories not contained below the new root directory.

Use of these security practices has the following effect on how `vsftpd` deals with requests:

- *The parent process runs with the least privileges required* — The parent process dynamically calculates the level of privileges it requires to minimize the level of risk. Child processes handle direct interaction with the FTP clients and run with as close to no privileges as possible.
- *All operations requiring elevated privileges are handled by a small parent process* — Much like the Apache HTTP Server, `vsftpd` launches unprivileged child processes to handle incoming connections. This allows the privileged, parent process to be as small as possible and handle relatively few tasks.
- *All requests from unprivileged child processes are distrusted by the parent process* — Communication with child processes are received over a socket, and the validity of any information from child processes is checked before being acted on.
- *Most interaction with FTP clients is handled by unprivileged child processes in a `chroot` jail* — Because these child processes are unprivileged and only have access to the

directory being shared, any crashed processes only allows the attacker access to the shared files.

15.2.3. Files Installed with `vsftpd`

The `vsftpd` RPM installs the daemon (`/usr/sbin/vsftpd`), its configuration and related files, as well as FTP directories onto the system. The following lists the files and directories related to `vsftpd` configuration:

- `/etc/rc.d/init.d/vsftpd` — The *initialization script* (*initscript*) used by the `systemctl` command to start, stop, or reload `vsftpd`. Refer to Section 15.2.4, *Starting and Stopping* `vsftpd` (page 345) for more information about using this script.
- `/etc/pam.d/vsftpd` — The Pluggable Authentication Modules (PAM) configuration file for `vsftpd`. This file specifies the requirements a user must meet to login to the FTP server. For more information on PAM, refer to the *Using Pluggable Authentication Modules (PAM)* chapter of the Fedora 15 *Managing Single Sign-On and Smart Cards* guide.
- `/etc/vsftpd/vsftpd.conf` — The configuration file for `vsftpd`. Refer to Section 15.2.5, `vsftpd` *Configuration Options* (page 346) for a list of important options contained within this file.
- `/etc/vsftpd/ftpusers` — A list of users not allowed to log into `vsftpd`. By default, this list includes the `root`, `bin`, and `daemon` users, among others.
- `/etc/vsftpd/user_list` — This file can be configured to either deny or allow access to the users listed, depending on whether the `userlist_deny` directive is set to `YES` (default) or `NO` in `/etc/vsftpd/vsftpd.conf`. If `/etc/vsftpd/user_list` is used to grant access to users, the usernames listed must *not* appear in `/etc/vsftpd/ftpusers`.
- `/var/ftp/` — The directory containing files served by `vsftpd`. It also contains the `/var/ftp/pub/` directory for anonymous users. Both directories are world readable, but writable only by the `root` user.

15.2.4. Starting and Stopping `vsftpd`

The `vsftpd` RPM installs the `/etc/rc.d/init.d/vsftpd` script, which can be accessed using the `systemctl` command.

To start the server, as `root` type:

```
systemctl start vsftpd.service
```

To stop the server, as `root` type:

```
systemctl stop vsftpd.service
```

The `restart` option is a shorthand way of stopping and then starting `vsftpd`. This is the most efficient way to make configuration changes take effect after editing the configuration file for `vsftpd`.

To restart the server, as `root` type:

```
systemctl restart vsftpd.service
```

The `condrestart` (*conditional restart*) option only starts `vsftpd` if it is currently running. This option is useful for scripts, because it does not start the daemon if it is not running.

To conditionally restart the server, as `root` type:

```
systemctl condrestart vsftpd.service
```

By default, the `vsftpd` service does *not* start automatically at boot time. To configure the `vsftpd` service to start at boot time, use a service manager such as `systemctl`. Refer to Chapter 7, *Services and Daemons* (page 120) for more information on how to configure services in Fedora.

15.2.4.1. Starting Multiple Copies of `vsftpd`

Sometimes one computer is used to serve multiple FTP domains. This is a technique called *multihoming*. One way to multihome using `vsftpd` is by running multiple copies of the daemon, each with its own configuration file.

To do this, first assign all relevant IP addresses to network devices or alias network devices on the system. Additional information about network configuration scripts can be found in Chapter 6, *Network Interfaces* (page 104).

Next, the DNS server for the FTP domains must be configured to reference the correct machine. For information about BIND and its configuration files, refer to Section 11.2, *BIND* (page 199).

If there is more configuration files present in the `/etc/vsftpd` directory, calling `systemctl start vsftpd.service` results in the `/etc/rc.d/init.d/vsftpd` initscript starting the same number of processes as the number of configuration files. Each configuration file must have a unique name in the `/etc/vsftpd/` directory and must be readable and writable only by `root`.

15.2.5. `vsftpd` Configuration Options

Although `vsftpd` may not offer the level of customization other widely available FTP servers have, it offers enough options to fill most administrator's needs. The fact that it is not overly feature-laden limits configuration and programmatic errors.

All configuration of `vsftpd` is handled by its configuration file, `/etc/vsftpd/vsftpd.conf`. Each directive is on its own line within the file and follows the following format:

`directive=value`

For each directive, replace *`directive`* with a valid directive and *`value`* with a valid value.

Do not use spaces

There must not be any spaces between the *`directive`*, equal symbol, and the *`value`* in a directive.

Comment lines must be preceded by a hash sign (`#`) and are ignored by the daemon.

For a complete list of all directives available, refer to the man page for `vsftpd.conf`.

Securing the vsftpd service

For an overview of ways to secure `vsftpd`, refer to the Fedora *Security Guide*.

The following is a list of some of the more important directives within `/etc/vsftpd/vsftpd.conf`. All directives not explicitly found or commented out within `vsftpd`'s configuration file are set to their default value.

15.2.5.1. Daemon Options

The following is a list of directives which control the overall behavior of the `vsftpd` daemon.

- `listen` — When enabled, `vsftpd` runs in stand-alone mode. Fedora sets this value to `YES`. This directive cannot be used in conjunction with the `listen_ipv6` directive.

  The default value is `NO`.

- `listen_ipv6` — When enabled, `vsftpd` runs in stand-alone mode, but listens only to `IPv6` sockets. This directive cannot be used in conjunction with the `listen` directive.

  The default value is `NO`.

- `session_support` — When enabled, `vsftpd` attempts to maintain login sessions for each user through Pluggable Authentication Modules (PAM). For more information, refer to the *Using Pluggable Authentication Modules (PAM)* chapter of the Red Hat Enterprise Linux 6 *Managing Single Sign-On and Smart Cards* and the PAM man pages. . If session logging is not necessary, disabling this option allows `vsftpd` to run with less processes and lower privileges.

  The default value is `YES`.

15.2.5.2. Log In Options and Access Controls

The following is a list of directives which control the login behavior and access control mechanisms.

- `anonymous_enable` — When enabled, anonymous users are allowed to log in. The usernames `anonymous` and `ftp` are accepted.

  The default value is `YES`.

  Refer to Section 15.2.5.3, *Anonymous User Options* (page 349) for a list of directives affecting anonymous users.

- `banned_email_file` — If the `deny_email_enable` directive is set to `YES`, this directive specifies the file containing a list of anonymous email passwords which are not permitted access to the server.

  The default value is `/etc/vsftpd/banned_emails`.

- `banner_file` — Specifies the file containing text displayed when a connection is established to the server. This option overrides any text specified in the `ftpd_banner` directive.

  There is no default value for this directive.

- `cmds_allowed` — Specifies a comma-delimited list of `FTP` commands allowed by the server. All other commands are rejected.

  There is no default value for this directive.

- `deny_email_enable` — When enabled, any anonymous user utilizing email passwords specified in the `/etc/vsftpd/banned_emails` are denied access to the server. The name of the file referenced by this directive can be specified using the `banned_email_file` directive.

  The default value is `NO`.

- `ftpd_banner` — When enabled, the string specified within this directive is displayed when a connection is established to the server. This option can be overridden by the `banner_file` directive.

  By default `vsftpd` displays its standard banner.

- `local_enable` — When enabled, local users are allowed to log into the system.

  The default value is `YES`.

  Refer to Section 15.2.5.4, *Local User Options* (page 350) for a list of directives affecting local users.

- `pam_service_name` — Specifies the PAM service name for `vsftpd`.

  The default value is `ftp`. Note, in Fedora, the value is set to `vsftpd`.

- The default value is `NO`. Note, in Fedora, the value is set to `YES`.

- `userlist_deny` — When used in conjunction with the `userlist_enable` directive and set to `NO`, all local users are denied access unless the username is listed in the file specified by the `userlist_file` directive. Because access is denied before the client is asked for a password, setting this directive to `NO` prevents local users from submitting unencrypted passwords over the network.

  The default value is `YES`.

- `userlist_enable` — When enabled, the users listed in the file specified by the `userlist_file` directive are denied access. Because access is denied before the client is asked for a password, users are prevented from submitting unencrypted passwords over the network.

  The default value is `NO`, however under Fedora the value is set to `YES`.

- `userlist_file` — Specifies the file referenced by `vsftpd` when the `userlist_enable` directive is enabled.

  The default value is `/etc/vsftpd/user_list` and is created during installation.

15.2.5.3. Anonymous User Options

The following lists directives which control anonymous user access to the server. To use these options, the `anonymous_enable` directive must be set to `YES`.

- `anon_mkdir_write_enable` — When enabled in conjunction with the `write_enable` directive, anonymous users are allowed to create new directories within a parent directory which has write permissions.

  The default value is `NO`.

- `anon_root` — Specifies the directory `vsftpd` changes to after an anonymous user logs in.

  There is no default value for this directive.

- `anon_upload_enable` — When enabled in conjunction with the `write enable` directive, anonymous users are allowed to upload files within a parent directory which has write permissions.

  The default value is `NO`.

- `anon_world_readable_only` — When enabled, anonymous users are only allowed to download world-readable files.

  The default value is `YES`.

- `ftp_username` — Specifies the local user account (listed in `/etc/passwd`) used for the anonymous `FTP` user. The home directory specified in `/etc/passwd` for the user is the root directory of the anonymous `FTP` user.

  The default value is `ftp`.

- `no_anon_password` — When enabled, the anonymous user is not asked for a password.

  The default value is `NO`.

- `secure_email_list_enable` — When enabled, only a specified list of email passwords for anonymous logins are accepted. This is a convenient way to offer limited security to public content without the need for virtual users.

  Anonymous logins are prevented unless the password provided is listed in `/etc/vsftpd/email_passwords`. The file format is one password per line, with no trailing white spaces.

  The default value is `NO`.

15.2.5.4. Local User Options

The following lists directives which characterize the way local users access the server. To use these options, the `local_enable` directive must be set to `YES`.

- `chmod_enable` — When enabled, the `FTP` command `SITE CHMOD` is allowed for local users. This command allows the users to change the permissions on files.

  The default value is `YES`.

- `chroot_list_enable` — When enabled, the local users listed in the file specified in the `chroot_list_file` directive are placed in a `chroot` jail upon log in.

  If enabled in conjunction with the `chroot_local_user` directive, the local users listed in the file specified in the `chroot_list_file` directive are *not* placed in a `chroot` jail upon log in.

  The default value is `NO`.

- `chroot_list_file` — Specifies the file containing a list of local users referenced when the `chroot_list_enable` directive is set to `YES`.

  The default value is `/etc/vsftpd/chroot_list`.

- `chroot_local_user` — When enabled, local users are change-rooted to their home directories after logging in.

  The default value is `NO`.

Avoid enabling the chroot_local_user option

Enabling `chroot_local_user` opens up a number of security issues, especially for users with upload privileges. For this reason, it is *not* recommended.

- `guest_enable` — When enabled, all non-anonymous users are logged in as the user `guest`, which is the local user specified in the `guest_username` directive.

  The default value is `NO`.

- `guest_username` — Specifies the username the `guest` user is mapped to.

  The default value is `ftp`.
- `local_root` — Specifies the directory `vsftpd` changes to after a local user logs in.

  There is no default value for this directive.
- `local_umask` — Specifies the umask value for file creation. Note that the default value is in octal form (a numerical system with a base of eight), which includes a "0" prefix. Otherwise the value is treated as a base-10 integer.

  The default value is `022`.
- `passwd_chroot_enable` — When enabled in conjunction with the `chroot_local_user` directive, `vsftpd` change-roots local users based on the occurrence of the `/./` in the home directory field within `/etc/passwd`.

  The default value is `NO`.
- `user_config_dir` — Specifies the path to a directory containing configuration files bearing the name of local system users that contain specific setting for that user. Any directive in the user's configuration file overrides those found in `/etc/vsftpd/vsftpd.conf`.

  There is no default value for this directive.

15.2.5.5. Directory Options

The following lists directives which affect directories.

- `dirlist_enable` — When enabled, users are allowed to view directory lists.

  The default value is `YES`.
- `dirmessage_enable` — When enabled, a message is displayed whenever a user enters a directory with a message file. This message resides within the current directory. The name of this file is specified in the `message_file` directive and is `.message` by default.

  The default value is `NO`. Note, in Fedora, the value is set to `YES`.
- `force_dot_files` — When enabled, files beginning with a dot (`.`) are listed in directory listings, with the exception of the `.` and `..` files.

  The default value is `NO`.
- `hide_ids` — When enabled, all directory listings show `ftp` as the user and group for each file.

  The default value is `NO`.
- `message_file` — Specifies the name of the message file when using the `dirmessage_enable` directive.

  The default value is `.message`.

- `text_userdb_names` — When enabled, text usernames and group names are used in place of UID and GID entries. Enabling this option may slow performance of the server.

  The default value is `NO`.
- `use_localtime` — When enabled, directory listings reveal the local time for the computer instead of GMT.

  The default value is `NO`.

15.2.5.6. File Transfer Options

The following lists directives which affect directories.

- `download_enable` — When enabled, file downloads are permitted.

  The default value is `YES`.
- `chown_uploads` — When enabled, all files uploaded by anonymous users are owned by the user specified in the `chown_username` directive.

  The default value is `NO`.
- `chown_username` — Specifies the ownership of anonymously uploaded files if the `chown_uploads` directive is enabled.

  The default value is `root`.
- `write_enable` — When enabled, `FTP` commands which can change the file system are allowed, such as `DELE`, `RNFR`, and `STOR`.

  The default value is `YES`.

15.2.5.7. Logging Options

The following lists directives which affect `vsftpd`'s logging behavior.

- `dual_log_enable` — When enabled in conjunction with `xferlog_enable`, `vsftpd` writes two files simultaneously: a `wu-ftpd`-compatible log to the file specified in the `xferlog_file` directive (`/var/log/xferlog` by default) and a standard `vsftpd` log file specified in the `vsftpd_log_file` directive (`/var/log/vsftpd.log` by default).

  The default value is `NO`.
- `log_ftp_protocol` — When enabled in conjunction with `xferlog_enable` and with `xferlog_std_format` set to `NO`, all `FTP` commands and responses are logged. This directive is useful for debugging.

  The default value is `NO`.

- `syslog_enable` — When enabled in conjunction with `xferlog_enable`, all logging normally written to the standard `vsftpd` log file specified in the `vsftpd_log_file` directive (`/var/log/vsftpd.log` by default) is sent to the system logger instead under the `FTPD` facility.

  The default value is `NO`.
- `vsftpd_log_file` — Specifies the `vsftpd` log file. For this file to be used, `xferlog_enable` must be enabled and `xferlog_std_format` must either be set to `NO` or, if `xferlog_std_format` is set to `YES`, `dual_log_enable` must be enabled. It is important to note that if `syslog_enable` is set to `YES`, the system log is used instead of the file specified in this directive.

  The default value is `/var/log/vsftpd.log`.
- `xferlog_enable` — When enabled, `vsftpd` logs connections (`vsftpd` format only) and file transfer information to the log file specified in the `vsftpd_log_file` directive (`/var/log/vsftpd.log` by default). If `xferlog_std_format` is set to `YES`, file transfer information is logged but connections are not, and the log file specified in `xferlog_file` (`/var/log/xferlog` by default) is used instead. It is important to note that both log files and log formats are used if `dual_log_enable` is set to `YES`.

  The default value is `NO`. Note, in Fedora, the value is set to `YES`.
- `xferlog_file` — Specifies the `wu-ftpd`-compatible log file. For this file to be used, `xferlog_enable` must be enabled and `xferlog_std_format` must be set to `YES`. It is also used if `dual_log_enable` is set to `YES`.

  The default value is `/var/log/xferlog`.
- `xferlog_std_format` — When enabled in conjunction with `xferlog_enable`, only a `wu-ftpd`-compatible file transfer log is written to the file specified in the `xferlog_file` directive (`/var/log/xferlog` by default). It is important to note that this file only logs file transfers and does not log connections to the server.

  The default value is `NO`. Note, in Fedora, the value is set to `YES`.

Maintaining compatibility with older log file formats

To maintain compatibility with log files written by the older `wu-ftpd` `FTP` server, the `xferlog_std_format` directive is set to `YES` under Fedora. However, this setting means that connections to the server are not logged.

To both log connections in `vsftpd` format and maintain a `wu-ftpd`-compatible file transfer log, set `dual_log_enable` to `YES`.

If maintaining a `wu-ftpd`-compatible file transfer log is not important, either set `xferlog_std_format` to `NO`, comment the line with a hash sign (`#`), or delete the line entirely.

15.2.5.8. Network Options

The following lists directives which affect how vsftpd interacts with the network.

- accept_timeout — Specifies the amount of time for a client using passive mode to establish a connection.

  The default value is 60.

- anon_max_rate — Specifies the maximum data transfer rate for anonymous users in bytes per second.

  The default value is 0, which does not limit the transfer rate.

- connect_from_port_20 When enabled, vsftpd runs with enough privileges to open port 20 on the server during active mode data transfers. Disabling this option allows vsftpd to run with less privileges, but may be incompatible with some FTP clients.

  The default value is NO. Note, in Fedora, the value is set to YES.

- connect_timeout — Specifies the maximum amount of time a client using active mode has to respond to a data connection, in seconds.

  The default value is 60.

- data_connection_timeout — Specifies maximum amount of time data transfers are allowed to stall, in seconds. Once triggered, the connection to the remote client is closed.

  The default value is 300.

- ftp_data_port — Specifies the port used for active data connections when connect_from_port_20 is set to YES.

  The default value is 20.

- idle_session_timeout — Specifies the maximum amount of time between commands from a remote client. Once triggered, the connection to the remote client is closed.

  The default value is 300.

- listen_address — Specifies the IP address on which vsftpd listens for network connections.

  There is no default value for this directive.

Running multiple copies of vsftpd

If running multiple copies of vsftpd serving different IP addresses, the configuration file for each copy of the vsftpd daemon must have a different value for this directive. Refer to Section 15.2.4.1, *Starting Multiple Copies of vsftpd* (page 346) for more information about multihomed FTP servers.

- `listen_address6` — Specifies the IPv6 address on which `vsftpd` listens for network connections when `listen_ipv6` is set to `YES`.

  There is no default value for this directive.

Running multiple copies of vsftpd

If running multiple copies of `vsftpd` serving different IP addresses, the configuration file for each copy of the `vsftpd` daemon must have a different value for this directive. Refer to Section 15.2.4.1, *Starting Multiple Copies of `vsftpd`* (page 346) for more information about multihomed FTP servers.

- `listen_port` — Specifies the port on which `vsftpd` listens for network connections.

  The default value is `21`.

- `local_max_rate` — Specifies the maximum rate data is transferred for local users logged into the server in bytes per second.

  The default value is `0`, which does not limit the transfer rate.

- `max_clients` — Specifies the maximum number of simultaneous clients allowed to connect to the server when it is running in standalone mode. Any additional client connections would result in an error message.

  The default value is `0`, which does not limit connections.

- `max_per_ip` — Specifies the maximum of clients allowed to connected from the same source IP address.

  The default value is `0`, which does not limit connections.

- `pasv_address` — Specifies the IP address for the public facing IP address of the server for servers behind Network Address Translation (NAT) firewalls. This enables `vsftpd` to hand out the correct return address for passive mode connections.

  There is no default value for this directive.

- `pasv_enable` — When enabled, passive mode connects are allowed.

  The default value is `YES`.

- `pasv_max_port` — Specifies the highest possible port sent to the FTP clients for passive mode connections. This setting is used to limit the port range so that firewall rules are easier to create.

  The default value is `0`, which does not limit the highest passive port range. The value must not exceed `65535`.

- `pasv_min_port` — Specifies the lowest possible port sent to the FTP clients for passive mode connections. This setting is used to limit the port range so that firewall rules are easier to create.

The default value is `0`, which does not limit the lowest passive port range. The value must not be lower `1024`.

- `pasv_promiscuous` — When enabled, data connections are not checked to make sure they are originating from the same `IP` address. This setting is only useful for certain types of tunneling.

Avoid enabling the pasv_promiscuous option

Do not enable this option unless absolutely necessary as it disables an important security feature which verifies that passive mode connections originate from the same `IP` address as the control connection that initiates the data transfer.

The default value is `NO`.

- `port_enable` — When enabled, active mode connects are allowed.

  The default value is `YES`.

15.2.6. Additional Resources

For more information about `vsftpd`, refer to the following resources.

15.2.6.1. Installed Documentation

- The `/usr/share/doc/vsftpd-`*`version-number`*`/` directory — Replace *`version-number`* with the installed version of the `vsftpd` package. This directory contains a `README` with basic information about the software. The `TUNING` file contains basic performance tuning tips and the `SECURITY/` directory contains information about the security model employed by `vsftpd`.
- `vsftpd` related man pages — There are a number of man pages for the daemon and configuration files. The following lists some of the more important man pages.

  Server Applications

  - `man vsftpd` — Describes available command line options for `vsftpd`.

  Configuration Files

  - `man vsftpd.conf` — Contains a detailed list of options available within the configuration file for `vsftpd`.
  - `man 5 hosts_access` — Describes the format and options available within the TCP wrappers configuration files: `hosts.allow` and `hosts.deny`.

15.2.6.2. Useful Websites

- *http://vsftpd.beasts.org/* — The `vsftpd` project page is a great place to locate the latest documentation and to contact the author of the software.

- *http://slacksite.com/other/ftp.html* — This website provides a concise explanation of the differences between active and passive mode `FTP`.
- *http://www.ietf.org/rfc/rfc0959.txt* — The original *Request for Comments* (*RFC*) of the `FTP` protocol from the IETF.

Part VI.
Monitoring and Automation

This part describes various tools that allow system administrators to monitor system performance, automate system tasks, and report bugs.

Chapter 16.

System Monitoring Tools

Before you learn how to configure your system, you should learn how to gather essential system information. For example, you should know how to find the amount of free memory, the amount of available hard drive space, how your hard drive is partitioned, and what processes are running. This chapter discusses how to retrieve this type of information from your Fedora system using simple commands and a few simple programs.

16.1. System Processes

The `ps ax` command displays a list of current system processes, including processes owned by other users. To display the owner alongside each process, use the `ps aux` command. This list is a static list; in other words, it is a snapshot of what was running when you invoked the command. If you want a constantly updated list of running processes, use `top` as described below.

The `ps` output can be long. To prevent it from scrolling off the screen, you can pipe it through less:

```
ps aux | less
```

You can use the `ps` command in combination with the `grep` command to see if a process is running. For example, to determine if **Emacs** is running, use the following command:

```
ps ax | grep emacs
```

The `top` command displays currently running processes and important information about them including their memory and CPU usage. The list is both real-time and interactive. An example of output from the `top` command is provided as follows:

```
top - 18:11:48 up 1 min,  1 user,  load average: 0.68, 0.30, 0.11
Tasks: 122 total,   1 running, 121 sleeping,   0 stopped,   0 zombie
Cpu(s):  0.0%us,  0.5%sy,  0.0%ni, 93.4%id,  5.7%wa,  0.2%hi,  0.2%si,  0.0
Mem:    501924k total,   376496k used,   125428k free,    29664k buffers
Swap:  1015800k total,        0k used,  1015800k free,   189008k cached

  PID USER      PR  NI  VIRT  RES  SHR S %CPU %MEM    TIME+  COMMAND
 1601 root      40   0 20172 1084  920 S  0.3  0.2   0:00.08 hald-addon-sto
 1998 silas     40   0 14984 1160  880 R  0.3  0.2   0:00.13 top
    1 root      40   0 19160 1412 1156 S  0.0  0.3   0:00.96 init
```

```
    2 root      40   0     0    0    0 S  0.0  0.0   0:00.01 kthreadd
    3 root      RT   0     0    0    0 S  0.0  0.0   0:00.05 migration/0
    4 root      20   0     0    0    0 S  0.0  0.0   0:00.00 ksoftirqd/0
    5 root      RT   0     0    0    0 S  0.0  0.0   0:00.00 watchdog/0
    6 root      RT   0     0    0    0 S  0.0  0.0   0:00.04 migration/1
    7 root      20   0     0    0    0 S  0.0  0.0   0:00.00 ksoftirqd/1
    8 root      RT   0     0    0    0 S  0.0  0.0   0:00.00 watchdog/1
    9 root      20   0     0    0    0 S  0.0  0.0   0:00.00 events/0
   10 root      20   0     0    0    0 S  0.0  0.0   0:00.01 events/1
   11 root      20   0     0    0    0 S  0.0  0.0   0:00.00 cpuset
   12 root      20   0     0    0    0 S  0.0  0.0   0:00.00 khelper
[output truncated]
```

To exit `top`, press the **q** key.

Table 16.1. Interactive top commands below contains useful interactive commands that you can use with `top`. For more information, refer to the `top`(1) manual page.

Command	Description
Space	Immediately refresh the display
h	Display a help screen
k	Kill a process. You are prompted for the process ID and the signal to send to it.
n	Change the number of processes displayed. You are prompted to enter the number.
u	Sort by user.
M	Sort by memory usage.
P	Sort by CPU usage.

Table 16.1. Interactive top commands

If you prefer a graphical interface for `top`, you can use the **GNOME System Monitor**. To start it from the desktop, select **Applications** → **System Tools** → **System Monitor** from the **Activities** menu, or execute `gnome-system-monitor` at a shell prompt. Select the **Processes** tab.

The **GNOME System Monitor** allows you to search for a process in the list of running processes. Using the **GNOME System Monitor**, you can also view all processes, your processes, or active processes.

The **Edit** menu item allows you to:

- Stop a process.
- Continue or start a process.
- End a processes.
- Kill a process.
- Change the priority of a selected process.

- Edit the System Monitor preferences. These include changing the interval seconds to refresh the list and selecting process fields to display in the System Monitor window.

The **View** menu item allows you to:

- View only active processes.
- View all processes.
- View my processes.
- View process dependencies.
- View a memory map of a selected process.
- View the files opened by the selected process.
- Refresh the list of processes.

To stop a process, select it and click **End Process**. Alternatively you can also stop a process by selecting it, clicking **Edit** on your menu and selecting **Stop Process**.

To sort the information by a specific column, click on the name of the column. This sorts the information by the selected column in ascending order. Click on the name of the column again to toggle the sort between ascending and descending order.

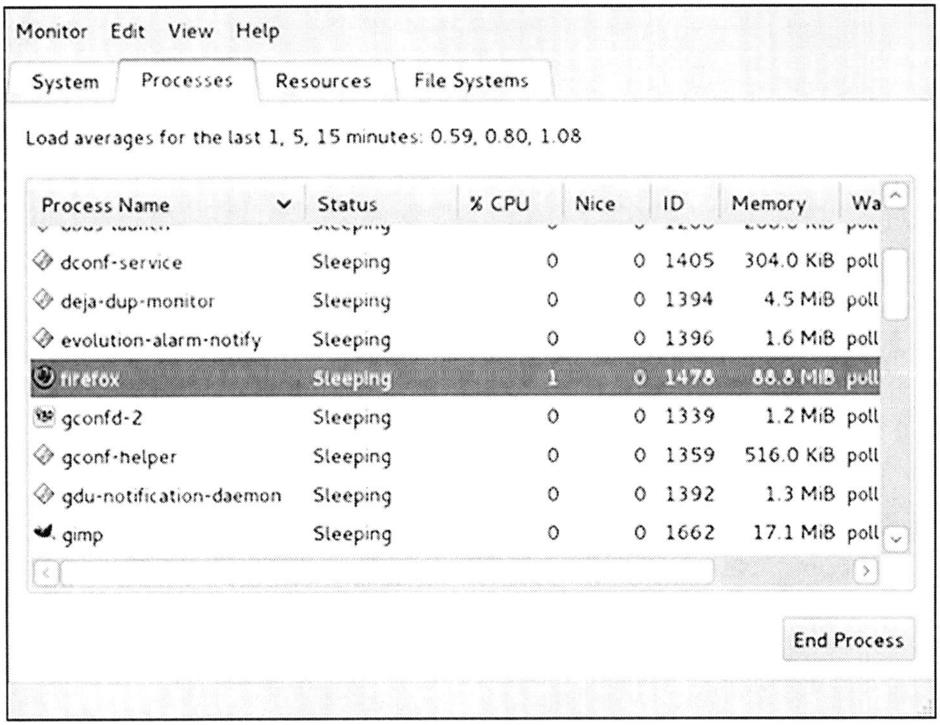

Figure 16.1. GNOME System Monitor — Processes tab

16.2. Memory Usage

The `free` command displays the total amount of physical memory and swap space for the system as well as the amount of memory that is used, free, shared, in kernel buffers, and cached.

```
             total       used       free     shared    buffers     cached
Mem:       4017660    1619044    2398616          0      59864     637968
-/+ buffers/cache:     921212    3096448
Swap:      3071996          0    3071996
```

The command `free -m` shows the same information in megabytes, which are easier to read.

```
             total       used       free     shared    buffers     cached
Mem:          3923       1569       2353          0         58        626
-/+ buffers/cache:        884       3038
Swap:         2999          0       2999
```

If you prefer a graphical interface for `free`, you can use the **GNOME System Monitor**. To start it from the desktop, select **Applications → System Tools → System Monitor** from the **Activities** menu, or execute `gnome-system-monitor` at a shell prompt. Click on the **Resources** tab.

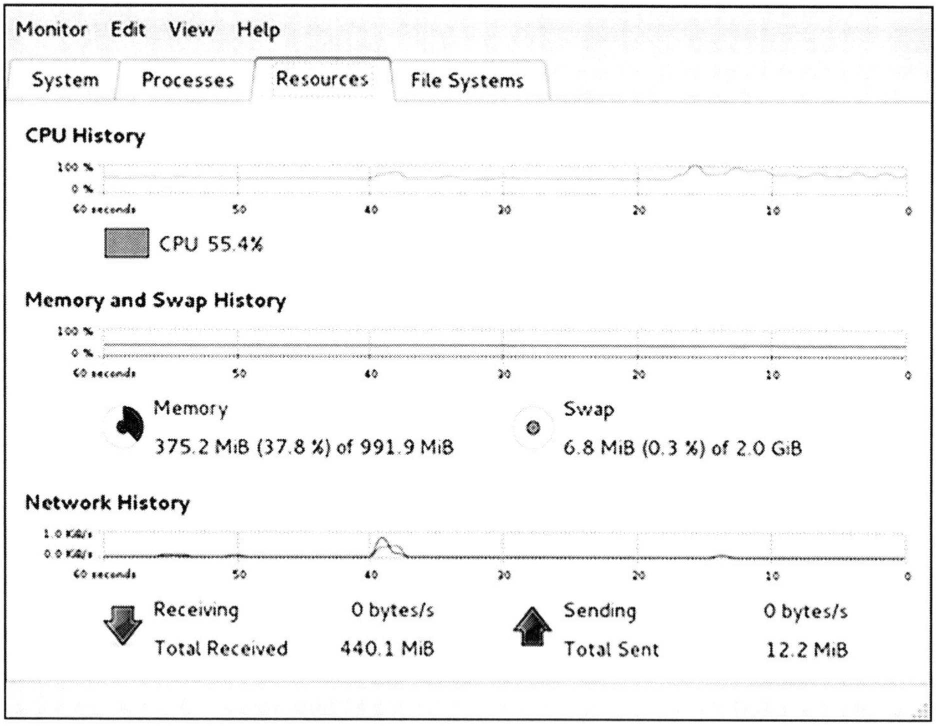

Figure 16.2. GNOME System Monitor — Resources tab

16.3. File Systems

The `df` command reports the system's disk space usage. If you Execute the command `df` at a shell prompt, the output looks similar to the following:

```
Filesystem          1K-blocks      Used Available Use% Mounted on
rootfs                6726160   3091216   3566620  47% /
udev                   500716         0    500716   0% /dev
tmpfs                  507840      2152    505688   1% /dev/shm
tmpfs                  507840       644    507196   1% /run
/dev/sda1             6726160   3091216   3566620  47% /
tmpfs                  507840         0    507840   0% /sys/fs/cgroup
tmpfs                  507840         0    507840   0% /media
/dev/sda4           139412616 105018908  27367684  80% /home
/dev/sda1             6726160   3091216   3566620  47% /tmp
/dev/sda1             6726160   3091216   3566620  47% /var/tmp
```

By default, this utility shows the partition size in 1 kilobyte blocks and the amount of used and available disk space in kilobytes. To view the information in megabytes and gigabytes, use the command `df -h`. The `-h` argument stands for human-readable format. The output looks similar to the following:

```
Filesystem            Size  Used Avail Use% Mounted on
rootfs                6.5G  3.0G  3.5G  47% /
udev                  489M     0  489M   0% /dev
tmpfs                 496M  2.2M  494M   1% /dev/shm
tmpfs                 496M  644K  496M   1% /run
/dev/sda1             6.5G  3.0G  3.5G  47% /
tmpfs                 496M     0  496M   0% /sys/fs/cgroup
tmpfs                 496M     0  496M   0% /media
/dev/sda4             133G  101G   27G  80% /home
/dev/sda1             6.5G  3.0G  3.5G  47% /tmp
/dev/sda1             6.5G  3.0G  3.5G  47% /var/tmp
```

In the list of mounted partitions, there is an entry for `/dev/shm`. This entry represents the system's virtual memory file system.

The `du` command displays the estimated amount of space being used by files in a directory. If you execute `du` at a shell prompt, the disk usage for each of the subdirectories is displayed in a list. The grand total for the current directory and subdirectories are also shown as the last line in the list. If you do not want to see the totals for all the subdirectories, use the command `du -hs` to see only the grand total for the directory in human-readable format. Use the `du --help` command to see more options.

To view the system's partitions and disk space usage in a graphical format, use the **GNOME System Monitor** by selecting **Applications** → **System Tools** → **System Monitor** from the **Activities** menu, or executing the `gnome-system-monitor` command at a shell prompt. Select the **File Systems** tab to view the system's partitions.

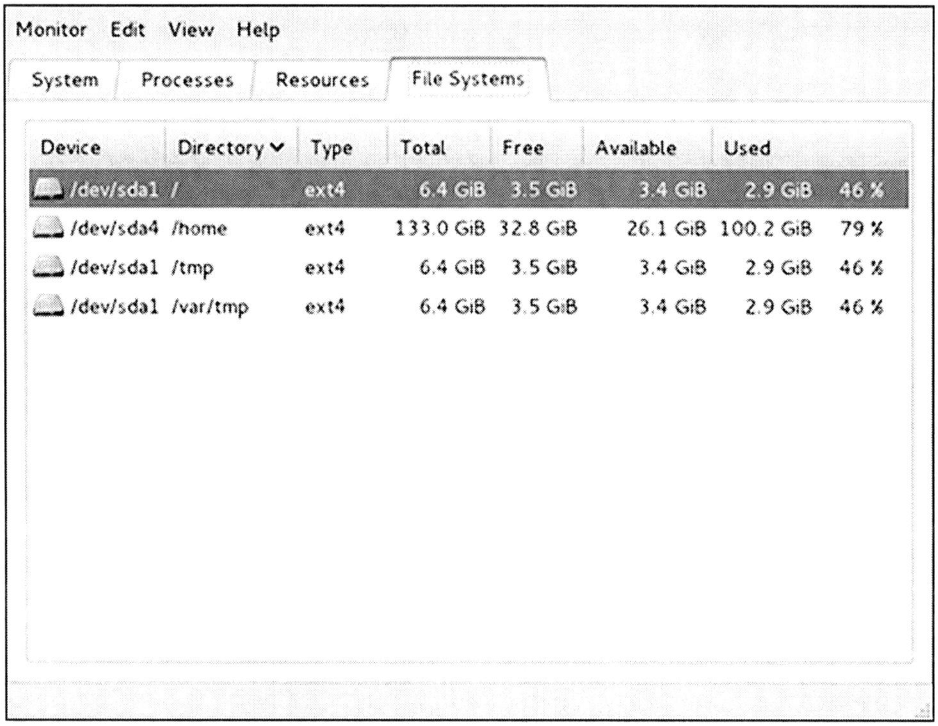

Figure 16.3. GNOME System Monitor — File Systems tab

16.4. Hardware

If you are having trouble configuring your hardware or just want to know what hardware is in your system, you can use the `lspci` command to list all PCI devices. Use the command `lspci -v` for more verbose information or `lspci -vv` for very verbose output.

For example, `lspci` can be used to determine the manufacturer, model, and memory size of a system's video card:

```
00:02.1 Display controller: Intel Corporation Mobile 4 Series Chipset Integrated
Graphics Controller (rev 07)
        Subsystem: Lenovo Device 20e4
        Flags: bus master, fast devsel, latency 0
        Memory at f4200000 (64-bit, non-prefetchable) [size=1M]
        Capabilities: [d0] Power Management version 3
```

The `lspci` is also useful to determine the network card in your system if you do not know the manufacturer or model number.

16.5. Additional Resources

To learn more about gathering system information, refer to the following resources.

16.5.1. Installed Documentation

- `ps --help` — Displays a list of options that can be used with `ps`.
- `top` manual page — Execute `man top` to learn more about `top` and its many options.
- `free` manual page — Execute `man free` to learn more about `free` and its many options.
- `df` manual page — Execute `man df` to learn more about the `df` command and its many options.
- `du` manual page — Execute `man du` to learn more about the `du` command and its many options.
- `lspci` manual page — Execute `man lspci` to learn more about the `lspci` command and its many options.
- `/proc/` directory — The contents of the `/proc/` directory can also be used to gather more detailed system information.

Chapter 17.
Viewing and Managing Log Files

Log files are files that contain messages about the system, including the kernel, services, and applications running on it. There are different log files for different information. For example, there is a default system log file, a log file just for security messages, and a log file for cron tasks.

Log files can be very useful when trying to troubleshoot a problem with the system such as trying to load a kernel driver or when looking for unauthorized login attempts to the system. This chapter discusses where to find log files, how to view log files, and what to look for in log files.

Some log files are controlled by a daemon called `rsyslogd`. A list of log files maintained by `rsyslogd` can be found in the `/etc/rsyslog.conf` configuration file.

rsyslog is an enhanced, multi-threaded syslog daemon which replaced the `sysklogd` daemon. **rsyslog** supports the same functionality as **sysklogd** and extends it with enhanced filtering, encryption protected relaying of messages, various configuration options, or support for transportation via the `TCP` or `UDP` protocols. Note that **rsyslog** is compatible with **sysklogd**.

17.1. Configuring rsyslog

The main configuration file for **rsyslog** is `/etc/rsyslog.conf`. It consists of *global directives*, *rules* or comments (any empty lines or any text following a hash sign (`#`)). Both, global directives and rules are extensively described in the sections below.

17.1.1. Global Directives

Global directives specify configuration options that apply to the `rsyslogd` daemon. They usually specify a value for a specific pre-defined variable that affects the behavior of the `rsyslogd` daemon or a rule that follows. All of the global directives must start with a dollar sign (`$`). Only one directive can be specified per line. The following is an example of a global directive that specifies the maximum size of the syslog message queue:

```
$MainMsgQueueSize 50000
```

The default size defined for this directive (`10,000` messages) can be overridden by specifying a different value (as shown in the example above).

You may define multiple directives in your `/etc/rsyslog.conf` configuration file. A directive affects the behavior of all configuration options until another occurrence of that same directive is detected.

A comprehensive list of all available configuration directives and their detailed description can be found in `/usr/share/doc/rsyslog-`*<version-number>*`/rsyslog_conf_global.html`.

17.1.2. Modules

Due to its modular design, **rsyslog** offers a variety of *modules* which provide dynamic functionality. Note that modules can be written by third parties. Most modules provide additional inputs (see *Input Modules* below) or outputs (see *Output Modules* below). Other modules provide special functionality specific to each module. The modules may provide additional configuration directives that become available after a module is loaded. To load a module, use the following syntax:

```
$ModLoad <MODULE>
```

where `$ModLoad` is the global directive that loads the specified module and *<MODULE>* represents your desired module. For example, if you want to load the `Text File Input Module` (`imfile` — enables **rsyslog** to convert any standard text files into syslog messages), specify the following line in your `/etc/rsyslog.conf` configuration file:

```
$ModLoad imfile
```

rsyslog offers a number of modules which are split into these main categories:

- Input Modules — Input modules gather messages from various sources. The name of an input module always starts with the `im` prefix, such as `imfile`, `imrelp`, etc.
- Output Modules — Output modules provide a facility to store messages into various targets such as sending them across network, storing them in a database or encrypting them. The name of an output module always starts with the `om` prefix, such as `omsnmp`, `omrelp`, etc.
- Filter Modules — Filter modules provide the ability to filter messages according to specified rules. The name of a filter module always starts with the `fm` prefix.
- Parser Modules — Parser modules use the message parsers to parse message content of any received messages. The name of a parser module always starts with the `pm` prefix, such as `pmrfc5424`, `pmrfc3164`, etc.
- Message Modification Modules — Message modification modules change the content of a syslog message. The message modification modules only differ in their implementation from the output and filter modules but share the same interface.

- String Generator Modules — String generator modules generate strings based on the message content and strongly cooperate with the template feature provided by **rsyslog**. For more information on templates, refer to Section 17.1.3.3, *Templates* (page 375). The name of a string generator module always starts with the `sm` prefix, such as `smfile`, `smtradfile`, etc.
- Library Modules — Library modules generally provide functionality for other loadable modules. These modules are loaded automatically by **rsyslog** when needed and cannot be configured by the user.

A comprehensive list of all available modules and their detailed description can be found at *http://www.rsyslog.com/doc/rsyslog_conf_modules.html*

Make sure you use trustworthy modules only

Note that when **rsyslog** loads any modules, it provides them with access to some of its functions and data. This poses a possible security threat. To minimize security risks, use trustworthy modules only.

17.1.3. Rules

A rule is specified by a *filter* part, which selects a subset of syslog messages, and an *action* part, which specifies what to do with the selected messages. To define a rule in your `/etc/rsyslog.conf` configuration file, define both, a filter and an action, on one line and separate them with one or more spaces or tabs. For more information on filters, refer to Section 17.1.3.1, *Filter Conditions* (page 368) and for information on actions, refer to Section 17.1.3.2, *Actions* (page 371).

17.1.3.1. Filter Conditions

rsyslog offers various ways how to filter syslog messages according to various properties. This sections sums up the most used filter conditions.

Facility/Priority-based filters

The most used and well-known way to filter syslog messages is to use the facility/priority-based filters which filter syslog messages based on two conditions: *facility* and *priority*. To create a selector, use the following syntax:

```
<FACILITY>.<PRIORITY>
```

where:

- *<FACILITY>* specifies the subsystem that produces a specific syslog message. For example, the `mail` subsystem handles all mail related syslog messages. *<FACILITY>* can be represented by one of these keywords: `auth`, `authpriv`, `cron`, `daemon`, `kern`, `lpr`, `mail`, `news`, `syslog`, `user`, `uucp`, and `local0` through `local7`.

- *<PRIORITY>* specifies a priority of a syslog message. *<PRIORITY>* can be represented by one of these keywords (listed in an ascending order): `debug`, `info`, `notice`, `warning`, `err`, `crit`, `alert`, and `emerg`.

By preceding any priority with an equal sign (`=`), you specify that only syslog messages with that priority will be selected. All other priorities will be ignored. Conversely, preceding a priority with an exclamation mark (`!`) selects all syslog messages but those with the defined priority. By not using either of these two extensions, you specify a selection of syslog messages with the defined or higher priority.

In addition to the keywords specified above, you may also use an asterisk (`*`) to define all facilities or priorities (depending on where you place the asterisk, before or after the dot). Specifying the keyword `none` serves for facilities with no given priorities.

To define multiple facilities and priorities, simply separate them with a comma (`,`). To define multiple filters on one line, separate them with a semi-colon (`;`).

The following are a few examples of simple facility/priority-based filters:

```
kern.*    # Selects all kernel syslog messages with any priority
```

```
mail.crit  # Selects all mail syslog messages with priority crit and higher.
```

```
cron.!info,!debug   # Selects all cron syslog messages except those with the
                                                          info or debug priority.
```

Property-based filters

Property-based filters let you filter syslog messages by any property, such as *timegenerated* or *syslogtag*. For more information on properties, refer to Section 17.1.3.3.2, *Properties* (page 376). Each of the properties specified in the filters lets you compare it to a specific value using one of the compare-operations listed in *Table 17.1, Property-based compare-operations* below.

Compare-operation	Description
contains	Checks whether the provided string matches any part of the text provided by the property.
isequal	Compares the provided string against all of the text provided by the property.
startswith	Checks whether the provided string matches a prefix of the text provided by the property.
regex	Compares the provided POSIX BRE (Basic Regular Expression) regular expression against the text provided by the property.
ereregex	Compares the provided POSIX ERE (Extended Regular Expression) regular expression against the text provided by the property.

Table 17.1. Property-based compare-operations

To define a property-based filter, use the following syntax:

```
:<PROPERTY>, [!]<COMPARE_OPERATION>, "<STRING>"
```

where:

- The *<PROPERTY>* attribute specifies the desired property (for example, *timegenerated*, *hostname*, etc.).
- The optional exclamation point (`!`) negates the output of the compare-operation (if prefixing the compare-operation).
- The *<COMPARE_OPERATION>* attribute specifies one of the compare-operations listed in *Table 17.1. Property-based compare-operations* above.
- The *<STRING>* attribute specifies the value that the text provided by the property is compared to. To escape certain character (for example a quotation mark (`"`)), use the backslash character (`\`).

The following are few examples of property-based filters:

- The following filter selects syslog messages which contain the string `error` in their message text:

  ```
  :msg, contains, "error"
  ```

- The following filter selects syslog messages received from the hostname `host1`:

  ```
  :hostname, isequal, "host1"
  ```

- The following filter selects syslog messages which do not contain any mention of the words `fatal` and `error` with any or no text between them (for example, `fatal lib error`):

  ```
  :msg, !regex, "fatal .* error"
  ```

Expression-based filters

Expression-based filters select syslog messages according to defined arithmetic, boolean or string operations. Expression-based filters use **rsyslog**'s own scripting language. The syntax of this language is defined in `/usr/share/doc/rsyslog-`*<version-number>*`/rscript_abnf.html` along with examples of various expression-based filters.

To define an expression-based filter, use the following syntax:

```
if <EXPRESSION> then <ACTION>
```

where:

- The *<EXPRESSION>* attribute represents an expression to be evaluated, for example: `$msg startswith 'DEVNAME'` or `$syslogfacility-text == 'local0'`.
- The *<ACTION>* attribute represents an action to be performed if the expression returns the value `true`.

Define an expression-based filter on a single line

When defining an expression-based filter, it must be defined on a single line.

Do not use regular expressions

Regular expressions are currently not supported in expression-based filters.

BSD-style blocks

rsyslog supports BSD-style blocks inside the `/etc/rsyslog.conf` configuration file. Each block consists of rules which are preceded with a program or hostname label. Use the '!*<PROGRAM>*' or '-*<PROGRAM>*' labels to include or exclude programs, respectively. Use the '+*<HOSTNAME>*' or '-*<HOSTNAME>*' labels include or exclude hostnames, respectively.

Example 17.1. BSD-style block below shows a BSD-style block that saves all messages generated by **yum** to a file.

```
!yum
*.*      /var/log/named.log
```

Example 17.1. BSD-style block

17.1.3.2. Actions

Actions specify what is to be done with the messages filtered out by an already-defined selector. The following are some of the actions you can define in your rule:

Saving syslog messages to log files

The majority of actions specify to which log file a syslog message is saved. This is done by specifying a file path after your already-defined selector. The following is a rule comprised of a selector that selects all **cron** syslog messages and an action that saves them into the `/var/log/cron.log` log file:

```
cron.* /var/log/cron.log
```

Use a dash mark (`-`) as a prefix of the file path you specified if you want to omit syncing the desired log file after every syslog message is generated.

Your specified file path can be either static or dynamic. Static files are represented by a simple file path as was shown in the example above. Dynamic files are represented by a template and a question mark (`?`) prefix. For more information on templates, refer to Section 17.1.3.3.1, *Generating dynamic file names* (page 376).

If the file you specified is an existing **tty** or `/dev/console` device, syslog messages are sent to standard output (using special **tty**-handling) or your console (using special `/dev/console`-handling) when using the X Window System, respectively.

Sending syslog messages over the network

rsyslog allows you to send and receive syslog messages over the network. This feature allows to administer syslog messages of multiple hosts on one machine. To forward syslog messages to a remote machine, use the following syntax:

```
@[(<OPTION>)]<HOST>:[<PORT>]
```

where:

- The at sign (@) indicates that the syslog messages are forwarded to a host using the UDP protocol. To use the TCP protocol, use two at signs with no space between them (@@).
- The *<OPTION>* attribute can be replaced with an option such as z*<NUMBER>* . This option enables **zlib** compression for syslog messages; the *<NUMBER>* attribute specifies the level of compression. To define multiple options, simply separate each one of them with a comma (,).
- The *<HOST>* attribute specifies the host which receives the selected syslog messages.
- The *<PORT>* attribute specifies the host machine's port.

When specifying an IPv6 address as the host, enclose the address in square brackets ([,]).

The following are some examples of actions that forward syslog messages over the network (note that all actions are preceded with a selector that selects all messages with any priority):

```
*.* @192.168.0.1        # Forwards messages to 192.168.0.1 via the UDP protocol
```

```
*.* @@example.com:18    # Forwards messages to "example.com" using port 18 and
                                                                    the TCP protocol
```

```
*.* @(z9)[2001::1]      # Compresses messages with zlib (level 9 compression)
                        # and forwards them to 2001::1 using the UDP protocol
```

Output channels

Output channels are primarily used for log file rotation (for more info on log file rotation, refer to Section 17.2.1, *Configuring logrotate* - page 379), that is, to specify the maximum size a log file can grow to. To define an output channel, use the following syntax:

```
$outchannel <NAME>, <FILE_NAME>, <MAX_SIZE>, <ACTION>
```

where:

- The *<NAME>* attribute specifies the name of the output channel.
- The *<FILE_NAME>* attribute specifies the name of the output file.

- The *<MAX_SIZE>* attribute represents the maximum size the specified file (in *<FILE_NAME>*) can grow to. This value is specified in *bytes*.
- The *<ACTION>* attribute specifies the action that is taken when the maximum size, defined in *<MAX_SIZE>*, is hit.

Example 17.2. Output channel log rotation below shows a simple log rotation through the use of an output channel. First, the output channel is defined via the *$outchannel* directive and then used in a rule which selects every syslog message with any priority and executes the previously-defined output channel on the acquired syslog messages. Once the limit (in the example `100 MB`) is hit, the `/home/joe/log_rotation_script` is executed. This script can contain anything from moving the file into a different folder, editing specific content out of it, or simply removing it.

```
$outchannel log_rotation,/var/log/test_log.log, 104857600,
/home/joe/log_rotation_script

*.* $log_rotation
```

Example 17.2. Output channel log rotation

Support for output channels is to be removed in the future

Output channels are currently supported by **rsyslog**, however, they are planned to be removed in the nearby future.

Sending syslog messages to specific users

rsyslog can send syslog messages to specific users by simply specifying a username of the user you wish to send the messages to. To specify more than one user, separate each username with a comma (`,`). To send messages to every user that is currently logged on, use an asterisk (`*`).

Executing a program

rsyslog lets you execute a program for selected syslog messages and uses the `system()` call to execute the program in shell. To specify a program to be executed, prefix it with a caret character (`^`). Consequently, specify a template that formats the received message and passes it to the specified executable as a one line parameter (for more information on templates, refer to Section 17.1.3.3, *Templates* - page 375). In the following example, any syslog message with any priority is selected, formatted with the *template* template and passed as a parameter to the **test-program** program, which is then executed with the provided parameter:

```
*.* ^test-program;template
```

Be careful when using the shell execute action

When accepting messages from any host, and using the shell execute action, you may be vulnerable to command injection. An attacker may try to inject and execute commands specified by the attacker in the program you specified (in your action) to be executed. To avoid any possible security threats, thoroughly consider the use of the shell execute action.

Inputting syslog messages in a database

Selected syslog messages can be directly written into a database table using the *database writer* action. The database writer uses the following syntax:

```
:<PLUGIN>:<DB_HOST>,<DB_NAME>,<DB_USER>,<DB_PASSWORD>;[<TEMPLATE>]
```

where:

- The *<PLUGIN>* calls the specified plug-in that handles the database writing (for example, the `ommysql` plug-in).
- The *<DB_HOST>* attribute specifies the database hostname.
- The *<DB_NAME>* attribute specifies the name of the database.
- The *<DB_USER>* attribute specifies the database user.
- The *<DB_PASSWORD>* attribute specifies the password used with the aforementioned database user.
- The *<TEMPLATE>* attribute specifies an optional use of a template that modifies the syslog message. For more information on templates, refer to Section 17.1.3.3, *Templates* (page 375).

Using MySQL and PostgreSQL

Currently, **rsyslog** provides support for `MySQL` (for more information, refer to `/usr/share/doc/rsyslog-`*<version-number>*`/rsyslog_mysql.html`) and `PostgreSQL` databases only. In order to use the `MySQL` and `PostgreSQL` database writer functionality, install the rsyslog-mysql and rsyslog-pgsql packages installed, respectively. Also, make sure you load the appropriate modules in your `/etc/rsyslog.conf` configuration file:

```
$ModLoad ommysql    # Output module for MySQL support
$ModLoad ompgsql    # Output module for PostgreSQL support
```

For more information on **rsyslog** modules, refer to Section 17.1.2, *Modules* (page 367).

Alternatively, you may use a generic database interface provided by the `omlibdb` module. However, this module is currently not compiled.

Discarding syslog messages

To discard your selected messages, use the tilde character (~). The following rule discards any cron syslog messages:

```
cron.* ~
```

For each selector, you are allowed to specify multiple actions. To specify multiple actions for one selector, write each action on a separate line and precede it with an ampersand character (&). Only the first action is allowed to have a selector specified on its line. The following is an example of a rule with multiple actions:

```
kern.=crit joe
& ^test-program;temp
& @192.168.0.1
```

In the example above, all kernel syslog messages with the critical priority (*crit*) are send to user `joe`, processed by the template *temp* and passed on to the *test-program* executable, and forwarded to `192.168.0.1` via the `UDP` protocol.

Specifying multiple actions improves the overall performance of the desired outcome since the specified selector has to be evaluated only once.

Note that any action can be followed by a template that formats the message. To specify a template, suffix an action with a semicolon (`;`) and specify the name of the template.

Using templates

A template must be defined before it is used in an action, otherwise, it is ignored.

For more information on templates, refer to Section 17.1.3.3, *Templates* (page 375).

17.1.3.3. Templates

Any output that is generated by **rsyslog** can be modified and formatted according to your needs through the use of templates. To create a template use the following syntax:

```
$template <TEMPLATE_NAME>,"text %<PROPERTY>% more text", [<OPTION>]
```

where:

- *$template* is the template directive that indicates that the text following it, defines a template.
- *<TEMPLATE_NAME>* is the name of the template. Use this name to refer to the template.
- Anything between the two quotation marks (`"…"`) is the actual template text. Within this text, you are allowed to escape characters in order to use their functionality, such as `\n` for new line or `\r` for carriage return. Other characters, such as `%` or `"`, have to be escaped in case you want to those characters literally.

The text specified within two percent signs (`%`) specifies a *property* that is consequently replaced with the property's actual value. For more information on properties, refer to Section 17.1.3.3.2, *Properties* (page 376).

- The *`<OPTION>`* attribute specifies any options that modify the template functionality. Do not mistake these for property options, which are defined inside the template text (between `"…"`). The currently supported template options are *`sql`* and *`stdsql`* used for formatting the text as an SQL query.

The sql and stdsql options

Note that the database writer (for more information, refer to section *Inputting syslog messages in a database* in Section 17.1.3.2, *Actions* - page 371) checks whether the *`sql`* and *`stdsql`* options are specified in the template. If they are not, the database writer does not perform any action. This is to prevent any possible security threats, such as SQL injection.

17.1.3.3.1. Generating dynamic file names

Templates can be used to generate dynamic file names. By specifying a property as a part of the file path, a new file will be created for each unique property. For example, use the *`timegenerated`* property to generate a unique file name for each syslog message:

```
$template DynamicFile,"/var/log/test_logs/%timegenerated%-test.log"
```

Keep in mind that the *`$template`* directive only specifies the template. You must use it inside a rule for it to take effect:

```
*.* ?DynamicFile
```

17.1.3.3.2. Properties

Properties defined inside a template (within two percent signs (`%`)) allow you to access various contents of a syslog message through the use of a *property replacer*. To define a property inside a template (between the two quotation marks (`"…"`)), use the following syntax:

```
%<PROPERTY_NAME>[:<FROM_CHAR>:<TO_CHAR>:<OPTION>]%
```

where:

- The *`<PROPERTY_NAME>`* attribute specifies the name of a property. A comprehensible list of all available properties and their detailed description can be found in `/usr/share/doc/rsyslog-<version-number>/property_replacer.html` under the section *Available Properties*.

- *<FROM_CHAR>* and *<TO_CHAR>* attributes denote a range of characters that the specified property will act upon. Alternatively, regular expressions can be used to specify a range of characters. To do so, specify the letter `R` as the *<FROM_CHAR>* attribute and specify your desired regular expression as the *<TO_CHAR>* attribute.
- The *<OPTION>* attribute specifies any property options. A comprehensible list of all available properties and their detailed description can be found in `/usr/share/doc/rsyslog-<version-number>/property_replacer.html` under the section *Property Options*.

The following are some examples of simple properties:

- The following property simply obtains the whole message text of a syslog message:
  `%msg%`
- The following property obtains the first two characters of the message text of a syslog message:
  `%msg:1:2%`
- The following property obtains the whole message text of a syslog message and drops its last line feed character:
  `%msg:::drop-last-lf%`
- The following property obtains the first 10 characters of the timestamp that is generated when the syslog message is received and formats it according to the RFC 3999 date standard.
  `%timegenerated:1:10:date-rfc3339%`

17.1.3.3.3. Template Examples

This section presents few examples of **rsyslog** templates.

Example 17.3. A verbose syslog message template below shows a template that formats a syslog message so that it outputs the message's severity, facility, the timestamp of when the message was received, the hostname, the message tag, the message text, and ends with a new line.

```
$template
verbose,"%syslogseverity%,%syslogfacility%,%timegenerated%,%HOSTNAME%,%syslogtag%,
                                                                       %msg%\n"
```

Example 17.3. A verbose syslog message template

Example 17.4. A wall message template below shows a template that resembles a traditional wall message (a message that is send to every user that is logged in and has their `mesg(1)` permission set to `yes`). This template outputs the message text, along with a hostname, message tag and a timestamp, on a new line (using `\r` and `\n`) and rings the bell (using `\7`).

```
$template wallmsg,"\r\n\7Message from syslogd@%HOSTNAME% at %timegenerated%
                                        ...\r\n %syslogtag% %msg%\n\r"
```

Example 17.4. A wall message template

Example 17.5. A database formatted message template below shows a template that formats a syslog message so that it can be used as a database query. Notice the use of the `sql` option at the end of the template specified as the template option. It tells the database writer to format the message as an MySQL SQL query.

```
$template dbFormat,"insert into SystemEvents (Message, Facility,FromHost, Priority,
DeviceReportedTime, ReceivedAt, InfoUnitID, SysLogTag) values ('%msg%',
%syslogfacility%, '%HOSTNAME%',%syslogpriority%, '%timereported:::date-mysql%',
'%timegenerated:::date-mysql%', %iut%, '%syslogtag%')",sql
```

Example 17.5. A database formatted message template

rsyslog also contains a set of predefined templates identified by the `RSYSLOG_` prefix. It is advisable to not create a template using this prefix to avoid any conflicts. The following list shows these predefined templates along with their definitions.

`RSYSLOG_DebugFormat`

```
"Debug line with all properties:\nFROMHOST: '%FROMHOST%', fromhost-ip:
'%fromhost-ip%', HOSTNAME: '%HOSTNAME%', PRI: %PRI%,\nsyslogtag '%syslogtag%',
programname: '%programname%', APP-NAME: '%APP-NAME%', PROCID: '%PROCID%',
MSGID: '%MSGID%',\nTIMESTAMP: '%TIMESTAMP%', STRUCTURED-DATA: '%STRUCTURED-
DATA%',\nmsg: '%msg%'\nescaped msg: '%msg:::drop-cc%'\nrawmsg: '%rawmsg%'\n\n\"
```

`RSYSLOG_SyslogProtocol23Format`

```
"<%PRI%>1 %TIMESTAMP:::date-rfc3339% %HOSTNAME% %APP-NAME% %PROCID% %MSGID%
%STRUCTURED-DATA% %msg%\n\"
```

`RSYSLOG_FileFormat`

```
"%TIMESTAMP:::date-rfc3339% %HOSTNAME% %syslogtag%%msg:::sp-if-no-1st-
sp%%msg:::drop-last-lf%\n\"
```

`RSYSLOG_TraditionalFileFormat`

```
"%TIMESTAMP% %HOSTNAME% %syslogtag%%msg:::sp-if-no-1st-sp%%msg:::drop-last-
lf%\n\"
```

`RSYSLOG_ForwardFormat`

```
"<%PRI%>%TIMESTAMP:::date-rfc3339% %HOSTNAME% %syslogtag:1:32%%msg:::sp-if-no-
1st-sp%%msg%\"
```

`RSYSLOG_TraditionalForwardFormat`

```
"<%PRI%>%TIMESTAMP% %HOSTNAME% %syslogtag:1:32%%msg:::sp-if-no-1st-sp%%msg%\"
```

17.1.4. rsyslog Command Line Configuration

Some of **rsyslog**'s functionality can be configured through the command line options, as **sysklogd**'s can. Note that as of version 3 of **rsyslog**, this method was deprecated. To enable some of these option, you must specify the compatibility mode **rsyslog** should run in. However, configuring **rsyslog** through the command line options should be avoided.

To specify the compatibility mode **rsyslog** should run in, use the `-c` option. When no parameter is specified, **rsyslog** tries to be compatible with **sysklogd**. This is partially achieved by activating configuration directives that modify your configuration accordingly. Therefore, it is advisable to supply this option with a number that matches the major version of **rsyslog** that is in use and update your `/etc/rsyslog.conf` configuration file accordingly. If you want to, for example, use **sysklogd** options (which were deprecated in version 3 of **rsyslog**), you can specify so by executing the following command:

```
~]# rsyslogd -c 2
```

Options that are passed to the `rsyslogd` daemon, including the backward compatibility mode, can be specified in the `/etc/sysconfig/rsyslog` configuration file.

For more information on various `rsyslogd` options, refer to `man rsyslogd`.

17.2. Locating Log Files

Most log files are located in the `/var/log/` directory. Some applications such as `httpd` and `samba` have a directory within `/var/log/` for their log files.

You may notice multiple files in the `/var/log/` directory with numbers after them (for example, `cron-20100906`). These numbers represent a timestamp that has been added to a rotated log file. Log files are rotated so their file sizes do not become too large. The `logrotate` package contains a cron task that automatically rotates log files according to the `/etc/logrotate.conf` configuration file and the configuration files in the `/etc/logrotate.d/` directory.

17.2.1. Configuring logrotate

The following is a sample `/etc/logrotate.conf` configuration file:

```
# rotate log files weekly
weekly
# keep 4 weeks worth of backlogs
rotate 4
# uncomment this if you want your log files compressed
compress
```

All of the lines in the sample configuration file define global options that apply to every log file. In our example, log files are rotated weekly, rotated log files are kept for the duration of

4 weeks, and all rotated log files are compressed by **gzip** into the `.gz` format. Any lines that begin with a hash sign (#) are comments and are not processed

You may define configuration options for a specific log file and place it under the global options. However, it is advisable to create a separate configuration file for any specific log file in the `/etc/logrotate.d/` directory and define any configuration options there.

The following is an example of a configuration file placed in the `/etc/logrotate.d/` directory:

```
/var/log/messages {
    rotate 5
    weekly
    postrotate
    /usr/bin/killall -HUP syslogd
    endscript
}
```

The configuration options in this file are specific for the `/var/log/messages` log file only. The settings specified here override the global settings where possible. Thus the rotated `/var/log/messages` log file will be kept for five weeks instead of four weeks as was defined in the global options.

The following is a list of some of the directives you can specify in your **logrotate** configuration file:

- *`weekly`* – Specifies the rotation of log files on a weekly basis. Similar directives include:
    - *`daily`*
    - *`monthly`*
    - *`yearly`*
- *`compress`* – Enables compression of rotated log files. Similar directives include:
    - *`nocompress`*
    - *`compresscmd`* – Specifies the command to be used for compressing.
    - *`uncompresscmd`*
    - *`compressext`* – Specifies what extension is to be used for compressing.
    - *`compressoptions`* – Lets you specify any options that may be passed to the used compression program.
    - *`delaycompress`* – Postpones the compression of log files to the next rotation of log files.

- *rotate <INTEGER>* — Specifies the number of rotations a log file undergoes before it is removed or mailed to a specific address. If the value `0` is specified, old log files are removed instead of rotated.
- *mail <ADDRESS>* — This option enables mailing of log files that have been rotated as many times as is defined by the *rotate* directive to the specified address. Similar directives include:
  - *nomail*
  - *mailfirst* — Specifies that the just-rotated log files are to be mailed, instead of the about-to-expire log files.
  - *maillast* — Specifies that the just-rotated log files are to be mailed, instead of the about-to-expire log files. This is the default option when *mail* is enabled.

For the full list of directives and various configuration options, refer to the `logrotate` man page (`man logrotate`).

17.3. Viewing Log Files

Most log files are in plain text format. You can view them with any text editor such as `Vi` or **Emacs**. Some log files are readable by all users on the system; however, `root` privileges are required to read most log files.

To view system log files in an interactive, real-time application, use the **Log File Viewer**.

Installing the gnome-system-log package

In order to use the **Log File Viewer**, first ensure the gnome-system-log package is installed on your system by running, as `root`:

```
yum install gnome-system-log
```

For more information on installing packages with Yum, refer to Section 4.2.4, *Installing Packages* (page 78).

After you have installed the gnome-system-log package, you can open the **Log File Viewer** by selecting **Applications** → **System Tools** → **Log File Viewer** from the **Activities** menu, or type the following command at a shell prompt:

```
gnome-system-log
```

The application only displays log files that exist; thus, the list might differ from the one shown in *Figure 17.1. Log File Viewer* below.

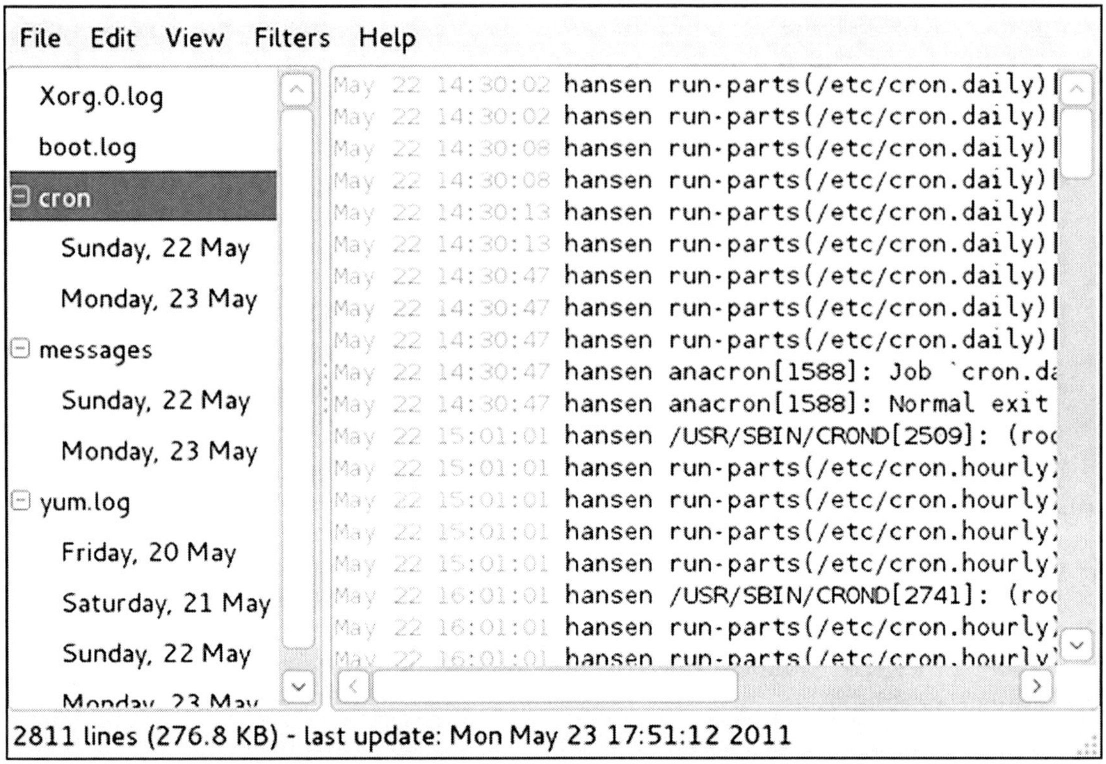

Figure 17.1. Log File Viewer

The **Log File Viewer** application lets you filter any existing log file. Click on **Filters** from the menu and select **Manage Filters** to define or edit your desired filter.

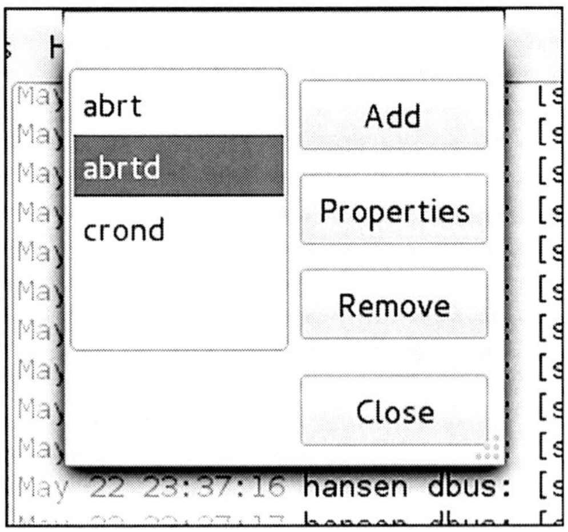

Figure 17.2. Log File Viewer — filters

Adding or editing a filter lets you define its parameters as is shown in *Figure 17.3. Log File Viewer — defining a filter* below

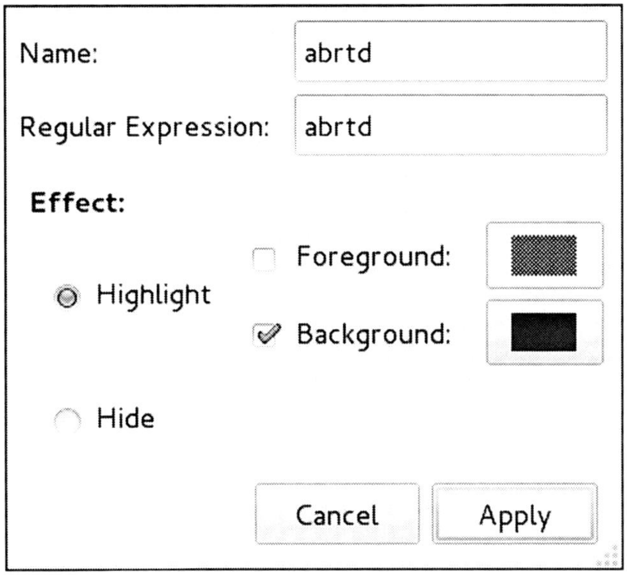

Figure 17.3. Log File Viewer — defining a filter

When defining a filter, you can edit the following parameters:

- **Name** — Specifies the name of the filter.
- **Regular Expression** — Specifies the regular expression that will be applied to the log file and will attempt to match any possible strings of text in it.
- **Effect**
  - **Highlight** — If checked, the found results will be highlighted with the selected color. You may select whether to highlight the background or the foreground of the text.
  - **Hide** — If checked, the found results will be hidden from the log file you are viewing.

When you have at least one filter defined, you may select it from the **Filters** menu and it will automatically search for the strings you have defined in the filter and highlight/hide every successful match in the log file you are currently viewing.

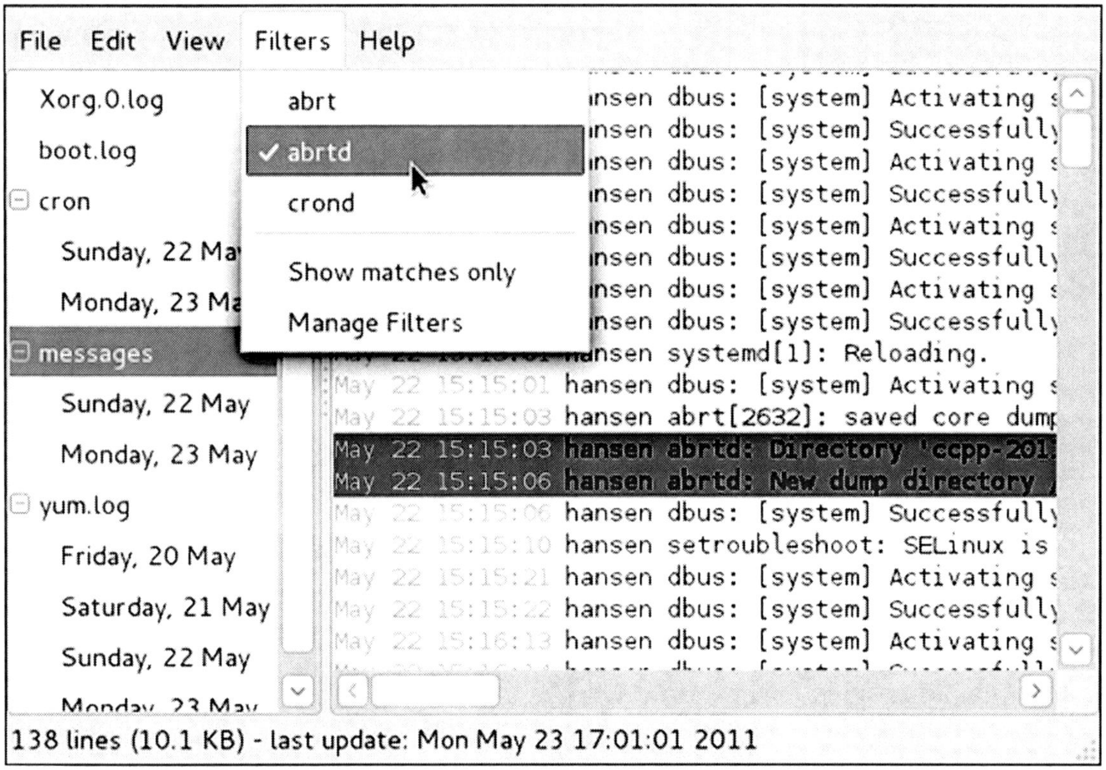

Figure 17.4. Log File Viewer — enabling a filter

When you check the **Show matches only** option, only the matched strings will be shown in the log file you are currently viewing.

17.4. Adding a Log File

To add a log file you wish to view in the list, select **File** → **Open**. This will display the **Open Log** window where you can select the directory and file name of the log file you wish to view. *Figure 17.5. Log File Viewer – adding a log file* below illustrates the **Open Log** window.

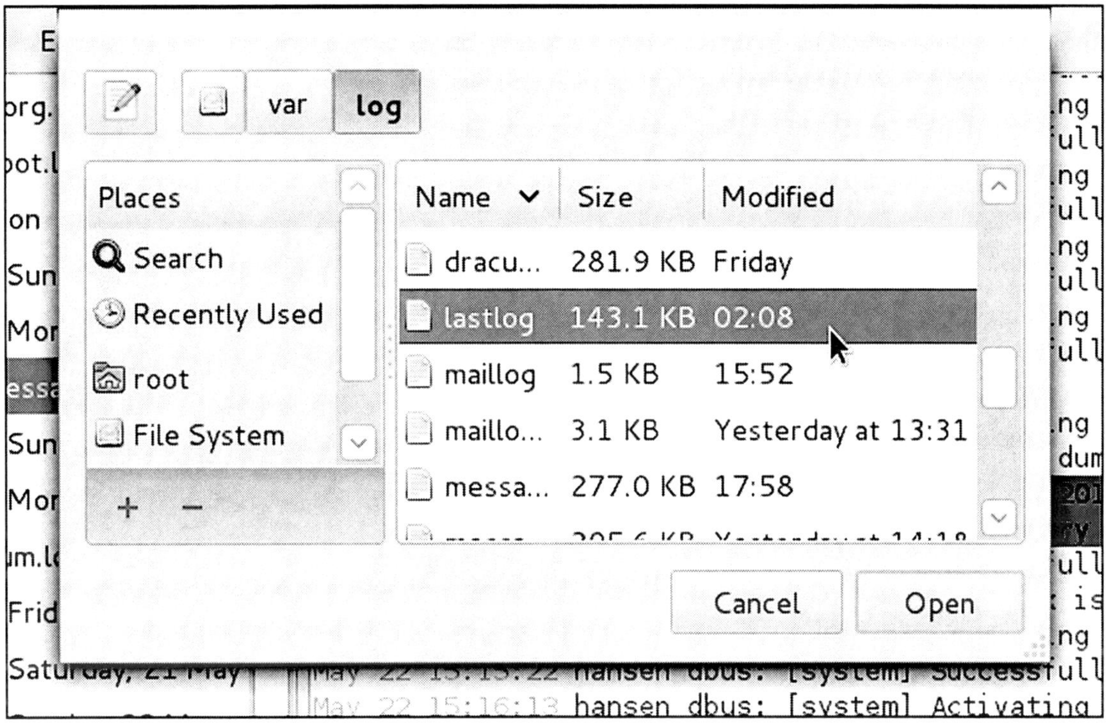

Figure 17.5. Log File Viewer – adding a log file

Click on the **Open** button to open the file. The file is immediately added to the viewing list where you can select it and view its contents.

Reading zipped log files

The **Log File Viewer** also allows you to open log files zipped in the `.gz` format.

17.5. Monitoring Log Files

Log File Viewer monitors all opened logs by default. If a new line is added to a monitored log file, the log name appears in bold in the log list. If the log file is selected or displayed, the new lines appear in bold at the bottom of the log file. *Figure 17.6. Log File Viewer – new log alert* below illustrates a new alert in the **yum.log** log file and in the **messages** log file. Clicking on the **messages** log file displays the logs in the file with the new lines in bold.

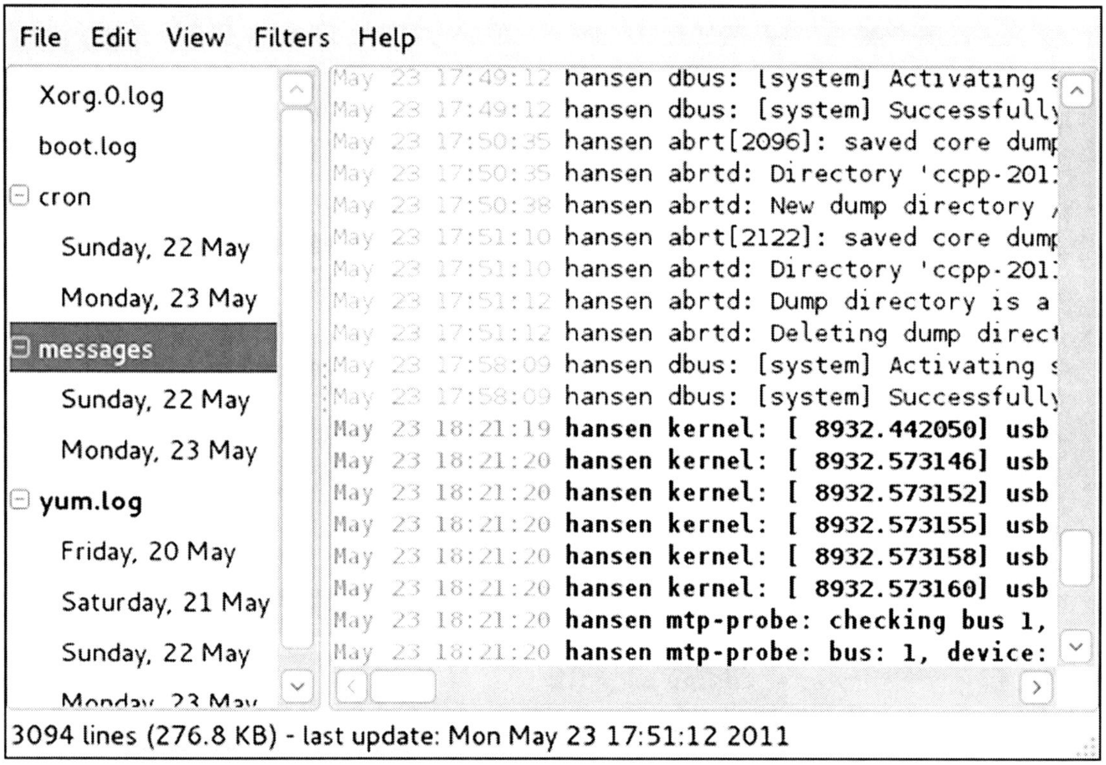

Figure 17.6. Log File Viewer — new log alert

17.6. Additional Resources

To learn more about **rsyslog**, **logrotate**, and log files in general, refer to the following resources.

17.6.1. Installed Documentation

- `rsyslogd` manual page — Type `man rsyslogd` to learn more about `rsyslogd` and its many options.
- `rsyslog.conf` manual page — Type `man rsyslog.conf` to learn more about the `/etc/rsyslog.conf` configuration file and its many options.

- `/usr/share/doc/rsyslog-<version-number>/` — After installing the rsyslog package, this directory contains extensive documentation in the `html` format.
- `logrotate` manual page — Type `man logrotate` to learn more about `logrotate` and its many options.

17.6.2. Useful Websites

- *http://www.rsyslog.com/* — Offers a thorough technical breakdown of rsyslog features, documentation, configuration examples, and video tutorials.
- *http://wiki.rsyslog.com/index.php/Main_Page* — Contains useful `/etc/rsyslog.conf` configuration examples.

Chapter 18.

Automating System Tasks

In Linux, tasks, which are also known as *jobs*, can be configured to run automatically within a specified period of time, on a specified date, or when the system load average is below a specified number. Fedora is pre-configured to run important system tasks to keep the system updated. For example, the slocate database used by the `locate` command is updated daily. A system administrator can use automated tasks to perform periodic backups, monitor the system, run custom scripts, and more.

Fedora comes with several automated tasks utilities: `cron`, `at`, and `batch`.

18.1. Cron and Anacron

Both, Cron and Anacron, are daemons that can be used to schedule the execution of recurring tasks according to a combination of the time, day of the month, month, day of the week, and week.

Cron assumes that the system is on continuously. If the system is not on when a job is scheduled, it is not executed. Cron allows jobs to be run as often as every minute. Anacron does not assume the system is always on, remembers every scheduled job, and executes it the next time the system is up. However, Anacron can only run a job once a day. To schedule recurring jobs, refer to Section 18.1.2, *Configuring Anacron Jobs* (page 389) or Section 18.1.3, *Configuring Cron Jobs* (page 391). To schedule one-time jobs, refer to Section 18.2, *At and Batch* (page 393).

To use the cron service, the `cronie` RPM package must be installed and the `crond` service must be running. `anacron` is a sub-package of `cronie`. To determine if these packages are installed, use the `rpm -q cronie cronie-anacron` command.

18.1.1. Starting and Stopping the Service

To determine if the service is running, use the following command:

```
systemctl is-active crond.service
```

To start the cron service, type the following at a shell prompt as `root`:

```
systemctl start crond.service
```

To stop the service, run the following command as `root`:

```
systemctl stop crond.service
```

It is recommended that you start the service at boot time. To do so, use the following command as `root`:

```
systemctl enable crond.service
```

Refer to Chapter 7, *Services and Daemons* (page 120) for more information on how to configure services in Fedora.

18.1.2. Configuring Anacron Jobs

The main configuration file to schedule jobs is `/etc/anacrontab` (only `root` is allowed to modify this file), which contains the following lines:

```
SHELL=/bin/sh
PATH=/sbin:/bin:/usr/sbin:/usr/bin
MAILTO=root
# the maximal random delay added to the base delay of the jobs
RANDOM_DELAY=45
# the jobs will be started during the following hours only
START_HOURS_RANGE=3-22

#period in days   delay in minutes   job-identifier   command
1         5      cron.daily     nice run-parts /etc/cron.daily
7         25     cron.weekly    nice run-parts /etc/cron.weekly
@monthly  45     cron.monthly   nice run-parts /etc/cron.monthly
```

The first three lines are variables used to configure the environment in which the anacron tasks are run. The `SHELL` variable tells the system which shell environment to use (in this example the bash shell). The `PATH` variable defines the path used to execute commands. The output of the anacron jobs are emailed to the username defined with the `MAILTO` variable. If the `MAILTO` variable is not defined, (i.e. is empty, `MAILTO=`), email is not sent.

The next two lines are variables that modify the time for each scheduled job. The `RANDOM_DELAY` variable denotes the maximum number of minutes that will be added to the `delay in minutes` variable which is specified for each job. The minimum delay value is set, by default, to 6 minutes. A `RANDOM_DELAY` set to 12 would therefore add, randomly, between 6 and 12 minutes to the `delay in minutes` for each job in that particular anacrontab. `RANDOM_DELAY` can also be set to a value below 6, or even 0. When set to 0, no random delay is added. This proves to be useful when, for example, more computers that share one network connection need to download the same data every day. The `START_HOURS_RANGE` variable defines an interval (in hours) when scheduled jobs can be run. In case this time interval is missed, for example, due to a power down, then scheduled jobs are not executed that day.

The rest of the lines in the `/etc/anacrontab` file represent scheduled jobs and have the following format:

```
period in days   delay in minutes   job-identifier   command
```

- `period in days` — specifies the frequency of execution of a job in days. This variable can be represented by an integer or a macro (`@daily`, `@weekly`, `@monthly`), where `@daily` denotes the same value as the integer 1, `@weekly` the same as 7, and `@monthly` specifies that the job is run once a month, independent on the length of the month.
- `delay in minutes` — specifies the number of minutes anacron waits, if necessary, before executing a job. This variable is represented by an integer where 0 means no delay.
- `job-identifier` — specifies a unique name of a job which is used in the log files.
- `command` — specifies the command to execute. The command can either be a command such as `ls /proc >> /tmp/proc` or a command to execute a custom script.

Any lines that begin with a hash sign (#) are comments and are not processed.

18.1.2.1. Examples of Anacron Jobs

The following example shows a simple `/etc/anacrontab` file:

```
SHELL=/bin/sh
PATH=/sbin:/bin:/usr/sbin:/usr/bin
MAILTO=root

# the maximal random delay added to the base delay of the jobs
RANDOM_DELAY=30
# the jobs will be started during the following hours only
START_HOURS_RANGE=16-20

#period in days   delay in minutes   job-identifier   command
1         20    dailyjob       nice run-parts /etc/cron.daily
7         25    weeklyjob      /etc/weeklyjob.bash
@monthly  45    monthlyjob     ls /proc >> /tmp/proc
```

All jobs defined in this `anacrontab` file are randomly delayed by 6-30 minutes and can be executed between 16:00 and 20:00. Thus, the first defined job will run anywhere between 16:26 and 16:50 every day. The command specified for this job will execute all present programs in the `/etc/cron.daily` directory (using the `run-parts` script which takes a directory as a command-line argument and sequentially executes every program within that directory). The second specified job will be executed once a week and will execute the `weeklyjob.bash` script in the `/etc` directory. The third job is executed once a month and runs a command to write the contents of the `/proc` to the `/tmp/proc` file (e.g. `ls /proc >> /tmp/proc`).

18.1.2.1.1. Disabling Anacron

In case your system is continuously on and you do not require anacron to run your scheduled jobs, you may uninstall the `cronie-anacron` package. Thus, you will be able to define jobs using crontabs only.

18.1.3. Configuring Cron Jobs

The configuration file to configure cron jobs, `/etc/crontab` (only `root` is allowed to modify this file), contains the following lines:

```
SHELL=/bin/bash
PATH=/sbin:/bin:/usr/sbin:/usr/bin
MAILTO=root
HOME=/
# For details see man 4 crontabs
# Example of job definition:
# .---------------- minute (0 - 59)
# | .------------- hour (0 - 23)
# | | .---------- day of month (1 - 31)
# | | | .------- month (1 - 12) OR jan,feb,mar,apr ...
# | | | | .---- day of week (0 - 6) (Sunday=0 or 7) OR sun,mon,tue,wed,thu,fri,sat
# | | | | |
# * * * * * user command to be executed
```

The first three lines contain the same variables as an `anacrontab` file, `SHELL`, `PATH` and `MAILTO`. For more information about these variables, refer to Section 18.1.2, *Configuring Anacron Jobs* (page 389). The fourth line contains the `HOME` variable. The `HOME` variable can be used to set the home directory to use when executing commands or scripts.

The rest of the lines in the `/etc/crontab` file represent scheduled jobs and have the following format:

```
minute   hour   day   month   day of week   user   command
```

- `minute` — any integer from 0 to 59
- `hour` — any integer from 0 to 23
- `day` — any integer from 1 to 31 (must be a valid day if a month is specified)
- `month` — any integer from 1 to 12 (or the short name of the month such as jan or feb)
- `day of week` — any integer from 0 to 7, where 0 or 7 represents Sunday (or the short name of the week such as sun or mon)
- `user` — specifies the user under which the jobs are run
- `command` — the command to execute (the command can either be a command such as `ls /proc >> /tmp/proc` or the command to execute a custom script)

For any of the above values, an asterisk (*) can be used to specify all valid values. For example, an asterisk for the month value means execute the command every month within the constraints of the other values.

A hyphen (-) between integers specifies a range of integers. For example, `1-4` means the integers 1, 2, 3, and 4.

A list of values separated by commas (,) specifies a list. For example, `3, 4, 6, 8` indicates those four specific integers.

The forward slash (/) can be used to specify step values. The value of an integer can be skipped within a range by following the range with `/integer`. For example, `0-59/2` can be used to define every other minute in the minute field. Step values can also be used with an asterisk. For instance, the value `*/3` can be used in the month field to run the task every third month.

Any lines that begin with a hash sign (#) are comments and are not processed.

Users other than `root` can configure cron tasks by using the `crontab` utility. All user-defined crontabs are stored in the `/var/spool/cron/` directory and are executed using the usernames of the users that created them. To create a crontab as a user, login as that user and type the command `crontab -e` to edit the user's crontab using the editor specified by the `VISUAL` or `EDITOR` environment variable. The file uses the same format as `/etc/crontab`. When the changes to the crontab are saved, the crontab is stored according to username and written to the file `/var/spool/cron/username` . To list the contents of your own personal crontab file, use the `crontab -l` command.

Do not specify a user

When using the `crontab` utility, there is no need to specify a user when defining a job.

The `/etc/cron.d/` directory contains files that have the same syntax as the `/etc/crontab` file. Only `root` is allowed to create and modify files in this directory.

Do not restart the daemon to apply the changes

The cron daemon checks the `/etc/anacrontab` file, the `/etc/crontab` file, the `/etc/cron.d/` directory, and the `/var/spool/cron/` directory every minute for any changes. If any changes are found, they are loaded into memory. Thus, the daemon does not need to be restarted if an anacrontab or a crontab file is changed.

18.1.4. Controlling Access to Cron

The `/etc/cron.allow` and `/etc/cron.deny` files are used to restrict access to cron. The format of both access control files is one username on each line. Whitespace is not permitted in either file. The cron daemon (`crond`) does not have to be restarted if the access control files are modified. The access control files are checked each time a user tries to add or delete a cron job.

The `root` user can always use cron, regardless of the usernames listed in the access control files.

If the file `cron.allow` exists, only users listed in it are allowed to use cron, and the `cron.deny` file is ignored.

If `cron.allow` does not exist, users listed in `cron.deny` are not allowed to use cron.

Access can also be controlled through Pluggable Authentication Modules (PAM). These settings are stored in `/etc/security/access.conf`. For example, adding the following line in this file forbids creating crontabs for all users except the `root` user:

```
-:ALL EXCEPT root :cron
```

The forbidden jobs are logged in an appropriate log file or, when using "crontab -e", returned to the standard output. For more information, refer to `access.conf.5` (i.e. `man 5 access.conf`).

18.1.5. Black/White Listing of Cron Jobs

Black/White listing of jobs is used to omit parts of the defined jobs that do not need to be executed. When calling the `run-parts` script on a cron folder, such as `/etc/cron.daily`, we can define which of the programs in this folder will not be executed by `run-parts`.

To define a black list, create a `jobs.deny` file in the folder that `run-parts` will be executing from. For example, if we need to omit a particular program from /etc/cron.daily, then, a file `/etc/cron.daily/jobs.deny` has to be created. In this file, specify the names of the omitted programs from the same directory. These will not be executed when a command, such as `run-parts /etc/cron.daily`, is executed by a specific job.

To define a white list, create a `jobs.allow` file.

The principles of `jobs.deny` and `jobs.allow` are the same as those of `cron.deny` and `cron.allow` described in section Section 18.1.4, *Controlling Access to Cron* (page 392).

18.2. At and Batch

While cron is used to schedule recurring tasks, the `at` command is used to schedule a one-time task at a specific time and the `batch` command is used to schedule a one-time task to be executed when the systems load average drops below 0.8.

To use `at` or `batch`, the `at` RPM package must be installed, and the `atd` service must be running. To determine if the package is installed, use the `rpm -q at` command. To determine if the service is running, use the following command:

```
systemctl is-active atd.service
```

18.2.1. Configuring At Jobs

To schedule a one-time job at a specific time, type the command `at time` , where `time` is the time to execute the command.

The argument `time` can be one of the following:

- HH:MM format — For example, 04:00 specifies 4:00 a.m. If the time is already past, it is executed at the specified time the next day.
- midnight — Specifies 12:00 a.m.
- noon — Specifies 12:00 p.m.
- teatime — Specifies 4:00 p.m.
- month-name day year format — For example, January 15 2002 specifies the 15th day of January in the year 2002. The year is optional.
- MMDDYY, MM/DD/YY, or MM.DD.YY formats — For example, 011502 for the 15th day of January in the year 2002.
- now + time — time is in minutes, hours, days, or weeks. For example, now + 5 days specifies that the command should be executed at the same time five days from now.

The time must be specified first, followed by the optional date. For more information about the time format, read the `/usr/share/doc/at-version/timespec` text file.

After typing the `at` command with the time argument, the `at>` prompt is displayed. Type the command to execute, press **Enter**, and press **Ctrl+D** . Multiple commands can be specified by typing each command followed by the **Enter** key. After typing all the commands, press **Enter** to go to a blank line and press **Ctrl+D** . Alternatively, a shell script can be entered at the prompt, pressing **Enter** after each line in the script, and pressing **Ctrl+D** on a blank line to exit. If a script is entered, the shell used is the shell set in the user's `SHELL` environment, the user's login shell, or `/bin/sh` (whichever is found first).

If the set of commands or script tries to display information to standard output, the output is emailed to the user.

Use the command `atq` to view pending jobs. Refer to Section 18.2.3, *Viewing Pending Jobs* (page 395) for more information.

Usage of the `at` command can be restricted. For more information, refer to Section 18.2.5, *Controlling Access to At and Batch* (page 395) for details.

18.2.2. Configuring Batch Jobs

To execute a one-time task when the load average is below 0.8, use the `batch` command.

After typing the `batch` command, the `at>` prompt is displayed. Type the command to execute, press **Enter**, and press **Ctrl+D** . Multiple commands can be specified by typing each command followed by the **Enter** key. After typing all the commands, press **Enter** to go to a blank line and press **Ctrl+D** . Alternatively, a shell script can be entered at the prompt, pressing **Enter** after each line in the script, and pressing **Ctrl+D** on a blank line to exit. If a script is entered, the shell used is the shell set in the user's `SHELL` environment, the user's login shell, or `/bin/sh` (whichever is found first). As soon as the load average is below 0.8, the set of commands or script is executed.

If the set of commands or script tries to display information to standard out, the output is emailed to the user.

Use the command `atq` to view pending jobs. Refer to Section 18.2.3, *Viewing Pending Jobs* (page 395) for more information.

Usage of the `batch` command can be restricted. For more information, refer to Section 18.2.5, *Controlling Access to At and Batch* (page 395) for details.

18.2.3. Viewing Pending Jobs

To view pending `at` and `batch` jobs, use the `atq` command. The `atq` command displays a list of pending jobs, with each job on a line. Each line follows the job number, date, hour, job class, and username format. Users can only view their own jobs. If the `root` user executes the `atq` command, all jobs for all users are displayed.

18.2.4. Additional Command Line Options

Additional command line options for `at` and `batch` include:

Option	Description
`-f`	Read the commands or shell script from a file instead of specifying them at the prompt.
`-m`	Send email to the user when the job has been completed.
`-v`	Display the time that the job is executed.

Table 18.1. `at` and `batch` Command Line Options

18.2.5. Controlling Access to At and Batch

The `/etc/at.allow` and `/etc/at.deny` files can be used to restrict access to the `at` and `batch` commands. The format of both access control files is one username on each line. Whitespace is not permitted in either file. The `at` daemon (`atd`) does not have to be restarted if the access control files are modified. The access control files are read each time a user tries to execute the `at` or `batch` commands.

The root user can always execute at and batch commands, regardless of the access control files.

If the file at.allow exists, only users listed in it are allowed to use at or batch, and the at.deny file is ignored.

If at.allow does not exist, users listed in at.deny are not allowed to use at or batch.

18.2.6. Starting and Stopping the Service

To start the at service, use the following command as root:

```
systemctl start atd.service
```

To stop the service, as root, type the following at a shell prompt:

```
systemctl stop atd.service
```

It is recommended that you start the service at boot time. To do so, run the following command as root:

```
systemctl enable atd.service
```

Refer to Chapter 7, *Services and Daemons* (page 120) for more information on how to configure services in Fedora.

18.3. Additional Resources

To learn more about configuring automated tasks, refer to the following resources.

18.3.1. Installed Documentation

- cron man page — contains an overview of cron.
- crontab man pages in sections 1 and 5 — The man page in section 1 contains an overview of the crontab file. The man page in section 5 contains the format for the file and some example entries.
- anacron man page — contains an overview of anacron.
- anacrontab man page — contains an overview of the anacrontab file.
- /usr/share/doc/at-*version*/timespec contains more detailed information about the times that can be specified for cron jobs.
- at man page — description of at and batch and their command line options.

Chapter 19.

Automatic Bug-Reporting Tool (ABRT)

19.1. Overview

ABRT is the **Automatic Bug-Reporting Tool**. **ABRT** consists of a daemon that runs silently in the background most of the time. It springs into action when an application crashes. It then collects the relevant crash data such as a core file if there is one, the crashing application's command line parameters, and other contextual puzzle pieces of forensic utility. Finally, **ABRT** is capable of reporting crash data to a relevant issue tracker, such as Red Hat Bugzilla. Reporting crash data to a relevant issue tracker can be configured to happen automatically at every detected crash, or crash dumps can be stored locally, reviewed, reported, and deleted manually by a user. **ABRT**'s various plugins analyze crash data from applications written in the C, C++ and Python language, as well as report crashes to relevant issue trackers.

The **ABRT** package consists of:

- `abrtd`, the system service
- **abrt-applet**, which runs in the user's Notification Area
- **abrt-gui**, the GUI application that shows collected crash dumps and allows you to edit, report, and delete them
- **abrt-cli**, the command line interface with functionality similar to **abrt-gui**.

You can open the **ABRT** GUI application by selecting **Applications** → **System Tools** → **Automatic Bug Reporting Tool** from the **Activities** menu.

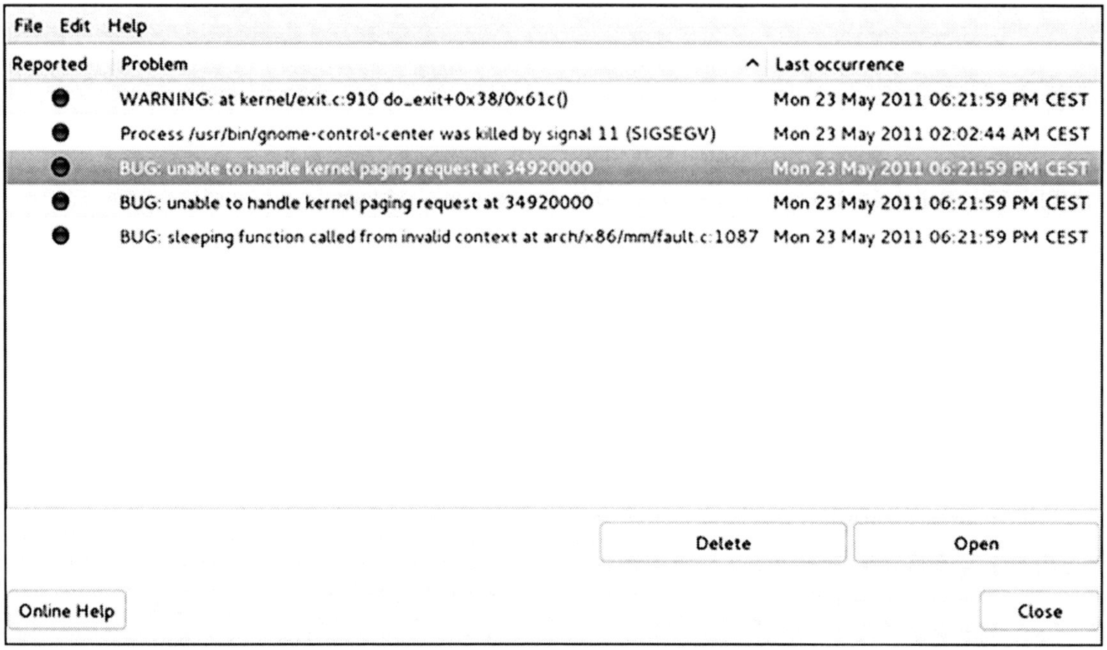

Figure 19.1. The Automatic Bug Reporting Tool main window

A number of additional packages can be installed to provide **ABRT** plugins and addons. To view all the available **ABRT** packages, type the following command:

```
yum list all | grep abrt
```

19.2. Installing and Running ABRT

By default, **ABRT** should be installed on your system, the `abrtd` daemon configured to run at boot time, and **abrt-applet** to run in the Notification Area of your desktop session.

Installing the ABRT packages

In order to use **ABRT**, first ensure the `abrt-desktop` package is installed on your system by running, as `root`:

```
yum install abrt-desktop
```

For more information on installing packages with Yum, refer to Section 4.2.4, *Installing Packages* (page 78).

ABRT is typically configured to start up at boot time. You can check that the `abrtd` daemon is running by running the following command, as `root`:

```
systemctl is-active abrtd.service
```

If you receive `abrt is stopped`, you can start the `abrtd` service by running, as `root`:

```
systemctl start abrtd.service
```

You can ensure that the `abrtd` service initializes at startup time by running the following command, as `root`:

```
systemctl enable abrtd.service
```

ABRT's applet can be started by hand by running the `abrt-applet` program as a normal user when logged into your desktop session, or by arranging for it to be started when the GUI session is initialized.

Figure 19.2. The ABRT problem report

When a crash is detected and saved, a broadcast `D-Bus` message is sent about this crash. If `abrt-applet` is running, it receives this message and displays an alarm icon in the Notification Area. You can open the GUI application by clicking on this icon.

Alternatively, you can open the **ABRT** GUI application by selecting **Applications** → **System Tools** → **Automatic Bug Reporting Tool** from the **Activities** menu.

19.3. ABRT Plugins

ABRT offers a variety of analyzer plugins and reporter plugins. These plugins are described in the following two sections. Not all of the plugins mentioned in the following sections are installed by default. To view all available plugins, run the following command:

```
yum list all | grep abrt-plugin-*
```

19.3.1. Analyzer Plugins

These plugins serve as analyzers and crash information collectors for specific types of crashes. For example, the **Kerneloops** analyzer plugin checks for crashes in the kernel only. These plugins can be enabled/disabled from loading at start-up in their corresponding configuration files placed in the `/etc/abrt/plugins/` directory. The following is a list of all analyzer plugins.

Kerneloops

— Checks for crashes in the kernel and consequently collects kernel crash information. It can be enabled/disabled from loading at start-up in the `/etc/abrt/plugins/Kerneloops.conf` file.

Python

— Checks for crashes in Python programs and consequently collects the crash information. It can be enabled/disabled from loading at start-up in the `/etc/abrt/plugins/Python.conf` file.

CCpp

— Checks for crashes in C and C++ programs and consequently collects the crash information. It can be enabled/disabled from loading at start-up in the `/etc/abrt/plugins/CCpp.conf` file.

19.3.2. Reporter Plugins

These plugins gather the crash data acquired by the analyzer plugins, combine the data with any user input (such as comments about the crash, reproducibility, etc.), and provide a specific output. Each of these plugins is configurable in its corresponding configuration file placed in the `/etc/abrt/plugins/` directory or in the **ABRT** GUI application (for more information on reporter plugin configuration in the **ABRT** GUI application, refer to Section 19.3.3, *Plugin Configuration in the GUI* - page 400).

MailX

— Sends a crash report via the **mailx** utility to a specified email address.

Report Uploader

— Uploads a tarball with crash data into a `FTP/SCP` server

Bugzilla

— Reports crashes into Bugzilla in the form of Bugzilla database entries.

Logger

— Creates a crash report and saves it to a specified local file.

19.3.3. Plugin Configuration in the GUI

You can override the system-wide plugin configuration in the `/etc/abrt/plugins/*.conf` configuration files on a per-user basis. Each of the plugins specified in section Section 19.3.2, *Reporter Plugins* (page 400) can be configured in the **ABRT** GUI application. Open the plugins window by clicking **Edit → Event configuration**. This window shows a list of all installed plugins. When you select one of the configurable plugins, you can click the **Configure Event** button and you will be able to configure your desired plugin. If you change any of the plugins' parameters, they are saved in the GNOME Keyring and will be used in the future GUI sessions.

Do not store sensitive data in global configuration files

All of the `/etc/abrt/plugins/*.conf` configuration files are world readable and are meant to be used as global settings. Thus, it is not advisable to store usernames, passwords or any other sensitive data in them. The per-user settings (set in the GUI application and readable by the owner of $HOME only) are stored in the Gnome keyring or can be stored in a text file in `$HOME/.abrt/*.conf` for use in `abrt-cli`.

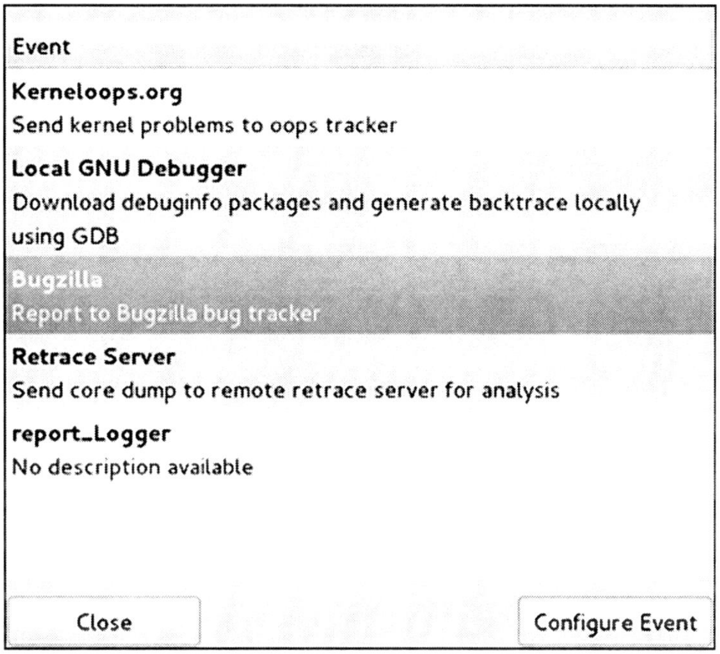

Figure 19.3. ABRT plugins

The following is a list of all configuration options available for each configurable plugin in the **ABRT** GUI application.

MailX

In the **MailX plugin configuration**, you can configure the following parameters:

- **Subject** — A string that appears in the `Subject` field of a crash report email sent by **mailx** (by default, set to `"[abrt] crash report"`).
- **Your Email** — A string that appears in the `From` field of a crash report email.
- **Recipient's Email** — Email address of the recipient of a crash report email.

When the **Send Binary Data** option is checked, the crash report email will also contain all binary files associated with the crash in an attachment. The core dump file is also sent as an attachment.

ReportUploader

In the **ReportUploader plugin configuration**, you can configure the following parameters:

- **Customer** — Specifies customer's identification.
- **Ticket** — Specifies the Ticket ID number in a specific issue tracker that collects crash reports.
- **URL** — Specifies the URL of the issue tracker used to collect crash reports.
- **Retry count** — Specifies the number of retries should an upload fail.
- **Retry delay** — Specifies the number or seconds between two retries.

When the **Use encryption** option is checked, the crash report sent to the issue tracker is encrypted.

When the **Upload** option is checked, all crash reports are uploaded to the specified issue tracker. If the option is unchecked, all crash reports are saved locally.

Bugzilla

In the **Bugzilla plugin configuration**, you can configure the following parameters:

- **Bugzilla URL** — Specifies the Bugzilla URL where crash dumps are sent (by default, set to *https://bugzilla.redhat.com*).
- **Login (email)** — User login which is used to log into Bugzilla and create a Bugzilla database entry for a reported crash.
- **Password** — Password used to log into Bugzilla.

When the **SSL verify** option is checked, the `SSL` protocol is used when sending the data over the network.

Logger

In the **Logger plugin configuration**, you can configure the following parameter:

- **Logger file** — Specifies a file into which the crash reports are saved (by default, set to `/var/log/abrt.log`).

When the **Append new logs** option is checked, the Logger plugin will append new crash reports to the log file specified in the **Logger file** option. When unchecked, the new crash report always replaces the previous one.

19.4. Generating Backtraces

In order to analyze a reported crash, developers need as much detail about the crash as possible. A *stack backtrace* is an important source of information when a crash in a binary program (caught by the `CCpp` analyzer plugin) occurs.

ABRT is configured to generate a backtrace whenever a crash is reported through the **ABRT** GUI application or the **ABRT** command line interface.

ABRT completes the following steps to generate a backtrace:

- It examines the core dump (which consists of the recorded contents of the memory of an application at a specific time), which is saved in the crash dump directory. From this file, **ABRT** extracts the information about the crashed binary program and information about every loaded dynamic library.
- It queries **Yum** to determine which debuginfo packages correspond to all the files extracted from the crash dump. This is the first potentially slow operation. **Yum** may need to refresh the *`filelists`* of various repositories in order to find the correct package names. This process may take a few minutes.
- It downloads the needed debuginfo packages, and extracts and saves the `debuginfo` files. In order to speed up future backtrace generation, `debuginfo` files are cached in the `/var/cache/abrt-di` directory.
- It generates a backtrace using **GDB** (the GNU Debugger) and saves it into the crash dump directory.

You can change the following backtrace generation parameters in the `/etc/abrt/plugins/CCpp.conf` file:

- `Backtrace = `*`yes/no`* — Enables/Disables backtrace generation.
- `BacktraceRemotes = `*`yes/no`* — For more information about this parameter, refer to Section 19.7, *Configuring Centralized Crash Collection* (page 409).
- `InstallDebugInfo = `*`yes/no`* — Enables/Disables the installation of debuginfo packages (useful if your network is not available or it is firewalled).
- `ReadonlyLocalDebugInfoDirs = /path1:/path2:...` — Specifies the paths of local repositories (available, for example, through a network mount) that contain pre-downloaded debuginfo packages.
- `DebugInfoCacheMB = 4000` — Specifies the maximum size of the cached debuginfo packages in the `/var/cache/abrt-di` directory.

19.4.1. Troubleshooting Backtrace Generation

In some cases, a long delay in the **ABRT** GUI application occurs after choosing a crash and pressing the **Report** button. In this case, open the **Details** in the **Generating backtrace** window and examine the messages.

The following is a typical output seen in the **Generating backtrace** window:

```
Starting the debuginfo installation
Getting list of build IDs
```

```
12 missing debuginfos, getting package list from cache
12 missing debuginfos, getting package list from repositories
Downloading 7 packages
Download 1/7: acl-debuginfo-2.2.49-6.fc13.x86_64
Unpacking: acl-debuginfo-2.2.49-6.fc13.x86_64.rpm
Caching debuginfo:
usr/lib/debug/.build-id/3d/e20df1db609bd9313b1dc440796004f95911fd.debug
Download 2/7: firefox-debuginfo-3.6.7-1.fc13.x86_64
Unpacking: firefox-debuginfo-3.6.7-1.fc13.x86_64.rpm
Caching debuginfo:
usr/lib/debug/.build-id/3d/b29c9308cb276431ce8854a2d88cf83518afc6.debug
Caching debuginfo:
usr/lib/debug/.build-id/a3/86884285365c8288e4e761ec034fafaa1daee1.debug
⋮
Download 7/7: zlib-debuginfo-1.2.3-23.fc12.x86_64
Unpacking: zlib-debuginfo-1.2.3-23.fc12.x86_64.rpm
Caching debuginfo:
usr/lib/debug/.build-id/f7/933750da80f555321576e72b375caf7a3cc075.debug
All needed debuginfos are present
Generating backtrace
```

This process is performed by the **/usr/bin/abrt-debuginfo-install** shell script. This script uses a temporary directory (e.g. `/var/run/abrt/tmp-29177-1283344373`) for its operations. Normally, this directory is removed when **abrt-debuginfo-install** exits.

If the debuginfo installation hangs, or is unable to download anything, you may debug the problem by editing the **abrt-debuginfo-install** script. Change the following parameters:

```
debug=false
keep_tmp=false
```

at the top of the script to:

```
debug=true
keep_tmp=true
```

The first parameter instructs **abrt-debuginfo-install** to be verbose, the second parameter instructs **abrt-debuginfo-install** to not delete the `/var/run/abrt/tmp-NNN-NNN` directory. You can examine the log files in this directory, they may contain useful error messages.

abrt-debuginfo-install uses **yum** and **yumdownloader** to handle the debuginfo packages. In order to quickly check that your **yum** configuration does not cause any problems which prevent **abrt-debuginfo-install** from working properly, change to the `/tmp` directory and run the following commands, as `root`:

```
tmp]# yum --enablerepo=*debuginfo* --quiet provides /usr/bin/true
tmp]# yumdownloader --enablerepo=*debuginfo* --quiet coreutils
```

Both of these commands should complete successfully, with no error messages. The second command should download the `coreutils-*.rpm` file. If any error messages appear, check your **yum** configuration files in the `/etc/yum.repos.d/*` directory and the `/etc/yum/*`

directory. If any of these commands hang, check that you do not have another instance of **yum** running, and that your network connection is working properly.

19.5. Using the Command Line Interface

Crashes detected by **ABRT** can be viewed, reported, and deleted using the command line interface.

19.5.1. Viewing Crashes

To get a list of all crashes, simply enter `abrt-cli --list` or `abrt-cli -l`:

```
~]$ abrt-cli --list
0.
   UID         : 500
   UUID        : 784b06666020e9f43718d99bf2649f19b4f251a9
   Package     : bash-4.1.2-3.el6
   Executable  : /bin/bash
   Crash Time  : Tue 20 Jul 2010 03:22:52 PM CEST
   Crash Count: 2
1.
   UID         : 500
   UUID        : 48007b98d65cca4530d99a564379e2609169239d
   Package     : coreutils-8.4-9.el6
   Executable  : /bin/sleep
   Crash Time  : Tue 20 Jul 2010 03:22:00 PM CEST
   Crash Count: 1
```

This output contains basic information for every crash. The `UID:` field shows the ID of the user which ran the program that caused the crash. The `Package` field shows the name and version of the Fedora package that contains the program, and the `Executable` field shows the location of the binary or script that crashed. The `Crash Count` field indicates how many times the same crash happened.

19.5.2. Reporting Crashes

To report a certain crash, enter `abrt-cli --report` *`UUID`* or `abrt-cli --r` *`UUID`*, where `UUID` is a Universally Unique Identifier of a crash from the list of crashes; to view this list, execute the `abrt-cli --list` command. You do not need to remember the exact `UUID`; either use a mouse to copy and paste it, or enter a unique prefix and press **ENTER**.

```
~]$ abrt-cli --report 480
<ENTER>
>> Starting report creation...
```

ABRT analyzes the crash and creates a report about it. This might take a while. When the report is ready, `abrt-cli` opens a text editor with the content of the report. You can see what is being reported, and you can fill in instructions on how to reproduce the crash and other comments. You should also check the backtrace, because the backtrace might be sent to a public server and viewed by anyone, depending on the plugin settings.

Selecting a preferred text editor

You can choose which text editor is used to check the reports. `abrt-cli` uses the editor defined in the `ABRT_EDITOR` environment variable. If the variable is not defined, it checks the `VISUAL` and `EDITOR` variables. If none of these variables is set, `vi` is used. You can set the preferred editor in your `.bashrc` configuration file. For example, if you prefer GNU Emacs, add the following line to the file:

```
export VISUAL=emacs
```

When you are done with the report, save your changes and close the editor. You will be asked which of the enabled **ABRT** plugins you want to use to send the report. Respond **Y** to send the report using your desired plugin or **N** to skip a plugin you wish not to use.

19.5.3. Deleting Crashes

If you know that you do not want to report a certain crash dump, you can delete it from the crash list. To delete a certain crash dump, enter the command: `abrt-cli --delete` *`UUID`* .

Note that **ABRT** performs a detection of duplicate crashes by comparing new crashes with all locally saved crashes. For a repeating crash, **ABRT** requires you to act upon it only once. However, if you delete the crash dump of that crash, the next time this specific crash occurs, **ABRT** will treat it as a new crash: **ABRT** will alert you about it, prompt you to fill in a description, and report it. This can be redundant, therefore, deleting a crash is not advisable.

19.6. Configuring ABRT

ABRT's main configuration file is `/etc/abrt/abrt.conf`. **ABRT** plugins can be configured through their configuration files, located in the `/etc/abrt/plugins/` directory.

Restart the abrtd daemon to apply the changes

After changing and saving the `/etc/abrt/abrt.conf` configuration file, you must restart the `abrtd` daemon—as `root`—for the new settings to take effect:

```
systemctl restart abrtd.service
```

The following configuration directives are currently supported in `/etc/abrt/abrt.conf`.

[Common] Section Directives

OpenGPGCheck = *`yes/no`*

Setting the `OpenGPGCheck` directive to **`yes`** (the default setting) tells **ABRT** to *only* analyze and handle crashes in applications provided by packages which are signed by the GPG keys whose locations are listed in the `/etc/abrt/gpg_keys` file. Setting *OpenGPGCheck* to **no** tells **ABRT** to catch crashes in all programs.

BlackList = nspluginwrapper, valgrind, strace, avant-window-navigator, [*additional_packages*]

Crashes in packages and binaries listed after the *BlackList* directive will not be handled by **ABRT**. If you want **ABRT** to ignore other packages and binaries, list them here separated by commas.

ProcessUnpackaged = *yes/no*

This directive tells **ABRT** whether to process crashes in executables that do not belong to any package.

BlackListedPaths = `/usr/share/doc/*, */example*`

Crashes in executables in these paths will be ignored by **ABRT**.

Database = SQLite3

This directive instructs **ABRT** to store its crash data in the **SQLite3** database. Other databases are not currently supported. However, **ABRT**'s plugin architecture allows for future support for alternative databases.

#WatchCrashdumpArchiveDir = /var/spool/abrt-upload/

This directive is commented out by default. Enable (uncomment) it if you want `abrtd` to auto-unpack crashdump tarballs which appear in the specified directory — in this case `/var/spool/abrt-upload/` — (for example, uploaded via `ftp`, `scp`, etc.). You must ensure that whatever directory you specify in this directive exists and is writable for `abrtd`. `abrtd` will not create it automatically.

MaxCrashReportsSize = *size_in_megabytes*

This option sets the amount of storage space, in megabytes, used by **ABRT** to store all crash information from all users. The default setting is `1000` MB. Once the quota specified here has been met, **ABRT** will continue catching crashes, and in order to make room for the new crash dumps, it will delete the oldest and largest ones.

ActionsAndReporters = SOSreport, [*additional_plugins*]

This option tells **ABRT** to run the specified plugin(s) immediately after a crash is detected and saved. For example, the **`SOSreport`** plugin runs the `sosreport` tool which adds the data collected by it to the created crash dump. You can turn this behavior off by commenting out this line. For further fine-tuning, you can add **`SOSreport`** (or any other specified plugin) to either the *CCpp* or *Python* options to make **ABRT** run `sosreport` (or any other specified plugin) after any C and C++ or Python applications crash, respectively. For more information on various Action and Reporter plugins, refer to Section 19.3, *ABRT Plugins* (page 399).

[AnalyzerActionsAndReporters] Section Directives

This section allows you to associate certain analyzer actions and reporter actions to run when **ABRT** catches kernel oopses or crashes in C, C++ or Python programs. The actions and reporters specified in any of the directives below will run only if you run `abrt-gui` or `abrt-cli` and report the crash that occurred. If you do not specify any actions and reporters in these directives, you will not be able to report a crash via `abrt-gui` or `abrt-cli`. The order of actions and reporters is important. Commenting out a directive, will cause **ABRT** not to catch the crashes associated with that directive. For example, commenting out the Kerneloops line will cause **ABRT** not to catch kernel oopses.

Kerneloops = Logger

This directive specifies that, for kernel oopses, the Logger reporter will be run.

CCpp = Logger

This directive specifies that, when C or C++ program crashes occur, the Logger reporter will be run.

Python = Logger

This directive specifies that, when Python program crashes occur, the Logger reporter will be run.

Each of these destinations' details can be specified in the corresponding `plugins/*.conf` file. All these options can also be configured through the `abrt-gui` application (for more information on plugin configuration refer to Section 19.3, *ABRT Plugins* - page 399).

[Cron] Section Directives

`time` = *`action_to_run`*

The `[ Cron ]` section of `abrt.conf` allows you to specify the exact time, or elapsed amount of time between, when **ABRT** should run a certain action, such as scanning for kernel oopses or performing file transfers. You can list further actions to run by appending them to the end of this section.

```
# Which Action plugins to run repeatedly
[ Cron ]
# h:m - at h:m
# s - every s seconds
120 = KerneloopsScanner
#02:00 = FileTransfer
```

Example 19.1. [Cron] section of /etc/abrt/abrt.conf

The format for an entry is either **`time_in_seconds = action_to_run`** or **`hh:mm = action_to_run`** , where **`hh`** (hour) is in the range `00-23` (all hours less than 10 should be zero-filled, i.e. preceded by a `0`), and **`mm`** (minute) is `00-59`, zero-filled likewise.

19.7. Configuring Centralized Crash Collection

You can set up **ABRT** so that crash reports are collected from multiple systems and sent to a dedicated system for further processing. This is useful when an administrator does not want to log into hundreds of systems and manually check for crashes found by **ABRT**. In order to use this method, you need to install the **abrt-plugin-reportuploader** plugin (`yum install abrt-plugin-reportuploader`).

The steps to configure **ABRT**'s centralized crash collection are:

1. Complete the following steps on a dedicated system ("server system"):
   - Create a directory to which you want the crash reports to be uploaded to. Usually, `/var/spool/abrt-upload/` is used (the rest of the document assumes you are using `/var/spool/abrt-upload/`). Make sure this directory is writable by the `abrt` user.

   > **The abrt user and group**
   >
   > When the abrt-desktop package is installed, it creates a new system user and a group, both named `abrt`. This user is used by the `abrtd` daemon for various things, for example, as the owner:group of `/var/spool/abrt/*` directories.

   - In the `/etc/abrt/abrt.conf` configuration file, set the `WatchCrashdumpArchiveDir` directive to the following:

     `WatchCrashdumpArchiveDir = /var/spool/abrt-upload/`
   - Determine your preferred upload mechanism; for example, `FTP` or `SCP`. For more information on how to configure `FTP`, refer to Section 15.2, *FTP* (page 342). For more information on how to configure `SCP`, refer to Section 9.3.2, *Using the scp Utility* (page 180).

     For security reasons, make sure that uploads can only be performed by a specific user and with a password. The rest of the document assumes that the username used for uploads is `USERNAME` and the password is `PASSWORD`. If you do not already have a suitable username which can be used to perform uploads under, you may use the `abrt` user which already exists on every system where **ABRT** is installed.

     It is advisable to check whether your upload method works. For more information, refer to Section 19.7.2, *Testing the Upload Method* (page 411).
   - It is advisable to check and modify the following parameters if needed:

- The *MaxCrashReportsSize* directive (in /etc/abrt/abrt.conf) needs to be set to a larger value if the expected volume of crash data is larger than the default 1000 MB.
- The *ProcessUnpackaged* directive (in /etc/abrt/abrt.conf) needs to be set to *yes* and the *BacktraceRemotes* (in /etc/abrt/plugins/CCpp.conf) needs to be set to *no* if the client system and the server system have significantly different sets of installed packages.

2. Complete the following steps on every client system which will use the central management method:
   - Modify the /etc/abrt/plugins/ReportUploader.conf configuration file so that the **ReportUploader** plugin knows where to copy the saved crash reports in the following way:

   ```
   Enabled = yes
   Upload = yes
   URL = ftp://USERNAME:PASSWORD@SERVERNAME/var/spool/abrt-upload/
   ```

   - To automatically send the crash reports to the server system immediately after the crash occurs, is detected, and saved, set the [ActionsAndReporters] directive in the /etc/abrt/abrt.conf configuration file to the following:

   ```
   ActionsAndReporters = ReportUploader
   ```

   - Alternatively, if user interaction is required before the crash dump is sent to the server system, set the *ReportUploader* to be a reporter plugin for a specific crash type in the [AnalyzerActionsAndReporters] section of the /etc/abrt/abrt.conf configuration file. The user will be required to run **abrt-cli** or **abrt-gui** and instruct the abrtd daemon to report the crash and send it to the server system. For example, if you want all crash types to use this method, edit the [AnalyzerActionsAndReporters] section in your /etc/abrt/abrt.conf configuration file in the following way:

   ```
   Kerneloops = ReportUploader
   CCpp = ReportUploader
   Python = ReportUploader
   ```

19.7.1. Testing ABRT's Crash Detection

After completing all the steps of the configuration process, the basic setup is finished. To test that this setup works properly use the `kill -s SEGV` *`PID`* command to terminate a process on a client system. For example, start a `sleep` process and terminate it with the `kill` command in the following way:

```
~]$ sleep 100 &
[1] 2823
~]$ kill -s SEGV 2823
```

ABRT should detect a crash shortly after executing the `kill` command. Check that the crash was detected by **ABRT** on the client system (this can be checked by examining the appropriate syslog file, by running the `abrt-cli --list --full` command, or by examining the crash dump created in the `/var/spool/abrt` directory), copied to the server system, unpacked on the server system and can be seen and acted upon using `abrt-cli` or `abrt-gui` on the server system.

19.7.2. Testing the Upload Method

Test your upload method from a client system to ensure that it works. For example, upload a file using the interactive `FTP` client:

```
~]$ ftp
ftp> open SERVERNAME
Name: USERNAME
Password: PASSWORD
ftp> cd /var/spool/abrt-upload
250 Operation successful
ftp> put TESTFILE
ftp> quit
```

Check whether `TESTFILE` appeared in the correct directory on the server system.

19.8. Configuring Automatic Reporting

ABRT can be configured to automatically report any detected issues or crashes. The following steps show how to enable this feature:

1. In your `/etc/abrt/abrt.conf` configuration file, for each analyzer, change the list of reporters according to your needs, for example:

   ```
   [ AnalyzerActionsAndReporters ]
   Kerneloops = Logger
   CCpp = Logger
   Python = Logger
   ```

2. In the configuration files corresponding to each analyzer plugin (that is, `/etc/abrt/plugins/CCpp.conf`, `/etc/abrt/plugins/Kerneloops.conf` and `/etc/abrt/plugins/Python.conf`), add the following line:

   ```
   AutoReportUIDs = USERNAME
   ```

   where *`USERNAME`* represents a user whose detected crashes and issues will be automatically reported via your specified reporters. You can specify multiple users by separating them with a comma (`,`).

Part VII.
Kernel, Module and Driver Configuration

This part covers various tools that assist administrators with kernel customization.

Chapter 20.

Manually Upgrading the Kernel

The Fedora kernel is custom-built by the Fedora kernel team to ensure its integrity and compatibility with supported hardware. Before a kernel is released, it must first pass a rigorous set of quality assurance tests.

Fedora kernels are packaged in the RPM format so that they are easy to upgrade and verify using the **Yum** or **PackageKit** package managers. **PackageKit** automatically queries the Yum repositories and informs you of packages with available updates, including kernel packages.

This chapter is therefore *only* useful for users who need to manually update a kernel package using the `rpm` command instead of `yum`.

Use Yum to install kernels whenever possible

Whenever possible, use either the **Yum** or **PackageKit** package manager to install a new kernel because they always *install* a new kernel instead of replacing the current one, which could potentially leave your system unable to boot.

For more information on installing kernel packages with **Yum**, refer to Section 4.1.2, *Updating Packages* (page 72).

20.1. Overview of Kernel Packages

Fedora contains the following kernel packages:

- kernel — Contains the kernel for single, multicore and multiprocessor systems.
- kernel-debug — Contains a kernel with numerous debugging options enabled for kernel diagnosis, at the expense of reduced performance.
- kernel-devel — Contains the kernel headers and makefiles sufficient to build modules against the kernel package.
- kernel-debug-devel — Contains the development version of the kernel with numerous debugging options enabled for kernel diagnosis, at the expense of reduced performance.

- kernel-doc — Documentation files from the kernel source. Various portions of the Linux kernel and the device drivers shipped with it are documented in these files. Installation of this package provides a reference to the options that can be passed to Linux kernel modules at load time.

  By default, these files are placed in the `/usr/share/doc/kernel-doc-`*`kernel_version`*`/` directory.
- kernel-headers — Includes the C header files that specify the interface between the Linux kernel and user-space libraries and programs. The header files define structures and constants that are needed for building most standard programs.
- linux-firmware — Contains all of the firmware files that are required by various devices to operate.
- perf — This package contains supporting scripts and documentation for the **perf** tool shipped in each kernel image subpackage.

20.2. Preparing to Upgrade

Before upgrading the kernel, it is recommended that you take some precautionary steps.

First, ensure that working boot media exists for the system in case a problem occurs. If the boot loader is not configured properly to boot the new kernel, the system cannot be booted into Fedora without working boot media.

USB media often comes in the form of flash devices sometimes called *pen drives, thumb disks,* or *keys,* or as an externally-connected hard disk device. Almost all media of this type is formatted as a `VFAT` file system. You can create bootable USB media on media formatted as `ext2`, `ext3`, `ext4`, or `VFAT`.

You can transfer a distribution image file or a minimal boot media image file to USB media. Make sure that sufficient free space is available on the device. Around `4 GB` is required for a distribution DVD image, around `700 MB` for a distribution CD image, or around `10 MB` for a minimal boot media image.

You must have a copy of the `boot.iso` file from a Fedora installation DVD, or installation CD-ROM#1, and you need a USB storage device formatted with the `VFAT` file system and around `16 MB` of free space. The following procedure will not affect existing files on the USB storage device unless they have the same path names as the files that you copy onto it. To create USB boot media, perform the following commands as the `root` user:

1. Install the **SYSLINUX** bootloader on the USB storage device:

   ```
   syslinux /dev/sdX1
   ```

   ...where *sdX* is the device name.

2. Create mount points for `boot.iso` and the USB storage device:

   `mkdir /mnt/isoboot /mnt/diskboot`

3. Mount `boot.iso`:

   `mount -o loop boot.iso /mnt/isoboot`

4. Mount the USB storage device:

   `mount /dev/;sdX1 /mnt/diskboot`

5. Copy the **ISOLINUX** files from the `boot.iso` to the USB storage device:

   `cp /mnt/isoboot/isolinux/* /mnt/diskboot`

6. Use the `isolinux.cfg` file from `boot.iso` as the `syslinux.cfg` file for the USB device:

   `grep -v local /mnt/isoboot/isolinux/isolinux.cfg > /mnt/diskboot/syslinux.cfg`

7. Unmount `boot.iso` and the USB storage device:

   `umount /mnt/isoboot /mnt/diskboot`

8. You should reboot the machine with the boot media and verify that you are able to boot with it before continuing.

Alternatively, on systems with a floppy drive, you can create a boot diskette by installing the mkbootdisk package and running the `mkbootdisk` command as `root`. Refer to `man mkbootdisk` man page after installing the package for usage information.

To determine which kernel packages are installed, execute the command `yum list installed "kernel-*"` at a shell prompt. The output will comprise some or all of the following packages, depending on the system's architecture, and the version numbers may differ:

```
~]# yum list installed "kernel-*"
Loaded plugins: langpacks, presto, refresh-packagekit
Installed Packages
kernel.x86 64                  2.6.38.6-27.fc15        installed
kernel-doc.noarch              2.6.38.6-27.fc15        installed
kernel-headers.x86_64          2.6.38.6-27.fc15        installed
```

From the output, determine which packages need to be downloaded for the kernel upgrade. For a single processor system, the only required package is the kernel package. Refer to Section 20.1, *Overview of Kernel Packages* (page 413) for descriptions of the different packages.

20.3. Downloading the Upgraded Kernel

There are several ways to determine if an updated kernel is available for the system.

- Security Advisories — Refer to *http://fedoraproject.org/wiki/FSA* for information on Security Advisories, including kernel upgrades that fix security issues.

- Via Fedora Update System — Download and install the kernel RPM packages. For more information, refer to *http://admin.fedoraproject.org/updates/*.

To install the kernel manually, continue to Section 20.4, *Performing the Upgrade* (page 416).

20.4. Performing the Upgrade

After retrieving all of the necessary packages, it is time to upgrade the existing kernel.

Keep the old kernel when performing the upgrade

It is strongly recommended that you keep the old kernel in case there are problems with the new kernel.

At a shell prompt, change to the directory that contains the kernel RPM packages. Use `-i` argument with the `rpm` command to keep the old kernel. Do *not* use the `-U` option, since it overwrites the currently installed kernel, which creates boot loader problems. For example:

```
rpm -ivh kernel-kernel_version.arch.rpm
```

The next step is to verify that the initial RAM disk image has been created. Refer to Section 20.5, *Verifying the Initial RAM Disk Image* (page 416) for details.

20.5. Verifying the Initial RAM Disk Image

The job of the initial RAM disk image is to preload the block device modules, such as for IDE, SCSI or RAID, so that the root file system, on which those modules normally reside, can then be accessed and mounted. On Fedora 15 systems, whenever a new kernel is installed using either the **Yum**, **PackageKit**, or **RPM** package manager, the **Dracut** utility is always called by the installation scripts to create an *initramfs* (initial RAM disk image).

On all architectures other than IBM eServer System i (see to Section 20.5, *Verifying the Initial RAM Disk Image* - page 416), you can create an `initramfs` by running the `dracut` command. However, you usually don't need to create an `initramfs` manually: this step is automatically performed if the kernel and its associated packages are installed or upgraded from RPM packages distributed by The Fedora Project.

You can verify that an `initramfs` corresponding to your current kernel version exists and is specified correctly in the `grub.conf` configuration file by following this procedure:

Procedure 20.1. Verifying the Initial RAM Disk Image

1. As `root`, list the contents in the `/boot/` directory and find the kernel (`vmlinuz-kernel_version`) and `initramfs-kernel_version` with the latest (most recent) version number:

   ```
   ~]# ls /boot/
   ```

```
config-2.6.38.6-26.fc15.x86_64
config-2.6.38.6-27.fc15.x86_64
efi
elf-memtest86+-4.10
grub
initramfs-2.6.38.6-26.fc15.x86_64.img
initramfs-2.6.38.6-27.fc15.x86_64.img
lost+found
memtest86+-4.10
System.map-2.6.38.6-26.fc15.x86_64
System.map-2.6.38.6-27.fc15.x86_64
vmlinuz-2.6.38.6-26.fc15.x86_64
vmlinuz-2.6.38.6-27.fc15.x86_64
```

The example above shows that:

- we have two kernels installed (or, more correctly, two kernel files are present in the `/boot/` directory),
- the latest kernel is `vmlinuz-2.6.38.6-27.fc15.x86_64`, and
- an `initramfs` file matching our kernel version, `initramfs-2.6.38.6-27.fc15.x86_64.img`, also exists.

initrd files in the /boot/ directory are not the same as initramfs files

In the `/boot/` directory you may find several `initrd-`*`version`*`kdump.img` files. These are special files created by the `kdump` mechanism for kernel debugging purposes, are not used to boot the system, and can safely be ignored. For more information on `kdump`, refer to Chapter 22, *The kdump Crash Recovery Service* (page 439).

2. (Optional) If your `initramfs-`*`kernel_version`* file does not match the version of the latest kernel in `/boot/`, or, in certain other situations, you may need to generate an `initramfs` file with the **Dracut** utility. Simply invoking `dracut` as `root` without options causes it to generate an `initramfs` file in the `/boot/` directory for the latest kernel present in that directory:

```
~]# dracut
```

You must use the `--force` option if you want `dracut` to overwrite an existing `initramfs` (for example, if your `initramfs` has become corrupt). Otherwise `dracut` will refuse to overwrite the existing `initramfs` file:

```
~]# dracut
F: Will not override existing initramfs (/boot/initramfs-2.6.38.6-
                                      26.fc15.x86_64.img) without --force
```

You can create an initramfs in the current directory by calling `dracut` *`initramfs_name kernel_version`*:

```
~]# dracut "initramfs-$(uname -r).img" $(uname -r)
```

If you need to specify specific kernel modules to be preloaded, add the names of those modules (minus any file name suffixes such as `.ko`) inside the parentheses of the `add_dracutmodules="module [more_modules]"` directive of the `/etc/dracut.conf` configuration file. You can list the file contents of an `initramfs` image file created by dracut by using the `lsinitrd initramfs_file` command:

```
~]# lsinitrd /boot/initramfs-2.6.38.6-26.fc15.x86_64.img
/boot/initramfs-2.6.38.6-26.fc15.x86_64.img:
========================================================================
dracut-009-10.fc15
========================================================================
drwxr-xr-x  23 root     root            0 May 20 14:45 .
drwxr-xr-x   2 root     root            0 May 20 14:45 bin
-rwxr-xr-x   1 root     root        38400 Feb  8 12:46 bin/rmdir
-rwxr-xr-x   1 root     root       116632 Feb  8 12:46 bin/ls
-rwxr-xr-x   1 root     root        39568 Feb  8 03:27 bin/setfont
[output truncated]
```

Refer to `man dracut` and `man dracut.conf` for more information on options and usage.

3. Examine the `grub.conf` configuration file in the `/boot/grub/` directory to ensure that an `initrd initramfs-kernel_version.img` exists for the kernel version you are booting. Refer to Section 20.6, *Verifying the Boot Loader* (page 418) for more information.

Verifying the Initial RAM Disk Image and Kernel on IBM eServer System i

On IBM eServer System i machines, the initial RAM disk and kernel files are combined into a single file, which is created with the `addRamDisk` command. This step is performed automatically if the kernel and its associated packages are installed or upgraded from the RPM packages distributed by The Fedora Project; thus, it does not need to be executed manually. To verify that it was created, use the command `ls -l /boot/` to make sure the `/boot/vmlinitrd-kernel_version` file already exists (the `kernel_version` should match the version of the kernel just installed).

20.6. Verifying the Boot Loader

When you install a kernel using `rpm`, the kernel package creates an entry in the boot loader configuration file for that new kernel. However, `rpm` does *not* configure the new kernel to boot as the default kernel. You must do this manually when installing a new kernel with `rpm`.

It is always recommended to double-check the boot loader configuration file after installing a new kernel with `rpm` to ensure that the configuration is correct. Otherwise, the system may not be able to boot into Fedora properly. If this happens, boot the system with the boot media created earlier and re-configure the boot loader.

In the following table, find your system's architecture to determine the boot loader it uses, and then click on the "Refer to" link to jump to the correct instructions for your system.

Architecture	Boot Loader	Refer to
x86	GRUB	Section 20.6.1, *Configuring the GRUB Boot Loader* (page 419)
AMD AMD64 *or* Intel 64	GRUB	Section 20.6.1, *Configuring the GRUB Boot Loader* (page 419)
IBM eServer System i	OS/400	Section 20.6.2, *Configuring the OS/400 Boot Loader* (page 421)
IBM eServer System p	YABOOT	Section 20.6.3, *Configuring the YABOOT Boot Loader* (page 421)
IBM System z	z/IPL	

Table 20.1. Boot loaders by architecture

20.6.1. Configuring the GRUB Boot Loader

GRUB's configuration file, `/boot/grub/grub.conf`, contains a few lines with directives, such as `default`, `timeout`, `splashimage` and `hiddenmenu` (the last directive has no argument). The remainder of the file contains 4-line *stanzas* that each refer to an installed kernel. These stanzas always start with a `title` entry, after which the associated `root`, `kernel` and `initrd` directives should always be indented. Ensure that each stanza starts with a `title` that contains a version number (in parentheses) that matches the version number in the `kernel /vmlinuz-version_number` line of the same stanza.

```
# grub.conf generated by anaconda
[comments omitted]
default=1
timeout=0
splashimage=(hd0,0)/boot/grub/splash.xpm.gz
hiddenmenu

title Fedora (2.6.38.6-27.fc15.x86_64)
        root (hd0,0)
        kernel /boot/vmlinuz-2.6.38.6-27.fc15.x86_64 ro root=UUID=e8148266-4a56-
4f4d-b6df-9eafea4586b2 rd_NO_LUKS rd_NO_LVM rd_NO_MD rd_NO_DM LANG=en_US.UTF-8
SYSFONT=latarcyrheb-sun16 KEYTABLE=us rhgb quiet
        initrd /boot/initramfs-2.6.38.6-27.fc15.x86_64.img
title Fedora (2.6.38.6-26.rc1.fc15.x86_64)
        root (hd0,0)
        kernel /boot/vmlinuz-2.6.38.6-26.fc15.x86_64 ro root=UUID=e8148266-4a56-
4f4d-b6df-9eafea4586b2 rd_NO_LUKS rd_NO_LVM rd_NO_MD rd_NO_DM LANG=en_US.UTF-8
SYSFONT=latarcyrheb-sun16 KEYTABLE=us rhgb quiet
        initrd /boot/initramfs-2.6.38.6-26.fc15.x86_64.img
```

Example 20.1. /boot/grub/grub.conf

If a separate `/boot/` partition was created, the paths to the kernel and the `initramfs` image are relative to `/boot/`. This is the case in *Example 20.1. /boot/grub/grub.conf* above, therefore the `initrd /initramfs-2.6.38.6-27.fc15.x86_64.img` line in the first kernel stanza means that the `initramfs` image is actually located at `/boot/initramfs-2.6.38.6-27.fc15.x86_64.img` when the root file system is mounted, and likewise for the kernel path (for example: `kernel /vmlinuz-2.6.38.6-27.fc15.x86_64`) in each stanza of `grub.conf`.

The initrd directive in grub.conf refers to an initramfs image

In kernel boot stanzas in `grub.conf`, the `initrd` directive must point to the location (relative to the `/boot/` directory if it is on a separate partition) of the *`initramfs`* file corresponding to the same kernel version. This directive is called `initrd` because the previous tool which created initial RAM disk images, `mkinitrd`, created what were known as `initrd` files. Thus the `grub.conf` directive remains `initrd` to maintain compatibility with other tools. The file-naming convention of systems using the `dracut` utility to create the initial RAM disk image is: `initramfs-`*`kernel_version`*`.img`

Dracut is a new utility available in Fedora 15, and much-improved over `mkinitrd`. For information on using **Dracut**, refer to Section 20.5, *Verifying the Initial RAM Disk Image* (page 416).

You should ensure that the kernel version number as given on the `kernel /vmlinuz-`*`kernel_version`* line matches the version number of the `initramfs` image given on the `initrd /initramfs-`*`kernel_version`*`.img` line of each stanza. Refer to *Procedure 20.1, "Verifying the Initial RAM Disk Image"* (page 416) for more information.

The `default=` directive tells GRUB which kernel to boot *by default*. Each `title` in `grub.conf` represents a bootable kernel. GRUB counts the `title`d stanzas representing bootable kernels starting with `0`. In *Example 20.1. /boot/grub/grub.conf* above, the line `default=1` indicates that GRUB will boot, by default, the *second* kernel entry, i.e. `title Fedora (2.6.38.6-26.fc15.x86_64)`.

In *Example 20.1. /boot/grub/grub.conf* above GRUB is therefore configured to boot an older kernel, when we compare by version numbers. In order to boot the newer kernel, which is the *first* `title` entry in `grub.conf`, we would need to change the `default` value to `0`.

After installing a new kernel with `rpm`, verify that `/boot/grub/grub.conf` is correct, change the `default=` value to the new kernel (while remembering to count from `0`), and reboot the computer into the new kernel. Ensure your hardware is detected by watching the boot process output.

If GRUB presents an error and is unable to boot into the default kernel, it is often easiest to try to boot into an alternative or older kernel so that you can fix the problem.

> **Causing the GRUB boot menu to display**
>
> If you set the `timeout` directive in `grub.conf` to `0`, GRUB will not display its list of bootable kernels when the system starts up. In order to display this list when booting, press and hold any alphanumeric key while and immediately after BIOS information is displayed, and GRUB will present you with the GRUB menu.

Alternatively, use the boot media you created earlier to boot the system.

20.6.2. Configuring the OS/400 Boot Loader

The `/boot/vmlinitrd-`*`kernel-version`* file is installed when you upgrade the kernel. However, you must use the `dd` command to configure the system to boot the new kernel.

1. As `root`, issue the command `cat /proc/iSeries/mf/side` to determine the default side (either A, B, or C).
2. As `root`, issue the following command, where *`kernel-version`* is the version of the new kernel and *`side`* is the side from the previous command:

```
dd if=/boot/vmlinitrd-kernel-version
                              of=/proc/iSeries/mf/side/vmlinux bs=8k
```

Begin testing the new kernel by rebooting the computer and watching the messages to ensure that the hardware is detected properly.

20.6.3. Configuring the YABOOT Boot Loader

IBM eServer System p uses YABOOT as its boot loader. YABOOT uses `/etc/aboot.conf` as its configuration file. Confirm that the file contains an `image` section with the same version as the kernel package just installed, and likewise for the `initramfs` image:

```
boot=/dev/sda1 init-message=Welcome to Fedora! Hit <TAB> for boot options
partition=2 timeout=30 install=/usr/lib/yaboot/yaboot delay=10 nonvram
image=/vmlinuz-2.6.32-17.EL
        label=old
        read-only
        initrd=/initramfs-2.6.32-17.EL.img
        append="root=LABEL=/"
image=/vmlinuz-2.6.32-19.EL
        label=linux
        read-only
        initrd=/initramfs-2.6.32-19.EL.img
        append="root=LABEL=/"
```

Notice that the default is not set to the new kernel. The kernel in the first image is booted by default. To change the default kernel to boot either move its image stanza so that it is the first one listed or add the directive `default` and set it to the `label` of the image stanza that contains the new kernel.

Begin testing the new kernel by rebooting the computer and watching the messages to ensure that the hardware is detected properly.

Chapter 21.

Working with Kernel Modules

The Linux kernel is modular, which means it can extend its capabilities through the use of dynamically-loaded *kernel modules*. A kernel module can provide:

- a device driver which adds support for new hardware; or,
- support for a file system such as `btrfs` or `NFS`.

Like the kernel itself, modules can take parameters that customize their behavior, though the default parameters work well in most cases. User-space tools can list the modules currently loaded into a running kernel; query all available modules for available parameters and module-specific information; and load or unload (remove) modules dynamically into or from a running kernel. Many of these utilities, which are provided by the module-init-tools package, take module dependencies into account when performing operations so that manual dependency-tracking is rarely necessary.

On modern systems, kernel modules are automatically loaded by various mechanisms when the conditions call for it. However, there are occasions when it is necessary to load and/or unload modules manually, such as when a module provides optional functionality, one module should be preferred over another although either could provide basic functionality, or when a module is misbehaving, among other situations.

This chapter explains how to:

- use the user-space module-init-tools package to display, query, load and unload kernel modules and their dependencies;
- set module parameters both dynamically on the command line and permanently so that you can customize the behavior of your kernel modules; and,
- load modules at boot time.

Installing the module-init-tools package

In order to use the kernel module utilities described in this chapter, first ensure the module-init-tools package is installed on your system by running, as `root`:

```
yum install module-init-tools
```

For more information on installing packages with Yum, refer to Section 4.2.4, *Installing Packages* (page 78).

21.1. Listing Currently-Loaded Modules

You can list all kernel modules that are currently loaded into the kernel by running the `lsmod` command, for example:

```
~]$ lsmod
Module                  Size  Used by
xfs                   803635  1
exportfs                3424  1 xfs
vfat                    8216  1
fat                    43410  1 vfat
tun                    13014  2
fuse                   54749  2
ip6table_filter         2743  0
ip6_tables             16558  1 ip6table_filter
ebtable_nat             1895  0
ebtables               15186  1 ebtable_nat
ipt_MASQUERADE          2208  6
iptable_nat             5420  1
nf_nat                 19059  2 ipt_MASQUERADE,iptable_nat
rfcomm                 65122  4
ipv6                  267017  33
sco                    16204  2
bridge                 45753  0
stp                     1887  1 bridge
llc                     4557  2 bridge,stp
bnep                   15121  2
l2cap                  45185  16 rfcomm,bnep
cpufreq_ondemand        8420  2
acpi_cpufreq            7493  1
freq_table              3851  2 cpufreq_ondemand,acpi_cpufreq
usb_storage            44536  1
sha256_generic         10023  2
aes_x86_64              7654  5
aes_generic            27012  1 aes_x86_64
cbc                     2793  1
dm_crypt               10930  1
kvm_intel              40311  0
kvm                   253162  1 kvm_intel
[output truncated]
```

Each row of `lsmod` output specifies:

- the name of a kernel module currently loaded in memory;
- the amount of memory it uses; and,
- the sum total of processes that are using the module and other modules which depend on it, followed by a list of the names of those modules, if there are any.

Using this list, you can first unload all the modules depending the module you want to unload. For more information, refer to Section 21.4, *Unloading a Module* (page 427).

Finally, note that `lsmod` output is less verbose and considerably easier to read than the content of the `/proc/modules` pseudo-file.

21.2. Displaying Information About a Module

You can display detailed information about a kernel module by running the `modinfo` *`module_name`* command.

Module names do not end in .ko

When entering the name of a kernel module as an argument to one of the module-init-tools utilities, do not append a `.ko` extension to the end of the name. Kernel module names do not have extensions: their corresponding files do.

To display information about the `e1000e` module, which is the Intel PRO/1000 network driver, run:

```
~]# modinfo e1000e
filename:       /lib/modules/2.6.32-
71.el6.x86_64/kernel/drivers/net/e1000e/e1000e.ko
version:        1.2.7-k2
license:        GPL
description:    Intel(R) PRO/1000 Network Driver
author:         Intel Corporation, <linux.nics@intel.com>
srcversion:     93CB73D3995B501872B2982
alias:          pci:v00008086d00001503sv*sd*bc*sc*i*
alias:          pci:v00008086d00001502sv*sd*bc*sc*i*
[some alias lines omitted]
alias:          pci:v00008086d0000105Esv*sd*bc*sc*i*
depends:
vermagic:       2.6.32-71.el6.x86_64 SMP mod_unload modversions
parm:           copybreak:Maximum size of packet that is copied to a new buffer
                                                            on receive (uint)
parm:           TxIntDelay:Transmit Interrupt Delay (array of int)
parm:           TxAbsIntDelay:Transmit Absolute Interrupt Delay (array of int)
parm:           RxIntDelay:Receive Interrupt Delay (array of int)
parm:           RxAbsIntDelay:Receive Absolute Interrupt Delay (array of int)
parm:           InterruptThrottleRate:Interrupt Throttling Rate (array of int)
parm:           IntMode:Interrupt Mode (array of int)
parm:           SmartPowerDownEnable:Enable PHY smart power down (array of int)
parm:           KumeranLockLoss:Enable Kumeran lock loss workaround (array of int)
parm:           WriteProtectNVM:Write-protect NVM [WARNING: disabling this can
                                        lead to corrupted NVM] (array of int)
parm:           CrcStripping:Enable CRC Stripping, disable if your BMC needs the
                                                               CRC (array of int)
parm:           EEE:Enable/disable on parts that support the feature (array of int)
```

Example 21.1. Listing information about a kernel module with lsmod

Here are descriptions of a few of the fields in `modinfo` output:

filename

The absolute path to the `.ko` kernel object file. You can use `modinfo -n` as a shortcut command for printing only the `filename` field.

description

A short description of the module. You can use `modinfo -d` as a shortcut command for printing only the description field.

alias

The `alias` field appears as many times as there are aliases for a module, or is omitted entirely if there are none.

depends

This field contains a comma-separated list of all the modules this module depends on.

Omitting the depends field

If a module has no dependencies, the `depends` field may be omitted from the output.

parm

Each `parm` field presents one module parameter in the form *`parameter_name`*`:`*`description`*, where:

- *`parameter_name`* is the exact syntax you should use when using it as a module parameter on the command line, or in an option line in a `.conf` file in the `/etc/modprobe.d/` directory; and,
- *`description`* is a brief explanation of what the parameter does, along with an expectation for the type of value the parameter accepts (such as int, unit or array of int) in parentheses.

You can list all parameters that the module supports by using the `-p` option. However, because useful value type information is omitted from `modinfo -p` output, it is more useful to run:

```
~]# modinfo e1000e | grep "^parm" | sort
parm:       copybreak:Maximum size of packet that is copied to a new buffer on
receive (uint)
parm:       CrcStripping:Enable CRC Stripping, disable if your BMC needs the
CRC (array of int)
parm:       EEE:Enable/disable on parts that support the feature (array of int)
parm:       InterruptThrottleRate:Interrupt Throttling Rate (array of int)
parm:       IntMode:Interrupt Mode (array of int)
parm:       KumeranLockLoss:Enable Kumeran lock loss workaround (array of int)
```

```
parm:           RxAbsIntDelay:Receive Absolute Interrupt Delay (array of int)
parm:           RxIntDelay:Receive Interrupt Delay (array of int)
parm:           SmartPowerDownEnable:Enable PHY smart power down (array of int)
parm:           TxAbsIntDelay:Transmit Absolute Interrupt Delay (array of int)
parm:           TxIntDelay:Transmit Interrupt Delay (array of int)
parm:           WriteProtectNVM:Write-protect NVM [WARNING: disabling this can lead
to corrupted NVM] (array of int)
```

Example 21.2. Listing module parameters

21.3. Loading a Module

To load a kernel module, run `modprobe` *`module_name`* as `root`. For example, to load the `wacom` module, run:

```
~]# modprobe wacom
```

By default, `modprobe` attempts to load the module from `/lib/modules/`*`kernel_version`*`/kernel/drivers/`. In this directory, each type of module has its own subdirectory, such as `net/` and `scsi/`, for network and SCSI interface drivers respectively.

Some modules have dependencies, which are other kernel modules that must be loaded before the module in question can be loaded. The `modprobe` command always takes dependencies into account when performing operations. When you ask `modprobe` to load a specific kernel module, it first examines the dependencies of that module, if there are any, and loads them if they are not already loaded into the kernel. `modprobe` resolves dependencies recursively: it will load all dependencies of dependencies, and so on, if necessary, thus ensuring that all dependencies are always met.

You can use the `-v` (or `--verbose`) option to cause `modprobe` to display detailed information about what it is doing, which may include loading module dependencies.

You can load the `Fibre Channel over Ethernet` module verbosely by typing the following at a shell prompt:

```
~]# modprobe -v fcoe
insmod /lib/modules/2.6.32-71.el6.x86_64/kernel/drivers/scsi/scsi_tgt.ko
insmod /lib/modules/2.6.32-71.el6.x86_64/kernel/drivers/scsi/scsi_transport_fc.ko
insmod /lib/modules/2.6.32-71.el6.x86_64/kernel/drivers/scsi/libfc/libfc.ko
insmod /lib/modules/2.6.32-71.el6.x86_64/kernel/drivers/scsi/fcoe/libfcoe.ko
insmod /lib/modules/2.6.32-71.el6.x86_64/kernel/drivers/scsi/fcoe/fcoe.ko
```

In this example, you can see that `modprobe` loaded the `scsi_tgt`, `scsi_transport_fc`, `libfc` and `libfcoe` modules as dependencies before finally loading `fcoe`. Also note that `modprobe` used the more "primitive" `insmod` command to insert the modules into the running kernel.

Example 21.3. modprobe -v shows module dependencies as they are loaded

Always use modprobe instead of insmod!

Although the `insmod` command can also be used to load kernel modules, it does not resolve dependencies. Because of this, you should *always* load modules using `modprobe` instead.

21.4. Unloading a Module

You can unload a kernel module by running `modprobe -r module_name` as `root`. For example, assuming that the `wacom` module is already loaded into the kernel, you can unload it by running:

```
~]# modprobe -r wacom
```

However, this command will fail if a process is using:

- the `wacom` module,
- a module that `wacom` directly depends on, or,
- any module that `wacom`—through the dependency tree—depends on indirectly.

Refer to Section 21.1, *Listing Currently-Loaded Modules* (page 423) for more information about using `lsmod` to obtain the names of the modules which are preventing you from unloading a certain module.

For example, if you want to unload the `firewire_ohci` module (because you believe there is a bug in it that is affecting system stability, for example), your terminal session might look similar to this:

```
~]# modinfo -F depends firewire_ohci
depends:        firewire-core
~]# modinfo -F depends firewire_core
depends:        crc-itu-t
~]# modinfo -F depends crc-itu-t
depends:
```

You have figured out the dependency tree (which does not branch in this example) for the loaded Firewire modules: `firewire_ohci` depends on `firewire_core`, which itself depends on `crc-itu-t`.

You can unload `firewire_ohci` using the `modprobe -v -r module_name` command, where `-r` is short for `--remove` and `-v` for `--verbose`:

```
~]# modprobe -r -v firewire_ohci
rmmod /lib/modules/2.6.32-71.el6.x86_64/kernel/drivers/firewire/firewire-ohci.ko
rmmod /lib/modules/2.6.32-71.el6.x86_64/kernel/drivers/firewire/firewire-core.ko
rmmod /lib/modules/2.6.32-71.el6.x86_64/kernel/lib/crc-itu-t.ko
```

The output shows that modules are unloaded in the reverse order that they are loaded, given that no processes depend on any of the modules being unloaded.

Example 21.4. Unloading a kernel module

Do not use rmmod directly!

Although the `rmmod` command can be used to unload kernel modules, it is recommended to use `modprobe -r` instead.

21.5. Setting Module Parameters

Like the kernel itself, modules can also take parameters that change their behavior. Most of the time, the default ones work well, but occasionally it is necessary or desirable to set custom parameters for a module. Because parameters cannot be dynamically set for a module that is already loaded into a running kernel, there are two different methods for setting them.

1. You can unload all dependencies of the module you want to set parameters for, unload the module using `modprobe -r`, and then load it with `modprobe` along with a list of customized parameters. This method is often used when the module does not have many dependencies, or to test different combinations of parameters without making them persistent, and is the method covered in this section.
2. Alternatively, you can list the new parameters in an existing or newly-created file in the `/etc/modprobe.d/` directory. This method makes the module parameters persistent by ensuring that they are set each time the module is loaded, such as after every reboot or `modprobe` command. This method is covered in Section 21.6, *Persistent Module Loading* (page 429), though the following information is a prerequisite.

You can use `modprobe` to load a kernel module with custom parameters using the following command line format:

```
modprobe module_name [parameter=value]
```

When loading a module with custom parameters on the command line, be aware of the following:

- You can enter multiple parameters and values by separating them with spaces.
- Some module parameters expect a list of comma-separated values as their argument. When entering the list of values, do *not* insert a space after each comma, or `modprobe` will incorrectly interpret the values following spaces as additional parameters.
- The `modprobe` command silently succeeds with an exit status of `0` if:
  - it successfully loads the module, *or*
  - the module is *already* loaded into the kernel.

  Thus, you must ensure that the module is not already loaded before attempting to load it with custom parameters. The `modprobe` command does not automatically reload the module, or alert you that it is already loaded.

Here are the recommended steps for setting custom parameters and then loading a kernel module. This procedure illustrates the steps using the `e1000e` module, which is the network driver for Intel PRO/1000 network adapters, as an example:

Procedure 21.1. Loading a Kernel Module with Custom Parameters

1. First, ensure the module is not already loaded into the kernel. For example:

   ```
   ~]# lsmod | grep e1000e
   ~]#
   ```

   Output indicates that the module is already loaded into the kernel, in which case you must first unload it before proceeding. Refer to Section 21.4, *Unloading a Module* (page 427) for instructions on safely unloading it.
2. Load the module and list all custom parameters after the module name. For example, if you wanted to load the Intel PRO/1000 network driver with the interrupt throttle rate set to 3000 interrupts per second for the first, second and third instances of the driver, and Energy Efficient Ethernet (EEE) turned on[1], you would run, as `root`:

   ```
   ~]# modprobe e1000e InterruptThrottleRate=3000,3000,3000 EEE=1
   ```

   This example illustrates passing multiple valued to a single parameter by separating them with commas and omitting any spaces between them.

21.6. Persistent Module Loading

As shown in *Example 21.1. Listing information about a kernel module with lsmod* above, many kernel modules are loaded automatically at boot time. You can specify additional modules to be loaded by creating a new `file_name.modules` file in the `/etc/sysconfig/modules/` directory, where `file_name` is any descriptive name of your choice. Your `file_name.modules` files are treated by the system startup scripts as shell scripts, and as such should begin with an *interpreter directive* (also called a "bang line") as their first line:

```
#!/bin/sh
```

Additionally, the `file_name.modules` file should be executable. You can make it executable by running:

```
modules]# chmod +x file_name.modules
```

The following `bluez-uinput.modules` script loads the `uinput` module:

```
#!/bin/sh
```

[1] Despite what the example might imply, Energy Efficient Ethernet is turned on by default in the `e1000e` driver.

```
if [ ! -c /dev/input/uinput ] ; then
        exec /sbin/modprobe uinput >/dev/null 2>&1
fi
```

The `if`-conditional statement on the third line ensures that the `/dev/input/uinput` file does *not* already exist (the `!` symbol negates the condition), and, if that is the case, loads the `uinput` module by calling `exec /sbin/modprobe uinput`. Note that the `uinput` module creates the `/dev/input/uinput` file, so testing to see if that file exists serves as verification of whether the `uinput` module is loaded into the kernel.

The following `>/dev/null 2>&1` clause at the end of that line redirects any output to `/dev/null` so that the `modprobe` command remains quiet.

Example 21.5. /etc/sysconfig/modules/bluez-uinput.modules

21.7. Specific Kernel Module Capabilities

This section explains how to enable specific kernel capabilities using various kernel modules.

21.7.1. Using Multiple Ethernet Cards

It is possible to use multiple Ethernet cards on a single machine. For each card there must be an `alias` and, possibly, `options` lines for each card in a user-created *`module_name`*`.conf` file in the `/etc/modprobe.d/` directory.

For additional information about using multiple Ethernet cards, refer to the *Linux Ethernet-HOWTO* online at *http://www.redhat.com/mirrors/LDP/HOWTO/Ethernet-HOWTO.html*.

21.7.2. Using Channel Bonding

Fedora allows administrators to bind NICs together into a single channel using the `bonding` kernel module and a special network interface, called a *channel bonding interface*. Channel bonding enables two or more network interfaces to act as one, simultaneously increasing the bandwidth and providing redundancy.

To channel bond multiple network interfaces, the administrator must perform the following steps:

1. As `root`, create a new file named *`bonding`*`.conf` in the `/etc/modprobe.d/` directory. Note that you can name this file anything you like as long as it ends with a `.conf` extension. Insert the following line in this new file:

   ```
   alias bondN bonding
   ```

   Replace `N` with the interface number, such as `0`. For each configured channel bonding interface, there must be a corresponding entry in your new `/etc/modprobe.d/`*`bonding`*`.conf` file.

2. Configure a channel bonding interface as outlined in Section 6.2.2, *Channel Bonding Interfaces* (page 109).
3. To enhance performance, adjust available module options to ascertain what combination works best. Pay particular attention to the `miimon` or `arp_interval` and the `arp_ip_target` parameters. Refer to Section 21.7.2.1, *Bonding Module Directives* (page 431) for a list of available options and how to quickly determine the best ones for your bonded interface.

21.7.2.1. Bonding Module Directives

It is a good idea to test which channel bonding module parameters work best for your bonded interfaces before adding them to the `BONDING_OPTS="bonding parameters"` directive in your bonding interface configuration file (`ifcfg-bond0` for example). Parameters to bonded interfaces can be configured without unloading (and reloading) the bonding module by manipulating files in the `sysfs` file system.

`sysfs` is a virtual file system that represents kernel objects as directories, files and symbolic links. `sysfs` can be used to query for information about kernel objects, and can also manipulate those objects through the use of normal file system commands. The `sysfs` virtual file system has a line in `/etc/fstab`, and is mounted under the `/sys/` directory. All bonding interfaces can be configured dynamically by interacting with and manipulating files under the `/sys/class/net/` directory.

In order to determine the best parameters for your bonding interface, create a channel bonding interface file such as `ifcfg-bond0` by following the instructions in Section 6.2.2, *Channel Bonding Interfaces* (page 109). Insert the `SLAVE=yes` and `MASTER=bond0` directives in the configuration files for each interface bonded to bond0. Once this is completed, you can proceed to testing the parameters.

First, bring up the bond you created by running `ifconfig bondN up` as `root`:

```
~]# ifconfig bond0 up
```

If you have correctly created the `ifcfg-bond0` bonding interface file, you will be able to see `bond0` listed in the output of running `ifconfig` (without any options):

```
~]# ifconfig
bond0     Link encap:Ethernet HWaddr 00:00:00:00:00:00
          UP BROADCAST RUNNING MASTER MULTICAST  MTU:1500  Metric:1
          RX packets:0 errors:0 dropped:0 overruns:0 frame:0
          TX packets:0 errors:0 dropped:0 overruns:0 carrier:0
          collisions:0 txqueuelen:0
          RX bytes:0  (0.0 b)  TX bytes:0  (0.0 b)
eth0      Link encap:Ethernet  HWaddr 52:54:00:26:9E:F1
          inet addr:192.168.122.251  Bcast:192.168.122.255  Mask:255.255.255.0
          inet6 addr: fe80::5054:ff:fe26:9ef1/64 Scope:Link
```

```
        UP BROADCAST RUNNING MULTICAST  MTU:1500  Metric:1
        RX packets:207 errors:0 dropped:0 overruns:0 frame:0
        TX packets:205 errors:0 dropped:0 overruns:0 carrier:0
        collisions:0 txqueuelen:1000
        RX bytes:70374 (68.7 KiB)  TX bytes:25298 (24.7 KiB)
[output truncated]
```

To view all existing bonds, even if they are not up, run:

```
~]# cat /sys/class/net/bonding_masters
bond0
```

You can configure each bond individually by manipulating the files located in the `/sys/class/net/bondN/bonding/` directory. First, the bond you are configuring must be taken down:

```
~]# ifconfig bond0 down
```

As an example, to enable MII monitoring on bond0 with a 1 second interval, you could run (as `root`):

```
~]# echo 1000 > /sys/class/net/bond0/bonding/miimon
```

To configure bond0 for *balance-alb* mode, you could run either:

```
~]# echo 6 > /sys/class/net/bond0/bonding/mode
```

...or, using the name of the mode:

```
~]# echo balance-alb > /sys/class/net/bond0/bonding/mode
```

After configuring options for the bond in question, you can bring it up and test it by running `ifconfig bondN up` . If you decide to change the options, take the interface down, modify its parameters using `sysfs`, bring it back up, and re-test.

Once you have determined the best set of parameters for your bond, add those parameters as a space-separated list to the *BONDING_OPTS=* directive of the `/etc/sysconfig/network-scripts/ifcfg-bondN` file for the bonding interface you are configuring. Whenever that bond is brought up (for example, by the system during the boot sequence if the *ONBOOT=yes* directive is set), the bonding options specified in the *BONDING_OPTS* will take effect for that bond. For more information on configuring bonding interfaces (and *BONDING_OPTS*), refer to Section 6.2.2, *Channel Bonding Interfaces* (page 109).

The following list provides the names of many of the more common channel bonding parameters, along with a descriptions of what they do. For more information, refer to the brief descriptions for each `parm` in `modinfo bonding` output, or the exhaustive descriptions in the `bonding.txt` file in the kernel-doc package (see Section 21.8, *Additional Resources* - page 437).

Bonding Interface Parameters

`arp_interval=`*`time_in_milliseconds`*

Specifies (in milliseconds) how often ARP monitoring occurs.

> **Make sure you specify all required parameters**
>
> It is essential that both `arp_interval` and `arp_ip_target` parameters are specified, or, alternatively, the `miimon` parameter is specified. Failure to do so can cause degradation of network performance in the event that a link fails.

If using this setting while in `mode=0` or `mode=1` (the two load-balancing modes), the network switch must be configured to distribute packets evenly across the NICs. For more information on how to accomplish this, refer to `/usr/share/doc/kernel-doc-`*`kernel_version`*`/Documentation/networking/bonding.txt`

The value is set to `0` by default, which disables it.

`arp_ip_target=`*`ip_address`*`[,`*`ip_address_2`*`,...`*`ip_address_16`*`]`

Specifies the target IP address of ARP requests when the `arp_interval` parameter is enabled. Up to 16 IP addresses can be specified in a comma separated list.

`arp_validate=`*`value`*

Validate source/distribution of ARP probes; default is **`none`**. Other valid values are **`active`**, **`backup`**, and **`all`**.

`debug=`*`number`*

Enables debug messages. Possible values are:

- `0` — Debug messages are disabled. This is the default.
- `1` — Debug messages are enabled.

`downdelay=`*`time_in_milliseconds`*

Specifies (in milliseconds) how long to wait after link failure before disabling the link. The value must be a multiple of the value specified in the `miimon` parameter. The value is set to `0` by default, which disables it.

lacp_rate=*`value`*

Specifies the rate at which link partners should transmit LACPDU packets in 802.3ad mode. Possible values are:

- **`slow`** or `0` — Default setting. This specifies that partners should transmit LACPDUs every 30 seconds.
- **`fast`** or `1` — Specifies that partners should transmit LACPDUs every 1 second.

`miimon=`*`time_in_milliseconds`*

Specifies (in milliseconds) how often MII link monitoring occurs. This is useful if high availability is required because MII is used to verify that the NIC is active. To verify that the driver for a particular NIC supports the MII tool, type the following command as `root`:

```
~]# ethtool interface_name | grep "Link detected:"
```

In this command, replace *`interface_name`* with the name of the device interface, such as **`eth0`**, not the bond interface. If MII is supported, the command returns:

```
Link detected: yes
```

If using a bonded interface for high availability, the module for each NIC must support MII. Setting the value to `0` (the default), turns this feature off. When configuring this setting, a good starting point for this parameter is `100`.

Make sure you specify all required parameters

It is essential that both `arp_interval` and `arp_ip_target` parameters are specified, or, alternatively, the `miimon` parameter is specified. Failure to do so can cause degradation of network performance in the event that a link fails.

`mode=`*`value`*

Allows you to specify the bonding policy. The *`value`* can be one of:

- **`balance-rr`** or `0` — Sets a round-robin policy for fault tolerance and load balancing. Transmissions are received and sent out sequentially on each bonded slave interface beginning with the first one available.
- **`active-backup`** or `1` — Sets an active-backup policy for fault tolerance. Transmissions are received and sent out via the first available bonded slave interface. Another bonded slave interface is only used if the active bonded slave interface fails.
- **`balance-xor`** or `2` — Sets an XOR (exclusive-or) policy for fault tolerance and load balancing. Using this method, the interface matches up the incoming request's MAC address with the MAC address for one of the slave NICs. Once this link is established, transmissions are sent out sequentially beginning with the first available interface.
- **`broadcast`** or `3` — Sets a broadcast policy for fault tolerance. All transmissions are sent on all slave interfaces.
- **`802.3ad`** or `4` — Sets an IEEE 802.3ad dynamic link aggregation policy. Creates aggregation groups that share the same speed and duplex settings. Transmits and receives on all slaves in the active aggregator. Requires a switch that is 802.3ad compliant.

- **`balance-tlb`** or **`5`** — Sets a Transmit Load Balancing (TLB) policy for fault tolerance and load balancing. The outgoing traffic is distributed according to the current load on each slave interface. Incoming traffic is received by the current slave. If the receiving slave fails, another slave takes over the MAC address of the failed slave.
- **`balance-alb`** or **`6`** — Sets an Active Load Balancing (ALB) policy for fault tolerance and load balancing. Includes transmit and receive load balancing for IPV4 traffic. Receive load balancing is achieved through ARP negotiation.

`num_unsol_na=`*`number`*

Specifies the number of unsolicited IPv6 Neighbor Advertisements to be issued after a failover event. One unsolicited NA is issued immediately after the failover.

The valid range is **`0 - 255`**; the default value is **`1`**. This parameter affects only the active-backup mode.

`primary=`*`interface_name`*

Specifies the interface name, such as **`eth0`**, of the primary device. The `primary` device is the first of the bonding interfaces to be used and is not abandoned unless it fails. This setting is particularly useful when one NIC in the bonding interface is faster and, therefore, able to handle a bigger load.

This setting is only valid when the bonding interface is in **`active-backup`** mode. Refer to `/usr/share/doc/kernel-doc-`*`kernel-version`*`/Documentation/networking/bonding.txt` for more information.

`primary_reselect=`*`value`*

Specifies the reselection policy for the primary slave. This affects how the primary slave is chosen to become the active slave when failure of the active slave or recovery of the primary slave occurs. This parameter is designed to prevent flip-flopping between the primary slave and other slaves. Possible values are:

- **`always`** or **`0`** (default) — The primary slave becomes the active slave whenever it comes back up.
- **`better`** or **`1`** — The primary slave becomes the active slave when it comes back up, if the speed and duplex of the primary slave is better than the speed and duplex of the current active slave.
- **`failure`** or **`2`** — The primary slave becomes the active slave only if the current active slave fails and the primary slave is up.

The `primary_reselect` setting is ignored in two cases:

- If no slaves are active, the first slave to recover is made the active slave.
- When initially enslaved, the primary slave is always made the active slave.

Changing the `primary_reselect` policy via `sysfs` will cause an immediate selection of the best active slave according to the new policy. This may or may not result in a change of the active slave, depending upon the circumstances

`updelay=`*`time_in_milliseconds`*

Specifies (in milliseconds) how long to wait before enabling a link. The value must be a multiple of the value specified in the `miimon` parameter. The value is set to **`0`** by default, which disables it.

`use_carrier=`*`number`*

Specifies whether or not `miimon` should use MII/ETHTOOL ioctls or `netif_carrier_ok()` to determine the link state. The `netif_carrier_ok()` function relies on the device driver to maintains its state with `netif_carrier_`*`on/off`* ; most device drivers support this function.

The MII/ETHROOL ioctls tools utilize a deprecated calling sequence within the kernel. However, this is still configurable in case your device driver does not support `netif_carrier_`*`on/off`* .

Valid values are:

- `1` — Default setting. Enables the use of `netif_carrier_ok()`.
- `0` — Enables the use of MII/ETHTOOL ioctls.

Note

If the bonding interface insists that the link is up when it should not be, it is possible that your network device driver does not support `netif_carrier_`*`on/off`*.

`xmit_hash_policy=`*`value`*

Selects the transmit hash policy used for slave selection in **`balance-xor`** and **`802.3ad`** modes. Possible values are:

- `0` or **`layer2`** — Default setting. This parameter uses the XOR of hardware MAC addresses to generate the hash. The formula used is:
- (*`source_MAC_address`* XOR *`destination_MAC`*) MODULO *`slave_count`*

  This algorithm will place all traffic to a particular network peer on the same slave, and is 802.3ad compliant.
- `1` or **`layer3+4`** — Uses upper layer protocol information (when available) to generate the hash. This allows for traffic to a particular network peer to span multiple slaves, although a single connection will not span multiple slaves.

  The formula for unfragmented TCP and UDP packets used is:

  `((`*`source_port`* `XOR` *`dest_port`*`) XOR`

```
((source_IP XOR dest_IP) AND 0xffff)
  MODULO slave_count
```

For fragmented TCP or UDP packets and all other IP protocol traffic, the source and destination port information is omitted. For non-IP traffic, the formula is the same as the `layer2` transmit hash policy.

This policy intends to mimic the behavior of certain switches; particularly, Cisco switches with PFC2 as well as some Foundry and IBM products.

The algorithm used by this policy is not 802.3ad compliant.

- `2` or **`layer2+3`** — Uses a combination of layer2 and layer3 protocol information to generate the hash.

  Uses XOR of hardware MAC addresses and IP addresses to generate the hash. The formula is:

  ```
  (((source_IP XOR dest_IP) AND 0xffff) XOR
    ( source_MAC XOR destination_MAC ))
      MODULO slave_count
  ```

  This algorithm will place all traffic to a particular network peer on the same slave. For non-IP traffic, the formula is the same as for the layer2 transmit hash policy.

  This policy is intended to provide a more balanced distribution of traffic than layer2 alone, especially in environments where a layer3 gateway device is required to reach most destinations.

  This algorithm is 802.3ad compliant.

21.8. Additional Resources

For more information on kernel modules and their utilities, refer to the following resources.

21.8.1. Installed Documentation

There is a number of manual pages for various utilities related to the kernel modules:

`man lsmod`
: The manual page for the `lsmod` command.

`man modinfo`
: The manual page for the `modinfo` command.

`man modprobe`
: The manual page for the `modprobe` command.

`man rmmod`
: The manual page for the `rmmod` command.

`man ethtool`
: The manual page for the `ethtool` command.

`man mii-tool`
: The manual page for the `mii-tool` command.

Additionally, you can refer to the documentation provided by the kernel-doc package:

`/usr/share/doc/kernel-doc-`*`kernel_version`*`/Documentation/`
: This directory contains information on the kernel, kernel modules, and their respective parameters. Note that before accessing the kernel documentation, you must run the following command as `root`:

```
yum install kernel-doc
```

21.8.2. Useful Websites

Linux Loadable Kernel Module HOWTO[2]

The *Linux Loadable Kernel Module HOWTO* from the Linux Documentation Project contains further information on working with kernel modules.

[2] *http://tldp.org/HOWTO/Module-HOWTO/*

Chapter 22.
The kdump Crash Recovery Service

`kdump` is an advanced crash dumping mechanism. When enabled, the system is booted from the context of another kernel. This second kernel reserves a small amount of memory, and its only purpose is to capture the core dump image in case the system crashes. Since being able to analyze the core dump helps significantly to determine the exact cause of the system failure, it is strongly recommended to have this feature enabled.

This chapter explains how to configure, test, and use the `kdump` service in Fedora, and provides a brief overview of how to analyze the resulting core dump using the **crash** debugging utility.

22.1. Configuring the kdump Service

This section covers two common means of configuring the `kdump` service: using the **Kernel Dump Configuration** graphical utility, and doing so manually on the command line. It also describes how to test the configuration to verify that everything works as expected.

Disable IOMMU on Intel chipsets

A limitation in the current implementation of the `Intel IOMMU` driver can occasionally prevent the `kdump` service from capturing the core dump image. To use `kdump` on Intel architectures reliably, it is advised that the IOMMU support is disabled.

Make sure you have relevant packages installed

To use the `kdump` service, you must have the kexec-tools and system-config-kdump packages installed. To do so, type the following at a shell prompt as `root`:

```
yum install kexec-tools system-config-kdump
```

For more information on how to install new packages in Fedora, refer to Section 4.2.4, *Installing Packages* (page 78).

22.1.1. Using the Kernel Dump Configuration Utility

To start the **Kernel Dump Configuration** utility, select **Applications → Other → Kernel crash dumps** from the **Activities** menu, or type `system-config-kdump` at a shell prompt. You will be presented with a window as shown in *Figure 22.1. Basic Settings* below.

The utility allows you to configure `kdump` as well as to enable or disable starting the service at boot time. When you are done, click **Apply** to save the changes. The system reboot will be requested, and unless you are already authenticated, you will be prompted to enter the superuser password.

Make sure the system has enough memory

Unless the system has enough memory, the utility will not start, and you will be presented with the following error message:

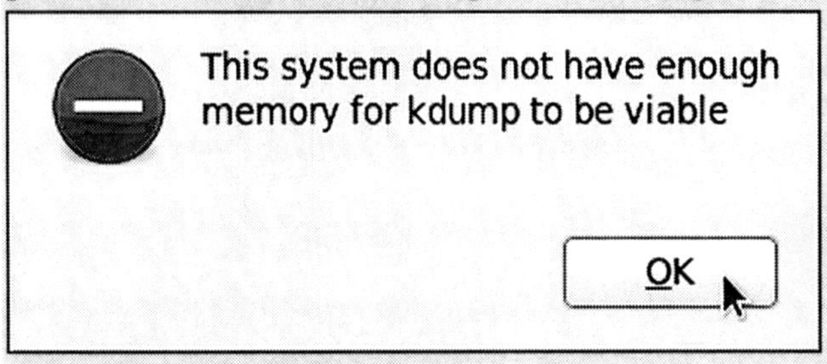

For the information on minimum memory requirements, refer to the *Hardware Overview* section of the *Fedora 15 Release Notes*[1]. Note that when the `kdump` crash recovery is enabled, the minimum memory requirements increase by the amount of memory reserved for it. This value is determined by a user, and defaults to 128MB.

22.1.1.1. Enabling the Service

To start the `kdump` daemon at boot time, click the **Enable** button on the toolbar. This will enable the service for runlevels `2`, `3`, `4`, and `5`, and start it for the current session. Similarly, clicking the **Disable** button will disable it for all runlevels and stop the service immediately.

For more information on runlevels and configuring services in general, refer to Chapter 7, *Services and Daemons* (page 120).

[1] *http://docs.fedoraproject.org/en-US/Fedora/15/html/Release_Notes/index.html*

22.1.1.2. The Basic Settings Tab

The **Basic Settings** tab enables you to configure the amount of memory that is reserved for the `kdump` kernel. To do so, select the **Manual kdump memory settings** radio button, and click the up and down arrow buttons next to the **New kdump Memory** field to increase or decrease the value. Notice that the **Usable Memory** field changes accordingly showing you the remaining memory that will be available to the system.

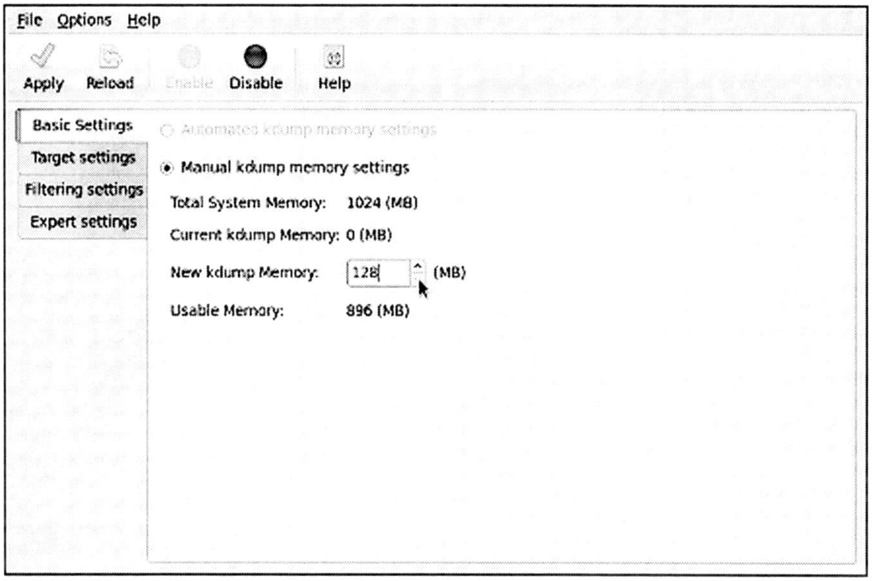

Figure 22.1. Basic Settings

22.1.1.3. The Target Settings Tab

The **Target Settings** tab enables you to specify the target location for the `vmcore` dump. It can be either stored as a file in a local file system, written directly to a device, or sent over a network using the NFS (Network File System) or SSH (Secure Shell) protocol.

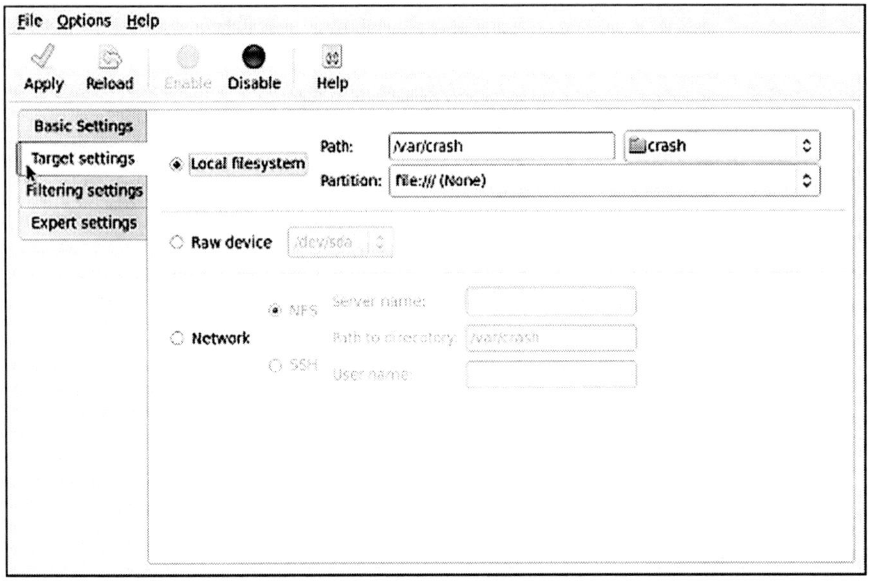

Figure 22.2. Target Settings

To save the dump to the local file system, select the **Local filesystem** radio button. Optionally, you can customize the settings by choosing a different partition from the **Partition**, and a target directory from the **Path** pulldown lists.

To write the dump directly to a device, select the **Raw device** radio button, and choose the desired target device from the pulldown list next to it.

To store the dump to a remote machine, select the **Network** radio button. To use the NFS protocol, select the **NFS** radio button, and fill the **Server name** and **Path to directory** fields. To use the SSH protocol, select the **SSH** radio button, and fill the **Server name**, **Path to directory**, and **User name** fields with the remote server address, target directory, and a valid remote user name respectively. Refer to Chapter 9, *OpenSSH* (page 168) for information on how to configure an SSH server, and how to set up a key-based authentication.

For a complete list of currently supported targets, see *Table 22.1. Supported kdump targets* below.

Type	Supported Targets	Unsupported Targets
Raw device	All locally attached raw disks and partitions.	—
Local file system	`ext2`, `ext3`, `ext4`, `minix` file systems on directly attached disk drives, hardware RAID logical drives, LVM devices, and `mdraid` arrays.	The `eCryptfs` file system.
Remote directory	Remote directories accessed using the `NFS` or `SSH` protocol over `IPv4`.	Remote directories on the `rootfs` file system accessed using the `NFS` protocol.
	Remote directories accessed using the `iSCSI` protocol over hardware initiators.	Remote directories accessed using the `iSCSI` protocol over software initiators.
	—	Remote directories accessed over `IPv6`.
		Remote directories accessed using the `SMB/CIFS` protocol.
		Remote directories accessed using the `FCoE` (*Fibre Channel over Ethernet*) protocol.
		Remote directories accessed using wireless network interfaces.
		Multipath-based storages.

Table 22.1. Supported kdump targets

Using the hpsa driver for a storage

Due to known issue with the `hpsa` driver, `kdump` is unable to save the dump to a storage that uses this driver for HP Smart Array Controllers. If this applies to your machine, it is advised that you save the dump to a remote system using the NFS or SSH protocol instead.

22.1.1.4. The Filtering Settings Tab

The **Filtering Settings** tab enables you to select the filtering level for the `vmcore` dump.

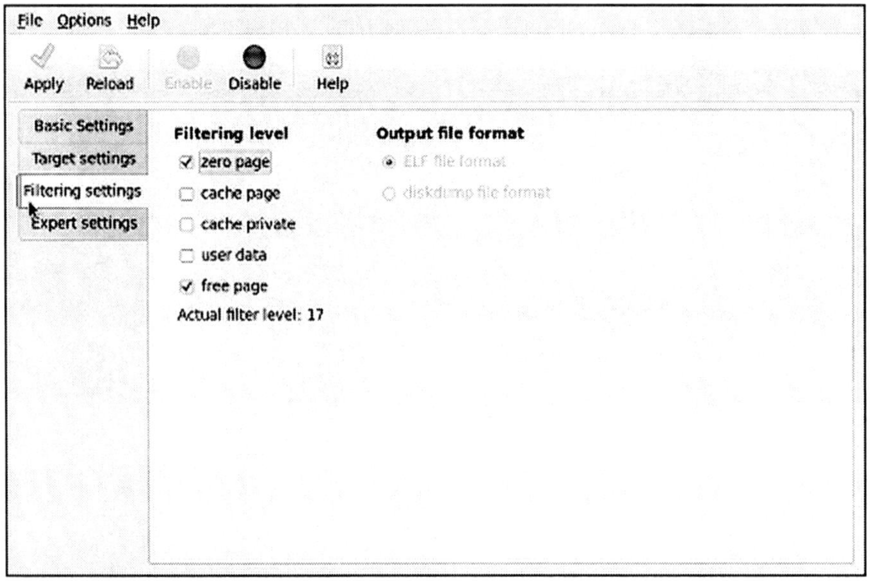

Figure 22.3. Filtering Settings

To exclude the **zero page**, **cache page**, **cache private**, **user data**, or **free page** from the dump, select the check box next to the appropriate label.

22.1.1.5. The Expert Settings Tab

The **Expert Settings** tab enables you to choose which kernel and initial RAM disk to use, as well as to customize the options that are passed to the kernel and the core collector program.

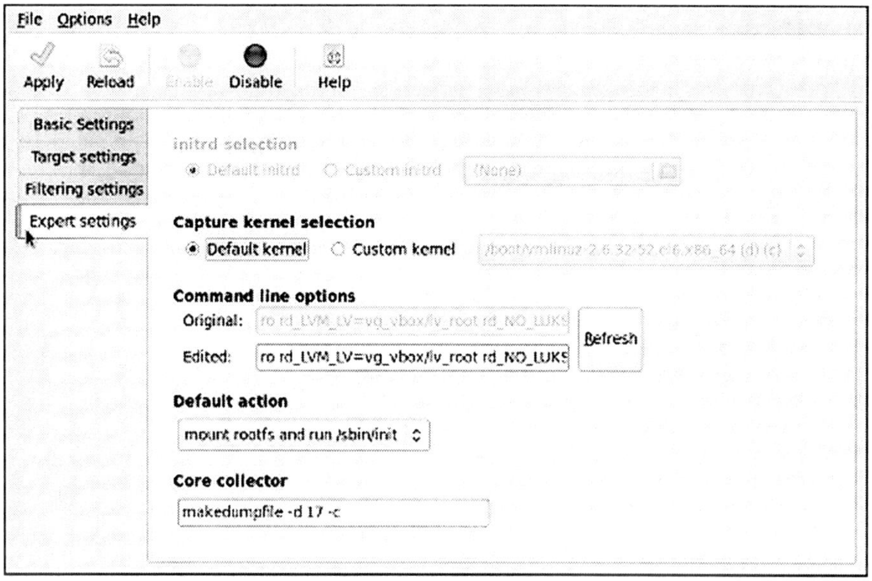

Figure 22.4. Expert Settings

To use a different initial RAM disk, select the **Custom initrd** radio button, and choose the desired RAM disk from the pulldown list next to it.

To capture a different kernel, select the **Custom kernel** radio button, and choose the desired kernel image from the pulldown list on the right.

To adjust the list of options that are passed to the kernel at boot time, edit the content of the **Edited** text field. Note that you can always revert your changes by clicking the **Refresh** button.

To choose what steps should be taken when the kernel crash is captured, select the appropriate option from the **Default action** pulldown list. Available options are **mount rootfs and run /sbin/init** (the default action), **reboot** (to reboot the system), **shell** (to present a user with an interactive shell prompt), **halt** (to halt the system), and **poweroff** (to power the system off).

To customize the options that are passed to the `makedumpfile` core collector, edit the **Core collector** text field; see Section 22.1.2.3, *Configuring the Core Collector* (page 447) for more information.

22.1.2. Configuring kdump on the Command Line

To perform actions described in this section, you have to be logged in as `root`. To do so, run the following command:

```
su -
```

22.1.2.1. Configuring the Memory Usage

To configure the amount of memory that is reserved for the `kdump` kernel, open the `/boot/grub/grub.conf` file in a text editor such as **vi** or **nano**, and add the `crashkernel=<size>M` parameter to the list of kernel options as shown in *Example 22.1. A sample /boot/grub/grub.conf file* below.

```
# grub.conf generated by anaconda
#
# Note that you do not have to rerun grub after making changes to this file
# NOTICE:  You have a /boot partition.  This means that
#          all kernel and initrd paths are relative to /boot/, eg.
#          root (hd0,0)
#          kernel /vmlinuz-version ro root=/dev/sda3
#          initrd /initrd
#boot=/dev/sda
default=0
timeout=5
splashimage=(hd0,0)/grub/splash.xpm.gz
hiddenmenu
title Red Hat Enterprise Linux (2.6.32-54.el6.i686)
        root (hd0,0)
        kernel /boot/vmlinuz-2.6.32-54.el6.i686 root=/dev/sda3 ro crashkernel=128M
        initrd /initramfs-2.6.32-54.el6.i686.img
```

Example 22.1. A sample /boot/grub/grub.conf file

Make sure the system has enough memory

When the `kdump` crash recovery is enabled, the minimum memory requirements increase by the amount of memory reserved for it. This value is determined by a user, and defaults to 128 MB, as lower values proved to be unreliable. For the information on minimum memory requirements, refer to the *Hardware Overview* section of the *Fedora 15 Release Notes*[2].

22.1.2.2. Configuring the Target Type

When a kernel crash is captured, the core dump can be either stored as a file in a local file system, written directly to a device, or sent over a network using the NFS (Network File

[2] *http://docs.fedoraproject.org/en-US/Fedora/15/html/Release_Notes/index.html*

System) or SSH (Secure Shell) protocol. Note that only one of these options can be set at the moment. The default option is to store the `vmcore` file in the `/var/crash/` directory of the local file system. To change this, open the `/etc/kdump.conf` configuration file in a text editor such as **vi** or **nano**, and edit the options as described below.

To change the local directory in which the core dump is to be saved, remove the hash sign ("#") from the beginning of the `#path /var/crash` line, and replace the value with a desired directory path. Optionally, if you wish to write the file to a different partition, follow the same procedure with the `#ext4 /dev/sda3` line as well, and change both the file system type and the device (a device name, a file system label, and UUID are all supported) accordingly. For example:

```
ext3 /dev/sda4
path /usr/local/cores
```

To write the dump directly to a device, remove the hash sign ("#") from the beginning of the `#raw /dev/sda5` line, and replace the value with a desired device name. For example:

```
raw /dev/sdb1
```

To store the dump to a remote machine using the NFS protocol, remove the hash sign ("#") from the beginning of the `#net my.server.com:/export/tmp` line, and replace the value with a valid hostname and directory path. For example:

```
net penguin.example.com:/export/cores
```

To store the dump to a remote machine using the SSH protocol, remove the hash sign ("#") from the beginning of the `#net user@my.server.com` line, and replace the value with a valid username and hostname. For example:

```
net john@penguin.example.com
```

Refer to Chapter 9, *OpenSSH* (page 168) for information on how to configure an SSH server, and how to set up a key-based authentication.

For a complete list of currently supported targets, see *Table 22.1. Supported kdump targets* above.

Using the hpsa driver for a storage

Due to known issue with the `hpsa` driver, `kdump` is unable to save the dump to a storage that uses this driver for HP Smart Array Controllers. If this applies to your machine, it is advised that you save the dump to a remote system using the NFS or SSH protocol instead.

22.1.2.3. Configuring the Core Collector

To reduce the size of the `vmcore` dump file, `kdump` allows you to specify an external application (that is, a core collector) to compress the data, and optionally leave out all irrelevant information. Currently, the only fully supported core collector is `makedumpfile`.

To enable the core collector, open the `/etc/kdump.conf` configuration file in a text editor such as **vi** or **nano**, remove the hash sign ("#") from the beginning of the `#core_collector makedumpfile -c --message-level 1 -d 31` line, and edit the command line options as described below.

To enable the dump file compression, add the `-c` parameter. For example:

```
core_collector makedumpfile -c
```

To remove certain pages from the dump, add the `-d value` parameter, where `value` is a sum of values of pages you want to omit as described in *Table 22.2. Supported filtering levels* below. For example, to remove both zero and free pages, use the following:

```
core_collector makedumpfile -d 17 -c
```

Refer to the manual page for `makedumpfile` for a complete list of available options.

Option	Description
1	Zero pages
2	Cache pages
4	Cache private
8	User pages
16	Free pages

Table 22.2. Supported filtering levels

22.1.2.4. Changing the Default Action

By default, when the kernel crash is captured, the root file system is mounted, and `/sbin/init` is run. To change this behavior, open the `/etc/kdump.conf` configuration file in a text editor such as **vi** or **nano**, remove the hash sign ("#") from the beginning of the `#default shell` line, and replace the value with a desired action as described in *Table 22.3. Supported actions* below. For example:

```
default halt
```

Option	Description
`reboot`	Reboot the system, losing the core in the process.
`halt`	After attempting to capture a core, halt the system no matter if it succeeded.
`poweroff`	Power off the system.
`shell`	Run the **msh** session from within the initramfs, allowing a user to record the core manually.

Table 22.3. Supported actions

22.1.2.5. Enabling the Service

To start the `kdump` daemon at boot time, type the following at a shell prompt:

```
systemctl enable kdump.service
```

Similarly, typing `systemctl disable kdump.service` will disable it. To start the service in the current session, use the following command:

```
systemctl start kdump.service
```

For more information on runlevels and configuring services in general, refer to Chapter 7, *Services and Daemons* (page 120).

22.1.3. Testing the Configuration

Be careful when using these commands

The commands below will cause the kernel to crash. Use caution when following these steps, and by no means use them on a production machine.

To test the configuration, reboot the system with `kdump` enabled, and make sure that the service is running (refer to Section 7.2, *Running Services* - page 121 for more information on how to run a service in Fedora):

```
systemctl is-active kdump.service
```

Then type the following commands at a shell prompt:

```
echo 1 > /proc/sys/kernel/sysrq
echo c > /proc/sysrq-trigger
```

This will force the Linux kernel to crash, and the *`address-YYYY-MM-DD-HH:MM:SS`*`/vmcore` file will be copied to the location you have selected in the configuration (that is, to `/var/crash/` by default).

```
~]# tree --charset=ascii /var/crash
/var/crash
`-- 127.0.0.1-2010-08-25-08:45:02
    `-- vmcore

1 directory, 1 file
```

Example 22.2. Listing a content of /var/crash/ after a crash

22.2. Analyzing the Core Dump

To determine the cause of the system crash, you can use the **crash** utility, which provides an interactive prompt very similar to the GNU Debugger (GDB). This utility allows you to interactively analyze a running Linux system as well as a core dump created by `netdump`, `diskdump`, `xendump`, or `kdump`.

Make sure you have relevant packages installed

To analyze the vmcore dump file, you must have the crash and kernel-debuginfo packages installed. To install these packages, type the following at a shell prompt as root:

```
yum install crash
debuginfo-install kernel
```

For more information on how to install new packages in Fedora, refer to Section 4.2.4, *Installing Packages* (page 78).

22.2.1. Running the crash Utility

To start the utility, type the command in the following form at a shell prompt:

```
crash /var/crash/timestamp/vmcore /usr/lib/debug/lib/modules/kernel/vmlinux
```

Note that the *kernel* version should be the same that was captured by kdump. To find out which kernel you are currently running, use the uname -r command.

```
~]# crash /usr/lib/debug/lib/modules/2.6.32-69.el6.i686/vmlinux \
/var/crash/127.0.0.1-2010-08-25-08:45:02/vmcore

crash 5.0.0-23.el6
Copyright (C) 2002-2010  Red Hat, Inc.
Copyright (C) 2004, 2005, 2006  IBM Corporation
Copyright (C) 1999-2006  Hewlett-Packard Co
Copyright (C) 2005, 2006  Fujitsu Limited
Copyright (C) 2006, 2007  VA Linux Systems Japan K.K.
Copyright (C) 2005  NEC Corporation
Copyright (C) 1999, 2002, 2007  Silicon Graphics, Inc.
Copyright (C) 1999, 2000, 2001, 2002  Mission Critical Linux, Inc.
This program is free software, covered by the GNU General Public License,
and you are welcome to change it and/or distribute copies of it under
certain conditions.  Enter "help copying" to see the conditions.
This program has absolutely no warranty.  Enter "help warranty" for details.

GNU gdb (GDB) 7.0
Copyright (C) 2009 Free Software Foundation, Inc.
License GPLv3+: GNU GPL version 3 or later <http://gnu.org/licenses/gpl.html>
This is free software: you are free to change and redistribute it.
There is NO WARRANTY, to the extent permitted by law.  Type "show copying"
and "show warranty" for details.
This GDB was configured as "i686-pc-linux-gnu"...

      KERNEL: /usr/lib/debug/lib/modules/2.6.32-69.el6.i686/vmlinux
    DUMPFILE: /var/crash/127.0.0.1-2010-08-25-08:45:02/vmcore  [PARTIAL DUMP]
        CPUS: 4
        DATE: Wed Aug 25 08:44:47 2010
      UPTIME: 00:09:02
LOAD AVERAGE: 0.00, 0.01, 0.00
```

```
      TASKS: 140
   NODENAME: hp-dl320g5-02.lab.bos.redhat.com
    RELEASE: 2.6.32-69.el6.i686
    VERSION: #1 SMP Tue Aug 24 10:31:45 EDT 2010
    MACHINE: i686  (2394 Mhz)
     MEMORY: 8 GB
      PANIC: "Oops: 0002 [#1] SMP " (check log for details)
        PID: 5591
    COMMAND: "bash"
       TASK: f196d560  [THREAD_INFO: ef4da000]
        CPU: 2
      STATE: TASK_RUNNING (PANIC)

crash>
```

Example 22.3. Running the crash utility

22.2.2. Displaying the Message Buffer

To display the kernel message buffer, type the `log` command at the interactive prompt.

```
crash> log
... several lines omitted ...
EIP: 0060:[<c068124f>] EFLAGS: 00010096 CPU: 2
EIP is at sysrq_handle_crash+0xf/0x20
EAX: 00000063 EBX: 00000063 ECX: c09e1c8c EDX: 00000000
ESI: c0a09ca0 EDI: 00000286 EBP: 00000000 ESP: ef4dbf24
 DS: 007b ES: 007b FS: 00d8 GS: 00e0 SS: 0068
Process bash (pid: 5591, ti=ef4da000 task=f196d560 task.ti=ef4da000)
Stack:
 c068146b c0960891 c0968653 00000003 00000000 00000002 efade5c0 c06814d0
<0> fffffffb c068150f b7776000 f2600c40 c0569ec4 ef4dbf9c 00000002 b7776000
<0> efade5c0 00000002 b7776000 c0569e60 c051de50 ef4dbf9c f196d560 ef4dbfb4
Call Trace:
 [<c068146b>] ? __handle_sysrq+0xfb/0x160
 [<c06814d0>] ? write_sysrq_trigger+0x0/0x50
 [<c068150f>] ? write_sysrq_trigger+0x3f/0x50
 [<c0569ec4>] ? proc_reg_write+0x64/0xa0
 [<c0569e60>] ? proc_reg_write+0x0/0xa0
 [<c051de50>] ? vfs_write+0xa0/0x190
 [<c051e8d1>] ? sys_write+0x41/0x70
 [<c0409adc>] ? syscall_call+0x7/0xb
Code: a0 c0 01 0f b6 41 03 19 d2 f7 d2 83 e2 03 83 e0 cf c1 e2 04 09 d0 88 41 03 f3
c3 90 c7 05 c8 1b 9e c0 01 00 00 00 0f ae f8 89 f6 <c6> 05 00 00 00 00 01 c3 89 f6
8d bc 27 00 00 00 00 8d 50 d0 83
EIP: [<c068124f>] sysrq_handle_crash+0xf/0x20 SS:ESP 0068:ef4dbf24
CR2: 0000000000000000
```

Example 22.4. Displaying the kernel message buffer

Type `help log` for more information on the command usage.

22.2.3. Displaying a Backtrace

To display the kernel stack trace, type the `bt` command at the interactive prompt. You can use `bt` *`pid`* to display the backtrace of the selected process.

```
crash> bt
PID: 5591   TASK: f196d560  CPU: 2   COMMAND: "bash"
 #0 [ef4dbdcc] crash_kexec at c0494922
 #1 [ef4dbe20] oops_end at c080e402
 #2 [ef4dbe34] no_context at c043089d
 #3 [ef4dbe58] bad_area at c0430b26
 #4 [ef4dbe6c] do_page_fault at c080fb9b
 #5 [ef4dbee4] error_code (via page_fault) at c080d809
    EAX: 00000063  EBX: 00000063  ECX: c09e1c8c  EDX: 00000000  EBP: 00000000
    DS:  007b      ESI: c0a09ca0  ES:  007b      EDI: 00000286  GS:  00e0
    CS:  0060      EIP: c068124f  ERR: ffffffff  EFLAGS: 00010096
 #6 [ef4dbf18] sysrq_handle_crash at c068124f
 #7 [ef4dbf24] __handle_sysrq at c0681469
 #8 [ef4dbf48] write_sysrq_trigger at c068150a
 #9 [ef4dbf54] proc_reg_write at c0569ec2
#10 [ef4dbf74] vfs_write at c051de4e
#11 [ef4dbf94] sys_write at c051e8cc
#12 [ef4dbfb0] system_call at c0409ad5
    EAX: ffffffda  EBX: 00000001  ECX: b7776000  EDX: 00000002
    DS:  007b      ESI: 00000002  ES:  007b      EDI: b7776000
    SS:  007b      ESP: bfcb2088  EBP: bfcb20b4  GS:  0033
    CS:  0073      EIP: 00edc416  ERR: 00000004  EFLAGS: 00000246
```

Example 22.5. Displaying the kernel stack trace

Type `help bt` for more information on the command usage.

22.2.4. Displaying a Process Status

To display status of processes in the system, type the `ps` command at the interactive prompt. You can use `ps` *`pid`* to display the status of the selected process.

```
crash> ps
   PID    PPID  CPU   TASK    ST  %MEM     VSZ    RSS  COMM
>     0      0   0  c09dc560  RU   0.0       0      0  [swapper]
>     0      0   1  f7072030  RU   0.0       0      0  [swapper]
      0      0   2  f70a3a90  RU   0.0       0      0  [swapper]
>     0      0   3  f70ac560  RU   0.0       0      0  [swapper]
      1      0   1  f705ba90  IN   0.0    2828   1424  init
... several lines omitted ...
   5566      1   1  f2592560  IN   0.0   12876    784  auditd
   5567      1   2  ef427560  IN   0.0   12876    784  auditd
   5587   5132   0  f196d030  IN   0.0   11064   3184  sshd
>  5591   5587   2  f196d560  RU   0.0    5084   1648  bash
```

Example 22.6. Displaying status of processes in the system

Type `help ps` for more information on the command usage.

22.2.5. Displaying Virtual Memory Information

To display basic virtual memory information, type the `vm` command at the interactive prompt. You can use `vm` *`pid`* to display information on the selected process.

```
crash> vm
PID: 5591   TASK: f196d560  CPU: 2   COMMAND: "bash"
   MM       PGD      RSS    TOTAL_VM
f19b5900  ef9c6000  1648k    5084k
  VMA       START      END    FLAGS  FILE
f1bb0310    242000    260000 8000875  /lib/ld-2.12.so
f26af0b8    260000    261000 8100871  /lib/ld-2.12.so
efbc275c    261000    262000 8100873  /lib/ld-2.12.so
efbc2a18    268000    3ed000 8000075  /lib/libc-2.12.so
efbc23d8    3ed000    3ee000 8000070  /lib/libc-2.12.so
efbc2888    3ee000    3f0000 8100071  /lib/libc-2.12.so
efbc2cd4    3f0000    3f1000 8100073  /lib/libc-2.12.so
efbc243c    3f1000    3f4000 100073
efbc28ec    3f6000    3f9000 8000075  /lib/libdl-2.12.so
efbc2568    3f9000    3fa000 8100071  /lib/libdl-2.12.so
efbc2f2c    3fa000    3fb000 8100073  /lib/libdl-2.12.so
f26af888    7e6000    7fc000 8000075  /lib/libtinfo.so.5.7
f26aff2c    7fc000    7ff000 8100073  /lib/libtinfo.so.5.7
efbc211c    d83000    d8f000 8000075  /lib/libnss_files-2.12.so
efbc2504    d8f000    d90000 8100071  /lib/libnss_files-2.12.so
efbc2950    d90000    d91000 8100073  /lib/libnss_files-2.12.so
f26afe00    edc000    edd000 4040075
f1bb0a18   8047000   8118000 8001875  /bin/bash
f1bb01e4   8118000   811d000 8101873  /bin/bash
f1bb0c70   811d000   8122000 100073
f26afae0   9fd9000   9ffa000 100073
... several lines omitted ...
```

Example 22.7. Displaying virtual memory information of the current context

Type `help vm` for more information on the command usage.

22.2.6. Displaying Open Files

To display information about open files, type the `files` command at the interactive prompt. You can use `files` *`pid`* to display files opened by the selected process.

```
crash> files
PID: 5591   TASK: f196d560  CPU: 2   COMMAND: "bash"
ROOT: /    CWD: /root
 FD    FILE      DENTRY     INODE    TYPE  PATH
  0  f734f640  eedc2c6c  eecd6048  CHR   /pts/0
  1  efade5c0  eee14090  f00431d4  REG   /proc/sysrq-trigger
  2  f734f640  eedc2c6c  eecd6048  CHR   /pts/0
 10  f734f640  eedc2c6c  eecd6048  CHR   /pts/0
255  f734f640  eedc2c6c  eecd6048  CHR   /pts/0
```

Example 22.8. Displaying information about open files of the current context

Type `help files` for more information on the command usage.

22.2.7. Exiting the Utility

To exit the interactive prompt and terminate **crash**, type `exit` or `q`.

```
crash> exit
~]#
```

Example 22.9. Exiting the crash utility

22.3. Additional Resources

22.3.1. Installed Documentation

`man kdump.conf`
: The manual page for the `/etc/kdump.conf` configuration file containing the full documentation of available options.

`man makedumpfile`
: The manual page for the `makedumpfile` core collector containing the full documentation on its usage.

`man kexec`
: The manual page for `kexec` containing the full documentation on its usage.

`man crash`
: The manual page for the **crash** utility containing the full documentation on its usage.

`/usr/share/doc/kexec-tools-`*`version`*`/kexec-kdump-howto.txt`
: An overview of the `kdump` and `kexec` installation and usage.

22.3.2. Useful Websites

http://people.redhat.com/anderson/
: The **crash** utility homepage.

Appendixes

Appendix A.
RPM

The *RPM Package Manager* (RPM) is an open packaging system , which runs on Fedora as well as other Linux and UNIX systems. Red Hat, Inc. and the Fedora Project encourage other vendors to use RPM for their own products. RPM is distributed under the terms of the *GPL* (*GNU General Public License*).

The RPM Package Manager only works with packages built to work with the *RPM format*. RPM is itself provided as a pre-installed rpm package. For the end user, RPM makes system updates easy. Installing, uninstalling and upgrading RPM packages can be accomplished with short commands. RPM maintains a database of installed packages and their files, so you can invoke powerful queries and verifications on your system.

The RPM package format has been improved for Fedora 15. RPM packages are now compressed using the XZ lossless data compression format, which has the benefit of greater compression and less CPU usage during decompression, and support multiple strong hash algorithms, such as SHA-256, for package signing and verification.

Use Yum Instead of RPM Whenever Possible

For most package management tasks, the **Yum** package manager offers equal and often greater capabilities and utility than RPM . **Yum** also performs and tracks complicated system dependency resolution, and will complain and force system integrity checks if you use RPM as well to install and remove packages. For these reasons, it is highly recommended that you use **Yum** instead of RPM whenever possible to perform package management tasks. Refer to Chapter 4, *Yum* (page 70).

If you prefer a graphical interface, you can use the **PackageKit** GUI application, which uses **Yum** as its back end, to manage your system's packages. Refer to Chapter 5, *PackageKit* (page 91) for details.

Install RPM packages with the correct architecture!

When installing a package, ensure it is compatible with your operating system and processor architecture. This can usually be determined by checking the package name. Many of the following examples show RPM packages compiled for the AMD64/Intel 64computer architectures; thus, the RPM file name ends in `x86_64.rpm`.

During upgrades, RPM handles configuration files carefully, so that you never lose your customizations—something that you cannot accomplish with regular `.tar.gz` files.

For the developer, RPM allows you to take software source code and package it into source and binary packages for end users. This process is quite simple and is driven from a single file and optional patches that you create. This clear delineation between *pristine* sources and your patches along with build instructions eases the maintenance of the package as new versions of the software are released.

Running rpm commands must be performed as root

Because RPM makes changes to your system, you must be logged in as root to install, remove, or upgrade an RPM package.

A.1. RPM Design Goals

To understand how to use RPM, it can be helpful to understand the design goals of RPM:

Upgradability

With RPM, you can upgrade individual components of your system without completely reinstalling. When you get a new release of an operating system based on RPM, such as Fedora, you do not need to reinstall a fresh copy of the operating system your machine (as you might need to with operating systems based on other packaging systems). RPM allows intelligent, fully-automated, in-place upgrades of your system. In addition, configuration files in packages are preserved across upgrades, so you do not lose your customizations. There are no special upgrade files needed to upgrade a package because the same RPM file is used to both install and upgrade the package on your system.

Powerful Querying

RPM is designed to provide powerful querying options. You can perform searches on your entire database for packages or even just certain files. You can also easily find out what package a file belongs to and from where the package came. The files an RPM package contains are in a compressed archive, with a custom binary header containing useful information about the package and its contents, allowing you to query individual packages quickly and easily.

System Verification

Another powerful RPM feature is the ability to verify packages. If you are worried that you deleted an important file for some package, you can verify the package. You are then notified of anomalies, if any—at which point you can reinstall the package, if necessary. Any configuration files that you modified are preserved during reinstallation.

Pristine Sources

A crucial design goal was to allow the use of *pristine* software sources, as distributed by the original authors of the software. With RPM, you have the pristine sources along with any patches that were used, plus complete build instructions. This is an important advantage for several reasons. For instance, if a new version of a program is released, you do not necessarily have to start from scratch to get it to compile. You can look at the patch to see what you *might* need to do. All the compiled-in defaults, and all of the changes that were made to get the software to build properly, are easily visible using this technique.

The goal of keeping sources pristine may seem important only for developers, but it results in higher quality software for end users, too.

A.2. Using RPM

RPM has five basic modes of operation (not counting package building): installing, uninstalling, upgrading, querying, and verifying. This section contains an overview of each mode. For complete details and options, try `rpm --help` or `man rpm`. You can also refer to Section A.5, *Additional Resources* (page 468) for more information on RPM.

A.2.1. Finding RPM Packages

Before using any RPM packages, you must know where to find them. An Internet search returns many RPM repositories, but if you are looking for Red Hat RPM packages, they can be found at the following locations:

- The Fedora installation media contain many installable RPMs.
- The initial RPM repositories provided with the YUM package manager . Refer to Chapter 4, *Yum* (page 70) for details on how to use the official Fedora package repositories.
- The active Fedora mirrors contains many installable RPMs: *http://mirrors.fedoraproject.org/publiclist/*.
- Unofficial, third-party repositories not affiliated with The Fedora Project also provide RPM packages.

Third-party repositories and package compatibility

When considering third-party repositories for use with your Fedora system, pay close attention to the repository's web site with regard to package compatibility before adding the repository as a package source. Alternate package repositories may offer different, incompatible versions of the same software, including packages already included in the Fedora repositories.

A.2.2. Installing and Upgrading

RPM packages typically have file names like `tree-1.5.3-2.fc15.x86_64.rpm`. The file name includes the package name (`tree`), version (`1.5.3`), release (`2`), operating system major version (`fc15`) and CPU architecture (`x86_64`).

You can use `rpm`'s `-U` option to:

- upgrade an existing but older package on the system to a newer version, or
- install the package even if an older version is not already installed.

That is, `rpm -U` *<rpm_file>* is able to perform the function of either *upgrading* or *installing* as is appropriate for the package.

Assuming the `tree-1.5.3-2.fc15.x86_64.rpm` package is in the current directory, log in as root and type the following command at a shell prompt to either upgrade or install the tree package as determined by `rpm`:

```
rpm -Uvh tree-1.5.3-2.fc15.x86_64.rpm
```

Use -Uvh for nicely-formatted RPM installs

The `-v` and `-h` options (which are combined with `-U`) cause **rpm** to print more verbose output and display a progress meter using hash signs.

If the upgrade/installation is successful, the following output is displayed:

```
Preparing...                ########################################### [100%]
   1:tree                   ########################################### [100%]
```

Always use the -i (install) option to install new kernel packages!

`rpm` provides two different options for installing packages: the aforementioned `-U` option (which historically stands for *upgrade*), and the `-i` option, historically standing for *install*. Because the `-U` option subsumes both install and upgrade functions, we recommend to use `rpm -Uvh` with all packages *except kernel packages*.

You should always use the `-i` option to simply *install* a new kernel package instead of upgrading it. This is because using the `-U` option to upgrade a kernel package removes the previous (older) kernel package, which could render the system unable to boot if there is a problem with the new kernel. Therefore, use the `rpm -i` *<kernel_package>* command to install a new kernel *without replacing any older kernel packages*. For more information on installing kernel packages, refer to Chapter 20, *Manually Upgrading the Kernel* (page 413).

The signature of a package is checked automatically when installing or upgrading a package. The signature confirms that the package was signed by an authorized party. For example, if the verification of the signature fails, an error message such as the following is displayed:

```
error: tree-1.5.2.2-4.fc15.x86_64.rpm: Header V3 RSA/SHA256 signature: BAD,
                                                               key ID d22e77f2
```

If it is a new, header-only, signature, an error message such as the following is displayed:

```
error: tree-1.5.2.2-4.fc15.x86_64.rpm: Header V3 RSA/SHA256 signature: BAD,
                                                               key ID d22e77f2
```

If you do not have the appropriate key installed to verify the signature, the message contains the word `NOKEY`:

```
warning: tree-1.5.2.2-4.fc15.x86_64.rpm: Header V3 RSA/SHA1 signature: NOKEY,
                                                               key ID 57bbccba
```

Refer to Section A.3, *Checking a Package's Signature* (page 465) for more information on checking a package's signature.

A.2.2.1. Package Already Installed

If a package of the same name and version is already installed , the following output is displayed:

```
Preparing...                ########################################### [100%]
        package tree-1.5.3-2.fc15.x86_64 is already installed
```

However, if you want to install the package anyway, you can use the `--replacepkgs` option, which tells RPM to ignore the error:

```
rpm -Uvh --replacepkgs tree-1.5.3-2.fc15.x86_64.rpm
```

This option is helpful if files installed from the RPM were deleted or if you want the original configuration files from the RPM to be installed.

A.2.2.2. Conflicting Files

If you attempt to install a package that contains a file which has already been installed by another package , the following is displayed:

```
Preparing... ##################################################
 file /usr/bin/foobar from install of foo-1.0-1.fc15.x86_64 conflicts
with file from package bar-3.1.1.fc15.x86_64
```

To make RPM ignore this error, use the `--replacefiles` option:

```
rpm -Uvh --replacefiles foo-1.0-1.fc15.x86_64.rpm
```

A.2.2.3. Unresolved Dependency

RPM packages may sometimes depend on other packages , which means that they require other packages to be installed to run properly. If you try to install a package which has an unresolved dependency, output similar to the following is displayed:

```
error: Failed dependencies:
    bar.so.3()(64bit) is needed by foo-1.0-1.fc15.x86_64
```

If you are installing a package from the Fedora installation media, such as from a CD-ROM or DVD, the dependencies may be available. Find the suggested package(s) on the Fedora installation media or on one of the active Fedora mirrors and add it to the command:

```
rpm -Uvh foo-1.0-1.fc15.x86_64.rpm    bar-3.1.1.fc15.x86_64.rpm
```

If installation of both packages is successful, output similar to the following is displayed:

```
Preparing...                ########################################### [100%]
   1:foo                    ########################################### [ 50%]
   2:bar                    ########################################### [100%]
```

You can try the `--whatprovides` option to determine which package contains the required file.

```
rpm -q --whatprovides "bar.so.3"
```

If the package that contains `bar.so.3` is in the RPM database, the name of the package is displayed:

```
bar-3.1.1.fc15.i586.rpm
```

Warning: Forcing Package Installation

Although we can *force* `rpm` to install a package that gives us a `Failed dependencies` error (using the `--nodeps` option), this is *not* recommended, and will usually result in the installed package failing to run. Installing or removing packages with `rpm --nodeps` can cause applications to misbehave and/or crash, and can cause serious package management problems or, possibly, system failure. For these reasons, it is best to heed such warnings; the package manager—whether **RPM, Yum** or **PackageKit**—shows us these warnings and suggests possible fixes because accounting for dependencies is critical. The **Yum** package manager can perform dependency resolution and fetch dependencies from online repositories, making it safer, easier and smarter than forcing `rpm` to carry out actions without regard to resolving dependencies.

A.2.3. Configuration File Changes

Because RPM performs intelligent upgrading of packages with configuration files , you may see one or the other of the following messages:

```
saving /etc/foo.conf as /etc/foo.conf.rpmsave
```

This message means that changes you made to the configuration file may not be *forward-compatible* with the new configuration file in the package, so RPM saved your original file and installed a new one. You should investigate the differences between the two configuration files and resolve them as soon as possible, to ensure that your system continues to function properly.

Alternatively, RPM may save the package's *new* configuration file as, for example, `foo.conf.rpmnew`, and leave the configuration file you modified untouched. You should still resolve any conflicts between your modified configuration file and the new one, usually by merging changes from the old one to the new one with a `diff` program.

If you attempt to upgrade to a package with an *older* version number (that is, if a higher version of the package is already installed), the output is similar to the following:

```
package foo-2.0-1.fc15.x86_64.rpm (which is newer than foo-1.0-1) is already installed
```

To force RPM to upgrade anyway, use the `--oldpackage` option:

```
rpm -Uvh --oldpackage foo-1.0-1.fc15.x86_64.rpm
```

A.2.4. Uninstalling

Uninstalling a package is just as simple as installing one. Type the following command at a shell prompt:

```
rpm -e foo
```

rpm -e and package name errors

Notice that we used the package *name* `foo`, not the name of the original package *file*, `foo-1.0-1.fc15.x86_64`. If you attempt to uninstall a package using the `rpm -e` command and the original full file name, you will receive a package name error.

You can encounter dependency errors when uninstalling a package if another installed package depends on the one you are trying to remove. For example:

```
rpm -e ghostscript
error: Failed dependencies:
      libgs.so.8()(64bit) is needed by (installed) libspectre-0.2.2-3.fc15.x86_64
      libgs.so.8()(64bit) is needed by (installed) foomatic-4.0.3-1.fc15.x86_64
      libijs-0.35.so()(64bit) is needed by (installed) gutenprint-5.2.4-5.fc15.x86_64
      ghostscript is needed by (installed) printer-filters-1.1-4.fc15.noarch
```

Similar to how we searched for a shared object library (i.e. a *<library_name>*.so.*<number>* file) in Section A.2.2.3, *Unresolved Dependency* (page 460) ,we can search for a 64-bit shared object library using this exact syntax (and making sure to quote the file name):

```
~]# rpm -q --whatprovides "libgs.so.8()(64bit)"
ghostscript-8.70-1.fc15.x86_64
```

Warning: Forcing Package Installation

Although we can *force* `rpm` to remove a package that gives us a `Failed dependencies` error (using the `--nodeps` option), this is *not* recommended, and may cause harm to other installed applications. Installing or removing packages with `rpm --nodeps` can cause applications to misbehave and/or crash, and can cause serious package management problems or, possibly, system failure. For these reasons, it is best to heed such warnings; the package manager—whether **RPM**, **Yum** or **PackageKit**—shows us these warnings and suggests possible fixes because accounting for dependencies is critical. The **Yum** package manager can perform dependency resolution and fetch dependencies from online repositories, making it safer, easier and smarter than forcing `rpm` to carry out actions without regard to resolving dependencies.

A.2.5. Freshening

Freshening is similar to upgrading, except that only existent packages are upgraded. Type the following command at a shell prompt:

```
rpm -Fvh foo-2.0-1.fc15.x86_64.rpm
```

RPM's freshen option checks the versions of the packages specified on the command line against the versions of packages that have already been installed on your system. When a newer version of an already-installed package is processed by RPM's freshen option, it is upgraded to the newer version. However, RPM's freshen option does not install a package if no previously-installed package of the same name exists. This differs from RPM's upgrade option, as an upgrade *does* install packages whether or not an older version of the package was already installed.

Freshening works for single packages or package groups. If you have just downloaded a large number of different packages, and you only want to upgrade those packages that are already installed on your system, freshening does the job. Thus, you do not have to delete any unwanted packages from the group that you downloaded before using RPM.

In this case, issue the following with the `*.rpm` glob:

```
rpm -Fvh *.rpm
```

RPM then automatically upgrades only those packages that are already installed.

A.2.6. Querying

The RPM database stores information about all RPM packages installed in your system. It is stored in the directory `/var/lib/rpm/`, and is used to query what packages are installed, what versions each package is, and to calculate any changes to any files in the package since installation, among other use cases.

To query this database, use the `-q` option. The `rpm -q package name` command displays the package name, version, and release number of the installed package *<package_name>*. For example, using `rpm -q tree` to query installed package `tree` might generate the following output:

```
tree-1.5.2.2-4.fc15.x86_64
```

You can also use the following *Package Selection Options* (which is a subheading in the RPM man page: see `man rpm` for details) to further refine or qualify your query:

- `-a` — queries all currently installed packages.
- `-f <file_name>` — queries the RPM database for which package owns `<file_name>`. Specify the absolute path of the file (for example, `rpm -qf /bin/ls` instead of `rpm -qf ls`).
- `-p <package_file>` — queries the uninstalled package `<package_file>`.

There are a number of ways to specify what information to display about queried packages. The following options are used to select the type of information for which you are searching. These are called the *Package Query Options*.

- `-i` displays package information including name, description, release, size, build date, install date, vendor, and other miscellaneous information.
- `-l` displays the list of files that the package contains.
- `-s` displays the state of all the files in the package.
- `-d` displays a list of files marked as documentation (man pages, info pages, READMEs, etc.) in the package.
- `-c` displays a list of files marked as configuration files. These are the files you edit after installation to adapt and customize the package to your system (for example, `sendmail.cf`, `passwd`, `inittab`, etc.).

For options that display lists of files, add `-v` to the command to display the lists in a familiar `ls -l` format.

A.2.7. Verifying

Verifying a package compares information about files installed from a package with the same information from the original package. Among other things, verifying compares the file size, MD5 sum, permissions, type, owner, and group of each file.

The command `rpm -V` verifies a package. You can use any of the *Verify Options* listed for querying to specify the packages you wish to verify. A simple use of verifying is `rpm -V tree`, which verifies that all the files in the `tree` package are as they were when they were originally installed. For example:

- To verify a package containing a particular file:

  ```
  rpm -Vf /usr/bin/tree
  ```

  In this example, `/usr/bin/tree` is the absolute path to the file used to query a package.
- To verify ALL installed packages throughout the system (which will take some time):

  ```
  rpm -Va
  ```

- To verify an installed package against an RPM package file:

  ```
  rpm -Vp tree-1.5.2.2-4.fc15.x86_64.rpm
  ```

  This command can be useful if you suspect that your RPM database is corrupt.

If everything verified properly, there is no output. If there are any discrepancies, they are displayed. The format of the output is a string of eight characters (a "`c`" denotes a configuration file) and then the file name. Each of the eight characters denotes the result of a comparison of one attribute of the file to the value of that attribute recorded in the RPM database. A single period (`.`) means the test passed. The following characters denote specific discrepancies:

- `5` — MD5 checksum
- `S` — file size
- `L` — symbolic link
- `T` — file modification time
- `D` — device
- `U` — user
- `G` — group
- `M` — mode (includes permissions and file type)
- `?` — unreadable file (file permission errors, for example)

If you see any output, use your best judgment to determine if you should remove the package, reinstall it, or fix the problem in another way.

A.3. Checking a Package's Signature

If you wish to verify that a package has not been corrupted or tampered with, you can examine just the md5sum by entering this command at the shell prompt: (where *<rpm_file>* is the file name of the RPM package):

```
rpm -K --nosignature <rpm_file>
```

The output `<rpm_file>: rsa sha1 (md5) pgp md5 OK` (specifically the *OK* part of it) indicates that the file was not corrupted during download. To see a more verbose message, replace `-K` with `-Kvv` in the command.

On the other hand, how trustworthy is the developer who created the package? If the package is *signed* with the developer's GnuPG *key*, you know that the developer really is who they say they are.

An RPM package can be signed using *Gnu Privacy Guard* (or GnuPG), to help you make certain your downloaded package is trustworthy.

GnuPG is a tool for secure communication; it is a complete and free replacement for the encryption technology of PGP, an electronic privacy program. With GnuPG, you can authenticate the validity of documents and encrypt/decrypt data to and from other recipients. GnuPG is capable of decrypting and verifying PGP 5.*x* files as well.

During installation, GnuPG is installed by default, which enables you to immediately start using it to verify any packages that you download from the Fedora Project. Before doing so, you first need to import the correct Fedora key.

A.3.1. Importing Keys

Fedora GnuPG keys are located in the `/etc/pki/rpm-gpg/` directory. To verify a Fedora Project package, first import the correct key based on your processor architecture:

```
rpm --import /etc/pki/rpm-gpg/RPM-GPG-KEY-fedora-x86_64
```

To display a list of all keys installed for RPM verification, execute the command:

```
rpm -qa gpg-pubkey*
```

For the Fedora Project key, the output states:

```
gpg-pubkey-57bbccba-4a6f97af
```

To display details about a specific key, use `rpm -qi` followed by the output from the previous command:

```
rpm -qi gpg-pubkey-57bbccba-4a6f97af
```

A.3.2. Verifying Signature of Packages

To check the GnuPG signature of an RPM file after importing the builder's GnuPG key, use the following command (replace *<rpm_file>* with the file name of the RPM package):

```
rpm -K <rpm_file>
```

If all goes well, the following message is displayed: `rsa sha1 (md5) pgp md5 OK`. This means that the signature of the package has been verified, that it is not corrupt, and is therefore safe to install and use.

For more information, including a list of currently-used Fedora Project keys and their fingerprints, refer to *http://fedoraproject.org/en/keys*.

A.4. Practical and Common Examples of RPM Usage

RPM is a useful tool for both managing your system and diagnosing and fixing problems. The best way to make sense of all its options is to look at some examples.

- Perhaps you have deleted some files by accident, but you are not sure what you deleted. To verify your entire system and see what might be missing, you could try the following command:

  ```
  rpm -Va
  ```

  If some files are missing or appear to have been corrupted, you should probably either re-install the package or uninstall and then re-install the package.

- At some point, you might see a file that you do not recognize. To find out which package owns it, enter:

  ```
  rpm -qf /usr/bin/ghostscript
  ```

  The output would look like the following:

  ```
  ghostscript-8.70-1.fc15.x86_64
  ```

- We can combine the above two examples in the following scenario. Say you are having problems with `/usr/bin/paste`. You would like to verify the package that owns that program, but you do not know which package owns `paste`. Enter the following command,

  ```
  rpm -Vf /usr/bin/paste
  ```

  and the appropriate package is verified.

- Do you want to find out more information about a particular program? You can try the following command to locate the documentation which came with the package that owns that program:

  ```
  rpm -qdf /usr/bin/free
  ```

  The output would be similar to the following:

  ```
  /usr/share/doc/procps-3.2.8/BUGS
  /usr/share/doc/procps-3.2.8/FAQ
  /usr/share/doc/procps-3.2.8/NEWS
  /usr/share/doc/procps-3.2.8/TODO
  /usr/share/man/man1/free.1.gz
  /usr/share/man/man1/pgrep.1.gz
  /usr/share/man/man1/pkill.1.gz
  /usr/share/man/man1/pmap.1.gz
  /usr/share/man/man1/ps.1.gz
  /usr/share/man/man1/pwdx.1.gz
  /usr/share/man/man1/skill.1.gz
  /usr/share/man/man1/slabtop.1.gz
  /usr/share/man/man1/snice.1.gz
  /usr/share/man/man1/tload.1.gz
  /usr/share/man/man1/top.1.gz
  /usr/share/man/man1/uptime.1.gz
  ```

```
/usr/share/man/man1/w.1.gz
/usr/share/man/man1/watch.1.gz
/usr/share/man/man5/sysctl.conf.5.gz
/usr/share/man/man8/sysctl.8.gz
/usr/share/man/man8/vmstat.8.gz
```

- You may find a new RPM, but you do not know what it does. To find information about it, use the following command:

  ```
  rpm -qip crontabs-1.10-31.fc15.noarch.rpm
  ```

  The output would be similar to the following:

  ```
  Name        : crontabs                    Relocations: (not relocatable)
  Size        : 2486                            License: Public Domain and GPLv2
  Signature   : RSA/SHA1, Tue 11 Aug 2009 01:11:19 PM CEST, Key ID 9d1cc34857bbccba
  Packager    : Fedora Project
  Summary     : Root crontab files used to schedule the execution of programs
  Description :
  The crontabs package contains root crontab files and directories.
  You will need to install cron daemon to run the jobs from the crontabs.
  The cron daemon such as cronie or fcron checks the crontab files to
  see when particular commands are scheduled to be executed.  If commands
  are scheduled, it executes them.
  Crontabs handles a basic system function, so it should be installed on
  your system.
  ```

- Perhaps you now want to see what files the `crontabs` RPM package installs. You would enter the following:

  ```
  rpm -qlp crontabs-1.10-31.fc15.noarch.rpm
  ```

  The output is similar to the following:

  ```
  /etc/cron.daily
  /etc/cron.hourly
  /etc/cron.monthly
  /etc/cron.weekly
  /etc/crontab
  /usr/bin/run-parts
  /usr/share/man/man4/crontabs.4.gz
  ```

These are just a few examples. As you use RPM, you may find more uses for it.

A.5. Additional Resources

RPM is an extremely complex utility with many options and methods for querying, installing, upgrading, and removing packages. Refer to the following resources to learn more about RPM.

A.5.1. Installed Documentation

- `rpm --help` — This command displays a quick reference of RPM parameters.
- `man rpm` — The RPM man page gives more detail about RPM parameters than the `rpm --help` command.

A.5.2. Useful Websites

- The RPM website — *http://www.rpm.org/*
- The RPM mailing list can be subscribed to, and its archives read from, here — *https://lists.rpm.org/mailman/listinfo/rpm-list*

A.5.3. Related Books

Maximum RPM — http://www.rpm.org/max-rpm/
: The *Maximum RPM* book, which you can read online, covers everything from general RPM usage to building your own RPMs to programming with rpmlib.

Appendix B.

The sysconfig Directory

This appendix outlines some of the files and directories found in the `/etc/sysconfig/` directory, their function, and their contents. The information in this appendix is not intended to be complete, as many of these files have a variety of options that are only used in very specific or rare circumstances.

The content of the /etc/sysconfig/ directory

The actual content of your `/etc/sysconfig/` directory depends on the programs you have installed on your machine. To find the name of the package the configuration file belongs to, type the following at a shell prompt:

```
~]$ yum provides /etc/sysconfig/filename
```

Refer to Section 4.2.4, *Installing Packages* (page 78) for more information on how to install new packages in Fedora.

B.1. Files in the /etc/sysconfig/ Directory

The following sections offer descriptions of files normally found in the `/etc/sysconfig/` directory.

B.1.1. /etc/sysconfig/arpwatch

The `/etc/sysconfig/arpwatch` file is used to pass arguments to the `arpwatch` daemon at boot time. By default, it contains the following option:

`OPTIONS=`*`value`*

Additional options to be passed to the `arpwatch` daemon. For example:

```
OPTIONS="-u arpwatch -e root -s 'root (Arpwatch)'"
```

B.1.2. /etc/sysconfig/authconfig

The `/etc/sysconfig/authconfig` file sets the authorization to be used on the host. By default, it contains the following options:

`USEMKHOMEDIR=`*`boolean`*

A boolean to enable (`yes`) or disable (`no`) creating a home directory for a user on the first login. For example:

```
USEMKHOMEDIR=no
```

`USEPAMACCESS=`*`boolean`*

A boolean to enable (`yes`) or disable (`no`) the PAM authentication. For example:

```
USEPAMACCESS=no
```

`USESSSDAUTH=`*`boolean`*

A boolean to enable (`yes`) or disable (`no`) the SSSD authentication. For example:

```
USESSSDAUTH=no
```

`USESHADOW=`*`boolean`*

A boolean to enable (`yes`) or disable (`no`) shadow passwords. For example:

```
USESHADOW=yes
```

`USEWINBIND=`*`boolean`*

A boolean to enable (`yes`) or disable (`no`) using Winbind for user account configuration. For example:

```
USEWINBIND=no
```

`USEDB=`*`boolean`*

A boolean to enable (`yes`) or disable (`no`) the FAS authentication. For example:

```
USEDB=no
```

`USEFPRINTD=`*`boolean`*

A boolean to enable (`yes`) or disable (`no`) the fingerprint authentication. For example:

```
USEFPRINTD=yes
```

`FORCESMARTCARD=`*`boolean`*

A boolean to enable (`yes`) or disable (`no`) enforcing the smart card authentication. For example:

```
FORCESMARTCARD=no
```

`PASSWDALGORITHM=`*`value`*

The password algorithm. The *`value`* can be `bigcrypt`, `descrypt`, `md5`, `sha256`, or `sha512`. For example:

```
PASSWDALGORITHM=sha512
```

`USELDAPAUTH=`*`boolean`*

A boolean to enable (`yes`) or disable (`no`) the LDAP authentication. For example:

```
USELDAPAUTH=no
```

`USELOCAUTHORIZE=`*`boolean`*

A boolean to enable (`yes`) or disable (`no`) the local authorization for local users. For example:

```
USELOCAUTHORIZE=yes
```

`USECRACKLIB=`*`boolean`*

A boolean to enable (`yes`) or disable (`no`) using the CrackLib. For example:

```
USECRACKLIB=yes
```

`USEWINBINDAUTH=`*`boolean`*

A boolean to enable (`yes`) or disable (`no`) the Winbind authentication. For example:

```
USEWINBINDAUTH=no
```

`USESMARTCARD=`*`boolean`*

A boolean to enable (`yes`) or disable (`no`) the smart card authentication. For example:

```
USESMARTCARD=no
```

`USELDAP=`*`boolean`*

A boolean to enable (`yes`) or disable (`no`) using LDAP for user account configuration. For example:

```
USELDAP=no
```

`USENIS=`*`boolean`*

A boolean to enable (`yes`) or disable (`no`) using NIS for user account configuration. For example:

```
USENIS=no
```

`USEKERBEROS=`*`boolean`*

A boolean to enable (`yes`) or disable (`no`) the Kerberos authentication. For example:

```
USEKERBEROS=no
```

`USESYSNETAUTH=`*`boolean`*

A boolean to enable (`yes`) or disable (`no`) authenticating system accounts with network services. For example:

```
USESYSNETAUTH=no
```

`USESMBAUTH=`*`boolean`*

A boolean to enable (`yes`) or disable (`no`) the SMB authentication. For example:

```
USESMBAUTH=no
```

`USESSSD=`*`boolean`*

A boolean to enable (`yes`) or disable (`no`) using SSSD for obtaining user information. For example:

```
USESSSD=no
```

`USEHESIOD=`*`boolean`*

A boolean to enable (`yes`) or disable (`no`) using the Hesoid name service. For example:

```
USEHESIOD=no
```

Refer to Chapter 8, *Configuring Authentication* (page 125) for more information on this topic.

B.1.3. /etc/sysconfig/autofs

The `/etc/sysconfig/autofs` file defines custom options for the automatic mounting of devices. This file controls the operation of the automount daemons, which automatically mount file systems when you use them and unmount them after a period of inactivity. File systems can include network file systems, CD-ROM drives, diskettes, and other media.

By default, it contains the following options:

`MASTER_MAP_NAME=`*`value`*

The default name for the master map. For example:

```
MASTER_MAP_NAME="auto.master"
```

`TIMEOUT=`*`value`*

The default mount timeout. For example:

```
TIMEOUT=300
```

`NEGATIVE_TIMEOUT=`*`value`*

The default negative timeout for unsuccessful mount attempts. For example:

```
NEGATIVE_TIMEOUT=60
```

`MOUNT_WAIT=`*`value`*

The time to wait for a response from `mount`. For example:

```
MOUNT_WAIT=-1
```

`UMOUNT_WAIT=`*`value`*

The time to wait for a response from `umount`. For example:

```
UMOUNT_WAIT=12
```

`BROWSE_MODE=`*`boolean`*

A boolean to enable (`yes`) or disable (`no`) browsing the maps. For example:

```
BROWSE_MODE="no"
```

`MOUNT_NFS_DEFAULT_PROTOCOL=`*`value`*

The default protocol to be used by `mount.nfs`. For example:

```
MOUNT_NFS_DEFAULT_PROTOCOL=4
```

`APPEND_OPTIONS=`*`boolean`*

A boolean to enable (`yes`) or disable (`no`) appending the global options instead of replacing them. For example:

```
APPEND_OPTIONS="yes"
```

`LOGGING=`*`value`*

The default logging level. The *`value`* has to be either `none`, `verbose`, or `debug`. For example:

```
LOGGING="none"
```

`LDAP_URI=`*`value`*

A space-separated list of server URIs in the form of *`protocol`*`://`*`server`* . For example:

```
LDAP_URI="ldaps://ldap.example.com/"
```

`LDAP_TIMEOUT=`*`value`*

The synchronous API calls timeout. For example:

```
LDAP_TIMEOUT=-1
```

`LDAP_NETWORK_TIMEOUT=`*`value`*

The network response timeout. For example:

```
LDAP_NETWORK_TIMEOUT=8
```

`SEARCH_BASE=`*`value`*

The base Distinguished Name (DN) for the map search. For example:

```
SEARCH_BASE=""
```

`AUTH_CONF_FILE=`*`value`*

The default location of the SASL authentication configuration file. For example:

```
AUTH_CONF_FILE="/etc/autofs_ldap_auth.conf"
```

`MAP_HASH_TABLE_SIZE=`*`value`*

The hash table size for the map cache. For example:

```
MAP_HASH_TABLE_SIZE=1024
```

`USE_MISC_DEVICE=`*`boolean`*

A boolean to enable (`yes`) or disable (`no`) using the autofs miscellaneous device. For example:

```
USE_MISC_DEVICE="yes"
```

`OPTIONS=`*`value`*

Additional options to be passed to the LDAP daemon. For example:

```
OPTIONS=""
```

B.1.4. /etc/sysconfig/clock

The `/etc/sysconfig/clock` file controls the interpretation of values read from the system hardware clock. It is used by the **Date and Time** configuration tool, and should not be edited by hand. By default, it contains the following option:

`ZONE=`*`value`*

The time zone file under `/usr/share/zoneinfo` that `/etc/localtime` is a copy of. For example:

```
ZONE="Europe/Prague"
```

Refer to Section 2.1, *Date and Time Configuration Tool* (page 39) for more information on the **Date and Time** configuration tool and its usage.

B.1.5. /etc/sysconfig/dhcpd

The `/etc/sysconfig/dhcpd` file is used to pass arguments to the `dhcpd` daemon at boot time. By default, it contains the following options:

`DHCPDARGS=`*`value`*

Additional options to be passed to the `dhcpd` daemon. For example:

```
DHCPDARGS=
```

Refer to Chapter 10, *DHCP Servers* (page 186) for more information on DHCP and its usage.

B.1.6. /etc/sysconfig/firstboot

The `/etc/sysconfig/firstboot` file defines whether to run the `firstboot` utility. By default, it contains the following option:

`RUN_FIRSTBOOT=`*`boolean`*

A boolean to enable (`YES`) or disable (`NO`) running the `firstboot` program. For example:

```
RUN_FIRSTBOOT=NO
```

The first time the system boots, the `init` program calls the `/etc/rc.d/init.d/firstboot` script, which looks for the `/etc/sysconfig/firstboot` file. If this file does not contain the `RUN_FIRSTBOOT=NO` option, the `firstboot` program is run, guiding a user through the initial configuration of the system.

You can run the firstboot program again

To start the `firstboot` program the next time the system boots, change the value of `RUN_FIRSTBOOT` option to `YES`, and type the following at a shell prompt as `root`:

```
~]# systemctl enable firstboot.service
```

B.1.7. /etc/sysconfig/i18n

The `/etc/sysconfig/i18n` configuration file defines the default language, any supported languages, and the default system font. By default, it contains the following options:

`LANG=`*`value`*

The default language. For example:

```
LANG="en_US.UTF-8"
```

`SUPPORTED=`*`value`*

A colon-separated list of supported languages. For example:

```
SUPPORTED="en_US.UTF-8:en_US:en"
```

`SYSFONT=`*`value`*

The default system font. For example:

```
SYSFONT="latarcyrheb-sun16"
```

B.1.8. /etc/sysconfig/init

The `/etc/sysconfig/init` file controls how the system appears and functions during the boot process. By default, it contains the following options:

`BOOTUP=`*`value`*

The bootup style. The value has to be either `color` (the standard color boot display), `verbose` (an old style display which provides more information), or anything else for the new style display, but without ANSI formatting. For example:

```
BOOTUP=color
```

`RES_COL=`*`value`*

The number of the column in which the status labels start. For example:

```
RES_COL=60
```

`MOVE_TO_COL=`*`value`*

The terminal sequence to move the cursor to the column specified in `RES_COL` (see above). For example:

```
MOVE_TO_COL="echo -en \\033[${RES_COL}G"
```

`SETCOLOR_SUCCESS=`*`value`*

The terminal sequence to set the success color. For example:

```
SETCOLOR_SUCCESS="echo -en \\033[0;32m"
```

`SETCOLOR_FAILURE=`*`value`*

The terminal sequence to set the failure color. For example:

```
SETCOLOR_FAILURE="echo -en \\033[0;31m"
```

`SETCOLOR_WARNING=`*`value`*

The terminal sequence to set the warning color. For example:

```
SETCOLOR_WARNING="echo -en \\033[0;33m"
```

`SETCOLOR_NORMAL=`*`value`*

The terminal sequence to set the default color. For example:

```
SETCOLOR_NORMAL="echo -en \\033[0;39m"
```

`LOGLEVEL=`*`value`*

The initial console logging level. The *`value`* has to be in the range from `1` (kernel panics only) to `8` (everything, including the debugging information). For example:

```
LOGLEVEL=3
```

`PROMPT=`*`boolean`*

A boolean to enable (`yes`) or disable (`no`) the hotkey interactive startup. For example:

```
PROMPT=yes
```

`AUTOSWAP=`*`boolean`*

A boolean to enable (`yes`) or disable (`no`) probing for devices with swap signatures. For example:

```
AUTOSWAP=no
```

`ACTIVE_CONSOLES=`*`value`*

The list of active consoles. For example:

```
ACTIVE_CONSOLES=/dev/tty[1-6]
```

`SINGLE=`*`value`*

The single-user mode type. The *`value`* has to be either `/sbin/sulogin` (a user will be prompted for a password to log in), or `/sbin/sushell` (the user will be logged in directly). For example:

```
SINGLE=/sbin/sushell
```

B.1.9. /etc/sysconfig/ip6tables-config

The `/etc/sysconfig/ip6tables-config` file stores information used by the kernel to set up IPv6 packet filtering at boot time or whenever the `ip6tables` service is started. Note that you should not modify it unless you are familiar with `ip6tables` rules. By default, it contains the following options:

`IP6TABLES_MODULES=`*`value`*

A space-separated list of helpers to be loaded after the firewall rules are applied. For example:

```
IP6TABLES_MODULES="ip_nat_ftp ip_nat_irc"
```

`IP6TABLES_MODULES_UNLOAD=`*`boolean`*

A boolean to enable (`yes`) or disable (`no`) module unloading when the firewall is stopped or restarted. For example:

```
IP6TABLES_MODULES_UNLOAD="yes"
```

`IP6TABLES_SAVE_ON_STOP=`*`boolean`*

A boolean to enable (`yes`) or disable (`no`) saving the current firewall rules when the firewall is stopped. For example:

```
IP6TABLES_SAVE_ON_STOP="no"
```

`IP6TABLES_SAVE_ON_RESTART=`*`boolean`*

A boolean to enable (`yes`) or disable (`no`) saving the current firewall rules when the firewall is restarted. For example:

```
IP6TABLES_SAVE_ON_RESTART="no"
```

`IP6TABLES_SAVE_COUNTER=`*`boolean`*

A boolean to enable (`yes`) or disable (`no`) saving the rule and chain counters. For example:

```
IP6TABLES_SAVE_COUNTER="no"
```

`IP6TABLES_STATUS_NUMERIC=`*`boolean`*

A boolean to enable (`yes`) or disable (`no`) printing IP addresses and port numbers in a numeric format in the status output. For example:

```
IP6TABLES_STATUS_NUMERIC="yes"
```

`IP6TABLES_STATUS_VERBOSE=`*`boolean`*

A boolean to enable (`yes`) or disable (`no`) printing information about the number of packets and bytes in the status output. For example:

```
IP6TABLES_STATUS_VERBOSE="no"
```

`IP6TABLES_STATUS_LINENUMBERS=`*`boolean`*

A boolean to enable (`yes`) or disable (`no`) printing line numbers in the status output. For example:

```
IP6TABLES_STATUS_LINENUMBERS="yes"
```

Use the ip6tables command to create the rules

You can create the rules manually using the `ip6tables` command. Once created, type the following at a shell prompt:

```
~]# service ip6tables save
```

This will add the rules to `/etc/sysconfig/ip6tables`. Once this file exists, any firewall rules saved in it persist through a system reboot or a service restart.

B.1.10. /etc/sysconfig/keyboard

The `/etc/sysconfig/keyboard` file controls the behavior of the keyboard. By default, it contains the following options:

`KEYTABLE=`*`value`*

The name of a keytable file. The files that can be used as keytables start in the `/lib/kbd/keymaps/i386/` directory, and branch into different keyboard layouts from there, all labeled *`value`*`.kmap.gz`. The first file name that matches the `KEYTABLE` setting is used. For example:

```
KEYTABLE="us"
```

`MODEL=`*`value`*

The keyboard model. For example:

```
MODEL="pc105+inet"
```

`LAYOUT=`*`value`*

The keyboard layout. For example:

```
LAYOUT="us"
```

`KEYBOARDTYPE=`*`value`*

The keyboard type. Allowed values are `pc` (a PS/2 keyboard), or `sun` (a Sun keyboard). For example:

```
KEYBOARDTYPE="pc"
```

B.1.11. /etc/sysconfig/ldap

The `/etc/sysconfig/ldap` file holds the basic configuration for the LDAP server. By default, it contains the following options:

`SLAPD_OPTIONS=`*`value`*

Additional options to be passed to the `slapd` daemon. For example:

```
SLAPD_OPTIONS="-4"
```

`SLURPD_OPTIONS=`*`value`*

Additional options to be passed to the `slurpd` daemon. For example:

```
SLURPD_OPTIONS=""
```

`SLAPD_LDAP=`*`boolean`*

A boolean to enable (`yes`) or disable (`no`) using the LDAP over TCP (that is, `ldap:///`). For example:

```
SLAPD_LDAP="yes"
```

`SLAPD_LDAPI=`*`boolean`*

A boolean to enable (`yes`) or disable (`no`) using the LDAP over IPC (that is, `ldapi:///`). For example:

```
SLAPD_LDAPI="no"
```

`SLAPD_LDAPS=`*`boolean`*

A boolean to enable (`yes`) or disable (`no`) using the LDAP over TLS (that is, `ldaps:///`). For example:

```
SLAPD_LDAPS="no"
```

`SLAPD_URLS=`*`value`*

A space-separated list of URLs. For example:

```
SLAPD_URLS="ldapi:///var/lib/ldap_root/ldapi ldapi:/// ldaps:///"
```

`SLAPD_SHUTDOWN_TIMEOUT=`*`value`*

The time to wait for `slapd` to shut down. For example:

```
SLAPD_SHUTDOWN_TIMEOUT=3
```

`SLAPD_ULIMIT_SETTINGS=`*`value`*

The parameters to be passed to `ulimit` before the `slapd` daemon is started. For example:

```
SLAPD_ULIMIT_SETTINGS=""
```

Refer to Section 14.1, *OpenLDAP* (page 302) for more information on LDAP and its configuration.

B.1.12. /etc/sysconfig/named

The `/etc/sysconfig/named` file is used to pass arguments to the `named` daemon at boot time. By default, it contains the following options:

`ROOTDIR=`*`value`*

The chroot environment under which the `named` daemon runs. The *`value`* has to be a full directory path. For example:

```
ROOTDIR="/var/named/chroot"
```

Note that the chroot environment has to be configured first (type `info chroot` at a shell prompt for more information).

`OPTIONS=`*`value`*

Additional options to be passed to `named`. For example:

```
OPTIONS="-6"
```

Note that you should not use the `-t` option. Instead, use `ROOTDIR` as described above.

`KEYTAB_FILE=`*`value`*

The keytab file name. For example:

```
KEYTAB_FILE="/etc/named.keytab"
```

Refer to Section 11.2, *BIND* (page 199) for more information on the BIND DNS server and its configuration.

B.1.13. /etc/sysconfig/network

The `/etc/sysconfig/network` file is used to specify information about the desired network configuration. By default, it contains the following options:

`NETWORKING=`*`boolean`*

A boolean to enable (`yes`) or disable (`no`) the networking. For example:

```
NETWORKING=yes
```

`HOSTNAME=`*`value`*

The hostname of the machine. For example:

```
HOSTNAME=penguin.example.com
```

`GATEWAY=`*`value`*

The IP address of the network's gateway. For example:

```
GATEWAY=192.168.1.0
```

Avoid using custom init scripts

Do not use custom init scripts to configure network settings. When performing a post-boot network service restart, custom init scripts configuring network settings that are run outside of the network init script lead to unpredictable results.

B.1.14. /etc/sysconfig/ntpd

The `/etc/sysconfig/ntpd` file is used to pass arguments to the `ntpd` daemon at boot time. By default, it contains the following option:

`OPTIONS=`*`value`*

Additional options to be passed to `ntpd`. For example:

```
OPTIONS="-u ntp:ntp -p /var/run/ntpd.pid -g"
```

Refer to Section 2.2.2, *Configuring the Network Time Protocol* (page 41) for more information on how to configure the `ntpd` daemon.

B.1.15. /etc/sysconfig/quagga

The `/etc/sysconfig/quagga` file holds the basic configuration for Quagga daemons. By default, it contains the following options:

`QCONFDIR=`*`value`*

The directory with the configuration files for Quagga daemons. For example:

```
QCONFDIR="/etc/quagga"
```

`BGPD_OPTS=`*`value`*

Additional options to be passed to the `bgpd` daemon. For example:

```
BGPD_OPTS="-A 127.0.0.1 -f ${QCONFDIR}/bgpd.conf"
```

`OSPF6D_OPTS=`*`value`*

Additional options to be passed to the `ospf6d` daemon. For example:

```
OSPF6D_OPTS="-A ::1 -f ${QCONFDIR}/ospf6d.conf"
```

`OSPFD_OPTS=`*`value`*

Additional options to be passed to the `ospfd` daemon. For example:

```
OSPFD_OPTS="-A 127.0.0.1 -f ${QCONFDIR}/ospfd.conf"
```

`RIPD_OPTS=`*`value`*

Additional options to be passed to the `ripd` daemon. For example:

```
RIPD_OPTS="-A 127.0.0.1 -f ${QCONFDIR}/ripd.conf"
```

`RIPNGD_OPTS=`*`value`*

Additional options to be passed to the `ripngd` daemon. For example:

```
RIPNGD_OPTS="-A ::1 -f ${QCONFDIR}/ripngd.conf"
```

`ZEBRA_OPTS=`*`value`*

Additional options to be passed to the `zebra` daemon. For example:

```
ZEBRA_OPTS="-A 127.0.0.1 -f ${QCONFDIR}/zebra.conf"
```

`ISISD_OPTS=`*`value`*

Additional options to be passed to the `isisd` daemon. For example:

```
ISISD_OPTS="-A ::1 -f ${QCONFDIR}/isisd.conf"
```

`WATCH_OPTS=`*`value`*

Additional options to be passed to the `watchquagga` daemon. For example:

```
WATCH_OPTS="-Az -b_ -r/sbin/service_%s_restart -s/sbin/service_%s_start -
k/sbin/service_%s_stop"
```

`WATCH_DAEMONS=`*`value`*

A space separated list of monitored daemons. For example:

```
WATCH_DAEMONS="zebra bgpd ospfd ospf6d ripd ripngd"
```

B.1.16. /etc/sysconfig/radvd

The `/etc/sysconfig/radvd` file is used to pass arguments to the `radvd` daemon at boot time. By default, it contains the following option:

`OPTIONS=value`

Additional options to be passed to the `radvd` daemon. For example:

```
OPTIONS="-u radvd"
```

B.1.17. /etc/sysconfig/samba

The `/etc/sysconfig/samba` file is used to pass arguments to the Samba daemons at boot time. By default, it contains the following options:

`SMBDOPTIONS=value`

Additional options to be passed to `smbd`. For example:

```
SMBDOPTIONS="-D"
```

`NMBDOPTIONS=value`

Additional options to be passed to `nmbd`. For example:

```
NMBDOPTIONS="-D"
```

`WINBINDOPTIONS=value`

Additional options to be passed to `winbindd`. For example:

```
WINBINDOPTIONS=""
```

Refer to Section 15.1, *Samba* (page 317) for more information on Samba and its configuration.

B.1.18. /etc/sysconfig/selinux

The `/etc/sysconfig/selinux` file contains the basic configuration options for SELinux. It is a symbolic link to `/etc/selinux/config`, and by default, it contains the following options:

`SELINUX=value`

The security policy. The `value` can be either `enforcing` (the security policy is always enforced), `permissive` (instead of enforcing the policy, appropriate warnings are displayed), or `disabled` (no policy is used). For example:

```
SELINUX=enforcing
```

`SELINUXTYPE=value`

The protection type. The `value` can be either `targeted` (the targeted processes are protected), or `mls` (the Multi Level Security protection). For example:

```
SELINUXTYPE=targeted
```

B.1.19. /etc/sysconfig/sendmail

The `/etc/sysconfig/sendmail` is used to set the default values for the **Sendmail** application. By default, it contains the following values:

`DAEMON=`*`boolean`*

A boolean to enable (`yes`) or disable (`no`) running `sendmail` as a daemon. For example:

```
DAEMON=yes
```

`QUEUE=`*`value`*

The interval at which the messages are to be processed. For example:

```
QUEUE=1h
```

Refer to Section 13.3.2, *Sendmail* (page 280) for more information on Sendmail and its configuration.

B.1.20. /etc/sysconfig/spamassassin

The `/etc/sysconfig/spamassassin` file is used to pass arguments to the `spamd` daemon (a daemonized version of **Spamassassin**) at boot time. By default, it contains the following option:

`SPAMDOPTIONS=`*`value`*

Additional options to be passed to the `spamd` daemon. For example:

```
SPAMDOPTIONS="-d -c -m5 -H"
```

Refer to Section 13.4.2.6, *Spam Filters* (page 296) for more information on Spamassassin and its configuration.

B.1.21. /etc/sysconfig/squid

The `/etc/sysconfig/squid` file is used to pass arguments to the `squid` daemon at boot time. By default, it contains the following options:

`SQUID_OPTS=`*`value`*

Additional options to be passed to the `squid` daemon. For example:

```
SQUID_OPTS=""
```

`SQUID_SHUTDOWN_TIMEOUT=`*`value`*

The time to wait for `squid` daemon to shut down. For example:

```
SQUID_SHUTDOWN_TIMEOUT=100
```

`SQUID_CONF=`*`value`*

The default configuration file. For example:

```
SQUID_CONF="/etc/squid/squid.conf"
```

B.1.22. /etc/sysconfig/system-config-users

The `/etc/sysconfig/system-config-users` file is the configuration file for the **User Manager** utility, and should not be edited by hand. By default, it contains the following options:

`FILTER=`*`boolean`*

A boolean to enable (`true`) or disable (`false`) filtering of system users. For example:

```
FILTER=true
```

`ASSIGN_HIGHEST_UID=`*`boolean`*

A boolean to enable (`true`) or disable (`false`) assigning the highest available UID to newly added users. For example:

```
ASSIGN_HIGHEST_UID=true
```

`ASSIGN_HIGHEST_GID=`*`boolean`*

A boolean to enable (`true`) or disable (`false`) assigning the highest available GID to newly added groups. For example:

```
ASSIGN_HIGHEST_GID=true
```

`PREFER_SAME_UID_GID=`*`boolean`*

A boolean to enable (`true`) or disable (`false`) using the same UID and GID for newly added users when possible. For example:

```
PREFER_SAME_UID_GID=true
```

Refer to Section 3.2, *User Manager Tool* (page 49) for more information on **User Manager** and its usage.

B.1.23. /etc/sysconfig/vncservers

The `/etc/sysconfig/vncservers` file configures the way the *Virtual Network Computing* (*VNC*) server starts up. By default, it contains the following options:

`VNCSERVERS=`*`value`*

A list of space separated *`display`*`:`*`username`* pairs. For example:

```
VNCSERVERS="2:myusername"
```

`VNCSERVERARGS[`*`display`*`]=`*`value`*

Additional arguments to be passed to the VNC server running on the specified *`display`*. For example:

```
VNCSERVERARGS[2]="-geometry 800x600 -nolisten tcp -localhost"
```

B.1.24. /etc/sysconfig/xinetd

The /etc/sysconfig/xinetd file is used to pass arguments to the xinetd daemon at boot time. By default, it contains the following options:

EXTRAOPTIONS=*value*

Additional options to be passed to xinetd. For example:

```
EXTRAOPTIONS=""
```

XINETD_LANG=*value*

The locale information to be passed to every service started by xinetd. Note that to remove locale information from the xinetd environment, you can use an empty string ("") or none. For example:

```
XINETD_LANG="en_US"
```

Refer to Chapter 7, *Services and Daemons* (page 120) for more information on how to configure the xinetd services.

B.2. Directories in the /etc/sysconfig/ Directory

The following directories are normally found in /etc/sysconfig/.

/etc/sysconfig/cbq/

This directory contains the configuration files needed to do *Class Based Queuing* for bandwidth management on network interfaces. CBQ divides user traffic into a hierarchy of classes based on any combination of IP addresses, protocols, and application types.

/etc/sysconfig/networking/

This directory is used by the **Network Administration Tool** (system-config-network), and its contents should not be edited manually.

/etc/sysconfig/network-scripts/

This directory contains the following network-related configuration files:

- Network configuration files for each configured network interface, such as ifcfg-eth0 for the eth0 Ethernet interface.
- Scripts used to bring network interfaces up and down, such as ifup and ifdown.
- Scripts used to bring ISDN interfaces up and down, such as ifup-isdn and ifdown-isdn.
- Various shared network function scripts which should not be edited directly.

For more information on the /etc/sysconfig/network-scripts/ directory, refer to Chapter 6, *Network Interfaces* (page 104).

B.3. Additional Resources

This chapter is only intended as an introduction to the files in the `/etc/sysconfig/` directory. The following source contains more comprehensive information.

B.3.1. Installed Documentation

`/usr/share/doc/initscripts-`*`version`*`/sysconfig.txt`
: A more authoritative listing of the files found in the `/etc/sysconfig/` directory and the configuration options available for them.

Appendix C.

The proc File System

The Linux kernel has two primary functions: to control access to physical devices on the computer and to schedule when and how processes interact with these devices. The `/proc/` directory (also called the `proc` file system) contains a hierarchy of special files which represent the current state of the kernel, allowing applications and users to peer into the kernel's view of the system.

The `/proc/` directory contains a wealth of information detailing system hardware and any running processes. In addition, some of the files within `/proc/` can be manipulated by users and applications to communicate configuration changes to the kernel.

The /proc/ide/ and /proc/pci/ directories

Later versions of the 2.6 kernel have made the `/proc/ide/` and `/proc/pci/` directories obsolete. The `/proc/ide/` file system is now superseded by files in `sysfs`; to retrieve information on PCI devices, use `lspci` instead. For more information on `sysfs` or `lspci`, refer to their respective `man` pages.

C.1. A Virtual File System

Linux systems store all data as *files*. Most users are familiar with the two primary types of files: text and binary. But the `/proc/` directory contains another type of file called a *virtual file*. As such, `/proc/` is often referred to as a *virtual file system*.

Virtual files have unique qualities. Most of them are listed as zero bytes in size, but can still contain a large amount of information when viewed. In addition, most of the time and date stamps on virtual files reflect the current time and date, indicative of the fact they are constantly updated.

Virtual files such as `/proc/interrupts`, `/proc/meminfo`, `/proc/mounts`, and `/proc/partitions` provide an up-to-the-moment glimpse of the system's hardware. Others, like the `/proc/filesystems` file and the `/proc/sys/` directory provide system configuration information and interfaces.

For organizational purposes, files containing information on a similar topic are grouped into virtual directories and sub-directories. Process directories contain information about each running process on the system.

C.1.1. Viewing Virtual Files

Most files within /proc/ files operate similarly to text files, storing useful system and hardware data in human-readable text format. As such, you can use cat, more, or less to view them. For example, to display information about the system's CPU, run cat /proc/cpuinfo. This will return output similar to the following:

```
processor         : 0
vendor_id         : AuthenticAMD
cpu family        : 5
model             : 9
model name        : AMD-K6(tm) 3D+
Processor stepping : 1 cpu
MHz               : 400.919
cache size        : 256 KB
fdiv_bug          : no
hlt_bug           : no
f00f_bug          : no
coma_bug          : no
fpu               : yes
fpu_exception     : yes
cpuid level       : 1
wp                : yes
flags             : fpu vme de pse tsc msr mce cx8 pge mmx syscall 3dnow k6_mtrr
bogomips          : 799.53
```

Some files in /proc/ contain information that is not human-readable. To retrieve information from such files, use tools such as lspci, apm, free, and top.

Certain files can only be accessed with root privileges

Some of the virtual files in the /proc/ directory are readable only by the root user.

C.1.2. Changing Virtual Files

As a general rule, most virtual files within the /proc/ directory are read-only. However, some can be used to adjust settings in the kernel. This is especially true for files in the /proc/sys/ subdirectory.

To change the value of a virtual file, use the following command:

```
echo value > /proc/file
```

For example, to change the hostname on the fly, run:

```
echo www.example.com > /proc/sys/kernel/hostname
```

Other files act as binary or Boolean switches. Typing cat /proc/sys/net/ipv4/ip_forward returns either a 0 (off or false) or a 1 (on or true). A 0 indicates that the kernel is not forwarding network packets. To turn packet forwarding on, run echo 1 > /proc/sys/net/ipv4/ip_forward.

The sysctl command

Another command used to alter settings in the `/proc/sys/` subdirectory is `/sbin/sysctl`. For more information on this command, refer to Section C.4, *Using the sysctl Command* (page 527).

For a listing of some of the kernel configuration files available in the `/proc/sys/` subdirectory, refer to Section C.3.9, */proc/sys/* (page 514).

C.2. Top-level Files within the `proc` File System

Below is a list of some of the more useful virtual files in the top-level of the `/proc/` directory.

The content of your files may differ

In most cases, the content of the files listed in this section are not the same as those installed on your machine. This is because much of the information is specific to the hardware on which Fedora is running for this documentation effort.

C.2.1. /proc/buddyinfo

This file is used primarily for diagnosing memory fragmentation issues. Using the buddy algorithm, each column represents the number of pages of a certain order (a certain size) that are available at any given time. For example, for zone *direct memory access* (DMA), there are 90 of $2^{(0*PAGE\_SIZE)}$ chunks of memory. Similarly, there are 6 of $2^{(1*PAGE\_SIZE)}$ chunks, and 2 of $2^{(2*PAGE\_SIZE)}$ chunks of memory available.

The `DMA` row references the first 16 MB on a system, the `HighMem` row references all memory greater than 4 GB on a system, and the `Normal` row references all memory in between.

The following is an example of the output typical of `/proc/buddyinfo`:

```
Node 0, zone      DMA     90      6      2      1      1      ...
Node 0, zone   Normal   1650    310      5      0      0      ...
Node 0, zone  HighMem      2      0      0      1      1      ...
```

C.2.2. /proc/cmdline

This file shows the parameters passed to the kernel at the time it is started. A sample `/proc/cmdline` file looks like the following:

```
ro root=/dev/VolGroup00/LogVol00 rhgb quiet 3
```

This tells us that the kernel is mounted read-only (signified by `(ro)`), located on the first logical volume (`LogVol00`) of the first volume group (`/dev/VolGroup00`). `LogVol00` is the equivalent of a disk partition in a non-LVM system (Logical Volume Management), just as `/dev/VolGroup00` is similar in concept to `/dev/hda1`, but much more extensible.

For more information on LVM used in Fedora, refer to *http://www.tldp.org/HOWTO/LVM-HOWTO/index.html*.

Next, `rhgb` signals that the `rhgb` package has been installed, and graphical booting is supported, assuming `/etc/inittab` shows a default runlevel set to `id:5:initdefault:`.

Finally, `quiet` indicates all verbose kernel messages are suppressed at boot time.

C.2.3. /proc/cpuinfo

This virtual file identifies the type of processor used by your system. The following is an example of the output typical of `/proc/cpuinfo`:

```
processor     : 0
vendor_id     : GenuineIntel
cpu family    : 15
model         : 2
model name    : Intel(R) Xeon(TM) CPU 2.40GHz
stepping      : 7 cpu
MHz           : 2392.371
cache size    : 512 KB
physical id   : 0
siblings      : 2
runqueue      : 0
fdiv_bug      : no
hlt_bug       : no
f00f_bug      : no
coma_bug      : no
fpu           : yes
fpu_exception: yes
cpuid level   : 2
wp            : yes
flags         : fpu vme de pse tsc msr pae mce cx8 apic sep mtrr pge mca  cmov pat
pse36 clflush dts acpi mmx fxsr sse sse2 ss ht tm
bogomips      : 4771.02
```

- `processor` — Provides each processor with an identifying number. On systems that have one processor, only a `0` is present.
- `cpu family` — Authoritatively identifies the type of processor in the system. For an Intel-based system, place the number in front of "86" to determine the value. This is particularly helpful for those attempting to identify the architecture of an older system such as a 586, 486, or 386. Because some RPM packages are compiled for each of these particular architectures, this value also helps users determine which packages to install.
- `model name` — Displays the common name of the processor, including its project name.
- `cpu MHz` — Shows the precise speed in megahertz for the processor to the thousandths decimal place.

- `cache size` — Displays the amount of level 2 memory cache available to the processor.
- `siblings` — Displays the number of sibling CPUs on the same physical CPU for architectures which use hyper-threading.
- `flags` — Defines a number of different qualities about the processor, such as the presence of a floating point unit (FPU) and the ability to process MMX instructions.

C.2.4. /proc/crypto

This file lists all installed cryptographic ciphers used by the Linux kernel, including additional details for each. A sample `/proc/crypto` file looks like the following:

```
name         : sha1
module       : kernel
type         : digest
blocksize    : 64
digestsize   : 20
name         : md5
module       : md5
type         : digest
blocksize    : 64
digestsize   : 16
```

C.2.5. /proc/devices

This file displays the various character and block devices currently configured (not including devices whose modules are not loaded). Below is a sample output from this file:

```
Character devices:
  1 mem
  4 /dev/vc/0
  4 tty
  4 ttyS
  5 /dev/tty
  5 /dev/console
  5 /dev/ptmx
  7 vcs
  10 misc
  13 input
  29 fb
  36 netlink
  128 ptm
  136 pts
  180 usb

Block devices:
  1 ramdisk
  3 ide0
  9 md
```

```
22 ide1
253 device-mapper
254 mdp
```

The output from `/proc/devices` includes the major number and name of the device, and is broken into two major sections: `Character devices` and `Block devices`.

Character devices are similar to *block devices*, except for two basic differences:

1. Character devices do not require buffering. Block devices have a buffer available, allowing them to order requests before addressing them. This is important for devices designed to store information — such as hard drives — because the ability to order the information before writing it to the device allows it to be placed in a more efficient order.
2. Character devices send data with no preconfigured size. Block devices can send and receive information in blocks of a size configured per device.

For more information about devices refer to the following installed documentation:

```
/usr/share/doc/kernel-doc-<kernel_version>/Documentation/devices.txt
```

C.2.6. /proc/dma

This file contains a list of the registered ISA DMA channels in use. A sample `/proc/dma` files looks like the following:

```
4: cascade
```

C.2.7. /proc/execdomains

This file lists the *execution domains* currently supported by the Linux kernel, along with the range of personalities they support.

```
0-0   Linux           [kernel]
```

Think of execution domains as the "personality" for an operating system. Because other binary formats, such as Solaris, UnixWare, and FreeBSD, can be used with Linux, programmers can change the way the operating system treats system calls from these binaries by changing the personality of the task. Except for the `PER_LINUX` execution domain, different personalities can be implemented as dynamically loadable modules.

C.2.8. /proc/fb

This file contains a list of frame buffer devices, with the frame buffer device number and the driver that controls it. Typical output of `/proc/fb` for systems which contain frame buffer devices looks similar to the following:

```
0 VESA VGA
```

C.2.9. /proc/filesystems

This file displays a list of the file system types currently supported by the kernel. Sample output from a generic `/proc/filesystems` file looks similar to the following:

```
nodev   sysfs
nodev   rootfs
nodev   bdev
nodev   proc
nodev   sockfs
nodev   binfmt_misc
nodev   usbfs
nodev   usbdevfs
nodev   futexfs
nodev   tmpfs
nodev   pipefs
nodev   eventpollfs
nodev   devpts
        ext2
nodev   ramfs
nodev   hugetlbfs
        iso9660
nodev   mqueue
        ext3
nodev   rpc_pipefs
nodev   autofs
```

The first column signifies whether the file system is mounted on a block device. Those beginning with `nodev` are not mounted on a device. The second column lists the names of the file systems supported.

The `mount` command cycles through the file systems listed here when one is not specified as an argument.

C.2.10. /proc/interrupts

This file records the number of interrupts per IRQ on the x86 architecture. A standard `/proc/interrupts` looks similar to the following:

```
  CPU0
  0:    80448940          XT-PIC  timer
  1:      174412          XT-PIC  keyboard
  2:           0          XT-PIC  cascade
  8:           1          XT-PIC  rtc
 10:      410964          XT-PIC  eth0
 12:       60330          XT-PIC  PS/2 Mouse
 14:     1314121          XT-PIC  ide0
 15:     5195422          XT-PIC  ide1
NMI:           0
ERR:           0
```

For a multi-processor machine, this file may look slightly different:

```
           CPU0       CPU1
  0: 1366814704          0          XT-PIC  timer
  1:        128        340    IO-APIC-edge  keyboard
  2:          0          0          XT-PIC  cascade
  8:          0          1    IO-APIC-edge  rtc
 12:       5323       5793    IO-APIC-edge  PS/2 Mouse
 13:          1          0          XT-PIC  fpu
 16:   11184294   15940594   IO-APIC-level  Intel EtherExpress Pro 10/100 Ethernet
 20:    8450043   11120093   IO-APIC-level  megaraid
 30:      10432      10722   IO-APIC-level  aic7xxx
 31:         23         22   IO-APIC-level  aic7xxx
NMI:          0
ERR:          0
```

The first column refers to the IRQ number. Each CPU in the system has its own column and its own number of interrupts per IRQ. The next column reports the type of interrupt, and the last column contains the name of the device that is located at that IRQ.

Each of the types of interrupts seen in this file, which are architecture-specific, mean something different. For x86 machines, the following values are common:

- `XT-PIC` — This is the old AT computer interrupts.
- `IO-APIC-edge` — The voltage signal on this interrupt transitions from low to high, creating an *edge*, where the interrupt occurs and is only signaled once. This kind of interrupt, as well as the `IO-APIC-level` interrupt, are only seen on systems with processors from the 586 family and higher.
- `IO-APIC-level` — Generates interrupts when its voltage signal is high until the signal is low again.

C.2.11. /proc/iomem

This file shows you the current map of the system's memory for each physical device:

```
00000000-0009fbff : System RAM
0009fc00-0009ffff : reserved
000a0000-000bffff : Video RAM area
000c0000-000c7fff : Video ROM
000f0000-000fffff : System ROM
00100000-07ffffff : System RAM
00100000-00291ba8 : Kernel code
00291ba9-002e09cb : Kernel data
e0000000-e3ffffff : VIA Technologies, Inc. VT82C597 [Apollo VP3] e4000000-e7ffffff
: PCI Bus #01
e4000000-e4003fff : Matrox Graphics, Inc. MGA G200 AGP
e5000000-e57fffff : Matrox Graphics, Inc. MGA G200 AGP
e8000000-e8ffffff : PCI Bus #01
e8000000-e8ffffff : Matrox Graphics, Inc. MGA G200 AGP
```

```
ea000000-ea00007f : Digital Equipment Corporation DECchip 21140 [FasterNet]
ea000000-ea00007f : tulip ffff0000-ffffffff : reserved
```

The first column displays the memory registers used by each of the different types of memory. The second column lists the kind of memory located within those registers and displays which memory registers are used by the kernel within the system RAM or, if the network interface card has multiple Ethernet ports, the memory registers assigned for each port.

C.2.12. /proc/ioports

The output of `/proc/ioports` provides a list of currently registered port regions used for input or output communication with a device. This file can be quite long. The following is a partial listing:

```
0000-001f : dma1
0020-003f : pic1
0040-005f : timer
0060-006f : keyboard
0070-007f : rtc
0080-008f : dma page reg
00a0-00bf : pic2
00c0-00df : dma2
00f0-00ff : fpu
0170-0177 : ide1
01f0-01f7 : ide0
02f8-02ff : serial(auto)
0376-0376 : ide1
03c0-03df : vga+
03f6-03f6 : ide0
03f8-03ff : serial(auto)
0cf8-0cff : PCI conf1
d000-dfff : PCI Bus #01
e000-e00f : VIA Technologies, Inc. Bus Master IDE
e000-e007 : ide0
e008-e00f : ide1
e800-e87f : Digital Equipment Corporation DECchip 21140 [FasterNet]
e800-e87f : tulip
```

The first column gives the I/O port address range reserved for the device listed in the second column.

C.2.13. /proc/kcore

This file represents the physical memory of the system and is stored in the core file format. Unlike most `/proc/` files, `kcore` displays a size. This value is given in bytes and is equal to the size of the physical memory (RAM) used plus 4 KB.

The contents of this file are designed to be examined by a debugger, such as `gdb`, and is not human readable.

Do not attempt to view the content of /proc/kcore

Do not view the `/proc/kcore` virtual file. The contents of the file scramble text output on the terminal. If this file is accidentally viewed, press **Ctrl+C** to stop the process and then type `reset` to bring back the command line prompt.

C.2.14. /proc/kmsg

This file is used to hold messages generated by the kernel. These messages are then picked up by other programs, such as `/sbin/klogd` or `/bin/dmesg`.

C.2.15. /proc/loadavg

This file provides a look at the load average in regard to both the CPU and IO over time, as well as additional data used by `uptime` and other commands. A sample `/proc/loadavg` file looks similar to the following:

```
0.20 0.18 0.12 1/80 11206
```

The first three columns measure CPU and IO utilization of the last one, five, and 15 minute periods. The fourth column shows the number of currently running processes and the total number of processes. The last column displays the last process ID used.

In addition, load average also refers to the number of processes ready to run (i.e. in the run queue, waiting for a CPU share.

C.2.16. /proc/locks

This file displays the files currently locked by the kernel. The contents of this file contain internal kernel debugging data and can vary tremendously, depending on the use of the system. A sample `/proc/locks` file for a lightly loaded system looks similar to the following:

```
1: POSIX  ADVISORY  WRITE 3568 fd:00:2531452 0 EOF
2: FLOCK  ADVISORY  WRITE 3517 fd:00:2531448 0 EOF
3: POSIX  ADVISORY  WRITE 3452 fd:00:2531442 0 EOF
4: POSIX  ADVISORY  WRITE 3443 fd:00:2531440 0 EOF
5: POSIX  ADVISORY  WRITE 3326 fd:00:2531430 0 EOF
6: POSIX  ADVISORY  WRITE 3175 fd:00:2531425 0 EOF
7: POSIX  ADVISORY  WRITE 3056 fd:00:2548663 0 EOF
```

Each lock has its own line which starts with a unique number. The second column refers to the class of lock used, with `FLOCK` signifying the older-style UNIX file locks from a `flock` system call and `POSIX` representing the newer POSIX locks from the `lockf` system call.

The third column can have two values: `ADVISORY` or `MANDATORY`. `ADVISORY` means that the lock does not prevent other people from accessing the data; it only prevents other attempts to lock it. `MANDATORY` means that no other access to the data is permitted while the lock is held. The fourth column reveals whether the lock is allowing the holder READ or WRITE access to the file. The fifth column shows the ID of the process holding the lock. The sixth column shows the ID of the file being locked, in the format of *MAJOR-DEVICE:MINOR-DEVICE:INODE-NUMBER* . The seventh and eighth column shows the start and end of the file's locked region.

C.2.17. /proc/mdstat

This file contains the current information for multiple-disk, RAID configurations. If the system does not contain such a configuration, then /proc/mdstat looks similar to the following:

```
Personalities :  read_ahead not set unused devices: <none>
```

This file remains in the same state as seen above unless a software RAID or md device is present. In that case, view /proc/mdstat to find the current status of md*X* RAID devices.

The /proc/mdstat file below shows a system with its md0 configured as a RAID 1 device, while it is currently re-syncing the disks:

```
Personalities : [linear] [raid1] read_ahead 1024 sectors
md0: active raid1 sda2[1] sdb2[0] 9940 blocks [2/2] [UU] resync=1% finish=12.3min
algorithm 2 [3/3] [UUU]
unused devices: <none>
```

C.2.18. /proc/meminfo

This is one of the more commonly used files in the /proc/ directory, as it reports a large amount of valuable information about the systems RAM usage.

The following sample /proc/meminfo virtual file is from a system with 256 MB of RAM and 512 MB of swap space:

```
MemTotal:     255908 kB
MemFree:       69936 kB
Buffers:       15812 kB
Cached:       115124 kB
SwapCached:        0 kB
Active:        92700 kB
Inactive:      63792 kB
HighTotal:         0 kB
HighFree:          0 kB
LowTotal:     255908 kB
LowFree:       69936 kB
SwapTotal:    524280 kB
SwapFree:     524280 kB
Dirty:             4 kB
Writeback:         0 kB
Mapped:        42236 kB
```

```
Slab:              25912 kB
Committed_AS:     118680 kB
PageTables:         1236 kB
VmallocTotal:    3874808 kB
VmallocUsed:        1416 kB
VmallocChunk:    3872908 kB
HugePages_Total:       0
HugePages_Free:        0
Hugepagesize:       4096 kB
```

Much of the information here is used by the `free`, `top`, and `ps` commands. In fact, the output of the `free` command is similar in appearance to the contents and structure of `/proc/meminfo`. But by looking directly at `/proc/meminfo`, more details are revealed:

- `MemTotal` — Total amount of physical RAM, in kilobytes.
- `MemFree` — The amount of physical RAM, in kilobytes, left unused by the system.
- `Buffers` — The amount of physical RAM, in kilobytes, used for file buffers.
- `Cached` — The amount of physical RAM, in kilobytes, used as cache memory.
- `SwapCached` — The amount of swap, in kilobytes, used as cache memory.
- `Active` — The total amount of buffer or page cache memory, in kilobytes, that is in active use. This is memory that has been recently used and is usually not reclaimed for other purposes.
- `Inactive` — The total amount of buffer or page cache memory, in kilobytes, that are free and available. This is memory that has not been recently used and can be reclaimed for other purposes.
- `HighTotal` and `HighFree` — The total and free amount of memory, in kilobytes, that is not directly mapped into kernel space. The `HighTotal` value can vary based on the type of kernel used.
- `LowTotal` and `LowFree` — The total and free amount of memory, in kilobytes, that is directly mapped into kernel space. The `LowTotal` value can vary based on the type of kernel used.
- `SwapTotal` — The total amount of swap available, in kilobytes.
- `SwapFree` — The total amount of swap free, in kilobytes.
- `Dirty` — The total amount of memory, in kilobytes, waiting to be written back to the disk.
- `Writeback` — The total amount of memory, in kilobytes, actively being written back to the disk.
- `Mapped` — The total amount of memory, in kilobytes, which have been used to map devices, files, or libraries using the `mmap` command.

- `Slab` — The total amount of memory, in kilobytes, used by the kernel to cache data structures for its own use.
- `Committed_AS` — The total amount of memory, in kilobytes, estimated to complete the workload. This value represents the worst case scenario value, and also includes swap memory.
- `PageTables` — The total amount of memory, in kilobytes, dedicated to the lowest page table level.
- `VMallocTotal` — The total amount of memory, in kilobytes, of total allocated virtual address space.
- `VMallocUsed` — The total amount of memory, in kilobytes, of used virtual address space.
- `VMallocChunk` — The largest contiguous block of memory, in kilobytes, of available virtual address space.
- `HugePages_Total` — The total number of hugepages for the system. The number is derived by dividing `Hugepagesize` by the megabytes set aside for hugepages specified in `/proc/sys/vm/hugetlb_pool`. *This statistic only appears on the x86, Itanium, and AMD64 architectures.*
- `HugePages_Free` — The total number of hugepages available for the system. *This statistic only appears on the x86, Itanium, and AMD64 architectures.*
- `Hugepagesize` — The size for each hugepages unit in kilobytes. By default, the value is 4096 KB on uniprocessor kernels for 32 bit architectures. For SMP, hugemem kernels, and AMD64, the default is 2048 KB. For Itanium architectures, the default is 262144 KB. *This statistic only appears on the x86, Itanium, and AMD64 architectures.*

C.2.19. /proc/misc

This file lists miscellaneous drivers registered on the miscellaneous major device, which is device number 10:

```
63 device-mapper 175 agpgart 135 rtc 134 apm_bios
```

The first column is the minor number of each device, while the second column shows the driver in use.

C.2.20. /proc/modules

This file displays a list of all modules loaded into the kernel. Its contents vary based on the configuration and use of your system, but it should be organized in a similar manner to this sample `/proc/modules` file output:

The content of /proc/modules

This example has been reformatted into a readable format. Most of this information can also be viewed via the `/sbin/lsmod` command.

```
nfs      170109  0 -              Live 0x129b0000
lockd    51593   1 nfs,           Live 0x128b0000
nls_utf8 1729    0 -              Live 0x12830000
vfat     12097   0 -              Live 0x12823000
fat      38881   1 vfat,          Live 0x1287b000
autofs4  20293   2 -              Live 0x1284f000
sunrpc   140453  3 nfs,lockd,     Live 0x12954000
3c59x    33257   0 -              Live 0x12871000
uhci_hcd 28377   0 -              Live 0x12869000
md5      3777    1 -              Live 0x1282c000
ipv6     211845 16 -              Live 0x128de000
ext3     92585   2 -              Live 0x12886000
jbd      65625   1 ext3,          Live 0x12857000
dm_mod   46677   3 -              Live 0x12833000
```

The first column contains the name of the module.

The second column refers to the memory size of the module, in bytes.

The third column lists how many instances of the module are currently loaded. A value of zero represents an unloaded module.

The fourth column states if the module depends upon another module to be present in order to function, and lists those other modules.

The fifth column lists what load state the module is in: `Live`, `Loading`, or `Unloading` are the only possible values.

The sixth column lists the current kernel memory offset for the loaded module. This information can be useful for debugging purposes, or for profiling tools such as `oprofile`.

C.2.21. /proc/mounts

This file provides a list of all mounts in use by the system:

```
rootfs / rootfs rw 0 0
/proc /proc proc rw,nodiratime 0 0 none
/dev ramfs rw 0 0
/dev/mapper/VolGroup00-LogVol00 / ext3 rw 0 0
none /dev ramfs rw 0 0
/proc /proc proc rw,nodiratime 0 0
/sys /sys sysfs rw 0 0
none /dev/pts devpts rw 0 0
usbdevfs /proc/bus/usb usbdevfs rw 0 0
/dev/hda1 /boot ext3 rw 0 0
none /dev/shm tmpfs rw 0 0
none /proc/sys/fs/binfmt_misc binfmt_misc rw 0 0
sunrpc /var/lib/nfs/rpc_pipefs rpc_pipefs rw 0 0
```

The output found here is similar to the contents of `/etc/mtab`, except that `/proc/mounts` is more up-to-date.

The first column specifies the device that is mounted, the second column reveals the mount point, and the third column tells the file system type, and the fourth column tells you if it is mounted read-only (`ro`) or read-write (`rw`). The fifth and sixth columns are dummy values designed to match the format used in `/etc/mtab`.

C.2.22. /proc/mtrr

This file refers to the current Memory Type Range Registers (MTRRs) in use with the system. If the system architecture supports MTRRs, then the `/proc/mtrr` file may look similar to the following:

```
reg00: base=0x00000000 (   0MB), size= 256MB: write-back, count=1
reg01: base=0xe8000000 (3712MB), size=  32MB: write-combining, count=1
```

MTRRs are used with the Intel P6 family of processors (Pentium II and higher) and control processor access to memory ranges. When using a video card on a PCI or AGP bus, a properly configured `/proc/mtrr` file can increase performance more than 150%.

Most of the time, this value is properly configured by default. More information on manually configuring this file can be found locally at the following location:

```
/usr/share/doc/kernel-doc-<kernel_version>/Documentation/<arch>/mtrr.txt
```

C.2.23. /proc/partitions

This file contains partition block allocation information. A sampling of this file from a basic system looks similar to the following:

```
major minor  #blocks  name
  3     0   19531250 hda
  3     1     104391 hda1
  3     2   19422585 hda2
253     0   22708224 dm-0
253     1     524288 dm-1
```

Most of the information here is of little importance to the user, except for the following columns:

- `major` — The major number of the device with this partition. The major number in the `/proc/partitions`, (`3`), corresponds with the block device `ide0`, in `/proc/devices`.
- `minor` — The minor number of the device with this partition. This serves to separate the partitions into different physical devices and relates to the number at the end of the name of the partition.

- `#blocks` — Lists the number of physical disk blocks contained in a particular partition.
- `name` — The name of the partition.

C.2.24. /proc/slabinfo

This file gives full information about memory usage on the *slab* level. Linux kernels greater than version 2.2 use *slab pools* to manage memory above the page level. Commonly used objects have their own slab pools.

Instead of parsing the highly verbose `/proc/slabinfo` file manually, the `/usr/bin/slabtop` program displays kernel slab cache information in real time. This program allows for custom configurations, including column sorting and screen refreshing.

A sample screen shot of `/usr/bin/slabtop` usually looks like the following example:

```
Active / Total Objects (% used)    : 133629 / 147300 (90.7%)
Active / Total Slabs (% used)      : 11492 / 11493 (100.0%)
Active / Total Caches (% used)     : 77 / 121 (63.6%)
Active / Total Size (% used)       : 41739.83K / 44081.89K (94.7%)
Minimum / Average / Maximum Object : 0.01K / 0.30K / 128.00K
OBJS  ACTIVE USE      OBJ   SIZE     SLABS  OBJ/SLAB CACHE SIZE NAME
44814 43159  96%    0.62K   7469         6    29876K ext3_inode_cache
36900 34614  93%    0.05K    492        75     1968K buffer_head
35213 33124  94%    0.16K   1531        23     6124K dentry_cache
7364  6463   87%    0.27K    526        14     2104K radix_tree_node
2585  1781   68%    0.08K     55        47      220K vm_area_struct
2263  2116   93%    0.12K     73        31      292K size-128
1904  1125   59%    0.03K     16       119       64K size-32
1666   768   46%    0.03K     14       119       56K anon_vma
1512  1482   98%    0.44K    168         9      672K inode_cache
1464  1040   71%    0.06K     24        61       96K size-64
1320   820   62%    0.19K     66        20      264K filp
678    587   86%    0.02K      3       226       12K dm_io
678    587   86%    0.02K      3       226       12K dm_tio
576    574   99%    0.47K     72         8      288K proc_inode_cache
528    514   97%    0.50K     66         8      264K size-512
492    372   75%    0.09K     12        41       48K bio
465    314   67%    0.25K     31        15      124K size-256
452    331   73%    0.02K      2       226        8K biovec-1
420    420  100%    0.19K     21        20       84K skbuff_head_cache
305    256   83%    0.06K      5        61       20K biovec-4
290      4    1%    0.01K      1       290        4K revoke_table
264    264  100%    4.00K    264         1     1056K size-4096
260    256   98%    0.19K     13        20       52K biovec-16
260    256   98%    0.75K     52         5      208K biovec-64
```

Some of the more commonly used statistics in `/proc/slabinfo` that are included into `/usr/bin/slabtop` include:

- `OBJS` — The total number of objects (memory blocks), including those in use (allocated), and some spares not in use.
- `ACTIVE` — The number of objects (memory blocks) that are in use (allocated).
- `USE` — Percentage of total objects that are active. ((ACTIVE/OBJS)(100))
- `OBJ SIZE` — The size of the objects.
- `SLABS` — The total number of slabs.
- `OBJ/SLAB` — The number of objects that fit into a slab.
- `CACHE SIZE` — The cache size of the slab.
- `NAME` — The name of the slab.

For more information on the `/usr/bin/slabtop` program, refer to the `slabtop` man page.

C.2.25. /proc/stat

This file keeps track of a variety of different statistics about the system since it was last restarted. The contents of `/proc/stat`, which can be quite long, usually begins like the following example:

```
cpu  259246 7001 60190 34250993 137517 772 0
cpu0 259246 7001 60190 34250993 137517 772 0
intr 354133732 347209999 2272 0 4 4 0 0 3 1 1249247 0 0 80143 0 422626 5169433
ctxt 12547729
btime 1093631447
processes 130523
procs_running 1
procs_blocked 0
preempt 5651840
cpu  209841 1554 21720 118519346 72939 154 27168
cpu0 42536 798 4841 14790880 14778 124 3117
cpu1 24184 569 3875 14794524 30209 29 3130
cpu2 28616 11 2182 14818198 4020 1 3493
cpu3 35350 6 2942 14811519 3045 0 3659
cpu4 18209 135 2263 14820076 12465 0 3373
cpu5 20795 35 1866 14825701 4508 0 3615
cpu6 21607 0 2201 14827053 2325 0 3334
cpu7 18544 0 1550 14831395 1589 0 3447
intr 15239682 14857833 6 0 6 6 0 5 0 1 0 0 0 29 0 2 0 0 0 0 0 0 0 94982 0 286812
ctxt 4209609
btime 1078711415
processes 21905
procs_running 1
procs_blocked 0
```

Some of the more commonly used statistics include:

- `cpu` — Measures the number of *jiffies* (1/100 of a second for x86 systems) that the system has been in user mode, user mode with low priority (nice), system mode, idle task, I/O wait, IRQ (hardirq), and softirq respectively. The IRQ (hardirq) is the direct response to a hardware event. The IRQ takes minimal work for queuing the "heavy" work up for the softirq to execute. The softirq runs at a lower priority than the IRQ and therefore may be interrupted more frequently. The total for all CPUs is given at the top, while each individual CPU is listed below with its own statistics. The following example is a 4-way Intel Pentium Xeon configuration with multi-threading enabled, therefore showing four physical processors and four virtual processors totaling eight processors.

- `page` — The number of memory pages the system has written in and out to disk.
- `swap` — The number of swap pages the system has brought in and out.
- `intr` — The number of interrupts the system has experienced.
- `btime` — The boot time, measured in the number of seconds since January 1, 1970, otherwise known as the *epoch*.

C.2.26. /proc/swaps

This file measures swap space and its utilization. For a system with only one swap partition, the output of `/proc/swaps` may look similar to the following:

```
Filename                           Type         Size     Used    Priority
/dev/mapper/VolGroup00-LogVol01    partition    524280   0       -1
```

While some of this information can be found in other files in the `/proc/` directory, `/proc/swap` provides a snapshot of every swap file name, the type of swap space, the total size, and the amount of space in use (in kilobytes). The priority column is useful when multiple swap files are in use. The lower the priority, the more likely the swap file is to be used.

C.2.27. /proc/sysrq-trigger

Using the `echo` command to write to this file, a remote root user can execute most System Request Key commands remotely as if at the local terminal. To `echo` values to this file, the `/proc/sys/kernel/sysrq` must be set to a value other than `0`. For more information about the System Request Key, refer to Section C.3.9.3, */proc/sys/kernel/* (page 516).

Although it is possible to write to this file, it cannot be read, even by the root user.

C.2.28. /proc/uptime

This file contains information detailing how long the system has been on since its last restart. The output of `/proc/uptime` is quite minimal:

```
350735.47 234388.90
```

The first number is the total number of seconds the system has been up. The second number is how much of that time the machine has spent idle, in seconds.

C.2.29. /proc/version

This file specifies the version of the Linux kernel, the version of `gcc` used to compile the kernel, and the time of kernel compilation. It also contains the kernel compiler's user name (in parentheses).

```
Linux version 2.6.8-1.523 (user@foo.redhat.com) (gcc version 3.4.1 20040714 \  (Red
Hat Enterprise Linux 3.4.1-7)) #1 Mon Aug 16 13:27:03 EDT 2004
```

This information is used for a variety of purposes, including the version data presented when a user logs in.

C.3. Directories within /proc/

Common groups of information concerning the kernel are grouped into directories and subdirectories within the `/proc/` directory.

C.3.1. Process Directories

Every `/proc/` directory contains a number of directories with numerical names. A listing of them may be similar to the following:

```
dr-xr-xr-x    3 root     root            0 Feb 13 01:28 1
dr-xr-xr-x    3 root     root            0 Feb 13 01:28 1010
dr-xr-xr-x    3 xfs      xfs             0 Feb 13 01:28 1087
dr-xr-xr-x    3 daemon   daemon          0 Feb 13 01:28 1123
dr-xr-xr-x    3 root     root            0 Feb 13 01:28 11307
dr-xr-xr-x    3 apache   apache          0 Feb 13 01:28 13660
dr-xr-xr-x    3 rpc      rpc             0 Feb 13 01:28 637
dr-xr-xr-x    3 rpcuser  rpcuser         0 Feb 13 01:28 666
```

These directories are called *process directories*, as they are named after a program's process ID and contain information specific to that process. The owner and group of each process directory is set to the user running the process. When the process is terminated, its `/proc/` process directory vanishes.

Each process directory contains the following files:

- `cmdline` — Contains the command issued when starting the process.
- `cwd` — A symbolic link to the current working directory for the process.
- `environ` — A list of the environment variables for the process. The environment variable is given in all upper-case characters, and the value is in lower-case characters.

- `exe` — A symbolic link to the executable of this process.
- `fd` — A directory containing all of the file descriptors for a particular process. These are given in numbered links:

```
total 0
lrwx------    1 root     root          64 May  8 11:31 0 -> /dev/null
lrwx------    1 root     root          64 May  8 11:31 1 -> /dev/null
lrwx------    1 root     root          64 May  8 11:31 2 -> /dev/null
lrwx------    1 root     root          64 May  8 11:31 3 -> /dev/ptmx
lrwx------    1 root     root          64 May  8 11:31 4 -> socket:[7774817]
lrwx------    1 root     root          64 May  8 11:31 5 -> /dev/ptmx
lrwx------    1 root     root          64 May  8 11:31 6 -> socket:[7774829]
lrwx------    1 root     root          64 May  8 11:31 7 -> /dev/ptmx
```

- `maps` — A list of memory maps to the various executables and library files associated with this process. This file can be rather long, depending upon the complexity of the process, but sample output from the `sshd` process begins like the following:

```
08048000-08086000 r-xp 00000000 03:03 391479     /usr/sbin/sshd
08086000-08088000 rw-p 0003e000 03:03 391479  /usr/sbin/sshd
08088000-08095000 rwxp 00000000 00:00 0
40000000-40013000 r-xp 0000000 03:03 293205   /lib/ld-2.2.5.so
40013000-40014000 rw-p 00013000 03:03 293205  /lib/ld-2.2.5.so
40031000-40038000 r-xp 00000000 03:03 293282  /lib/libpam.so.0.75
40038000-40039000 rw-p 00006000 03:03 293282  /lib/libpam.so.0.75
40039000-4003a000 rw-p 00000000 00:00 0
4003a000-4003c000 r-xp 00000000 03:03 293218  /lib/libdl-2.2.5.so
4003c000-4003d000 rw-p 00001000 03:03 293218  /lib/libdl-2.2.5.so
```

- `mem` — The memory held by the process. This file cannot be read by the user.
- `root` — A link to the root directory of the process.
- `stat` — The status of the process.
- `statm` — The status of the memory in use by the process. Below is a sample `/proc/statm` file:

```
263 210 210 5 0 205 0
```

The seven columns relate to different memory statistics for the process. From left to right, they report the following aspects of the memory used:

1. Total program size, in kilobytes.
2. Size of memory portions, in kilobytes.
3. Number of pages that are shared.
4. Number of pages that are code.
5. Number of pages of data/stack.
6. Number of library pages.
7. Number of dirty pages.

- `status` — The status of the process in a more readable form than `stat` or `statm`. Sample output for `sshd` looks similar to the following:

```
Name:  sshd
State: S (sleeping)
Tgid:  797
Pid:   797
PPid:  1
TracerPid:     0
Uid:   0       0       0       0
Gid:   0       0       0       0
FDSize:        32
Groups:
VmSize:        3072 kB
VmLck:            0 kB
VmRSS:          840 kB
VmData:         104 kB
VmStk:           12 kB
VmExe:          300 kB
VmLib:         2528 kB
SigPnd:        0000000000000000
SigBlk:        0000000000000000
SigIgn:        8000000000001000
SigCgt:        0000000000014005
CapInh:        0000000000000000
CapPrm:        00000000fffffeff
CapEff:        00000000fffffeff
```

  The information in this output includes the process name and ID, the state (such as `S (sleeping)` or `R (running)`), user/group ID running the process, and detailed data regarding memory usage.

C.3.1.1. /proc/self/

The `/proc/self/` directory is a link to the currently running process. This allows a process to look at itself without having to know its process ID.

Within a shell environment, a listing of the `/proc/self/` directory produces the same contents as listing the process directory for that process.

C.3.2. /proc/bus/

This directory contains information specific to the various buses available on the system. For example, on a standard system containing PCI and USB buses, current data on each of these buses is available within a subdirectory within `/proc/bus/` by the same name, such as `/proc/bus/pci/`.

The subdirectories and files available within `/proc/bus/` vary depending on the devices connected to the system. However, each bus type has at least one directory. Within these bus directories are normally at least one subdirectory with a numerical name, such as `001`, which contain binary files.

For example, the `/proc/bus/usb/` subdirectory contains files that track the various devices on any USB buses, as well as the drivers required for them. The following is a sample listing of a `/proc/bus/usb/` directory:

```
total 0 dr-xr-xr-x    1 root     root            0 May  3 16:25 001
-r--r--r--    1 root     root            0 May  3 16:25 devices
-r--r--r--    1 root     root            0 May  3 16:25 drivers
```

The `/proc/bus/usb/001/` directory contains all devices on the first USB bus and the `devices` file identifies the USB root hub on the motherboard.

The following is a example of a `/proc/bus/usb/devices` file:

```
T:  Bus=01 Lev=00 Prnt=00 Port=00 Cnt=00 Dev#=  1 Spd=12  MxCh= 2
B:  Alloc=  0/900 us ( 0%), #Int=  0, #Iso=  0
D:  Ver= 1.00 Cls=09(hub  ) Sub=00 Prot=00 MxPS= 8 #Cfgs=  1
P:  Vendor=0000 ProdID=0000 Rev= 0.00
S:  Product=USB UHCI Root Hub
S:  SerialNumber=d400
C:* #Ifs= 1 Cfg#= 1 Atr=40 MxPwr=  0mA
I:  If#= 0 Alt= 0 #EPs= 1 Cls=09(hub  ) Sub=00 Prot=00 Driver=hub
E:  Ad=81(I) Atr=03(Int.) MxPS=   8 Ivl=255ms
```

C.3.3. /proc/bus/pci

Later versions of the 2.6 Linux kernel have obsoleted the `/proc/pci` directory in favor of the `/proc/bus/pci` directory. Although you can get a list of all PCI devices present on the system using the command `cat /proc/bus/pci/devices`, the output is difficult to read and interpret.

For a human-readable list of PCI devices, run the following command:

```
~]# /sbin/lspci -vb
00:00.0 Host bridge: Intel Corporation 82X38/X48 Express DRAM Controller
        Subsystem: Hewlett-Packard Company Device 1308
        Flags: bus master, fast devsel, latency 0
        Capabilities: [e0] Vendor Specific Information <?>
        Kernel driver in use: x38_edac
        Kernel modules: x38_edac

00:01.0 PCI bridge: Intel Corporation 82X38/X48 Express Host-Primary PCI Express
Bridge (prog-if 00 [Normal decode])
        Flags: bus master, fast devsel, latency 0
        Bus: primary=00, secondary=01, subordinate=01, sec-latency=0
        I/O behind bridge: 00001000-00001fff
        Memory behind bridge: f0000000-f2ffffff
        Capabilities: [88] Subsystem: Hewlett-Packard Company Device 1308
        Capabilities: [80] Power Management version 3
        Capabilities: [90] MSI: Enable+ Count=1/1 Maskable- 64bit-
        Capabilities: [a0] Express Root Port (Slot+), MSI 00
        Capabilities: [100] Virtual Channel <?>
        Capabilities: [140] Root Complex Link <?>
```

```
        Kernel driver in use: pcieport
        Kernel modules: shpchp

00:1a.0 USB Controller: Intel Corporation 82801I (ICH9 Family) USB UHCI Controller
#4 (rev 02) (prog-if 00 [UHCI])
        Subsystem: Hewlett-Packard Company Device 1308
        Flags: bus master, medium devsel, latency 0, IRQ 5
        I/O ports at 2100
        Capabilities: [50] PCI Advanced Features
        Kernel driver in use: uhci_hcd
[output truncated]
```

The output is a sorted list of all IRQ numbers and addresses as seen by the cards on the PCI bus instead of as seen by the kernel. Beyond providing the name and version of the device, this list also gives detailed IRQ information so an administrator can quickly look for conflicts.

C.3.4. /proc/driver/

This directory contains information for specific drivers in use by the kernel.

A common file found here is `rtc` which provides output from the driver for the system's *Real Time Clock (RTC)*, the device that keeps the time while the system is switched off. Sample output from `/proc/driver/rtc` looks like the following:

```
rtc_time        : 16:21:00
rtc_date        : 2004-08-31
rtc_epoch       : 1900
alarm           : 21:16:27
DST_enable      : no
BCD             : yes
24hr            : yes
square_wave     : no
alarm_IRQ       : no
update_IRQ      : no
periodic_IRQ    : no
periodic_freq   : 1024
batt_status     : okay
```

For more information about the RTC, refer to the following installed documentation:

`/usr/share/doc/kernel-doc-<kernel_version>/Documentation/rtc.txt.`

C.3.5. /proc/fs

This directory shows which file systems are exported. If running an NFS server, typing `cat /proc/fs/nfsd/exports` displays the file systems being shared and the permissions granted for those file systems. For more on file system sharing with NFS, refer to the *Network File System (NFS)* chapter of the *Storage Administration Guide*.

C.3.6. /proc/irq/

This directory is used to set IRQ to CPU affinity, which allows the system to connect a particular IRQ to only one CPU. Alternatively, it can exclude a CPU from handling any IRQs.

Each IRQ has its own directory, allowing for the individual configuration of each IRQ. The `/proc/irq/prof_cpu_mask` file is a bitmask that contains the default values for the `smp_affinity` file in the IRQ directory. The values in `smp_affinity` specify which CPUs handle that particular IRQ.

For more information about the `/proc/irq/` directory, refer to the following installed documentation:

`/usr/share/doc/kernel-doc-`*`kernel_version`*`/Documentation/filesystems/proc.txt`

C.3.7. /proc/net/

This directory provides a comprehensive look at various networking parameters and statistics. Each directory and virtual file within this directory describes aspects of the system's network configuration. Below is a partial list of the `/proc/net/` directory:

- `arp` — Lists the kernel's ARP table. This file is particularly useful for connecting a hardware address to an IP address on a system.
- `atm/` directory — The files within this directory contain *Asynchronous Transfer Mode (ATM)* settings and statistics. This directory is primarily used with ATM networking and ADSL cards.
- `dev` — Lists the various network devices configured on the system, complete with transmit and receive statistics. This file displays the number of bytes each interface has sent and received, the number of packets inbound and outbound, the number of errors seen, the number of packets dropped, and more.
- `dev_mcast` — Lists Layer2 multicast groups on which each device is listening.
- `igmp` — Lists the IP multicast addresses which this system joined.
- `ip_conntrack` — Lists tracked network connections for machines that are forwarding IP connections.
- `ip_tables_names` — Lists the types of `iptables` in use. This file is only present if `iptables` is active on the system and contains one or more of the following values: `filter`, `mangle`, or `nat`.
- `ip_mr_cache` — Lists the multicast routing cache.
- `ip_mr_vif` — Lists multicast virtual interfaces.
- `netstat` — Contains a broad yet detailed collection of networking statistics, including TCP timeouts, SYN cookies sent and received, and much more.

- `psched` — Lists global packet scheduler parameters.
- `raw` — Lists raw device statistics.
- `route` — Lists the kernel's routing table.
- `rt_cache` — Contains the current routing cache.
- `snmp` — List of Simple Network Management Protocol (SNMP) data for various networking protocols in use.
- `sockstat` — Provides socket statistics.
- `tcp` — Contains detailed TCP socket information.
- `tr_rif` — Lists the token ring RIF routing table.
- `udp` — Contains detailed UDP socket information.
- `unix` — Lists UNIX domain sockets currently in use.
- `wireless` — Lists wireless interface data.

C.3.8. /proc/scsi/

The primary file in this directory is `/proc/scsi/scsi`, which contains a list of every recognized SCSI device. From this listing, the type of device, as well as the model name, vendor, SCSI channel and ID data is available.

For example, if a system contains a SCSI CD-ROM, a tape drive, a hard drive, and a RAID controller, this file looks similar to the following:

```
Attached devices:
Host: scsi1
Channel: 00
Id: 05
Lun: 00
Vendor: NEC
Model: CD-ROM DRIVE:466
Rev: 1.06
Type:   CD-ROM
ANSI SCSI revision: 02
Host: scsi1
Channel: 00
Id: 06
Lun: 00
Vendor: ARCHIVE
Model: Python 04106-XXX
Rev: 7350
Type:   Sequential-Access
ANSI SCSI revision: 02
Host: scsi2
Channel: 00
Id: 06
```

```
Lun: 00
Vendor: DELL
Model: 1x6 U2W SCSI BP
Rev: 5.35
Type:   Processor
ANSI SCSI revision: 02
Host: scsi2
Channel: 02
Id: 00
Lun: 00
Vendor: MegaRAID
Model: LD0 RAID5 34556R
Rev: 1.01
Type:   Direct-Access
ANSI SCSI revision: 02
```

Each SCSI driver used by the system has its own directory within `/proc/scsi/`, which contains files specific to each SCSI controller using that driver. From the previous example, `aic7xxx/` and `megaraid/` directories are present, since two drivers are in use. The files in each of the directories typically contain an I/O address range, IRQ information, and statistics for the SCSI controller using that driver. Each controller can report a different type and amount of information. The Adaptec AIC-7880 Ultra SCSI host adapter's file in this example system produces the following output:

```
Adaptec AIC7xxx driver version: 5.1.20/3.2.4
Compile Options:
TCQ Enabled By Default : Disabled
AIC7XXX_PROC_STATS     : Enabled
AIC7XXX_RESET_DELAY    : 5
Adapter Configuration:
SCSI Adapter: Adaptec AIC-7880 Ultra SCSI host adapter
Ultra Narrow Controller     PCI MMAPed
I/O Base: 0xfcffe000
Adapter SEEPROM Config: SEEPROM found and used.
Adaptec SCSI BIOS: Enabled
IRQ: 30
SCBs: Active 0, Max Active 1, Allocated 15, HW 16, Page 255
Interrupts: 33726
BIOS Control Word: 0x18a6
Adapter Control Word: 0x1c5f
Extended Translation: Enabled
Disconnect Enable Flags: 0x00ff
Ultra Enable Flags: 0x0020
Tag Queue Enable Flags: 0x0000
Ordered Queue Tag Flags: 0x0000
Default Tag Queue Depth: 8
Tagged Queue By Device array for aic7xxx
host instance 1:
{255,255,255,255,255,255,255,255,255,255,255,255,255,255,255,255}
Actual queue depth per device for aic7xxx host instance 1:
{1,1,1,1,1,1,1,1,1,1,1,1,1,1,1,1}
```

```
Statistics:

(scsi1:0:5:0) Device using Narrow/Sync transfers at 20.0 MByte/sec, offset 15
Transinfo settings: current(12/15/0/0), goal(12/15/0/0), user(12/15/0/0)
Total transfers 0 (0 reads and 0 writes)
              < 2K      2K+     4K+     8K+    16K+    32K+    64K+   128K+
Reads:          0        0       0       0       0       0       0       0
Writes:         0        0       0       0       0       0       0       0

(scsi1:0:6:0) Device using Narrow/Sync transfers at 10.0 MByte/sec, offset 15
Transinfo settings: current(25/15/0/0), goal(12/15/0/0), user(12/15/0/0)
Total transfers 132 (0 reads and 132 writes)
              < 2K      2K+     4K+     8K+    16K+    32K+    64K+   128K+
Reads:          0        0       0       0       0       0       0       0
Writes:         0        0       0       1     131       0       0       0
```

This output reveals the transfer speed to the SCSI devices connected to the controller based on channel ID, as well as detailed statistics concerning the amount and sizes of files read or written by that device. For example, this controller is communicating with the CD-ROM at 20 megabytes per second, while the tape drive is only communicating at 10 megabytes per second.

C.3.9. /proc/sys/

The `/proc/sys/` directory is different from others in `/proc/` because it not only provides information about the system but also allows the system administrator to immediately enable and disable kernel features.

Be careful when changing the content of /proc/sys/

Use caution when changing settings on a production system using the various files in the `/proc/sys/` directory. Changing the wrong setting may render the kernel unstable, requiring a system reboot.

For this reason, be sure the options are valid for that file before attempting to change any value in `/proc/sys/`.

A good way to determine if a particular file can be configured, or if it is only designed to provide information, is to list it with the `-l` option at the shell prompt. If the file is writable, it may be used to configure the kernel. For example, a partial listing of `/proc/sys/fs` looks like the following:

```
-r--r--r--    1 root     root            0 May 10 16:14 dentry-state
-rw-r--r--    1 root     root            0 May 10 16:14 dir-notify-enable
-rw-r--r--    1 root     root            0 May 10 16:14 file-max
-r--r--r--    1 root     root            0 May 10 16:14 file-nr
```

In this listing, the files `dir-notify-enable` and `file-max` can be written to and, therefore, can be used to configure the kernel. The other files only provide feedback on current settings.

Changing a value within a /proc/sys/ file is done by echoing the new value into the file. For example, to enable the System Request Key on a running kernel, type the command:

```
echo 1 > /proc/sys/kernel/sysrq
```

This changes the value for sysrq from 0 (off) to 1 (on).

A few /proc/sys/ configuration files contain more than one value. To correctly send new values to them, place a space character between each value passed with the echo command, such as is done in this example:

```
echo 4 2 45 > /proc/sys/kernel/acct
```

Changes made using the echo command are not persistent

Any configuration changes made using the echo command disappear when the system is restarted. To make configuration changes take effect after the system is rebooted, refer to Section C.4, *Using the sysctl Command* (page 527).

The /proc/sys/ directory contains several subdirectories controlling different aspects of a running kernel.

C.3.9.1. /proc/sys/dev/

This directory provides parameters for particular devices on the system. Most systems have at least two directories, cdrom/ and raid/. Customized kernels can have other directories, such as parport/, which provides the ability to share one parallel port between multiple device drivers.

The cdrom/ directory contains a file called info, which reveals a number of important CD-ROM parameters:

```
CD-ROM information, Id: cdrom.c 3.20 2003/12/17
drive name:             hdc
drive speed:            48
drive # of slots:       1
Can close tray:         1
Can open tray:          1
Can lock tray:          1
Can change speed:       1
Can select disk:        0
Can read multisession:  1
Can read MCN:           1
Reports media changed:  1
Can play audio:         1
Can write CD-R:         0
Can write CD-RW:        0
Can read DVD:           0
Can write DVD-R:        0
Can write DVD-RAM:      0
Can read MRW:           0
```

```
Can write MRW:          0
Can write RAM:          0
```

This file can be quickly scanned to discover the qualities of an unknown CD-ROM. If multiple CD-ROMs are available on a system, each device is given its own column of information.

Various files in /proc/sys/dev/cdrom, such as autoclose and checkmedia, can be used to control the system's CD-ROM. Use the echo command to enable or disable these features.

If RAID support is compiled into the kernel, a /proc/sys/dev/raid/ directory becomes available with at least two files in it: speed_limit_min and speed_limit_max. These settings determine the acceleration of RAID devices for I/O intensive tasks, such as resyncing the disks.

C.3.9.2. /proc/sys/fs/

This directory contains an array of options and information concerning various aspects of the file system, including quota, file handle, inode, and dentry information.

The binfmt_misc/ directory is used to provide kernel support for miscellaneous binary formats.

The important files in /proc/sys/fs/ include:

- dentry-state — Provides the status of the directory cache. The file looks similar to the following:

  ```
  57411  52939  45     0      0      0
  ```

  The first number reveals the total number of directory cache entries, while the second number displays the number of unused entries. The third number tells the number of seconds between when a directory has been freed and when it can be reclaimed, and the fourth measures the pages currently requested by the system. The last two numbers are not used and display only zeros.
- file-max — Lists the maximum number of file handles that the kernel allocates. Raising the value in this file can resolve errors caused by a lack of available file handles.
- file-nr — Lists the number of allocated file handles, used file handles, and the maximum number of file handles.
- overflowgid and overflowuid — Defines the fixed group ID and user ID, respectively, for use with file systems that only support 16-bit group and user IDs.

C.3.9.3. /proc/sys/kernel/

This directory contains a variety of different configuration files that directly affect the operation of the kernel. Some of the most important files include:

- `acct` — Controls the suspension of process accounting based on the percentage of free space available on the file system containing the log. By default, the file looks like the following:

  ```
  4    2    30
  ```

  The first value dictates the percentage of free space required for logging to resume, while the second value sets the threshold percentage of free space when logging is suspended. The third value sets the interval, in seconds, that the kernel polls the file system to see if logging should be suspended or resumed.
- `ctrl-alt-del` — Controls whether **Ctrl+Alt+Delete** gracefully restarts the computer using `init` (`0`) or forces an immediate reboot without syncing the dirty buffers to disk (`1`).
- `domainname` — Configures the system domain name, such as `example.com`.
- `exec-shield` — Configures the Exec Shield feature of the kernel. Exec Shield provides protection against certain types of buffer overflow attacks.

  There are two possible values for this virtual file:

  - `0` — Disables Exec Shield.
  - `1` — Enables Exec Shield. This is the default value.

Using Exec Shield

If a system is running security-sensitive applications that were started while Exec Shield was disabled, these applications must be restarted when Exec Shield is enabled in order for Exec Shield to take effect.

- `hostname` — Configures the system hostname, such as `www.example.com`.
- `hotplug` — Configures the utility to be used when a configuration change is detected by the system. This is primarily used with USB and Cardbus PCI. The default value of `/sbin/hotplug` should not be changed unless testing a new program to fulfill this role.
- `modprobe` — Sets the location of the program used to load kernel modules. The default value is `/sbin/modprobe` which means `kmod` calls it to load the module when a kernel thread calls `kmod`.
- `msgmax` — Sets the maximum size of any message sent from one process to another and is set to `8192` bytes by default. Be careful when raising this value, as queued messages between processes are stored in non-swappable kernel memory. Any increase in `msgmax` would increase RAM requirements for the system.
- `msgmnb` — Sets the maximum number of bytes in a single message queue. The default is `16384`.

- `msgmni` — Sets the maximum number of message queue identifiers. The default is `4008`.
- `osrelease` — Lists the Linux kernel release number. This file can only be altered by changing the kernel source and recompiling.
- `ostype` — Displays the type of operating system. By default, this file is set to `Linux`, and this value can only be changed by changing the kernel source and recompiling.
- `overflowgid` and `overflowuid` — Defines the fixed group ID and user ID, respectively, for use with system calls on architectures that only support 16-bit group and user IDs.
- `panic` — Defines the number of seconds the kernel postpones rebooting when the system experiences a kernel panic. By default, the value is set to `0`, which disables automatic rebooting after a panic.
- `printk` — This file controls a variety of settings related to printing or logging error messages. Each error message reported by the kernel has a *loglevel* associated with it that defines the importance of the message. The loglevel values break down in this order:
    - `0` — Kernel emergency. The system is unusable.
    - `1` — Kernel alert. Action must be taken immediately.
    - `2` — Condition of the kernel is considered critical.
    - `3` — General kernel error condition.
    - `4` — General kernel warning condition.
    - `5` — Kernel notice of a normal but significant condition.
    - `6` — Kernel informational message.
    - `7` — Kernel debug-level messages.

  Four values are found in the `printk` file:

  ```
  6     4     1     7
  ```

  Each of these values defines a different rule for dealing with error messages. The first value, called the *console loglevel*, defines the lowest priority of messages printed to the console. (Note that, the lower the priority, the higher the loglevel number.) The second value sets the default loglevel for messages without an explicit loglevel attached to them. The third value sets the lowest possible loglevel configuration for the console loglevel. The last value sets the default value for the console loglevel.
- `random/` directory — Lists a number of values related to generating random numbers for the kernel.
- `sem` — Configures *semaphore* settings within the kernel. A semaphore is a System V IPC object that is used to control utilization of a particular process.

- `shmall` — Sets the total amount of shared memory that can be used at one time on the system, in bytes. By default, this value is `2097152`.
- `shmmax` — Sets the largest shared memory segment size allowed by the kernel, in bytes. By default, this value is `33554432`. However, the kernel supports much larger values than this.
- `shmmni` — Sets the maximum number of shared memory segments for the whole system, in bytes. By default, this value is `4096`
- `sysrq` — Activates the System Request Key, if this value is set to anything other than zero (`0`), the default.

  The System Request Key allows immediate input to the kernel through simple key combinations. For example, the System Request Key can be used to immediately shut down or restart a system, sync all mounted file systems, or dump important information to the console. To initiate a System Request Key, type **Alt+SysRq+** ***`system request code`***. Replace *`system request code`* with one of the following system request codes:

  - `r` — Disables raw mode for the keyboard and sets it to XLATE (a limited keyboard mode which does not recognize modifiers such as **Alt**, **Ctrl**, or **Shift** for all keys).
  - `k` — Kills all processes active in a virtual console. Also called *Secure Access Key* (*SAK*), it is often used to verify that the login prompt is spawned from `init` and not a trojan copy designed to capture usernames and passwords.
  - `b` — Reboots the kernel without first unmounting file systems or syncing disks attached to the system.
  - `c` — Crashes the system without first unmounting file systems or syncing disks attached to the system.
  - `o` — Shuts off the system.
  - `s` — Attempts to sync disks attached to the system.
  - `u` — Attempts to unmount and remount all file systems as read-only.
  - `p` — Outputs all flags and registers to the console.
  - `t` — Outputs a list of processes to the console.
  - `m` — Outputs memory statistics to the console.
  - `0` through `9` — Sets the log level for the console.
  - `e` — Kills all processes except `init` using SIGTERM.
  - `i` — Kills all processes except `init` using SIGKILL.

   - `l` — Kills all processes using SIGKILL (including `init`). *The system is unusable after issuing this System Request Key code.*
   - `h` — Displays help text.

  This feature is most beneficial when using a development kernel or when experiencing system freezes.

  Be careful when enabling the System Request Key feature

  The System Request Key feature is considered a security risk because an unattended console provides an attacker with access to the system. For this reason, it is turned off by default.

  Refer to `/usr/share/doc/kernel-doc-`*`kernel_version`*`/Documentation/sysrq.txt` for more information about the System Request Key.

- `tainted` — Indicates whether a non-GPL module is loaded.
   - `0` — No non-GPL modules are loaded.
   - `1` — At least one module without a GPL license (including modules with no license) is loaded.
   - `2` — At least one module was force-loaded with the command `insmod -f`.
- `threads-max` — Sets the maximum number of threads to be used by the kernel, with a default value of `2048`.
- `version` — Displays the date and time the kernel was last compiled. The first field in this file, such as `#3`, relates to the number of times a kernel was built from the source base.

C.3.9.4. /proc/sys/net/

This directory contains subdirectories concerning various networking topics. Various configurations at the time of kernel compilation make different directories available here, such as `ethernet/`, `ipv4/`, `ipx/`, and `ipv6/`. By altering the files within these directories, system administrators are able to adjust the network configuration on a running system.

Given the wide variety of possible networking options available with Linux, only the most common `/proc/sys/net/` directories are discussed.

The `/proc/sys/net/core/` directory contains a variety of settings that control the interaction between the kernel and networking layers. The most important of these files are:

- `message_burst` — Sets the amount of time in tenths of a second required to write a new warning message. This setting is used to mitigate *Denial of Service* (*DoS*) attacks. The default setting is `10`.

- message_cost — Sets a cost on every warning message. The higher the value of this file (default of 5), the more likely the warning message is ignored. This setting is used to mitigate DoS attacks.

  The idea of a DoS attack is to bombard the targeted system with requests that generate errors and fill up disk partitions with log files or require all of the system's resources to handle the error logging. The settings in message_burst and message_cost are designed to be modified based on the system's acceptable risk versus the need for comprehensive logging.
- netdev_max_backlog — Sets the maximum number of packets allowed to queue when a particular interface receives packets faster than the kernel can process them. The default value for this file is 1000.
- optmem_max — Configures the maximum ancillary buffer size allowed per socket.
- rmem_default — Sets the receive socket buffer default size in bytes.
- rmem_max — Sets the receive socket buffer maximum size in bytes.
- wmem_default — Sets the send socket buffer default size in bytes.
- wmem_max — Sets the send socket buffer maximum size in bytes.

The /proc/sys/net/ipv4/ directory contains additional networking settings. Many of these settings, used in conjunction with one another, are useful in preventing attacks on the system or when using the system to act as a router.

Be careful when changing these files

An erroneous change to these files may affect remote connectivity to the system.

The following is a list of some of the more important files within the /proc/sys/net/ipv4/ directory:

- icmp_echo_ignore_all and icmp_echo_ignore_broadcasts — Allows the kernel to ignore ICMP ECHO packets from every host or only those originating from broadcast and multicast addresses, respectively. A value of 0 allows the kernel to respond, while a value of 1 ignores the packets.
- ip_default_ttl — Sets the default *Time To Live (TTL)*, which limits the number of hops a packet may make before reaching its destination. Increasing this value can diminish system performance.
- ip_forward — Permits interfaces on the system to forward packets to one other. By default, this file is set to 0. Setting this file to 1 enables network packet forwarding.
- ip_local_port_range — Specifies the range of ports to be used by TCP or UDP when a local port is needed. The first number is the lowest port to be used and the

second number specifies the highest port. Any systems that expect to require more ports than the default 1024 to 4999 should use a range from 32768 to 61000.

- `tcp_syn_retries` — Provides a limit on the number of times the system re-transmits a SYN packet when attempting to make a connection.
- `tcp_retries1` — Sets the number of permitted re-transmissions attempting to answer an incoming connection. Default of `3`.
- `tcp_retries2` — Sets the number of permitted re-transmissions of TCP packets. Default of `15`.

The file called

```
/usr/share/doc/kernel-doc-kernel_version/Documentation/networking/
                                                      ip-sysctl.txt
```

contains a complete list of files and options available in the `/proc/sys/net/ipv4/` directory.

A number of other directories exist within the `/proc/sys/net/ipv4/` directory and each covers a different aspect of the network stack. The `/proc/sys/net/ipv4/conf/` directory allows each system interface to be configured in different ways, including the use of default settings for unconfigured devices (in the `/proc/sys/net/ipv4/conf/default/` subdirectory) and settings that override all special configurations (in the `/proc/sys/net/ipv4/conf/all/` subdirectory).

The `/proc/sys/net/ipv4/neigh/` directory contains settings for communicating with a host directly connected to the system (called a network neighbor) and also contains different settings for systems more than one hop away.

Routing over IPV4 also has its own directory, `/proc/sys/net/ipv4/route/`. Unlike `conf/` and `neigh/`, the `/proc/sys/net/ipv4/route/` directory contains specifications that apply to routing with any interfaces on the system. Many of these settings, such as `max_size`, `max_delay`, and `min_delay`, relate to controlling the size of the routing cache. To clear the routing cache, write any value to the `flush` file.

Additional information about these directories and the possible values for their configuration files can be found in:

```
/usr/share/doc/kernel-doc-kernel_version/Documentation/filesystems/proc.txt
```

C.3.9.5. /proc/sys/vm/

This directory facilitates the configuration of the Linux kernel's virtual memory (VM) subsystem. The kernel makes extensive and intelligent use of virtual memory, which is commonly referred to as swap space.

The following files are commonly found in the `/proc/sys/vm/` directory:

- `block_dump` — Configures block I/O debugging when enabled. All read/write and block dirtying operations done to files are logged accordingly. This can be useful if diagnosing disk spin up and spin downs for laptop battery conservation. All output when `block_dump` is enabled can be retrieved via `dmesg`. The default value is `0`.

Stopping the klogd daemon

If `block_dump` is enabled at the same time as kernel debugging, it is prudent to stop the `klogd` daemon, as it generates erroneous disk activity caused by `block_dump`.

- `dirty_background_ratio` — Starts background writeback of dirty data at this percentage of total memory, via a pdflush daemon. The default value is `10`.
- `dirty_expire_centisecs` — Defines when dirty in-memory data is old enough to be eligible for writeout. Data which has been dirty in-memory for longer than this interval is written out next time a pdflush daemon wakes up. The default value is `3000`, expressed in hundredths of a second.
- `dirty_ratio` — Starts active writeback of dirty data at this percentage of total memory for the generator of dirty data, via pdflush. The default value is `20`.
- `dirty_writeback_centisecs` — Defines the interval between pdflush daemon wakeups, which periodically writes dirty in-memory data out to disk. The default value is `500`, expressed in hundredths of a second.
- `laptop_mode` — Minimizes the number of times that a hard disk needs to spin up by keeping the disk spun down for as long as possible, therefore conserving battery power on laptops. This increases efficiency by combining all future I/O processes together, reducing the frequency of spin ups. The default value is `0`, but is automatically enabled in case a battery on a laptop is used.

  This value is controlled automatically by the acpid daemon once a user is notified battery power is enabled. No user modifications or interactions are necessary if the laptop supports the ACPI (Advanced Configuration and Power Interface) specification.

  For more information, refer to the following installed documentation:
  `/usr/share/doc/kernel-doc-`*`kernel_version`*`/Documentation/laptop-mode.txt`
- `max_map_count` — Configures the maximum number of memory map areas a process may have. In most cases, the default value of `65536` is appropriate.
- `min_free_kbytes` — Forces the Linux VM (virtual memory manager) to keep a minimum number of kilobytes free. The VM uses this number to compute a `pages_min` value for each `lowmem` zone in the system. The default value is in respect to the total memory on the machine.

- nr_hugepages — Indicates the current number of configured hugetlb pages in the kernel.

  For more information, refer to the following installed documentation:

  /usr/share/doc/kernel-doc-*kernel_version*/Documentation/vm/hugetlbpage.txt

- nr_pdflush_threads — Indicates the number of pdflush daemons that are currently running. This file is read-only, and should not be changed by the user. Under heavy I/O loads, the default value of two is increased by the kernel.
- overcommit_memory — Configures the conditions under which a large memory request is accepted or denied. The following three modes are available:
  - 0 — The kernel performs heuristic memory over commit handling by estimating the amount of memory available and failing requests that are blatantly invalid. Unfortunately, since memory is allocated using a heuristic rather than a precise algorithm, this setting can sometimes allow available memory on the system to be overloaded. This is the default setting.
  - 1 — The kernel performs no memory over commit handling. Under this setting, the potential for memory overload is increased, but so is performance for memory intensive tasks (such as those executed by some scientific software).
  - 2 — The kernel fails requests for memory that add up to all of swap plus the percent of physical RAM specified in /proc/sys/vm/overcommit_ratio. This setting is best for those who desire less risk of memory overcommitment.

Using this setting

This setting is only recommended for systems with swap areas larger than physical memory.

- overcommit_ratio — Specifies the percentage of physical RAM considered when /proc/sys/vm/overcommit_memory is set to 2. The default value is 50.
- page-cluster — Sets the number of pages read in a single attempt. The default value of 3, which actually relates to 16 pages, is appropriate for most systems.
- swappiness — Determines how much a machine should swap. The higher the value, the more swapping occurs. The default value, as a percentage, is set to 60.

All kernel-based documentation can be found in the following locally installed location:

/usr/share/doc/kernel-doc-*kernel_version*/Documentation/, which contains additional information.

C.3.10. /proc/sysvipc/

This directory contains information about System V IPC resources. The files in this directory relate to System V IPC calls for messages (`msg`), semaphores (`sem`), and shared memory (`shm`).

C.3.11. /proc/tty/

This directory contains information about the available and currently used *tty devices* on the system. Originally called *teletype devices*, any character-based data terminals are called tty devices.

In Linux, there are three different kinds of tty devices. *Serial devices* are used with serial connections, such as over a modem or using a serial cable. *Virtual terminals* create the common console connection, such as the virtual consoles available when pressing **Alt+<F-key>** at the system console. *Pseudo terminals* create a two-way communication that is used by some higher level applications, such as XFree86. The `drivers` file is a list of the current tty devices in use, as in the following example:

```
serial               /dev/cua       5  64-127 serial:callout
serial               /dev/ttyS      4  64-127 serial
pty_slave            /dev/pts     136   0-255 pty:slave
pty_master           /dev/ptm     128   0-255 pty:master
pty_slave            /dev/ttyp      3   0-255 pty:slave
pty_master           /dev/pty       2   0-255 pty:master
/dev/vc/0            /dev/vc/0      4       0 system:vtmaster
/dev/ptmx            /dev/ptmx      5       2 system
/dev/console         /dev/console   5       1 system:console
/dev/tty             /dev/tty       5       0 system:/dev/tty
unknown              /dev/vc/%d     4    1-63 console
```

The `/proc/tty/driver/serial` file lists the usage statistics and status of each of the serial tty lines.

In order for tty devices to be used as network devices, the Linux kernel enforces *line discipline* on the device. This allows the driver to place a specific type of header with every block of data transmitted over the device, making it possible for the remote end of the connection to a block of data as just one in a stream of data blocks. SLIP and PPP are common line disciplines, and each are commonly used to connect systems to one other over a serial link.

C.3.12. /proc/PID/

Out of Memory (OOM) refers to a computing state where all available memory, including swap space, has been allocated. When this situation occurs, it will cause the system to panic and stop functioning as expected. There is a switch that controls OOM behavior in `/proc/sys/vm/panic_on_oom`. When set to `1` the kernel will panic on OOM. A setting of `0` instructs the kernel to call a function named `oom_killer` on an OOM. Usually, `oom_killer` can kill rogue processes and the system will survive.

The easiest way to change this is to echo the new value to `/proc/sys/vm/panic_on_oom`.

```
# cat /proc/sys/vm/panic_on_oom
1

# echo 0 > /proc/sys/vm/panic_on_oom

# cat /proc/sys/vm/panic_on_oom
0
```

It is also possible to prioritize which processes get killed by adjusting the `oom_killer` score. In `/proc/PID/` there are two tools labeled `oom_adj` and `oom_score`. Valid scores for `oom_adj` are in the range -16 to +15. To see the current `oom_killer` score, view the `oom_score` for the process. `oom_killer` will kill processes with the highest scores first.

This example adjusts the oom_score of a process with a *PID* of 12465 to make it less likely that `oom_killer` will kill it.

```
# cat /proc/12465/oom_score
79872

# echo -5 > /proc/12465/oom_adj

# cat /proc/12465/oom_score
78
```

There is also a special value of -17, which disables `oom_killer` for that process. In the example below, `oom_score` returns a value of 0, indicating that this process would not be killed.

```
# cat /proc/12465/oom_score
78

# echo -17 > /proc/12465/oom_adj

# cat /proc/12465/oom_score
0
```

A function called `badness()` is used to determine the actual score for each process. This is done by adding up 'points' for each examined process. The process scoring is done in the following way:

1. The basis of each process's score is its memory size.
2. The memory size of any of the process's children (not including a kernel thread) is also added to the score
3. The process's score is increased for 'niced' processes and decreased for long running processes.

4. Processes with the CAP_SYS_ADMIN and CAP_SYS_RAWIO capabilities have their scores reduced.
5. The final score is then bitshifted by the value saved in the oom_adj file.

Thus, a process with the highest oom_score value will most probably be a non-priviliged, recently started process that, along with its children, uses a large amount of memory, has been 'niced', and handles no raw I/O.

C.4. Using the sysctl Command

The /sbin/sysctl command is used to view, set, and automate kernel settings in the /proc/sys/ directory.

For a quick overview of all settings configurable in the /proc/sys/ directory, type the /sbin/sysctl -a command as root. This creates a large, comprehensive list, a small portion of which looks something like the following:

```
net.ipv4.route.min_delay = 2 kernel.sysrq = 0 kernel.sem = 250   32000   32   128
```

This is the same information seen if each of the files were viewed individually. The only difference is the file location. For example, the /proc/sys/net/ipv4/route/min_delay file is listed as net.ipv4.route.min_delay, with the directory slashes replaced by dots and the proc.sys portion assumed.

The sysctl command can be used in place of echo to assign values to writable files in the /proc/sys/ directory. For example, instead of using the command

```
echo 1 > /proc/sys/kernel/sysrq
```

use the equivalent sysctl command as follows:

```
sysctl -w kernel.sysrq="1"
kernel.sysrq = 1
```

While quickly setting single values like this in /proc/sys/ is helpful during testing, this method does not work as well on a production system as special settings within /proc/sys/ are lost when the machine is rebooted. To preserve custom settings, add them to the /etc/sysctl.conf file.

Each time the system boots, the init program runs the /etc/rc.d/rc.sysinit script. This script contains a command to execute sysctl using /etc/sysctl.conf to determine the values passed to the kernel. Any values added to /etc/sysctl.conf therefore take effect each time the system boots.

C.5. References

Below are additional sources of information about proc file system.

C.6. Installed Documentation

Some of the best documentation about the `proc` file system is installed on the system by default.

- `/usr/share/doc/kernel-doc-`*`kernel_version`*`/Documentation/filesystems/proc.txt` — Contains assorted, but limited, information about all aspects of the `/proc/` directory.
- `/usr/share/doc/kernel-doc-`*`kernel_version`*`/Documentation/sysrq.txt` — An overview of System Request Key options.
- `/usr/share/doc/kernel-doc-`*`kernel_version`*`/Documentation/sysctl/` — A directory containing a variety of `sysctl` tips, including modifying values that concern the kernel (`kernel.txt`), accessing file systems (`fs.txt`), and virtual memory use (`vm.txt`).
- `/usr/share/doc/kernel-doc-`*`kernel_version`*`/Documentation/networking/ip-sysctl.txt` — A detailed overview of IP networking options.

C.7. Useful Websites

- *http://www.linuxhq.com/* — This website maintains a complete database of source, patches, and documentation for various versions of the Linux kernel.

Revision History

Revision History	Data	Author
Revision 1-2 Corrected a command synopsis in Section 10.2.3, *Starting and Stopping the Server* (page 190). Added missing information to Section 7.2.1, *Checking the Service Status* (page 122).	Tue Jul 12 2011	Jaromír Hradílek
Revision 1-1 Added missing `via` keywords to Section 6.4, *Configuring Static Routes* (page 115). Described the `HOTPLUG` configuration option in Section 6.2.1, *Ethernet Interfaces* (page 105). Corrected a typing error in Section 6.2.1, *Ethernet Interfaces* (page 105).	Mon Jun 20 2011	Jaromír Hradílek
Revision 1-0 Fedora 15 release of the *Deployment Guide*.	Tue May 24 2011	Jaromír Hradílek

Index

Linbrary™ Advertising Club (LAC)

Linbrary™ Official Docs as a Real Books http://www.linbrary.com Linux Library

LAC™

Linbrary Advertising Club

The Linux Documentation Project

Linux Documentation Project - Machtelt Garrels

http://www.tldp.org

Version	Title	Edition	ISBN-10	ISBN-13
TLDP	Introduction to Linux (Third Edition)	paperback	1-59682-199-X	978-1-59682-199-6
		eBook (pdf)	1-59682-200-7	978-1-59682-200-9
	Bash Guide for Beginners (Second Edition)	paperback	1-59682-201-5	978-1-59682-201-6
		eBook (pdf)	1-59682-202-3	978-1-59682-202-3
http://www.linbrary.com/linux-tldp/				

LAC™

Linbrary Advertising Club

fedora

Fedora Project Official Documentation

http://docs.fedoraproject.org

Version	Title	Edition	ISBN-10	ISBN-13
Fedora 15	Fedora 15 Installation Guide	paperback	1-59682-231-7	978-1-59682-231-3
		eBook (pdf)	1-59682-236-8	978-1-59682-236-8
	Fedora 15 Deployment Guide	paperback	1-59682-232-5	978-1-59682-232-0
		eBook (pdf)	1-59682-237-6	978-1-59682-237-5
Fedora 14	Fedora 14 Installation Guide	paperback	1-59682-228-7	978-1-59682-228-3
		eBook (pdf)	1-59682-233-3	978-1-59682-233-7
	Fedora 14 User Guide	paperback	1-59682-229-5	978-1-59682-229-0
		eBook (pdf)	1-59682-234-1	978-1-59682-234-4
	Fedora 14 Security Guide	paperback	1-59682-230-9	978-1-59682-230-6
		eBook (pdf)	1-59682-235-X	978-1-59682-235-1
Fedora 13	Fedora 13 Installation Guide	paperback	1-59682-212-0	978-1-59682-212-2
		eBook (pdf)	1-59682-217-1	978-1-59682-217-7
	Fedora 13 User Guide	paperback	1-59682-213-9	978-1-59682-213-9
		eBook (pdf)	1-59682-218-X	978-1-59682-218-4
	Fedora 13 Security Guide	paperback	1-59682-214-7	978-1-59682-214-6
		eBook (pdf)	1-59682-219-8	978-1-59682-219-1
	Fedora 13 SE Linux User Guide	paperback	1-59682-215-5	978-1-59682-215-3
		eBook (pdf)	1-59682-220-1	978-1-59682-220-7
	Fedora 13 Virtualization Guide	paperback	1-59682-216-3	978-1-59682-216-0
		eBook (pdf)	1-59682-221-X	978-1-59682-221-4
http://www.linbrary.com/fedora/				

LAC™

Linbrary Advertising Club

fedora

Fedora Project Official Documentation

http://docs.fedoraproject.org

Version	Title	Edition	ISBN-10	ISBN-13
Fedora 12	Fedora 12 Installation Guide	paperback	1-59682-179-5	978-1-59682-179-8
		eBook (pdf)	1-59682-184-1	978-1-59682-184-2
	Fedora 12 User Guide	paperback	1-59682-180-9	978-1-59682-180-4
		eBook (pdf)	1-59682-185-X	978-1-59682-185-9
	Fedora 12 Security Guide	paperback	1-59682-181-7	978-1-59682-181-1
		eBook (pdf)	1-59682-186-8	978-1-59682-186-6
	Fedora 12 SE Linux User Guide	paperback	1-59682-182-5	978-1-59682-182-8
		eBook (pdf)	1-59682-187-6	978-1-59682-187-3
	Fedora 12 Virtualization Guide	paperback	1-59682-183-3	978-1-59682-183-5
		eBook (pdf)	1-59682-188-4	978-1-59682-188-0
Fedora 11	Fedora 11 Installation Guide	paperback	1-59682-142-6	978-1-59682-142-2
		eBook (pdf)	1-59682-146-9	978-1-59682-146-0
	Fedora 11 User Guide	paperback	1-59682-143-4	978-1-59682-143-9
		eBook (pdf)	1-59682-147-7	978-1-59682-147-7
	Fedora 11 Security Guide	paperback	1-59682-144-2	978-1-59682-144-6
		eBook (pdf)	1-59682-148-5	978-1-59682-148-4
	Fedora 11 SE Linux User Guide	paperback	1-59682-145-0	978-1-59682-145-3
		eBook (pdf)	1-59682-149-3	978-1-59682-149-1
http://www.linbrary.com/fedora/				

LAC™

Linbrary Advertising Club

ubuntu
linux for human beings

Ubuntu Official Documentation

http://www.ubuntu.com

Version	Title	Edition	ISBN- 10	ISBN- 13
Ubuntu 11.04	Ubuntu 11.04 Installation Guide	paperback	1-59682-257-0	978-1-59682-257-3
		eBook (pdf)	1-59682-262-7	978-1-59682-262-7
	Ubuntu 11.04 Unity Desktop Guide	paperback	1-59682-258-9	978-1-59682-258-0
		eBook (pdf)	1-59682-263-5	978-1-59682-263-4
	Ubuntu 11.04 Classic Desktop Guide	paperback	1-59682-259-7	978-1-59682-259-7
		eBook (pdf)	1-59682-264-3	978-1-59682-264-1
	Ubuntu 11.04 Server Guide	paperback	1-59682-260-0	978-1-59682-260-3
		eBook (pdf)	1-59682-265-1	978-1-59682-265-8
Ubuntu 10.10	Ubuntu 11.04 Packaging Guide	paperback	1-59682-261-9	978-1-59682-261-0
		eBook (pdf)	1-59682-266-X	978-1-59682-266-5
	Ubuntu 10.10 Installation Guide	paperback	1-59682-238-4	978-1-59682-238-2
		eBook (pdf)	1-59682-242-2	978-1-59682-242-9
	Ubuntu 10.10 Desktop Guide	paperback	1-59682-239-2	978-1-59682-239-9
		eBook (pdf)	1-59682-243-0	978-1-59682-243-6
	Ubuntu 10.10 Server Guide	paperback	1-59682-240-6	978-1-59682-240-5
		eBook (pdf)	1-59682-244-9	978-1-59682-244-3
http://www.linbrary.com/ubuntu/				

LAC™

Linbrary Advertising Club

ubuntu
linux for human beings

Ubuntu Official Documentation

http://www.ubuntu.com

Version	Title	Edition	ISBN- 10	ISBN- 13
Ubuntu 10.04 LTS	Ubuntu 10.04 LTS Installation Guide	paperback	1-59682-203-1	978-1-59682-203-0
		eBook (pdf)	1-59682-207-4	978-1-59682-207-8
	Ubuntu 10.04 LTS Desktop Guide	paperback	1-59682-204-X	978-1-59682-204-7
		eBook (pdf)	1-59682-208-2	978-1-59682-208-5
	Ubuntu 10.04 LTS Server Guide	paperback	1-59682-205-8	978-1-59682-205-4
		eBook (pdf)	1-59682-209-0	978-1-59682-209-2
	Ubuntu 10.04 LTS Packaging Guide	paperback	1-59682-206-6	978-1-59682-206-1
		eBook (pdf)	1-59682-210-4	978-1-59682-210-8
Ubuntu 9.10	Ubuntu 9.10 Installation Guide	paperback	1-59682-171-X	978-1-59682-171-2
		eBook (pdf)	1-59682-175-2	978-1-59682-175-0
	Ubuntu 9.10 Desktop Guide	paperback	1-59682-172-8	978-1-59682-172-9
		eBook (pdf)	1-59682-176-0	978-1-59682-176-7
	Ubuntu 9.10 Server Guide	paperback	1-59682-173-6	978-1-59682-173-6
		eBook (pdf)	1-59682-177-9	978-1-59682-177-4
	Ubuntu 9.10 Packaging Guide	paperback	1-59682-174-4	978-1-59682-174-3
		eBook (pdf)	1-59682-178-7	978-1-59682-178-1
Ubuntu 9.04	Ubuntu 9.04 Installation Guide	paperback	1-59682-150-7	978-1-59682-150-7
		eBook (pdf)	1-59682-154-X	978-1-59682-154-5
	Ubuntu 9.04 Desktop Guide	paperback	1-59682-151-5	978-1-59682-151-4
		eBook (pdf)	1-59682-155-8	978-1-59682-155-2
	Ubuntu 9.04 Server Guide	paperback	1-59682-152-3	978-1-59682-152-1
		eBook (pdf)	1-59682-156-6	978-1-59682-156-9
	Ubuntu 9.04 Packaging Guide	paperback	1-59682-153-1	978-1-59682-153-8
		eBook (pdf)	1-59682-157-4	978-1-59682-157-6

http://www.linbrary.com/ubuntu/

LAC™

Linbrary Advertising Club

PostgreSQL

PostgreSQL Official Documentation

http://www.postgresql.org

Version	Title	Edition	ISBN- 10	ISBN- 13
PostgreSQL 9.0	PostgreSQL 9.0 Volume I. The SQL Language	paperback	1-59682-246-5	978-1-59682-246-7
		eBook (pdf)	1-59682-251-1	978-1-59682-251-1
	PostgreSQL 9.0 Volume II. Server Administration	paperback	1-59682-247-3	978-1-59682-247-4
		eBook (pdf)	1-59682-252-X	978-1-59682-252-8
	PostgreSQL 9.0 Volume III. Server Programming	paperback	1-59682-248-1	978-1-59682-248-1
		eBook (pdf)	1-59682-253-8	978-1-59682-253-5
	PostgreSQL 9.0 Volume IV. Reference	paperback	1-59682-249-X	978-1-59682-249-8
		eBook (pdf)	1-59682-254-6	978-1-59682-254-2
	PostgreSQL 9.0 Volume V. Internals & Appendixes	paperback	1-59682-250-3	978-1-59682-250-4
		eBook (pdf)	1-59682-255-4	978-1-59682-255-9
PostgreSQL 8.04	PostgreSQL 8.04 Volume I. The SQL Language	paperback	1-59682-158-2	978-1-59682-158-3
		eBook (pdf)	1-59682-163-9	978-1-59682-163-7
	PostgreSQL 8.04 Volume II. Server Administration	paperback	1-59682-159-0	978-1-59682-159-0
		eBook (pdf)	1-59682-164-7	978-1-59682-164-4
	PostgreSQL 8.04 Volume III. Server Programming	paperback	1-59682-160-4	978-1-59682-160-6
		eBook (pdf)	1-59682-165-5	978-1-59682-165-1
	PostgreSQL 8.04 Volume IV. Reference	paperback	1-59682-161-2	978-1-59682-161-3
		eBook (pdf)	1-59682-166-3	978-1-59682-166-8
	PostgreSQL 8.04 Volume V. Internals & Appendixes	paperback	1 59682-162-0	978-1-59682-162-0
		eBook (pdf)	1-59682-167-1	978-1-59682-167-5
http://www.linbrary.com/postgresql/				

LAC™

Linbrary Advertising Club

The Apache Software Foundation Official Documentation

http://www.apache.org

Version	Title	Edition	ISBN- 10	ISBN- 13
Apache Web Server 2.2	Apache HTTP Server 2.2 Vol.I. Server Administration	paperback	1-59682-191-4	978-1-59682-191-0
		eBook (pdf)	1-59682-195-7	978-1-59682-195-8
	Apache HTTP Server 2.2 Vol.II. Security & Server Programs	paperback	1-59682-192-2	978-1-59682-192-7
		eBook (pdf)	1-59682-196-5	978-1-59682-196-5
	Apache HTTP Server 2.2 Vol.III. Modules (A-H)	paperback	1-59682-193-0	978-1-59682-193-4
		eBook (pdf)	1-59682-197-3	978-1-59682-197-2
	Apache HTTP Server 2.2 Vol.IV. Modules (I-V)	paperback	1-59682-194-9	978-1-59682-194-1
		eBook (pdf)	1-59682-198-1	978-1-59682-198-9
http://www.linbrary.com/apache-http/				

Version	Title	Edition	ISBN- 10	ISBN- 13
Subversion 1.6	Subversion 1.6 Version Control with Subversion	paperback	1-59682-169-8	978-1-59682-169-9
		eBook (pdf)	1-59682-170-1	978-1-59682-170-5
SUBVERSION				
http://www.linbrary.com/subversion/				

LAC™

Linbrary Advertising Club

LAC™

Linbrary Advertising Club

Your Advertising Here

More Books Coming Soon!!!

Please Feel Free to Contact Us at

production@fultus.com

CPSIA information can be obtained at www.ICGtesting.com
Printed in the USA
BVOW06030426101l
274547BV00003B/191/P

9 781596 822320